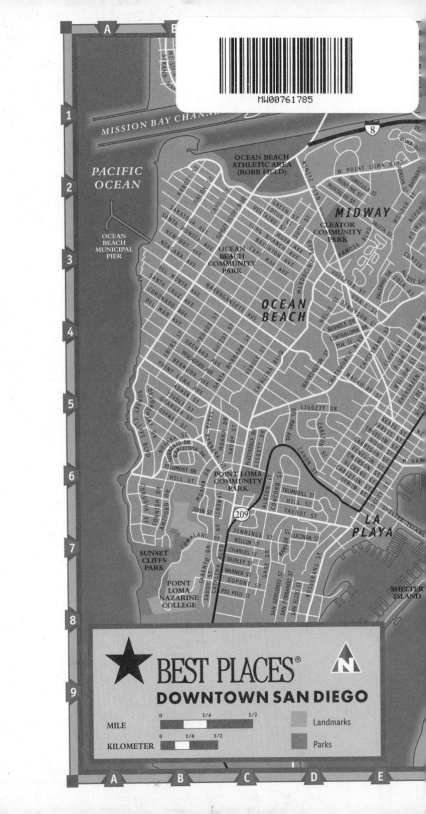

MW00761785

PACIFIC
OCEAN

MISSION BAY CHANNEL

OCEAN BEACH
ATHLETIC AREA
(ROBB FIELD)

MIDWAY

CLEATOR
COMMUNITY
PARK

OCEAN
BEACH
COMMUNITY
PARK

OCEAN
BEACH

OCEAN
BEACH
MUNICIPAL
PIER

NARRAGANSETT AVE

LIGGETT DR

SUNSET
CLIFFS
PARK

POINT LOMA
COMMUNITY
PARK

LA
PLAYA

TRUMBULL ST

HILL ST

TALBOT ST

209

JENNINGS ST

WILCOX ST

CHARLES ST

DUDLEY ST

WARNER ST

DUPONT ST

PIO PICO ST

POINT
LOMA
NAZARINE
COLLEGE

SHELTER
ISLAND

★ BEST PLACES®

DOWNTOWN SAN DIEGO

MILE
0   1/4   1/2

KILOMETER
0   1/4   1/2

Landmarks

Parks

A   B   C   D   E

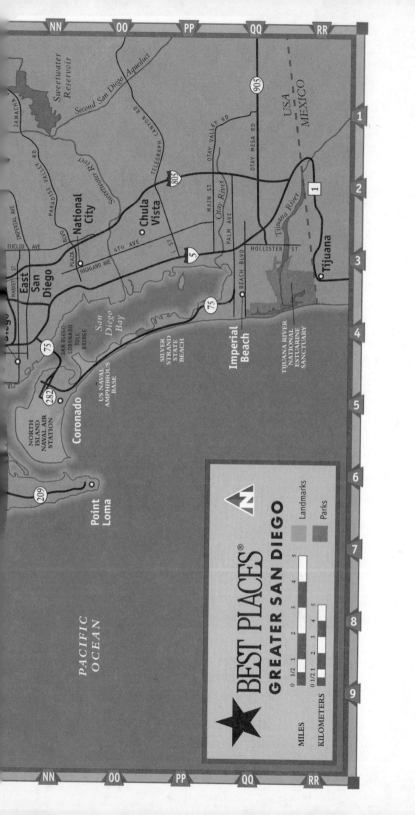

BEST PLACES®

SAN DIEGO

BEST PLACES®

SAN DIEGO

Edited by
MARIBETH MELLIN

EDITION 1

SASQUATCH BOOKS
SEATTLE

Printed in the United States of America
Distributed in Canada by Raincoast Books Ltd.

First edition.
02 01 00 99   5 4 3 2 1

ISSN: 1524-9247
ISBN: 1-57061-197-1

Series editor: Kate Rogers
Cover and interior design: Nancy Gellos
Cover photograph: Grant V. Faint/The Image Bank
Fold-out and interior maps: GreenEye Design

SPECIAL SALES

BEST PLACES° guidebooks are available at special discounts on bulk purchases for corporate, club, or organization sales promotions, premiums, and gifts. Special editions, including personalized covers, excerpts of existing guides, and corporate imprints, can be created in large quantities for specific needs. For more information, contact your local bookseller or Special Sales, BEST PLACES° Guidebooks, 615 Second Avenue, Suite 260, Seattle, Washington 98104, 800/775-0817.

SASQUATCH BOOKS
615 Second Avenue
Seattle, WA 98104
206/467-4300
books@SasquatchBooks.com
www.SasquatchBooks.com

CONTENTS

Introduction and Acknowledgments viii
Contributors ix
About Best Places® Guidebooks xi
How to Use This Book xii
Best Places® Star Ratings xiii

PLANNING A TRIP 1
How to Get Here 2
When to Visit 5
General Costs 6
Tips for Special Travelers 8
Calendar of Events 12
Freeway Frenzy 4
Phone Alert 9
In the Beginning 10

LAY OF THE CITY 19
Orientation 20
Visitor Information 22
Getting Around 23
Essentials 25
Local Resources 30
Important Telephone Numbers 33
How to Pass for a Local 21
Places of Worship 26
Holes in the Ground 31

TOP 160 RESTAURANTS 35
Restaurants by Star Rating 36
Restaurants by Neighborhood 38
Restaurants by Food and Other Features 40
Restaurant Reviews 44
Doggie Dining 47
Fresh from the Sea 104

LODGINGS 115
Downtown 116
Airport Area 121
Coronado 121
Point Loma/Shelter Island 123
Old Town 124
Mission Valley 126
Mission Bay 127

Pacific Beach 129
La Jolla 130
Del Mar 135
Rancho Santa Fe 136
Carlsbad 137
Rancho Bernardo 137
Julian 138
Borrego Springs 139
  Love, San Diego Style 119
  San Diego Ciné 131

EXPLORING 141
Top 25 Attractions 142
Neighborhoods 166
Museums 181
Art in Public Places 186
Galleries 189
Gardens 193
Beaches and Parks 194
Organized Tours 202
  Top 25 Attractions 143
  A Maze of Neighborhoods 170
  Tide Pool Tango 195

SHOPPING 207
Shops from A to Z 210
  Designer Shopping 213
  Growth and Dreams 237

PERFORMING ARTS 245
Theater 246
Classical Music and Opera 252
Dance 256
Film 257
Literature 259
  Ticket Alert 247
  The Symphony Is Back . . . and Looking Good 253
  Airport Art 258

NIGHTLIFE 261
Nightlife by Features 262
Nightlife by Neighborhood 263
Music and Clubs 264
Bars, Pubs, and Taverns 270

Desserts, Coffees, and Teas 275
  Local Gold 267
  On the Small Screen 276

ITINERARIES 279
Days One Through Seven 280
  Kids' Play 281
  Mister Horton Builds a City 283

DAY TRIPS 287
North Coast 288
Carlsbad and Environs 290
Escondido and Environs 293
Palomar Mountain and Julian 295
Anza-Borrego Desert and Borrego Springs 297
Temecula 300
Disneyland 302
  Beautiful View 291
  Gambling Goes Native 298

BAJA 305
Tijuana 307
Rosarito 312
Puerto Nuevo (Newport) 315
Ensenada 316
  Border Sense 310
  The Whole Enchilada 317

RECREATION 321
Outdoor Activities 322
Spectator Sports 343
  Weird Sports 329
  Above It All 336
  Contamination Blues 341

CONFERENCES, MEETINGS, AND RECEPTIONS 347

Index xxx
Money-back Guarantee xxx
Best Places® Report Form xxx

Introduction and Acknowledgments

I was in Peru researching a travel book when news of *San Diego Best Places* came my way. What a wonderful concept, I thought. No planes. No stumbling over foreign tongues. No strange currency. I could explore my hometown, using local critics and writers as my guides.

Thus, I lobbied eagerly to become the editor of this definitive tome. Many months later, I thank series editor Kate Rogers for her tenacious faith in my abilities. This project has been my anchor through tumultuous times; my co-workers have become valued friends.

I'm delighted to say San Diego is my home. This youthful, exuberant, sunny city is subtly seductive. It soothes the senses with its warm climate and lack of pretension. Stuffy rules and prissy conventions have no place here; it seems everyone is intent on having fun. Yet San Diego encourages amazing creativity. Scientists, artists, bankers, and military commanders all thrive in this laid-back community. They toil in research institutes perched above the Pacific Ocean and compose stratagems while walking by the sea. They surf, bike, skate, and swim while structuring plots and schemes. The natural realm forms a palette for the imagination here.

Discovering the best of San Diego is a slippery matter. Favorite restaurants, shops, and activities are easily discarded when something new comes along. It takes a seasoned eye to find the stars that endure whimsical trends. The writers, researchers, experts, and friends who have contributed to this book are both perceptive and flexible. They know which businesses are likely to succeed with San Diegans, and which deserve recognition for their staying power. It takes a healthy dose of bravado to assume one has found all the best places in San Diego. I'm sure some readers will disagree with our choices; others will be thrilled to find their favorites included (or overlooked, if you want to keep them a secret).

Some of the best insights came from those who joined my own excursions throughout the region. Patrick Mellin approached downtown, Ocean Beach, and Tijuana with an infectious enthusiasm. Gary Grimaud never ceased to expound on the merits of sportfishing and Coronado. Others who deserve acknowledgment include the Humphrey and Grimaud families, Carol Drummond, and music critic George Varga. I am most fortunate to be working with Sasquatch Books, and thank Kate Rogers and assistant editor Laura Gronewold for their patience, guidance, and kindness.

Finally, I dedicate this book to my mother, who passed away as this project was evolving. I will forever cherish her sense of curiosity, source of my own creativity. —*Maribeth Mellin, Editor*

Contributors

ALISON ASHTON wrote about San Diego's mountains, deserts, and neighborhoods and offered her insights on hotels and restaurants throughout the county. She is a freelance travel writer and author of a weekly travel column syndicated by Copley News Service.

Longtime downtown resident **VIRGINIA BUTTERFIELD** is the Executive Editor of *San Diego Magazine*. She covered performing arts and the ever-changing downtown scene.

MOLLIE GLASSER, who hates getting into her car without knowing exactly where she is going, used her unceasing curiosity to write the Lay of the City chapter.

SUSAN HUMPHREY carted her three kids around the county to cover San Diego's beaches, parks, and "kid-friendly" attractions. She contributed to all the chapters as a writer, editor, and organizational whiz. Her assistance was invaluable.

Freelance writer **PETER JENSEN** covered his neighborhood of Del Mar, California, along with restaurants, design shops, and San Diego history. Jensen contributes regularly to *Sunset, This Old House, Coastal Living, San Diego Home/Garden* and other periodicals. He is the author of several books regarding travel destinations in the West.

MARAEL JOHNSON is an award-winning freelance travel writer whose interests range from fine restaurants and North County neighborhoods to the amusements at Disneyland. She has authored or contributed to many travel guidebooks, and is currently working on a guide to Los Angeles.

Dedicated shopper **LISA KALLERMAN** spent eight years as the prop buyer for the Old Globe Theatre in San Diego. She is a veteran antique dealer, bargain hound, and yard sale assassin.

Our primary restaurant critic **ROBIN KLEVEN** is a native San Diegan with a discerning attitude toward dining, fine wine, and world travel. She was a reporter and editor for the *San Diego Union-Tribune* and restaurant critic for San Diego sidewalk.com. She freelances for a variety of online and print publications.

PRISCILLA LISTER is a freelance travel and features writer in San Diego. A native San Diegan, she has written extensively on conference venues in the West.

Over the past two decades **MARIBETH MELLIN** has covered San Diego as a Senior Editor, Travel Editor, and Contributing Editor for *San Diego Magazine*. She contributed to every chapter in this book, and has authored travel tomes on Argentina, Peru, Mexico, Hawaii, and California.

Writer and artist **JANE ONSTOTT** divides her time between San Diego and Latin America. She contributed to several chapters, including Baja, Performing Arts, Recreation, and Shopping. She is currently writing a Mexico guide.

KY PLASKON is a reporter for the *San Diego Gay and Lesbian Times* and a freelance writer who lost many hours of sleep while covering the nightlife scene.

About Best Places® Guidebooks

People trust us. BEST PLACES® guidebooks, which have been published continuously since 1975, represent one of the most respected regional travel series in the country. Each guide is written completely independently: no advertisers, no sponsors, no favors. Our reviewers know their territory, work incognito, and seek out the very best a city or region has to offer. Because we accept no free meals, accommodations, or other complimentary services, we are able to provide tough, candid reports about places that have rested too long on their laurels, and to delight in new places that deserve recognition. We describe the true strengths, foibles, and unique characteristics of each establishment listed.

San Diego Best Places is written by and for locals, and is therefore coveted by travelers. It's written for people who live here and who enjoy exploring the city's bounty and its out-of-the-way places of high character and individualism. It is these very characteristics that make San Diego Best Places ideal for tourists, too. The best places in and around the city are the ones that denizens favor: independently owned establishments of good value, touched with local history, run by lively individuals, and graced with natural beauty. With this premier edition of San Diego Best Places, travelers will find the information they need: where to go and when, what to order, which rooms to request (and which to avoid), where the best music, art, nightlife, shopping, and other attractions are, and how to find the city's hidden secrets.

We're so sure you'll be satisfied with our guide, we guarantee it.

NOTE: *The reviews in this edition are based on information available at press time and are subject to change. Readers are advised that places listed may have closed or changed management, and, thus, may no longer be recommended by this series. The editors welcome information conveyed by users of this book. A report form is provided at the end of the book, and feedback is also welcome via email: books@ SasquatchBooks.com.*

How to Use This Book

This book is divided into thirteen chapters covering a wide range of establishments, destinations, and activities in and around San Diego. All evaluations are based on numerous reports from local and traveling inspectors. BEST PLACES' reporters do not identify themselves when they review an establishment, and they accept no free meals, accommodations, or any other services. Final judgments are made by the editors. Every place featured in this book is recommended.

STAR RATINGS *(for Top 160 Restaurants and Lodgings only)* Restaurants and lodgings are rated on a scale of one to four stars (with half stars in between), based on uniqueness, loyalty of local clientele, performance measured against the establishment's goals, excellence of cooking, cleanliness, value, and professionalism of service. Reviews are listed alphabetically, and every place is recommended.

★★★★ The very best in the city

★★★ Distinguished; many outstanding features

★★ Excellent; some wonderful qualities

★ A good place

[unrated] New or undergoing major changes

(For more on how we rate places, see the BEST PLACES' Star Ratings box, below.)

PRICE RANGE *(for Top 160 Restaurants and Lodgings only)* Prices for lodgings are based on peak season rates for one night's lodging for two people (i.e., double occupancy). Off-season rates vary but can sometimes be significantly less. Prices for restaurants are based primarily on dinner for two, including dessert, tax, and tip. When prices range between two categories (for example, moderate to expensive), the lower one is given. Call ahead to verify, as all prices are subject to change.

$$$ Expensive (more than $80 for dinner for two; more than $125 for one night's lodgings for two)

$$ Moderate (between expensive and inexpensive)

$ Inexpensive (less than $30 for dinner for two; $85 or less for one night's lodgings for two)

RESERVATIONS We used one of the following terms for our reservations policy: reservations required, reservations recommended, no reservations, or reservations accepted. "No reservations" means either that they're not necessary or not accepted.

ADDRESSES AND PHONE NUMBERS Every attempt has been made to provide accurate information on an establishment's location and phone number. But it's always a good idea to call ahead and confirm. For establishments with two or more locations, we try to provide information on the original or most recommended branches.

CHECKS AND CREDIT CARDS Most establishments that accept checks also require a major credit card for identification. Note that some places accept only local checks. Credit cards are abbreviated in this book as

BEST PLACES® STAR RATINGS

Any travel guide that rates establishments is inherently subjective—and BEST PLACES® is no exception. We rely on our professional experience, yes, but also on a gut feeling. And, occasionally, we even give in to a soft spot for a favorite neighborhood hangout. Our star-rating system is not simply a AAA-checklist; it's judgmental, critical, sometimes fickle, and highly personal. And unlike most other travel guides, we pay our own way and accept no freebies: no free meals or accommodations, no advertisers, no sponsors, no favors.

For each new edition, we send local food and travel experts out to review restaurants and lodgings anonymously, and then to rate them on a scale of one to four, based on uniqueness, loyalty of local clientele, performance measured against the establishment's goals, excellence of cooking, cleanliness, value, and professionalism of service. That doesn't mean a one-star establishment isn't worth dining or sleeping at—far from it. When we say that *all* the places listed in our books are recommended, we mean it. That one-star pizza joint may be just the ticket for the end of a whirlwind day of shopping with the kids. But if you're planning something more special, the star ratings can help you choose an eatery or hotel that will wow your new clients or be a stunning, romantic place to celebrate an anniversary or impress a first date.

We award four-star ratings sparingly, reserving them for what we consider truly the best. And once an establishment has earned our highest rating, everyone's expectations seem to rise. Readers often write us letters specifically to point out the faults in four-star establishments. With changes in chefs, management, styles, and trends, it's always easier to get knocked off the pedestal than to ascend it. Three-star establishments, on the other hand, seem to generate healthy praise. They exhibit outstanding qualities, and we get lots of love letters about them. The difference between two and three stars can sometimes be a very fine line. Two-star establishments are doing a good, solid job and gaining attention, while one-star places are often dependable spots that have been around forever.

The restaurants and lodgings described in *San Diego Best Places* have earned their stars from hard work and good service (and good food). They're proud to be included in this book—look for our BEST PLACES® sticker in their windows. And we're proud to honor them in this, the first edition of *San Diego Best Places*.

follows: American Express (AE); Carte Blanche (CB); Diners Club (DC); Discover (DIS); Japanese credit card (JCB); MasterCard (MC); Visa (V).

EMAIL AND WEB SITE ADDRESSES With the understanding that more people are using email and the internet to access information and to plan trips, BEST PLACES' has included email and Web site addresses for establishments, where available. Please note that the World Wide Web is a fluid and evolving medium, and that Web pages are often "under construction" or, as with all time-sensitive information, may no longer be valid.

MAP INDICATORS The letter-and-number codes appearing at the end of most listings refer to coordinates on the fold-out map included in the front of the book. Single letters (for example, F7) refer to the downtown San Diego map; double letters (FF7) refer to the Greater San Diego map on the flip side. If an establishment does not have a map code listed, its location falls beyond the boundaries of these maps.

HELPFUL ICONS Watch for these quick-reference symbols throughout the book:

 FAMILY FUN Family-oriented places that are great for kids—fun, easy, not too expensive, and accustomed to dealing with young ones.

 GOOD VALUE While not necessarily cheap, these places offer you the best value for your dollars—a good deal within the context of the city.

 ROMANTIC These spots offer candlelight, atmosphere, intimacy, or other romantic qualities—kisses and proposals are encouraged!

 UNIQUELY SAN DIEGO These are places that are unique and special to the city, such as a restaurant owned by a beloved local chef or a tourist attraction recognized around the globe. (Hint: If you want to hit several of these special spots at once, turn to the Top 25 Attractions in the Exploring chapter. They're all uniquely San Diego!)

 Appears after listings for establishments that have wheelchair-accessible facilities.

INDEXES In addition to a general index at the back of the book, there are five specialized indexes: restaurants are indexed by star-rating, features, and location at the beginning of the Restaurants chapter, and nightspots are indexed by features and location at the beginning of the Nightlife chapter.

READER REPORTS At the end of the book is a report form. We receive hundreds of reports from readers suggesting new places or agreeing or disagreeing with our assessments. They greatly help in our evaluations, and we encourage you to respond.

MONEY-BACK GUARANTEE See "We Stand by Our Reviews" at the end of this book.

PLANNING A TRIP

PLANNING A TRIP

How to Get Here

BY AIRPLANE

SAN DIEGO INTERNATIONAL AIRPORT AT LINDBERGH FIELD (3707 N Harbor Drive, downtown; 619/231-2100; map:I5) is smack in the middle of the city, 3 miles northwest of downtown, paralleling San Diego Bay. A $238 million, two-year renovation of the airport, completed in January 1998, has increased flight options for the estimated 15 million yearly passengers. The airport includes Terminal 1, Terminal 2, and a Commuter Terminal. Large road signs on Harbor Drive list the different airlines served by each terminal. The **RED BUS SHUTTLE** travels between terminals, and though it is possible to walk between Terminals 1 and 2, the Commuter Terminal is in a separate complex with no pedestrian access. If you're flying on a small regional airline or one of the large airlines' commuter carriers, ask the airlines for the terminal and gate info in advance; many passengers get to the airport only to find their flight is departing quite a ways down the road.

TRAVELERS AID stations in Terminals 1 and 2 open daily from 8am to 11pm, providing services for disabled or elderly passengers and children traveling alone as well as free information and referrals for getting around town. The lost and found office is at Terminal 2 (619/686-8002). The recent expansion has brought an abundance of new shops and eating establishments; La Salsa and Rubio's Mexican eateries are especially good.

Unfortunately, the expansion has made the airport less user-friendly in some ways. Passengers must hike long distances to get to baggage claim; then to reach cabs, shuttles, and parking lots, they must retrace their steps and use escalators and elevators to return to the second floor, walk across a skybridge, descend again, and cross streets (one or more, depending on the terminal). Airport planners are rethinking the situation, and some crosswalks are in the works, but it's still a bit of a mess for travelers. Drivers picking up passengers can still wait in front of the baggage claim areas, but taxis dropping off passengers can not pick up passengers here. For comprehensive information on flight arrivals and departures, and parking, car rental, and paging services, call the airport information line (619/231-2100).

PARKING at the airport can be challenging, so allow enough time to cruise for one of the 3,000 spots. Rates are per hour; for example, 1 hour costs $1, 7 to 8 hours $10, 8 to 24 hours $12, 24 to 48 hours $18, and so on, for up to thirty days. Major credit cards are accepted. The parking lots are fenced; a skybridge provides terminal access.

Airport Transportation
A convenient way to get to and from San Diego's Lindbergh Field is by shuttle, accessible at the transportation plazas across from Terminals 1 and 2 (by way of the skybridge) and curbside at the Commuter Terminal. Airport personnel there can assist you. Shuttle service to and from the airport is available through Cloud 9 Shuttle (outside California, 619/278-8877; within California, 800/974-8885), Coastline's Shuttle (800/816-3520), Access Shuttle (619/282-1515), or Supreme Shuttle (619/295-1863). San Diego is a big county, and the price will vary considerably depending on where you are coming from.

TAXIS from the airport to downtown (or vice versa) run $7–$10.

By Charter or Private Airplane
Most charter airplane and helicopter companies are based at the smaller airports in San Diego County: Palomar Airport (760/431-4640; map:CC8), Montgomery Field (619/573-1440; map:KK4), and Gillespie Field (619/596-3900; map:JJ1). Services include aircraft rentals and flying lessons. Call the San Diego flight service station (800/992-7433) for up-to-date weather reports and flight-related information.

BY BUS
GREYHOUND BUS LINES (120 W Broadway, downtown; 619/239-3266, 800/231-2222; map:N7) offers low-cost transportation to San Diego from all over the country. The terminal, open 24 hours a day, is located in downtown San Diego, just up the street from the Santa Fe train depot and conveniently close to trolley stops. Many bus companies offer charter services to local and long-distance points of interest. GRAY LINE SAN DIEGO (800/331-5077) is a good bet.

BY TRAIN
AMTRAK's Santa Fe depot (1050 Kettner Blvd, downtown; 800/872-7245; www.amtrak.com; map:M7) near the harbor is a beautiful Spanish colonial-style building, with high ceilings and walls decorated with lovely old tiles. Train service up the coast to Los Angeles and on to Santa Barbara is offered several times daily. Local train service is also available via the COASTER, a commuter train with five stops in North County. Fares vary depending on the distance traveled; most are between $3 and $3.75. Parking is free at all stations except Santa Fe and Sorrento Valley.

BY CAR
Our first advice: get a good map. Until you become accustomed to it, the freeway system in San Diego is a quagmire of looping roads and intimidating on- and off-ramps. Interstate 8 is San Diego's main artery, moving people and their vehicles east and west from its starting point in Ocean Beach, through Mission Valley and El Cajon, over the mountains and down into the California desert, culminating in Arizona. Connecting

points north and south is Interstate 5, commencing at the border with Mexico and carving through San Diego County to Los Angeles (120 miles away) and on to Oregon and Washington. The beach communities of Imperial Beach, Mission Beach, Pacific Beach, La Jolla, and Del Mar are all accessed from Interstate 5; it is also your connection to the Coronado Bay Bridge. Interstate 805 is another main drag through the county—and a drag it is to those hapless commuters caught during rush hour. Like salmon fighting their way upstream, morning and late-afternoon drivers struggle mightily on 805 to reach their destinations. From its southern end near the Mexican border to its connection with Interstate 5 in Sorrento Valley, this freeway gets more congested every year. Interstate 15 is another north-to-south route, farther inland than the 5, running up to Escondido and the Wild Animal Park and on to Temecula. Highway 163 is a small but important stretch of road, with an especially pretty section called the Cabrillo Freeway, which runs through Balboa Park. The recently completed Highway 52, going east and west with connections to the 5, 805, 163, and 15, has relieved some of the congestion on Interstate 8.

During the peak hours of 7–9am and 4–6pm, do your best to avoid the freeways altogether, especially Interstate 8 heading east through Mission Valley, Interstate 805 from the Interstate 8 connector going north, and the 15 from Mira Mesa to Escondido.

FREEWAY FRENZY

San Diego runs on wheels. You must have a car, unless you're a first-time visitor content with packaged tours. Convertibles are nice; so are Range Rovers and Jeeps. Maps are an absolute necessity. San Diegans are ruthless drivers. They act as if mellowness is best left at the beach. Forget slowing down for merging traffic; locals love to speed up and challenge anyone with temerity. Study your entrances and exits before hitting the freeways, especially during rush hour. In fact, stay off major byways when workers and students are hell-bent on following their daily schedules. If you're a tourist, take the surface streets. San Diegans also have a blind spot when it comes to using turn signals to change lanes; cutting off traffic is part of the game. Keep your defenses finely tuned, but don't express outrage. The tangle of freeways is a confounding source of frustration even for locals—everyone has a story of driving in circles on three or four interchanges before reaching their destination. Directions sound like this: "Take the 8 to the 5 to the 163 to the 15 and go east." Take our advice and get detailed directions before hitting the road. If you do get lost, ask for help immediately unless you want an extended high-speed tour of San Diego's baffling freeways.

—Maribeth Mellin

When to Visit

There is no bad season to visit San Diego. The weather is pleasant and balmy most of the year, and interesting events are held year-round. Keep in mind when you look at the temperature chart below that these averages were derived from the weather at the coast; some parts of northern and eastern San Diego county positively sizzle during the summer. Visitors to the Wild Animal Park in Escondido will find the heat fairly blistering during August and September. Call the local weather service's recorded forecast (619/289-1212) before venturing out, and dress appropriately.

WEATHER

Tired of sunshine? Head to the coast, where sea breezes and low-lying clouds can cast a gray chill until noon. Tired of gloom? Head 5 miles east toward blue skies. Though San Diego's climate is temperate, there's enough variety to please everyone. While surfers in wet suits are riding the waves in January, kids are sledding down snow-covered hills just 50 miles east in the Laguna Mountains. As beach dwellers shiver in the chill winter dampness, desert rats run about in shades and shorts. The ocean is rarely as warm as the air, and only surfers in wetsuits and pale out-of-towners venture into the water in winter. The best months for swimming are August and September, when the water nears 70 degrees. Rain, a great cause of celebration for farmers and gardeners, seems to baffle drivers, whose windshield wipers have cracked and dried in the sunshine. Commonsense warnings to drive slowly are utterly ignored; thus, disabled vehicles from all sorts of fender benders litter the streets. High winds can also wreak havoc with traffic in the mountains and deserts.

Average temperature and precipitation by month

Month	Daily Maximum Temp. degrees F	Daily Minimum Temp. degrees F	Monthly Precipitation in inches
JANUARY	66	49	1.80
FEBRUARY	67	51	1.53
MARCH	66	53	1.77
APRIL	68	56	.79
MAY	69	59	.19
JUNE	72	62	.07
JULY	76	66	.02
AUGUST	78	67	.10
SEPTEMBER	77	66	.24
OCTOBER	75	61	.37
NOVEMBER	70	51	1.45
DECEMBER	66	49	1.57

Source: National Weather Service

TIME

San Diego is on Pacific Standard Time (PST)—three hours behind New York, two hours behind Chicago, one hour behind Denver, one hour ahead of Alaska, and two hours ahead of Hawaii. Daylight Saving Time is observed, beginning in early April and ending in late October.

WHAT TO BRING

Sunscreen and sunglasses are essential accouterments year-round in sunny San Diego, as are comfortable walking/running shoes and slip-on thongs. Everything else is up for grabs in this anything-goes clime. Shorts are worn everywhere—but please don't wear them with calf-high socks. Stockings are also verboten, unless you must work in some staid office. Think a summer afternoon in your backyard and you'll have your wardrobe nailed. A light jacket or sweater comes in handy even in summer, when night winds can be chilly (especially when wafting across sunburned skin). Only a few restaurants have dress codes beyond "no shirt, no shoes, no service"; for men, sport jackets with jeans serve most special occasions nicely. Women will do well with sundresses of any length (some think shorter is better), paired with sexy sandals. Kids need clothes that withstand rough play (bring plenty of premoistened towelettes and Band-Aids).

General Costs

San Diego's economy rarely falters. It seems the natural climate encourages good luck for businesses. The county outperformed the state and nation in 1998 with an economic growth rate of 4.1 percent. Forecasters predict continued growth into the new millennium, as the region continues to adapt to changing economic forces. San Diego's prosperity originated with the presence of the military and an abundance of defense industries. Peace and base closures haven't harmed the economy, however: San Diego is still home to United States Navy and Marine bases stationing more than 100,000 military personnel, and manufacturing has diversified to include everything from golf clubs to supercomputers. Carlsbad, in north San Diego County, is home to three big-name golf equipment manufacturers: Callaway, Taylor Made, and Cobra. Gateway Computers secured San Diego's place in high-technology by moving their headquarters here in 1999. An educated work force (over 22 percent of San Diego's residents have graduated from college) and an abundance of research centers, including the Salk Institute, fuel the scientific community. Health-care manufacturers abound, and over 200 local companies specialize in biotechnology. San Diego county has become one of the largest telecommunications centers in the world, dominated by Qualcomm (the football stadium now bears the company's name), and two

Fortune 500 companies—Sempra Energy and Gateway—help lead the way for the region. Venture capital investors found San Diego so promising that they spent $199 million on local Internet and biotech startups in the second quarter of 1999 alone.

Though manufacturing and high-tech industries attract the most attention, tourism is San Diego's largest employer and greatest economic indicator. And thanks to the service industries, the unemployment rate hovers around 3.4 percent, far lower than California's 5.3 percent. The San Diego Convention and Visitors Bureau reported that in 1998, 14.5 million overnight visitors stayed in the county, breaking all previous records. Many of those visitors return to stay, forming the base of an ongoing real estate boom. New communities multiply like rabbits in the few undeveloped regions of the county, and housing prices continue to rise. In June 1999, the median price of all homes sold in the first six months of that year was a staggering $201,000. As a result, only about 55 percent of San Diego's householders own their homes, compared to a national rate of 66 percent. Affordable housing is one of the largest drawbacks for companies looking to relocate in San Diego. But that doesn't seem to discourage newcomers from moving to the region: forecasters predict the county's population will hit 3 million by the year 2000.

Average costs for lodging and food

Double room:

INEXPENSIVE	$50–$80
MODERATE	$80–$150
EXPENSIVE	$150 AND UP

Lunch for one:

INEXPENSIVE	$8–$12
MODERATE	$12–$18
EXPENSIVE	$19 AND UP

Beverages in a restaurant:

GLASS OF WINE	$4–$10
PINT OF BEER	$3–$5
COCA-COLA	$1.50
DOUBLE TALL ICED MOCHA	$2.50

Other common items:

MOVIE TICKET	$8.50
ROLL OF FILM	$5.50
TAXI PER MILE	$1.75
RAY-BANS	$50–$200
SAN DIEGO SOUVENIR T-SHIRT	$8–$15

Tips for Special Travelers

FAMILIES WITH CHILDREN

In an emergency, dial 911, day or night. If you fear that your child has swallowed a toxic substance, call the San Diego division of the California Poison Control System, located at UCSD Medical Center (800/876-4766). For general questions about your child's health or development, call the parent resource information line at Children's Hospital of San Diego (619/576-4000). Several local publications offer information on events for families, as well as articles geared to parents. *San Diego Parent* (www.san-diego-parent.com) is distributed free at many stores, libraries, schools, and attractions around town. *The Reader* (www.sdreader.com), published weekly, is another good source for info on family activities.

Families are as important as conventioneers to local hoteliers, even downtown. Though the hotels closest to the Convention Center are packed with business travelers, they still have kids' pools and game rooms. Hotels in Mission Bay and the beaches seem completely geared to families; many have in-room refrigerators and joysticks for video games (for an additional fee that can add up quickly) along with water- and land-toy rentals. Some of the larger chains have supervised children's programs, freeing parents for adult pleasures. Most restaurants have children's menus.

 Watch for this icon throughout the book; it indicates places and activities that are great for families.

SENIORS

Aging and Independent Services, a County of San Diego department (858/560-2500 or 800/510-2020), offers information for seniors on health and welfare resources, as well as transportation and leisure opportunities. San Diego public transportation is offered to senior citizens 60 years and older at a reduced rate (75 cents) with a transit ID card, available for $2.50 at the Transit Store (102 Broadway, downtown; 619/234-1060; map:N7).

PEOPLE WITH DISABILITIES

Accessible San Diego (858/279-0704) is a nonprofit information center for people with disabilities traveling or living in San Diego. This group provides a wealth of information, from restaurants that provide menus in Braille to which tour operators can accommodate a wheelchair. It also provides a calendar of events. Check out their Web site at www.accessandiego.com. For information on public transportation, call the Metro Info line at 619/233-3004 (TTY-TDD 619/234-5005).

PHONE ALERT

San Diego's far-ranging 619 area code is a thing of the past. Calls from downtown to La Jolla, for example, are no longer free. Instead, Pacific Bell has divided the county into four districts; the central portion of the city retaining the 619 code is the smallest of the lot. In June 1999, the area code for parts of central San Diego (including some parts of Pacific Beach), La Jolla, Del Mar, and adjacent inland communities changed to 858. After a six-month introduction period, the new area code becomes mandatory. In June 2000, Coronado, Imperial Beach, and much of East and South Counties will take on the 935 area code, mandatory in December 2000. Another code, 760, is currently in effect through much of the inland county.   —*Maribeth Mellin*

WOMEN

San Diego is safer than most cities its size, though of course women should use the same precautions they would anywhere. For health and reproductive services call Planned Parenthood at 619/683-7526. The Rape Crisis Hotline is at 858/272-1767.

PET OWNERS

Dogs are pampered nearly as much as kids in this outdoor-oriented community. They're even invited to afternoon tea at the U. S. Grant Hotel (see "Doggie Dining" in the Restaurants chapter). Beach dogs tend to sport bandannas and carry Frisbees in their mouths; the annual Frisbee-catching contest (see Calendar of Events in this chapter) is as competitive as any major sport. Dog owners have become far more responsible about cleaning up after their pets; plastic bags and pooper-scoopers are essential accouterments when walking your pet along neighborhood sidewalks. Here are San Diego's off-leash areas:

DOG BEACH at Ocean Beach, next to the jetty.

FIESTA ISLAND at Mission Bay.

the westernmost section of the **CITY BEACH** in Coronado.

DEL MAR (Camino del Mar at 29th St), but only September through June.

MORLEY FIELD DOG PARK, at Balboa Park behind the tennis club.

GAYS AND LESBIANS

San Diego's gay community has evolved into a visible part of the civic scene; there is even a lesbian county supervisor (unheard of a decade ago). The gay scene is centered around Hillcrest, with a plethora of gay-focused bars, clubs, bookshops, and cafes. The *Gay and Lesbian Times*, a weekly newspaper, is distributed on Fridays and available free at most coffee shops and bookstores. The Greater San Diego Business Association

IN THE BEGINNING

Juan Rodríguez Cabrillo, a Portuguese explorer in the employ of Spain, discovered San Diego Bay in 1542. Cabrillo sailed on north, leaving the indigenous **La Jolla and Kumeyaay Indians** alone in their warm, food-rich home. The La Jolla peoples stuck close to the coast in small settlements. Discarded shells and fish bones, some still visible today as white layers in the crumbling cliff edges of Point Loma, Pacific Beach, La Jolla, and Del Mar, attest to these early residents' bountiful harvests from the sea and coastal marshes. The Kumeyaay, who began forcing the La Jollans out as the dominant populace around 1000 B.C., arrived from the Colorado River region to hunt deer, harvest acorns, and spend summers at cooler elevations in the mountain ranges 50 miles from the coast. Their grinding rocks can still be found beside most shady San Diego County streams wherever oak trees spread their limbs in neighboring groves.

Everything changed when the Spaniards settled in with great determination after 1769, giving San Diego its own equivalent of Plymouth Rock, now lying beneath earthen mounds on Presidio Hill above Mission Valley. The ruins of the first European garrison and settlement in California sit atop grassy hills beside the Junipero Serra Museum (2727 Presidio Dr, Old Town; 619/297-3258). Father Junipero Serra established the first California mission, **Basilica San Diego de Alcalá**, on the hill in 1769. The soldiers and missionaries brought new agricultural methods and beliefs to the region, as well as deadly European diseases that killed many of the Indians. The padres moved the mission away from the coast in 1774 to place it closer to the freshwater rivers in Mission Valley, where the **Mission Basilica San Diego de Alcalá** (10818 San Diego Mission Rd, Mission Valley; 619/281-8449) now stands.

The original, presidio-protected settlement gradually expanded down the hill into what today is called **Old Town**. San Diego was still considered a part of Mexico, and when Mexico won its independence from Spain in 1821, the Spanish influence began to dwindle. The Mexican flag rose over the Presidio, and a new system of enormous, 10,000-acre-plus ranchos took hold to encourage colonization. The ranch owners were called the Silver Dons (for their silver-decorated saddles), and a Mexican-European *Californio* culture took hold. The Dons lived lavishly and raised large, extended families in grand sprawling houses made of sun-hardened adobe walls roofed with tile. The Californios' forte was cattle ranching, and the sweet grasses of San Diego's valleys and nearby mountains became some of the most productive lands for raising beef cattle in the world. A hide trade flourished, with Yankee trading ships arriving regularly from around Cape Horn, a journey immortalized in Richard Henry Dana's sensational account of an 1834 voyage, *Two Years Before The Mast*.

During the Mexican-American War in 1846, Californio forces—mounted vaqueros armed with lances—easily trapped the 300-strong "American Army of the West," led by General Stephen Kearny, at a site in the San Pasqual Valley. Kearny's force had left Fort Leavenworth, Kansas, only six months before on foot and horseback and were now exhausted. With many unable to fire their guns because of damp gunpowder, 18 of the weary Yankees died on the ends of long lances. But victory was brief for the Californios. In San Diego, American warships held the harbor. A new Yankee fort was erected above Old Town. Other settlements up north were also besieged, and California fell from Mexican hands in 1847.　　　　　　　　　　　　　　　　　　　*—Peter Jensen*

(3737 5th Ave, Ste 207, downtown; 619/296-4543; www.gsdba.org; map:N3) provides a business directory, and a calendar of events that include gay-oriented establishments and activities. The Lesbian and Gay Men's Community Center (3916 Normal St, North Park; 619/692-2077; map:P2) sponsors nightly activities as well as discussion and support groups. One of the largest selections of gay and lesbian books and magazines can be found at Obelisk Books (1029 University Ave, Hillcrest; 619/297-4171; map:O2).

FOREIGN VISITORS

Since few international flights land in San Diego—only a few from Mexico and one daily flight from London—most foreign visitors arrive in Southern California via Los Angeles. For foreign currency exchange, try Travelex America at the airport (Terminal 1, lower level; 619/295-1501), or the Thomas Cook Foreign Exchange office downtown in Horton Plaza (800/287-7362; map:N7). The International Visitors Center (11 Horton Plaza at 1st Ave and F St, downtown; 619/236-1212; map:N7) is well staffed with bilingual clerks and can contact translators for most languages. Most foreign consulates are located in Los Angeles; the only full consulate in San Diego is the Consulate General de Mexico (1549 India St, downtown; 619/231-8414; map:M7).

WEB INFORMATION

San Diego is well connected and represented on the Internet, with Web sites for many local businesses and attractions. The City of San Diego's site is www.sannet.gov. The San Diego Convention & Visitors Bureau maintains a site at www.sandiego.org. Other helpful sites are:

WWW.SIGNONSANDIEGO.COM (Union-Tribune Publishing)
WWW.SDREADER.COM (The Reader)
WWW.SANDIEGO-ONLINE.COM (San Diego Magazine)
WWW.UCSD.EDU/ (University of California at San Diego)
WWW.SDSU.EDU/ (San Diego State University)

11

Calendar of Events

JANUARY

PENGUIN DAY SKI FEST / De Anza Cove, De Anza Bay Dr off N Mission Bay Dr, Mission Bay; 619/270-0840 Water-skiers sans wet suits earn Penguin patches during the ultimate New Year's Day hangover cure—a bracing race through 50-degree water at 9am.

FEBRUARY

WILDFLOWERS BLOOM IN THE DESERT / Anza-Borrego Desert State Park, Borrego Springs; 760/767-4684 (24-hour information line) or 760/767-4205 Winter rains bring spring blooms to desert wildflowers and cacti starting in late February and usually lasting into April. The flowers attract hordes of people, especially when the blossoms are most abundant. Call in advance to find out what's blooming.

CHINESE NEW YEAR / 3rd Ave and J St, Downtown; 619/234-4447 Held in February or March (depending on the lunar calendar), the annual celebration includes martial arts performances, cooking demonstrations, lion dancers, and plenty of firecrackers jangling the nerves.

MARCH

CARLSBAD FLOWER FIELDS / I-5 at Palomar Airport Rd, Carlsbad; 760/431-0352 Starting in early March, thousands of ranunculus flowers stripe hillsides with red, yellow, and white blossoms at Carlsbad Ranch. Tour the fields on foot or in a vintage biplane; bring plenty of film.

OCEAN BEACH KITE FESTIVAL / 4726 Santa Monica Ave, Ocean Beach; (619)224-0189 Schoolkids and amateur kite makers gather at the Ocean Beach Recreation Center before parading to the beach, kites in tow, for awards ceremonies, concerts, and the inevitable tangled strings. Particularly impressive when viewed from the OB Pier.

ST. PATRICK'S DAY PARADE / From 6th Ave and Juniper Street to 5th Avenue and Upas Street, ending at 6th Avenue and Laurel Street, Downtown; 619/298-9111 or 619/299-7812 You don't have to be Irish to wear the green and join in the merriment at this annual bash, which ends on the lawns of Balboa Park amid revelers quaffing green beer.

SAN DIEGO CREW CLASSIC / Crown Point Shores, Mission Bay; 858/488-0700 University alumni groups and international fans stake out picnic spots along Mission Bay to watch more than 3,000 rowers from Europe, the United States, and Canada compete while Navy parachutists sail overhead.

APRIL

LA JOLLA EASTER HAT SIDEWALK PROMENADE / Prospect St and Herschel Ave, La Jolla; 858/454-2600 Proper La Jollans don fancy chapeaus covered in tulips and daffodils, baby bonnets with bunnies, and outrageous headgear to compete for prizes and attention at this lighthearted gathering.

CORONADO FLOWER SHOW WEEKEND / Spreckles Park, 601 Orange Ave, Coronado; 619/437-8788 One of the West Coast's largest tent-covered flower shows takes place in mid-April in the gardenlike setting of Coronado, where neighbors try to outdo each other with front-yard beds of delphiniums, larkspur, and hollyhocks beside rose-laden trellises. At the show, horticulturists and floral designers display perfect blossoms in arrangements both gorgeous and amusing.

EARTH DAY / 2125 Park Blvd, Balboa Park, Downtown; 619/496-6666 All things natural are celebrated all over San Diego on Earth Day; the biggest gathering is at Balboa Park, where exhibits, children's craft demonstrations, and bundles of info on recycling and protecting the environment attract thousands of nature lovers.

ARTWALK FESTIVAL / Throughout Downtown; 619/615-1090 Artists open their studios, galleries expand their collections, and performance artists stage their most outrageous works on the sidewalks. Self-guided tours and maps are provided at all participating businesses, and restaurants get in the act with specials and sidewalk stands.

DAY AT THE DOCKS / San Diego Sportfishing Landing, Harbor Dr and Scott St, Point Loma; 800/944-FISH Anglers practice their casts, kids fish for free, vendors hawk the latest lures, and sunglass vendors do a booming business at the dock in Point Loma, where four sportfishing landings and two excellent seafood restaurants attract crowds throughout the year. www.sportfishing.org

ART ALIVE / San Diego Museum of Art, 2125 Park Blvd, Balboa Park, Downtown; 619/232-7931 Floral artists re-create the museum's collection with whimsical or literal interpretations; the ikebana arrangements are particularly intriguing. The floral portraits fill galleries for four days as docents adapt their descriptions and lecturers expound on the links between nature and the arts.

MAY

CINCO DE MAYO / Throughout Old Town; 619/296-3161 or 619/220-5422 Mexico commemorates an 1862 victory over French invaders on May 5; San Diegans use the date as an excuse to party hearty with tacos, tequila, cervezas, and margaritas. Old Town's festivities are a bit more subdued than those at local bars; count on hearing excellent mariachis and sampling Mexican delicacies throughout the area. Mexican musicians, folk dancers, and artists provide an endless fiesta in Bazaar del Mundo.

ROCK 'N' ROLL MARATHON / Route goes from 6th Ave at Balboa Park along Hwy 163 to Friars Rd and west to Mission Bay, Downtown; 619/450-6510 There are dozens of marathons in San Diego each year, but this 26.2-mile race brings much of the city to a grinding halt as bands perform along the route and celebrations last for two days at Mission Bay.

ETHNIC FOOD FAIR / House of Pacific Relations International Cottages, 2125 Park Blvd, Balboa Park, Downtown; 619/234-0736 or 619/239-0512 Music and food from 30 nations draw San Diegans of every ethnic persuasion to this oft-overlooked section of the park. The aromas of Portuguese sausage, Swedish cookies, Chinese dim sum, and pad thai lure museum visitors onto crowded lawns, where amateur linguists have a field day figuring out tongues.

CANINE FRISBEE CHAMPIONSHIPS / War Memorial Lawn, 3325 Zoo Dr, Balboa Park, Downtown; 619/573-1392 Shepherds, collies, Jack Russells, and motley mutts leap in the air when their masters spin Frisbees and call their names. The dogs put on a spectacular show; the owners are pretty funny as well. The 1999 event was the 25th anniversary—some '70s fads have endured.

JUNE

INDIAN FAIR / Museum of Man, 2125 Park Blvd, Balboa Park, Downtown; 619/239-2001 Native American tribes from throughout the Southwest gather at the museum for a weekend of tribal dances, art exhibits, and plenty of down-home cooking.

OB STREET FAIR / Newport Ave, Ocean Beach; 619/226-2193 Pull on your tie-dyed T-shirt and straw hat and wander among the holdout hippies selling crystals, incense, Balinese sundresses, and wind chimes. A special area features kids' rides and games; bands perform on several stages throughout the day. A chili cook-off spices up the scene, and food stalls sell everything from rice and veggie bowls to hot dogs and perfectly greasy burgers.

DEL MAR FAIR / 2260 Jimmy Durante Blvd, Del Mar Fairgrounds, Del Mar; 858/755-1161; 24-hour hot line 858/793-5555 This San Diego County fair is one of the largest in California and a source of ongoing amusement for locals. In addition to acres of hobby shows, food booths, and 4-H exhibits, concerts are held at the racetrack, featuring top-name rock, country, and Latin performers.

TWILIGHT IN THE PARK / Spreckels Organ Pavilion, 1549 El Prado, Balboa Park, Downtown; 619/239-0512 Evening band and choral concerts are held Tuesday through Thursday in one of the loveliest settings in town; if you can't find a seat, spread a blanket on one of the nearby lawns.

JULY

CORONADO INDEPENDENCE DAY CELEBRATION / Orange Ave, Spreckels Park, and Glorietta Bay, Coronado; 619/437-8788 Spread over one or two days, Coronado's July 4th festivities include an impressive parade with military vehicles of every imaginable sort, plus all the bands, horses, and antique cars you'd ever want to see. The Navy (which has a huge presence on the island) puts on an astonishing air and sea demonstration at the bay; a concert is held in Spreckels Park at 4pm; and fireworks explode over the bay at dark. If the 4th falls on a Sunday, the parade is held the next day.

OVER THE LINE TOURNAMENT / Fiesta Island, Mission Bay; 619/688-0817 A truly bizarre gathering for fans of bawdy revelry takes place in early July at Fiesta Island. Three-member quasi-softball teams (most bearing off-color names) eschew running bases and simply hit balls over a line; the opposing team must catch the ball while it's in flight for an "out." Hundreds of teams compete wearing next to nothing—or even in their birthday suits—while scantily clad onlookers wander about.

DEL MAR RACING SEASON / 2260 Jimmy Durante Blvd, Del Mar Fairgrounds, Del Mar; 858/755-1161 or 858/792-4242 Thoroughbreds race six days a week; opening day is like a coming-out party for local denizens and race fans. Bring a lawn chair and sit on the lawn inside the track for a more casual perspective.

LESBIAN & GAY PRIDE PARADE / University and 6th Aves, Hillcrest; 619/297-7683 Closets crack open for this ever-expanding celebration in conservative San Diego's gay enclave of Hillcrest. Though not as flamboyant as similar events in Los Angeles or San Francisco, the parade and the subsequent festival at Marston Point in Balboa Park are heartfelt, amusing, and occasionally outrageous.

U.S. OPEN SAND CASTLE COMPETITION / Imperial Beach Pier in the 900 block of Seacoast Drive, Imperial Beach; 619/424-6663 Forget your typical towers; these castles rise 4 feet high and come replete with sea dragons and moats. The three-day celebration includes a Sand Castle Ball on Friday night, a parade and fireworks on Saturday, and judging of the engineering marvels on Sunday.

GRUNION FESTIVAL / Crystal Pier, Ocean Blvd and Garnet Ave, Pacific Beach; 858/274-1326 Slippery, silvery grunion flip-flop on the sand late at night, following an internal calendar that has endured ever since local Indians lived simply along coastal coves. Grunion hunters armed with buckets and flashlights take great delight in chasing the tiny fish under the moonlight. The daytime festival includes performances by Native American dancers and musicians relating native lore about the tenacious grunion.

MIRAMAR AIR SHOW / Between the I-5 and I-15 freeways, Miramar; 619/537-1000 The Blue Angels rattle windows throughout the county when they perform in this wildly popular air show at the Marine Corps Air Station. Aerial acrobatics thrill ticket holders baking in the sun; wise locals park along nearby streets, crank on the AC, and angle their necks out sunroofs to catch the fly boys in action.

AUGUST

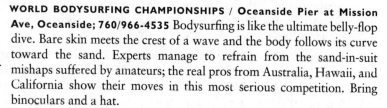

WORLD BODYSURFING CHAMPIONSHIPS / Oceanside Pier at Mission Ave, Oceanside; 760/966-4535 Bodysurfing is like the ultimate belly-flop dive. Bare skin meets the crest of a wave and the body follows its curve toward the sand. Experts manage to refrain from the sand-in-suit mishaps suffered by amateurs; the real pros from Australia, Hawaii, and California show their moves in this most serious competition. Bring binoculars and a hat.

SEPTEMBER

SAN DIEGO STREET SCENE / Gaslamp Quarter, Downtown; 619/557-0505 Top-name zydeco, blues, jazz, and country musicians perform on stages throughout the Quarter on an early September weekend. Food stands match the many musical moods with everything from double espresso to Cajun spice. The crowds are enormous; park away from downtown and take the trolley.

ADAMS AVENUE STREET FAIR / Adams Ave between 32nd and 35th Sts, Kensington; 619/282-7329 This oft-overlooked urban neighborhood party (see Kensington/Adams Avenue in the Exploring chapter) attracts grassroots circuses, mimes, and folksingers to its sidewalks in late September, when quirky antique shops and book stores move their wares to the street amid carnival rides and ethnic food stands.

CABRILLO FESTIVAL / Cabrillo National Monument at the end of Cabrillo Memorial Dr, Point Loma; 619/557-5450 Juan Rodríguez Cabrillo sailed into San Diego Bay in 1542; his arrival is reenacted annually at Cabrillo Monument with a performer in period costume.

OCTOBER

ZOO FOUNDER'S DAY / San Diego Zoo, 2920 Zoo Dr, Balboa Park, Downtown; 619/234-3153 Only the foolhardy show up to see the animals and brave the crowds on October 4, when admission is free to all in honor of Dr. Harry Wegeforth, who founded the zoo in 1916. Still, it's great fun for locals to reclaim the park for a day without forking out the big bucks.

HARVEST FESTIVAL / Community Concourse, 202 C St, Downtown; 619/615-4100 Artisans from throughout the United States have packed downtown's old convention center in mid-October for years, offering a massive array of tempting handcrafted holiday gifts.

UNDERWATER PUMPKIN CARVING CONTEST / 8200 Camino del Oro, La Jolla Shores; 858/565-6054 Scuba divers feed seed and pulp to the fish as they carve Halloween pumpkins underwater. Crowds gather to enjoy the sun and wait for a glimpse of the divers who pop up every so often to show off their pumpkins. Creations are later displayed on the beach—the results are truly surreal.

NOVEMBER

THANKSGIVING DIXIELAND JAZZ FESTIVAL / Town & Country Hotel, 500 Hotel Circle N, Mission Valley; 619/297-5277 Big bands from the United States and Canada set toes a tappin' with a brassy noise that reverberates in the hotel's ballroom.

DECEMBER

CHRISTMAS ON THE PRADO / 2125 Park Blvd, Balboa Park, Downtown; 619/239-0512 The holidays begin with this early December celebration throughout the park. Lights twinkle on trees, Christmas carols fill the air, and ethnic groups prepare their favorite seasonal treats. Don't miss this one.

OLD TOWN'S LAS POSADAS / Procession from Heritage Park (Juan St at Harney St) to Old Town State Park (San Diego Ave at Twiggs St), Old Town; 619/297-1183 In Mexico, Mary and Joseph's search for a manger is reenacted with candlelight processions from home to home; hosts provide food and drink, but no shelter. The tradition is replicated in Old Town's lovely annual event, as San Diegans carry candles past businesses and historic houses to the center of the park, where a giant piñata bursts with candies.

MISSION BAY BOAT PARADE OF LIGHTS / Quivera Basin to Crown Point, Mission Bay; 619/488-8788 Locals lay claim to fire rings on Fiesta Island and at Crown Point by dawn, though the flotilla of decorated boats doesn't begin chugging through the bay till twilight. Onlookers huddle in blankets on shore (many a bonfire is crashed) as boaters party, wave, and broadcast holiday carols from loudspeakers.

SAN DIEGO HARBOR PARADE OF LIGHTS / Shelter Island, Harbor Island, Seaport Village, and Coronado Usually held the second weekend in December, this more elaborate version of the Mission Bay Parade includes tugboats, Navy and Coast Guard vessels, and a motley crew of boats in full regalia. The rowboats and kayaks are always amusing.

LAY OF THE CITY

LAY OF THE CITY

Orientation

Desert, mountains, canyons, and mesas shape San Diego's landscape and character. Don't be fooled by tropical palms and birds-of-paradise; this place is dry, dry, dry, and a major drain on the distant Colorado River and Northern California. Fresh water is sometimes so precious that people are cautioned against irrigating gardens or flushing toilets, and rainstorms bring transplanted residents outdoors to celebrate moist air and damp earth. Most times, the wind is scented with salt and suntan oil. Transplants bemoan the lack of seasons in this idyllic and idiosyncratic climate. It takes years to catch on to the subtle changes. Summer begins with the dreaded June Gloom, gray low-lying clouds that block out the sun till noon. The ocean doesn't get tolerably warm until August—at least for those who won't dabble a toe in the water until it hits 68 degrees. In fact, beach devotees are fond of September, when the water reaches its warmest and the summer hordes have left the sand to its natural beauty. Fall is heralded by mystical Santa Ana winds, so hot and dry and swift they topple power lines and crack sensitive lips.

Locals are always surprised when they have to ignite gas pilots on their wall heaters in November and are horrified when the thermometer dips into the 50s around January. We actually do have a winter, marked by days of chilly rain, fog, and floods. February brings snow to the **LAGUNA MOUNTAINS** 50 miles east of downtown, while wildflowers and cacti burst into bloom in the desert. Then comes spring, full of blue skies and the fragrance of orange blossoms and night-blooming jasmine. Yes, we do have seasons, though our median temperature is a steady 72 degrees.

San Deigns live in clusters of microclimates (a favorite term among bored weather announcers). **SAN DIEGO BAY** casts a coastal coolness over downtown, where the **EMBARCADERO** (Harbor Dr and Grape St, downtown; map:M6) serves as host to massive cruise ships, navy freighters, and all manner of watercraft. The waterfront sidewalk runs south from the tall-sailed *Star of India* to the Cruise Ship Pier and **SEAPORT VILLAGE**, a treasure trove for tourists and entrepreneurs. Next, after a series of high-rise hotels, is the San Diego Convention Center, topped with white sails. Built with considerable expense and heated debate, the Convention Center shifted the focus of downtown to the waterfront. Its success and current expansion have changed downtown forever.

The financial, legal, and civic center of downtown lies along Broadway, where a series of 1980s office towers and hotels lead to **HORTON PLAZA**, a phantasmagoric (some say garish) shopping mall. East of the plaza, the historic **GASLAMP QUARTER** runs along Fourth and Fifth Avenues back toward the waterfront. Much of San Diego's history lies in this once-derelict neighborhood, where 19th-century Victorian mansions and erstwhile clapboard brothels now house offices, cafes, and hotels.

The **SAN DIEGO–CORONADO BRIDGE** spans the bay, connecting the south side of downtown to the picture-perfect city of Coronado. Steep

HOW TO PASS FOR A LOCAL

A San Diego native is a rare gem indeed; it seems everyone has moved here from somewhere else. The U.S. Navy and Marines have done their part to swell the population, as have émigrés from Portugal, France, Vietnam, Laos, Cambodia, Mexico, Brazil, and Guatemala. On the surface, the city looks pure WASP. But its food, music, and culture are so much of a melting pot, locals hardly notice outside influence. It's easy to blend in if you use the right mix of style and flexibility.

The Look: Casual and trendy, with lots of bare skin. No cutoff jeans or garish Aloha shirts (collared shirts with muted fish themes are fine). Thongs (a.k.a. flip-flops) or running shoes. No socks. Polarized sunglasses in every imaginable shape (keep the cartoon characters on the kids). Baseball caps and hats with enormous straw brims.

The Lingo: Many San Diegans speak Spanglish, a mix of Spanish and English that comes naturally after you've been here a few years. Gracias (thank you), hasta luego (see you later), adiós (good-bye), and cerveza (beer) are all part of the local tongue. Surf slang sprinkles beach and all other talk. Waves are gnarly and form tubes at their crest; on a nice day everybody "shines on" all practical tasks.

The Attitude: Yes, we're a laid-back, fun-loving lot, but we're also quite driven in a round-about way. Scholars, scientists, researchers, writers, and actors all behave as if they're in a mini LA, striving for great achievements while jogging at Mission Bay. Conservatives reign on talk radio; salutes are common in many parts of town. The flag is treated with respect. And despite San Diego's mellow image, many locals are ruthless drivers. Study your maps.

The Snacks: Ketchup ranks second to salsa on most kitchen tables, and guacamole and corn chips are far more common than potato chips and dip. Sushi and fish tacos are served at the ballpark. Everyone carries a water bottle nearly everywhere.

The Wheels: Skateboards are ubiquitous on beach city streets; unfortunately, they also rumble along sidewalks and occasionally lash out at pedestrians. Beach cruiser bikes with fat tires have surfboard clamps on their frames; bike helmets are the law. The resurgence of convertibles makes sun lovers crave new cars, though you'll see plenty of old VW buses with custom paint jobs. "Suburban Assault Vehicles" (or S.U.V.s to those of you who drive them) are as common as Mercedes coupes. Blessed are those who live in pedestrian-friendly neighborhoods. —*Mollie Glasser* hills climb east to Mission Hills and Hillcrest, both chic and trendy neighborhoods. Train and trolley tracks, freeways and side streets head north to Old Town, where Spanish soldiers and missionaries were once garrisoned in the late 1700s on Presidio Hill overlooking the San Diego River and Mission Valley.

Beach towns line the coast north of downtown, starting with the promontory at **POINT LOMA** through **OCEAN BEACH, MISSION BEACH,** and **PACIFIC BEACH**: three funky communities with individual quirks. **LA JOLLA** goes the opposite direction attitudinally, with the class and cultured air of a Mediterranean coast town. **DEL MAR** marks the beginning of the North Coast, a lineup of small towns and burgeoning cities that runs into Camp Pendleton Marine Base, a natural greenbelt between San Diego and Orange Counties.

Though it seems coastal San Diego could easily tip into the ocean under the weight of its popularity (a few natural earthquake-inclined faults in the area make this possibility not so far-fetched), plenty of San Diegans are lured inland by clean, dry air, a bit of a break on real estate, and a topography laced with boulder-strewn mountains and fishing lakes. All locals take pride in the proximity of the piney Cuyamaca and Laguna Mountains and seemingly endless desert; many of them head east to witness meteor showers and snow.

San Diego's southern border is its most controversial. An invisible line stretches east from the ocean to the desert, separating what once was called Alta (higher) California from Baja (lower) California in Mexico. Said to be the busiest border crossing in the world, the line between San Diego and **TIJUANA** is blurred in many ways. Commuters pass back and forth, families visit relatives, shoppers search for bargains on both sides of the border, and San Diegans think nothing of driving down Baja to Tijuana, Rosarito, and Ensenada on day and overnight escapes.

Visitor Information

San Diego can be downright confusing if you wander off the beaten track—which you undoubtedly will, since exploring is what a visit to this city is all about. If you're staying downtown, start your visit at the **SAN DIEGO CONVENTION AND VISITORS BUREAU** (1st Ave and F St, downtown; 619/232-3101; www.sandiego.org; map:N7) storefront office adjacent to Horton Plaza. It's open for tickets and general information Monday through Saturday from 8:30am to 5pm, Sundays 1–5pm in June, July, and August. The bureau has an impressive array of multilingual personnel, though how multi depends on who's on duty that day. If you're staying near the Convention Center, stop at the **INTERNATIONAL INFORMATION CENTER** (170 6th Ave at L St, downtown; 619/232-8583;

map:N8) open Tuesday through Saturday 10am to 5pm, closed Sunday and Monday, for tickets to local attractions, reservations, and referral services. Call ahead for bilingual assistance. If you're wandering the beach areas, stop by the **SAN DIEGO VISITOR INFORMATION CENTER** (2688 East Mission Bay Dr, Mission Bay; 619/276-8200; map:KK6); open 9am to dusk daily. The center sits on a slight hill by the Interstate 5 Mission Bay exit; plenty of parking is usually available (even for RVs), and the playground and picnic tables are perfect spots for reviewing your brochures.

Getting Around

BY BUS

San Diego has an excellent bus system running through the city and county. Granted, it can take hours to get where you're going, but at least you're not dodging freeway traffic. **THE SAN DIEGO TRANSIT COMPANY** (619/233-3004 or www.sdcommute.com for bus route information) operates the **TRANSIT STORE** (102 Broadway, downtown; 619/234-1060; map:N7), open 8:30am to 5pm Monday through Friday and 12–4pm Saturday and Sunday. Here you'll find a wealth of information on any and all public transportation from the border through North and East Counties. Also available are discounted frequent-rider coupons, bus passes, and route maps. Bus fare is $1.75 or 75 cents for seniors; children under 5 ride free; on weekends children 6 to 18 ride free with one paid adult fare. A one-day pass for all buses and trolleys is $5; two-day is $8; three-day is $10; four-day is $12. All San Diego buses are wheelchair accessible; routes number 1 to 299 and all 900-numbered routes have bike racks. Bus stops are marked with a blue-and-white sign designating which routes they serve. For bus tours, see "Guided Tours" in the Exploring chapter.

BY TROLLEY

The bright red electric **SAN DIEGO TROLLEY** (619/595-4949; fares and schedule information also available at the Transit Store, see By Bus, above) has become a model for transit systems worldwide. The first route ran from downtown San Diego to the border with Mexico. Additional routes now run to various points in downtown, Old Town, Mission Valley, Qualcomm Stadium, and East County. Fares range from $1 to $2.25, bicycles are an additional 50 cents and require a permit, available at the Transit Store. Unlimited trolley passes for one month are $50 and $25 for just the downtown area. Ticket machines for trolley tickets are available at all stops. On board, trolley cops check for tickets; a passenger sans ticket will pay a fine.

BY CAR

California and cars are synonymous; without wheels you're not really taking in the whole experience. You needn't have a car for your whole stay, but will likely wish you had one for at least a couple of days. Most of the major **RENTAL CAR COMPANIES** have courtesy shuttle buses that will take you from the San Diego Airport to their locations. Alamo (800/327-9633), Avis (800/831-2847), Budget (800/527-0700), Hertz (800/654-3131), and National (800/227-7368) all have offices throughout the city. **AAA SOUTHERN CALIFORNIA** (815 Date St, downtown; 619/233-1000, 800/400-4222 for roadside assistance, 800/222-5000 for travel services; map:O6) has excellent **ROAD MAPS** available to members and can help plan your routes to outlying areas. Locals rely on Thomas Brothers Maps (800/899-6277; www.thomas.com) to find beach streets and the new communities that sprout about the county like crabgrass.

PARKING is relatively easy downtown except during special events. Public lots charge $5–$10 a day, depending on location; those closest to Horton Plaza, Seaport Village, the Gaslamp Quarter, and the Embarcadero tend to be expensive (though some honor validation). Side streets are cheaper—try Ash and B Streets and J through L Streets. Parking meters cost 25 cents per 15 minutes, with a two-hour limit. You must move your car after two hours or risk getting a ticket.

Beach parking is another story. There are free parking lots along W Mission Bay Drive and at Belmont Park, but lucky is the fellow who grabs a spot after 10am on a sunny summer Sunday. All the main beaches have free lots—cruising around for a space will afford you the time to check out the surfers and families. Neighborhood side streets are a good bet, as long as you arrive early. If you're unlucky enough to return and find no car, begin by calling the San Diego Police Department's **AUTO IMPOUND** (619/531-2844) to see if it has been impounded or towed. Car theft, alas, is relatively common in San Diego, as are car break-ins. Take your valuables with you. Report stolen cars at 619/531-2000.

BY TAXI

Here's the deal: Cab drivers have to cover significant distance to get you from downtown to the beach. The fare from the airport to downtown is $7 to $10; from downtown to Ocean Beach, $12 to $15; and $30 to $40 from downtown to La Jolla. Cabs are metered; rates range from $1.40 to $1.90 per mile. Local companies include Yellow Cab (619/234-6161), San Diego Cab (619/226-8294), and Direct Ride (619/281-4686).

BY BICYCLE

Bikes are the perfect touring vehicle within parts of San Diego, including Coronado, Mission Bay, Shelter and Harbor Islands, and the beaches. Bike rentals are available at all these locations. For suggestions on scenic bike circuits, see the Recreation chapter. Biking downtown is not enjoyable on weekdays, but can be great fun on a Sunday morning. *A Map of Bike Routes in San Diego County* is available from **CALTRANS** (2829 Juan St, Old Town; 619/688-6785; map:I1) Monday through Friday from 8am to 5pm. Bike Tours of San Diego (509 5th Ave, downtown; 619/238-2444; map:N8) delivers rental bikes; daily rates are $15. Open 8am to 7pm daily. Call 619/231-BIKE for locker information. **BIKE RACKS** are available at tourist attractions, the Convention Center, and in beach parking lots. Use a good lock. **TO RENT A BIKE** try Hamel's (704 Ventura Pl; 858/488-5050; map:LL7) near the boardwalk in Mission Beach or Play It Again Sports (1401 Garnet Ave; 858/490-0222; map:KK7) in Pacific Beach. For descriptions and pointers on particularly pleasant trails, see the Recreation chapter.

BY FERRY

Until the San Diego-Coronado Bridge opened in 1969, ferries were the only transport between the island (actually it's an isthmus) and downtown. Ferry service was suspended for nearly two decades until the bridge debt was paid off. Service was reinstated in the late 1980s, much to the delight of islanders and sightseers. **THE SAN DIEGO–CORONADO BAY FERRY** (San Diego Harbor Excursions; 619/234-4111) departs from the Broadway Pier downtown daily on the hour from 9am to 9pm Sunday through Thursday, and 9am to 10pm on Friday and Saturday. The ferry departs Ferry Landing on First Street in Coronado on the half hour from 9:30 am to 9:30pm Sunday through Thursday, and 9:30 am to 10:30pm Friday and Saturday. The fare is $2 each way; bicycles are an additional 50 cents. Bike rentals are available at the Coronado Ferry Landing, as are public buses.

Essentials

PUBLIC REST ROOMS

Public rest rooms are available downtown at Horton Plaza, Seaport Village, and the Embarcadero. Government buildings are a good choice as well. In many park and beach facilities, the doors have been removed from the stalls and the toilets are chilly metal contraptions. The rest rooms are usually clean, except for the sand, grass, and dirt tracked on the floors; some, such as those at La Jolla Cove, have showers and dressing areas.

MAJOR BANKS

ATMs are as abundant as parking meters throughout San Diego, though neighborhood banks still have friendly tellers who know their customers. Currency exchange is not available at all branches; a Thomas Cook office

PLACES OF WORSHIP

Though it often seems that San Diego's main place of worship is the beach, those in search of more conventional religious environs can find everything under the sun. Padre Junípero Serra's first mission, **Mission Basilica San Diego de Alcalá** (10818 San Diego Mission Rd, Mission Valley; 619/283-7319), established in 1769, continues to hold mass each day in the simple wooden chapel. **Mary Star of the Sea** (7727 Girard Ave, La Jolla; 858/454-2631) offers more elegant surroundings and is convenient to après-prayer shopping. The Jewish community gathers at the conservative **Congregation Beth El** (8660 Gilman Dr, La Jolla; 858/587-1967), and the reform temple **Congregation Beth Israel** (2512 3rd Ave, downtown; 619/239-0149). The **Cathedral Church of St. Paul** (2728 6th Ave, downtown; 619/298-7261) is an exquisite edifice for Episcopalians, with an exceptionally fine chorus. Methodists need look no further than the **United Methodist Church** (6063 La Jolla Blvd, La Jolla; 858/454-1418), a Mission-style conglomeration of buildings that also includes a former trolley depot, Mexican restaurant, and bar. The 1890 Victorian-Gothic **Graham Memorial Church** (975 C Ave, Coronado; 619/435-6860) was designed by architect James Reid, of Hotel del Coronado fame. The 10-foot gold-leaf statue of the angel Moroni and 10 alabaster spires rising from the blindingly white, temple of the **Church of Jesus Christ of Latter-Day Saints** (9527 La Jolla Farms Rd, La Jolla; 858/452-7256), are enough to hypnotize anyone off of the freeway and into the Mormon religion. The **Self-Realization Fellowship** (215 W K St, Encinitas; 760/753-2888), combining Eastern and Western teachings with enough meditation and Indian inferences to please any New Ager, shelters an ashram, hermitage, koi ponds, and ethereal gardens within a white-walled compound with golden lotus-flower spires. —*Marael Johnson*

(800/287-7362, in San Diego call 619/235-0901) downtown in Horton Plaza is open Monday through Friday from 10am to 6pm, Saturday from 10am to 4pm. For information on bank services and branches, call the downtown offices of Bank of America (450 B St; 619/452-8400; map:N7), Union Bank (1201 5th Ave; 619/230-4666; map:N7), Washington Mutual (101 W Broadway; 619/615-0600; map:N7), or Wells Fargo (401 B St; 619/699- 3070).

POLICE AND SAFETY

In serious, life-threatening emergencies, call 911. In non-emergency situations call the San Diego Police Department at 619/531-2000. San Diego is far safer than other cities of its size; with 1.2 million people (the county has 2.8 million residents), it's the sixth largest in the nation. But pickpockets, auto thieves, and threatening elements do exist, particularly downtown and in seedier parts of beach towns. Keep hold of your possessions when wandering about, and keep an eye on them at the beach. Don't put everything in your trunk at your parking space—that's way too enticing for petty thieves.

HOSPITAL AND MEDICAL/DENTAL SERVICES

World-class science and research centers have inspired renowned surgeons and physicians to settle in San Diego; as a result, San Diegans have an abundance of excellent medical facilities from which to choose. UCSD Medical Center (200 W Arbor Dr, Hillcrest; 619/543-8273 for physician referral or 619/543-6222 for general info; map:N1) is the teaching and research hospital for the University of Southern California at San Diego. Clinics in every imaginable specialty are available. Most area hospitals are part of a conglomerate, with branch hospitals and clinics around the county. The major chains are Sharp (Sharp Memorial Hospital, 7901 Frost St, Kearny Mesa; 858/541-3000; map:KK5) and Scripps (10666 North Torrey Pines Rd, La Jolla; 858-455-9100; map:II7). In non-emergency situations, call ahead to find out if your insurance is accepted. Kaiser (4647 Zion Ave, Mission Gorge; 619/528-5000; map:KK3) serves members from its nationwide program. Physician Finder (619/229-3333 or 858/483-7777) can help you find a specialist in your area. Dental Referral Service (800/511-8669) and Dental Referral Network (619/283-5644) can refer you to a local dentist.

POST OFFICE

San Diego's main U.S. Post Office (11251 Rancho Carmel Dr, Miramar; general information 800/275-8777 for all branches; map:GG3) is inconveniently located far from downtown. The neighborhood offices are much more accessible; some are open Saturdays. Send your postcards from any box on the street or the downtown branch (815 E St; map:O7); the large Midway office near Point Loma(2535 Midway Dr; map:H2), or Pacific Beach (4640 Cass St; map:KK7).

GROCERY STORES

The major chains in San Diego are Vons, Ralph's, and Lucky, with branches all over the county. Downtown, the only large-scale supermarket is Ralph's (101 G St; 619/595-1581; map:N8) near Horton Plaza, open 24 hours.

PHARMACIES

Several of the major chains in the area have toll-free numbers to help you locate the branch nearest you or one that's open 24 hours. Try Rite Aid (800/748-3243), Sav-On (888/443-5701), or Longs (800/TO-LONGS). Longs has a branch downtown in Horton Plaza (619/231-9135). Park Boulevard Pharmacy (3904 Park Blvd, Hillcrest; 619/295-3109; map:P2) has delivery service for most of the San Diego area.

DRY CLEANERS AND LAUNDROMATS

Many of the local hotels either offer room-service dry cleaning at a reasonable premium or will recommend one. Johnny Valet (945 Market St, downtown; 619/234-4200; map:O8) has pick-up and delivery within the downtown and neighboring areas and a two-day turnaround; they can also help with alterations or repairs. In the Mission Valley area, try Royal Touch Cleaners (4242 Camino Del Rio N; 619/624-0989; map:LL3) for pick-up service or alterations. Most laundromats are located within strip malls so you can run other errands while your laundry finishes. Take lots of quarters. Some have full-time attendants and offer a fluff-and-fold service. At the One Stop Laundry in Pacific Beach (4617 Cass St; 858/483-1344; map:KK7), you can have them do your laundry while you head across the street to the Cass Street Bar and Grill for a bite and a beer.

LEGAL SERVICES

The Attorney Referral Service of Consumer Attorneys of San Diego (800/660-2251) and the Lawyer Referral & Information Service (619/231-8585) offer a free initial consultation of up to 30 minutes and are non-profit services. Both have low-income programs available.

BUSINESS, COPY, AND MESSENGER SERVICES

Kinko's, that wonder of a 24-hour instant office, has 15 branches in neighborhoods and downtown. Three convenient locations are downtown (532 C St; 619/645-3300; map:N7), Pacific Beach (1934 Garnet Ave; 858/483-1852; map:KK7), and Mission Valley (7510 Hazard Center Dr; 619/294-3877; map:LL4). Storefronts offering mailing services are nearly as common as gas stations. Mail Boxes Etc. (501 W Broadway, downtown; 619/232-0332 or 800/789-4623; map:O7) has an automated locator to help find your nearest location. Postal Annex has roughly 35 outlets in the greater San Diego area. Convenient locations include downtown (660 K St, 619/231-6245; map:O8; and 1010 2nd Ave, 619/234-9997; map:N7), Pacific Beach (1666 Garnet Ave; 858/483-6001; map:KK7), and Mission Valley (7710 Hazard Center Dr; 619/295-8810; map:LL4). There are several messenger services available, including CMX (619/758-0555), Hesco (858/571-7395), and Messenger Express (858/550-1400).

PHOTOGRAPHY EQUIPMENT AND SERVICES

The best all-around shop for photographic supplies and high-level service is Nelson Photo Supplies (2909 India St, downtown; 619/234-6621; map:L4).They've been open since 1950, yet keep current on the latest equipment, as well as selling used equipment on consignment. The pros take their slide film to Chrome Photo Labs & Digital (2345 Kettner Blvd, downtown; 619/233-3456; map:M5); Gaslamp Photo (422 Market St, downtown; 619/696-8733; map:N8) is a favorite for one-hour film processing of color and black-and-white prints; and repairs are available at Professional Photographic Repair (7910 Raytheon Rd, Kearny Mesa; 619/277-3700; map:JJ5). And although it's out of the way, the competent staff of Kurt's Camera Repair (7811 Mission Gorge Rd, Ste P, Navajo; 619/286-1810; map:KK3) can usually find the fix when your camera refused to operate—and they're patient with novices, a real bonus.

COMPUTER REPAIRS AND RENTAL

Radio Shack advertises that it can fix anything no matter where you bought it. To find the location nearest you, call 1-800/THE-SHACK. Same day, on-site service is offered at many locations, but there are few in the immediate downtown area. Computer Care (3769 32nd St; 619/281-5551, Normal Heights; map:MM4) is near downtown and has some loaners available. Computer Clinic (9340 Carmel Mountain Rd, Poway; 858/484-7314; map:GG5) provides free pick-up and delivery. According to the Convention and Visitors Bureau, San Diego has upward of 1,000 conventions, trade shows, and the like each year. If you need to rent equipment, there are several companies that can help: try Computer Rentals by RBC (800/479-2000), Macrentals (800/756-6227), or Electro Rent (858/622-0065). If you can't resist checking out nifty computer shops, try Datel (4611 Mercury St, Kearny Mesa; 619/571-3100; map:JJ5).

PETS AND STRAY ANIMALS

Call San Diego Animal Control (619/236-4250) to report a lost pet or stray animal. The San Diego Humane Society (887 Sherman St, Bay Park; 619/299-7012; map:LL5) also gets a fair share of lost pets and has plenty of abandoned animals available for adoption. The VCA Emergency Animal Hospital and Referral Service (2317 Hotel Circle S, Mission Valley; 619/299-2400; map:K1) is centrally located in Mission Valley and has 24-hour service.

SPAS AND SALONS

Day spas and full-service salons abound in image-conscious San Diego. Some of the finest in convenient locations include Primo (500 Hotel Circle N; 619/220-0014; map:M1) in the Town & Country Hotel in Mission Valley; Aida Grey (7643 Girard Ave; 858/454-1660; map:JJ7) in La Jolla; Beauty Kliniek (3628 Governor Dr; 858/457-0191; map:JJ6) in the Golden Triangle; Ashe Walden (930 W Washington St; 619/295-7302; map:M2) in Mission Hills; and Details (4993 Niagra St; 619/222-6777; map:B3) in Ocean Beach.

Local Resources

NEWSPAPERS

San Diego has an appalling lack of local newspapers. **THE SAN DIEGO UNION-TRIBUNE** (350 Camino de la Reina, Mission Valley; 619/299-3131; map:LL5) once published two papers with separate editors and reporters—the *Union* in the morning, and the *Tribune* in the afternoon. Now the two have merged into one paper, with San Diego, North County, and East County editions. The *Union*'s Thursday Night & Day section is packed with reviews and listings up-to-date events listings. The **LOS ANGELES TIMES** (530 B St, #1820, downtown; 619/544-6001; map:N7) provided much-needed competition when it opened a San Diego bureau and local edition in the 1980s; today, San Diego is largely overlooked in the paper's coverage but many locals still subscribe for more thorough international reports. The free weekly **READER** (1703 India St, Middletown; 619/235-3000; map:M6) offers some investigative reporting and full coverage of the arts, entertainment, and restaurants, along with listings of local events. The **SAN DIEGO DAILY TRANSCRIPT** (2131 3rd Ave, downtown; 619/232-4381; map:N5) covers business and legal affairs. Local business issues get more in-depth coverage in the **SAN DIEGO BUSINESS JOURNAL** (4909 Murphy Canyon Rd, Mission Valley; 858/277-6359; map:JJ4). Most neighborhoods have weeklies of varying journalistic quality; check out the **METROPOLITAN MAGAZINE** (1250 6th Ave, downtown; 619/687-3868; map:N7) for downtown news and events and the **LA JOLLA LIGHT** (450 Pearl St, La Jolla; 858/459-2651; map:JJ7) for a view of society soirees. **NORTH COUNTY TIMES** has offices in Escondido (760/745-6611), Solana Beach (858/755-1127), and Vista (760/631-6600).

PUBLIC LIBRARIES

The San Diego main library (820 E St, downtown; 619/236-5800; map:O7) is open Monday to Thursday 10am to 9pm, Friday and Saturday 9:30am to 5:30pm, and Sunday 1pm to 5pm, and boasts 2.1 million volumes. It also has current subscriptions to papers in over 50 cities across the United States, in case you want to catch up on the home front while you are away, along with international papers covering news from London, Vancouver, Philippines, Russia, and Mexico. If you need to do research on local or statewide issues, use the California Room. Internet access is free at the library; you can sign up for time up to seven days in advance. Free movies are shown every Monday night at 6pm and the first and third Sunday of the month at 2pm. At the branch libraries, you might want to check out the children's story-telling programs. Most branch libraries are open Monday and Wednesday 12pm to 8pm, and Tuesday,

HOLES IN THE GROUND

If you've ever tried navigating a city under construction, you'll feel right at home in San Diego. For the next three to five years, downtown will truly be a construction site—but for a good cause.

San Diego has great plans for expansion into a city of the future. Harbor Drive will be closed off for at least a year to accommodate the building of a new **Convention Center addition** (111 W Harbor Dr; 619/525-5000), which will equal the magnificence and scope of the present facility. Next door, at the site of the Campbell Shipyards, a new hotel will rise. Permission to develop this hotel shifts among prominent San Diegans, with the current contenders listed as Douglas Manchester, developer of the nearby Hyatt Hotel, and John Moores, owner of the Padres.

The **Hyatt**, at One Market Place, is scheduled for an additional tower, and the last undeveloped section of downtown, a region now called East Village, is slated for a new baseball stadium. To make way for the $700 million, 1,500-acre ballpark, 69 businesses and 27 residential properties (26 blocks in all) are earmarked for condemnation. The ballpark itself will be at approximately K Street and Eighth Avenue, surrounded by hotels, office buildings, stores, and parks.

Meanwhile, eight development proposals—mostly condominiums and rental housing—have been approved for the **Marina District**, along Market and Island Streets just south of Horton Plaza. In a few cases, the land has been scraped and holes dug; in others, signs on the property herald the future dwelling units. **Cortez Hill**, at 8th and Date Streets, will see new condos and rentals. The historic **El Cortez Hotel**, a San Diego landmark that now stands vacant, will be renovated for upscale occupancy.

In **Little Italy**, along Kettner Boulevard and India Street, row homes and lofts have already been completed; 37 low- and moderate-income apartment units, plus 42 loft apartments, are planned for the near future.

So expect a cloud of dust, a proliferation of holes in the ground, the constant presence of earthmovers and cranes, and as many blocked-off streets as it will take to make it all happen. It won't be a pretty sight—for a while. But come the early years of the new century, you won't recognize this new city of San Diego.　　—*Virginia Butterfield*

Thursday, Friday, and Saturday 9:30am to 5:30pm. Some are open Sundays. The County of San Diego public library system (858/694-2414) has 31 different branches and two bookmobiles. Each branch offers different programs and hours.

MAJOR DOWNTOWN BOOKSTORES

The major booksellers have shunned downtown, opting instead for Mission Valley and other urban neighborhoods. Everyone interested in travel info stops by Le Travel (739 4th Ave, downtown; 619/544-0005; map:O8). The Rand McNally Map & Travel Store (243 Horton Plaza, downtown; 619/234-3341; map:N7) is a good source for guide books and maps. Upstart Crow Bookstore & Coffeehouse (835 West Harbor Dr, Seaport Village, downtown; 619/232-4855; map:M8) is your best choice for children's books, local history, and vacation novels. For more bookstores, see the Shopping chapter.

RADIO AND TV

San Diego's radio scene changes frequently as large conglomerates gobble up local stations. The best stations for news, weather, and traffic reports are KSDO and KPBS, the local PBS station.

Several cable operators reign TV land in San Diego, making channel-surfing confusing. Channels are mostly consistent for the major networks, but everything else is up for grabs. Check the extensive chart in the front pages of the *Union*'s TV listings for the right numbers in your area.

Radio Stations

NEWS, TALK	1130	KSDO AM
NEWS, TALK	600	KOGO AM
JAZZ	98.1	KIFM
EASY LISTENING	94.1	KJOY FM
OLDIES	94.9	KBEST FM
PUBLIC BROADCASTING	89.5	KPBS FM
CLASSICAL	92.1	KFSD FM
ROCK	101.5	KGB FM
COUNTRY	97.3	KSON FM
SPANISH CONTEMPORARY	104.5	XLTN FM
CUTTING-EDGE ROCK	91.1	XTRA FM
R&B/SOUL	92.5	XHRM FM
SPANISH POP	97.7	XTIJ FM
TIJUANA PUBLIC RADIO	88.7	XHITT

TV Stations

ABC	10	KGTV
NBC	39/7	KNSD
CBS	8	KFMB
FOX	6	XETV
PBS	15	KPBS

INTERNET ACCESS

At the CINE CAFÉ (412 K St, downtown; 619/595-1929; map:O8) you can get a sandwich and espresso with your Internet access. Machines are coin operated, giving you 10 minutes for your buck. Movies are shown here in the evening; cafe hours are Sunday through Thursday 7am to

9pm, Friday and Saturday until midnight. KINKO'S offers Internet access (see Business, Copy, and Messenger Services, above) on Macs and PCs. THE SAN DIEGO MAIN PUBLIC LIBRARY has free Internet access; see "Public Libraries" above, for hours.

UNIVERSITIES

San Diego is said to have more Nobel laureates than any other city in the United States; many are affiliated with the University of California at San Diego (Gilman and La Jolla Village Dr, La Jolla; 858/534-2230; map:JJ7). San Diego State University (Campanile Dr, Kensington; 619/594-5200; map:LL3) has an active local alumni association and a popular football team, the Aztecs. Lovingly designed in the Spanish revival style, the University of San Diego (5998 Alcala Park, Normal Heights; 619/260-4600; map:LL6) is a private Catholic college with an excellent law school. Career development classes are available at the University of Phoenix (3870 Murphy Canyon Rd, Mission Valley; 619/576-7469; map:JJ4) and National University (4141 Camino del Rio S, Mission Valley; 619/563-7100; map:LL3).

Important Telephone Numbers

AAA SAN DIEGO (TRAVEL SERVICES)	800/222-5000
AAA EMERGENCY ROAD SERVICE (24 HOURS)	800/400-4222
AIDS HOTLINE	800/367-2437
AARP	619/641-7020
ALCOHOLICS ANONYMOUS	619/265-8762
AMBULANCE	858/974-9706
AMTRAK	800/872-7245
ANIMAL CONTROL	619/236-4250
AUTO IMPOUND	619/531-2844
BALBOA PARK INFORMATION	619/239-0512
BETTER BUSINESS BUREAU	858/496-2131
BIRTH AND DEATH RECORDS	619/237-0502
BLOOD BANK	619/296-6393
CALIFORNIA HIGHWAY PATROL	858/467-3300
CHAMBER OF COMMERCE	619/544-1300
CHILD ABUSE HOT LINE	800/344-6000
CHILD CARE REFERRALS	800/481-2151
CITY OF SAN DIEGO INFORMATION	619/236-5555
CITY PARKS VISITOR INFORMATION	619/239-0512
COAST GUARD	619/683-6320
COAST GUARD EMERGENCY	619/295-3121
COMMUNITY INFORMATION LINE	619/236-5990
CUSTOMS (U.S.)	619/557-5360

DIRECTORY ASSISTANCE	619/555-1212
DOMESTIC VIOLENCE HOT LINE	619/234-3164
FBI	858/565-1255
FIRE DEPARTMENT	619/974-9706
GASLAMP HISTORICAL FOUNDATION	619/233-4692
GREYHOUND BUS SAN DIEGO TERMINAL	800/231-2222
IMMIGRATION AND NATURALIZATION SERVICE	619/557-5570
LOST PETS	619/236-4250
MARRIAGE LICENSES	619/237-0502
METROLINK	800/371-5465
MISSING PERSONS	619/531-2000
PASSPORTS	619/758-7122
PLANNED PARENTHOOD	619/683-7526
POISON CONTROL HOT LINE	800/876-4766
POST OFFICE INFORMATION	800/275-8777
RAPE CRISIS HOT LINE	858/272-1767
RED CROSS	619/542-7400
SAN DIEGO CONVENTION AND VISITORS BUREAU	619/232-3101
SAN DIEGO DEPARTMENT OF PUBLIC HEALTH	619/515-6770
SENIOR SOCIAL SERVICES	619/236-6905
SURF REPORT	619/221-8824
SUICIDE HOT LINE	800/479-3339
TICKETMASTER	619/220-8497
TRAVELERS AID SOCIETY	619/295-8393
WEATHER	800/985-3040
ZIP CODE INFORMATION	800/275-8777

TOP 160 RESTAURANTS

Restaurants by Star Rating

★★★★

Mille Fleurs

★★★⯪

Azzura Point
Belgian Lion
Delicias
The Marine Room
Rancho Valencia Resort
The Sky Room

★★★

California Cuisine
Dobson's Bar &
   Restaurant
El Agave
El Bizcocho
Laurel
Le Fontainebleau
Star of the Sea
Top o' the Cove
Trattoria Acqua
Winesellar & Brasserie

★★⯪

Azul La Jolla
Cafe Pacifica
Chameleon Cafe
Cilantro's
Fish Market Restaurant
George's at the Cove
Hob Nob Hill
Jasmine
Joe's Crab Shack
Kemo Sabe
Korea House
La Provence
La Salsa
Market Cafe
MiXX
Morton's of Chicago
150 Grand Cafe
Pamplemousse Grille
Primavera Ristorante
The Prince of Wales
   Grill
Red Sails Inn
Saffron Noodles &
   Saté
Spices Thai Cafe
Taste of Thai
Thee Bungalow

Tori Tori New
   Japanese Cuisine
Tutto Mare Ristorante
Twins
Via Italia Trattoria
Vigilucci's
The Whaling Bar
When in Rome

★★

Aladdin Mediterranean
   Cafe
Athens Market Taverna
Bai Yook Thai Cuisine
Bali Authentic
   Indonesian
Bayou Bar and Grill
Bella Luna
Bellefleur Winery &
   Restaurant
Bombay
The Brigantine
Cafe Japengo
Café Sevilla
Cafe Zinc
Cafe Zucchero
Cass Street Bar & Grill
Chez Loma
Chilango's Mexico City
   Grill
Cody's at the Cove
Epazote
Fio's Cucina Italiana
French Pastry Shop
Gulf Coast Grill
Il Fornaio
Jake's Del Mar
Jyoti Bihanga
Kaiserhof
Karl Strauss Brewery
   & Grill
Mission Hills Cafe
Mission Hills Market
   Cafe
Montanas
Nick's at the Beach
Ortega's
Pacifica Del Mar
Panda Inn Chinese
   Restaurant
Pizza Nova
Sally's

Sammy's California
   Woodfired Pizza
Samson's Restaurant
Santé Ristorante
St. James Bar at
   Triangles
Trattoria Mama Ana
Yoshino

★★⯪

Berta's Latin American
   Restaurant
Blue Point Coastal
   Cuisine
Bread & Cie
Bully's North
Cafe Del Mar
Cecil's Cafe & Fish
   Market
D.Z. Akin's
Del Mar Pizza
Don's Country Kitchen
Downtown Johnny
   Brown's
El Indio Shop
Embers Grille
Gourmet Bagger
Greek Islands Cafe
Hodad's
Ichiban PB
Kensington Grill
La Especial Norte
La Fresqueria
Mimmo's Italian Village
Olé Madrid
Parkhouse Eatery
Piatti
Pizza Port
Point Loma Seafoods
Qwiigs Bar & Grill
Ricky's Family
   Restaurant
Roppongi Restaurant,
   Bar, and Cafe
Rubio's
Ruby's Diner
Sushi on the Rock
Tip Top Meats
Tony's Jacal
T's Cafe
The Vegetarian Zone

★

Adam's Steak & Eggs
Alfonso's
The Big Kitchen
Cafe 222
Cafe Athena
Chart House
The Cheese Shop
Crest Cafe
Fairouz Restaurant &
  Gallery
Fidel's
Filippi's Pizza Grotto
Firehouse Beach Cafe

Greek Town Restaurant
  and Taverna
Hamburger Mary's
Jose's Courtroom
Ki's
Kono's Cafe
Mission Café & Coffee
  Shop
Old Venice Italian
  Restaurant Caffe &
  Bar
On the Border
The Original Pancake
  House
Porkyland
Rainwater's

Roberto's
Roxy
Shakespeare Pub and
  Grille
Souplantation
South Beach Bar and
  Grill
Sushi Deli
Trophy's
Turf Supper Club
The Venetian
The Waterfront

UNRATED
The Grant Grill

Restaurants by Neighborhood

CARDIFF
Ki's

CARLSBAD
Bellefleur Winery &
Restaurant
Don's Country Kitchen
Tip Top Meats

CLAIREMONT
Aladdin Mediterranean
Cafe
Via Italia Trattoria

CORONADO
Azzura Point
Chameleon Cafe
Chez Loma
Market Cafe
Primavera Ristorante
The Prince of Wales Grill

DEL MAR
Bully's North
Cafe Del Mar
Cilantro's
Del Mar Pizza
Epazote
Il Fornaio
Jake's Del Mar
Pacifica Del Mar
Taste of Thai

DOWNTOWN
Athens Market Taverna
Bayou Bar and Grill
Bella Luna
Blue Point Coastal
Cuisine
Cafe 222
Café Sevilla
Cafe Zucchero
Chart House
The Cheese Shop
Dobson's Bar &
Restaurant
Downtown Johnny
Brown's
Filippi's Pizza Grotto
Fio's Cucina Italiana
Fish Market Restaurant
The Grant Grill
Greek Islands Cafe

Greek Town Restaurant
and Taverna
Hob Nob Hill
La Fresqueria
La Provence
La Salsa
Laurel
Le Fontainebleau
Mimmo's Italian Village
Morton's of Chicago
Olé Madrid
Panda Inn Chinese
Restaurant
Rainwater's
Sally's
Star of the Sea
Sushi Deli
Trattoria Mama Anna
The Waterfront

ENCINITAS
Roxy
Twins
Vigilucci's
When in Rome

ESCONDIDO
150 Grand Cafe

GOLDEN HILL
The Big Kitchen
Turf Supper Club

HILLCREST
Bai Yook Thai Cuisine
Bombay
Bread & Cie
California Cuisine
Chilango's Mexico City
Grill
Crest Cafe
Hamburger Mary's
Kemo Sabe
MiXX
Montanas
The Vegetarian Zone

KEARNY MESA
Jasmine
Korea House
The Original Pancake
House

KENSINGTON
Kensington Grill

LA JOLLA
Alfonso's
Azul La Jolla
Bali Authentic
Indonesian
Cafe Japengo
Cody's at the Cove
French Pastry Shop
George's at the Cove
Jose's Courtroom
The Marine Room
Piatti
Porkyland
Roppongi Restaurant,
Bar, and Cafe
Sammy's California
Woodfired Pizza
Samson's Restaurant
Santé Ristorante
The Sky Room
St. James Bar at Triangles
Sushi on the Rock
Top o' the Cove
Trattoria Acqua
Tutto Mare Ristorante
The Whaling Bar

LA MESA
D.Z. Akin's

LEUCADIA
La Especial Norte

MIDDLETOWN
El Indio Shop
Saffron Noodles & Saté
Shakespeare Pub and
Grille
Yoshino

MIDWAY
Embers Grille
Fairouz Restaurant &
Gallery
Souplantation

MISSION BEACH
Mission Café & Coffee
Shop

MISSION HILLS
Mission Hills Cafe
Mission Hills Market
  Cafe

MISSION VALLEY
Adam's Steak & Eggs
Gourmet Bagger
Joe's Crab Shack
On The Border
Ricky's Family
  Restaurant
Ruby's Diner
Trophy's

NORMAL HEIGHTS
Jyoti Bihanga

OCEAN BEACH
Belgian Lion
Cecil's Cafe & Fish
  Market
Hodad's
Kaiserhof
Ortega's
Qwiigs Bar & Grill
South Beach Bar and
  Grill

Thee Bungalow

OLD TOWN
Berta's Latin American
  Restaurant
Cafe Pacifica
El Agave

PACIFIC BEACH
Cafe Athena
Cass Street Bar & Grill
Firehouse Beach Cafe
Ichiban PB
Kono's Cafe
Nick's at the Beach
Roberto's
Rubio's

POINT LOMA
Old Venice Italian
  Restaurant Caffe &
  Bar
Pizza Nova
Point Loma Seafoods
The Venetian

RANCHO BERNARDO
El Bizcocho

RANCHO SANTA FE
Delicias
Mille Fleurs
Rancho Valencia Resort

SHELTER ISLAND
The Brigantine
Red Sails Inn

SOLANA BEACH
Cafe Zinc
Fidel's
Pamplemousse Grille
Pizza Port
Tony's Jacal
T's Cafe

SORRENTO VALLEY
Karl Strauss Brewery &
  Grill
Spices Thai Cafe
Winesellar & Brasserie

UNIVERSITY HEIGHTS
Gulf Coast Grill
Parkhouse Eatery
Tori Tori New Japanese
  Cuisine

Restaurants by Food and Other Features

BAKERY
Bread & Cie
Il Fornaio
D.Z. Akin's

BREAKFAST
Adam's Steak & Eggs
Cafe 222
Cafe Del Mar
Cafe Zinc
Cecil's Cafe & Fish
Market
Cody's at the Cove
Don's Country Kitchen
French Pastry Shop
Kono's Cafe
Market Cafe
Mission Café & Coffee
Shop
Mission Hills Cafe

BREAKFAST ALL DAY
The Big Kitchen
The Original Pancake
House
Ricky's Family
Restaurant

BRUNCH
Chez Loma
Epazote
Il Fornaio
Jake's Del Mar
Le Fontainebleau
The Marine Room
Pacifica Del Mar
Qwiigs Bar & Grill

BURGERS
The Brigantine
Bully's North
Cass Street Bar & Grill
Crest Cafe
Downtown Johnny
Brown's
Hamburger Mary's
Hodad's
Karl Strauss Brewery &
Grill
Kensington Grill
Trophy's
The Waterfront

CAJUN/CREOLE
Blue Point Coastal
Cuisine
Bayou Bar and Grill
Gulf Coast Grill

CALIFORNIA CUISINE
California Cuisine
Cecil's Cafe & Fish
Market
Chameleon Cafe
Delicias
Dobson's Bar &
Restaurant
El Bizcocho
George's at the Cove
Kemo Sabe
La Provence
Mille Fleurs
Mission Hills Market
Cafe
Montanas
Rancho Valencia Resort
Sally's
The Sky Room
Star of the Sea
Thee Bungalow

CHINESE
Panda Inn Chinese
Restaurant
Jasmine

COFFEE SHOP
Ricky's Family
Restaurant
Mission Café & Coffee
Shop

CONTINENTAL
Azzura Point
The Grant Grill
The Marine Room
Mission Hills Market
Cafe
Parkhouse Eatery
Santé Ristorante
The Sky Room
St. James Bar at Triangles
Thee Bungalow
The Whaling Bar

**DESSERTS
(EXCELLENT)**
Cafe Pacifica
Cafe Zucchero
French Pastry Shop
George's Ocean Terrace
Morton's of Chicago
Pamplemousse Grille
The Sky Room
When in Rome

DINER
Hob Nob Hill
Ruby's Diner

FAMILY 🏃🏃
Adam's Steak & Eggs
The Big Kitchen
D.Z. Akin's
El Indio Shop
Filippi's Pizza Grotto
Fish Market Restaurant
Greek Islands Cafe
Ichiban PB
Jasmine
Korea House
La Especial Norte
Market Cafe
Mimmo's Italian Village
The Original Pancake
House
Red Sails Inn
Ricky's Family
Restaurant
Ruby's Diner
Samson's Restaurant
Souplantation
Tony's Jacal
The Venetian

FIREPLACE
Delicias
Parkhouse Eatery
150 Grand Cafe
Rancho Valencia Resort
Santé Ristorante
T's Cafe
Twins
The Whaling Bar

FRENCH
Azzura Point
Belgian Lion

Chez Loma
Delicias
El Bizcocho
French Pastry Shop
Laurel
La Provence
Le Fontainebleau
Mille Fleurs
Pamplemousse Grille
Rancho Valencia Resort
The Sky Room
Thee Bungalow
Top o' the Cove

GERMAN
Kaiserhof
Karl Strauss Brewery &
   Grill

GOOD VALUE 🐷
Adam's Steak & Eggs
The Brigantine
Bully's North
Cafe Athena
Cass Street Bar & Grill
Cecil's Cafe & Fish
   Market
The Cheese Shop
Fairouz Restaurant &
   Gallery
Gourmet Bagger
Hob Nob Hill
Ichiban PB
Jake's Del Mar
Joe's Crab Shack
Ki's
Kono's Cafe
La Especial Norte
Mimmo's Italian Village
Mission Hills Cafe
Parkhouse Eatery
Pizza Nova
Porkyland
Roberto's
Roxy
Rubio's
Sammy's California
   Woodfired Pizza
Souplantation
South Beach Bar and
   Grill
Spices Thai Cafe
Sushi Deli
Tip Top Meats
Tori Tori New Japanese
   Cuisine

T's Cafe
Vigilucci's
The Waterfront
Yoshino

GOURMENT TAKEOUT
D.Z. Akin's
French Pastry Shop
Il Fornaio
Mission Hills Market
   Cafe
Sushi on the Rock

GREEK
Aladdin Mediterranean
   Cafe
Athens Market Taverna
Cafe Athena
Fairouz Restaurant &
   Gallery
Greek Islands Cafe
Greek Town Restaurant
   and Taverna

GRILL
Bayou Bar and Grill
Cass Street Bar & Grill
Kensington Grill
Montanas
Qwiigs Bar & Grill

HEALTH CONSCIOUS
Jyoti Bihanga
Ki's
La Fresqueria
Roxy
Souplantation
Sushi on the Rock

INDIAN
Bombay

INDONESIAN
Bali Authentic
   Indonesian

INVENTIVE ETHNIC
Cafe Pacifica
California Cuisine
Chameleon Cafe
Embers Grille
Kemo Sabe
MiXX
Roppongi Restaurant,
   Bar, and Cafe

ITALIAN
Bella Luna

Del Mar Pizza
Fio's Cucina Italiana
Il Fornaio
Mimmo's Italian Village
Old Venice Italian
   Restaurant Caffe &
   Bar
Piatti
Pizza Nova
Pizza Port
Primavera Ristorante
Trattoria Acqua
Trattoria Mama Anna
Via Italia Trattoria
The Venetian
Vigilucci's
When in Rome

JAPANESE
Ichiban PB
Sushi Deli
Sushi on the Rock
Tori Tori New Japanese
   Cuisine
Yoshino

KITSCH
Cafe 222
Hodad's
Mission Café & Coffee
   Shop
Turf Supper Club

KOREAN
Korea House

LATE NIGHT
Crest Cafe
Nick's at the Beach

LATIN
Berta's Latin American
   Restaurant

MEDITTERANEAN
Azul La Jolla
Azzura Point
Cafe Pacifica
Laurel
150 Grand Cafe
Rancho Valencia Resort
Sally's
Star of the Sea
Thee Bungalow
Top o' the Cove
Trattoria Acqua

MEXICAN
Alfonso's
Berta's Latin American
  Restaurant
Chilango's Mexico City
  Grill
El Agave
El Indio Shop
Fidel's
Jose's Courtroom
La Especial Norte
La Fresqueria
La Salsa
Old Town Mexican Cafe
On the Border
Ortega's
Porkyland
Rubio's
Tony's Jacal

MIDDLE EASTERN
Aladdin Mediterranean
  Cafe
Fairouz Restaurant &
  Gallery

OUTDOOR DINING
Adam's Steak & Eggs
Alfonso's
Bayou Bar and Grill
Bombay
Bread & Cie
The Brigantine
Cafe Del Mar
Cafe Zinc
Cafe Zucchero
California Cuisine
Cody's at the Cove
Downtown Johnny
  Brown's
Greek Islands Cafe
Fish Market Restaurant
MiXX
Nick's at the Beach
150 Grand Cafe
Parkhouse Eatery
Sally's
Shakespeare Pub and
  Grille
Market Cafe
Tony's Jacal
Trattoria Acqua
The Vegetarian Zone

PAN ASIAN/PACIFIC
  RIM
Cafe Japengo

Kemo Sabe
150 Grand Cafe
Pacifica Del Mar
Roppongi Restaurant,
  Bar, and Cafe
Top o' the Cove

PIZZA
Aladdin Mediterranean
  Cafe
Del Mar Pizza
Embers Grille
Filippi's Pizza Grotto
Old Venice Italian
  Restaurant Caffe &
  Bar
Pizza Nova
Pizza Port
Sammy's California
  Woodfired Pizza
Trattoria Acqua
The Venetian

PRIVATE ROOMS
La Provence
Laurel
Morton's of Chicago
Roppongi Restaurant,
  Bar, and Cafe
T's Cafe

ROMANTIC 💘
Athens Market Taverna
Azzura Point
Belgian Lion
Cafe Del Mar
Cafe Pacifica
California Cuisine
Chez Loma
Delicias
El Bizcocho
Fish Market Restaurant
George's at the Cove
Il Fornaio
Le Fontainebleau
The Marine Room
Market Cafe
Mille Fleurs
Old Venice Italian
  Restaurant Caffe &
  Bar
150 Grand Cafe
Primavera Ristorante
The Prince of Wales Grill
Rancho Valencia Resort
Santé Ristorante
The Sky Room

Star of the Sea
Thee Bungalow
Top o' the Cove
Trattoria Acqua
Vigilucci's
The Whaling Bar

SEAFOOD
Azul La Jolla
Azzura Point
Blue Point Coastal
  Cuisine
The Brigantine
Cafe Pacifica
Chart House
Delicias
Fish Market Restaurant
The Grant Grill
George's at the Cove
Jake's Del Mar
Joe's Crab Shack
Mille Fleurs
Pacifica Del Mar
Point Loma Seafoods
Qwiigs Bar & Grill
Red Sails Inn
Sally's
South Beach Bar and
  Grill
Star of the Sea
Top o' the Cove
Top of the Market
Tutto Mare Ristorante

SPANISH
Café Sevilla
Olé Madrid

SOUP/SALAD/
  SANDWICH
Bread & Cie
Cafe Zinc
Cass Street Bar & Grill
The Cheese Shop
Crest Cafe
Downtown Johnny
  Brown's
D.Z. Akin's
Gourmet Bagger
Hamburger Mary's
Samson's Restaurant
Souplantation
Tip Top Meats

SOUTH AMERICAN
Berta's Latin American
  Restaurant

SOUTHWEST
Bellefleur Winery &
  Restaurant
Blue Point Coastal
  Cuisine
Chameleon Cafe
Cilantro's
Epazote
Kemo Sabe
Montanas
On The Border

STEAK
The Brigantine
Bully's North
Chart House
The Grant Grill
Morton's of Chicago
Rainwater's
Turf Supper Club

SUSHI
Ichiban PB
Sushi Deli
Sushi on the Rock
Tori Tori New Japanese
  Cuisine

TAPAS
Café Sevilla
Olé Madrid
Roppongi Restaurant,
  Bar, and Cafe

TAKEOUT
Chilango's Mexico City
  Grill
Downtown Johnny
  Brown's

Del Mar Pizza
El Indio Shop
Embers Grille
Filippi's Pizza Grotto
Firehouse Beach Cafe
Gourmet Bagger
Ichiban PB
La Salsa
Mimmo's Italian Village
Pizza Nova
Pizza Port
Point Loma Seafoods
Porkyland
Rubio's
Saffron Noodles & Saté
Samson's Restaurant
Tip Top Meats
Tori Tori New Japanese
  Cuisine
The Vegetarian Zone

THAI
Bai Yook Thai Cuisine
Blue Point Coastal
  Cuisine
Saffron Noodles & Saté
Taste of Thai
Spices Thai Cafe

UNIQUELY SAN DIEGO
Azzura Point
The Brigantine
California Cuisine
Cass Street Bar & Grill
Cecil's Cafe & Fish
  Market
El Indio Shop
Epazote

Firehouse Beach Cafe
George's at the Cove
Hodad's
Ki's
Kono's Cafe
The Marine Room
MiXX
Point Loma Seafoods
Qwiigs Bar & Grill
Red Sails Inn
Roxy
Rubio's
South Beach Bar and
  Grill
Tony's Jacal

VEGETARIAN
Bombay
Jyoti Bihanga
Cafe Zinc
The Vegetarian Zone

VIEW
Cecil's Cafe & Fish
  Market
George's at the Cove
Jake's Del Mar
Jose's Courtroom
The Marine Room
Market Cafe
Nick's at the Beach
Pacifica Del Mar
Pizza Nova
Point Loma Seafoods
Qwiigs Bar & Grill
Sally's
Star of the Sea
Top o' the Cove

RESTAURANTS

Adam's Steak & Eggs / ★

1201 HOTEL CIRCLE S, MISSION VALLEY; 619/291-1103
Go on a weekday at 10am and you might not have to wait for a table at what may be the best breakfast hangout in town. Yes, you can get a plump, perfect steak and eggs here, with fresh, crispy fried potatoes, but regulars who stop by for a quick meal or full family celebration have more discerning tastes. They order the down-home corn fritters with honey butter, the homemade sausage patty, the enormous Spanish omelet smothered in spicy sauce and sour cream, or the meal-size cinnamon bun. Kids love the fruit smoothies and pancakes. Check out the daily specials, including the Philly steak and eggs covered with sautéed onions—order it with melted cheese on top. The wood tables are tightly packed, and strangers end up sharing sugar, cream, and local tidbits. Adam's is only open till 11:30am (1pm on Saturday and Sunday), but some of the breakfast items are served throughout the day at Albie's, the adjacent steak house. *$; AE, DC, DIS, MC, V; no checks; breakfast everyday; full bar; no reservations; map:L1* &

Aladdin Mediterranean Cafe / ★★

5420 CLAIREMONT MESA BLVD, CLAIREMONT; 619/573-0000
Despite its suburban strip mall location, this delightful restaurant provides a great escape for anyone craving Middle Eastern fare. The menu is extensive, ranging from the usual hummus, tabbouleh, and gyros to wood-fired pizzas on deliciously puffy crusts. Standout dishes are the stuffed grape leaves, lamb kebabs, generous Greek salads, succulent chicken shawerma, and fat pita sandwiches. And don't pass up those pizzas: they're worth a visit all by themselves. Sample one of these pies topped with juicy bites of chicken shawerma or smoky grilled veggies and lots of fresh herbs, and you may never settle for plain pepperoni again. The place has a casual, comfy feel, with a shaded front patio (facing the parking lot, but still pleasant) and lots of indoor seating. It's equally popular with local workers and families (kids, especially, love all these finger foods). A market area inside the restaurant sells imported olive oil, Middle Eastern spices, and assorted groceries. *$; MC, V; no checks; lunch, dinner every day; beer and wine; reservations required for large parties; map:JJ5* &

Alfonso's / ★

1251 PROSPECT ST, LA JOLLA; 858/454-2232
Margaritas by the pitcher, chips, hot bean dip, carne asada burritos, and guacamole are the perfect ingredients for an afternoon gossip session at this prime people-watching cafe. La Jollans have been hanging out at the sidewalk tables since 1971, and many a family celebration has graced the

overcrowded, dark dining rooms. The cooks firmly resist trends, relying on basic enchiladas, burritos, and tacos to please the crowds. Don't spend the big bucks on fancy entrees; stick with the old standards, appetizers, and drinks for a rewarding shopping break. *$; AE, DC, DIS, MC, V; no checks; lunch, dinner every day; full bar; no reservations for patio; map:JJ7*

Athens Market Taverna / ★★

109 WEST F ST, DOWNTOWN; 619/234-1955
This Greek restaurant is a favorite with lawyers and other downtown professionals for lunch, dinner, and after-work cocktails; their well-heeled, well-dressed demeanor goes nicely with the understated, elegant white linen tablecloths and napkins, tiny candles, and dried flowers gracing each table. Owner Mary Pappas has been cooking up sublime Greek food downtown since 1974, and her devoted clientele followed her from her first location at Fourth Avenue and E Street to the current digs just south of Horton Plaza. Among the most succulent dishes is the fall-off-the-bone baked lemon chicken, served with rice pilaf, roasted potato wedge, vegetable, and soup or salad. The lentil soup is zesty, though the egg-lemon soup is almost too subtle, and the salad greens at last visit were gasping for oxygen. Still, there's something so chic yet comfortable about Athens Market Taverna that occasional wilted lettuce is almost instantly forgiven. *$$; AE, DC, DIS, MC, V; no checks; lunch, dinner Mon–Sat, dinner Sun; full bar; reservations recommended; map:N8* &

Azul La Jolla / ★★★

1250 PROSPECT ST, LA JOLLA; 858/454-9616
If location can ensure success, this new venture by the Brigantine Restaurant Corporation ought to be a hit. Azul (Spanish for blue) is anchored on the hill above La Jolla Cove with a see-forever view of the Pacific. An extensive renovation has turned this site of many a failed restaurant into a gorgeous grottolike room, dramatically lit and decorated. The best tables are along the windows, of course, but the two-level dining room assures an ocean view from many of the booths farther back. Early visits found a menu that offers a number of Mediterranean-influenced dishes that are fresh and appealing, if a bit on the bland side. Right now, the best items are the roasted John Dory, a firm white-fleshed fish, and the free-range chicken with an outstanding potato gratin. Service is unfailingly pleasant, and there's a special menu just for kids. Given Brigantine's success with its more casual restaurants throughout the county (such as Old Town and Point Loma), it's worth watching the youthful Azul to see how it matures. *$$; AE, CB, DC, MC, V; no checks; lunch, dinner every day; full bar; reservations recommended; map:JJ7* &

Azzura Point / ★★★⯪

4000 CORONADO BAY RD (LOEWS CORONADO BAY RESORT), CORONADO; 619/424-4477

A strong contender for best restaurant in San Diego, this dining room at the Loews Coronado Bay Resort is a star. A multimillion-dollar renovation turned the harbor-view restaurant into a vision of safari chic that perfectly reflects the resort atmosphere. Service is polished and knowledgeable, the wine list extensive (and expensive). Chef de cuisine Michael Stebner and his talented staff consistently turn out fantastic dishes incorporating Pacific Rim, classic French, and Mediterranean flavors. Pristinely fresh fish and shellfish imported from around the world always sparkle; particular standouts are the oysters splashed with sake vinaigrette, the lobster risotto, and France's rare *loup de mer*. Nightly prix fixe dinners offer multicourse tasting menus that are a signature of this dining room and a fine way to sample the cuisine. Save room for dessert—a melted chocolate truffle cake makes you feel like you've won the Lotto. *$$$; AE, MC, V; no checks; dinner Tues–Sun; full bar; reservations recommended; map:NN5* &

Bai Yook Thai Cuisine / ★★

1260 UNIVERSITY AVE, HILLCREST; 619/296-2700

Typical of many a local restaurant, this stellar Thai kitchen is tucked into a nondescript mall. But don't miss it: the green papaya salad redolent of garlic and fish sauce just might be the best version in town. After that, chow down on one of the curry or noodle dishes, all of which come with meats, seafood, or vegetables. Don't have a favorite dish? Try the red curry with green beans (pad prik khing); the panang curry flavored with basil, green peppers, and coconut; or the familiar pad thai sprinkled with peanuts and bean sprouts. The small dining room is very casual and doesn't offer much privacy, but the soft blue walls and Asian art add a touch of serenity that's all too rare on the informal dining scene. *$; AE, CB, DC, DIS, MC, V; no checks; lunch Mon–Sat, dinner every day; beer and wine; reservations recommended; map:O2*

Bali Authentic Indonesian / ★★

7660 FAY AVE, LA JOLLA; 858/454-4540

San Diego's first (and only) Indonesian restaurant is a charmer, from the gracious servers to the fascinating cuisine. Settle into the two-level dining room filled with Balinese artifacts and prepare to be delighted by a beautifully presented meal. You'll quickly learn why Indonesia earned the name Spice Islands: predominant flavors include ginger, nutmeg, lemongrass, cinnamon, and a variety of chilies. For starters, try the fiery tamarind soup or the *lemper*, a blend of chicken, sticky rice, and assorted spices cooked in a banana leaf. Then move on to any of the entrees that

DOGGIE DINING

When it comes to pets and restaurants, San Diego isn't as progressive as Paris, where the bearded guest sitting next to you might be an Airedale. *La belle France* understands that well-behaved dogs, much like well-mannered children, deserve to go out for a good meal. (Of course, one never encounters a poorly behaved French dog *or* child in Paris.) While the San Diego health department prohibits canines (except for service dogs) in restaurant interiors, a number of enlightened eateries offer pup-friendly patios. Many places, including Bread & Cie, Greek Islands Cafe, The Roxy, and Pizza Port, even keep a water bowl filled for their four-legged guests. The U.S. Grant Hotel goes so far as to invite the pooches to high tea. Although it's mostly casual places that welcome dogs, several upscale places with outdoor dining areas also permit them. Both Mille Fleurs and the Market Cafe at Loews Coronado Bay Resort, each known for top-notch atmosphere and fine cuisine, offer terraces where mannerly mutts and polite purebreds are welcome. A word to the wise: help keep local restaurants pet-friendly by making sure your dog is quiet and under control. And remember to bring some clean-up supplies, just in case. —*Robin Kleven*

sound intriguing; we haven't found a loser in the bunch. Need a recommendation? Ask the batik-clad staff, or try the tofu curry, the pork with ginger, the chicken saté, or one of the rijsttafel combinations. The latter, a feast of various dishes and condiments, is a fun and instructive way to sample the best of Indonesian cooking all at once. *$$; AE, DC, DIS, MC, V; no checks; lunch Fri–Sun, dinner every day; beer and wine; reservations recommended; map:JJ7* &

Bayou Bar and Grill / ★★

329 MARKET ST, DOWNTOWN; 619/696-8747

Bringing a little bit of Bourbon Street to Market Street—that's what San Diego's best Cajun restaurant is about. Between the Dixieland jazz (including live performances for New Year's Eve and Mardi Gras), the Big Easy posters, and the huge selection of chili sauces for sale, it's easy to imagine yourself in the French Quarter. The Southern cooking delivers authentic punch as well, generating lots of requests for the jambalaya, shrimp po'boy, fiery blackened fish, and soft-shell crab. Save a little room for dessert because the place is famous for a chilled peanut butter mousse pie and a bourbon-spiked bread pudding. In addition to the bar area and dining rooms, there's patio seating on the sidewalk fronting Market Street, a favorite vantage point on busy weekend nights. If you're in town during Mardi Gras season, this is the place to be for hearty partying and hurricanes that go down smooth and cold. *$$; AE, CB, DC, DIS, MC,*

V; *no checks; lunch, dinner every day; full bar; reservations recommended; bayoubar@aol.com; map:N8* &

Belgian Lion / ★★★☆

2265 BACON ST, OCEAN BEACH; 619/223-2700
Chef/owner Don Coulon is the heart and soul of this exquisite French restaurant, which he runs with several members of his family. A star on the local scene for more than 15 years, the Belgian Lion continues to wow critics, longtime customers, and first-time visitors with a mix of traditional and contemporary fare. There's not a disappointing dish on the menu, but over the years the following have become true classics: salmon sauced with sorrel, hearty cassoulet, chicken Normande with apples and turnip soufflé. Lacy curtains, old-fashioned decor, a cozy bar, and flattering lighting make this a favorite choice for couples; larger groups can be accommodated in a separate dining room with advance notice. Be sure to spend some time perusing the wine list, which includes rarely seen imports and many little-known California treasures chosen by the chef, a committed connoisseur. The small staff treats repeat visitors practically like family, and while entrees average at least $20, the personal service and Old World ambience make the Belgian Lion one of our special occasion faves. *$$$; AE, DC, DIS, MC, V; no checks; dinner Thurs–Sat; beer and wine; reservations recommended; map:C2*

Bella Luna / ★★

748 5TH AVE, DOWNTOWN; 619/239-3222
Downtown's Gaslamp Quarter offers a staggering number of trattorias, but those in the know keep going back to this eye-catching Italian restaurant whose name means "beautiful moon." The dining room is one of the Gaslamp's most striking; the ceiling evokes blue sky and clouds and has dozens of artworks celebrating the moon. There's also seating at the bar and on the sidewalk patio, a prime vantage point for Fifth Avenue people-watching. The tempting menu is strong on appetizers, with five different carpaccios (try the smoked duck with truffle oil) and a particularly nice salad of arugula, radicchio, and shaved Parmesan. Main courses of note include the veal saltimbocca, tagliatelle with salmon and leeks, penne with eggplant, and risottos that change with the season. Along with a decent wine selection, the restaurant serves six varieties of grappa and a number of fine aged tequilas. Service is skilled, and the restaurant has a distinctively European cachet that sets it apart from the crowd. *$$; AE, DC, MC, V; no checks; lunch Mon–Fri, dinner every day; full bar; reservations recommended; map:O7*

Bellefleur Winery & Restaurant / ★★

5610 PASEO DEL NORTE, CARLSBAD; 760/603-1919

Looking somewhat like a beautiful fish out of water, this upscale restaurant/bar anchors one end of an outlet store mall (the Carlsbad Company Stores) just off Interstate 5. It's a welcome presence among the fast food joints, the discount shoe stores, and the displays of last year's fashions. Inside the villa-esque building, soaring ceilings and graceful architecture provide a chic showcase for often innovative American cuisine, ranging from roasted poblano chili appetizers to a marvelous chocolate peanut butter torte. Other standout dishes are a quickly seared sea bass, and red-meat specials such as hanger steak and baby back ribs. An in-house bakery provides exceptional breads, and a petite gift shop offers wine paraphernalia and other souvenirs. At lunch, the place has a casual feeling; a dressier, older crowd shows up at night. Some customers may enjoy the wines sold under the Bellefleur label, but discerning drinkers will want to shell out some extra dough for the better-known California brands on the list. *$$$; AE, DIS, MC, V; no checks; lunch, dinner every day; beer and wine; reservations recommended; map:CC7* &

Berta's Latin American Restaurant / ★★☆

3928 TWIGGS ST, OLD TOWN; 619/295-2343

Low ceilings, lace curtains, soft lighting, and a red-tile floor conspire to make this one of Old Town's most intimate restaurants. Berta's doesn't overdo the Mexican theme as do some other eateries in San Diego's historic district; instead, there are representative dishes from the best-known Latin American countries. One of the best ways to sample various cuisines is ordering tapas as starters. Try the Colombian *tostones* (smashed and fried plantain slices); Guatemalan *rellenitos de plátano* (sweet bananas stuffed with black bean paste, lightly fried, and dusted with sugar); or the delightfully different orange salad from Mexico, expertly seasoned with garlic, parsley, and a hint of rosemary. Entrees include grilled flank steak marinated in lime (Argentina), tender chicken served with a sauce of smoky chipotle chilies, cilantro, and tomatillos (Mexico); and from the mother country, Spanish paella. *$$; AE, MC, V; no checks; lunch, dinner Tues–Sun; beer and wine; reservations accepted; map:I2* &

The Big Kitchen / ★

3003 GRAPE ST, GOLDEN HILL; 619/231-9441

Judy the Beauty on Duty, the irrepressible owner of this neighborhood icon, has rules for her patrons printed on the first page of the menu. Rule number two is "Do not deliver your baby in my cafe." Other than that, Judy's darn accommodating, and she's garnered a colorful following over two decades. Whoopi Goldberg used to eat here when she was in town, and her favorite breakfast now bears her name. (If you must know, it's eggs, potatoes, and a large OJ.) Other meals honor lesser-known, quirky patrons. Check out Lily's Special—a bowl of rice with cheese, a small fruit plate, and a homemade muffin. Most people come for the enormous, fluffy omelets or spinach and eggs, both served with golden-brown home fries and toast. Regulars slide onto their favorite seats at the three-sided bar, holding forth on liberal politics while holding out their mugs for a refill. Daily lunch specials are straight out of *American Graffiti*: there's chicken with biscuits and gravy on Tuesdays and turkey 'n fixin's on Wednesdays. A plant-filled, kid-friendly back patio and a second dining room (filled with original art) are packed on weekend mornings. Breakfast may not be the cheapest in town, but they're friendly enough to keep 'em coming back. *$; no credit cards; checks OK; breakfast, lunch every day; no alcohol; no reservations; map:MM4*

Blue Point Coastal Cuisine / ★★☆

565 5TH AVE, DOWNTOWN; 619/233-6623

Chalk up this Gaslamp Quarter restaurant's success to a number of factors. Prime among them is the dynamite location on busy Fifth Avenue, where the comings and goings of the after-dark crowd provide constant entertainment. Blue Point is also one of the rare seafood houses in the area offering an oyster bar along with a multicultural menu that leans heavily on fish. This is one spot in the Gaslamp where pasta doesn't rule; instead, in-the-know diners choose Baja-style clam chowder, ahi sashimi, southwestern scampi with cilantro pesto, or salmon rolled in sesame seeds. The setting is both flashy and attractive, offering big, cushy booths, bold flower arrangements, and some of the best-looking bartenders around. These guys know their stuff, whipping up smooth, shaken-not-stirred martinis that would make Dean Martin purr. The food isn't always as consistent as the drinks, but Blue Point's still a fun place to drop anchor. *$$$; AE, DC, DIS, MC, V; no checks; dinner every day; full bar; reservations recommended; www.cohnrestaurants.com; map:O8* &

Bombay / ★★

3975 5TH AVE, HILLCREST; 619/298-3155

This Indian restaurant is a pleasing place to pass the time over lunch or dinner, especially if you sit near the trickling indoor fountain or on the sheltered outdoor patio. It's a peaceful refuge from bustling Fifth Avenue, with unobtrusive service and calming earth-toned decor. The wide-ranging menu is designed to please just about everyone. Top selections for carnivores are the excellent lamb stews (the red-hot vindaloo with ginger is a standout) and the moist tandoori-style chicken prepared in a real tandoor oven. Vegetarians will be delighted with a choice of more than 20 meat-free dishes, especially the curries and the delicious puree of fresh spinach. And everyone should love the breads, especially a garlicky naan that's just right for sopping up any last bits of sauce. The best deal here is a luncheon buffet for around $8; it's all-you-can-eat and includes basmati rice, various stews and curries, condiments, soups, and that terrific tandoori chicken. *$$; AE, DIS, MC, V; no checks; lunch, dinner every day; beer and wine, reservations recommended; map:N2* &

Bread & Cie / ★★☆

350 UNIVERSITY AVE, HILLCREST; 619/683-9322
If Wonder and Roman Meal aren't quite your slice of bread, check out the superb selection of loaves at this upscale neighborhood bakery. Owner Charles Kaufman toured Europe in search of the perfect bread before opening the business, and his legwork shows: the beauties baked here taste as divine as they look. Varieties range from simple sourdough baguettes and rustic whole-grain loaves to gourmet breads flavored with black olives, sun-dried tomatoes, various cheeses, or nuts. Buy loaves to go, or settle into the cafe for a sandwich, a caffe latte, and one of the bakery's fabulous Paradise bars for dessert. Bonus for dog owners: a small patio out front—complete with water bowl—allows pets and their humans a place to sit, dine, and watch the Hillcrest world wander by. *$; no credit cards; checks OK; breakfast, lunch, dinner every day (closes by 7pm); no alcohol; no reservations; map:N2* &

The Brigantine / ★★

2725 SHELTER ISLAND DR, SHELTER ISLAND (AND BRANCHES); 619/224-2871
San Diego's nicest restaurant chain offers multiple locations and a crowd-pleasing menu heavy on fresh seafood. Decor might be called Nautical Fern Bar, with dark wood, lush greenery, and fresh-faced servers. Young singles, early bird retirees, and entire families gather in Brig bars, dining rooms, and patios from Old Town to Del Mar. Steaks, pastas, and the chicken tequila are best bets if you don't care for fish. Otherwise, take advantage of the fresh swordfish, salmon, mahimahi, and ono grilled or broiled. Both the shrimp cocktail and the deep-fried coconut-crusted shrimp are first rate. Dinners include a choice of soup or salad (the Italian/blue cheese house dressing is outstanding) and rice pilaf or baked potatoes. The burger is always good—have it served on a toasted bolillo (crusty Mexican roll). The wine list is extensive and well priced. *$$; AE, CB, DC, MC, V; checks OK; lunch, dinner every day; full bar; reservations recommended; map:E7*

Bully's North / ★★☆

1404 CAMINO DEL MAR, DEL MAR; 858/755-1660
 Though the atmosphere is not quite the same since California's no–smoking law went into effect (some places are just meant to have clouds), Bully's still exudes plenty of character (and characters). Del Mar residents and the summer racetrack crowd have been patronizing this

dark and clubby restaurant with its deep red booths since the 1960s—making it their preferred haunt for a meat fix. The full- or half-cut prime rib, filet mignon, New York, porterhouse, and prime top sirloin steaks are renowned among local meat lovers (the prime rib is hand-selected USDA Choice, prime-grade Midwestern, corn-fed aged beef). Both top sirloin and prime rib can be ordered as a combo plate with lobster, crab leg, or shrimp, and every meal comes with soup or salad and baked potato, French fries, rice pilaf, or Spanish rice. Other favorites include the steadfast Bully Burger, French dip, New York steak sandwich, and baby back ribs. Non-bovine eaters can select from various seafood or chicken dishes, or daily specials that might feature fresh sea bass or halibut. The bar is a local institution, particularly during summer. *$$; AE, DC, MC, V; local checks only; breakfast, lunch, dinner every day; full bar; no reservations; map:GG7* &

Cafe 222 / ★

222 ISLAND AVE, DOWNTOWN; 619/236-9902

"The man who gets breakfast in bed is probably in the hospital," reads the menu at this irreverent egg-and-waffle eatery. The cafe is tiny—a corner storefront with a half dozen tables and whimsical decor such as chandeliers made of teacups and spoons. The menu is hearty: "big, fat, golden brown waffles" leads the list. "Hash and eggs, ask about it—not that crappy corned beef," we are assured. But despite the lighthearted prose and the rubber chickens hanging on the wall, the food is great and attracts a waiting line of hungry downtowners. For breakfast, order pumpkin or sweet corn waffles, or Joe's special—"a frittata-ish thing with toast." Green Eggs (spinach) and Spam Scramble is just as basic as it sounds. For lunch, choose grilled turkey, goat cheese, and pesto on rosemary focaccia or one of 222's other trendy sandwiches. *$; cash only; breakfast, lunch every day; no alcohol; no reservations; map:N8* &

Cafe Athena / ★

1846 GARNET AVE, PACIFIC BEACH; 858/274-1140

Service has always been the Achilles heel of this comfy, casual Greek eatery in one of Pacific Beach's wood-shingled strip malls, but the food makes up for it. Locals in casual clothes amble in to eat and converse, not to see and be seen. The restaurant's interior, although architecturally uninspired, is gladdened by oil paintings of the Greek isles crowding the walls. In addition to satisfying dishes such as lemon chicken soup (a bit chunky with lots of rice) and cinnamon-laced moussaka with a side of rice pilaf, there are some memorable house specialties. Try the Shrimp Scorpio: shrimp grilled and then baked in a spicy sauce of garlic, olive oil, parsley, and tomatoes. Spinach pastitsio is another house specialty; it's a creamy casserole of penne pasta, spinach, and bechamel sauce. For an appetizer, split an order of four delicately flavored bourekia, fried rolls of filo stuffed with flavorful ground lamb, onion, and pine nuts. The hummus, tzatziki, and taramasalata are all inspired. There's a brisk business in takeout and catering service too. *$; AE, CB, DC, DIS, MC, V; no checks; lunch, dinner every day; beer and wine; reservations recommended for groups of six or more; map:KK7* &

Cafe Del Mar / ★★

1247 CAMINO DEL MAR, DEL MAR; 858/481-1133
For almost two decades, Cafe Del Mar has been the delightful, romantic (yet also casual and friendly) neighborhood restaurant every beach town deserves. Twinkling lights festoon fig trees overhead, and the patio areas are reminiscent of a Mediterranean bistro. There's nothing diminutive about the food, however. The filet mignon, served on a large, deep plate, swims in a rich roasted shallot sauce. A grilled pork loin chop is accompanied by herbed mashed potatoes. At least nine specials are offered nightly, ranging from sautéed sea scallops with a roasted red pepper sauce to wild mushrooms in wine over fettuccine. Hot, crusty baguettes are perfect for mopping up. Owner Steve Kranhold ("Kranny") is often on hand—he's also been involved with larger successful restaurants in town, but Cafe Del Mar remains his baby. *$$; AE, MC, V; no checks; lunch, dinner every day, brunch Sat–Sun; full bar; reservations recommended; map:GG7* &

Cafe Japengo / ★★

8960 UNIVERSITY CENTER LN, LA JOLLA; 858/450-3355
Owned by the adjacent Hyatt Regency La Jolla, Cafe Japengo is one of the most stylish and sophisticated restaurants in San Diego County, catering to the unabashedly trendy who relish attitude along with their order. The decor is a marvelous combination of industrial chic, Asian design, and California cliché—exposed-duct ceilings, Japanese-pebble flooring, Chinese paper lanterns, bamboo and birds of paradise, an exhibition kitchen, and showpiece sushi bar. The menu is well-coordinated with the environment—an eclectic blend of Asian inspiration and North and South American influences. Dinners include imaginative miso marinated halibut over Israeli couscous (with straw mushrooms, soy mirin, and crispy sweet potato), tamarind-honey glazed swordfish (with citrus black bean sauce, wok-mixed vegetables, and crispy leeks), grilled beef filet on garlic-chili mashed potatoes (with Chinese broccoli, cipolline onions, and black bean demi-glace), and ten-ingredient wok-fried rice. And for dessert? What else but warm gingerbread. *$$$; AE, DC, DIS, MC, V; no checks; lunch Mon–Fri, dinner every day; full bar; reservations required; map:II6* &

Cafe Pacifica / ★★☆

2414 SAN DIEGO AVE, OLD TOWN; 619/291-6666

When it opened in 1980, Cafe Pacifica was one of the first places in town to offer exotic dishes like New Zealand green-lipped mussels. Today, this culinary pioneer continues to present fresh, carefully prepared versions of everything from catfish to seafood-studded pastas. The clam chowder makes a fine starter, as does a portobello mushroom stuffed with crab. Signature dishes include lobster bouillabaisse, seared ahi (often served with a ginger butter), and crab-stuffed sole. And don't miss the crème brûlée for dessert; it's one of the best in the area. Best seating is in the upper dining room, which has an airy, patiolike ambience, though the see-and-be-seen crowd prefers to be seated by the front door. Although the place has a sophisticated menu with wine prices to match, there's no need to dress up; service and ambience are pretty low-key. Take advantage of the valet service, as parking is notoriously tight in this tourist-heavy neighborhood. *$$; AE, DC, DIS, MC, V; no checks; dinner every day; full bar; reservations recommended; map:J2*

Café Sevilla / ★★

555 4TH AVE, DOWNTOWN; 619/233-5979

After a long, hard day, downtown office workers unwind at this Spanish tapas bar in the Gaslamp district, and empty bar stools are a rarity after 5pm. The ambience is the main draw. Bullfight posters and oil paintings of Andalusian beauties surround the mirrored bar, where two bartenders dispense plates of Spanish olives stuffed with anchovies and glasses of Spanish and domestic wine. Although you can make a dinner of such tapas as tortilla española, fried calamari, or mushrooms in white wine garlic sauce at either of the two bars (serenaded by live flamenco guitar after 9:30pm), you might head to the dining room, El Patio Andaluz, which is dressed up like a courtyard from southern Spain. Wrought-iron grills and potted geraniums decorate make-believe windows, and a black light brings out a ceiling full of stars. The most popular dish here is traditional paella valenciana—seafood, sausage, and chicken in saffron rice—but you can also get seafood-only and vegetarian versions. Some of the desserts (all made on the premises) really do shine, like the sinful crema catalana, a chocolate espresso crème brûlée topped with whipped cream, with a bottom layer of chocolate chips. In the downstairs Club Sevilla, there's a different brand of live Latino music nightly, with samba and lambada lessons, Spanish rock, salsa, and on Fridays and Saturdays, a so-so flamenco dinner show for $35. *$$; AE, DC, DIS, MC, V; no checks; dinner every day; full bar; reservations recommended; sevilla@ cafesevilla.com; www.cafesevilla.com; map:O8* &

Cafe Zinc / ★★

132 S CEDROS AVE, SOLANA BEACH; 858/793-5436

The first eatery to set up shop in the Cedros Design District was destined to be a hit just by virtue of location. The fact that the food is terrific is a happy bonus. Though several tables are positioned indoors, dining is mainly alfresco on the people-watching front patio, the sunny side area, or the reclusive rear yard (where tables teeter precariously atop gravel). Breakfast items run from simple bagels and muffins to oatmeal with sour cherry and nut topping and frittata with cucumber salsa; ever-comforting fruit crisp or bread pudding are available on weekends. Lunch entrees, salad samplers, and specialty soups change daily, and all creations are meatless. Good bets are the vegetarian Zinc burger and the colorful mixed vegetable sandwich (pain rustique bread filled with thinly sliced fennel, aioli, red and green bell peppers, radish, celery, arugula, hard-boiled egg, olive tapenade, and vinaigrette). Personal pizzas are nouvelle hard-liners with pesto, Mexican, or southwestern toppings. *$; No credit cards; checks OK; breakfast, lunch every day; no alcohol; no reservations; map:FF7* &

Cafe Zucchero / ★★

1731 INDIA ST, DOWNTOWN; 619/531-1731

Arguably the best Italian restaurant in Little Italy, Cafe Zucchero gets the nod for stylish decor, pleasant service, and some outstanding dishes. The place is small but inviting, with marble tables and floors inside, a few tables on the sidewalk, and a charming patio out back. Lunch is this cafe's strong point, and diners in the know order the panini (sandwiches) filled with grilled vegetables and Gorgonzola or chicken and feta cheese. On the lighter side, the kitchen also turns out appealing salads and a nice assortment of antipasti. At night, go for pastas: either the chicken pesto or the spaghetti dressed with truffle-flavored oil and mozzarella cheese. And save room for dessert: they make marvelous cannoli here, and the cafe is famous throughout town for its expertly made gelati. The smooth, intense Italian ice cream comes in classic flavors including hazelnut, chocolate, vanilla, and mascarpone. Sit out on the patio on a sunny day, and you might as well be in Siena. *$; AE, DIS, MC, V; no checks; breakfast, lunch, dinner every day; beer and wine; reservations accepted; map:M6* &

California Cuisine / ★★★

1027 UNIVERSITY AVE, HILLCREST; (619)543-0790

Consistently at the top of the charts when it comes to innovative fare, Cal Cuisine (as locals say) is a foodie's delight—not to mention a favorite haunt of the trendy and tuned in. Executive chef Chris Walsh keeps the ever-changing menu fresh by using the best seasonal produce available, and whether he's offering tiny grilled eggplant stuffed with goat cheese, a fat chile relleno in a pool of cilantro crème fraîche, or a soup puréed from assorted squash, his daily inventions are always worth a spin. So are the warm chicken salad with nuts, the bitter and mellow greens (both helped build the restaurant's reputation), and the seafood pasta strewn with mussels, rock shrimp, and feta cheese. Service is well informed and attentive without being intrusive and the staff is good about letting diners linger. The dining room is sleek and compact with a chic, stylish feeling, accented with contemporary art and a good-looking clientele. Out back, a multileveled patio decorated with greenery and fountains offers one of the coziest outdoor dining venues in town. *$$$; AE, DC, DIS, MC, V; no checks; lunch Tues–Fri, dinner Tues–Sun; beer and wine; reservations recommended; map:N2* &

Cass Street Bar & Grill / ★★

4612 CASS ST, PACIFIC BEACH; 858/270-1320

No fussy yuppie bar this. Cass Street Bar and Grill caters to locals, who drop by for the camaraderie, the pool tables, the connoisseur's beer selection, and the best bar fare at the beach. Burgers are a customer favorite, and those in the know choose a topping of sautéed onions and melted cheese. The chicken sandwich decorated with avocado and served on a baguette is pretty impressive, and there's a reason that huge marlin is hanging on the wall: the fish is great. Get a fish taco platter with grilled or fried fish, or the fresh fish of the day served with two side dishes, and you'll have plenty to cheer about besides the low prices, microbrews, and congenial crowd. Lose the tie and the high heels before you drop by; this is a shorts and T-shirt kind of a place. *$; cash only; breakfast, lunch, dinner every day; beer and wine; no reservations; map:KK7* &

Cecil's Cafe & Fish Market / ★⯪

5083 SANTA MONICA AVE, OCEAN BEACH; 619/222-0501

Even if this ultracasual cafe with the weathered, lived-in look weren't right across from the beach, we'd come here often. (Of course, the unobstructed views of surfers, seagulls, and the Ocean Beach Pier are a nice touch, as is the westerly sea breeze you get at the outside tables.) Diners of all ages jam the place during weekend breakfasts—arguably the best meal of the day here—to feast on good old-timey oatmeal, spicy Mexican egg scrambles, substantial pancakes, and Belgian waffles. The coffee refills are timely, the short-order cooks fast, and the wait staff friendly. At lunch or dinner, choose the lobster bisque, the excellent chili, or one of the simply prepared seafood dishes or sandwiches. Parking can be difficult, so be prepared to park on a side street and walk at least a block or two. Watch for no-parking signs that mention specific street-cleaning days; you don't want a ticket to ruin such a laid-back, beachy experience. *$; AE, CB, DC, DIS, MC, V; no checks; breakfast, lunch, dinner every day; full bar; reservations recommended; map:B2* &

Chameleon Cafe / ★★☆

1301 ORANGE AVE, CORONADO; 619/437-6677
Folks in this prosperous neighborhood could choose to eat just about anywhere they like. That makes it doubly impressive that so many locals show up at this striking cafe, marked by a flamboyant neon sign and filled with designer touches such as custom-made plates and enormous flower arrangements. Lucky are the tourists who find this little treasure, whose offbeat menu incorporates Pacific Rim, Southwest, and the various whims of executive chef/owner Ken Irvine. Think crab and lobster pot stickers, tea-smoked duck, pork prime rib and smoked chili "smashed" potatoes, and you'll have a pretty good idea of the Chameleon's ever-shifting lineup. For dessert, chocolate banana bread pudding is worth each guilt-filled calorie. Best seating is in the large, cushy booths at the edges of the noisy, open dining room with a view of the kitchen, or at the window tables; dress ranges from polo shirts to Zegna ties. An adjacent bar specializes in martinis and is a good place to drop in for a quick bite or quaff. *$$; AE, CB, DC, DIS, MC, V; no checks; lunch, dinner every day; full bar; reservations recommended; map:NN5* &

Chart House / ★

525 HARBOR DR, DOWNTOWN (AND BRANCHES); 619/233-7391
Weary conventioneers rely on soothing breaks at this dependable steak and seafood restaurant perched atop 30 wood pilings above San Diego Bay. The peaked-roof white building was dedicated as headquarters for the San Diego Rowing Club in 1900; club members held firm to their home until 1974, when they moved to Mission Bay. The Chart House chain then renovated the sagging building into a charming restaurant filled with nautical memorabilia. The prime rib, grilled fish, salad bar, and killer mud pie are the menu's best offerings. Though the quality of the cooking doesn't match that of other downtown steak houses, the views of the bay and nostalgic setting are worth a visit and a sunset drink. The Coronado branch is housed in the Hotel del Coronado's original 1887 boathouse; the La Jolla site overlooks the cove. *$$; AE, CB, DC, DIS, MC, V; no checks; lunch, dinner every day; full bar; reservations recommended; map:N9* &

The Cheese Shop / ★

627 4TH AVE, DOWNTOWN; 619/232-2303
2165 AVENIDA DE LA PLAYA, LA JOLLA; 858/459-3921
 Can a downtown restaurant thrive on the simple premise of putting thinly sliced meats between two slices of bread? The Cheese Shop can because it makes every sandwich into a teetering tower of Dagwoodian generosity. Heaps of roasted-on-the-premises turkey breast or rare beef aren't enough: the sandwich makers here love adding at least another

inch of fresh avocado, plus plenty of tomato, onion, and lettuce. In short, the slippery, fresh, gooey "works." Imported and domestic cheeses allow you to customize sandwiches to a higher gourmet standard. Ask owner Dave for his thoughts on peanut butter sandwiches (he likes 'em with Dijon mustard!). Lunchtime here is a scene: suited executives next to blue-jeaned artists. Each knows this is the best value in the Gaslamp. The La Jolla location is a great place to pick up a quick lunch for a beach picnic. *$; MC, V; local checks only; breakfast, lunch every day; beer and wine; no reservations; map:N8 and JJ7* &

Chez Loma / ★★

1132 LOMA AVE, CORONADO; 619/435-0661

Before you even enter this restaurant, you'll be charmed by the handsome Victorian house and old-money elegance of the Coronado neighborhood. Inside, chef Ken Irvine's graceful mix of classic and updated French cuisine is sure to impress. The small menu emphasizes seasonal seafood and usually includes stellar preparations of duck, salmon, and filet mignon (including a signature steak in a heady blue cheese sauce). The servers here are particularly well-trained—always available when needed, but never intrusive. Add a carefully chosen wine list, romantic enclosed patio, and very fair prices for the quality, and you've got one of Coronado's most delightful eateries. It's an especially good choice for couples celebrating anniversaries. Although children are welcome, this is one of the more grown-up-feeling establishments in town. *$$; AE, DC, DIS, MC, V; no checks; dinner every day, brunch Sun; full bar; reservations recommended; map:NN5*

Chilango's Mexico City Grill / ★★

142 UNIVERSITY AVE, HILLCREST; 619/294-8646

Some of the most interesting and authentic Mexican fare in San Diego is served here in the heart of Hillcrest. The restaurant is small and so are the prices, but the flavors are big, bold, and irresistible. Bring an asbestos palate for the super-spicy chicken-tortilla soup, a particular favorite here (for something milder, choose the black bean porridge). Move on to entrees such as roasted chicken, distinctively flavored with citrus juice and achiote paste; huaraches (thick corn tortillas topped with pork, salsa, and Mexican cheese); and chilaquiles, the comfort-food casserole fashioned from tortillas, chicken, onion, and cilantro. Need a palate quencher? Sample the fresh fruit salad laced with lime juice and cilantro, and you'll never touch fruit cocktail again. *$; cash only; lunch, dinner every day; no alcohol; no reservations; map:N2*

Cilantro's / ★★⯪

3702 VIA DE LA VALLE, DEL MAR; 858/259-8777

Cilantro's popularity has yet to diminish, even though other "Southwest-oriented" establishments have sprung up nearby (including Epazote, under the same ownership). Coastal dwellers and visiting celebs—as well as the horsey set—gather at this surprisingly unpretentious restaurant with its warm, inviting dining room and very cool bar. The menu offers a crowd-pleasing selection of spit-roasted and grilled meats and fish. Delicious dishes include seafood enchiladas (shrimp, crab, scallops, and Swiss chard with roasted tomato sauce and sautéed seasonal vegetables) and Cilantro's fajitas (fresh flour tortillas, black beans, guacamole, and spicy carrots, with a choice of steak, chicken, or shrimp). The tapas menu offers creative (and less costly) mini-meals. The benign-sounding tricolored tortilla chips are such a treat that consummate homemaker Martha Stewart requested the recipe from chef Tim Sullivan. Whatever you eat, try to save room for the house dessert—profiteroles stuffed with Häagen-Dazs cappuccino ice cream and drizzled with caramel sauce. *$$; AE, DC, MC, V; no checks; lunch, dinner every day; full bar; reservations accepted; www.cilantros.com; map:GG7* ♿

Cody's at the Cove / ★★

8030 GIRARD AVE, LA JOLLA; 858/459-0040

Cody's menu is creative enough to intrigue adventurous eaters and portions are hearty enough to satisfy big appetites—it's cutting-edge without being prissy. Breakfast is a good bet, especially if you splurge on one of the egg dishes. Our favorite is scrambled eggs with goat cheese and French chicken sausage—served with a generous side of tasty home fries. You'll find plenty of temptations at lunch and dinner, too. Entree salads and burgers are reliably good, but fish dishes are a specialty. For lunch, try the grilled albacore tuna sandwich dressed up with arugula, roasted tomato, and a spicy chipotle marinade. For dinner, start with an order of Cody's Crab Potato Cake, then move on with herb-braised Pacific cod or, for big appetites, a cracked pepper sirloin with roasted-garlic mashed potatoes. The ambience at Cody's is casual. Naturally, the patio tables with a view of La Jolla Cove are the best. The only drawback is the service. It's friendly, but tends to be slow when the place is full. *$$; MC, V; local checks only; breakfast Fri–Sun, lunch, dinner every day; beer and wine; reservations accepted; map:JJ7* ♿

Crest Cafe / ★

425 ROBINSON AVE, HILLCREST; 619/295-2510

Although prices have been creeping up over the years, the funky Crest Cafe remains a favorite destination for upscale but reasonable diner fare in enormous portions. The lengthy menu is best known for its burger selection: juicy, jumbo-size patties with imaginative toppings and excellent french fries on the side. Other specialties include the grilled vegetable sandwich, spicy Mexican machaca, and the notorious onion loaf (think of thin, lightly battered onion rings baked in a meat loaf pan). Bonus: the cafe is open until midnight, a plus in this town that tends to close down early, and the energetic staff is always cheerful. Tables are close together and eavesdropping is unavoidable, but with this collection of young and old, gay and straight, liberal and conservative, the listening is just as good as the food. *$; AE, D, MC, V; no checks; breakfast, lunch, dinner every day; beer and wine; reservations recommended; map:N2*

D. Z. Akin's / ★★☆

6930 ALVARADO RD, LA MESA; 619/265-0218

When it comes to delicatessens, San Diego is no New York or Los Angeles. Luckily, there's D. Z. Akin's, which legions of fans consider the best deli in town. Owners Debbie and Zvika Akin have created a deli faithful to the classic model: leatherette booths, a crock of dill pickles on every table, hardworking waitresses, and a dizzying lineup of sandwiches, smoked fish, entrees, and desserts. The piled-high triple-decker sandwiches here have been known to make first-time visitors gasp, and even the regular-size sandwiches can stupefy those with smaller appetites. Sharing the spotlight with pastrami on rye are matzo ball soup, excellent knishes, and chopped liver. The casual, bustling atmosphere attracts lots of families, and it's not uncommon to see three or four generations seated at the Formica tables. On your way out, check out the bakery and counter area for sliced meats and cheeses, salads, side dishes, and freshly baked breads and pastries to go. *$$; MC, V; no checks; breakfast, lunch, dinner every day; beer and wine; reservations recommended for groups of six or more; map:LL2* &

Delicias / ★★★☆

6106 PASEO DELICIAS, RANCHO SANTA FE; 858/756-8000

Named for the tony street that runs through Rancho Santa Fe's chic village center, Delicias is definitely a celebrity on the San Diego County dining scent. For one thing, it's drop-dead gorgeous, and not a single designer touch has been neglected. Spectacular flower arangements punctuate the bar and adjacent dining room, which is bedecked with intricate tapestries. The place even has miniature footstools for ladies' purses, so that Vuitton bag never has to be slung over a chair. The visibly affluent, well-groomed clientele comes as much for the scene as the cuisine, and you'd better not walk in unless you're dressed to impress and ready to turn heads. The cuisine defies easy description, but tends to be a well-balanced mix of new California and classic French. The kitchen has a winning way with fish, and regulars here have learned that you can never go wrong with any of the seafood specials. Swordfish, salmon, escolar, and ahi make regular appearances, generally grilled and served with anything from tropical fruit salsa to polenta to garlic- or truffle-mashed potatoes. Hearty risottos are another specialty, and if they're serving the over-sized veal chop, go for it. Desserts are simpler than the rest of the menu, with homey selections like apple bread pudding or chocolate baby cakes. Prime seating is at the bar near the entrance, at the edges of the grand dining room, or in the flower-filled patio near the wood-burning fireplace. Definitely a place for those with Dom Perignon tastes and titanium credit cards, this gorgeous restaurant is a delicious find indeed. *$$$; AE, CB, DC, DIS, MC, V; no checks; lunch Wed–Sat, dinner Tues–Sat; full bar; reservations recommended; map:EE5* &

Del Mar Pizza / ★★☆

211 15TH ST, DEL MAR; 858/481-8088

A neon sign posted in the window of this simple storefront operation proclaims Tony, the proprietor, "King of the Crust." New Yorkers homesick for real pizza pies as well as anyone just wondering what all the fuss is about make a beeline for this Del Mar hideaway, with its dozen or so little tables covered in red-and-white-checkered cloths. Even the most critical aficionados agree the pizza tastes like the real thing, as they munch away on that fabulous crisp crust, served with classic ingredients including sausage, pepperoni, anchovies, mushrooms, and Canadian bacon. The pizzas come in small or large, and cheese or pepperoni pies are available by the slice. Other menu items include straightforward stuffed eggplant parmigiana, lasagne, pastas, hot sandwiches, and Italian subs. *$; cash only; lunch, dinner every day; beer and wine; no reservations; map:GG7* &

Dobson's Bar & Restaurant / ★★★

956 BROADWAY CIRCLE, DOWNTOWN; 619/231-6771

One of San Diego's classiest watering holes, Dobson's has a big-city ambience and a clientele to match. Downstairs, the local mover-and-shaker crowd congregates at the polished bar for well-made martinis and smart conversation. Upstairs, a smallish dining room offers marvelous American and French cuisine. Specialties of the house include a rich-as-sin mussel bisque flavored with lobster stock and crowned with puff pastry, sautéed sweetbreads with a texture "like buttah," fresh fish specials, and rack of lamb. For lunch, try the Greek salad or the soup du jour, along with several refills of the warm house sourdough. This is a popular place for pre-theater dining and a good destination for a business lunch or dinner. The favored tables are upstairs overlooking the ever-bustling bar (where you can also dine). For a romantic evening, request the tiny upstairs alcove that's perfect for two. *$$; AE, CB, DC, MC, V; no checks; lunch Mon–Fri, dinner Mon–Sat; full bar; reservations recommended; map:N7*

61

Don's Country Kitchen / ★★

2885 ROOSEVELT ST, CARLSBAD; 760/729-2274

Welcome to an old-fashioned diner straight out of central casting, complete with chatty, down-to-earth waitresses and a fast-moving short-order cook. Take a seat at the well-worn counter and prepare for some difficult choices: buttermilk biscuits with sausage gravy, or eggy, moist French toast? Apple-topped flapjacks, or an extra side of home fries? The choices multiply at lunch, when you're forced to choose between the likes of homemade chicken soup, piled-high sandwiches, marvelous meat loaf, or just-roasted turkey with mashed potatoes. Whatever you choose, save some room for bread pudding or fruit pie. Soft drinks are served in the can, there's a bottle of maple syrup on each table, and half the crowd is seated in high chairs. Nouvelle? No way, and that's what we love about Don's. *$; MC, V; no checks; breakfast, lunch every day; no alcohol; no reservations; map:CC7* &

Downtown Johnny Brown's / ★★

1220 3RD AVE, DOWNTOWN; 619/232-8414

Comfortable, casual, and cool, Johnny's is a roll-up-your-shirtsleeves, shoot-some-pool-over-lunch kind of place. The perennially popular bar and grill overlooks the plaza of the busy community concourse, a center for activities ranging from purebred cat shows to opera premieres. Lots of local office folks come by for lunch or happy hour as well. That leads to a pretty eclectic crowd at Johnny's, and everybody knows the drill: line up, place your order at the counter, then snag a table inside or on the patio. When your meal's ready, they'll call you. Good-sized burgers are hot sellers here, and come with a mountain of french fries so tasty it's worth trying to eat them all. Grilled chicken and taco salads are a sure bet too, and if they're serving grilled ahi, go for it—it's awesome. The setting is nothing fancy, but there's a rockin' loud jukebox and plenty of great beer on tap and by the bottle. *$; AE, DIS, MC, V; no checks; lunch, dinner every day; full bar; no reservations; www.sandiegobars.com; map:N7*

El Agave / ★★★

2304 SAN DIEGO AVE, OLD TOWN; 619/220-0692

Notorious for its incredible selection of fine tequilas, El Agave is also considered the city's top destination for regional Mexican cuisine. It's a welcome change from most of the other eateries in Old Town, where gringo-style chimichangas and gooey enchiladas reign. This is the place to savor real mole sauce ladled over chicken or pork (the dark, smoky mole poblano here is a standout), rarely seen Mexican soups (the squash soup shouldn't be missed); and other artful dishes, including quesadillas stuffed with vegetables, Mexican cheeses, or shredded seasoned poultry. Force us to choose a favorite and it would be the marinated shrimp tossed with beans, cactus strips, and orange. For dessert, authentic versions of flan, a custardlike dish, showcase the sweeter side of Latin cuisine. Now, about that tequila: the restaurant offers more than 100 varieties by the shot, ranging in price from around $4 for familiar brands to well over $100 for rare aged tequilas smoother than old sippin' whiskey. *$$; AE, MC, V; no checks; lunch, dinner every day; full bar; reservations recommended; map:J2*

El Bizcocho / ★★★

17550 BERNARDO OAKS DR (RANCHO BERNARDO INN), RANCHO BERNARDO; 858/675-8500

One of the most consistent dining rooms in the county, El Bizcocho charms diners with artful service, gifted chefs, and understated elegance. The spacious room evokes an upmarket country inn, with fireplace, well-spaced tables, and a view of the carefully groomed golf course. Updated French cuisine has always been a signature here, with classics like escargot topped with puff pastry and quickly seared foie gras sharing billing with more innovative creations. Depending on the season, these inventions could be fingertip-sized scallops arranged on ravioli and drizzled with vanilla, or a napoleon of lobster and caviar amid layers of phyllo. Fresh fish is treated with special reverence, so don't miss the roasted monkfish or sautéed John Dory. Roasted free-range chicken and braised duckling paired with fresh fruit are other standouts. Order the dessert soufflés at the beginning of a meal, and they'll arrive airy and perfect, right on schedule, just as you're ready for espresso. Waiters are personable yet professional and the wine list is superb, with several hundred top-notch brands from California and France from which to choose. An adjoining bar often features live piano music, providing an extra touch of class to this stately hacienda. Sunday brunch is an elegant affair, worth an extra night's stay at the hotel so you can take a proper siesta afterward. *$$$; AE, CB, DC, DIS, MC, V; checks OK; dinner every day, brunch Sun; full bar; reservations recommended; www.ranchobernardoinn.com; map:FF3* &

El Indio Shop / ★★☆

3695 INDIA ST, MIDDLETOWN; 619/299-0333
409 F ST, DOWNTOWN; 619/239-8151

In San Diego, the name El Indio is pretty much synonymous with Mexican food. Just about everyone in town knows this little shop, which has built a reputation on tortilla chips, fresh salsa, beef taquitos, and combo plates. The chili-dusted tortilla chips and freshly prepared corn or flour tortillas are favorite souvenirs—locals regularly mail these as care packages to less-fortunate East Coast dwellers. In a nod to the times, a vegetarian menu was added a few years ago, offering surprisingly tasty items such as mashed potato tacos and vegetarian tamales. At the original location on India Street, you can dine inside or across the street on a patio in the shadow of Interstate 5. The downtown location offers a more urban setting in the busy Gaslamp Quarter. To order, head for the counter, then wait until your number is called. Be prepared at lunch: some days it seems as though everyone in town is lined up and ready to place their order. Catering is available too—many a local wedding reception has featured El Indio selections—and many items on the menu are available refrigerated or frozen for bulk orders. *$; MC, V; checks OK; breakfast, lunch, dinner every day; beer and wine; no reservations; map:L3* &

Embers Grille / ★☆

3924 W POINT LOMA BLVD, MIDWAY; 619/222-6877

Goat feta, roasted eggplant, grilled chicken, and smoky gouda cheese consort to create a SoCal palate of flavors in Embers' pizzas and pastas. For a taste that sings, try the Sun Dried Tomato Lovers Pizza, a delicious blend of sun-dried tomatoes, kalamata olives, fontina, roasted garlic, pine nuts, fresh basil, and Romano and goat cheeses. In all, choose from 23 different 10-inch pizzas. Several pasta dishes (some more interesting than others), salads, grilled chicken and fish, and a few sandwiches fill out the menu. Popular with office crews, this large place positively roars at lunchtime, when you have to shout to be heard. The big open space, exposed heating ducts and all, is painted a flat aubergine and decorated with large-format, unframed oil paintings and a sprinkling of green plants. The exhibition kitchen is set in the middle of the restaurant, which itself is set in the middle of a strip mall. It's not chic or trendy, but a good place to grab a pizza or healthy pasta and salad combo for lunch or dinner. *$; AE, DIS, MC, V; no checks; lunch, dinner Tues–Sun; beer and wine; reservations recommended; map:F1* &

Epazote / ★★

1555 CAMINO DEL MAR, DEL MAR; 858/259-9966

Like Cilantro's, its sibling up the road, Epazote features southwestern decor and cuisine with an ocean view. The dining room is bright, light, and chic, though most diners clamor for seats on the patio-with-a-view. The vast assortment of tapas grabs top honors, and the wait staff doesn't sniff at those who make a meal out of green corn tamales with lime cream, Dungeness crab corn cakes with chipotle aioli and tropical fruit salsa, coconut curry shrimp with guava barbecue sauce, or Navajo flatbread pizza. Favorite entrees include sesame-honey seared ahi with plantains and ginger-chili sauce, turkey and wild mushroom enchiladas with apricot-melon chutney and Swiss chard, and spit-roasted chicken with chipotle aioli, roasted garlic and peppers, and mashed potatoes. The bar is a happening spot at sunset, and live jazz is featured every Wednesday night. *$$; AE, DC, MC, V; no checks; lunch, dinner every day, brunch Sun; full bar; reservations recommended; www.epazote.com; map:GG7* &

Fairouz Restaurant & Gallery / ★

3166 MIDWAY DR #102, MIDWAY; 619/225-0308

Fairouz is an oasis of fine Greek and Lebanese cuisine and contemporary art in the wasteland of car washes and strip joints that line Midway Drive. Dark blue carpet and wood-grain Formica tables provide a simple backdrop for owner Ibrahim Al Nashashibi's stylized acrylic paintings, which completely fill two dining rooms. Al Nashashibi runs the restaurant with his Moroccan wife Hasida; his sister Sawzia does the cooking. Lovers of Greek food will recognize their favorites, including a very lemony avgolemono (chicken and rice soup), admirable tabbouleh, hummus, tzatziki, and gyros. It's hard to resist the daily lunch and dinner buffets: both are excellent values for carnivores or vegetarians, and a big hit with kids. The problem is, even if you try just half of the offerings in small portions, you come away significantly stuffed. Buffets consist of lots of salad ingredients, hot and cold potatoes, saffron rice, moussaka, lamb meat balls, and much more—in addition to the foods already mentioned. If humanly possible, save room for a dessert of rice pudding with rose water. Fairouz also caters. *$; AE, DC, DIS, MC, V; no checks; lunch, dinner every day; beer and wine; no reservations; map:H2* &

Fidel's / ★

607 VALLEY AVE, SOLANA BEACH; 858/755-5292

Unlike the more stalwart Tony's Jacal next door, Fidel's has a touristy feel and real appeal to anyone who wants Mexican-party ambience without crossing the border. The sprawl of dining rooms, bars, and patios, combined with Mexican tile, dangling piñatas, and norteño music, all contribute to the atmosphere. Accordingly, the place is a frenzied melange of first dates, celebratory groups, families, and fair and racetrack goers, not counting the buoyant students and surfers who show up for happy hour and the cheap taco bar. Standard Mexican favorites top the menu and nachos remain the appetizer of choice. Specialties include various renditions of chiles rellenos, carne and chicken asada, tortas, and tostadas. For something different, try nopales (nopal cactus in a spicy tomato and chile serrano sauce, topped with Monterey Jack cheese), or pescado ranchero (grilled dorado, topped with semispicy ranchero sauce). Burgers and fries are at the ready for kids, and logo T-shirts and baseball caps are for sale. *$; MC, V; no checks; breakfast, lunch, dinner every day; full bar; reservations recommended for 8 or more; map:FF7*

Filippi's Pizza Grotto / ★

1747 INDIA ST, DOWNTOWN (AND BRANCHES); 619/232-5094

 Mom and Pop are long gone, but seven sisters and brothers run this string of dependable Italian restaurants, situated all over San Diego. The original is in Little Italy and is the only one with a store. (That's how Filippi's began.) To enter, customers pass in single file past cases of cheese, sliced meats, a barrel of salted and filleted cod, breads from three bakeries, oils, vinegars, and every kind of pasta imaginable. The fragrance is overwhelmingly parmesan. The restaurant itself is huge, with an open kitchen and pizza oven, grotto-dark and busy-noisy. Tables are covered with red checkered cloths; Chianti bottles (hundreds, maybe thousands) hang from the rafters. The same theme prevails in other Filippi's locations in Pacific Beach and outlying neighborhoods. Specialties are lasagne, pizza, ravioli, spaghetti, hot sausage (made on the premises), and a variety of sandwiches on freshly crisp buns. Servings are ample; most diners leave with leftovers. Customers are clearly regulars, addressed by name by waitresses who seem to have been there forever. *$; AE, DC, DIS, MC, V; no checks; lunch, dinner every day; beer and wine; no reservations; map:M6* &

Fio's Cucina Italiana / ★★

801 5TH AVE, DOWNTOWN; 619/234-3467
Although it's only 10 years old, Fio's is both culinary landmark and downtown pioneer. It opened on a lonely corner in the Gaslamp Quarter long before the run-down neighborhood blossomed into a popular nighttime destination. While its upscale Italianate menu has been much copied by surrounding restaurants, Fio's still draws a faithful crowd that includes the occasional celebrity. Pastas rule the roost; both the wild mushroom ravioli and ravioli stuffed with pumpkin and squash are consistently good. There's a reliable chicken pesto dish too, and the kitchen is adept with seared salmon and peppery rare-cooked ahi. (Skip the lamb chops and the tiramisu, however.) The back dining rooms tend to be crowded and a bit noisy; ask to sit near the windows or out on the sidewalk patio for a more enjoyable evening. Along with a full bar, Fio's offers a fair wine selection, including some gorgeous Tuscan reds like Sassicaia. *$$; AE, CB, DC, DIS, MC, V; no checks; dinner every day; full bar; reservations recommended; map:O7* &

Firehouse Beach Cafe / ★

722 GRAND AVE, PACIFIC BEACH; 619/272-1999
Arrive early, skip the interior dining rooms, and head upstairs to the open-air deck overlooking the boardwalk and beach at this funky and immensely popular cafe. The view and casual ambience are the main draws, though you can't beat the unusual avocado omelet and spicy Bloody Marys as a perfect start for a day at the beach. Breakfast is the best meal, though hungry surfers have no trouble scarfing down the fresh fish tacos and burgers at lunch. The Pacific Beach firehouse is right next door; be prepared for sirens on busy weekends. Takeout is available for impromptu picnics on the sand. *$; AE, MC, V; no checks; breakfast, lunch, dinner every day; full bar; reservations recommended; map:KK7*

Fish Market Restaurant / ★★☆
Top of the Market / ★★

750 N HARBOR DR, DOWNTOWN; 619/232-3474

The panoramic views of San Diego Bay are as much an attraction as the huge menu of fresh catches at the Fish Market Restaurant and its upstairs, upscale sister, Top of the Market. Downstairs you'll find a full-service bar, a busy oyster bar, a counter displaying fresh fish to go, and the friendly, casual Fish Market Restaurant. Be prepared to wait for a table (have a drink in the bar or visit the oyster bar for an appetizer). Seating overlooks the bay; the best tables are the ones on the outdoor patio, directly over the water. The menu features a huge selection of fresh-caught seafood prepared grilled, Cajun style, or fried, according to your preference. Fish is served with a side of rice or au gratin potatoes (a sinfully delicious choice) and steaming hot sourdough bread. For the money and bustling ambience, the downstairs restaurant is the better bet. Upstairs, the more formal Top of the Market serves more exotic fresh seafood with more refined presentation and service and price tags to match. The list of offerings is astounding; you can tour the seven seas with Norwegian salmon, Alaskan halibut, New Zealand mussels, and Chilean sea bass, all flown in daily. The linen and candlelight setting is sublimely soothing; window tables present a romantic view of twinkling lights on boats floating in the bay. The wine list is excellent; servers will assist in matching grape and sea flavors. Save this one for a special night. *$$$; AE, CB, DC, DIS, MC, V; no checks; lunch, dinner every day; full bar; reservations recommended for large groups; map:M7* &

French Pastry Shop / ★★

5550 LA JOLLA BLVD, LA JOLLA; 858/454-9094

Reminiscent of neighborhood bakeries in Montparnasse or the Marais, this delightful restaurant features sit-down dining as well as a large takeout selection. Possible picnic fixings range from excellent pâtés (the coarse country variety is a standout) and a dozen types of bread to imported cheeses, assorted pastries, and gorgeous desserts. In addition to the informal dining room, there's an enclosed sidewalk patio that's just right for leisurely weekend breakfasts (our favorite meal here). Sit down with some good strong coffee, a selection of breakfast rolls or a *fines herbes* omelet (filled with fresh herbs like chervil, chives, parsley, and tarragon) and some of the cafe's fresh jam—then daydream your way all the way to the Right Bank. *$$; MC, V; checks OK; breakfast, lunch, dinner every day (closes by 6pm Monday); beer and wine; no reservations; map:KK7*

George's at the Cove / ★★☆

1250 PROSPECT ST, LA JOLLA; 858/454-4244

This popular restaurant on La Jolla's chic Prospect Street has been making local top-10 dining lists for more than a decade. Without a doubt, the three-level property has one of the finest views in the city—a panorama of La Jolla Cove and miles of Pacific coast. But unlike many a view restaurant in town, George's offers some terrific eating as well. The formal downstairs dining room is best for inventive fresh fish dishes that incorporate the flavors of California, France, and the Pacific Rim. The must-have starter is a smoked chicken and broccoli soup that's probably the most-requested recipe in the county (and yes, they'll share it). Follow

that with the likes of crab cakes with shiitake "hash browns," diver-harvested scallops partnered with caramelized cauliflower, or local mussels roasted at high heat for a bold, smoky flavor. Upstairs, in the bar (a top destination for singles) and on the rooftop terrace, the menu is a lower-priced affair that features excellent seafood salads, a gourmet meat loaf sandwich, very good focaccia, and splendid desserts. Two more reasons to drop by: the ever-changing collection of contemporary art in the main dining rooms, and owner George Hauer's thoughtfully chosen wine list. Note: Reservations aren't accepted on the upstairs terrace, which is open daily for lunch and dinner, but the open-air setting and throngs of swell-looking diners make it worth the wait. *$$$; AE, DC, DIS, MC, V; no checks; lunch Mon–Sat, dinner every day; full bar; reservations recommended downstairs; www.georgesatthecove.com; map:JJ7* &

Gourmet Bagger / ★☆

1400 CAMINO DE LA REINA, MISSION VALLEY; 619/299-1246
3357 ROSECRANS (AT LOMA SQUARE), POINT LOMA; 619/523-0590

Just as the name implies, this upscale takeout joint specializes in feeding the lunch crowd with style and speed. Sandwiches are the big draws, with dozens of options for meat lovers and vegetarians alike. If you're looking for the crème de la crème, choose one of the grilled chicken breast sandwiches with a variety of seasonings, the Bagger cheesesteak, or the classic grilled cheese on sourdough. The busy staff always manages to get special orders right, and customers are encouraged to specify whether they'd like extra cream cheese or nonfat mayo instead of regular. Main-dish salads are also very good, especially the Santa Fe Chicken or Baja Chicken creations. Orders, which are served in a brown bag, come with a chocolate chip cookie that adds the perfect childhood touch to a deliciously grown-up sack lunch. *$; no credit cards; checks OK; lunch Mon–Fri; no alcohol; no reservations; map:LL4 and H2*

The Grant Grill / unrated

326 BROADWAY (U.S. GRANT HOTEL), DOWNTOWN; 619/232-3121
With its dark-paneled walls, quaint hunting prints, and formally clad waiters, the Grant Grill resembles an old-fashioned gentlemen's club. Indeed, this hotel dining room, opened in 1910, once barred females from entering before 3pm. That all changed in 1969, when a group of San Diego women demanded a table for lunch. Since then, the restaurant has alternately thrived and languished as executive chefs have arrived, made their mark on the menu, and departed. Currently the kitchen is undergoing some changes, but the service remains consistent, and the Grant still attracts faithful legions in search of red meat, well-made martinis, and old-fashioned elegance. Signature dishes (and best bets) are the simply sautéed sweetbreads, rare-cooked rack of lamb, and a light-handed lobster bisque. The spacious booths are generally filled with businesspeople at lunch and concert- or opera-goers at night, so dress up a bit. The adjacent bar is every bit as handsome as the dining room, though it's modern enough to sport a wide-screen TV. The bar also offers a selection of sandwiches, pizzas, and salads for under $10. *$$$; AE, CB, DC, DIS, MC, V; checks OK; breakfast, lunch, dinner every day; full bar; reservations recommended; map:N7* &

Greek Islands Cafe / ★★

879 W HARBOR DR (SEAPORT VILLAGE), DOWNTOWN; 619/239-5216
Should you find yourself in tourist mecca Seaport Village, you're largely better off shopping than eating. Fortunately, there are a few exceptions to this rule. The friendly service and sunny bayfront patio at this modest Greek restaurant are bright enough to attract locals on their lunch hours, as well as out-of-towners with a yen for good gyros and pita bread. In addition to fat, juicy gyros and chicken sandwiches, the cafe offers a generous Greek salad and several combo plates. Order at the counter, then pick up your meal and choose a picnic table outside—or simply sit on the waterfront wall along the boardwalk. It's the best show around, with joggers, dog walkers, Rollerbladers, and conventioneers—not to mention a fabulous view of the harbor for the price of a $5 sandwich. *$; ash only; lunch, dinner every day; beer and wine; no reservations; map:M8* &

Greek Town Restaurant and Taverna / ★

431 E ST, DOWNTOWN; 619/232-0461
Among Greek Town's best features are the live music offered nightly from its tiny, second-story indoor balcony, the dependable Mediterranean menu, and the tenacity with which it has clung to this prime downtown location. Within seconds from Horton Plaza, the restaurant-tavern has featured hip-shaking belly dancers and Greek music on weekend nights since 1980. During the week you might hear slide guitar, blues, or jazz.

Tourists and downtowners squeeze into small booths or choose a table for four or more in the intimate dining room, adorned with fake frescoes and plastic grape clusters. Meats here are cooked to perfection: the enormous half chicken is crispy outside and succulent within, and accompanied by soup or salad, rice pilaf, potato wedge, and a side of institutional peas and carrots. The gyros are also tender, and vegetarians will be glad to know that the Extra Special Greek Salad is teeming with feta cheese, pepperoncini, artichoke hearts, red onion, and kalamata olives in addition to green leaf lettuce and fresh tomatoes. The restaurant stays open until 10pm; the bar until midnight. *$$; AE, DC, DIS, MC, V; no checks; lunch Tues–Fri, dinner Tues–Sun; full bar; reservations accepted; map:N7*

Gulf Coast Grill / ★★

4130 PARK BLVD, UNIVERSITY HEIGHTS; 619/295-2244
If you like feisty, fun-loving Cajun food, head to Gulf Coast Grill, home to some mighty fine southern cooking. This good-looking catery captivates on a number of levels. There's the spacious dining area: a two-level arrangement with golden walls, whimsical fish sculptures, and paintings of jazz musicians. There's the convivial bar, home to expertly mixed martinis and more than a dozen food-friendly beers. And of course, there's the hot stuff coming out of the kitchen, guaranteed to send you on a quick taste trip to the Big Easy. For starters, the barbecued shrimp in the shell are a messy must-have (dip into the spicy herb butter for maximum flavor). Signature entrees are the crawfish linguine, smoked pork chops, and homey breaded catfish. Dessert, anyone? Might as well get fat on the bourbon-sloshed bread pudding. Mmmm good. *$$; AE, CB, DC, DIS, MC, V; no checks; dinner every day, brunch Sun; full bar; reservations recommended; map:P1* &

Hamburger Mary's / ★

308 UNIVERSITY AVE, HILLCREST (AND BRANCHES); 619/491-0400
There's rarely a dull moment at this Hillcrest watering hole, where a lively, largely gay crowd drops in for dining, drinking, and socializing. Given the name, it's no surprise that hamburgers dominate the menu, with about a dozen toppings and variations on tap. They're always dependable, but other highlights of the menu are the chicken breast sandwiches, the onion rings, and several salads (who could resist the "Carmen Miranda," a fruit number served in a pineapple shell?). Sunday brunch draws fans of the custom-made omelets, desserts, and free-flowing coffee, orange juice, and bubbly. Prime seating is on the patio, where people-watching is every bit as important as dining—maybe more so. *$; AE, MC, V; no checks; breakfast, lunch, dinner every day, brunch Sun; full bar; no reservations; www.hamburgermarys.com; map:N2* &

Hob Nob Hill / ★★☆

2271 IST AVE, DOWNTOWN; 619/239-8176
One of the city's longest-running success stories, Hob Nob Hill is a throwback to the good ol' days. You know the ones: when nobody counted fat grams, butter was the spread of choice, and cholesterol wasn't a household word. This proudly old-fashioned eatery has satisfied San Diegans for over 50 years, and while these days you can order an egg-white-only omelet, why would you bother? This is the place for corned beef hash with eggs over easy, or a big stack of pancakes with real bacon on the side. Breakfast isn't the only highlight; lunch and dinner feature roasted turkey with gravy, stuffed bell peppers, club sandwiches, and three-bean salad. Don't come by too late, though; the place closes up around 9pm. Service is pure diner, with efficient, fast-moving waitresses in sensible shoes who are always ready with a coffee refill and a smile. The decor probably hasn't changed since the place opened in the 1940s, and that's just fine. Hob Nob is a classic example of if it ain't broke, don't fix it. *$$; AE, CB, DIS, MC, V; checks OK; breakfast, lunch, dinner every day; beer and wine; reservations recommended; map:N5* &

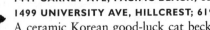

Hodad's / ★★☆

5010 NEWPORT AVE, OCEAN BEACH; 619/224-4623
Hodad's hamburger shop in Ocean Beach may have served slightly fewer than a billion burgers, but it's almost as famous as the place with the Golden Arches. Here's why: the juicy, jumbo-size burgers come heaped with enough condiments to rate a half dozen napkins (you'll need twice that many for the infamous double bacon burger). The onion rings are fat and fresh-tasting, the french fries crisp and hot. And you can see why the place is especially popular with the surfing crowd: they can check the breaks around the O.B. Pier just by stepping out the door. As for the decor, it's pure seaside retro, consisting mostly of old license plates, surf memorabilia, and a booth fashioned from a VW bus. Servers are fast and friendly, the beer's always plenty cold, and the dress code, if you could call it that, is minimal. All in all, Hodad's is every bit as much a San Diego institution as the zoo. *$; AE, DC, DIS, MC, V; no checks; lunch, dinner every day; beer and wine; no reservations; map:B3*

Ichiban PB / ★★☆
Ichiban / ★★☆

1441 GARNET AVE, PACIFIC BEACH; 858/270-5755
1499 UNIVERSITY AVE, HILLCREST; 619/299-7203

A ceramic Korean good-luck cat beckons from the window—heed his call and enter. This update of the original Japanese restaurant in Hillcrest serves the same superb food in a spruced-up environment. Order at the counter before slipping into one of the big, comfortable, C-shaped black naugahyde booths, or choose a tiny table for two. There are usually at least seven chefs, prep cooks, and servers bustling about the open kitchen, and two sushi chefs at the small bar. Everything at Ichiban (which means "number one" in Japanese) is delicious and authentic. The teriyaki chicken is an intense trio of chicken, fresh mushrooms, and zucchini in a thick, powerful teriyaki. It's accompanied by perfect sticky rice, a small seafood salad, marinated bean sprouts, and green salad with a delicious ginger dressing. The Fried Seafood Mixed has the same side dishes and arrives piping hot. Every day brings four new lunch and dinner specials, usually including a noodle dish and a sushi or sashimi combo.

The original Ichiban, in Hillcrest, serves equally delicious food in a more cramped setting, although now with an outdoor patio on busy Washington Street. It's sometimes hard to get a table, but one usually miraculously opens up just when you need it. *$; cash only; lunch Mon–Sat, dinner every day (Ichiban PB); lunch, dinner every day (Ichiban); beer and wine (Ichiban PB); no alcohol (Ichiban); no reservations; map:KK7 and P2*

Il Fornaio / ★★

1555 CAMINO DEL MAR, DEL MAR; 858/755-8876
When Il Fornaio opened its doors in the newly established Del Mar Plaza, this outpost of the popular California chain instantly became the hottest table in town for the upwardly mobile crowd, even rousting uppity La Jollans from their enclave. Reservations for dinner were backlogged for weeks, and it seemed nothing short of a miracle to garner a seat on the coveted ocean-view patio. The place still attracts crowds, though some of the excitement has worn off. The elegantly designed dining room is an instant transport to Italy with plenty of Carrara marble, terra-cotta flooring, vaulted ceilings, hand-painted trompe l'oeil friezes, and an open oven where meats and signature breads are baked to perfection (breads, pastries, and all food items are available for takeout). Most of the pasta dishes are excellent (ravioli di verdura al funghi is filled with Swiss chard, pine nuts, basil, parmesan, mixed mushrooms, and marinara), and the pizzas are fabulous (try pizza quattro stagioni with prosciutto cotto, asparagus, artichokes, and mushrooms). Other specialties include well-executed renditions of veal, steaks, chicken, and lamb. For dessert, the tiramisu is a must. For two weeks, every month of the year, the menu and wine list focus on a different region—enabling you to eat your way through Italy, from Trentino–Alto Adige all the way to Sicily. The chic bar is a favorite hangout for the beautiful people. *$$; AE, DC, MC, V; no checks; lunch, dinner every day, brunch Sun; full bar; reservations recommended; www.ilfornaio.com; map:GG7* &

Jake's Del Mar / ★★

1660 COAST BLVD, DEL MAR; 858/755-2002

Jake's has a laid-back rhythm, from the steady drumbeat of surf sounds to the endless parade of beachcombers seen through the big dining room windows. It's the quintessential place for a sunset cocktail followed by a hearty fish dinner. And seafood is Jake's strong suit, with the choices and preparations changing daily depending on chef Dan Castillo's selection from local purveyors. One favorite is a thick fillet of sea bass in a light tortilla crust, accompanied by an avocado aioli. Ahi gets a spicy (but not fiery) chili-heated crust. Other dinner entrees run the gamut from grilled chicken to roasted leg of lamb with herb Dijon mustard and mint-mango chutney. Steaks are generous and perfectly grilled, salads excellent, and the hot baguettes almost too tasty—you'll fill up on bread if you're not careful. The great value here is Jake's little-known policy of half-price "dinners" in the bar area (if ordered before 6pm). *$$; AE, DIS, MC, V; no checks; lunch Tues–Sun, dinner every day, brunch Sun; full bar; reservations recommended; www.hulapie.com; map:GG7* &

Jasmine / ★★★⯪

4609 CONVOY ST, KEARNY MESA; 858/268-0888

With seating for 800 diners, Jasmine at first glance might resemble a vast Chinese food factory. But don't be scared away. This handsome eatery specializing in Cantonese cooking manages to couple high quality with sheer quantity. Dim sum is served every day of the week, with the crowds peaking on Saturday and Sunday when the selection is at its most staggering. From sticky rice steamed in a lotus leaf to crispy chicken feet and barbecued pork, everybody's favorites show up on the fully laden carts. Dinner entrees include steamed fresh fish pulled live from large tanks just minutes before it hits your plate, excellent prawns the size of small lobsters, a marvelous shellfish stir-fry, and top-notch Peking duck. The place is equally popular with businesspeople and large families. While it's often packed, the skilled servers handle everyone with speed and aplomb. *$$; AE, MC, V; no checks; lunch, dinner every day; full bar; reservations recommended; map:JJ5*

Joe's Crab Shack / ★★★⯪

7610 HAZARD CENTER DR, MISSION VALLEY; 619/260-1111

One look at Joe's over-the-top nautical decor and wacky, fun-loving staff, and discriminating diners might assume that food takes a backseat to hilarity here. Wrong: the fish and seafood served in this every-day's-a-party-place is fresh and carefully prepared. Settle in among the plastic seagulls, sports memorabilia, stuffed fish, and other junk, and start off with a bowl of buttery-rich clam chowder. Or choose the crab cakes or deep-fried spicy shrimp; both make fine snacking before you take a mallet and start attacking a big batch of steamed king crab legs. Equally tasty, but a lot less messy, are the grilled halibut, the salmon, and the crawfish étouffée. Staffers are cheerful and enthusiastic (especially when they break into a chorus or two of "Macarena"), and there's an ample beer selection that might encourage you to join in as well. Consider the sunny patio for an offbeat business lunch—wouldn't you love to see the boss wearing Ray-Bans and a crab bib? *$$; AE, DC, DIS, MC, V; no checks; lunch, dinner every day; beer and wine; reservations recommended; www.joescrabshack.com; map:LL4* &

Jose's Courtroom / ★

1037 PROSPECT ST, LA JOLLA; 858/454-7655
Jose's is a fixture on La Jolla's busy Prospect Street, serving casual, hearty Mexican fare. The bar is ferociously busy on weekends, when it's often standing room only for the under-30 crowd. But don't let that deter you. Jose's menu offers a selection of reliably good burritos, tacos, quesadillas, and other dishes from south of the border. When ordering, keep in mind that portions are huge—splitting a combination plate is ideal for two, especially if you tend to fill up on the free tortilla chips and salsa. On a sunny spring or summer day, nibble nachos at one of the window tables for a view of La Jolla Cove and the passing parade. Weekday lunch or dinner is a saner time to visit, with friendlier service. *$; AE, CB, DC, DIS, MC, V; no checks; lunch, dinner every day; full bar; no reservations; map:JJ7* &

Jyoti Bihanga / ★★

3351 ADAMS AVE, NORMAL HEIGHTS; 619/282-4116
Surprisingly, San Diego has only a handful of vegetarian restaurants, an odd situation in a town where health and fitness keep a pretty high profile. But just when you've decided there's a fast food joint on every corner, you discover the soothing presence of Jyoti Bihanga, one of the city's oldest and best meat-free eateries. The serene, pastel-painted dining room has a definite New Age feeling that helps erase any type A tendencies at the door. Settle in with one of the many metaphysical publications distributed here for free. Savor the simple, satisfying cuisine, which ranges from enormous salads and excellent smoothies to overstuffed veggie burritos and cornbread chili. We've been hooked for years on the Infinite Blue Salad, a meal in itself of green beans, brown rice, cucumbers, blue cheese, and veggies. Stir-fries and curries are other perennial favorites, and the place even offers some simple dairy-free desserts such as pies and tofu-based cheesecake. The schedule here can change with little notice, so it's always best to call ahead. *$; AE, MC, V; checks OK; breakfast, lunch Mon–Sat, dinner Mon–Tues, Thurs–Sat; no alcohol; no reservations; map:LL4* &

Kaiserhof / ★★

2253 SUNSET CLIFFS BLVD, OCEAN BEACH; 619/224-0606

German food is done to perfection at this unpretentious biergarten just an oom-pah-pah from the beach. From authentic Wiener schnitzel to oh-so-tender beef rouladen to a dozen or so hearty side dishes, everything here is worthy of Oktoberfest in the Old Country. Portions are ridiculously large, and you may notice a waddle in your walk after a dinner that includes a choice of soup or salad, two side dishes, and plenty of bread. Of course, a number of German beers are available on tap, which makes up for a decided lack of wine selections. Best seating is in the dining room with the fireplace or on the shaded patio, depending on the weather. Customers range from fresh-faced young couples on first dates to white-haired regulars who've been Kaiserhof fans for decades. *$$; AE, CB, DC, DIS, MC, V; no checks; lunch, dinner every day; full bar; reservations recommended; map:C2* &

Karl Strauss Brewery & Grill / ★★

9675 SCRANTON RD, SORRENTO VALLEY (AND BRANCHES); 858/587-2739

Part of a locally founded chain that's become wildly popular over the last decade, this casual brewery-restaurant is set in a deceptively elegant Japanese garden. Half the fun of visiting here is winding along the paths and through the greenery to the koi pond and inviting deck; the other is knocking back well-made ales (along with an impressive selection of wines by the glass) and chowing down on filling traditional bar fare. Specialties of the house include plump, spicy sausages, well-made burgers, sandwiches from Philly-style steak to portobello mushroom, filet mignon, and grilled salmon. Given the sizeable business crowd that populates Sorrento Valley and the nearby Golden Triangle area, this can be heaven for yuppie singles, especially during happy hour. Keep in mind that the restaurant is closed on Saturdays, when it's often booked for wedding receptions and corporate parties. *$; MC, V; no checks; lunch, dinner Sun–Fri (closed Sat for private parties); beer and wine; reservations recommended; map:II7*

Kemo Sabe / ★★★✫

3958 5TH AVE, HILLCREST; 619/220-6802

Forget any references to the Lone Ranger. In this part of town, Kemo Sabe simply means Wow, referring equally to this eatery's spicy fusion fare and the chic, confident decor. From the metal-inlaid tables to the intricate ironworks inspired by primitive Native American art, the look is smashing indeed. The faint of palate need not drop by; chef Deborah Scott's cuisine is fashioned from the fiery personalities of Thailand, Mexico, and the American Southwest. Typical dishes include a grilled fish napoleon layered with pesto, goat cheese, and grilled vegetables; Asian-style dim sum served as a platter for two; and a grilled skirt steak that ought to be served with a fire extinguisher. A good selection of food-friendly wines and bold microbrew beers accompanies the food with style, and service is hip and accommodating. The location in a happening part of Hillcrest (near the Hillcrest Cinemas, one of the best movie theaters in town) keeps Kemo Sabe hopping; make reservations if you're looking to dine on the weekends. *$$; AE, DIS, MC, V; no checks; lunch, dinner every day; full bar; reservations recommended; map:N2* &

Kensington Grill / ★☆

4055 ADAMS AVE, KENSINGTON; 619/281-4014
Kensington Grill strikes just the right balance between a great neighborhood hangout and a hip hot spot—friendly and cool at the same time. The terrific bar, with a giant mirror to reflect the lively scene of 20- and 30-something professionals, features some great local microbrews and an extensive menu of wine by the glass. The purple-felt-covered pool table invites patrons to rack 'em up and shoot a few before dinner. Beyond the bar area is the main dining room, which has warm, butter-yellow walls that glow by candlelight. Deliciously spicy black linguine topped with rock shrimp shares the menu with hearty mixed grills and burgers. Among the salads, opt for baby spinach with roasted walnuts and chunks of fresh pear. This place is crowded on the weekends, so it's best to call for reservations. But if you can't get a table, you can always snag a seat at the bar and order from the menu. An ideal spot if you're catching a movie revival at the Ken movie theater next door. *$$; AE, DIS, MC, V; no checks; dinner every day; full bar; reservations recommended; map:LL3* &

Ki's / ★

2591 S COAST HWY 101, CARDIFF; 760/436-5236

Up until a few years ago, Ki's was just another hole-in-the-wall health-food cafe, where local surfers and the organic crowd congregated for smoothies, wheat grass juice, and Ki burgers. Making its move down the road to a decidedly more visible coastal location, Ki's has managed to up the ambience and the menu considerably, while holding prices way down. Both indoor and patio seating are plentiful, though the best seats in the house are at the long bar facing the ocean. Grab a New Age magazine from the stack near the door, place your order at the counter, then find a seat and await your meal. Organic fruits, veggies, and grains are incorporated into the mostly low-fat dishes, though cholesterol-laden eggs, avocados, and nuts are visible on the menu. The sizeable chicken or salmon salads combine baby greens, roasted red bell peppers, tomatoes, and cucumbers, topped with either a grilled chicken breast or salmon fillet and orange-basil vinaigrette. Veggie lasagne remains a perennial favorite, and Mexican stand-bys such as burritos, tostadas, and fish tacos have been improved with whole wheat tortillas, organic rice, and lard-free beans. The fruit smoothies are filling, delicious, and healthy. *$; AE, MC, V; checks OK; breakfast, lunch, dinner every day; beer and wine; reservations recommended for dinner; map:EE7* ᚼ

Kono's Cafe / ★

704 GARNET AVE, PACIFIC BEACH; 858/483-1669

Fans of Kono's say it offers the best seaside dining in town, where the eye candy comes free with the meal. The high-profile location right on the boardwalk by Crystal Pier ensures diners a front-row view of enough beach babes, hunks, Rollerbladers, cyclists, and other characters to induce whiplash. This easy-going cafe also serves up darn good food, especially at breakfast, when you can always expect a wait on the weekends. Regulars swear by the breakfast burritos (stuffed with a scramble of eggs, bacon, cheese, and much more), as well as notable home fries. For lunch, we recommend the burgers and hot dogs, along with the BLT layered with avocado. An espresso stand offers a quick energy fix for those who don't have time to relax over a meal on the deck. Between the view and the quality fare, the proprietors could charge a small fortune for eating here, but Kono's is known for its cheap eats; it's hard to spend over five bucks for your meal. *$; cash only; breakfast, lunch every day; no alcohol; no reservations; map:KK7*

Korea House / ★★☆

4620 CONVOY ST, KEARNY MESA; 858/560-0080

Although this popular ethnic restaurant serves a variety of entrees, the majority of diners prefer to feast on the traditional Korean barbecue. It's a strictly do-it-yourself affair, which is part of the charm. Settle into a comfy booth with a miniature grill right at the table, then cook flavorful strips of marinated beef exactly to your liking. The meat is served with a variety of accompaniments, including rice, assorted veggies, and kimchi—the fiery pickled cabbage that's used as a condiment. Along with beef, diners can order eel, tripe, and various kinds of fish (ask about any specials of the day). Some of the spiciest Korean fare in town can be found here, and the restaurant also offers such Japanese fare as sashimi and teriyaki dishes. This is a fine place for families; kids are intrigued by the barbecue process, and the staff is both gracious and helpful in explaining the menu. *$$; AE, MC, V; no checks; lunch, dinner every day; full bar; reservations recommended; map:JJ5*

La Especial Norte / ★★☆

664 N HWY 101, LEUCADIA; 760/942-1040

It's hard to believe that this downscale joint, stashed along funky Leucadia's main drag, could be such a wild favorite with locals. Owner Angel Salazar swears he does not advertise. Still, word of mouth brings a steady flow of surfers, seniors, blue-collar workers, young professionals, families,

77

and couples to this tired-looking dining room with institutional-like furnishings, hard booths, and decor consisting of several rickety gumball machines. The service is maddeningly slow—almost nonexistent—yet no one seems to mind as they wait for combo plates, tacos, or the Mexican soups that steal the show: chicken, tortilla, bean, hot shrimp cocktail, tlalpeño, albóndigas, eggplant caldo, and caldo de pescado, among others. Salazar tags his Caldo 7 Mares (shrimp, fish, clams, octopus, black mussels, crab legs, and scallops) the "king of all soups," promising that after downing a bowl, "today will be the first day of the rest of your life, sí Señor." Maybe so, but be prepared to wait almost a lifetime for that bowl to arrive. *$; MC, V; no checks; breakfast, lunch, dinner every day; full bar; no reservations; map:DD8* &

La Fresqueria / ★★☆

1125 6TH AVE, DOWNTOWN; 619/235-0655
550 W C ST, DOWNTOWN; 619/235-6816
Small enough to be dubbed a hole-in-the-wall, La Fresqueria is best known as a juice bar with fantastic smoothies. The place is a favorite of downtown workers seeking a healthy alternative to fast food. It's not strictly vegetarian, but offers several meat-free dishes and an emphasis on fresh, healthfully prepared foods. The smoothies alone can make a meal. Freshly blended with frozen fruit such as bananas or cantaloupe, they're smooth, slushy, and come in great combos like kiwi–orange and passion fruit–peach. On the more substantial side, the Chinese chicken salad with honey-sesame dressing is a winner. Sandwiches include subs, stuffed pita bread, and wraps, as well as tortas (Mexican style sandwiches served on a thick roll called a bolillo). Torta lovers tout the Special—with avocado, cucumbers, cheese, and other good stuff—as the best sandwich downtown. The very narrow dining room offers limited seating, and there's a small patio out front, but most people grab lunch to go. *$; cash only; breakfast Mon–Fri, lunch Mon–Sat; no alcohol; no reservations; map:O7 and M7*

La Provence / ★★★☆

708 4TH AVE, DOWNTOWN; 619/544-0661
Downtown's Gaslamp District is overflowing with Italian restaurants—just one reason this French bistro is such a welcome presence. The setting is delightful, capturing the sunny hues and carelessly chic decor of a small, family-run brasserie. Settle in among the fresh flowers, blue and yellow pottery, and cheerful fabrics, and prepare to take your time. In true French style, service is unhurried and courses are meant to be lingered over. The kitchen does well with much of the authentic cuisine served here, with gratinéed onion soup a particular standout. Other highly recommended dishes are the stew of veal and wild mushrooms, a generous cassoulet, and a bourride made with salmon and other fish and served with pungent aioli. The wine list includes some higher-priced pre-

mium French wines, as well as earthier, less expensive choices like Côtes-du-Rhône. In addition to the main dining room, a separate area with a huge wooden table can accommodate groups of up to about 40 guests. *$$; AE, CB, DC, DIS, MC, V; no checks; lunch, dinner every day; beer and wine; reservations recommended; map:N8* ⅙

La Salsa / ★★⯪

415 HORTON PLAZA, DOWNTOWN (AND BRANCHES); 619/234-6906
Fast, fresh, spicy, and not too expensive: that's the La Salsa spin on Mexican cooking. In these bustling kitchens, lard is a four-letter word, can openers are supposedly verboten, and your food arrives steaming hot because it's just been prepared—not microwaved. This stylish purveyor of fast food has branches throughout the county; two of the best are this one, in shoppers' paradise, and at the San Diego International Airport, on the second floor of Terminal 2. The latter provides a welcome respite from all-too predictable, disappointing airport food. In the morning, don't miss the huevos rancheros, the classic Mexican eye-opener made with sunny-side-up eggs, fresh tortillas, and salsa. Best bets at lunch and dinner are the gourmet chicken burrito, packed with well-seasoned chicken and guacamole, the carne asada burrito, and the grilled vegetable tacos. A serve-yourself salsa bar offers a variety of fresh garnishes and sauces, from mild to three-alarm hot. *$; DIS, MC, V; no checks; lunch, dinner every day; beer and wine; no reservations; map:N7* ⅙

Laurel Restaurant & Bar / ★★★

505 LAUREL ST, DOWNTOWN; 619/239-2222
Laurel is so lovely and sophisticated you might think you've strolled into some chic new spot in San Francisco or New York. After you've valet-parked, make an entrance down the staircase into the main dining room and adjacent bar. Be graceful; this is the kind of place where heads turn each time the door is opened. While it's true that many come to Laurel simply for the panache of pricey furnishings, flattering light, and exquisite martinis, many more are drawn by the memorable fare. Chef Doug Organ, who also oversees the kitchen at the WineSellar & Brasserie, keeps palates entertained with an ever-changing mix of Mediterranean, North African, Provençal, and classic French cuisine. Organ is especially well-known for his rustic Provençal chicken stewed in a pot with a flurry of fragrant herbs and his masterful duck confit with silken meat and crackly skin. Lamb and Moroccan spices, long-simmered osso buco, and roasted wild boar are all favorites on his oft-changing menu. An outstanding wine list offers many an unfamiliar bottle from various regions of France, although the list by the glass is somewhat lacking. Service is generally quite good, but it's the genial bartenders who really set the standard for Laurel's staff. Maybe that's why so many regulars drop by for a

quick bite at the bar. *$$$; AE, DC, DIS, MC, V; no checks; dinner every day; full bar; reservations recommended; map:N5*

Le Fontainebleau / ★★★

1055 2ND AVE (WESTGATE HOTEL), DOWNTOWN; 619/557-3655
Chef René Herbeck has breathed new life into the menu and attitude at this once-outdated French restaurant. Yes, the waiters still wear tuxedos and white gloves and the maître d' can be a bit haughty. But the setting is très elegant, all dolled up with chandeliers, crystal wall sconces, and lush carpeting that matches the roses on each table. Suits and ties are a must, as are hushed conversation and a yen for romance. Start with the brochette of duck with Anjou pear or the golden tomato soup with zucchini blossoms, followed by veal with a divine spinach flan. Nightly specials include lamb tenderloin with lemongrass, roasted gray pheasant stuffed with morels, or sautéed ostrich with blackberry sauce—surely a leap from traditional French cuisine. The oft-requested chilled Grand Marnier soufflé is worth every sinful yet light bite. The Sunday brunch is equally elegant and sublime. *$$$; AE, CB, DC, DIS, MC, V; checks OK; dinner Mon–Sat, brunch Sun; full bar; reservations recommended; map:N7* &

The Marine Room / ★★★☆

2000 SPINDRIFT DR, LA JOLLA; 858/459-7222
Between the unparalleled oceanfront location, the special-occasion ambience, and the talents of executive chef Bernard Guillas, the Marine Room is a true original. Descend the staircase into this dining room built right on the sand, and you'll see why generations of San Diegans come here for romantic evenings of dining and dancing. The north and south dining rooms offer unrestricted views of the coastline; the central bar has the cozy buzz of locals relaxing over the week's gossip with a gin and tonic. Light colored decor and crisp white linens create an airy, open feel. The cuisine came into its own when chef Guillas arrived on the scene a few years ago; today, a formerly good restaurant is outstanding. The French native infuses his brand of Mediterranean/Pacific Rim/California fare with imaginative flavors, from sambuca and fresh lavender to candied shallots and crunchy greens from the sea. Halibut, foie gras, ahi, and sweetbreads are some of the standouts on the menu, which changes according to the season and the chef's whims. Recent highlights have been the halibut poached in pinot Noir, the dry-aged strip steak with truffle-based potatoes, and the goose liver paired with preserved cherries and cognac. Be sure to check out the restaurant's dramatic High Tide Breakfasts during the winter, complete with a luxurious buffet and waves misting the windows. Since the dining room is connected to the La Jolla Beach and Tennis Club, you'll see some casually clad folks here, but it's really much more fun to dress to the nines, make an entrance, and get the

other diners wondering which Who's Who you're listed in. *$$$; AE, CB, DC, DIS, MC, V; no checks; lunch, dinner every day, brunch Sun; full bar; reservations recommended; www.marineroom.com; map:JJ7*

Market Cafe / ★★☆

4000 CORONADO BAY RD (LOEWS CORONADO BAY RESORT), CORONADO; 619/424-4000
Travelers tired of hotel fare are delighted to find crusty macaroni and cheese, crab cakes, and veggie calzones on the comfort-food menu. Locals fill the cafe on Sunday mornings, since brunch doesn't get much better than this. Sushi, crab claws, giant shrimp, smoked salmon, pot stickers, carved lamb and roast beef, fresh blueberries and whipped cream—need we say more? OK. Unlimited fresh-squeezed orange juice and subtle French champagne, served with a view of sailboats drifting through the Coronado Cays. Forget brunching here on Mother's Day, and be sure to make reservations no matter when you choose to serve yourself gourmet style. There are other meals to consider, and we're not talking typical hotel coffee-shop fare: the tortilla soup is a savory, spicy blend of chicken, tomatoes, avocado, and fried tortilla strips; the cobb salad is a work of art. The salmon is grilled to moist perfection; the surf-and-turf giant prawns and filet mignon can easily feed two. Even the club sandwich stands apart with its slices of white chicken, avocado, tomato, and crisp bacon strips. You may be so sated you'll spend the night at the Loews—not a bad idea. *$$; AE, MC, V; no checks; breakfast, lunch, dinner every day, brunch Sun; full bar; brunch reservations recommended; map:NN5* &

Mille Fleurs / ★★★★

6009 PASEO DELICIAS, RANCHO SANTA FE; 858/756-3085
Possibly the most rarefied and romantic of all San Diego restaurants, Mille Fleurs manages to combine a fabulously lush atmosphere with spectacular cuisine. Tucked into a quiet courtyard in the heart of Rancho Santa Fe's little village, Mille Fleurs attracts with a seductive whisper rather than a flashy wink. Much of its allure is due to the winning team of Bertrand Hug, the legendary host/proprietor who never seems to forget a face, and Martin Woesle, the stunningly talented chef who's a stickler for using only the very finest ingredients. The cuisine leans toward updated French, with typical dishes including truffle-oil-dressed salads made from a variety of organic greens, sautéed sweetbreads, artful duck creations, and game specials such as venison and quail. One might start with delicate cream of parsley soup, fragrant as a patch of herbs, followed by sautéed soft-shell crab nestled on a salsa of local white corn and tiny tomatoes. Entree choices vary, but Woesle's best creations include venison medallions punched up with a juniper berry marinade, stuffed quail sauced with red currants, and monkfish flown in from

France—and tastier than lobster. For dessert, there's a selection of imported cheese—surprisingly hard to find as a finale in this area—as well as pastries and sorbets often based on the season's best local fruit. Wine selections are limited only by your pocketbook, as Mille Fleurs offers one of the most impressive lists in town. The sophisticated service, understated Mediterranean decor, and welcoming piano bar all serve to show that gastronomically speaking, at least, money *can* buy happiness. *$$$; AE, CB, DC, MC, V; no checks; lunch Mon–Fri, dinner every day; full bar; reservations recommended; milfleurs@aol.com; www.mille fleurs. com; map:EE5*

Mimmo's Italian Village / ★☆

1743 INDIA ST, DOWNTOWN; 619/239-3710

Drop by this deli/restaurant during lunchtime, and it's busy enough to make you think they're giving food away. Well, they practically are—Mimmo's prices for deli salads and sandwiches are bargain basement, much like the decor in the dining room. Subs here are loaded with meats and cheeses heaped on good soft (but not too soft) rolls and start at under $3. There's a vegetarian number too. But the very best value here is the sampler of four deli salads plus garlic bread for about $4. You have more than a dozen options, including freshly prepared pasta salads, excellent caponata, a seafood ceviche, and several meatless creations. Get lunch in a box to go, or brave the crowds and pick out a table near the battered but popular piano. If the playing isn't up to snuff, head out the back door to a pleasant patio. Whatever you do, don't miss Mimmo's if you're a connoisseur of cheap eats. *$; cash only; lunch, dinner Mon–Sat; beer and wine; no reservations; map:M6*

Mission Café & Coffee Shop / ★

3795 MISSION BLVD, MISSION BEACH; 858/488-9060

Longtime fans of this admittedly funky cafe don't mind the faded decor, the thrift-shop furnishings, or the tough parking situation during summer. They're interested in one thing: good food, and lots of it. The menu at this beachy eatery (just a block from the Mission Beach board-walk) makes a big deal of breakfast—well worth a long, calorie-burning stroll afterwards. Pancakes, waffles, smoothies, breakfast burritos, and other morning foods shine; standouts include banana-blackberry pancakes, rosemary roasted potatoes, thick French toast, and low-fat fruit smoothies. Be prepared to wait quite a while on the weekends for a table, and don't dress up: sandals, tanks, and shorts fit this place to a tee. *$; AE, MC, V; no checks; breakfast, lunch every day; beer and wine; no reservations; map:LL7* &

Mission Hills Cafe / ★★

808 W WASHINGTON ST, MISSION HILLS; 619/296-8010

This bistro was a well-kept neighborhood secret until a glowing review by a popular food critic made it hard to get a table. Breakfast is reliably good, while lunch features a menu of salads, sandwiches, and daily specials. You can't go wrong with half an eggplant, pesto, and provolone sandwich served with a cup of homemade carrot soup. Evenings, however, have a special buzz, when locals arrive for the bargain-price prix-fixe dinner menu that includes an appetizer, entree, and dessert, with plenty of choices in all three categories. On weekend evenings, there's a wait for the candlelit tables in two large dining rooms. It's tempting to fill up on the Italian flatbread, but do save room for the meal which might begin with the house spinach salad served with a wonderful warm dressing laced with crumbled bacon. Entrees vary from fresh fish to osso buco and are served with choice of rice or potatoes. When it's time for dessert, always opt for the crepes, which arrive filled with fruit or ice cream. A fair selection of domestic wines is available, along with bottled beers. *$$; AE, DIS, MC V; no checks; breakfast, lunch, dinner Tues–Sun; beer and wine; reservations recommended for dinner; map:M2* &

Mission Hills Market Cafe / ★★

1037-C FORT STOCKTON DR, MISSION HILLS; 619/295-5353

It seems only fitting that Mission Hills should have a bistro that is every bit as tasteful and secluded as the neighborhood it serves. Family-run Mission Hills Market Cafe has only been open since 1998, but has already carved out a niche as a quiet spot for affordable fine dining. Every dish is prepared with a fine flair for taste and presentation. Soups made from scratch such as chilled gazpacho and corn chowder are particularly delightful, and the menu changes daily, determined by what's in season. Some days you'll find fresh, plump crab cakes or maybe lobster tail served on a bed of linguine. Lunchtime treats include the best panini in San Diego, especially a turkey version set off with caramelized onions. The cafe's casually elegant interior is light and airy by day, warmly romantic by candlelight at night. A good choice of wines and beers accompanies the ever-changing menu, and there is a fine selection of gourmet teas, brewed with precision. *$; AE, DIS, MC, V; checks OK; breakfast Sat–Sun, lunch Tues–Sun, dinner Tues–Sat; beer and wine; no reservations; map:M2* &

MiXX / ★★☆

3671 5TH AVE, HILLCREST; 619/299-6499
One of San Diego's most exciting eateries, trendy MiXX is a place where innumerable culinary influences and ingredients blossom into a nightly kaleidoscope of flavors. The kitchen's goal, as stated on the menu, is "cuisine with no ethnic boundaries." That would explain the bold mix of southwestern, Pacific Rim, traditional French, Vietnamese, and fusion cooking that attracts a steady stream of customers to this lively, dinner-only establishment. Daily specials featuring lamb, pork tenderloin, or fish are always worth a try, but don't ignore the regular lineup: a French burnt walnut salad, peppered seared ahi, and duck ravioli helped make MiXX an instant hit on the local dining scene. The two-level restaurant offers a trio of seating options: the piano bar downstairs, a very see-and-be-seen dining room on the second level, and a plant-filled patio offering a bit more privacy at the back. In addition to the good-looking clientele, talented chefs, and skilled servers, MiXX is known as a showcase for contemporary art—much of it available for sale. *$$; AE, CB, DC, DIS, MC, V; no checks; dinner every day; full bar; reservations recommended; map:N3* &

Montanas / ★★

1421 UNIVERSITY AVE, HILLCREST; 619/297-0722
Ever since its splashy appearance on the dining scene some years back, Montanas has been packing 'em in with a sassy blend of spicy cooking, sleek environs, trés cool crowd, and contemporary art. Business types often crowd the dining room during lunch, while an eclectic mix of young and old clad in anything from khaki pants to spandex keep the room busy right up to closing time. The appealing menu handles classic American cuisine with style, updating standards like grilled chicken and skirt steak with the flavors of the Southwest. Standout dishes include chili made with wild game or venison; barbecued ribs; a citrus-dressed salad tossed with pinenuts, perfectly ripe strawberries, and blackberries; and a silky chocolate caramel tart. Large parties can reserve a semiprivate room lined with wine bottles; prime seating for couples or foursomes is in the front booths overlooking the sidewalk. Often noisy and always interesting, Montanas is a great stop for a single perfectly made martini or an entire meal. *$$; AE, DC, DIS, MC, V; no checks; lunch Mon–Fri, dinner every day; full bar; reservations recommended; map:P2* &

Morton's of Chicago / ★★☆

285 J ST (HARBOR CLUB), DOWNTOWN; 619/696-3369
Welcome to the land of expense-account dinners, prime midwestern beef, expertly shaken martinis, and baked potatoes almost the size of footballs. Morton's offers steak house dining at its best, which means all the wood-

paneled ambience and waiterly ceremony you can handle. The crowd is much less formal, however; this national chain draws a mix of Hawaiian-shirted tourists, name-tagged conventioneers, and others dressed in everything from Gap to Gucci. Steaks, vegetables, and other items (including outsized live lobsters) are presented for your approval at the table before being turned into some truly top-notch all-American fare. Black bean soup and Caesar salad are the appetizers of choice; then it's a toss-up between the New York strip, the double-thick lamb chops, or the lightly breaded Veal Sicilian as your main course. Portions are enormous, but you'll still want to indulge in one of the fabulous dessert souf-flés or the Godiva chocolate truffle cake that takes the current rage for warm, gooey, melted-center desserts to new heights. A pricey but well-chosen wine list offers top California cabernets and double magnums of premium champagnes. Be ready to spend some money, and prepare for a splendid evening of excess. *$$$; AE, DC, MC, V; no checks; dinner every day; full bar; reservations recommended; www.mortons.com; map:N8* &

Nick's at the Beach / ★★

809 THOMAS ST, PACIFIC BEACH; 619/270-1730
Nick's is really two restaurants in one, both of them fun. On the first floor, a small bar area and spacious dining room offer a wide variety of well-priced, well-prepared meals ranging from meat loaf to Cajun gumbo. We're certain that the mussels steamed with tomatillos and lime juice take top honors here, but the competition is stiff from Nick's Caesar salad, the quesadilla stuffed with garlic mashed potatoes, the well-sea-soned crab cakes, and the fresh fish specials. The seafood pasta dressed with feta cheese and basil is also a special treat. Upstairs, a young crowd parties with a CD jukebox, four pool tables, lots of TVs, and a terrific late-night menu served daily till 1am. A recent remodel has added an ocean-view patio upstairs, while creating a needed bit of soundproofing and intimacy in the main dining room below. In addition to a stellar col-lection of beers on tap, the wine list offers lots of selections by both glass and bottle at user-friendly prices. No one under 21 is allowed upstairs. *$; AE, DIS, MC, V; no checks; lunch, dinner every day (bar menu until 1am); full bar; reservations recommended; map:KK7* &

Old Venice Italian Restaurant Caffe & Bar / ★

2910 CANON ST, POINT LOMA; 619/222-5888
The two best things about Old Venice are the pizza and ambience. The former has a delicious thin crust (both the recipe and the cooks came with the highly successful business when it was purchased in 1972 from Sicilian-American Vice Giacalone). The decor is simple yet elegant, with linen napkins and tablecloths—so what if the latter are covered with butcher paper? (A carton of crayons on each table solves the butcher-paper

85

mystery and provides recreation for the kids as they wait for the meal.) Lighting is furnished primarily by candles on the tables and in delicate wrought iron scones on the walls. The dining room gets a bit noisy when full; you can retire to the quieter back patio, dotted with potted plants. Avoid the house salad, which consists mainly of green-leaf lettuce, with a few red onion rings, one tomato chunk, and a bland house vinaigrette. The honey-baked salmon is a good choice—tender and moist—and is accompanied by a medley of grilled veggies julienne. La Linguine di Kathleen is a powerful combo of sun-dried tomatoes, pine nuts, pesto, and feta on egg-and-pepper linguine, which is a bold (some might say brash) conglomeration of spices and flavors: tasty, but not for the faint of palate. There's a fairly extensive wine list; drinks come from the adjacent White Bar, under the same management. With the same graceful, airy decoration as Old Venice and a friendly clientele of Point Loma residents this is a comfortable, upscale version of the neighborhood bar. *$$; AE, MC, V; no checks; lunch Mon–Sat, dinner every day; full bar; reservations accepted; map:E7* &

Olé Madrid / ★★

755 5TH AVE, DOWNTOWN; 619/557-0146

One of the Gaslamp Quarter's most enduring clubs, Olé Madrid attracts an A-list crowd arriving late on Friday and Saturday to drink and dance the night away. On weekends, this is truly the home of the young and the restless. But although the sangria here is fabulous, the music cutting-edge, and the young male bartenders downright sexy, Olé Madrid manages to be a pretty good Spanish restaurant as well. Tapas range from basics like manchego cheese and chorizo sausage to garlicky grilled shrimp and chicken croquettes. Main dishes include well-made paellas and grilled fish and meats, and the wine list features some noteworthy Spanish reds. The bar and dining rooms at this three-level hangout are attractive, with enormous flower arrangements, velvet curtains creating private spaces, and curving stairways. On balmy nights, the sidewalk patio offers a front-row view of the passing scene and the less fortunate in line waiting to get in. *$$; AE, MC, V; no checks; lunch Saturday, dinner Tues–Sun; full bar; reservations recommended; map:O8* &

On the Border / ★

1770 CAMINO DE LA REINA, MISSION VALLEY; 619/209-3700

Sure, the Tex-Mex food at this bustling Mission Valley restaurant is somewhat gringo-ized—when's the last time you saw a sizzling fajita salad south of the border? But the faux-rustic space complete with fireplace is casual and comfy, and the place is spacious enough that you could drop in practically any time sans reservations and not have to wait. Order the luncheon special of tortilla soup garnished with avocado plus a quesadilla, or the well-made carnitas with extra-tender pork, and you'll be a happy compadre indeed. Enchiladas and tamales are other crowd-pleasers, as are the honey-drizzled sopapillas made with deep-fried, puffy dough (they taste much lighter than they sound). The chicken fajitas tend to arrive looking a bit singed, and the chips and salsa are pretty pedestrian, but overall, this is one of the better dining destinations in the Valley. Thirsty? Check out the selection of tequilas, as well as assorted margaritas and potent Acapulco rum punch. *$$; AE, DIS, MC, V; no checks; lunch, dinner every day; full bar; reservations recommended; map:LL4* &

150 Grand Cafe / ★★☆

150 W GRAND AVE, ESCONDIDO; 760/738-6868
Not known as a culinary haven, the East County city of Escondido now has a restaurant worth seeking out. This casual yet classy cafe is overseen by Chef Riko Bartlome, who has a special way with fresh seafood—try the blackened salmon salad or escolar and sea bass over baked red and blue tortillas. Mediterranean, Asian, and American flavors are blended in the pork, black beans, and goat cheese entree, while the chocolate cake and fudge brownie are all-American and worth every bite. The cafe sits near the California Center of Performing Arts; make reservations if you're stopping by before a performance. The indoor fireplace, classical guitarist, and candlelit patio make this a delightful spot to linger over California chardonnay. *$$; AE, CB, MC, V; checks OK; lunch Mon-Fri, dinner Mon-Sat; full bar; reservations recommended; map:CC2* &

The Original Pancake House / ★

3906 CONVOY ST, KEARNY MESA (AND BRANCHES); 619/565-1740
Since the first one opened in Portland, Oregon, in 1953, "OPH" has thrived on a kind of anti-gravity approach to classic breakfast favorites. Omelets here are puffy-light oven-baked soufflés loaded with hidden treasures such as sharp cheddar and bacon chunks. A superb right-out-of-the-oven apple pancake arrives at the table awash in molten cinnamon and brown sugar. It slowly vents steam and settles onto a giant plate, still large enough to satisfy a family of four as a side dish to eggs. Same for the German pancake dusted with powdered sugar and a squeeze of lemon; in all, OPH offers over a dozen different kinds of airy pancakes, including unusual thin versions such as lacy Swedish with lingonberries and a chewy but still soft forty-niner style. Super-fresh eggs are scrambled into golden mounds, perfect with hickory-smoked bacon that has a candylike cured sweetness. An obsession with freshness and quality rules here, supported by an oven-mittened wait staff that runs from kitchen to table carrying food just off the grill. *$; DIS, MC, V; no checks; breakfast every day through mid-afternoon; no alcohol; no reservations; map:JJ5* &

Ortega's / ★★

4888 NEWPORT AVE, OCEAN BEACH; 619/222-4205

Neighborhood Mexican restaurants abound in San Diego; this small cafe with barely a dozen tables is a local favorite. The Ortega family comes from Puebla, one of Mexico's culinary capitals, and they've created the perfect homeland ambience by including much of the extended family in the operation. The family specializes in steamed tamales, which are served at a sidewalk stand during street fairs and farmer's bazaars. Sons and cousins work at an open grill by the front door, letting the savory smells of marinated pork, spiced shrimp, and corn tortillas tempt passersby. Regulars show up during off hours to feast on huevos rancheros drenched in salsa verde and melted cheese, enchiladas topped with mole (a blend of a dozen or more spices guaranteed to challenge the palate), and the best tacos al pastor (corn tortillas filled with grilled pork) this side of Tijuana. Specials include fresh tuna, calamari, or dorado and those incomparable tamales. *$; AE, DIS, MC, V; no checks; breakfast, lunch, dinner every day; beer only; no reservations; map:B3*

Pacifica Del Mar / ★★

1555 CAMINO DEL MAR, DEL MAR; 858/792-0476

"Pacific Rim" may be a term that's getting a little tired, but the concept remains fresh and exciting at this ocean-view restaurant in Del Mar. Given the proximity to the sea, it's only fitting that seafood dominates the extensive menu. The signature kimchi shrimp appetizer, served in an oversize martini glass, is one of the best items here. But don't rule out the likes of wok-seared catfish, ginger-marinated salmon, seafood pastas, and imaginative sandwiches, as well as some truly inspired Sunday brunch dishes. The dining room is pretty, but the real treat here is a seat on the patio. Don't just drop by for the food; the list of martinis and wines by the glass here is impressive, and the singles scene in the eye-catching bar is legendary. Troll here on a Friday night and you might end up with the catch of the day. And no, we don't mean catfish. *$$; AE, CB, DC, DIS, MC, V; no checks; lunch, dinner every day, brunch Sun; full bar; reservations recommended; kipp@pacificadelmar.com; www.pacifica delmar.com; map:GG7* &

Pamplemousse Grille / ★★★

514 VIA DE LA VALLE, SOLANA BEACH; 858/792-9090

High rollers, socialites, businessfolk, and trophy spouses abound at this stylish bistro across from the Del Mar racetrack. While many are no doubt drawn by the ambience—a chic, sophisticated take on country French with beautiful people in every corner—others undoubtedly come for the imaginative fare. The food isn't always Triple Crown material, but the kitchen delivers artfully garnished, creatively conceived variations on nouvelle American and classic French cuisine. The foie gras usually served as a special is always outstanding, as are the grilled fish specials prepared with your choice of a half dozen sauces. Salads and side dishes make fine use of the vegetables from Chino's produce farm (favored by chefs from L.A. and S.F.) just down the road, and desserts—especially the semibaked, melting chocolate truffle cake or the trio of three crème brûlées—are always worth an extra hour on the StairMaster. Pamplemousse is particularly busy during the racing season (linger in the bar and you might get a hot tip), but the prosperous mood and society gossip stay in the air year-round. $$$; AE, CB, DC, DIS, MC, V; checks OK; lunch Wed–Fri, dinner Tues–Sun; full bar; reservations recommended; map:FF7 &

Panda Inn Chinese Restaurant / ★★

506 HORTON PLAZA, DOWNTOWN; 619/233-7800
Hungry mall-goers and folks headed to nearby movie theaters or stage productions would be smart to remember this spacious Chinese restaurant on the top level of the Horton Plaza shopping center, where there's rarely a wait, even on weekend evenings. The decor is rather smashing, although casual attire is the norm, and the back dining room offers a view of downtown. Check the blackboard at the reception desk for daily specials, which tend to feature fresh seasonal ingredients like green beans or eggplant. On the regular menu, standouts are the smoky pan-fried noodles topped with a variety of meats, any of the chicken-based stir-fries, sweet 'n' sour pork, and incomparable white-chocolate-dipped fortune cookies for dessert. Service is always attentive and polite, and the reasonable prices and full bar may help to ease the pain of shoppers' maxed-out credit cards. $$; AE, DC, DIS, MC, V; no checks; lunch, dinner every day; full bar; reservations recommended; map:N7 &

Parkhouse Eatery / ★☆

4574 PARK BLVD, UNIVERSITY HEIGHTS; 619/295-7275
On the north end of Park Boulevard, Parkhouse Eatery is a cheerful beacon in the now-happening University Heights neighborhood. You can't miss that antique neon clock out front. The Eatery, open for breakfast, lunch, and dinner, is a great, cozy spot for hearty appetites. All the items on the menu are huge; you'll likely come away with a doggie bag. The restaurant is a converted house, with outdoor patio dining and a more intimate dining room inside (on a chilly evening ask for a table by the fireplace). Traditional American meat loaf rubs shoulders with some creative concoctions. For breakfast, opt for a filling pizza topped with egg and cheese or a plate of pumpkin pancakes. Lunch features fresh salads and hearty sandwiches. For dinner, the salmon cooked and served on a cedar plank makes for a delicious meal and a spectacular presentation. Service tends to be a bit leisurely, so let them know if you're on a tight schedule. $$; AE, CB, DC, DIS, MC, V; no checks; breakfast, lunch, dinner every day; beer and wine; reservations recommended for dinner; map:P1 &

Piatti / ★★☆

2182 AVENIDA DE LA PLAYA, LA JOLLA; 858/454-1589
The fashionable neighborhood of La Jolla Shores makes the perfect setting for this ever-trendy Italian restaurant where air-kissing has developed into an art form. Dressed-up socialites, wealthy vacationers, casually clad regulars, and cell phone-toting businessfolk keep the place hopping at lunch and dinner, and the bar and dining rooms can be cacophonous. Repeat visitors seeking a little peace and quiet ask to sit in the walled-in patio reminiscent of a Tuscan courtyard. Dominated by an enormous tree and loads of greenery, it's a charming spot to savor a Pinot Grigio or Barolo from the wine list. Consistent best sellers include the fancy wood-fired pizzas, roasted chicken, risotto, vegetable lasagne, and beautiful salads. And for an appetizer, the garlicky bruschetta heaped with tomatoes and basil chiffonade can't be beat—it's one of the best versions in town. To fit in with the crowd, keep one eye on your plate, the other constantly surveying the room to see who's doing what with whom. *$$; AE, DC, MC, V; no checks; lunch, dinner every day; full bar; reservations recommended; map:JJ7* ᕦ

Pizza Nova / ★★

5120 N HARBOR DR, POINT LOMA (AND BRANCHES); 619/226-0268
The mountainous salads at Pizza Nova can easily be split between two diners—at least! Grilled chicken tops several variations, such as a chipotle-lime version sprinkled with yellow corn and roasted peppers. Pasta portions are also generous, and adding goat cheese to shrimp nested in tomato-basil angel hair yields rich veins of molten cheese (at less than a dollar it's a real bargain). The Thai chicken pizza sports a colorful landscape of shredded carrots, peanuts, scallions, and cilantro in ginger sauce. Every pizza here gets a great head start thanks to spectacular dough that bubbles and crisps in a true wood-burning oven. Three other Pizza Nova branches have the same menu. The original location at Harbor Drive has the best view: its upstairs room overlooks San Diego Harbor. *$; AE, DIS, DC, MC, V; local checks only; lunch, dinner every day; beer and wine; reservations recommended; map:E6* ᕦ

Pizza Port / ★★☆

135 N HWY 101, SOLANA BEACH; 858/481-7332
Is this the area's best pizza? Probably. Is it the coolest pizzeria? For sure. It's close enough to the beach to attract the surf, skate, and sun-loving crowd, and the place also serves top-notch microbrew beers, made right on the premises. Pale ales, wheat beers, special seasonal brews, and more—they're all fresh and frosty and a perfect complement to pizza. And what pies these are: puff-crusted, chewy, and topped with goodies from trendy to traditional. Best bets are the spicy number topped with

Canadian bacon and jalapeños; the seafood pizza loaded with clams, shrimp, and onions; and the more classic pie topped with artichoke hearts, olives, and mushrooms. You even get a choice of crusts, either traditional or whole-grain beer batter. The crowd here is predominantly young, but anybody is welcome: families, seniors, even yuppies, as long as they're into video games, surf films, brewskis, and good food. *$; MC, V; no checks; lunch, dinner every day; beer and wine; no reservations; map:FF7* ⅃

Point Loma Seafoods / ★★

2805 EMERSON ST, POINT LOMA; 619/223-1109
Generations of San Diegans have lined up at the counter of this seafood market, purchasing fresh fish to prepare for dinner or ordering takeout. The place is almost always jammed, and with good reason: year after year, the quality of the goods and service here are superior to anyplace like it in San Diego. Fish and seafood (including live clams, crabs, and lobsters) are expensive, but always divinely fresh. The shop is also known for moist, just-smoked fish (which makes terrific picnic fixings), appealing seafood salads, sourdough bread, and a decent selection of wine. Top takeout foods (which you can eat on the harborside patio) are the excellent clam chowder, seafood ceviche, fresh tuna sandwich, and shrimp or crab cocktails. Service is knowledgeable and cheerful, even during rush hours. The location adjacent to the busy sportsfishing docks can make parking a pain, but one bite of this restaurant's smoked swordfish or fried calamari and you'll be glad you dropped by. *$; No credit cards; local checks only; lunch, dinner every day (until 7pm); beer and wine; no reservations; map:E6* ⅃

Porkyland / ★

1030 TORREY PINES RD, LA JOLLA; 858/459-1708
2196 LOGAN AVE, LOGAN HEIGHTS; 619/233-5139
Despite the lighthearted name, the people at this Mexican takeout spot turn out well-made, authentic fare. And the price is right, with lots of tacos, burritos, and combo plates under $3. You'll find the usual south-of-the-border specialties here, like quesadillas and enchiladas, but it's pork that puts Porkyland in our culinary hall of fame. This is the place to find first-rate carnitas: the tender, long-cooked pork is heaven in a warm tortilla with onions and cilantro. Pork or chicken tamales are also outstanding, and Porky fans have been known to make pilgrimages across town for the pork al pastor. Service is fast, the setting ultracasual with a do-it-yourself salsa bar. In addition to hot takeout, the shop sells fresh corn and flour tortillas and fixings like rice and beans. *$; cash only; lunch, dinner every day; no alcohol; no reservations; map:JJ7 and NN4* ⅃

Primavera Ristorante / ★★☆

932 ORANGE AVE, CORONADO; 619/435-0454

Islanders who prefer a bit of tradition with their dining return repeatedly to the tasteful marbleized edifice at Primavera. They request waiters by name and settle into favored banquettes facing the multi-tiered dining room. The service is courtly and efficient without being obsequious. Crumbs from the crusty bread are discreetly brushed from sight, and the maître d' clarifies menu selections with great charm. You can make a meal from the antipasti alone, soaking up the anchovy-scented oil from the roasted peppers piemontese or carpaccio with mozzarella-topped bruschetta. But you'll want to save room for linguine frutti di mare filled with seafood morsels or the tangy filleto di manzo al pepe verde, tender beef medallions with gorgonzola and green peppercorn sauce. If your appetite is small, sit in the sedate bar and split an order of simply sublime linguine with clams. *$$; AE, DC, DIS MC, V; local checks only; lunch, dinner every day; full bar; no reservations; map:NN5* &

The Prince of Wales Grill / ★★☆

1500 ORANGE AVE (HOTEL DEL CORONADO), CORONADO; 619/522-8819

Recently remodeled with plenty of art deco glamour, The Prince of Wales Grill takes its name from the Duke of Windsor, who, legend has it, rendezvoused with Wallis Simpson at the hotel in 1920. Decorated in warm, rich golds, the dining room offers tables and booths (reserve a booth for privacy), and a predinner visit to the piano bar calls for a martini to get you in the right mood. While a tie isn't mandatory, it certainly isn't out of place and makes for a nice change of pace in laid-back San Diego. This is the place to come for the special celebration—or just to revel in the good life for an evening. Like the decor, the updated menu offers a nod to tradition with rich dishes like lamb chops, yet caters to lighter, contemporary tastes with pastas and fresh seafood. A wonderful wine selection complements the menu and impeccable service. *$$$; AE, CB, DC, DIS, MC, V; no checks; dinner every day; full bar; reservations recommended; map:NN5* &

Qwiigs Bar & Grill / ★☆

5083 SANTA MONICA AVE, OCEAN BEACH; 619/222-1101

Snag a window table at sunset for the ultimate Ocean Beach dining experience right across from the water. Qwiigs offers spectacular views of surfers, joggers, seagulls, and the O.B. Pier. Locals gather for steamed artichokes, bountiful house salads, fried calamari, and gourmet pizzas in the upper-level cocktail lounge or hover around the busy little sushi bar. The dining room features cozy ocean-view tables with prized window seats and raised U-shaped booths that also face the outdoor spectacle. The place is packed at sunset, naturally. Enormous fresh cobb salads (we prefer the chicken version over the seafood salad) and thick burgers are good bets at lunch. Dinner specials might include rack of lamb or penne pesto with Japanese breaded chicken breast along with the fresh fish and blackened prime rib. A sit-down Sunday brunch includes average-to-good breakfast fare. The ambience and service are fairly low-key; while some people show up in ties and work suits at lunch, this is definitely one of those "come-as-you-are" neighborhood haunts. Use the underground parking lot if possible; spots on the street can be tough to find. *$$; AE, DC, DIS, MC, V; no checks; lunch Mon–Fri, dinner every day, brunch Sun; full bar; reservations recommended; map:B2*

Rainwater's / ★

1202 KETTNER BLVD, DOWNTOWN; 619/233-5757

Power brokers need some place to power down steaks, chops, and bountiful spinach salads at lunch. They tend to favor this clubby steak house well-hidden from the normal conventioneer route. Politicians, attorneys, and bankers settle down to business over black bean soup, cobb salads, grilled chicken, chicken pot pie, and those mind-numbingly delicious steaks in the main dining room, where tables and big, high-backed booths are set far apart for private conversations. Those in a rush stop in the bar for oysters or salads. The wine list (with several good vintages by the glass) is another plus, along with the unobtrusive yet efficient service. Rainwater is more crowded at lunch than at dinner, when the mood is more subdued. *$$; AE, MC, V; no checks; lunch, dinner every day; full bar; reservations recommended; map:M7* &

Rancho Valencia Resort / ★★★½

5921 VALENCIA CIRCLE, RANCHO SANTA FE; 858/756-1123

Rancho Valencia, in the new-money enclave of Rancho Santa Fe known as Fairbanks Ranch, is far enough off the usual restaurant rows to feel like a secret destination. It could easily have been custom-built for lovers, boasting a secluded and exclusive setting in a world-class tennis resort. The dining room is at once rustic and upscale, and although it's spacious, there's a definite intimacy to the place. Glowing fireplaces, artful flower arrangements, high-beamed ceilings, and highly polished service all compliment the meals and add an air of effortless sophistication. Don't rush through a meal here. Instead, bask in the country club ambience while lingering over a well-chosen wine list and a menu inspired by France, California, and the Mediterranean. A number of notable chefs have passed through the kitchen here, each leaving a trademark dish or two. The cuisine is consistently well-prepared, with top honors going to the golden squash ravioli flavored with sage, pancetta-wrapped monkfish, and a quickly sautéed foie gras that could hold its own in a French kitchen. For dessert, choose the perfectly caramelized tarte tatin. After dinner, take a stroll through the bougainvillea-bedecked courtyards. If you'd like to stay at the resort, call well in advance to book one of the private casitas here. Yes, it will cost a small fortune, but this verdant retreat is worth the extra green. *$$$; AE, DC, MC, V; no checks; breakfast, lunch, dinner every day; full bar; reservations recommended; map:EE5* ⟨&⟩

Red Sails Inn / ★★☆

2614 SHELTER ISLAND DR, SHELTER ISLAND; 619/223-3030

OK, so the decor is some of the oddest in town, complete with stuffed crabs and fish mounted on the walls and a vintage diving suit that looks left over from Halloween. Just don't let that or the humble 50s-esque setting sway you from trying some of San Diego's best old-fashioned seafood at decidedly old-fashioned prices. You won't find any fancy stuff, but the kitchen does a good job with grilled swordfish, mahimahi, monkfish, and sea bass for under $20 a plate. That includes soup or salad and a baked potato on the side. In addition to the two spacious dining rooms, which include a fireplace and harbor view along with those mounted fish, there's a delightful patio right on the water of San Diego Bay. Cheerful servers and basic breakfast and lunch items such as pancakes and tuna sandwiches make this a favorite of locals on the weekends. A huge fountain, boats coming and going, and lots of slumming seagulls keep kids entertained while you eat. *$$; AE, DC, MC, V; no checks; breakfast, lunch, dinner every day; full bar; reservations recommended; map:F7*

Ricky's Family Restaurant / ★☆

2181 HOTEL CIRCLE S, MISSION VALLEY; 619/291-4498

Coffee shops abound in San Diego, but the proudly old-fashioned Ricky's is considered one of the best. It's the kind of place where the waitresses wear name tags and patient smiles. The spacious eatery serves breakfast all day long, so there's no excuse to miss Ricky's famous apple pancake. This enormous puff of cinnamon, sugar, apples, and a custardlike batter will easily serve two, and it's well worth the 20-minute wait. Crispy hash browns are another breakfast favorite. Lunchtime specialties are the tuna melt, the stacked-high club sandwich, and an excellent clam chowder. For dinner, Ricky's has typically retro diner fare: liver and onions, roast beef, fried chicken. Booths are well spaced and comfortable, service generally fast. *$; AE, MC, V; no checks; breakfast, lunch, dinner every day; full bar; no reservations; map:K1* ⟨&⟩

Roberto's / ★

3202 MISSION BLVD, PACIFIC BEACH (AND BRANCHES); 619/488-1610

It's 3am and you're ravenous after a heavy dancing binge. What do you do in a town that shuts down by midnight? Easy—you pull into the most legendary of all local taco stands and order a giant quesadilla stuffed with cheese and guacamole, chicken tacos, carne asada burritos, and a plastic bag full of lip-tingling spicy marinated carrot, onion, and jalapeño slices.

Sure, there's a bit of lard in the mix and you wouldn't want to eat this stuff cold, but Roberto's uses fresh, warm tortillas and just the right amount of heat to bring you back to life. It sure beats Taco Bell. The Ocean Beach and Hillcrest branches are particularly popular with the late-night crowd. Though all stands have a few rusty tables in the parking lot, you might want to take your feast home. *$; cash only; breakfast, lunch, dinner every day; no alcohol; no reservations; map:KK7*

Roppongi Restaurant, Bar, and Cafe / ★★

875 PROSPECT ST, LA JOLLA; 858/551-5252
Local restaurateur Sami Ladeki, founder of the hugely popular, family-friendly Sammy's Woodfired Pizza chain, has gone upmarket with this flashy La Jolla endeavor. It's a sight to behold, from the expensive bric-a-brac to the spectacular aquarium with Day-Glo tropical fish. And the requisitely trendy menu, colored with influences from cutting-edge Pacific Rim to classic Americana, has plenty to dazzle as well—as long as you stick to the appetizers and skip the so-so entrees. The key to dining at Roppongi is to graze, tapas-style, through the list of superbly made starters. A multilayered crab napoleon; skewered scallops, plump and pretty as South Pacific pearls; fiery kung pao calamari; pot stickers filled with shrimp; and more—each is an exquisite, if expensive, little treat. The open dining room includes booth and table seating, as well as a semiprivate dining room for large parties. Out front, a raised fire pit keeps diners comfortable on the coolest evenings. Service ranges from adept to iffy, and the wine list is overpriced, but those top-notch tapas keep us coming back. *$$$; AE, DIS, MC, V; no checks; lunch, dinner every day; full bar; reservations recommended; map:JJ7* &

Roxy / ★

517 S HWY 101, ENCINITAS; 760/436-5001
The Roxy began as a simple ice cream parlor in the 1970s, when Encinitas was a simple seaside community. The ice cream counter still stands where it always has, though the business has expanded into a two-room extravaganza serving pizzas, pastas, omelets, hot casserole dinners, and house specialties. The portions are humongous, the prices low, and the quality fresh as a backyard garden. The menu caters to the surf-and-yoga crowd's vegetarian appetite, though fish and chicken are featured in a number of dishes. A blackboard menu advertises daily specials such as Hawaiian mahimahi and eggplant parmesan. Try the Avotaco (avocado, cheese, olives, onions, tomatoes, and alfalfa sprouts in a corn tortilla). Appetizers have a Mediterranean punch (hummus, baba ghanouj), while entrees range from falafel and pizzas to enchiladas and burritos. *$; AE, DIS, MC, V; no checks; lunch, dinner every day; full bar, no reservations; map:EE7* &

Rubio's / ★☆

4504 MISSION BAY DR, PACIFIC BEACH (AND BRANCHES); 858/272-2801
What a success story: local boy visits Baja, falls in love with the fish tacos there, opens a tiny restaurant in Pacific Beach selling same, and gains fortune and fame. Millions of battered-and-fried fish tacos later, founder Ralph Rubio has extended the menu at this thriving chain of restaurants, which numbers more than two dozen in San Diego County alone and is rapidly spreading through the West. These days, you'll find fresh, flavorful takes on Mexican cuisine: everything from grilled mahimahi tacos and shrimp burritos to Baja Bowls (a beans 'n' rice spin on the ubiquitous Asian rice bowl). A special HealthMex menu offers entrees with less than 22 percent of their calories from fat. But it's the original fish taco, made with a plump white fillet, a flurry of shredded cabbage, and a ranchlike dressing folded into a corn tortilla, that keeps Rubio's ardent fans coming back for takeout or a quick bite in the informal, sparkling-clean dining rooms. *$; AE, DC, DIS, MC, V; no checks; lunch, dinner every day; beer and wine; no reservations; www.rubios.com; map:KK7* &

Ruby's Diner / ★☆

1640 CAMINO DEL RIO N, MISSION VALLEY; 619/294-7829
5630 PASEO DEL NORTE, CARLSBAD; 760/931-7829
Ruby's is that classic soda fountain from It's a Wonderful Life morphed into a sleek, modern diner straight out of the 22nd century. The snappy red-and-white decor makes for a cheery, welcoming feeling that's reinforced by the lengthy menu of old-time comfort foods. This is the place to bring the kids for real milk shakes, offered in a rainbow of flavors and served from the blender in all their slushy splendor. Then it's on to burgers, onion rings, and fries; club sandwiches and home-style meat loaf; fish and chips; even a turkey pot pie. In a nod to vegetarians, there's a decent garden burger on the menu. Ruby's is the place to come for lunch and a matinee at the nearby multiplex, or for a nostalgic hot fudge sundae after the show. Even if you don't have kids, it's worth dropping in for a taste of the past. The noise level rises in proportion to the number of young children in the crowd, but this diner still owns a little piece of our heart. *$; AE, DC, DIS, MC, V; no checks; breakfast, lunch, dinner every day; beer and wine; no reservations; map:LL4 and CC7* &

Saffron Noodles and Saté / ★★☆

3737 INDIA ST, MIDDLETOWN; 619/574-7737
Nobody has done more to introduce San Diegans to the pleasures of Thai cuisine than owner/chef Su-Mei Yu, who founded the tiny original Saffron next door (still a favorite takeout joint). Today, she's expanded her original rotisserie chicken shop into a full-scale noodle house, with dozens of choices that explore a range of styles from mild to incendiary.

Classic noodle dishes such as pad thai and spicy noodles are done well, but it's the exotic daily specials flavored with pickled vegetables or fried shallots and the silken curries that are the true stars of this aromatic show. In addition to the artful food, the restaurant features works by glass sculptor Dale Chihuly and painter Italo Scanga. The place is a feast for the eyes as well as the palate, and the low prices make it an affordable treat. *$; MC, V; no checks; lunch, dinner every day; beer and wine; no reservations; map:L3* &

Sally's / ★★

1 MARKET PL, DOWNTOWN; 619/687-6080

With a prime location in Seaport Village overlooking the harbor and Coronado, Sally's would probably draw plenty of business for the view alone. Between the outdoor tables lining the bayside boardwalk and the great vantage points in the bar, this is one of the prime places in town to watch the world go by. But Sally's doesn't depend solely on its looks; the seafood served up with Mediterranean and Cal-Cuisine influences can be inviting as well. Fresh oysters are a house specialty, and we've found their fresh, salty goodness is further enhanced by one of the frosty Bombay Sapphire martinis prepared by the resident mixologists. Main-dish salads topped with grilled fish or chicken are top sellers for good reason, as are seared scallops, spicy crab cakes, and linguine heaped with sweet, flavorful rock shrimp. Along with the patio seating and comfortable booths in the dining room, a chef's table in the kitchen may be reserved in advance for up to a dozen diners, who get to watch the staff whip up their custom-designed meal. *$$; AE, CB, DC, DIS, MC, V; no checks; lunch, dinner every day; full bar; reservations recommended; map:M8*

Sammy's California Woodfired Pizza / ★★

565 PEARL ST, LA JOLLA (AND BRANCHES); 858/259-6600

San Diego has never been the same since Sami Ladeki brought wood-fired pizza to town. Savor varieties such as LaDou's Barbeque Chicken (with cilantro, smoked Gouda, and red onion), Artichokes (with tomato sauce, mozzarella, and gorgonzola cheese), or Smoked Duck Sausage (with spinach, Roma tomatoes, garlic, and smoked Gouda). Other mouthwatering offerings include Norwegian salmon fillet, grilled chicken salad, and some exquisite pasta dishes (the Spinach Ricotta Tortelloni in cream sauce with wild mushrooms is an artery-clogging trip to heaven). The open kitchen lets you keep a close eye on your order. A full take-out menu is offered. *$; AE, DC, MC, V; no checks; breakfast, lunch, dinner every day; full bar; no reservations; sammys@connectnet.com; www.sammys pizza.com; map:JJ7* &

Samson's Restaurant / ★★

8861 VILLA LA JOLLA DR, LA JOLLA; 858/455-1461

Samson's is one of San Diego's legends when it comes to bounteous portions of classic deli fare. You're guaranteed to roll out feeling satisfied, most likely carrying a box of leftovers for the next day. This is the place to find platters of lox, smoked whitefish, and chopped liver (call ahead to ask about catering and local delivery). All the standard deli sandwiches are here, including piled-high versions served with your choice of potato pancakes, coleslaw, french fries, or potato salad. The bowl of chicken soup complete with oversize matzo ball is Jewish comfort food at its best, as is beef brisket served with a side of noodle kugel. An on-site bakery prepares German chocolate cake, rugelach, and cheesecakes, as well as traditional challah and bagels. The informal atmosphere, spacious dining room, and reasonable prices attract lots of families as well as patrons from the nearby movie theaters. Just remember: bring a hearty appetite. *$; AE, DC, DIS, MC, V; checks OK; breakfast, lunch, dinner every day; beer and wine; reservations recommended; map:JJ7* &

Santé Ristorante / ★★

7811 HERSCHEL AVE, LA JOLLA; 858/454-1315

With a smart La Jolla address and a coterie of devoted fans, Santé has a New York neighborhood feel to it. It's the kind of place where the owner greets regulars and people tend to dress up—for San Diego at least. Along with the rather formal dining room (which includes a fireplace), seating options include the intimate bar with a couple of tables, a courtyard lit with tiny lights, and two additional patios. The kitchen is known for a variety of veal specials—grilled chops, scaloppine sauced with lemon or topped, saltimbocca-style, with fresh herbs and prosciutto—as well as pastas such as fettucine tossed with smoked salmon and finished with caviar. Wild game is occasionally featured on the menu, and both quail and breast of duck garnished with a rosemary glaze are especially well prepared here. Service is attentive, adding to the "everyone's a VIP" feeling. Whether you're looking for a classy place for a business dinner or a romantic setting for a hot date, Santé definitely delivers. *$$$; AE, CB, DC, DIS, MC, V; no checks; lunch Mon–Fri, dinner every day; full bar; reservations recommended; map:JJ7* &

Shakespeare Pub and Grille / ★

3701 INDIA ST, MIDDLETOWN; 619/299-0230

The most authentic British pub in all of San Diego, the Shakespeare (or "Shakey's" to the regulars) draws a crowd of expats in search of a bit o' Britain. Families come with the kids in tow for Sunday dinner, while lads gather at other times of the week to catch soccer matches on the telly. Indoors at the wooden bar, British brews dominate the tap—sample the likes of Boddington's and Fuller's by the half- and full pint. On a sunny afternoon, the outdoor deck overlooking the airport and bay is a fine spot to while away a few hours. A full menu is available too, featuring bangers and mash, shepherd's pie and, of course, chips (french fries), best enjoyed smothered with malt vinegar and salt. Sunday lunch is a feast of roast beef, but in a nod to its American patrons, the management has added fish tacos to the menu. Check with the waitresses for the daily beer specials. Insiders like to welcome the new year at Shakey's, a time when kilted bagpipers march around at 4pm (midnight in England). Not to be missed. *$; AE, MC, V; no checks; lunch, dinner every day; full bar; no reservations; map:L3* &

The Sky Room / ★★★☆

1132 PROSPECT ST (LA VALENCIA HOTEL), LA JOLLA; 858/454-0771
Saying La Valencia's The Sky Room is a romantic place to dine is like calling Placido Domingo a pretty good singer. This ocean-view dining room atop La Jolla's venerable pink palace of a hotel is *the* place in town to pop the question (whatever it might be), celebrate an important birthday or anniversary, or simply treat yourself to an evening of elegance and pomp. Gorgeous flower arrangements, tuxedo-clad servers, Wedgwood china, and long-stemmed roses for the ladies provide a feeling of old-world elegance and a lovely showcase for distinctly well-prepared California and French cuisine turned out by a cadre of experienced sous chefs. Selections range from contemporary (free-range chicken with morels; a trio of grilled Gulf fish with fruit relishes) to classic (delicate smoked salmon paired with julienned cucumber; cream of mushroom soup). If they're offering the filet mignon finished with a Merlot demiglace, it's a must have. So is the dessert plate, a selection of sweets that generally includes tidbits of tiramisu, cookies, and sublime chocolate truffles. An extensive wine list is particularly strong in California cabernet and chardonnay, but high rollers will also find plenty of premium French labels, including vintage champagnes. The courtly waiters and helpful sommelier, along with the rarefied ambience, leave you feeling like royalty. Stop by the piano bar in the lobby after dinner for a nightcap of good music in one of La Jolla's loveliest rooms. *$$$; AE, CB, DC, DIS, MC, V; no checks; dinner every day; full bar; reservations required; map:JJ7* &

Souplantation / ★

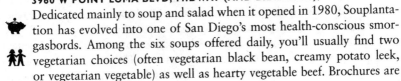

3960 W POINT LOMA BLVD, MIDWAY (AND BRANCHES); 619/222-7404
Dedicated mainly to soup and salad when it opened in 1980, Souplantation has evolved into one of San Diego's most health-conscious smorgasbords. Among the six soups offered daily, you'll usually find two vegetarian choices (often vegetarian black bean, creamy potato leek, or vegetarian vegetable) as well as hearty vegetable beef. Brochures are

99

available to spell out nutritional contents of the multitude of prepared salads, pizza, focaccia, pastas, and four kinds of homemade muffins. It's a favorite with families—kids enjoy concocting their own salads, selecting among chopped, shredded, diced, and sliced ingredients, and they live for preparing their own soft-serve or frozen yogurt desserts at the end of the meal. Parents love the pricing system: kids under 3 eat for free, 3- to 5-year-olds for just 99 cents. The space is very '70s, with knotty pine paneled walls and ceilings and an abundance of live green plants as the only decorative elements. An army of young employees is on patrol to remove trays from tables and wipe up spills at the long salad bar. *$; DC, DIS, MC, V; no checks; lunch, dinner every day; beer and wine; no reservations; map:F2 &*

South Beach Bar and Grill / ★

5059 NEWPORT AVE, OCEAN BEACH; 619/226-4577
At the end of Ocean Beach's Newport Avenue, ultracasual South Beach Bar and Grill hops with activity. The beach bar's open windows look out onto the Pacific and the Ocean Beach pier, but the real attraction is at the *back* of the bar where the stove is always cookin'. Sit here and watch as

the short-order cooks conduct their own culinary symphony, preparing the tastiest seafood tacos around. A broad menu offers tacos (and burritos, salads, and nachos) stuffed with grilled or fried mahimahi, wahoo, shrimp, lobster, and more. Our hands-down favorite: the succulent lobster tacos—an inexpensive treat filled with a generous helping of the sweet crustacean. Washed down with a microbrew, it's pure San Diego heaven. *$; cash only; lunch, dinner every day; full bar; no reservations; map:B3 &*

Spices Thai Cafe / ★★☆

3810 VALLEY CENTRE DR, STE 903, SORRENTO VALLEY; 858/259-0889
Locals tried valiantly to keep Spices a sort of unofficial secret, but word spread rapidly and now the place is almost always packed. Nonetheless, this soothing dining room decked out in pastel paint, black lacquer, and fresh flowers still feels like a calm oasis. A bad meal here is unheard of, the service is gracious, and even the large lunch and dinner crowds don't diminish the serene vibes. Starters range from Thai spring rolls to dumplings, calamari, tempura, and satés. The list of entrees is long and thought-provoking, including myriad curries, vegetables, noodle and rice dishes (prepared with or without meat and fish), and seafood. House specialties include Sizzling Lemon Grass Chicken, Choo-Chee Duck, and Pattaya Pineapple (pineapple stuffed with chicken, shrimp, and cashew nuts in special house sauce). All dishes are individually prepared, MSG is a no-no, and you can regulate the spiciness by using the restaurant's 1-to-10 scale (10 is for fire-breathing dragons). The lunch specials are a terrific value, with soup of the day, tossed salad, spring roll, fried wonton,

steamed rice, and choice of entree thrown into one very inexpensive package. Go after the power lunchers return to their cubicles. *$$; AE, DC, DIS, MC, V; no checks; lunch, dinner every day; beer and wine; reservations recommended; map:II7* &

St. James Bar at Triangles / ★★

4370 LA JOLLA VILLAGE DR, LA JOLLA; 858/453-6650
One of the classiest restaurants in this singles-bar-heavy neighborhood, St. James tends to attract a well-dressed, sophisticated crowd that takes food and wine quite seriously. The elegant dining room practically glows with subtle lighting, gleaming wood, and a general air of well-being, and it's stylish without being fussy. The varied menu offers something for just about everyone, and a well-chosen wine list ventures far beyond chardonnay and cabernet, with plenty of selections by the bottle or glass. Many patrons choose to eat right at the bar, either at the counter or the nearby tables; for more privacy, request one of the spacious booths in the dining room. In addition to a snazzy mussel bisque (topped with a puff pastry crust and spiked with sherry, if you like), the restaurant is known for deftly grilled salmon and rack of lamb, and main-dish salads topped variously with goat cheese, marinated chicken, or roasted vegetables. During happy hour (4–7pm, Monday through Friday), the bar offers appetizers for half price, along with numerous wine specials by the glass. *$$; AE, CB, MC, V; no checks; lunch Mon–Fri, dinner Mon–Sat; full bar; reservations recommended; map:JJ7* &

Star of the Sea / ★★★

1360 HARBOR DR, DOWNTOWN; 619/232-7408
Since opening in 1966, this crown jewel in the Anthony's family restaurant chain has drawn a well-heeled crowd with its elegant seafood preparations. The dramatic wharfside location always kept the place busy, but over the last couple of years, both the cuisine and decor have taken a quantum leap forward. Top-notch chef Jonathan Pflueger started working magic in the kitchen upon his arrival in 1995, earning raves from dining critics and longtime fans alike with innovative recipes and updated classics; the menu ranges from spicy macadamia-crusted scallops to halibut teamed with spectacular risotto to steamy chocolate soufflé. And in 1999, the building received a fabulous update as well. A complete renovation and stylish redesign transformed the dark, shingled dining room into a showcase, with floor-to-ceiling windows overlooking the bay, views from just about every table, lots of artistic flourishes (a jewelry designer created the silverware), and a dramatic over-the-water entryway. The kitchen has undergone some transitions as well, although there's every reason to believe this Star will continue shining brightly. Chef Pflueger has moved to the east coast and been replaced by Brian Johnson, whose local cooking credits include the well-regarded El Bizcocho

in Rancho Bernardo. Johnson will eventually turn the menu into his own creation; for the time being he's doing a fine job with appetizers like crab-stuffed calamari in a bell pepper broth and entrees ranging from halibut paired with a garnet-colored beet couscous to swordfish presented on an insanely rich baby artichoke risotto. Dessert anyone? Order the puffy Belgian chocolate soufflé garnished with three sauces at least 20 minutes before you'd like to dig in. The wide-ranging wine list offers lots of fish-friendly sauvignon blancs and chardonnays, along with a dozen lesser-seen whites and reds from California, Australia, France, Italy, and the Pacific Northwest. One caveat: this once-formal dining room no longer has a dress code, so you'll see more than your share of T-shirts and shorts along with evening dresses and suits and ties. *$$$; AE, DC, DIS, MC, V; no checks; dinner every day; full bar; reservations recommended; www.staroftthesea.com; map:O9* &

Sushi Deli / ★
Sushi Deli Too / ★

828 BROADWAY AVE, DOWNTOWN; 619/231-9597
339 W BROADWAY AVE, DOWNTOWN; 619/233-3072

The original Sushi Deli, at 8th and Broadway, is noisy with '80s and '90s rock, the ceilings and walls are halfway painted, and the main location is on the less fashionable end of Broadway. Yet Sushi Deli receives a steady stream of the faithful young, tripping in after work or after working out, and staggering out happy and full an hour or so later. Waiters glide among the mauve Formica tables and teal-cushioned chairs, delivering bar treats such as edamade (steamed soy beans), sunomono (a salad of clear noodles, cukes, and carrots), or chopped cucumbers with chili sauce. Sample many different dishes by ordering "small plates" (most under $4) such as the Dynamite—red snapper, octopus, crab, and shrimp baked with a spicy cream sauce—or the fried gyoza (wonderfully ungreasy), fried pickles, or tofu teriyaki. Japanese paper lanterns cast a pink glow at the sushi bar, presided over by the slow but steady Chef Amaya. At $12, the Shogun (a sampling of many different items) is the most expensive sushi plate. On Mondays it's all the sushi you can swallow—sashimi excepted—for $15. Sushi Deli Too, on lower Broadway, has a greater variety of cooked food, is a bit more expensive, and caters to the courthouse crowd. *$; MC, V; no checks; dinner Mon–Sat (Sushi Deli); lunch Mon–Fri, dinner Thurs–Sat (Sushi Deli Too); beer and wine; reservations accepted for dinner (Sushi Deli Too); map:O7 and N7* &*(Sushi Deli Too)*

Sushi on the Rock / ★☆

7734 GIRARD AVE, LA JOLLA; 858/456-1138

After a move from its tiny original space on Prospect, this Cal–Asian sushi bar has a longer menu and room to accommodate a lot more fans.

Good thing, since the place is generally packed on weekend evenings with a youngish, cell-phone-wielding crowd. They're obviously coming as much for the upscale-industrial setting and the affable, black-clad sushi chefs as the fare, since the menu ranges from merely average to outstanding. The lineup includes both classic and nouvelle-style sushi (both done quite nicely) as well as hot entrees. Best bets on this eclectic menu are the warm specialty sushis with fanciful names like Maui Wowie and Monkey Balls. The chilled vegetable-only rolls are also excellent, making this a vegetarian-friendly destination. Skip the limp tempura, however. The place is loud, with high, hard-edged ceilings and a concrete floor, and the animated conversations tend to drown out even the trendy music on the sound system. *$$; MC, V; no checks; lunch Mon–Fri, dinner every day; beer and wine; no reservations; map:JJ7* &

Taste of Thai / ★★☆

15770 SAN ANDREAS RD, DEL MAR; 858/793-9695

This former bank building behind the Flower Hill Mall is now the prettiest Thai restaurant in town. The whimsically decorated dining room is a visual feast, with squiggly cardboard lamps, colorful walls, and intricate tiled floors. Above, star-shaped cutouts in the ceiling change hue with the indirect lighting behind them. As for the fare, it's every bit as appealing as the setting. The lengthy menu ranges from the usual curries, soups, and appetizers to a number of stir-fries and grilled meats. Curries are particular standouts—try the panang version for a sweet 'n' spicy epiphany on what curry is all about. Seafood, noodles, and grilled or steamed fish are handled adeptly as well. A small wine list offers some spice-friendly selections like gewürztraminer at very reasonable prices. In addition to the two main dining rooms, there's a heated patio and a tiny bar where you can wait for to-go orders. *$$; AE, MC, V; no checks; lunch, dinner every day; beer and wine; reservations recommended; map:GG7* &

Thee Bungalow / ★★☆

4996 W POINT LOMA BLVD, OCEAN BEACH; 619/224-2884

For over 25 years, this family-run restaurant in a converted bungalow home has kept a faithful clientele while attracting new fans all the time. Some diners stick with classics that have been on the menu since the beginning: roast duck garnished with green peppercorns or à l'orange, sea bass served in a luscious seafood sauce, and rack of lamb. Others are attracted by chef/owner Ed Moore's newer creations, which include superb steamed mussels, black-pepper-crusted salmon, and handsome grilled halibut. Since you get soup or salad with your entree (we adore the smoked tomato soup and the tarragon-dressed house salad), you don't need to order a starter. But if you're extra ravenous, do start with the simple cream-sauced tortellini. And wrap up the evening with a

FRESH FROM THE SEA

San Diego's seafood restaurants rely on exotic imports for their menus, receiving fresh shipments of New Zealand mussels, Hawaiian swordfish, and Alaskan salmon and king crab. But residents keep local seafood calendars in mind when dining out or cooking at home. Pacific lobsters are in season from October through March; though less sweet than the Maine variety, these crustaceans bear meaty bodies with a tangy, saltwater taste. Yellowfin, bluefin, and albacore tuna swim by in the summer's warm waters; count on superb sashimi and seared ahi in July and August. Abalone were once common in local waters, but have become endangered; they're legally scooped from underwater habitats in small amounts from March through October. When pounded into tender submission, local abalone are far more flavorful than imported calamari or farmed abalone. The noble dorado (called mahimahi on many menus) still leap and fight on the hook in area waters in late summer. Though anglers deride what they call "bottom fish" (which require endurance at the reel), local bass and halibut make for fine eating in the winter months. Sometimes, when the moon, tides, and water temperatures coincide perfectly, a swordfish will snag its beak on a hook—an occasion for celebration among local cooks. Crustacean collectors know to be wary of poisons in local shellfish collected in spring and summer, so they treasure the winter months, when mussels and clams cling to easily accessible rocks and sand beds. Check out the local selection at Point Loma Seafoods before dining out, then order accordingly. Nothing beats the flavor of the catch of the day.

—*Maribeth Mellin*

crackle-topped crème brûlée, a Bungalow specialty. The lengthy wine list earns praise for both depth of selection and excellent prices, and the restaurant regularly hosts reasonably priced, heavily attended wine dinners that are some of the liveliest around. Although the service and menu are a tad on the formal side, the setting is casual and comfy. Show up in jeans or in jewels—the good people of Thee Bungalow will welcome you just the same. *$$; AE, DC, DIS, MC, V; no checks; dinner every day; full bar; reservations recommended; bungalow@adnc.com; www.thee bungalow.com; map:C2* &

Tip Top Meats / ★★☆

6118 PASEO DEL NORTE, CARLSBAD ; 760/438-2620

This North County butcher shop, grocery, and deli definitely deserves the moniker Tip Top. It's one of the few stores in the San Diego area that regularly carries prime grade beef, and it's even better known as home to a great selection of freshly made sausages. This is where to find the best of the wursts: bratwurst, liverwurst, English bangers, Portuguese linguica, and more, along with excellent hot dogs. In addition to the butcher shop, an adjacent cafe offers made-to-order sandwiches, several deli salads, and rib-sticking entrees like meat loaf, stuffed cabbage, and barbecued ribs. There's plenty of seating, or you can get orders to go. Looking for some exotic groceries or imported beer? The market sells over 100 varieties of beer from around the world, as well as lots of wine, imported condiments and cookies, and assorted fancy snacks and crackers. *$; AE, DIS, MC, V; checks OK; breakfast, lunch, dinner every day; beer and wine; no reservations; map:CC7* &

Tony's Jacal / ★★☆

621 VALLEY AVE, SOLANA BEACH; 858/755-2274

Family-owned and operated since 1946, Tony's Jacal has obviously been doing everything right. Even if you overlook the autographed photos of celebrity diners, you can't miss the long lines—up to an hour on weekends and during Del Mar's racing season. Hang out at the bar with a margarita while listening for your name to be sung out over the loudspeaker. A waitress in blue ruffles will show you to an aqua-upholstered booth in a cavernous room with wood paneling, open beams, Mexican knickknacks, and half-moon-shaped stained-glass windows, or to a table on the outdoor patio with small pond, gurgly waterfall, and flowering plants. Customary Mexican combination plates fill a big chunk of the menu, featuring pork and turkey along with the ubiquitous chicken. Special entrees include chili con carne, steak ranchero, and chicken mole, and the *platillos speciales* include various enchiladas, carnitas, tortas, quesadillas, and carne asada. *$; AE, MC, V; no checks; lunch Mon–Sat, dinner Wed–Mon; full bar; reservations recommended for 10 or more; map:FF7* &

Top o' the Cove / ★★★

1216 PROSPECT ST, LA JOLLA; 858/454-7779

Widely considered one of the county's most romantic restaurants, this La Jolla landmark attracts couples of all ages and is a notorious site for marriage proposals. With its lushly planted courtyard entrance, piano bar, and several tables overlooking the Pacific, Top o' the Cove is indeed a lovers' dream, as well as a top spot for upscale business dining. But there's more to the story than beauty; the kitchen's blend of classic French, Pacific Rim, and Mediterranean flavors is as impressive as the view. An appetizer of risotto and white truffles is exquisite (and should be, for the price). Entree-wise, grilled swordfish or salmon, often sauced with a cabernet sauvignon reduction that's perfect for these full-flavored fish, are our top choices. A rare-roasted Muscovy duck breast is another standout. The restaurant's wine list is breathtaking in depth and price; you can easily drop $100 or more on a bottle. Note that reservations are confirmed with a credit card; for parties of six or larger, you'll be charged unless you cancel 48 hours in advance of your reservation. *$$$; AE, CB, DC, MC, V; no checks; lunch, dinner every day, brunch Sun; full bar; reservations recommended; www.topothecove.com; map:JJ7* &

Tori Tori New Japanese Cuisine / ★★★

1905 EL CAJON BLVD, UNIVERSITY HEIGHTS; 619/295-2902

This marriage of a fast-food joint and a traditional Japanese restaurant is a happy one indeed. Ignore the drab strip mall setting, crowded parking lot, and simple decor. Once you've sampled Tori Tori's sparkling fresh sushi, stir-fried noodles, and spicy curries, you'll be a convert. Especially at these prices: it's hard to spend more than $5 on a meal, unless you get carried away with sushi specialties like the caterpillar roll with eel. Most sushi items and appetizers (including terrific spicy scallop rolls and yummy pot stickers) are about $3. Big spenders (here, that would be someone with five or six bucks to spare) should choose one of the entrees like the ginger chicken or teriyaki chicken rice bowls, the Tori Tori fried rice, or the combo meals served with three appetizers, a salad, and rice. To-go foods are just as carefully presented as those eaten on the premises, a boon for anyone in search of a nice take-home dinner. This is a no-tablecloths, no-frills kind of place, but the sushi chef is adept, the servers are pleasant, and the price is certainly right. *$; AE, DIS, MC, V; no checks; lunch, dinner Mon–Sat; beer and wine; no reservations; map:P1* &

Trattoria Acqua / ★★★

1298 PROSPECT ST, LA JOLLA; 858/454-0709

Opened in 1994, Trattoria Acqua is one of San Diego's best-known, best-regarded dining destinations. Part of the notoriety is due to a stunning setting; this indoor/outdoor restaurant, located in the Coast Walk building, is nestled into a La Jolla Cove hillside with ocean views that won't quit. But pretty views are a nickel a dozen in this seaside town; Acqua stands apart for actually delivering high-quality food and service too. The Mediterranean-influenced menu roams gracefully from Tuscany to Provence to Tangiers, with stops along the way for excellent designer pizzas, a variety of antipasti and salads, about a dozen pastas, and lots of grilled fish and meats. Start your meal with the complimentary spicy hummus dip while you peruse the lengthy wine list, where notable names from California and Italy are sold at most reasonable prices. Must-have dishes are the grilled portobello mushroom or bruschetta for starters; among the pastas, the lobster ravioli, penne Piemontese, or rigatoni with eggplant; and for main dishes, the veal shank or herb-crusted halibut. Prime seating is on the patio or one of the inside tables with a view of the water (reserve these well in advance). Validated parking is available in the garage under the building, or angle for a spot on busy Prospect Street. *$$; AE, MC, V; no checks; lunch, dinner every day; full bar; reservations recommended; map:JJ7* &

Trattoria Mama Anna / ★★

655 5TH AVE, DOWNTOWN; 619/235-8144
Downtown's Gaslamp Quarter is awash with Italian trattorias. Mama Anna's is not the glitziest, but it's certainly among the very best. All the dishes are prepared fresh, including the addictive fresh bread served with extra-virgin olive oil and balsamic vinegar for dipping. At lunchtime, focaccia sandwiches come with a green salad and are big enough to share with a friend. Our favorite: thin focaccia stuffed with goat cheese, basil, and sliced tomatoes. The pasta dishes are equally delicate and delicious. The restaurant has a nice bar stocked with Italian beers and wines. In addition to the large dining room, there is a small patio out front from which you can watch passersby on Fifth Avenue; the walls are adorned with photographs of the notables who have dined here. Let the trendies flock to the more expensive Italian restaurants up the street—those who know go to Mama's. *$$; AE, DIS, MC, V; no checks; lunch, dinner every day; beer and wine; reservations recommended for dinner; map:O7* &

Trophy's / ★

7510 HAZARD CENTER DR, MISSION VALLEY (AND BRANCHES); 619/296-9600
Not your typical sports bar—the Trophy's chain has something to please everyone from serious fans to those who don't know a first down from a fumble. Sure, there's the requisite memorabilia and big-screen TV, along with cadres of baseball and football cognoscenti cheering for the home teams. But there's also a fun combination of friendly service and good food. Generous, fresh-tasting salads are always a fine choice, as are a variety of burgers, wood-fired pizzas, and some extra-spicy chicken wings. The house chili flavored with hot salsa is another winner. Of course, there's a full bar, with a multitude of beers and several decent wines. Servers tend to be young, cute, and perky—as well as hard-working and efficient. The ambience is happy and noisy, with a thriving singles scene most nights. *$; AE, MC, V; no checks; lunch, dinner every day; full bar; no reservations; map:LL4* &

T's Cafe / ★★☆

271 N HWY 101, SOLANA BEACH; 858/755-7642
Locals have had a love affair with Mr. T's (as it's more commonly referred to) since it opened in 1978. Tucked unobtrusively as it is into one side of Solana Beach's rather uninteresting boardwalk, you'd never guess that lurking within are a spacious dining room with cozy bar area and small private function room (local artists' groups have staged Wednesday morning breakfasts here for years). The woodsy feel and large open fireplace (blazing during the rare Southern California drizzle or foggy chill)

lull patrons into dreams of Montana mountain lodges as they linger a salty breath away from the Pacific, enjoying enormous omelets with king crab, homemade chili, and roasted turkey, as well as various scrambles, Benedicts, bagels, pancakes, waffles, and potato skillet dishes. Although breakfasts are the claim to fame here (and are served until closing), the lunch menu offers a lengthy assortment of deli and veggie sandwiches, burgers, soups, and New York steak sandwiches. *$; AE, MC, V; no checks; breakfast, lunch every day; full bar; reservations accepted for 6 or more; map:FF7* &

Turf Supper Club / ★

1116 25TH ST, GOLDEN HILL; 619/234-6363
Why would you want to cook your own dinner at a restaurant grill? Because that's the way regulars have been doing it for decades at this neighborhood hangout. Burgers and steaks are served raw; patrons belly up to the coals and watch their meat sizzle while sipping Scotch or whiskey. The beef is basic grocery-store quality and the baked potatoes sometimes stick to their foil jackets, but it's the experience diners savor rather than the food. Settle into a Naughahyde booth, check out the photos of '50s-era celebs, throw a slab on the barbie, and chat with barflies who wouldn't drink anywhere else. *$; cash only; dinner every day; full bar; no reservations; map:Q7*

Tutto Mare Ristorante / ★★☆

4365 EXECUTIVE DR, LA JOLLA; 858/597-1188
The name means, basically, "everything from the sea," and that's what the menu at this glossy Golden Triangle destination is all about. The fish fest starts with the appetizers: a delicate lobster salad with baby lettuces, deep-fried calamari, and slivers of salmon flavored with grappa, to name just a few. Next come pastas, many of them starring fish or shellfish (pasta stuffed with smoked trout is a standout, but the penne with duck sausage is no slouch either). Entrees include grilled chicken and New York steaks; grilled sea scallops, their sweetness highlighted by tiny artichokes; boutique pizzas topped with clams and shrimp; and the best pasta in the neighborhood: Maine lobster in a feisty tomato sauce. There's a well-selected wine list and a full bar for appropriate libations. A well-dressed business crowd tends to frequent Tutto Mare at lunch (prime seating on nice days is on the enclosed terrace), and many of the same people come back for dinner. The ambience is stylish without being snobbish, with a sleek, contemporary look softened by displays of fresh ingredients like colorful handmade pastas hung to dry. Leave the little ones at home; Tutto Mare is meant for dates and power dinners. *$$; AE, DC, MC, V; no checks; lunch Mon–Fri, dinner every day; full bar; reservations recommended; map:JJ7*

Twins / ★★☆

9377 S HWY 101, ENCINITAS; 760/635-1962
A very pretty new face on the North County restaurant scene, Twins has plenty of personality and style. Don't let the plain exterior fool you. Inside, this Euro-inspired restaurant and bar exudes class, from meticulously finished ceilings and expensive table settings to a waterfall wall and a fire pit near the entrance. Exotic flower arrangements grace each table, while sconces provide flattering light. All this beauty would be for naught if the fare wasn't notable, but so far the chefs are every bit as talented as the decorators. French onion soup, scallops paired with a fluffy scallop mousse, pan-roasted halibut, filet mignon dotted with peppercorns—all are must-have dishes. Follow up with one of the berry or chocolate desserts. We'll be keeping an eye on how Twins develops. *$$$; AE, DIS, MC, V; no checks; lunch, dinner every day; full bar; reservations recommended; map:EE7* &

The Vegetarian Zone / ★☆

2949 5TH AVE, HILLCREST; 619/298-7302
Previously known as Kung Food, this vegetarian restaurant underwent a name change a couple of years ago. But the menu hasn't been altered too much; this is still a mellow, meat-free eatery with an emphasis on healthful dining. The kitchen takes an international approach, offering dishes ranging from Indian to Mediterranean to Mexican. Greek spinach pie is one of the best dishes here, along with vegetable lasagne, several quesadillas (available with rennetless cheese), and a bean sprout salad. Soups change daily and are always worth ordering. The open dining room is pretty but can get a bit noisy; sit in the shaded patio out back when the weather allows. Although the service tends to be as laid-back as the clientele, servers are pleasant and well-informed about meals and preparation methods. Along with the sit-down restaurant, an adjacent shop offers food to go and a fascinating array of books, music, jewelry, and skin care products. *$$; DIS, MC, V; no checks; breakfast Sat–Sun, lunch, dinner every day; beer and wine; no reservations; map:N4*

The Venetian / ★

3663 VOLTAIRE ST, POINT LOMA; 619/223-8197
Most of the peninsula's residents agree that The Venetian, near Point Loma High School, has the best thin-crust pizza in the city. First-generation Sicilian-American Vince Giacalone opened the business in 1965 as a small family pizza parlor. After years on Canon Street in Point Loma, he opened this second location, now run by sons Joe and Frank. (The original location, sold in 1972, is now called Old Venice.) Point Lomans and Obecians who ate here as kids now tuck their own offspring into the booths lining the walls of the original dining room, or head for the

peaceful covered patio in the back, with potted shrubs dusted in tiny white lights. If you're not in a pizza mood (unthinkable!), try the tasty seafood pasta: shrimp, clams, scallops, and calamari in a tomato-based sauce over linguine. *$; AE, DC, DIS, MC, V; no checks; lunch Mon–Fri, dinner every day; full bar; no reservations; map:E4* &

Via Italia Trattoria / ★★☆

4705-A CLAIREMONT DR, CLAIREMONT; 858/274-9732

A chorus of *buona seras* greets customers who enter this Italian gem tucked into an otherwise unremarkable mall. The accents are authentic (the entire staff is Italian), and so is the cooking, much of it based on regional specialties rarely seen in San Diego. While the thin-crusted, wood-fired pizzas are certainly a fine reason to visit, the nightly specials set this little dining room apart. Look for venison simmered in brandy, polenta flavored with truffle oil, bread-spinach dumplings (called *strozzapretti*) in a lush porcini sauce, and a memorable dessert pairing mascarpone cheese and fresh berries run under the broiler. On the regular menu, the stewed Italian sausage, Gorgonzola-topped greens, and penne with pancetta and vodka lead an eclectic parade that mixes the familiar with the unusual. While the restaurant is small and plainly decorated, candles glow on every table and the service is warm and sincere, making otherwise informal meals feel like special occasions. It's smart to make reservations for dinner, as the nearby movie theater draws plenty of pre- and post-show diners. *$$; AE, MC, V; no checks; lunch, dinner every day; beer and wine; reservations recommended; map:KK6* &

Vigilucci's / ★★☆

505 S HWY 101, ENCINITAS; 760/942-7332

When Roberto Vigilucci opened his Italian restaurant in 1993, he not only brought his delectable hometown Milano recipes to North County, but also managed to turn one corner of an innocuous intersection into an elegant and intimate haven. Most afternoons and evenings the place is swamped with the well heeled looking to be well fed. Tables swathed in crisp linens and topped with fresh flowers are laden with gnocchi al gorgonzola e nocchi (potato dumplings with gorgonzola cheese sauce and walnuts), pollo alla florentina (chicken breast stuffed with spinach and ricotta cheese in a creamy white sauce), and saltimbocca alla romana (veal scaloppini topped with prosciutto, sage, and mozzarella in white wine sauce). Portions are large, and all entrees come with fresh vegetables and spaghetti aglio e olio. Lunch specials are quite reasonable, and the wine list is extraordinary, from $15 bottles of California chardonnay to a 1990 Château Lafite Rothschild (going for a whopping $900). Vigilucci's chef has changed recently but the charming all-Italian staff remains much the same, offering unpretentious and welcoming service. *$$; AE, DIS, MC, V; no checks; lunch Mon–Fri, dinner every day; beer and wine; reservations accepted for 4 or more; map:EE7* &

The Waterfront / ★

2044 KETTNER BLVD, DOWNTOWN; 619/232-9656

A workingman's retreat since the 1930s, the Waterfront combines all the best qualities of dive bar, pool hall, burger joint, and neighborhood hangout. It's best known as a watering hole (and one that opens at 6am, at that), but savvy regulars know that the Waterfront offers darn good eatin' as well. Case in point: some of the best bargain burgers in town. They're a little bit greasy, but these half-pound beauties topped with grilled onions are some of the city's prime cheap eats. Fish tacos, excellent bean chili, and assorted sandwiches round out the menu, which also includes Mexican-style breakfasts on the weekends. Leave the little ones at home, and forget asking for a wine list; the preferred accompaniment to anything you eat here is beer. Prime seating is at the open windows that survey the sidewalk, but no matter where you sit, you'll get cheery service and an eclectic crowd that ranges from well-dressed businessfolk at lunch to night-shifters coming in for breakfast and a brew. *$; AE, MC, V; no checks; breakfast, lunch, dinner every day; full bar; no reservations; map:M6*

The Whaling Bar / ★★☆

1332 PROSPECT ST, LA JOLLA; 858/454-0771

Straight out of a Raymond Chandler mystery, the Whaling Bar is as close as San Diego gets to an old boy's club. The bar's character has hardly changed since the '50s, despite lengthy renovations in 1998. The tufted leather booths are cushier, the whaling mural has been restored, and the walls have a fresh rose-tinted glow. Though never trendy, the menu has been freshened a bit, offering upscale comfort food with a few twists. Oysters taste sparkling-fresh with a dash of horseradish vinaigrette; baby spinach salads sport pistachios with their feta; truffle essence provides a soupçon of earthy flavor to veal. Loyalists swear by the steaks, sautéed calf liver, and crisp coating on the rack of lamb, and this may well be the best place in town to order swordfish. Tuck your knees under a red tablecloth, order a single-malt Scotch, and watch maître d' Manny Silva greet old friends. Makes you want to tuck a rosebud in your honey's lapel. *$$$; AE, DIS, MC, V; no checks; lunch, dinner every day; full bar; reservations recommended; map:JJ7* &

When in Rome / ★★☆

1108 1ST ST, ENCINITAS; 760/944-1771

Restaurateurs Joe and Rosemary Ragone run this fine Italian restaurant the old-fashioned way, by doing just about everything themselves. They grow many of their own herbs, do much of the cooking, choose produce and meats with finicky precision, and even prepare their own breads and desserts. The results show in the perfect tomato and basil salad, the falling-off-the-bone osso buco, a velveteen fusilli with vodka, and each of the nightly fish specials. If they're serving halibut, mussels, or salmon, you're in for a particular treat. Desserts rate an equal rave, especially Rosemary's tiramisu, crème brûlée, and fluffy fresh fruit mousses. The spacious restaurant offers an especially cozy dining room with a fireplace, as well as a covered patio complete with bar and piano next to a larger room that's good for private parties. All in all, a visit to When in Rome means spending the evening in the company of very talented, very gracious people who make you want to return. *$$$; AE, MC, V; no checks; dinner every day; full bar; reservations recommended; map:EE7* &

Winesellar & Brasserie / ★★★

9550 WAPLES ST, SORRENTO VALLEY; 858/450-9576

Here's an upstairs/downstairs bit of heaven for wine connoisseurs and food worshippers alike. This nationally acclaimed restaurant may be miles from fashionable dining neighborhoods like downtown and La Jolla, but it's definitely center stage when it comes to the art of gastronomy. The incredible wine selection showcases little-known, hard-to-find boutique wines as well as heavy hitters from Bordeaux and Burgundy. The first floor of the restaurant, in fact, is a retail wine shop with an international selection; owner Gary Parker often buys entire cellars from collectors and offers many a rare bottle for sale. Upstairs, chef Doug Organ—one of the visionaries who helped lead San Diego out of the culinary dark ages—continues to impress diners with both traditional European and new-wave cuisine in a stylish, bistro-like setting with bar and table seating. Offbeat combos like foie gras sauced with lime and mangos or ginger-cured pork loin are every bit as good as classic roasted lamb with herbes de Provence. Although the lineup changes constantly, some of Organ's favorite inventions return again and again. For a taste of the city's most consistently interesting cuisine, look for angus beef teamed with shallots and Stilton, duck confit with fresh herbs, and roasted monkfish scented with curry and presented over green lentils. The dynamic Parker/Organ team also runs Laurel downtown; both restaurants certainly rate a visit. *$$$; AE, CB, DC, DIS, MC, V; no checks; lunch Sat, dinner Tues–Sun; beer and wine; reservations required; www.winesellar.com; map:II7* &

Yoshino / ★★

1790 W WASHINGTON ST, MIDDLETOWN; 619/295-2232

If you really love sashimi, forget all those sleek sushi bars and head to this luncheonette-style Japanese old-timer amid a centrally located (yet obscure) patch of offices and salons. Fresh tuna is Yoshino's forte. The chef chooses his catch with great wisdom, finding the perfect fillets for the thin, diagonal slices of rosy fish centered on a plain white plate. They're not chintzy here either—nothing of this charging by the slice.

One serving with white rice and plenty of soy and wasabi fills you up. Have your table-mate order the sesame chicken, a pile of chicken strips with a crisp, seed-filled crust, and share a great meal. Keep hold of your teacups, though; they tend to slip toward the edge of the slick plastic tables. *$; AE, MC, V; no checks; lunch, dinner Wed–Mon; beer and sake; no reservations; map:L3* &

LODGINGS

LODGINGS

Location, location, location. It's the most important consideration when you're choosing accommodations in San Diego. Downtown is largely the province of business travelers, conventioneers, and visitors doing their touring by public transportation. Old Town's moderately priced inns and Mission Valley's modest chains and full-scale resorts are favorites with families. Boaters and bicyclists prefer the quiet feel of Shelter Island and Point Loma. Vacationers with sun and fun in mind head for Mission Bay and Pacific Beach. The more aesthetically minded prefer the Mediterranean flair of La Jolla and the small-town feeling in Coronado.

San Diego County, in fact, is made up of 17 distinct cities with varied natural attractions—many of them destinations in their own right. Horse racing, dining, shopping, and hiking trails by the sea make Del Mar a sensible choice, and it's only 20 miles from downtown. Farther north on the coast, Carlsbad has made a big splash with Legoland. It's also the closest San Diego resort town to Disneyland: first-class golf resorts lay carpets of green east of Interstate 5, while Carlsbad's classy town center sits by the sea.

Visitors who've been to San Diego a few times tend to base their vacations even farther from the city center. They head to Julian and other mountain communities in the fall and Borrego Springs and the desert from March to June. Several out-of-the-way resorts have a devoted local clientele who love to escape to the hinterlands on weekends and holidays. Trains, trolleys, and freeways connect much of the county; it's easy to stay even 60 miles outside the city and take day trips to Mission Bay, Balboa Park, and Old Town.

Downtown

Balboa Park Inn / ★★

3402 PARK BLVD, DOWNTOWN; 619/298-0823 OR 800/938-8181
If you want to stay near the urban Eden of Balboa Park yet close to downtown, check out funky Balboa Park Inn. Located on the edge of the park, the inn has 26 rooms in a series of pink adobe Mission-style buildings. Be sure to ask for detailed room descriptions, or check out the Web site, since all rooms and suites are individually decorated. Some are truly charming, though others veer toward kitsch. Some are definitely for grown-ups on a romantic play date, while others are ideal for small families. If you prefer rooms in tasteful, soft pastels, ask for the Monet suite or the Las Palomas suite, which boasts a roomy private balcony overlooking the park and a cozy glass-enclosed sunroom. Go all the way and ask about the specialty suites. The Tara suite has a *Gone With the Wind*

theme (though you may or may not appreciate the portrait of Vivien Leigh as Scarlett O'Hara staring down at you), while you can get jungle-funky in the Tarzan-themed *Greystoke* suite. Some rooms have working fireplaces, and many have whirlpool tubs. Rates include continental breakfast for two, delivered to your room. *$$; AE, DC, DIS, MC, V; checks OK (2 weeks in advance); info@BalboaParkInn.com; www.balboapark inn.com; map:P3*

Embassy Suites San Diego Bay / ★★

610 PACIFIC HWY, DOWNTOWN; 619/239-2400 OR 800/EMBASSY
Families and conventioneers alike are enamored with this chain's sensible layout; the 337 suites all have separate living rooms, kitchenettes, and desk space outside the bedrooms. Though the rooms face a sky-high atrium, noise here is not a drawback; instead, the lively conversation from the lobby draws guests down to the complimentary breakfast buffet. Though the hotel lacks individuality, it more than makes up for that with its location, within steps of Seaport Village and the Gaslamp Quarter. Advance bookings are essential, no matter what time of year. *$$$; AE, DC, MC, V; checks OK; map:M8* &

Gaslamp Plaza Suites / ★★

520 E ST, DOWNTOWN; 619/232-9500 OR 800/874-8700
San Diego's first skyscraper, built in 1913, is now one of downtown's most attractive hotels. The 11-story building is listed on the National Register of Historic Places, and its Australian gumwood, Corinthian marble, mosaic tiles, and bronze and brass embellishments have all been lovingly restored. The 58 suites are small but charming, and complimentary breakfast is served on the rooftop terrace. The location, in the middle of the Gaslamp, is both a benefit and a drawback. You can party all night and walk back to your room, but if you're a light sleeper, the street noise may get on your nerves. This hotel books up quickly; make reservations early. *$$; AE, DC, DIS, MC, V; no checks; map:O7*

Horton Grand Hotel / ★★

311 ISLAND AVE, DOWNTOWN; 619/544-1886 OR 800/542-1886
Offering a nice antidote to downtown's cookie-cutter convention hotels, the Horton Grand Hotel is a touch of Victorian-era gentility in the heart of the historic Gaslamp Quarter. Composed of two historic Victorian hotels rescued from demolition, the Horton Grand has quite a colorful history. Wyatt Earp slept here when he lived in San Diego, and the management named the hotel's restaurant in honor of Ida Bailey, a notorious turn-of-the-century madam whose bordello once occupied this site. Outside, the hotel is a fantasy of blue-and-white gingerbread. Inside, all 108 rooms are individually decorated with period antiques, lace curtains, and working gas fireplaces. But we'll bet Wyatt Earp never had a microwave

or a hair dryer. For more space, request one of the 600-square-foot mini-suites. Sunday brunch at the Horton Grand is a sumptuous affair; for smaller appetites, make reservations for English afternoon or high tea served on Thursday, Friday, and Saturday afternoons. While the hotel has plenty of its own quirky charm, its location is the real bonus. You can live it up at the Gaslamp's many clubs and bars, then stroll or catch a pedicab back to the hotel. *$$$; AE, DC, DIS, MC, V; checks OK; info@ hortongrand.com; www.hortongrand.com; map:N8*

Hyatt Regency San Diego / ★★

I MARKET PL, DOWNTOWN; 619/232-1234 OR 800/233-1234
Local wags call this bayside tower "the screwdriver," thanks to its sleek obelisk shape narrowing to angular points. The Skidmore, Owings & Merrill architectural firm won the task of designing an 875-room hotel on a tiny lot wedged into the jam-packed waterfront; they succeeded by carving out gardens and pedestrian walkways past shops and restaurants, and put the pool on the third story overlooking the sails drifting under Coronado Bay Bridge. The rooms are undersize and the hallways noisy when conventioneers return from partying. The restaurants and bars are often packed with downtown workers and tourists. *$$$; AE, DC, DIS, JCB, MC, V; checks OK; map:M8* &

La Pensione Hotel / ★★

1700 INDIA ST, DOWNTOWN; 619/236-8000 OR 800/232-4683
This modern, architecturally innovative hotel is a boon for budget travelers. Most of the 80 rooms have kitchen facilities and large tables or desks; some have views of San Diego Bay; all have windows opening to

sea breezes and sunlight, and high ceilings that add a sense of space. Laundry facilities, a tiled courtyard, a marble fireplace in the lobby, and two adjacent restaurants are added perks, as is the colorful cast of multilingual travelers. The neighborhood has good Italian restaurants and bakeries, and the trolley runs nearby. *$; AE, DC, DIS, MC, V; no checks; www.lapensionehotel.com; map:M6*

San Diego Marriott Hotel & Marina / ★★☆

333 W HARBOR DR, DOWNTOWN; 619/234-1500 OR 800/228-9290
Twin mirrored towers reflect the cityscape and San Diego Bay backdrop at the grandest hotel beside San Diego's Convention Center. Despite its 1,355 rooms, all with spectacular views, this place doesn't overwhelm its guests. Instead, it calms them with a central tropical lagoon replete with waterfalls and swimming pools. The marina shelters 446 of the most handsome yachts and sailboats this side of Newport Beach; guests sleeping aboard their seaworthy homes can order room service delivered on deck. The rooms and suites are geared more to business travelers than to vacationers, with fax and modem ports, desks, two-line phones, and

LOVE, SAN DIEGO STYLE

San Diego may have a *Gidget* reputation as a wholesome surfside city, but its balmy Mediterranean climate, vivid sunsets, and natural beauty make it the perfect backdrop for any romance. Our picks for a great date—whether it's your 1st or your 50th—include:

Watch the sunset from a bench at **La Jolla Cove.**

Take a sunset stroll along Torrey Pines State Reserve's flat, cliff-top **Guy Fleming Trail** for endless views of the Pacific.

Hike to the top of **Cowles Mountain** in Mission Trails Regional Park to watch the sun rise over the East County mountains.

Picnic by the fountain in Balboa Park's **Alcazar Garden**, then stroll through the cool **Botanical Building** and explore the shady **Palm Canyon**.

Sip champagne and cuddle in a gondola on the Coronado Cays with the **Gondola Company** (619/429-6317; $60 per couple); hourlong cruises depart from the marina at Loews Coronado Bay Resort.

Take to the sky on a balloon ride with **Skysurfer Balloon Company** (858/481-6800; $135–$145 per person). Or soar over the coast in a vintage biplane with **Barnstorming Adventures** (800/759-5667; $98–$298 per couple).

Explore the 30-acre **Quail Botanical Gardens** (230 Quail Gardens Dr; 760/436-3036). Check out the lavender-scented Mediterranean garden and the lush jungle of the Tropical Rainforest Exhibit.

For a nostalgic thrill, ride the **Belmont Park Giant Dipper** (3190 Mission Blvd), an old-school roller coaster in Mission Beach.

Take a moonlit horse-drawn carriage ride along the downtown waterfront with **Cinderella Carriage Company** (619/239-8080).   *—Alison Ashton*

coffeemakers. The regular rooms are small and have a disconcerting mix of plaid and floral fabrics, and the hallways are noisy when merry conventioneers return from their revelries. Suites on the Concierge Levels are larger and more serene. The Marriott is nearly always filled with corporate hotshots commandeering the best digs for their convention bigwigs. Book far in advance of your trip. *$$$$; AE, DC, MC, V; checks OK; map:N8* &

U. S. Grant Hotel / ★★☆

326 BROADWAY, DOWNTOWN; 619/ 232-3121 OR 800/237-5029

Ulysses S. Grant Jr. thought of San Diego as a grand spot for a monument to his more famous dad, and commissioned Harrison Albright to design an Italian Renaissance palace in the heart of downtown. The hotel opened in 1910 amid much fanfare; after all, how many urban inns could boast a saltwater swimming pool and ladies' billiard hall amid marble pillars? Fortunes rose and fell in this hotel over the decades. It seems anyone who purchased the property felt like the poor offspring of a British duke saddled with the family mansion. The 340 rooms and suites are visions of far nobler times, with two-poster beds, Victorian chairs, and fireplaces (in some suites). Still, the lobby and bar are popular gathering spots for San Diegans, and the restaurant is a treasured landmark. *$$$; AE, DC, MC, V; checks OK; map:N7* &

The Westgate Hotel / ★★★☆

1055 2ND AVE, DOWNTOWN; 619/238-1818 OR 800/221-3802
Versailles meets SoCal in the lobby of this elegant hotel, financed in 1970 by San Diego's legendary character C. Arnholt Smith. Banker, politician, and misguided visionary, Smith was a civic booster and millionaire with questionable financial practices. He poured over $16 million into the white palace with gold-tinted windows and gave his wife carte blanche to tour Europe for many months, collecting Louis XV chairs, couches, and Baccarat chandeliers. The lobby remains a gracious museum staffed by courteous courtiers. Suited waiters serve coffee and port in the Plaza Bar to European guests on shopping and business trips. Gracious concierges acquire theater seats when none can be found; maître d's keep track of their guests' desires. The Westgate's 223 rooms and suites could be considered a bit stuffy. Satin negligees and silk pajamas are in order here; gold-and-white theme prevails; antique chairs demand proper use; and armoires hide the TVs. Cocktail dresses and suits are the attire of choice in the Le Fontainebleau restaurant, the Westgate dining room is both comfortable and classy, the perfect spot for a proper lunch. The hotel's facilities include a fitness center, barber shop, and gourmet deli; several airlines have offices on the Broadway side of the building. *$$$; AE, DC, MC, V; no checks; map:N7* &

Westin Hotel at Horton Plaza / ★★

910 BROADWAY CIRCLE, DOWNTOWN; 619/239-2200 OR 800/693-7846
A truly bizarre blue obelisk marks the circular drive and entryway to this mall hotel, which is often booked by groups of shoppers from Mexico City who are hooked on Nordstrom and Horton Plaza's specialty shops. The 450-room hotel is squished between the plaza's shops and restaurants, yet it has a calm, relaxed ambience. The rooms are decorated in soft pastels and offer all the business and vacation amenities; some top-floor rooms have good views of San Diego Bay. Several chains have claimed the hotel over the years; Westin has spit-and-polished the brass rails and knobs, and service is top-notch. *$$; AE, DC, DIS, JCB, MC, V; checks OK; www.westin.com; map:N7*

Airport Area

Sheraton Harbor Island San Diego / ★★

1380 HARBOR ISLAND DR, HARBOR ISLAND; 619/291-2900 OR 800/325-3535
Long before the convention center and luxury hotels drew travelers into downtown, this well-situated Sheraton was considered the best hotel in the area. The 700-room tower was completely renovated in 1994; the lobby is particular impressive, with ceiling frescoes lit by a computerized system that replicates the sky at various times of the day. The rooms are small but perfectly adequate and comfortable; the spa and fitness center is large and body treatments and massages are reasonably priced. Other pluses are bayside pools, tennis courts, bike and boat rentals, and trails leading along the island's edge to Spanish Landing, a long, narrow park beside San Diego Bay. The restaurants, while not stellar, are very good, and quick meals at the lobby Aroma Café keep dining costs down. *$$$; AE, DC, DIS, MC, V; checks OK; www.sheraton.com; map:I6*

Westin Harbor Island / ★★★☆

1590 HARBOR ISLAND DR, HARBOR ISLAND; 619/291-6400 OR 800/228-5000
The Westin chain took over the west tower of the Sheraton in 1999. Business travelers have long preferred this 346-room hotel; it's quieter than the Sheraton and more attuned to the needs of harried execs. The oversized rooms have large desks, separate seating areas, and formal French renaissance decor; phones have data ports, and the busy business center is well equipped with Internet access, fax machines, and all the services worker bees demand. In-room coffeemakers stocked with Starbucks and large baths with herbal soaps and gels comfort the weary. The tower has its own pool and restaurants, and guests have use of all the Sheraton's facilities. Best of all, the airport is minutes away. *$$$; AE, DC, DIS, MC, V; checks OK; www.westin.com; map:H6*

Coronado

El Cordova Hotel / ★★

1351 ORANGE AVE, CORONADO; 619/435-4131 OR 800/229-2032
In a beach town dominated by grand resorts, El Cordova Hotel is an affordable alternative. The salmon adobe building presiding over Coronado's bustling Orange Avenue is redolent of California in the 1930s. The airy, terra-cotta-tiled lobby sets just the right tone with a melodious fountain, intricate tile work, rustic carved-wood furnishings, and wrought-iron decorative touches. The inn's 36 rooms were recently redone, but still have a simple decor with carved wood furniture and Mexican tiles. Most rooms are accessed from the lush inner courtyard.

We have a couple of quibbles, though. Noise is a factor, emanating from both busy Orange Avenue and the patio tables of Miguel's Cocina, which occupies El Cordova's courtyard. The inn also has a dinky pool, so plan to hit the beach instead. *$$; AE, MC, V; no checks; map:NN5*

Glorietta Bay Inn / ★★

1630 GLORIETTA BLVD, CORONADO; 619/435-3101 OR 800/283-9383
John Spreckels, the sugar baron fond of all things grand and glorious for his vision of Coronado, hired architect Harrison Albright to design his family mansion on a sloping lawn facing the bay in 1908. The mansion now houses 11 of the hotel's rooms; the rest are in less glamorous (and less expensive) buildings with balconies and gardens above the bay. The original house is a wonder of polished wood, brass, glass, swooping marble stairways, and eye-boggling antiques. The rooms are the perfect beginning for a tour through Coronado's history. *$$; AE, DC, MC, V; checks OK; map:NN5* &

Hotel del Coronado / ★★★☆

1500 ORANGE AVE, CORONADO; 619/435-6611 OR 800/HOTEL-DEL
"The Del" presides over Coronado—indeed, over San Diego—like the grand empress she is. Opened in 1888, this sprawling, white-frame Victorian confection of red-roofed turrets, stained glass, and crown-shaped chandeliers is a National Historic Landmark and much-beloved hub of local activity. The hotel has hosted just about every dignitary and celebrity to roll through town, including 14 U.S. presidents. It also played a starring role—alongside Marilyn Monroe, Jack Lemmon, and Tony Curtis—in *Some Like It Hot*. With all this history, the public areas can get overwhelmed with sightseers, hotel guests, and conventioneers. Still, if you like the bustling activity of a full-service resort, with its scheduled activities, shopping arcade, and such, The Del should fit the bill. Rooms in the original building are scheduled for some renovations, including installation of air conditioning as part of a five-year, $50 million restoration project. Rooms in the original building have a classic Victorian theme. For more privacy, look to the newer Ocean Tower. Its spacious, comfortable rooms overlook the Pacific or the bay, and have been decorated like country cottages in shades of blue and green, with wicker chairs and chintz fabrics; the tower has its own pool and a nice stretch of beach. The intimate Prince of Wales Grill (see Restaurants chapter) has a jazzy 1930s-inspired decor; the menu was recently revamped with a Continental-California theme. In addition, the entire hotel is being restored to enhance the views of the sea. Though the grill's menu will remain the same, it will soon have an outdoor terrace. *$$$; AE, DC, DIS, MC, V; checks OK; www.hoteldel.com; map:NN5*

Loews Coronado Bay Resort / ★★★★

4000 CORONADO BAY RD, CORONADO; 619/424-4000 OR 800/81-LOEWS
At first, it seems strange to choose this isolated resort for a San Diego stay. Far removed from the bustle of downtown, the self-contained compound sprawls beside the west side of San Diego Bay at the southern end of Coronado. The neighboring Coronado Cays housing complex is an enclave of pricey homes on private canals; Silver Strand State Beach is right across the street. Why leave when you're stranded in paradise?

That's exactly what many guests think, especially San Diegans and frequent visitors on short escapes. The resort's Azzura Point restaurant consistently rates among the top five restaurants in the county; the Market Cafe facing the marina serves the most spectacular brunch this side of Hawaii. Energized souls sign up at Action Sports for sailboats, paddleboats, and all kinds of bikes for self-guided tours; lovers drift under the setting sun in gondolas stocked with champagne. The 438 rooms and suites all have water views and balconies; especially fine ones sit at the tip of the resort facing the 80-slip marina, where floating travelers throw casual cocktail parties on their prows. The rooms leave nothing to be desired. Kids get rubber ducks and bubbles in the giant bathtubs—although first they have to kick out the grown-ups. Chairs, couches, and beds are all comfy; it's hard to leave them for the padded pool chairs—though the idea of Häagen-Dazs bars sold poolside is enticing. Leave if you must; shuttles run regularly to downtown's Horton Plaza, and driving nearly anywhere is a breeze (literally, as you soar atop the arcing Coronado Bay Bridge to the mainland). *$$$; AE, DC, MC, V; checks OK; www.loewshotels.com; map:NN5* &

Point Loma/Shelter Island

The Bay Club / ★★

2131 SHELTER ISLAND DR, SHELTER ISLAND; 619/224-8888 OR 800/833-6565
Rattan furnishings, tropical fabrics, and plenty of windows open to the sea air make this 105-room low-rise hotel a good choice for adults on a grown-up getaway. Rooms face the yacht basin or the street, though views from those on the ground level, street side, are obstructed by traffic. Guests mingle at the complimentary breakfast buffet and beside the shaded pool when not off on excursions around the city. Service is personal, friendly, and accommodating; you can arrange nearly anything with the concierges. *$$; AE, DC, DIS, MC, V; checks OK; www.bayclubhotel.com; map:F7*

Best Western Island Palms Hotel & Marina / ★

2051 SHELTER ISLAND DR, SHELTER ISLAND; 619/222-0561 OR 877/484-3725
Boaters appreciate the nautical ambience and 188-slip marina; families delight in the six-person suites with full kitchens. The 97 rooms are unremarkable and designed to withstand tough wear and tear. But the heated pool and hot tub are set by the bay, where paths lead along the island's leeward shore and marinas. Children under 18 stay free. The dockmaster gives kids tours of the marina (grown-ups can tag along), and there is a fishing pier nearby. *$$$; AE, DC, DIS, MC, V; no checks; www.best western.com; map:F8* ⅃

Shelter Pointe Hotel and Marina / ★★★

1551 SHELTER ISLAND DR, SHELTER ISLAND; 619/221-8000 OR 800/566-2524
Tiki torches and mai tais were mainstays at this island resort when it opened as the Kona Kai in 1952. The original shingled bungalows facing Point Loma and San Diego Bay remained intact until the early '90s, when a Mexican conglomerate purchased the property and reconstructed most of the facilities with a hacienda theme. New owners took over in 1998, adding further amenities to one of the loveliest escapes near downtown. The resort faces a private marina at the south tip of the man-made island; rooms on the street side face the bay, Coronado, and downtown. A waterfront sidewalk runs the length of the property, past low-rise buildings housing the rooms and suites. The two-story units are particularly spectacular. Breakfast in the king-size bed in the second-story master bedroom comes with a water view, while downstairs living rooms, sleeper sofas, and full kitchens and baths give families plenty of room to spread out in comfort. Even the regular rooms are satisfying, with their terraces on the lawn within steps of the pool. Tennis courts, a fitness club, decent restaurants, and marina facilities provide entertainment; walkers and joggers appreciate the paths along the edge of Shelter Island. *$$$; AE, DC, DISC, MC, V; checks OK (if mailed in advance); www.shelterpointe.com; map:E8*

Old Town

Best Western Hacienda Suites–Old Town / ★

4041 HARNEY ST, OLD TOWN; 619/298-4707 OR 800/888-1991
White stucco buildings are staggered down a steep hill at this compact 169-room hotel, where it takes some time to figure out which stairway or ramp leads to the pool and your room. The rooms don't rate as suites in our book, and foldout couches and writing tables take up space. A southwest style (think wood, striped fabrics, and clay ornaments) prevails, and all rooms are stocked with microwaves, coffeemakers, VCRs, and refrigerators. There's limited room service from the adjacent Acapulco

restaurant (a good spot for sunset cocktails). The street is fairly quiet, and all of Old Town's attractions are within walking distance. Save energy for the hike back to your room. *$$; AE, DC, DIS, MC, V; no checks; www. haciendahotel-oldtown.com; map:J2*

Heritage Park Inn / ★★

2470 HERITAGE PARK ROW, OLD TOWN; 619/299-6832 OR 800/995-2470
Nestled in a cluster of lovingly restored Victorian homes overlooking Old Town, Heritage Park Inn is true to its elegant, old-time roots. Twelve rooms are contained in two historic homes—the circa 1889 Christian House and the Italianate Bushyhead House. With a formal Victorian parlor (where classic films are screened every evening) and period antiques and stained-glass windows throughout, the inn transports guests back to San Diego's early days. It doesn't take long to slow your pace—maybe sit for a spell in one of the wicker rockers on the veranda. We recommend the romantic Turret Room, high in a tower overlooking the gardens, or the Garret, with its own secret staircase. For more luxury, reserve one of the three rooms in Bushyhead House, with whirlpool tubs for two. Rates include a gourmet breakfast, served by candlelight in the dining room, plus a filling afternoon tea of finger sandwiches and sweet goodies. The location is a plus too. You're a short stroll from Old Town's shops and restaurants and the trolley stop for rides to downtown or Mission Valley. *$$$; AE, DC, DIS, MC, V; checks OK; innkeeper@heritage parkinn.com; www.heritageparkinn.com; map:J2*

Ramada Limited Old Town / ★

3900 OLD TOWN AVE, OLD TOWN; 619/299-7400 OR 800/451-9846
Several chain hotels edge the I-5 freeway on the outskirts of Old Town; this one is quieter than most, and is popular with business travelers wanting easy access to downtown and plenty of good restaurants within walking distance. The 125 rooms are decorated with Mexican wood furniture and have modem lines along with microwaves, fridges, and coffeemakers. The pool is on the small side but it is heated; a nearby hot tub helps relieve the kinks of the day. Complimentary continental breakfast and afternoon snacks are served in the lobby. *$$; AE, DC, DIS, MC, V; no checks; map:J2*

Mission Valley

Doubletree San Diego Mission Valley / ★★

7450 HAZARD CTR DR, MISSION VALLEY; 619/297-5466 OR 800/222-8733
Located in a relatively new section of Mission Valley away from the interstate, the Doubletree faces a small dining and shopping plaza called Hazard Center. Fashion Valley and Mission Valley malls are nearby, as is Highway 163. The 294 rooms and 6 suites are spacious and decorated in light pastels; in-room coffeemakers, irons and ironing boards, large work tables with good lighting, and modem phone lines are assets for business travelers. Suites on the executive floors all have balconies, as do some of the standard rooms. Families enjoy the hotel's light, airy style, the indoor and outdoor pools and hot tub, and the free giant chocolate chip cookies. The neighborhood isn't particularly scenic, but there are shopping and dining options galore. Best of all, the trolley stops just across the street from the hotel, so guests can visit downtown and Old Town and even reach the border with Mexico without driving. *$$; AE, DC, DIS, MC, V; no checks; www.doubletreehotels.com/DoubleT/ Hotel121/122; map:LL4* &

Hanalei Hotel / ★★

2270 HOTEL CIRCLE N, MISSION VALLEY; 619/297-1101 OR 800/882-0858
One of the better choices in the busy Mission Valley area, the Hanalei is Polynesian through and through. Guests who delighted in the tropical scene were concerned when the hotel was remodeled in 1998. But the fresh pale cream exterior and updated edifice don't detract from the palms, hibiscus flowers, waterfalls, koi ponds, and tiki torches. With 402 rooms and 14 suites in high-rise towers, the hotel isn't exactly peaceful; noise rises from the pool area and nearby freeways, causing recluses to shut their windows and crank on the AC. Guests become instant friends while lounging by the pool, and can schedule tours to all the local highlights using tips from the friendly staff. *$$; AE, DC, DIS, MC, V; checks OK (if mailed in advance); www.hanaleihotel.com; map:LL5*

Hotel Circle Inn / ★

2201 HOTEL CIRCLE S; 619/291-2711 OR 800/772-7711
Mission Valley has many small motels used by budget travelers who care more about price than luxury. This small inn is one of the nicest, since it is set back a bit from Interstate 8, behind Ricky's Family Restaurant. Ricky's apple pancake alone is a good reason to stay here; some guests never bother to eat elsewhere. The inn's basic rooms have a neutral,

western theme; those at the far back are the quietest. Rooms with kitchenettes are nearly twice as expensive as those without. The outdoor pool and hot tub are small and shaded; all rooms have satellite TV with movie channels. *$; MC, V; no checks; map:K1*

San Diego Marriott Mission Valley / ★★

8757 RIO SAN DIEGO DR, MISSION VALLEY; 619/692-3800 OR 800/842-5329
Close to Qualcomm Stadium on the north side of Mission Valley, this standard Marriott manages to satisfy all types of travelers. Families like the self-service laundry facilities and child-care services—and they can even bring their pets (check in advance, as there may be an added charge). Those mixing pleasure and business like the 17 rooms filled with work necessities including fax machines and oversize desks. All 355 rooms have two phone lines, coffeemakers, and minibars. The pool is tucked between the buildings beside the well-equipped fitness center. One additional claim to fame: athletes and musicians in town for sporting events and concerts at the nearby stadium often stay here. There is a trolley stop within walking distance. *$$; AE, DC, DIS, MC, V; no checks; www. marriott/SANMV; map:LL4*

Mission Bay

Bahia Resort Hotel / ★★

998 W MISSION BAY DR, MISSION BAY; 858/488-0551 OR 800/288-0770
The Evans family, owners of several classic San Diego hotels, opened the Bahia on 14 acres along Mission Bay in 1953. Generations have spent their vacations here, returning annually for family reunions and weekend escapes. The 325-room resort is located within walking distance of Mission Beach in one of the busiest areas of Mission Bay Park. Within the grounds, rooms are widely spaced, most in low-lying buildings around lawns, flower gardens, and beaches; they feature a common-sense, contemporary design, and many have kitchen facilities. Pools, tennis courts, water toys, bike rentals, and casual cafes and bars all offer incentive to stay put for weeks, despite the background shrieks from Belmont Park's roller-coaster riders and general beach cacophony. Drift away from shore during a moonlit cruise on the *Bahia Belle*, an opulent stern-wheeler used for weddings, parties, and romantic dinners. If you're looking for plenty of family action combined with comfortable quarters, this is your place. *$$$; AE, DC, DIS, MC, V; checks OK (if mailed in advance); www. bahiahotel.com; map:LL6*

Dana Inn / ★

1710 W MISSION BAY DR, MISSION BAY; 619/222-6440 OR 800/445-3339
Among the overpriced resorts at Mission Bay, this simple hotel stands out as a family-friendly and affordable hangout. The 196 rooms are spread about the property in two-story wood buildings facing parking lots, the bay, and the pool. Sensible rather than picturesque, the rooms all have small refrigerators, coffeemakers, and single or double beds; the wood-veneer and plastic furniture is designed to withstand sandy bodies and wet towels. All family members stay entertained with shuffleboard and tennis courts; two pools; bike, skate, and water-sports rentals; and all the parks and playgrounds on the bay. Sea World sits just across the water, providing free entertainment with the nighttime fireworks exploding overhead. The coffee shop does a decent job with basic breakfasts and sandwiches. *$$; AE, MC, V; no checks; map:LL6*

Paradise Point Resort / ★★★

1404 W VACATION RD, MISSION BAY; 858/274-4630 OR 800/334-2626
Originally opened by a Hollywood producer in the 1960s as Vacation Village South Seas Paradise, this sprawling 44-acre resort has gone through several transformations. New ownership and considerable renovations have only enhanced the private island setting in Mission Bay. The 462 rooms and suites are housed in single-level buildings with private patios, refrigerators, and coffeemakers. All are being gradually refurbished with dark patterned carpeting (to hide the marks of sandy feet), red, white, and blue linens, and marble baths. Guests are kept ultra-busy with the six swimming pools, 18-hole putting course, tennis courts, croquet lawns, and volleyball nets on the sand. The marina offers sailboat, Hobie Cat, and powerboat rentals; the activities center provides bikes for those wishing to cruise the bay on land. Restaurants include the ever-popular Barefoot Bar on the sand, along with the upscale Dockside dining room and the casual Village Cafe. The summer months bring Kids Kamp, filled with activities. You can easily stay put for days, but if the itch to wander attacks, Mission Beach, Sea World, Old Town, and other attractions are just a few minutes away. *$$$; AE, MC, V; no checks; www.paradisepoint.com; map:LL6*

San Diego Hilton Beach and Tennis Resort / ★★

1775 E MISSION BAY DR, MISSION BAY; 619/276-4010 OR 800/221-2424
Craving action and adventure with massage and spa treatments on the side? You belong at this swath of beach, bike paths, lawns, and private terraces beside Mission Bay. Hotel facilities include several swimming pools, tennis courts, fitness center, and equipment rentals for nearly every water or land sport you can imagine. The 357 tropical-style rooms and suites, with tables and chairs for group snacks and games (or laptops if

you must), are scattered through Mediterranean-style low-rise buildings (complete with terraces and balconies) beside the bay and one eight-story building facing Interstate 5. Rollerbladers whiz by from dawn to dusk, following trails for miles along the bay. Kites of every shape float in the sky. Multigenerational families celebrate weddings, birthdays, and sunny Sundays with elaborate picnics all around the hotel, and visitors are completely immersed in the SoCal scene. *$$$; AE, DC, MC, V; checks OK; map:LL5* &

Pacific Beach

Beach Haven Inn / ★

4740 MISSION BLVD, PACIFIC BEACH; 858/272-3812

Though it's little more than a motel near the sand, families young and old find affordable lodgings, security, and conveniences at this small complex. The 23 units range from tiny, dark rooms to family suites with kitchenettes. The '70s reign in the brown-on-brown decor; couches, chairs, and carpets can withstand sand and vacation messes. Coin-operated laundry machines are an additional plus, as is the free parking. *$$; AE, DC, DIS, MC, V; no checks; map:KK7*

The Catamaran Resort Hotel / ★★★

3999 MISSION BLVD, PACIFIC BEACH; 858/488-1081 OR 800/288-0770

Another venerable resort on Mission Bay, this self-contained oasis has a tropical South Seas style much loved by locals and return guests. The aquariums, rare plant gardens, waterfalls, and ponds provide a cool, shaded retreat from the Pacific Beach scene, yet those staying in one of the 312 rooms and suites can walk to most of PB's restaurants and attractions. The hotel's 12-story tower rises above busy Mission Boulevard; though ocean views are spectacular from the top floor, street noise and helicopter lights can distract from a peaceful retreat. The rest of the rooms in the tower and cottage-type buildings face gardens, pools, and a quiet stretch of Mission Bay. The rooms echo the hotel's tropical decor, with pastel fabrics and light wood furnishings, and feature such vacation necessities as refrigerators, coffeemakers, and irons and ironing boards. The bars and restaurants are as popular with locals as with guests, and the activities center offers kayaks, boogie boards, wave runners, sailboards, and tandem bikes with baby seats. Park your car, rent a bike, and live like a beach bum in paradise. *$$$; AE, DC, DISC, MC, V; checks OK (if mailed in advance); map:KK7*

Crystal Pier Hotel / ★★

4500 OCEAN BLVD, PACIFIC BEACH; 858/483-6983

Drive your car across the boardwalk and onto the pier. Park in front of a blue-and-white country cottage with flowers abloom beneath shuttered windows. Open the front door; gaze across the living room and kitchen to your back porch perched over the sea. Check out the bedroom; lie flat on your back atop a patchwork quilt. Feel the surge of the surf and sense the white noise of water and wind. Return to the hotel's office and request another night or more. The 26 Crystal Pier cottages are claimed months in advance by families from Arizona to Canada who set out barbecue grills, fill the fridge, and hang their beach towels over lounge chairs and wood railings. The scene is more peaceful during the off seasons, when couples and singles claim the cottages as private escapes. Winter nights are particularly exciting when the surf is high and the air has a salty chill. One longs for a fireplace to complete the ambience; sadly, there aren't any. The boardwalk scene is just a few steps away if you want to grab a great meal, rent a bike or boogie board, or mingle with humanity. After all, you'll be over the water from dark to dawn, sleeping above the sea. *$$; AE, MC, V; no checks; map:KK7*

La Jolla

The Bed & Breakfast Inn of La Jolla / ★★★

7753 DRAPER AVE, LA JOLLA; 858/456-2066 OR 800/582-2466

It's easy to miss the ivy-covered entrance to this pleasant hideaway just a few blocks from the busy thoroughfares of Girard Avenue and Prospect Street. Designed by architect Irving Gill in 1913 as a private home, it's a historic treasure once occupied by John Philip Sousa in the '20s. Kate Sessions, San Diego's grande dame of horticulture, designed the original gardens. Today, the 16 rooms offer guests a taste of genteel living. You'll find plenty of nice touches—fresh flowers, sherry, and fruit in the rooms, antiques and original artworks that lend the air of a private home. The first-floor Holiday Room is a romantic retreat with a four-poster bed and working fireplace. If you want a view of the water, reserve the Irving Gill Penthouse Suite, which has a private deck. The upstairs Peacock Room has a private balcony for sunbathing—you'll feel like you're at an elegant Côte d'Azur pension. Breakfast of homemade granola, crepes, quiche, and the like is served on Royal Albert bone china in the dining room or by the fountain on the patio. *$$; AE, MC, V; no checks; bed+breakfast@innlajolla.com; www.innlajolla.com; map:JJ7*

SAN DIEGO CINÉ

Ever since Cecil B. DeMille's *The Virginian* was partially filmed in San Diego in 1914, this natural stage set just 130 miles south of Hollywood has provided palm groves, desert scenery, and urban sophistication for filmmakers eager for a break from Los Angeles. The military has provided ample fodder for war flicks: James Cagney came to town to star in *Here Comes the Navy* in 1934, Errol Flynn stopped by for *Dive Bomber* in 1941, Lloyd Nolan saluted his way through *Guadalcanal Diary* in 1943, and Gregory Peck toured the world in *MacArthur* in 1971—all without ever leaving San Diego's bases, which served as the backdrop for scenes in Korea and the Philippines. More recently, Charlie Sheen treated San Diego to his antics while filming *Navy Seals* in 1990. The most famous of all San Diego's military movies has to be *Top Gun*, shot at the Marine Corps Air Station Mirimar in 1986. Tom Cruise became a hometown hero during production, and is still honored with movie memorabilia at Kansas City Barbecue, the downtown dive where the flyboys hung out in the film. Marilyn Monroe is also considered a San Diego star by those who recall watching her skirts rise and fall with ocean breezes in *Some Like it Hot*, filmed almost entirely at the Hotel del Coronado in 1959. But the biggest fanfare took place 30 miles south of downtown San Diego in the Mexican coastal town of Rosarito. Locals crossed the border by the hundreds in 1996 to work as extras in *Titanic*, filmed in all its grandeur at a Twentieth Century Fox studio constructed especially for the screen epic. There's no local scenery in the movie, but San Diegans delight in spotting familiar faces in crowd scenes . . . bobbing in the sea.

—Virginia Butterfield

The Grande Colonial / ★

910 PROSPECT ST, LA JOLLA; 858/454-2181 OR 800/832-5525, 800/826-1278 IN CA

In operation since 1913, the Grande Colonial (formerly the Colonial Inn) is overshadowed by its fancier neighbors, though it has a loyal following. The lobby and reception area have been freshly renovated, but this four-story, low-key Victorian-style establishment still offers traditional decor with original touches, antique furnishings, rich tapestries, an open fireplace, and flowers everywhere. A small pool area sits outside the lobby, and the beach is just a block away. All 75 guest rooms are scheduled for complete renovation by press time, including new furnishings, fabrics, and fresh paint. Most have ocean or village views. Putnam's Restaurant is a snazzy upmarket bistro and a popular gathering spot for local movers and shakers. Valet and overnight parking are available for a fee. *$$$; AE, DC, MC, V; checks OK; map:JJ7* &

Hilton La Jolla Torrey Pines / ★★★

10950 N TORREY PINES RD, LA JOLLA; 858/558-1500 OR 800/762-6160

We blinked one day and the Sheraton Grande Torrey Pines had suddenly metamorphosed into a Hilton. Designed to blend into the existing palisades, this Mediterranean white glory sits on the 18th hole of the championship Torrey Pines Golf Course, looking out to the blue Pacific beyond. Two lobby areas are positioned on either side of the entry—one with a large, glass-enclosed fireplace, the other offering cozy seating and a grand piano—and both overlook the enticing pool area. Downstairs, the Torreyana Grille serves excellent seasonal fare in a large, light-filled dining room fitted with fountains, foliage, art, sculpture, an exhibition kitchen, and copper-topped bar. All 394 rooms feature private balconies or patios and many have ocean and golf course views. The decor is sophisticated yet understated, with contemporary furnishings and fabrics in muted tones. Every room offers personalized butler service wherein your own man Friday can be summoned for tasks like shoe shines and fax retrieval, and a business center is on the property. Cavort in the on-site exercise room and on the three tennis courts, or pay a pittance for entry to the adjacent Shiley Sports and Health Center with its mind-boggling array of toning and training facilities. *$$$; AE, CB, DC, DIS, JCB, MC, V; checks OK; www.lajollatorreypines.hilton.com; map:HH7* &

Hyatt Regency La Jolla / ★★★

3777 LA JOLLA VILLAGE DR, GOLDEN TRIANGLE; 858/552-1234 OR 800/233-1234

Though its name includes "La Jolla," this Hyatt is actually in the Golden Triangle area, just off Interstate 5, about 10 minutes drive from La Jolla village and 20 minutes from the airport. Housed within the Aventine mixed-use complex of office towers, a health club, and several restaurants, architect Michael Graves' postmodern design has managed to delight locals and visitors alike. Rome meets Southern California is the theme throughout the 16-story property, with a two-level balcony, square marble columns, plush velvet seating groups, and a plethora of amenities. Four diverse restaurants are located in the complex, including Cafe Japengo (see Restaurants chapter), one of the coolest, slickest dining spots in town. Michael's Lounge, adjacent to the main lobby, offers a clubby ambience for cocktails, billiards, satellite TV, and those de rigueur cigars, while an espresso bar serves coffee drinks. All 400 guest rooms are extra-spacious, with high-end yet homey furnishings, down comforters, and round-the-clock room service. Business and Regency Club floors offer a variety of extra perks, including complete office workstations. Unwind in the pool, on two lighted tennis courts, or in the 32,000-square-foot Sporting Club, with its array of exercise equipment and facilities. *$$$; AE, CB, DC, DIS, JCB, MC, V; checks OK; www.hyatt. com; map:JJ6* &

La Jolla Cove Suites / ★★☆

1155 COAST BLVD, LA JOLLA; 858/459-2621 OR 800/248-2683
It never ceases to amaze locals and visitors alike that such a plain motel-like structure should sit right across from beautiful La Jolla Cove. All the better, we say. The simplicity of the accommodations allows for some of the lowest room rates you'll find in La Jolla, yet many rooms have direct views of magnificent Ellen Browning Scripps Park and the sea. There are 117 rooms and suites in a compound of drab buildings; the best have water views, kitchenettes, and a separate bedroom. Free parking is available—a major treat in this clogged area. The pool is a simple, square affair, and there is no restaurant (though continental breakfast is served on the rooftop terrace). But all of La Jolla's excellent restaurants, shops, museums, and clubs are within easy walking distance, and nothing beats the serenity of spending less than $175 to sleep right by the sea. *$$; AE, DC, DIS, MC, V; no checks; map:JJ7*

La Valencia Hotel / ★★★

1132 PROSPECT ST, LA JOLLA; 858/454-0771 OR 800/451-0772
To many residents and visitors, La Valencia Hotel *is* La Jolla. The Mediterranean-style "Pink Lady" has reigned over Prospect Street since 1926. And it's always been a hub of activity for well-heeled guests and local bigwigs. The hotel's 100 rooms and suites are individually decorated and have been "refreshed" over the last few years. Some have a green floral motif; others boast a beachy blue-and-white seashell theme. Naturally, rooms with million-dollar views of La Jolla Cove are the most desirable. "La V" is delightfully old-fashioned in that its public spaces are well trafficked, which gives the place a pleasant hum of activity. Every afternoon, the Mediterranean Room patio is filled with ladies who lunch, and the recently restored Whaling Bar is once again a favorite local hangout. At sunset, head to La Sala Lounge, sink into a sofa, and enjoy the view while you're serenaded by a pianist. Be sure to check out the hand-painted ceiling overhead. *$$$; AE, DC, DIS, MC, V; checks OK; info@lavalencia.com; www.lavalencia.com; map:JJ7*

Hotel Parisi / ★★

1111 PROSPECT ST, LA JOLLA; 858/454-1511
More urban and hip than what you'd normally expect in San Diego, the new Hotel Parisi is a 20-room boutique property in the heart of La Jolla. The hotel's spare, contemporary high-design concept seems to float above the hubbub of Prospect Street. Indeed, the hotel occupies the top floor of a mixed-use retail building. Guests are greeted by a calming lobby with a natural stone fountain and a fireplace. Although the Parisi

bills itself as an all-suite property, standard suites are really oversize rooms. No matter; they're still restful cocoons in shades of sand and taupe, outfitted with simple custom-made furnishings and beds dressed in inviting white-linen duvets. Flame-cut steel and wood nightstands are offset by cozy, slipcovered chairs; the overall effect is serenely uncluttered without being cold. Rates include continental breakfast. Rooms overlooking Prospect Street have a view of La Valencia Hotel just across the street, as well as a partial ocean view. Traditionalists will still prefer La Valencia, but if new-millennium modernity suits your style, make reservations at the Parisi. *$$$; AE, DIS, JCB, MC, V; no checks; www.hotel parisi.com; map:JJ7*

Scripps Inn / ★★☆

555 COAST BLVD S, LA JOLLA; 858/454-3391

Guests check in to this tiny hotel for weeks, setting up housekeeping just steps from the coastline and stately Ellen Browning Scripps Park. Two buildings face each other in a narrow lot; some privacy is lost, but the location and reasonable room rate are worth the close quarters. Most of the 13 rooms have views of the sea; the best have working fireplaces and ocean-view balconies. Rooms and suites (some with two bedrooms) have refrigerators, sitting areas, and fold out sofas; white walls, pale tan furnishings, and French doors give the rooms a breezy, relaxed feel. A complimentary breakfast of pastries and coffee is served on the lobby terrace. There's no pool—but who needs one when the best snorkeling spot on the coast is just a few steps away? Book a room at this little gem way in advance of your trip, and consider splurging on rooms 6 or 12, both with fireplaces and full views. *$$$; AE, DIS, MC, V; no checks; www.jc resorts.com/scripips-inn/; map:JJ7*

Sea Lodge / ★★

8110 CAMINO DEL ORO, LA JOLLA; 858/459-8271

Lucky are those who happen upon this hidden beachfront hotel, tucked down a side street at La Jolla beach. Low-rise tiled roof buildings frame a central courtyard and pool; Mexican painted tiles and terra-cotta fountains add a Spanish feel to the 130-room complex. Floral plants and light rattan furnishings lighten up the rooms facing the courtyard; those with a view of the sea are filled with sunlight. The restaurant has a full ocean view, and a sidewalk just outside the door leads to a playground area and the beach. The staff is like family to the many returning guests, who don't mind a bit of sand in their carpets and a casual ambience. The courtyard pool is a cool retreat from the beach, and underground parking protects cars from the salt air. There's a four-night minimum stay during the summer. *$$$; AE, DC, DIS, MC, V; no checks; www.sealodge.com/ sealodge.html; map:JJ7*

Del Mar

L'Auberge Del Mar / ★★★

1540 CAMINO DEL MAR, DEL MAR; 858/259-1515 OR 800/505-9043

This deluxe 120-room resort may be right on Del Mar's main drag, but you'll find ample privacy for any rendezvous. Small and wonderful, L'Auberge has all the elements of a great getaway. Rooms are decorated in an upscale Provençal theme, and all have a private balcony or patio. Bring your swimsuit, because the inn has two pools—one for lounging, another for lap swimming—and the beach is a short stroll away. There are also tennis courts, a small but well-equipped fitness room, and a terrific little spa where you'll want to indulge in a treatment or two. L'Auberge's central location means you can explore Del Mar's shops and restaurants on foot. The only drawback: it's so close to the beach, yet doesn't offer much in the way of an ocean view. For the most privacy, request a top-floor corner room from which you can gaze at the treetops and get a glimpse of the Pacific. *$$$; AE, DC, DIS, MC, V; checks OK; map:GG7*

Les Artistes / ★☆

944 CAMINO DEL MAR, DEL MAR; 858/755-4646

Don't let the Old Village Motel sign fool you. After extensive renovations in 1993, this rambling, pink adobe inn just south of Del Mar's main drag was transformed into a little treasure. True to its name, Les Artistes' 12 rooms are filled with unique touches. Behind the magenta bougainvillea, purple wisteria, and gurgling fountains out front, rooms boast creative tile work and prints, *objets d'art*, and original paintings to fit the room's theme. Seven "designer" rooms are larger than standard accommodations, and each is decorated to commemorate a different artist. The Diego Rivera room is a large upstairs unit with an ocean view and cozy, rustic Mexican decor. Similarly, with its wood beams and white stucco walls, the spacious Georgia O'Keeffe room befits its namesake. Other choices include the cowboy-inspired Remington room, the art-deco Erte room, and the South Pacific flair of the Gauguin. The hotel is walking distance from Del Mar's hopping restaurants and shops, yet set far back enough from busy Camino Del Mar that you'll enjoy some peace and privacy. If you like your accommodations on the bohemian side, you'll appreciate Les Artistes' offbeat charm. *$$; AE, DIS, MC, V; no checks; map:GG7*

Rancho Santa Fe

The Inn at Rancho Santa Fe / ★★

5951 LINEA DEL CIELO, RANCHO SANTA FE; 858/756-1131 OR 800/654-2928
In the heart of Rancho Santa Fe's tony but low-key village, The Inn at Rancho Santa Fe is an unassuming charmer that doesn't rush to embrace every trend. Eighty-seven rooms are spread throughout a cluster of white adobe buildings and cottages, surrounded by carefully manicured grounds. The inn's cool, wood-beamed main building was designed in 1923 by Lillian Rice, the architect responsible for Rancho Santa Fe's genteel Spanish-Colonial look. All rooms are individually decorated with gingham couches and Windsor chairs in a retro-1940s take on American Colonial. The result is a homey, unpretentious feel. About half the rooms have wood-burning fireplaces—a nice touch to chase away the evening chill. For extra privacy, request one of the garden cottages with a private patio. Still, you'll want to hang out on a chaise longue by the pool or borrow equipment for a rousing round of croquet on the front lawn. You could check in and never leave the premises—decent, if traditional, fare is served in the Vintage Room and the Library restaurants—but boutiques and more interesting restaurants are just a short stroll away. If you want to put in some time at the beach, the inn conveniently maintains a private day cottage on the sand in nearby Del Mar. *$$$; AE, DC, MC, V; no checks; map:EE5*

Rancho Valencia Resort / ★★★☆

5921 VALENCIA CIRCLE, RANCHO SANTA FE; 858/756-1123 OR 800/548-3664
You never know whom you might see on the tennis court or in the dining room at this deluxe hideaway—maybe Bill Gates and his family or Bob and Dolores Hope. They're among the well-heeled regulars who come for the resort's first-rate pampering. The 43 suites here are no bargain, but the staff certainly knows how to treat all guests like royalty. The smaller Del Mar suites are each a roomy 850 square feet of airy, Mediterranean elegance—terra-cotta floors, fireplaces, custom-made furnishings, and spacious private patios. The one-bedroom Rancho Santa Fe suites offer even more room to relax. Days here have a civilized start: a tray with fresh-squeezed orange juice, morning newspaper, and a rosebud is left just outside your door. Couples should ask about the one-night "Romantic Getaway." It includes lodging, a bottle of bubbly, a candlelit dinner and breakfast served in the room, plus in-room, one-hour massage for both. The resort's only drawback: while the 18 tennis courts and first-rate teaching staff make this a dream escape for tennis buffs, golfers must find fairways off-property. *$$$; AE, CB, DC, MC, V; checks OK; www.ranchovalencia.com; map:EE5*

Carlsbad

Four Seasons Resort–Aviara / ★★★★

7100 FOUR SEASONS PT, CARLSBAD; 760/603-6800 OR 800/332-7100

Yes, the Four Seasons is sleek, swank, and serene. But we love it best for its beds, which feel like fluffy clouds. The mattresses are plenty firm, and the smooth, ironed sheets, puffy white duvets, and pillows cushion weary bodies in womb-like comfort. Soft green walls, understated furnishings (including a large desk with comfortable chair), perfect lighting, marble baths with soaking tubs, huge closets, and a wet bar with coffee machine make it hard to leave the room, though it is nice to settle on the private balcony's cushioned deck chairs for sunset cocktails. There are plenty of other diversions in this 331-room hotel overlooking Batiquitos Lagoon and the ocean. Floral arrangements rival the artwork in the public spaces. The spa is filled with sensory delights from gentle chamomile scrubs to lavender wraps and will also send a masseuse to your room for pampering. The Jose Eber Salon is the perfect place to primp for dinner at Vivace, where Chef Pascal Vignau presents culinary wonders in a Mediterranean-style, ocean-view dining room. A to-die-for brunch (with a separate serving table overflowing with treats for kids) is displayed at the California Bistro; afternoon tea is graciously presented in the flower-filled Lobby Lounge. Golfers rave about the Arnold Palmer-designed Aviara Golf Course that sprawls over 180 acres of canyons and lagoons. Tennis buffs head for the six lighted courses; swimmers delight in a seemingly endless pool. Special programs include a jazz series on summer nights. You don't really need to know about nearby attractions—most guests refuse to leave the grounds. *$$$; AE, DC, DIS, JCB, MC, V; checks OK; www.fourseasons.com; map:CC7* &

Rancho Bernardo

Rancho Bernardo Inn / ★★★

17550 BERNARDO OAKS DR, RANCHO BERNARDO; 858/675-8400 OR 800/770-7482

Gourmands, golfers, business bigwigs, and vacationing families all feel at home in this hacienda-style inn set amid rolling fairways and clear valley air. Sculptures, fountains, and flowers mark the entrance to the lobby, where hand-painted tiles, hardwood beams, and blazing fireplaces evoke early California style at its most gracious. The best of the 288 rooms and suites have living room fireplaces, bedroom whirlpool tubs, and patios the size of an urban backyard. The rest are comfortable, though it's best to ask for a view of the grounds or distant mountain peaks. Guests in the know make time for at least one dinner and Sunday brunch at El Bizcocho, one of the county's finest restaurants (see Restaurants chapter). They can always work off the calories at the inn's championship golf course (along with four others in the neighborhood), 12 tennis courts, and fitness center, or vegetate beside the two pools, both so ensconced in flowering bushes and trees they feel like country lakes. The Wild Animal Park, several wineries, and the mountains and desert are all nearby, and downtown San Diego is just a 25-minute drive south. *$$$; AE, DC, DIS, MC, V; no checks; map:FF3*

Julian

The Artists' Loft / ★★

4811 PINE RIDGE AVE, JULIAN; 760/765-0765
For those weary of country-kitschy B&Bs, the Artists' Loft is a breath of fresh air. Owner-artists Nanessence and Chuck Kimball's serene 11-acre oasis outside the town of Julian is just the place to kick back and listen to the wind rustle through the manzanita trees. Two rooms in the main house are decorated with carefully chosen rustic antiques, Persian rugs, eclectic objets d'art and, of course, the Kimballs' own artwork. The Manzanita Room is a cozy retreat, complete with a working antique parlor stove to chase away the evening chill. The Gallery Room is a spacious, cheerful, yellow-hued hideaway. For added privacy, reserve one of the two separate cabins. The Cabin at Strawberry Hill, named for the wild strawberries that surround it, was hand-built by the Kimballs. You can't miss its delightful blue-tin roof. Inside, it boasts every comfort—an inviting couch, a wood-burning stove, a king-size bed, and a fully equipped kitchen. The cabin's huge screened porch is a special treat on warm summer evenings. The Kimballs' latest acquisition is the 70-year-old Big Cat Cabin, named for a mountain lion that hides nearby. They've lavishly remodeled this one-bedroom gem, which features a massive stone fireplace, fully equipped kitchen with countertops made of local oak, and a bathroom with a wood-paneled shower and a vintage cast-iron tub. You'll drift to sleep in an antique Balinese wedding bed, and the bedroom's screened study area is the ideal spot to curl up with a book or start working on that novel you always meant to write. *$$; MC, V; checks OK; www.artistsloft.com*

Orchard Hill Country Inn / ★★

2502 WASHINGTON ST, JULIAN; 760/765-1700 OR 800/716-7242
Upscale and elegant, Orchard Hill Country Inn offers an ideal combination of privacy and proximity to Julian's shops and restaurants. The inn opened in 1994 and is a loving reproduction of a California Craftsman lodge. There are 10 delightful rooms in the main lodge—all decorated

with genteel country flair—but the best rooms are the 12 cottage suites. Each is named for an apple variety and has its own theme. You can delight in the soft, feminine pinks of the Sweet Bough cottage or relax among the warm plaids of McIntosh. The Cortland suite is a romantic refuge of blue toile fabric. Some rooms have a fireplace and/or whirlpool tub. Owners Pat and Darrell Staube attend to every detail—room amenities include a half-bottle of local merlot, a mason jar filled with fresh-baked oatmeal cookies, and luxuriously soft robes. They also thoughtfully provide magazines, board games, and a terrific video library of classic movies. While you'll be reluctant to venture away from your room, the inn's four acres have plenty of private benches and hammocks—perfect for dozing with a book or gazing at the stars. *$$$; AE, MC, V; checks OK; www.orchardhill.com*

Borrego Springs

Borrego Valley Inn / ★★

405 PALM CANYON DR, BORREGO SPRINGS; 760/767-0311
Borrego Valley Inn's low-slung, Santa Fe–style adobe buildings are right at home in the Anza–Borrego Desert. Appropriately, the inn's 14 rooms are done in an unfussy, southwestern look with cool, terra-cotta-tiled floors, rough-hewn pine furnishings, and vibrant Indian fabrics. Most rooms also have fireplaces, kitchenettes, and private patios, making them a casual and warm place to unwind after a day exploring the desert's trails and oases. If it's hot out, you can always cool off in your choice of two pools and spas. In fact, either is a great spot from which to watch the sun set behind the Vallecito Mountains. In the evening, check out the stars through the inn's telescope. Room rates include a hearty breakfast buffet of granola, baked goodies, and locally grown citrus fruit. *$$; AE, CB, DIS, MC, V; checks OK; www.borregovalleyinn.com*

La Casa del Zorro / ★★★☆

3845 YAQUI PASS RD, BORREGO SPRINGS; 760/767-5323 OR 800/824-1884
There's no need to suffer and sweat in the desert. Instead, book a room or casita at this lush oasis buried in date palms set against a mountain backdrop. The casitas, with one to four bedrooms, are spread about in clusters throughout the 42-acre property. Some have fireplaces and private pools; all have kitchen facilities and living and dining rooms. Families book large casitas for reunions; couples hide out in one-bedroom settings with private hot tubs. Two-story white buildings with tiled roofs house the large, lodgelike guest rooms, most with fireplaces (the desert gets mighty chilly on winter nights). Several pools, one reserved for adult use only, are scattered about the gardens, and a river flows over boulders

between the buildings. Prices are high in the restaurant, but you can get lots of touring tips from the staff. Big-name jazz groups play on summer weekends. Tours of the desert are available, in jeeps or on foot. Visit in spring when ocotillo plants thrust spires of red blossoms into the sky. *$$$; AE, DC, DIS, MC, V; no checks; www.lacasadelzorro.com;* &

EXPLORING

EXPLORING

Top 25 Attractions

1) BALBOA PARK

2125 Park Blvd, Downtown; 619/239-0512 Spread over 1,200 acres in the heart of San Diego, Balboa Park has been an exemplary setting for city planners since 1909, when the first jacaranda and pepper trees appeared atop canyons and mesas just east of downtown. Garden lover Kate Sessions, long dubbed the "mother of Balboa Park," was given the honor and responsibility of turning a barren tract of seemingly uninhabitable land into a park, and her early plantings remain among the city's many treasures.

Today, more than 14,000 trees representing 350 different species grow here amid rolling lawns; the twisted limbs and gnarled roots of the 60-foot-tall Moreton Bay fig, north of the Natural History Museum, are a natural work of art. The **BOTANICAL BUILDING**, a large wood lath structure located on El Prado west of the Museum of Art, houses thousands of tropical plants as well as seasonal flowers. Just south of the Botanical Building children peer into the **LILY POND**, looking for goldfish and Japanese koi. The **ALCAZAR GARDEN**, with its ornate fountains adorned with turquoise, yellow, and green tiles, is replanted seasonally; the **INEZ GRANT PARKER MEMORIAL ROSE GARDEN** makes an idyllic wedding backdrop; and the **ZORO GARDEN**, a stone grotto planted with lantana, pincushion flowers, and verbena, is a paradise for monarch, sulphur, and swallowtail butterflies.

Best known as the home of the superb **SAN DIEGO ZOO**, Balboa Park is also the soul of San Diego's cultural legacy. Many of its buildings date back to the 1915–1916 Panama-California Exposition, held to honor the completion of the Panama Canal (and, domestically, to boost the new city's image among potential investors). Yellow and blue tiles gleam in the sun atop the ornate **CALIFORNIA TOWER**, the finest example of the Spanish colonial revival style of architecture favored by the exposition's sponsors. A second burst of construction occurred prior to the 1935–36 California Pacific International Exposition, which led to another financial boom for San Diego. Many of the park's 15 museums are housed in decades-old buildings covered with bas-relief carvings and baroque stone ornamentation. They weren't designed to last this long, but generations of San Diego families and civic entities have guaranteed their survival. Today, the city's Park and Recreation department does a commendable job of maintaining and restoring these marvelous old structures.

For the culturally minded and the artistically inclined, Balboa Park's attractions are varied and diverse. Start your sojourn at the **VISITORS**

TOP 25 ATTRACTIONS

1) Balboa Park
2) San Diego Zoo
3) Mission Bay Park
4) Cabrillo National Monument
5) Sea World
6) Hotel del Coronado
7) Downtown Waterfront
8) Gaslamp Quarter
9) Seaport Village
10) Horton Plaza
11) Reuben H. Fleet Space Theater & Science Center
12) Bazaar del Mundo

13) Wild Animal Park
14) Legoland California
15) San Diego Museum of Man
16) La Jolla Cove
17) Birch Aquarium at Scripps
18) Silver Strand State Beach
19) Belmont Park
20) Boardwalk
21) Ocean Beach Pier
22) Mission Trails Regional Park
23) Torrey Pines State Reserve
24) Mission Basilica San Diego de Alcalá
25) Museum of Contemporary Art San Diego

CENTER, located at the **HOUSE OF HOSPITALITY** near the middle of the park. Pick up a map and purchase a Passport to Balboa Park coupon book, valid for one week and entitling the bearer to admission to 12 museums, including the San Diego Aerospace Museum, San Diego Natural History Museum, San Diego Museum of Man, Reuben H. Fleet Space Theater and Science Center, and Mingei International Museum. Investigate the free tours offered or inquire about the varied cultural activities going on at the **CENTRO CULTURAL DE LA RAZA** and the **HOUSE OF PACIFIC RELATIONS.** If you happen to visit on a Sunday afternoon, go by the **SPRECKELS ORGAN PAVILION,** home to one of the world's largest outdoor pipe organs, and treat yourself to a free concert. Performances are from 2–3pm.

The youngsters will want to check out the **CAROUSEL,** located near the zoo. Built in 1910, the carousel has been at the park since 1922. Riders whirling around on tigers and ostriches hand-carved by European craftsmen try to catch the brass ring and win another go-round. From the third week in June through Labor Day, the carousel runs daily from 11am to 6pm. Winter hours are Saturdays, Sundays, and school holidays, 11am to 5:30pm. The price of a ticket is $1.25.

When hunger strikes, there are several remedies. **THE GALILEO CAFÉ** at the Reuben H. Fleet Science Center has tables set out next to the fountain; sandwiches, soups, and pastries are available daily after 9:30am. Or if you prefer a little more elegance with your meal, the **SAN DIEGO MUSEUM OF ART SCULPTURE GARDEN CAFE & BISTRO** offers a relaxing dining experience amid masterful sculptures by Rodin, Miro, and Calders. The Bistro serves light meals and desserts, but the food's not cheap; a

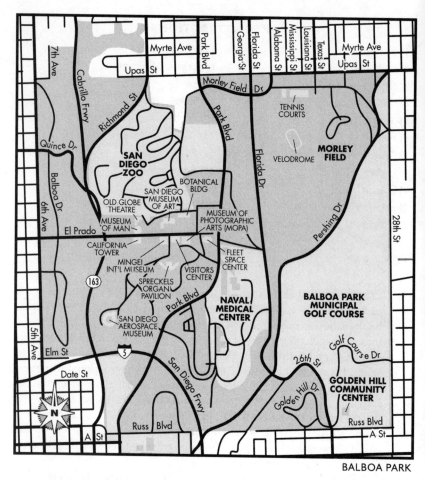

salad runs between $6.25 and $10. *Free; every day (Visitors Center open daily 9–4pm); www.ci.san-diego.ca.us/park-and-recreation/parks/balboa. html; map:P5* ♿

2) SAN DIEGO ZOO

2920 Zoo Dr, Balboa Park, Downtown; 619/234-3153 The world-famous San Diego Zoo began humbly with a handful of animals left over from Balboa Park's 1915–16 Panama-California Exposition. A local surgeon, Harry M. Wegeforth, sought to protect the lions, tigers, and bears and spearheaded the Zoological Society of San Diego in 1916. This not-for-profit organization has grown into one of the finest examples of its kind in the world while overseeing the zoo and its sister attraction, the San Diego Wild Animal Park (see Attraction number 13 in this chapter).

Nestled on 100 acres in the heart of Balboa Park, the zoo's rare and exotic creatures flourish in San Diego's temperate climate. Among the most unique and popular specimens are giant pandas Bai Yun and Shi Shi, on long-term loan from the People's Republic of China. You can see the only pair of these critically endangered animals in the United States nibbling bamboo at the **GIANT PANDA RESEARCH STATION**. The zoo is also home to the largest colony of koalas outside Australia, including Ghost Boy, the only albino koala living in a zoological facility.

Recently designed enclosures resemble the natural homes of the animals, with moats or thick glass to protect them from us. The **POLAR BEAR PLUNGE** simulates the arctic tundra with polar bears, Siberian reindeer, and arctic foxes in residence. A 130,000-gallon pool—cooled to 55°—is a playground for the frolicsome bears; a special indoor underwater viewing room, with a 5-inch-thick acrylic panel, allows an unusual perspective on their agile antics. **HIPPO BEACH** features a similar observation room, this one for viewing the surprisingly graceful 2-ton hippos as they slowly bounce along the bottom of their pool at viewers' eye level. The newly refurbished **GORILLA TROPICS** transports you into an African rain forest, haven to a gregarious troop of western lowland gorillas and thousands of jungle plants. Nearby is the **SCRIPPS AVIARY**, like a giant birdcage with splashing waterfalls, exotic plants, and hundreds of native African birds.

If scales and forked tongues are your forte, check out the **REPTILE HOUSE**. Slithering safely behind glass is a wondrous collection of snakes and lizards. A huge albino python hangs out in its tree or wallows lazily in its mini-pool. Thelma and Louise, an aptly named two-headed corn snake, elicits shrieks of amazement from the kids. Just past the Reptile House, the **CHILDREN'S ZOO** has several nurseries where you can watch a hairy baby with its bottle. Visit the **PETTING PADDOCK** and come face to snout with a pot-bellied pig.

A good introduction to the zoo is the 40-minute bus tour; informative and entertaining drivers are your guides. Double-decker buses leave the station every few minutes for the meandering 3-mile journey through much of the park, giving you a good idea of what warrants your further investigation and how far you'll have to hoof it to get there. If you don't suffer from acrophobia, try the Skyfari, an aerial tramway dangling 180 feet above ground.

General admission for adults is $16, $7 for children age 3 to 11; children 2 and under are free. Deluxe admission, which includes the bus tour and Skyfari aerial tram ride, is $24 for an adult and $13 for a child, with a senior rate of $21.60. If you are also interested in visiting the Wild Animal Park, a Two-Park Ticket (admission to both attractions) costs an adult $35.15; for a child it's $20.75. Parking at the zoo is free. *Every day, webmaster@sandiegozoo.org; www.sandiegozoo.org; map:P4* &

3) MISSION BAY PARK

Bordered by I-5, I-8, Grand Ave, and Mission Blvd, Mission Beach; 619/221-8900 Back before World War II, Mission Bay Park was a swamp originally named False Bay by the Spanish conquistadors. After the war (which vastly increased the military presence in San Diego and changed its character and landscape forever), the Army Corps of Engineers diverted the river, dredged channels, and carved a 4,600-acre swath of lawns and beaches between Interstate 5 and the ocean. The park has since evolved into a giant playground for all manner of San Diegans. Boaters and anglers head for Quivira Basin (Quivira Rd) within a stone's throw of Ocean Beach and Sea World. Charter boats carry herds of anglers from

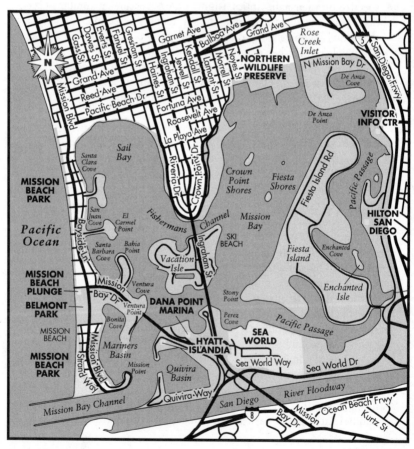

MISSION BAY

the marina at **SEAFORTH SPORTFISHING** (1717 Quivira Rd; 619/224-3383); boats bring back the catch around noon and 4pm. **THE LANDING** (1729 Quivira Rd; 619/222-3317), where crews fuel up on hearty pancakes, ham and eggs, and burgers, is a good place to listen to fish tales, as is **SPORTSMEN'S SEAFOODS** (1617 Quivira Rd; 619/224-3551), where seagulls beg for scraps at patio tables.

SEA WORLD (see Attraction number 5 in this chapter) sprawls along the southeast side of the bay; its frequent fireworks can be spotted from nearly everywhere in the park. **FIESTA ISLAND** (Fiesta Island Rd at Sea World Dr) is a man-made plot of dredged dirt and sand that serves as party central for jet-skiers, water-skiers, and powerboat fanatics. Eucalyptus groves, quiet picnic areas, and lawns favored by kite flyers lie along the south edge of the bay; here, kids delight in the latest play equipment at **TECOLOTE PLAYGROUND**, the largest disabled-accessible play area in the city.

Mission Bay's main entrance and **VISITOR'S INFORMATION CENTER** (see Lay of the City chapter) are located just off Interstate 5 at the E Mission Bay Drive exit; on summer weekends, huge awnings and tents provide shade for corporate picnics and waterfront weddings around the center. Cyclists, roller skaters, joggers, and power walkers love this section of the park, with its wide sidewalks swooping past the action around the **HILTON BEACH AND TENNIS RESORT** (1775 E Mission Bay Dr; 619/276-4010). Families and friends set up daylong carne asada and hot dog barbecue parties with volleyball games and bonfires (in cement fire rings), presenting all the SoCal action one could desire. **CROWN POINT** (Crown Point Dr at Ingraham St) also has fire rings, playgrounds, and idyllic picnic areas facing Sea World.

The shoreline curves around Crown Point, cupping the calm waters of **SAIL BAY** (near Briarfield Dr) and backed by private homes lining **BAYSIDE WALK**. Kayaks, canoes, Windsurfers, and other water toys are clustered about **SANTA CLARA POINT**, where classes and rentals are available at **MISSION BAY SPORTCENTER** (1010 Santa Clara Pl; 858/488-1004). West Mission Bay Drive parallels the most populated areas of the park close to Mission Beach, where wheel-borne sightseers run into traffic jams on the approach to Belmont Park.

The entire Mission Beach Bay area becomes utterly congested on holidays throughout the year—what could be more San Diegan than Christmas amid palms and kites? On some summer weekends, the park's 700 parking spots fill by noon; locals arrive at dawn to stake out prime party spots. Some areas can be reserved in advance. Check with the officials at the **MISSION BAY PARK HEADQUARTERS** (2581 Quivira Ct; 619/221-8901) for information on permits and maps; the office is open Monday through Friday 8am to 5pm. *Every day; map:LL6* &.

4) CABRILLO NATIONAL MONUMENT

At the end of Cabrillo Memorial Dr, Point Loma; 619/557-5450 Few vistas compare with those from atop the cliffs of Point Loma, jutting into the Pacific on the north side of San Diego Bay. Telescopes, charts, and hiking trails enhance the views at Cabrillo National Monument at the very tip of the point, 400 feet above sea level. The park was a scant half acre when established by President Woodrow Wilson in 1913; today it covers more than 80 acres of relatively undisturbed coastal habitat. Set on the highest point in the park is the Cape Cod-style **OLD POINT LOMA LIGHTHOUSE,** which served as the southernmost beacon along the U.S. Pacific Coast from 1855 to 1891. The lighthouse is closed to the public, but its dramatic architecture and setting serve as a focal point for the park. Nearby is the visitor center, where slide shows on whales, tide pools, and other oceanic subjects are presented throughout the day. The gift shop next door is one of the best in San Diego, with a plethora of books on boating and sea creatures, as well as souvenirs in every imaginable sea theme.

Behind the building is a lookout point with telescopes and charts describing the naval vessels in the bay. **NORTH ISLAND NAVAL AIR STATION** on Coronado is directly across the water; carriers, subs, destroyers, and all sorts of monstrous gray ships sit peacefully in the water off the island as fighter jets and helicopters lift off on maneuvers. On a clear day the view encompasses downtown, Coronado, and the sea as far as Mexico; in the winter months visitors sometimes catch glimpses of spouting gray whales migrating south from the Bering Sea to the birthing grounds in Baja California.

The best part of the park for nature lovers is the **BAYSIDE TRAIL,** a winding path down the cliff past native plants. At the west side of the park, Cabrillo Road leads down to more hiking trails above natural tide pools. Most of Point Loma near the monument is controlled by the U.S. Navy, but the public is welcome to wander the lawns at **FORT ROSECRANS NATIONAL CEMETERY,** where solemn lines of white headstones spread for 71 acres overlooking San Diego Bay. Admission is $5 per car or $2 per person for walk-ins; the pass into the park is good for seven days. *Every day 9am–5:15pm; map:OO6*

5) SEA WORLD

500 Sea World Dr, Mission Bay; 619/226-3901 Never content to rest on Shamu's laurels, the corporate owners of this 100-acre aquatic park constantly add exhibits and rides to its repertoire, reeling in locals bearing annual passes and tourists who wouldn't dream of a San Diego vacation without a visit. New in 1999, the **SHIPWRECK RAPIDS** ride adds watery thrills to the experience as passengers swirl about in inner-tube vehicles during a simulated storm at sea; hardy types then visit the 1,000-seat

SHIPWRECK CAFE, where real-life penguins and sea otters wander under the buffet. Other rides captivate some, but the real joys at the park come from watching white-tipped sharks glide by in the **SHARK ENCOUNTER AQUARIUM**, emperor penguins strutting about in the glass-enclosed icy **PENGUIN ENCOUNTER**, and bat rays and eels slinking through the **FORBIDDEN REEF**. Visitors stand in line patiently for a chance to pet the slippery snouts of bottlenose dolphins at **ROCKY POINT PRESERVE** or sling slimy fish to barking sea lions at the **FEEDER POOL**. One lucky kid gets chosen to pet a 10,000-pound Orca whale during each **SHAMU THE ADVENTURE SHOW**, which never fails to thrill onlookers (and drench those in the front rows).

You can easily spend a full day and evening at Sea World and still feel there wasn't enough time to watch sea otters at play, gaze at graceful sea turtles swimming in shallow tanks, and study cumbersome manatees with gentle faces. Park hours vary with the season; if you've only got one day, start when the park opens and stay till the fireworks show (every summer evening) at the end. Kids can unleash their energies at several theme playgrounds while parents sprawl on benches and catnap. Sit-down restaurants serve barbecued ribs, grilled seafood (horrors!), and decent Italian cuisine. For an additional fee, you can splurge on **DINING WITH SHAMU** and eat with the whale trainers beside the leviathans' pool. Admission is $38 for adults, $29 for children 3 to 11; parking is $6. *Every day, www.seaworld.com; map:F1*

6) HOTEL DEL CORONADO

1500 Orange Ave, Coronado; 619/435-6611 The red-shingled turrets, dormers, and peaked roofs of the Hotel del Coronado are a point of pride for all San Diegans, who delight in the oohs and aahs of first-time visitors. Designed by architects James and Merritt Reid in the late 1800s for visionary developers Elisha Babcock and H. L. Story, the hotel was meant to be the most lavish resort on the Pacific Coast. One could argue that it still is; filmmakers certainly find it the perfect backdrop. Billy Wilder chose the hotel as the idyllic headquarters for the antics of Marilyn Monroe, Tony Curtis, and Jack Lemmon in *Some Like it Hot*; Peter O'Toole dangled from its turrets in *The Stunt Man*.

Begin your tour in the magnificent lobby, where walls of Illinois oak and Honduran mahogany gleam in the glow from crystal lights. Take a peak at the **CROWN ROOM**, with its sugar-pine-domed ceiling and crown-shaped chandeliers; consider booking a table for Sunday brunch, an over-priced but lavish affair that entices guests to dress to the nines and act like royalty. Stroll through the central courtyard, beloved by brides, who pose in the white gazebo surrounded by roses and palms. The **HISTORY GALLERY** and collections of historical photos lining the hallways offer a fascinating perspective on the hotel's construction—laborers spent less than a year shaping this giant confection out of redwood, cedar, pine, and oak. Head into the sunlight at the pool deck overlooking a perfect stretch of sand and calm seas, and imagine sharing cocktails at the **OCEAN TER-RACE** with your favorite dignitaries. It seems they've all stayed here at least one night. Hourlong guided tours are offered Monday through Saturday at 11am and 1pm, Sunday at 3pm; the $15 charge proceeds the Coronado Historical Society. *Every day; www.hoteldel.com; map:NN5*

7) DOWNTOWN WATERFRONT

N Harbor Dr and Ash St to W Harbor Dr and 5th Ave, Downtown The indigenous Kumeyaay Indians, living in simple camps by the water, might well have considered San Diego Bay to be the region's downfall. Were it not for this placid deep-water pool buffeted from winds by Point Loma, European explorers might have continued north without stopping to plant the Spanish flag on the bay's shores. But Juan Rodriguez Cabrillo found the bay in 1542, and less than a century later, settlers and missionaries were building forts and missions on hills overlooking the water. Today, the natural curve of land against blue water is the focal point of downtown's revitalization and one of the most exciting parts of the city.

A waterfront walkway called the **EMBARCADERO** runs along the water's edge beside Harbor Drive. The first focal point is the **MARITIME MUSEUM** (N Harbor Dr at Ash St; 619/234-9153), home to the noble *Star of India*, a square-rigged, three-masted, steel-hulled ship that circled the globe many times after its construction in 1863. Sails unfurled, it's a stunning sight to visitors, who are welcome to explore below decks. The ship is preserved (and occasionally taken out to sea) by devoted volunteers. The museum also maintains the *Berkeley*, an ornate, unwieldy 1898 ferry built to shuttle passengers from Oakland to San Francisco. The museum's offices are on the ferry's first deck. Across Harbor Drive from the ships is one of San Diego's most beautiful buildings, the **SAN DIEGO COUNTY ADMINISTRATION CENTER** (1600 Pacific Hwy; 619/531-5880), dedicated by FDR in 1938. Architect Sam Hamill designed the structure in a colonial/beaux arts fashion; sculptor Donal Hord created the graceful *Guardian of the Water* statue of a woman bearing a water jug, which rises gracefully from the lawn. The building is open to the public during work hours; wander through to see the elaborately tiled floors and the view from the 10th-floor cafeteria.

The Embarcadero becomes packed with office workers striding in suits and sneakers during their lunch hours; those who arrive early enough stop by casual waterfront eateries for lunch. Visitors with plenty of time to spare escape the crowds by boarding a boat tour offered by **SAN DIEGO HARBOR EXCURSION BOATS** (1050 N Harbor Dr; 619/234-4111). Ride around the bay for an hour or two and you'll get a whole different sense of downtown. The city skyline, once drab and insignificant, now glistens with steel and glass towers forming a backdrop behind fluttering sails. You'll see shipyards, naval aircraft carriers, and private sailboats, as well as the curving span of the **SAN DIEGO-CORONADO BAY BRIDGE**. If you're too short on time for a complete tour, take the **SAN DIEGO BAY FERRY** (1050 N Harbor Dr; 619/234-4111) across to Coronado and back ($2, 15 minutes each way); it leaves downtown on the hour, Coronado on the half hour. You'll get a sense of the beauty of the bay without spending much time or money.

At the **CRUISE SHIP TERMINAL** (N Harbor Dr at B St) you'll likely see a Princess or Holland America cruise ship tied up for the day. Both lines include San Diego in their regular stopovers. Because the cruise trade is booming in San Diego, the terminal building is one of the first on the waterfront scheduled to be enlarged. Already the crowds are staggering when ships arrive and discharge thousands of passengers onto the Embarcadero—hop on a ferry and escape. Plans are under way to dock the **USS MIDWAY**, a retired aircraft carrier, just south of Broadway and parallel to the Navy Pier. The Navy presence is strong here, with the big, square buildings on the left of Harbor Drive housing supply units. Eventually, these buildings will be razed and replaced by office towers, but at present, the walk past them is parklike, with benches for strollers. Fishing boats, nets, and equipment line the dock and provide a glimpse of fishermen at work.

Further along the shore, **SEAPORT VILLAGE** (849 W Harbor Dr; 619/235-4013; see Attraction number 9 in this chapter) comes into view, with picturesque shops, restaurants, and a carousel. A bandstand in the middle of the village is the site of magic shows, clown acts, and free musical performances. Visitors eat ice cream cones, wander in and out of shops, and stroll past an elaborate marina containing shiny white yachts. This is the bayside yachting harbor of the elegant **MARRIOTT HOTEL AND MARINA** (333 W Harbor Dr; 619/234-1500), a mirrored, double-towered building that was one of the first hotels constructed on the downtown waterfront. It's now joined by the **HYATT REGENCY** (1 Market Pl; 619/232-1234), a luxury hotel that provides a stunning view of the city from its 40th floor, the highest spot downtown. You can stand at the hall windows without spending a penny, but there's a bar right there with high-backed club chairs. It's a great way to familiarize yourself with the geography of the city.

Looking south and east, you'll see San Diego's pride, the 760,000-square-foot **CONVENTION CENTER** (111 W Harbor Dr; 619/525-5000), topped with enormous Teflon-coated sails. Because city leaders feel the center is already insufficient to meet conventioneers' demands (it opened in 1990), a twin will soon be built; construction will impede traffic along Harbor Drive for at least a year. By the year 2001, look for a new $400 million baseball park too, which will be located a few blocks east of the Convention Center, surrounded by urbanization of what is now an industrial area.

There have also been suggestions for a bayside opera house like Sydney's, a Space Needle like Seattle's, an offshore botanical sphere, a promenade for bikers and pedestrians extending clear to the airport. Some of this will occur; some might not. Whatever happens, it's exciting to watch this beautiful waterfront in transition. *Map:L6–O9*

8) GASLAMP QUARTER

Bordered by W Harbor Dr, Broadway, 4th Ave, and 6th Ave, Downtown Covering a stretch of more than 16 downtown blocks, the Gaslamp is a living reminder of turn-of-the-century San Diego. At one time it was a red-light district known as the Stingaree, where Wyatt Earp is said to have operated three gambling halls in the 1880s. Today's Gaslamp contains some of San Diego's finest Victorian-style buildings, constructed between the Civil War and World War I. The **GASLAMP QUARTER HISTORIC FOUNDATION**, protector of this priceless pocket of history, is located in the historic Cape Cod-style **WILLIAM HEATH DAVIS HOUSE** (410 Island Ave; 619/233-4692; www.gqht). The house contains a museum with old photographs and room displays, and offers audiocassette rentals for self-guided tours of the neighborhood. Call in advance for opening times, as the house is staffed by volunteers and sometimes closes unexpectedly. The nearby **HORTON GRAND HOTEL** (311 Island Ave; 619/544-1886) is one of the best examples of the ingenuity and industry of today's Gaslamp entrepreneurs. Constructed from two 19th-century hotels, the Horton Grand is both Victorian and baroque, and is said to be haunted by a resident ghost.

The success of the Gaslamp Quarter is a phenomenon that surprised San Diegans, who just two decades ago were inclined to view downtown's oldest neighborhoods as run-down and dangerous. But visionaries and preservationists fiercely defended their city's oldest buildings, and the quarter was declared a National Historic District in 1980. Perhaps evoking the spirit of Wyatt Earp, modern-day gamblers renovated run-down Victorian, frontier, Italian Romanesque, and Spanish Renaissance buildings, transforming them into restaurants, shops, and office buildings, and awaited success with determination. Their bet paid off handsomely, though it took several years to lure San Diegans downtown after dark.

FIFTH AVENUE, downtown's original Main Street, has developed into the hub of San Diego's nightlife scene, with gaslamp-style street lamps illuminating hordes of stylish pedestrians. **FOURTH AVENUE** is nearly as crowded, with shoppers who browse through the books, luggage, and gadgets at **LE TRAVEL STORE** (745 4th Ave; 619/544-0005) until midnight on Fridays and Saturdays. During the day, crowds clog the aisles at **SAN DIEGO HARDWARE** (840 5th Ave; 619/232-7123), the oldest independent hardware store in the city. Movie fans head to the theaters at the **GASLAMP STADIUM 15** (701 5th Ave; 619/232-0400), which shows films from noon till midnight.

Today's Gaslamp Quarter is also home to more than 70 restaurants, offering Spanish tapas and paella, mesquite-grilled chicken, and Italian specialties. Dixieland jazz and Cajun cooking entice passersby into **BAYOU BAR AND GRILL** (329 Market St; 619/696-8747); flamenco music and the fragrance of olive oil and garlic draw a hip crowd to **OLÉ MADRID** (755 5th Ave; 619/557-0146) and **CAFÉ SEVILLA** (555 4th Ave; 619/233-5979). Diners can choose from among at least a dozen Italian trattorias: try **BELLA LUNA** (748 5th Ave; 619/239-3222) for a culinary splurge, or **TRATTORIA MAMA ANNA** (655 5th Ave; 619/235-8144) for less expensive yet delicious pasta. (For reviews of these eateries, see the Restaurants chapter) Throughout the neighborhood, diners enter intimate indoor spaces or sit at sidewalk cafes to catch a view of the passing crowds. And crowded it is, especially on weekend nights; lines are long and reservations are wise. Infectious rhythms of swing, country, jazz, and rock spill from the doorways as popular groups perform in bars and nightclubs. **CROCE'S JAZZ BAR** (818 5th Ave; 619/233-4355) and the adjacent **CROCE'S TOP HAT BAR & GRILL** (818 5th Ave; 619/233-6945) are among the most popular clubs, thanks to the indefatigable energy of Ingrid Croce, wife of the late folk-rock star Jim Croce.

Driving and parking in the Gaslamp is a nightmare best avoided, especially on weekends. City planners are working on developing new garages east of Sixth Avenue, and there are several public lots on Island Avenue and Market and G Streets. Horse-drawn carriages and bicycle-powered coaches called pedicabs ply the streets, offering rides through downtown and the waterfront. *Map:N7–O7*

9) SEAPORT VILLAGE

849 W Harbor Dr, Downtown; 619/235-4013 Long before the convention center and high-rise hotels marred the bay view from Harbor Drive, crafty entrepreneurs set out to design a mock coastal village along 14 acres of prime waterfront turf. Seaport Village opened in 1980 and has outlasted every dire prediction of imminent demise. Despite its decidedly tourist-trap bent, it remains a constant source of fun and entertainment for locals and visitors from throughout the world.

Shops and restaurants are housed in clusters of buildings resembling Swiss chalets, Cape Cod cottages, and Caribbean pirates' dens. The place is a veritable vision for souvenir shoppers, who browse kites, wind chimes, hammocks, handblown glass, sculptures, sportswear, and windup toys.

Nonshoppers hide out in cushy armchairs at **UPSTART CROW AND COMPANY**, one of the best bookshops downtown, or rest on benches facing San Diego Bay. Boat buffs peer through telescopes to examine aircraft carriers, sailboats, and cruise ships on the water; kids are diverted by face-painters, cartoonists, clowns, and balloon artists wandering about. Periodically, the central gazebo hosts a musical interlude, or perhaps a magic show. Kazoo the clown has been there for years; he hands out kazoos to the children in his audience and they form a musical parade. Everyone loves the 1890 hand-carved **BROADWAY FLYING HORSES CAROUSEL**; with its magical unicorns and chipper serenades, it adds to a sense of wonder to the entire experience.

Naturally, food is a major element in such environs. Visitors pause in front of restaurants to read menus, then choose shrimp cocktails and cold beers at one of the fancier seafood houses, or pick up a Greek salad, pizza, hot dog, or Ben and Jerry's ice-cream sundae and eat alfresco at picnic tables scattered between take-out eateries. Cookies, candies, fudge, popcorn—you name it, you eat it, then hike it off by strolling to the end of a long grassy jetty jutting into the bay. The jetty is the site of summer concerts, fireworks, and family picnics and provides a much-needed break from the crowds, which can be utterly overwhelming.

It's possible to remain entranced even after leaving Seaport Village by boarding a **CINDERELLA CARRIAGE** (619/239-8090) next to the Harbor House restaurant. As families step into the open carriages, the spiels begin. You can hear the patter of the drivers, the clip-clop of horse hooves, and the excited laughter of children all through the neighboring streets. **PEDI-CABS**, with young men on bicycles steering the wheeled carts, are a great way to get around Seaport Village and downtown. One cyclist assured us his last customers were two Olympic weightlifters, each measuring 6-foot-8, while he is only 5-foot-4. But he had no trouble pulling them along the city streets, away from fantasyland and back to their hotel. *Every day; www.spvillage.com; map:M8*

10) HORTON PLAZA

Entrances on Broadway, 4th Ave, G St, and 1st Ave, Downtown; 619/238-1596 A Disneyesque group of pink and purple buildings with Spanish domes and medieval banners, Horton Plaza was one of the prime catalysts for the recent growth of downtown. Before the mall opened, fearless and resilient downtown residents had few places to shop, and most San Diegans considered downtown a vast worker-bee nest best avoided at night. The plaza opened in 1985 beside a statue of city founder Alonzo Horton at the center of Broadway. The architecture was outlandish, but it brought curious locals downtown and became an instant gathering spot for visitors from all over the world.

The plaza was purchased by an enormous conglomerate that's gobbling up many malls in Southern California, and the name has officially been changed to Westfield Shoppingtown Horton Plaza—an awkward moniker sure to be ignored by locals. The current anchor department stores are **MACY'S** (619/231-4747), **MERVYN'S** (619/231-8800), and **NORDSTROM** (619/239-1700); all have escalators and elevators you can use as shortcuts to the various mall levels.

Given the plaza's theme-park appeal, several big names have fittingly entered the scene. **FAO SCHWARTZ** (619/702-7500), the **DISNEY STORE** (619/595-0404), and **WARNER BROS STUDIO STORE** (619/233-3058) are magnets for kids. The **DISCOVERY CHANNEL STORE** (619/231-1185), **RAND MCNALLY** (619/234-3341), and the local PBS channel's **KPBS STORE OF KNOWLEDGE** (619/233-1711) attract those with an intellectual bent; hikers and the safari-bound hit **ADVENTURE 16** (619/234-1751) and **ABERCROMBIE & FITCH** (619/234-1144). Upscale shops include **LOUIS VUITTON** (619/237-1882), **VERSAILLES** (619/232-2696), **ANN TAYLOR** (619/233-0705), and **JESSICA MCCLINTOCK** (619/233-9937).

If you're not into shopping, you can duck into the **UNITED ARTISTS THEATRE** (619/234-4661) with 14 movie screens on the plaza's fourth level. For stage plays, the underground **LYCEUM THEATER** (619/544-1000) is home to the San Diego Repertory Company, which draws a loyal following.

Groups of professional singers gather on the steps, and small bands set up their instruments in strategic spots. In Horton Plaza, there is always music in the air and a sense of confused bedazzlement among first-time shoppers. It's hard to find your way around the plaza's maze-like configuration: you can stand on one level and see the store you want . . . and have no idea how to get there. The elevators at each end of the mall are tiny and slow; the designers made sure visitors would pass by every establishment while following ramps, bridges, and stairways tucked beside plants and trees. Horton Plaza recently made its floor plan even more complex by adding a host of carts where sellers display crystals, jewelry, T-shirts, and sunglasses. The entire Plaza level has almost as many individual carts as it does specialty stores, which adds to the bustle and sense of haste.

One highlight: the irresistible sugary aroma escaping from **CLAUDIA'S CINNAMON ROLLS** (619/233-1529). It's right next to the movie theaters, along with a dozen other fast-food outlets serving Greek, Mexican, and all-American treats that attract a younger crowd. On other levels, restaurants for mature tastes abound: **CALIFORNIA CAFE BAR & GRILL** (619/238-5440), **PANDA INN** (619/233-7800; see Restaurants chapter), **MARIE CALLENDER'S** (619/239-4743), and **GALAXY GRILL** (619/234-7211) are all on the Plaza's uppermost level, with tables set under the clear sky. The celebrity theme restaurant **PLANET HOLLYWOOD** (619/702-7827) has overtaken the entryway on Broadway, attracting a steady lineup of customers more interested in show-biz props than gourmet dining.

The push is on to develop the area around Horton Plaza, which borders the Gaslamp Quarter on Fourth Avenue. Downtowners even have a major grocery store now, **RALPH'S** (101 G St; 619/595-1581), just across from the mall.

Horton Plaza's parking garage is another puzzle—even for frequent visitors. It's important to remember whether you parked at "tomatoes" or "avocados," "beets" or "pineapples"—and whether you're on the Fourth Avenue side or the G Street side. Security staff will drive you around until you find your car, but it's embarrassing to be lost. Three-hour validation is available at all plaza businesses; theaters have four-hour stamps. After that, the fees add up quickly. *Every day; www.horton-plaza. com; map:N7* &

11) REUBEN H. FLEET SPACE THEATER & SCIENCE CENTER

1875 El Prado, Balboa Park, Downtown; 619/238-1233 A space-age theater, child-size interactive exhibits, and an irresistible gift shop draw hordes to one of the most exciting museums in Balboa Park. Gadgets, gizmos, and computerized games fascinate the scientifically inclined at the **SCIENCE CENTER**, where even those who can't tell a computer from a calculator are hooked by whisper chambers, bolts of electricity zapping across terminals, and giant kaleidoscopes. The museum's resident astronomer, Dennis Mammana, displays his photographs of streaking stars and planets in the **SKYSCAPES** gallery on the second floor, rotating his favorite shots through the exhibit. The biggest draw is the domed **SPACE THEATER**, one of the first built in the world. Dizzying IMAX films take viewers up Mount Everest or into the depths of shark-filled seas; don't sit in the front rows if you are the type who tends to get seasick even on dry land. The middle rows actually provide better viewing, and you needn't get a crick in your neck trying to take in the highest images. The theater's 152 speakers get a workout during laser shows accompanying Pink Floyd's *Dark Side of the Moon* (scheduled intermittently throughout the year).

Try keeping your wallet in your pocket while touring the **NORTH STAR SCIENCE** retail shop; chances are you won't succeed. You needn't splurge on a $10,000 telescope (though if you'd like to, the shop provides classes in using such fancy toys), but you might want an old-fashioned gyroscope, a wall-sized poster of planets and stars, or a watch showing the phases of the moon. Plan on spending considerable time in this space-age complex; if it all gets to be too overwhelming, you can always wander out the front door and gaze at Balboa Park's centerpiece fountain, then return for more stimulation. *Mon–Tues 9:30am–6pm, Wed–Sat 9:30am–9pm, Sun 9:30am–8:30pm; www.rhfleet.org; map:O5* &

12) BAZAAR DEL MUNDO

2754 Calhoun St, Old Town; 619/296-3161 Yes, it's a tourist trap where you're sure to drop plenty of dollars into cashiers' palms, but few can resist the charms of this pseudo-Mexican village in Old Town. Blazing scarlet bougainvillea tumble over white stucco cottages framing a broad lawn where folkloric dancers twirl about the central gazebo, their ruffled blue and yellow skirts fluttering beneath them. Marimba and mariachi musicians compete for attention beside fiesta-themed restaurants; parrots and macaws squawk from their perches in giant cages; and the aromas of fresh tortillas, sautéed chilis, and steaming hot chocolate fill the air.

The Bazaar is the creation of Diane Powers, a savvy businesswoman with a passion for all things Latin. Powers leased part of **OLD TOWN HIS-TORIC PARK** in 1971; her creation has become one of San Diego's leading attractions. After renovating an 1824 wood and adobe hacienda into a dining and shopping complex framing the central courtyard, Powers installed some of San Diego's finest folk art, jewelry, and clothing shops. San Diegans looking for that special gift know they can rely on the selection of Italian platters and bowls; Guatemalan fabrics and clothes; and Mexican tin-framed mirrors and fanciful hand-carved dragons, called *alebrijes* in their native state of Oaxaca.

Giant margaritas are a major draw at Bazaar del Mundo's restaurants; diners stand in line up to an hour for a table at **CASA DE PICO** (619/296-3267). The spiced-for-tourists enchiladas, chimichangas, tortilla salads, and carnitas (see "The Whole Enchilada" in the Baja chapter) are sometimes overcooked or cold, although the portions are as large as the drinks. Stick with nachos, spiked or virgin flavored margaritas and piña coladas, and guacamole and chips. Other restaurants are tucked in corners about the bazaar; take a break from shopping and order hot chocolate and pan dulce (Mexican pastries) from **LA PANADERIA** (619/291-7662).

Artists from Mexico, New Mexico, and South America are featured in frequent shows in the courtyard; call for schedules. Though there are several free lots in the Old Town area, parking can be horrendous. Consider taking the trolley from Mission Valley or downtown. *Every day 10am–9pm; www.bazaardelmundo.com/bazaar/; map:J1* &

13) WILD ANIMAL PARK

15500 San Pasqual Valley Rd, Escondido; 760/747-8702 or 619/234-6541 The closest you may ever come to the African plains or the Mongolian steppe is just 30 miles north of downtown. The "WAP," with more than 3,200 mammals and birds, ranges over 2,200 acres in northern San Diego County. This part of the prestigious San Diego Zoological Society serves as a wildlife refuge and breeding center for endangered and rare animals who appear to thrive in surroundings replicating their natural homes.

There are several ways to appreciate the distinct environments carved into North County's dry, hot terrain. One is the slow-moving **WGASA BUSH LINE MONORAIL**, an elevated, electricity-driven journey around 5 miles of African- and Asian-style habitats where herds of antelope, rhinoceros, and giraffe roam in illusionary freedom. An Asian lion lazes in the protective shade of a tree. Flocks of pink flamingos perch one-legged around a watering hole. Drivers narrate the 55-minute trip with tasty tidbits of information. Did you know an elephant has 100,000 muscles in its trunk? Ever seen a white rhino? The WAP's Center for Reproduction of Endangered Species has bred 85 white rhinos; small herds of the beautiful and rare Przewalski's horse have also been successfully reproduced and returned to the Mongolian range.

If you want to get up close and personal with the fauna, the **HEART OF AFRICA** exhibit is the ticket. A circuitous trail leads hikers through varying African-style terrains. Forest hides shy opaki, kin to the giraffe. Lower wetlands reveal hairy warthogs and bat-eared foxes. Thomson's gazelles undulate in herds across the savanna. Two crashing waterfalls empty into a large lagoon with five islands, each harboring its own animal population. The center island, accessible by a floating bridge, has an interactive research center and simulated field camp.

The shows are always a hit with the kids and a good excuse to rest your feet for half an hour: there are amusing and educational bird performances, and others with those ever-popular elephants. If birds are your bag, feed the parrotlike lorikeets at Lorikeet Landing.

Some visitors ignore the creatures and study the WAP's accredited **BOTANICAL GARDEN** with over 3,500 species of plants, seeking out the North African cypress, one of only 12 left in the world. There are 10 specialty gardens in the northeast corner of the park; the **BONSAI PAVILION**, **FUCHSIA HOUSE**, and **OLD WORLD SUCCULENT GARDEN** are especially fascinating.

NAIROBI VILLAGE, close to the entrance, contains most of the visitor emenities. The Thorn Tree Terrace serves up hamburgers, sandwiches, and salads. The shops stock an irresistible array of Asian and African art, animal photos, cards, books and toys, and other gifts worth browsing.

The WAP offers still other temptations. The **PHOTO CARAVAN** tour takes visitors in open-backed trucks into the animal habitats for once-in-a-lifetime shots of giraffes, lions, and gazelles. Other behind-the-scenes educational tours and programs include overnight camping available from mid-April through October. Reservations are required; call 760/738-5049. Adult admission is $19.95; ages 3 to 11, $12.95; ages 2 and younger are free. Parking is $3 per vehicle. *Every day 9am to seasonal closing times (call for information); webmaster@sandiegozoo.org; www.sandiegozoo.org; map:CC2* &

14) LEGOLAND CALIFORNIA

1 Lego Dr, Carlsbad; 760/918-LEGO Young kids enamored with those knobby yellow, blue, green, and red plastic bricks (which originated in the tiny country of Denmark) are completely captivated by San Diego County's latest theme park. Spread over 128 acres in Carlsbad (the fastest-growing city in California), Legoland California opened with predictable fanfare in the spring of 1999 and the expected capacity-level crowds arrived. Parents with toddlers in tow now wait an hour to ride the **KID POWER TOWER** with its seats built from real Legos and its 30-foot free-fall drop, or to view miniature power brokers striding to work in Washington, DC, one of five U.S. regions depicted in **MINILAND**. It's astonishing to realize that every piece of the park is constructed from the same pieces kids use at home; reality hits home when the young ones enter the **BIG SHOP** and peruse the Lego selection, intent on building the city of their dreams. Science-oriented displays incorporating Legos with computer chips are a big hit with school groups, and the park can be packed even on the odd rainy Tuesday when you'd think nobody would be around. Admission is $32 for adults, $25 for seniors and children 3 to 16; ages 2 and younger are free. Parking is $6. *Every day, 10am to seasonal closing time (call for information); www.legolandca.com; map:CC7* &

15) SAN DIEGO MUSEUM OF MAN

1350 El Prado, Balboa Park, Downtown; 619/239-2001 Pleasing to the eye and intellect, the San Diego Museum of Man is one of Balboa Park's greatest treasures. Its edifice alone is worthy of close examination—from the 200-foot-high **CALIFORNIA TOWER** to the stone carvings of California's founders in the facade. The buildings now housing the museum were designed by Bertram Goodhue and Carleton Winslow as the entryway to the 1915–1916 Panama-California Exposition; their Spanish-colonial/baroque theme set the architectural standard for dozens of historic buildings scattered about the park.

The museum's collection began with artifacts displayed at the exposition and has since grown to encompass human cultures from around the world. Though the largest permanent exhibit is called **LIFE AND DEATH ON THE NILE** and features a genuine Egyptian mummy, much of the museum's focus is on the Americas. Rotating exhibits feature folk art and artifacts from Peru, Venezuela, Mexico, and other Latin countries. The annual **SAN DIEGO AMERICAN INDIAN CULTURAL DAYS** in May brings tribal leaders, musicians, dancers, and artists to the cement court-yard between the museum's buildings and the arched portals leading to Alcazar Gardens. Ghostly skeletons and skulls add to the ever-eerie air of the annual **HAUNTED HOUSE** around Halloween. The gift shop is excellent for memorable souvenirs, from Guatemalan purses to Egyptian cloth. Admission is $5 adults, $3 for children 6 to 17, children under 6 free. *Every day 10am–4:30pm; www.museumofman.org; map:O5*

16) LA JOLLA COVE

1100 Coast Blvd, La Jolla; 858/221-8900 True beach connoisseurs think they've reached nirvana at La Jolla Cove. This 150-foot-long smidgen of sand carved beneath crumbling sandstone cliffs is arguably one of the most beautiful beaches on the California coast. **ELLEN BROWNING SCRIPPS PARK** (see Beaches and Parks section in this chapter) creates a tableau of soul-satisfying lawns, twisted pines, and sky-high palms between the cove and the street. Million-dollar condos and homes pack every inch of turf on the hillside between Coast Boulevard and Prospect Street, the center of tony La Jolla's shopping and dining district. Rocks, boulders, spits of sand, and tide pools sculpt the coastline from the north-facing cove to La Jolla Shores. During the summer, La Jolla Cove is jam-packed with bodies by noon; arrive early and stake your turf near the cliffs. At high tide, the calm water edges upward and swallows towels and gear set close to its edge. The cove is a favorite launching site for scuba divers, who can be seen surreptitiously wiggling into their wet suits on Coast Boulevard above the beach. On a good day, underwater visibility reaches 30 feet; scuba divers and snorkelers use those stellar conditions to investigate the **SAN DIEGO–LA JOLLA UNDERWATER PARK.** Created in 1970, this 6,000-acre underwater sanctuary extends from La Jolla Cove north to the Torrey Pines State Reserve. Included in the park are an **ECOLOGICAL RESERVE** and a **MARINE LIFE REFUGE**, designed to protect the native marine and geological resources. Fishing is allowed farther offshore but not in the ecological reserve, where "look but don't touch" is the prevailing dictate. Golden Garibaldis, blue neons, angelfish, and the occasional misguided seal are at home in the preserve's safe waters, and grow in size and numbers as they would in a giant aquarium.

Lifeguards are on duty at the Cove year-round but the hours vary. There are rest rooms and showers by the steps down to the sand, next to the private **LA JOLLA SHUFFLEBOARD CLUB**, an idyllic wedding setting. Parking will probably be the most frustrating part of your day. Places on the street fill up fast, so bone up on your parallel-parking skills and cruise the residential streets nearest the beach. *Every day; map:JJ7*

17) BIRCH AQUARIUM AT SCRIPPS

2300 Expedition Way, La Jolla; 858/534-3474 Fond of fish? Glad about groupers? Ecstatic about eels? Well then, the Birch Aquarium at Scripps is just the place for you. Set high above the shores of the Pacific Ocean in La Jolla, the Aquarium offers a fascinating look into the wet and wavy part of our planet. Start your aquatic adventure in the cool, dark **HALL OF FISHES**, with 33 tanks full of various sea life and categorized by region. Pacific Salmon and a giant Pacific octopus occupy the **NORTH-WEST COAST** exhibit; a 150-pound grouper floats along in the warm water of **MEXICO'S GULF OF CALIFORNIA** tank; and 10-inch thick glass holds back 70,000 gallons of water in the massive **KELP FOREST** show-case exhibit. The latter is the only tank open at the top, a feature neces-sary for the kelp, which can grow a phenomenal 10 inches a day. Wander around and see the hilarious garden eels, their bottom halves burrowed in the sand, their upper halves up and waving at each other like silent guests at an underwater tea party. Darling little sea horses and brown polka-dotted clown triggerfish bring squeals of delight from the hordes of children visiting on school field trips.

Outside at the **PREUSS PLAZA**, tear yourself away from the fabulous ocean view to check out the demonstration tide pool, stocked with local marine plants and animals. Children aren't allowed to touch these crea-tures, but are encouraged to gently handle the sea cucumber and starfish in a nearby tank. Finish up your visit with a walk through the other side of the aquarium housing the **BLUE PLANET THEATER**, learning center, and educational exhibits. The **NEW PERSPECTIVES GALLERY** features short-term exhibits and travelling collections from around the world. Aquarium admission is $7.50 for adults, $4 for children 3 to 17, ages 2 and younger are free. *Every day 9am–5pm; www.aquarium.ucsd.edu/; map:JJ7* &

18) SILVER STRAND STATE BEACH

5000 Hwy 75, Coronado; 619/435-5184 This beach could be considered the quintessential Southern California beach, with its three miles of sand along the ocean and an array of laudable characteristics. A state park since 1932, the Silver Strand derives its name from the tiny silvery seashells found in great numbers near the water. Parents of young chil-dren prefer this spot to other county beaches, as the waves are generally calm. The same feature attracts surf fishermen, hoping to catch a Cali-fornia halibut, white croaker, or perch for dinner. Unfortunately, the water is sometimes polluted: obey warning signs when fishing or swim-ming. Grunion—funny little fish that flounce onto the sand to mate after dark—are found in abundance during the spring and summer months. The best time to spot them is at high tide four days after a full or new moon (check the events page of the local paper). Their capture is per-mitted with bare hands only. Hot summer days find teenagers flocking around the snack stand or chasing a volleyball on the sand. State life-guards protect beachgoers all year round. Parking is $4 per car and the lots are big. Camping aficionados can bring in an RV and stay overnight for a $16 fee. *Every day; map:NN5*

19) BELMONT PARK

3146 Mission Blvd, Mission Beach; 619/491-2988 Back when San Diego was booming in the wake of World War I, crafty developers created elab-orate theme parks on area beaches, replete with seawater pools and flashy ballrooms. Belmont Park is the only survivor from this era. Though it's been transformed into a shopping, dining, and amusement center, the park has retained its centerpiece, the 1925 **GIANT DIPPER** roller coaster. The coaster is modest by modern standards, but screams echo throughout nearby streets as the cars dip and swerve on wooden tracks. Also preserved from more glamorous times is the **PLUNGE** (3115 Ocean Front Walk; 619/488-3110), a 175-foot-long swimming pool encased in a Spanish Renaissance palace. The pool and building were remodeled in 1988; a whale mural covers a two-story-high wall the length of the pool, and a fitness club has opened on the second floor. The Plunge has been open to the public since 1925; call for hours and fees. **DIVE-IN MOVIES** are occasionally projected on large screens; viewers are encouraged to float in the water while viewing the many sequels to *Jaws*.

Other amusement rides, fast-food stands, and souvenir shops are clustered about the commercial area of Belmont Park, which borders the **BOARDWALK** (see Attraction number 20 in this chapter). This area is a fine spot for family fun during daylight hours, but can be a bit risky at night. Hold on to your possessions no matter what the hour, and take the kids home before dark. *Every day 11am–10pm; map:LL7* &

20) BOARDWALK

South Mission Beach Park to Law St, Mission and Pacific Beaches Bikini-clad bicyclists, tattooed oglers, roller skaters in neon spandex, and cops in shorts populate the 3-mile-long concrete boardwalk running between the ocean and the communities of Mission Beach and Pacific Beach, creating a classic SoCal beach scene. The walk begins in South Mission Beach, where pricey private homes built on postage-stamp lots face beach areas with fire rings and sand volleyball courts. Action central begins at the intersection of Mission Boulevard, W Mission Drive, and Ventura Place at Belmont Park. Day-trippers pick up rental bikes and skates at **HAMEL'S** (704 Ventura Pl; 619/488-5050), and approach the stream of traffic with respectful temerity. Though the city imposed an 8 mph speed limit on wheel-borne traffic in 1994, novices still feel like they're entering a speedway when on the Boardwalk. The congestion along this stretch is incredible on summer days; if you're not a confident, savvy athlete, stick to your feet and pass by the rental houses crammed with eager customers eyeing the babes on the beach.

Classic bars like **LAHAINA** (619/270-3888) and **THE GREEN FLASH** (619/270-7715) attract bronzed and buff sunbathers with cold beer, iced tea, moderately priced eats, and shaded tables overlooking the scene; if you're into good food check out **KONO'S CAFE** (858/483-1669; see Restaurants chapter) at the foot of **CRYSTAL PIER**. The 400-foot-long wood pier first opened in 1925, and led the way to the Crystal Ballroom perched atop the waves. The ballroom disappeared early on, as the sea proved too powerful for such lavish construction, but the pier remains one of the most treasured landmarks in Pacific Beach. The New England-style cottages of the **CRYSTAL PIER HOTEL** (4500 Ocean Blvd; 858/483-6983) now line the wood slats to the end T, where anglers dangle their lines in hopes of catching mackerel or sea bass.

The boardwalk action quiets down north of the pier, and walkers can actually link arms and lower their speed to a stroll as they approach the end of the walkway at **PALISADES PARK**, a small pocket of grass and benches perfect for watching the sun drop into the sea. *Every day; map:LL7*

21) OCEAN BEACH PIER

Foot of Niagra St, Ocean Beach; 619/226-3474 A series of piers pokes into the sea from Imperial Beach to North County; the liveliest stretches a half mile over prime surf breaks in Ocean Beach. Perched high above the sand just north of downtown OB, the pier is favored by photographers thrilled by close-ups of neon-clad surfers posing atop wave-slicked boards and panoramas of the wild coastline leading to Sunset Cliffs. Families set up coolers, stools, and radios along the railings and dangle lines and hooks into the surf. Cod, sea bass, perch, and the occasional sandal or wad of kelp are their rewards. **THE OCEAN BEACH PIER CAFE** and the **BAIT SHOP** (near the end of the pier; 619/226-3474) are the only concessions above the sea. The cafe is in one of its more successful stages (in the past it was pretty grungy). The tables out front are perfect when the sun is out; those inside by the windows are well suited to chilly, foggy mornings. Slippery anchovies, squid, and shrimp fill the tanks at the Bait Shop, which sells a bit of everything, from sunblock to soda. On July 4, fireworks streak into the sky from the T at the end of the pier, while OB's famed sparkling waterfall drips into the ocean over the pilings. OBceans bored with constant sunlight long for the winter days, when storms power the waves over the pier's railings; the pier is closed when the surf reigns supreme. *Every day (except during storms); map:B3* &

22) MISSION TRAILS REGIONAL PARK

I Father Junípero Serra Trail, Tierra Santa; 619/668-3275 Just 8 miles northeast of downtown San Diego, Mission Trails Regional Park is reminiscent of an era before urban sprawl and freeway crawl, when much of San Diego County was the domain of the Kumeyaay Indians. At 5,760 acres (one of the largest urban parks in the country), this unpolished gem is a well-kept secret, surprisingly enough, even to most locals. Those in the know start their day's adventure at the marvelous and modern **VISITOR AND INTERPRETIVE CENTER**, open every day from 9am to 5pm. An architectural delight set amid native chaparral and sagebrush, the center features an auditorium, library, and small gift shop with authentic local Kumeyaay Indian crafts for sale. Interactive exhibits instruct young and old alike about the geology, history, plants, and animals of the area. Beyond a wall of windows to the northeast is a stunning view of Cowles and Fortuna Mountains, sliced down the middle by Mission Gorge and the San Diego River. Maps showing biking and hiking trails and their respective degrees of difficulty, as well as information on the best fishing holes in the park, are also provided. Helpful volunteers and park rangers can direct you to the **OLD MISSION DAM**, a National Historic Landmark, where Spanish missionaries enlisted the Kumeyaay's help in building the dam to provide water for the **MISSION BASILICA SAN DIEGO DE ALCALÁ** (see Attraction number 24 in this chapter) in the early 19th century. Also part of Mission Trails Regional Park is nearby **LAKE MURRAY** (619/465-3474), where fishing and boating are permitted on Wednesday, Saturday, and Sunday. If golf is your game, **MISSION TRAILS GOLF COURSE**, an 18-hole, par-71 course is included in the park. Call 619/460-5400 for more information. *Every day; map:JJ2*

23) TORREY PINES STATE RESERVE

11000 N Torrey Pines Rd, La Jolla; 858/755-2063 Once owned in part by one of San Diego's most generous philanthropists, Torrey Pines State Reserve has been part of California's park system since 1959. Ellen Browning Scripps, a remarkable and magnanimous woman who died in 1932 at age 95, was instrumental in the formation of this natural preserve. Native only to this strip on the San Diego coast and on Santa Rosa Island (off the coast of Santa Barbara), the torrey pine is one of the rarest pines in the world. It grows in abundance here amid a rich plant community rife with brilliant wildflowers in the spring. A series of authorized trails leads through the reserve, and visitors are warned against leaving the sanctioned paths, to guard against erosion of crumbling earth or a disastrous tumble from an unstable cliff. Glorious views of the beach below and the ocean beyond can be seen from the safe havens of **YUCCA** and **RAZOR POINTS**, both of which can be accessed from trails intersecting with the popular **BEACH TRAIL**. Near the top of the road that climbs up into the reserve are a parking lot and the **VISITOR CENTER**. Built as a restaurant in 1922 and known as the Torrey Pines Lodge, this adobe brick structure now houses the ranger station. A cozy little fire warms the central room during the winter months, and guests are encouraged to wander around the exhibits. Kids get a kick out of the "Please Touch" signs next to the genuine (albeit stuffed) coyote, mountain lion, and red-tailed hawk; a sleek, plump stuffed skunk stands sentry on the greeter's desk near the door. The rangers here are friendly and happy to answer questions. Guided tours leave from the visitor center weekends and holidays at 11:30am and 1:30pm. *Every day 9am–sunset; map:HH7*

24) MISSION BASILICA SAN DIEGO DE ALCALÁ

10818 San Diego Mission Rd, Mission Valley; 619/281-8449 A peaceful retreat at the edge of the once-fertile Mission Valley, Mission San Diego de Alcalá is San Diego's oldest parish church and the oldest mission in California. The classic **CAMPANARIO** (bell tower) with five iron-cast bells set in white arches rises 46 feet above the grounds where Spanish Franciscan missionaries and indigenous Kumeyaay laborers farmed corn in the 18th century. The locals never developed a fondness for their patrons; California's first Christian martyr was killed here during a 1775 uprising. The small **FATHER LUIS JAYME MUSEUM** on the mission grounds includes the original records of disputes that still linger. Archaeologists and Native Americans who say the mission was built on sacred turf now explore Indian burial grounds. The church still has an active congregation; Sunday mass in the simple wood pews can evoke a sense of serenity. A statue of Saint Francis of Assisi sits amid gardens of native shrubs that attract hummingbirds and butterflies. If your interest in missions is sparked at Alcalá, be sure to check out the **MISSION SAN LUIS REY DE FRANCIA** (www.san luisrey.org; see Neighborhoods section in this chapter) in Oceanside. Admission to the museum is $4 for adults, $1 for ages 8 to 14, and free for children under 7. *Every day 10am–4:30pm; map:KK3*

25) MUSEUM OF CONTEMPORARY ART SAN DIEGO (MCA)

700 Prospect St, La Jolla; 858/454-3541 ▪ 1001 Kettner Blvd, Downtown; 619/234-1001 Designed by Irving Gill in 1916 and originally the home of nature preservationist Ellen Browning Scripps, the La Jolla MCA underwent extensive renovation and expansion between 1992 and 1996. The revamped building is both solid and simple, with lots of unadorned columns and arches. The redesign (by architect Robert Venturi) expanded and improved the exhibition space, now 60,000 square feet, and added a coffeehouse and a sculpture garden. Private parties and group meetings are held in rooms overlooking the Pacific. MCA's permanent collection of 3,000 contemporary works runs the gamut of media, placing particular emphasis on California artists. Symposiums and lectures are presented regularly at **SHERWOOD AUDITORIUM**; docent-led tours are scheduled weekends at 2pm, Wednesdays at 6pm.

The museum's downtown venue, across from the Santa Fe train depot, forms part of the small, triangular **AMERICA PLAZA**, designed by Helmut Jahn. There are docent-led tours weekends at 2pm; underground parking is $2 with validation, or better yet, take the train or trolley. Both locations have a museum store with an eclectic assortment of trendy gifts, as well as books about architecture, photography, and contemporary art. Adult admission is $4 ($2 downtown); students, seniors, and military pay $2 ($1 downtown); members and children under 12 are free; free first Tuesday and Sunday of the month. *Tues–Sat 10am–5pm, Sun 12–5pm; La Jolla Wed until 8pm; downtown Fri until 8pm; www.mcasandiego. org; map:JJ7 and M7* ᕫ

Neighborhoods

OLD TOWN

Old Town is at once San Diego's humble historical birthplace and a thriving tourist attraction. At the heart of it is the lively **BAZAAR DEL MUNDO** (2754 Calhoun; see Top 25 Attractions in this chapter), which was built on the remains of an authentic 19th-century Mexican casa. The bazaar is a parade of 18 interconnected stores surrounding a courtyard where mariachis strike up festive tunes and colorfully costumed dancers perform on weekends. It's that kind of harmonious blend of historic preservation and tourist commercialism that makes Old Town work.

The main pedestrian section of **OLD TOWN SAN DIEGO STATE HISTORIC PARK** is a 6-block area featuring the original restored 19th-century structures. It looks like a Wild West movie set, but these buildings are the real McCoy and offer a glimpse of the way life was for the city's first residents. Especially charming, **LA CASA DE ESTUDILLO** (4001 Mason St; 619/220-5422) is a traditional Mexican hacienda built in 1829 that's been restored to its original glory. Rooms furnished with period items open onto the central courtyard. Right across from La Casa de Estudillo, **CASA DE BANDINI RESTAURANT** (2754 Calhoun; 619/297-8211) is a wildly popular Mexican eatery (i.e., prepare for a wait) housed in the circa 1829 mansion of the Bandini family. Another don't-miss treat in Old Town is the **WHALEY HOUSE** (2482 San Diego Ave; 619/298-2482). The stately two-story house built in 1857 is an interesting glimpse at San Diego's early days, but the real treat is the docents' ghost stories. Apparently the Whaleys loved the place so much that their spirits continue to haunt the halls.

San Diego Avenue, the main road through Old Town, is home to more Mexican restaurants, including the **OLD TOWN MEXICAN CAFE** (2489 San Diego Ave; 619/297-4330) where you can watch tortillas being slapped into shape by the cooks. If you crave more upscale fare, try the fresh seafood at **CAFE PACIFICA** (2414 San Diego Ave; 619/291-6666; see Restaurants chapter). Right next door is the dinky **EL CAMPO CEMETERY**, the final resting place of the city's early denizens.

Just off Juan Street, **HERITAGE PARK VICTORIAN VILLAGE** (247 Heritage Park Row; 619/565-3600) is an enclave of seven lavishly restored Victorian homes that look like colorful dollhouses. Now housing shops, law offices, and a fine bed-and-breakfast inn, these fanciful structures are a departure from the Spanish colonial buildings that dominate Old Town. Sitting above Old Town and worth the short trek up Presidio Drive, **PRESIDIO PARK** stands guard over the city. This is California's birthplace, since it's where Father Junipero Serra established his first mission in 1769. The original mission is long gone (though you can watch archaeologists excavate its remains); the gleaming white adobe building on the hill is a replica that was built in 1929. Inside, you can check out the historic objects and exhibits of the **JUNIPERO SERRA MUSEUM** (2727 Presidio Dr; 619/297-3258). *Map:J1*

CORONADO

Just across the bay from downtown's skyscrapers, Coronado is an old-fashioned oasis of small-town living. This is a town so wholesome that the biggest controversy in the local weekly paper may be a teen reader protesting the enforcement of an anti-skateboarding ordinance. At once down-home and grand, Coronado marches at its own graceful pace. It's blessed with fine beaches, from which you can glimpse dolphins in the surf and watch Navy planes make their long, low descent to **NAVAL AIR STATION AT NORTH ISLAND**. The military base, which amiably shares this golden isthmus with residents, has a special place in aviation history—in 1927 Charles Lindbergh departed from North Island on the first leg of his historic solo flight across the Atlantic.

No exploration of the town is complete without a turn through the **HOTEL DEL CORONADO** (1500 Orange Ave; 619/435-6611). The red-roofed, white-frame Victorian masterpiece has been a local landmark since it opened in 1888. Countless celebrities have stayed, dined, and played at "The Del." To learn more about the town's past, spend an hour in the free **CORONADO BEACH HISTORICAL MUSEUM** (1126 Loma Ave; 619/435-7242), or join **CORONADO TOURING** (619/435-5993) for a 90-minute stroll through the island's historic neighborhoods. Tours cost $6 per person and depart on Tuesday, Thursday, and Saturday mornings at 11am from the music room of the **GLORIETTA BAY INN** (1630 Glorietta Blvd; 619/435-3101). The inn was formerly the summer mansion of sugar magnate John D. Spreckels, who considered the grand Italianate estate overlooking Glorietta Bay to be, well, modest.

On busy Orange Avenue, join the locals at a number of favored hangouts. **CLAYTON'S COFFEE SHOP** (979 Orange Ave; 619/435-5425) serves diner fare alongside original 1950s tabletop jukeboxes. **CAFE 1134** (1134 Orange Ave; 619/437-1134) is the local coffeehouse that's taking on Starbucks up the street, while the **CORONADO BAKERY** (1206 Orange Ave; 619/435-9272) has a strong following for its freshly baked breads. For Mexican food, find a patio table at **MIGUEL'S COCINA** (1351 Orange Ave; 619/437-4237), hidden away in the shaded courtyard of El Cordova Hotel.

But don't miss the action on Coronado's bayside. **FERRY LANDING MARKETPLACE** (1201 1st St; 619/435-8895) is *the* place to go at the end of the day, when the setting sun paints the high-rise buildings of downtown in fiery golden hues. Stop for a cocktail or a romantic dinner at **PEOHE'S** (1201 1st St; 619/437-4474).

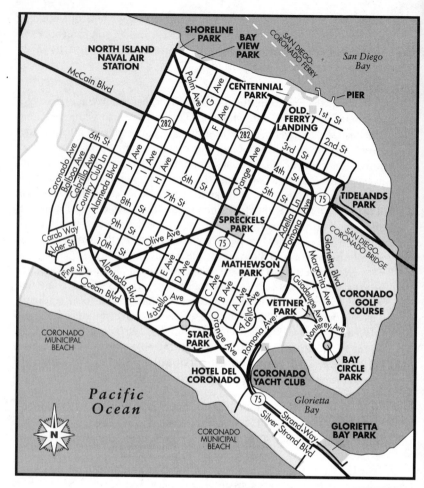

CORONADO

Coronado may be a casual resort community, but residents know how to step out in style. For fine dining, make reservations at Loews Coronado Bay Resort's signature restaurant **AZZURA POINT** (4000 Coronado Bay Rd; 619/424-4000). **PRINCE OF WALES GRILL** (1500 Orange Ave; 619/522-8496), downstairs at the Hotel del Coronado, is a step back in time to the art deco elegance of the 1920s. For a romantic French dinner, book a table at **CHEZ LOMA** (1132 Loma Ave; 619/435-0661), which is housed in a historic Queen Anne cottage. In the mood for elegant Northern Italian fare? Visit **PRIMAVERA RISTORANTE** (932 Orange Ave; 619/435-0454). (For reviews of these eateries, see the Restaurants chapter.) For entertainment, Coronado has the old-fashioned, single-screen **VILLAGE THEATRE** (820 Orange Ave; 619/435-6161), as well as two live stage theaters. The intimate **CORONADO PLAYHOUSE** (on the Silver Strand; 619/435-4856) offers amateur theatrical productions, while the professional repertory company, the **LAMBS PLAYERS THEATRE** (1142 Orange Ave; 619/437-6000), stages revivals and new plays on a stage in the remodeled Spreckels Building. *Map:NN5*

MISSION HILLS

Los Angeles has Hancock Park, San Francisco has St. Francis Woods. In San Diego, Mission Hills is the old, upscale neighborhood where house-proud residents guard a rich architectural heritage of Craftsman bunga-lows, Spanish colonial-style estates and Italianate mansions. Your best bet is to explore the neighborhood on foot or bicycle. That way you won't miss the quiet charms—carefully tended gardens, a cat lounging on an inviting porch, a cafe tucked away on a residential street.

The top of Washington Street, at the corner of Goldfinch, is the com-mercial heart of the neighborhood. Here you'll find a mix of hair salons, shops, galleries, and restaurants. If it's early, join the locals at the counter of **THE HUDDLE** (4023 Goldfinch St; 619/291-5950), an old-style diner where you can fill up on breakfast for under a buck. Right next door, **A LA FRANÇAISE** (4029 Goldfinch St; 619/294-4425) draws weekend crowds for omelets and fresh-baked croissants. In fine weather, choose a table on the patio. The neighborhood's Francophile influence is carried through in two shops that peddle fine housewares. **MAISON EN PROVENCE** (820 Fort Stockton Dr; 619/298-5318) is a red Craftsman bungalow filled with imported linens, pottery, and furnishings from the south of France. Two blocks down the street, the **FRENCH GARDEN SHOPPE** (3951 Goldfinch St; 619/295-4573) has an equally tempting, and slightly more affordable, selection of decor and garden wares.

Heading west on Fort Stockton Drive, you come to **MISSION HILLS NURSERY** (1525 Fort Stockton Dr; 619/295-2808). This urban jungle has served local green thumbs since 1910. Even if you're not in the market for a new gardenia bush, it's a treat to stroll through rows of trees, flowers, and fountains. Just behind the nursery is tiny **PIONEER PARK**, next to Grant Elementary School on Washington Place, at the foot of Randolph Street. Not only is it a favorite spot for locals to lounge and exercise under the eucalyptus trees, but there's some cool playground equipment too. Kids and grown-ups will be intrigued by the cluster of gravestones in the park's southeast corner. They're the remnants of the graveyard that once occupied this space.

Continue west along Fort Stockton or West Lewis Street to explore Mission Hills' sunny, friendly residential streets and join the locals at two favorite hangouts. **MISSION HILLS MARKET CAFE** (1922-C Fort Stockton Dr; 619/295-5353; see Restaurants chapter) is a great spot for a lunch of

A MAZE OF NEIGHBORHOODS

San Diego is composed of a series of small towns and neighborhoods connected by a maze of highways and surface streets. The city blends into San Diego County without warning. Boundaries are indistinct in many cases; in others, street signs proclaim a community's sense of pride. Personality-filled neighborhoods packed with shops, attractions, and restaurants are described in this chapter. But don't miss the gems that are tucked in less distinguished enclaves.

India Street runs north of downtown into **Middletown** (also known as Little Italy), a pocket of commercial and residential streets home to fine Italian restaurants. From there, Washington Street climbs through Mission Hills to **University Heights**, **North Park**, and **Normal Heights**; look for Asian eateries and antiques shops.

Broadway travels east of downtown to **Golden Hill**, where streets are lined with fine old Victorian houses and some notable nightlife spots. Follow Interstate 94 out of downtown to **East San Diego** (check out the ethnic markets) and **Lemon Grove** (home to one of the best bakeries in all San Diego). Interstate 8 provides an eastern link to **Mission Valley** (think shopping malls) and **La Mesa** and one of several entrances to Lake Murray and Mission Trails Regional Park, which sprawl north to Tierra Santa.

Harbor Drive runs along the north edge of San Diego Bay and then wraps southward to **Harbor** and **Shelter Islands** and **Point Loma**, where hills rise from the bay to Cabrillo National Monument. Neighborhoods spread beneath Point Loma, with businesses concentrated around the Midway Drive area. Interstate 5 runs north and south, skirting the lawns and playgrounds of Mission Bay. Though beach dwellers joke that there's no life east of Interstate 5, off ramps lead in that direction to **Bay Park**, where markets and bars cater to an eclectic crowd. Take Balboa Avenue and climb east to **Clairemont** and **Kearny Mesa**, with several good restaurants and interesting shops.

La Jolla also has spawned popular offshoot communities east of the coast: **University City**, **Golden Triangle**, **Sorrento Valley**, and **Sorrento Mesa** (all east of I-5) are filled with upscale hotels, malls, and fine restaurants. Farther east, Interstate 15 runs past the golf courses and inns of Rancho Bernardo to **Escondido**, home of the Wild Animal Park and the East County Performing Arts Center. Dozens of other communities beckon the curious; grab a map and start cruising. —*Maribeth Mellin*

homemade soup, gourmet sandwiches, and salads. If the weather is nice, sit on the back balcony under the shade of eucalyptus trees and overlooking a canyon carpeted with nasturtiums. If all you want is to refuel with cappuccino and a pastry, pop into **ESPRESSO MÍO** (1920 Fort Stockton Dr, Ste B; 619/296-3037) right next door.

Other eateries also include **MISSION HILLS CAFE** (808 W Washington St; 619/296-8010; see Restaurants chapter), where lunch and dinner specials change daily, or, for more casual fare, line up with the locals at **PHIL'S BBQ** (4030 Goldfinch St; 619/688-0559). In the summertime, you can nosh on ribs, then walk over to the **GARDEN CABARET CINEMA** (4040 Goldfinch St; 619/295-4221) to catch a classic movie under the stars. *Map:K1*

HILLCREST

Hillcrest may be the heart of San Diego's gay community, but it welcomes everyone with a lively blend of shops and cafes. Mainstream meets the cutting edge in this busy neighborhood that stretches along University Avenue all the way east to Park Boulevard and takes in the parade of stores on Fifth Avenue.

Perhaps the best place to watch the passing parade is from a sidewalk table at **BREAD & CIE** (350 University Ave; 619/683-9322; see Restaurants chapter), where the aroma of fresh gourmet bread attracts crowds on weekends. From there, you can walk over to **COLUMN ONE** (401 University Ave; 619/299-9074) to browse at a huge selection of neoclassical plaster objets d'art and statuary. A few doors up, **BABETTE SCHWARTZ** (421 University Ave; 619/220-7048) has latest in hip kitsch tchotchkes, and **CATHEDRAL** (435 University Ave; 619/296-4046) offers scented candles and accessories in a romantically gothic setting. Around the corner, on Fifth Avenue, is a string of new and used bookstores. For new reads, browse the stacks at **BLUE DOOR LITERARY BOOKSTORE** (3823 5th Ave; 619/298-8610), which specializes in small-press and gay/lesbian literature. **JOSEPH TABLER BOOKS** (3833 5th Ave; 619/296-1424) is one of the better secondhand book shops, especially for art books.

Many come to Hillcrest for its lively restaurant scene. You can grab a casual meal on the run or relax over a gourmet repast. The stalwart **CITY DELICATESSEN & BAKERY** (535 University Ave; 619/295-2747) stays open till the wee hours for the late-night crowd in search of an after-bar snack. The relative newcomer **LA VACHE & CO.** (420 Robinson; 619/295-0214) has already won regulars with its deliciously unpretentious French country cuisine. Moving east along University Avenue, **CALIFORNIA CUISINE** (1027 University Ave; 619/543-0790; see Restaurants chapter) was thrust into the limelight as the place where notorious serial killer Andrew Cunanan ate his last meal in San Diego. Don't let that put you off—the back patio is still one of the most romantic dinner spots in town. The Fifth Avenue restaurant row includes the '50s-style **CORVETTE DINER BAR & GRILL** (3946 5th Ave; 619/542-1001), where the servers put on a cheerful, in-your-face performance; the exotic fusion fare of **KEMO SABE** (3958 5th Ave; 619/220-6802; see Restaurants chapter); and the best Indian restaurant in town, **BOMBAY** (3975 5th Ave; 619/298-3155;

see Restaurants chapter). And while you wait for a table at one of these busy eateries, pop into the **WINE LOVER** (3968 5th Ave; 619/295-0456) to sample some California vintages. Across the street, you can catch an art house release at the **HILLCREST CINEMAS** (3965 5th Ave; 619/299-2100).

But Hillcrest isn't all shopping and eating. Nothing beats a stroll across the cobalt-blue **VERMONT STREET PEDESTRIAN BRIDGE** (foot of Vermont St), which spans Washington Street to link Hillcrest with neighboring University Heights. Built in 1994, it's a whimsical piece of functional public art and a shining example of Hillcrest's gift for urban renewal. Pithy quotations from the likes of Dr. Seuss and Kate Sessions (San Diego's grande dame of horticulture) are carved into its steel-and-glass panels and invite you to linger. "I am thankful that I wear sensible shoes and can walk with comfort all day long," Sessions comments. Sounds like good advice for anyone exploring a new neighborhood. *Map:N2*

KENSINGTON/ADAMS AVENUE

Perched high on the hills above the intersection of Interstates 805 and 8, Kensington and busy Adams Avenue are throwbacks to an earlier era, with San Diego Mission-style architecture, lovingly tended historic homes, and a funky collection of shops. In the 1920s, Kensington was a fashionable address; silent film star Norma Talmadge and her sisters bought some property in the eponymous subdivision, where the streets Norma, Constance, and Natalie Drives still bear their names. Today, Kensington is home to a diverse population of artists, writers, young families, professionals, and longtime residents.

Adams Avenue, which runs from Park Boulevard in University Heights, through Normal Heights, and east into Kensington, is the neighborhood's main artery. Working your way east toward Kensington, there's plenty to catch your attention. Proudly billing itself as **ANTIQUES ROW**, Adams Avenue offers a compelling melange of antique stores, used-furniture shops, vintage clothing boutiques, and secondhand book shops. Serious browsers are bound to find a few bargains. Check out **QUICK-SILVER STAINED GLASS & ANTIQUES** (2946 Adams Ave; 619/283-3638) to see what treasures are being sold on consignment. **REFINDERY ANTIQUES & COLLECTIBLES** (3463 Adams Ave; 619/563-0655) specializes in housewares and furnishings from the 1920s and 1930s. **PRINCE AND THE PAUPER** (3201 Adams Ave; 619/284-9408) is dedicated to old and new children's books, but **ADAMS AVENUE BOOKSTORE** (3502 Adams Ave; 619/281-3330) is the neighborhood's giant, with rooms full of bargain books as well as expensive first editions.

Restaurants run from the hip neighborhood hangout **KENSINGTON GRILL** (4055 Adams Ave; 619/281-4014) to the inexpensive, health-conscious vegetarian fare at **JYOTI BIHANGA** (3351 Adams Ave; 619/282-4116; see reviews in Restaurants chapter). It also seems there's at least one

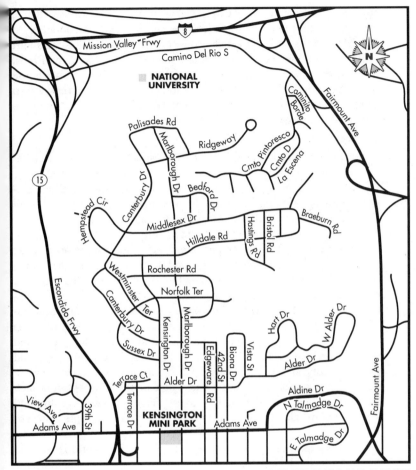

KENSINGTON/ADAMS AVENUE

coffeehouse per block on Adams, from the wonderfully named **LESTAT'S COFFEE HOUSE** (3343 Adams Ave; 619/282-0437) which offers live music a few evenings a week, to **JAVA BAR & GARDEN CAFE** (3562 Adams Ave; 619/281-6729), which features an urban jungle of plants and flowers. But on a sunny day, nothing beats a sidewalk table and the friendly service at **KENSINGTON COFFEE CO.** (4141 Adams Ave; 619/280-5153).

You may want to order that latte to go and take a stroll through Kensington's residential streets. From Adams Avenue, walk north on Marlborough Drive into a network of winding roads lined with delightful Spanish-style bungalows, Tudor-style villas, and other architectural gems—all fronted by carefully manicured lawns, of course. With street names like Hempstead Circle, Canterbury Drive, and Bristol Road, there's little doubt Kensington's developers were serious Anglophiles.

Movie buffs are well treated by the **KEN THEATER** (4061 Adams Ave; 619/283-5909), which has been entertaining San Diego since the 1940s. The old theater screens a repertoire of classics and modern art house films. Next door, the small neighborhood store **KENSINGTON VIDEO** (4067 Adams Ave; 619/584-7725) boasts a diverse selection that puts the likes of Blockbuster to shame. *Map:LL4*

OCEAN BEACH

A beach town with attitude, OB is a cult destination and home to independent souls of every age. OBceans, as the residents are called, are a tenacious and friendly lot. They love their community and all its freedoms with a passionate fanaticism. Some wouldn't mind turning the San Diego River (which feeds into the ocean at OB) into a moat.

A seedy, scurrilous reputation protects Ocean Beach from the tentacles of development. If newcomers aren't scared off by rumors of drug pushers, shopping-cart denizens, and mad bikers, they're deafened by the roar of planes taking off from nearby Lindbergh Field. It takes stamina to live in OB, but the rewards are incredible.

The ocean pounds with all its might on the sand and against the pilings under the **OCEAN BEACH PIER**. Residents a dozen blocks from the beach hear crashing waves and haunting foghorns as they sleep, and awaken to chimes from at least four of the town's many churches. Wild green parrots and blue macaws (who purportedly escaped from a burning pet shop a dozen years back) nest in and atop 100-foot-high palm trees lining neighborhood streets. Their flashes of color and squawks of delight are a constant joy (or major pain) to those closest to the nests.

OB begins at the intersection of Interstate 8, Sea World Drive, and Sunset Cliffs Boulevard, the westernmost point in the continental United States. Of late, town activists have been planting the entryway with palms, vivid pink ice plant, and Pride of Madeira bushes, whose purple blooms spike three feet high. Those bound for the beach follow West Point Loma Boulevard to the parking lot beside the river channel, where bird-watching enthusiasts delight in sighting herons and egrets. The first section of beach at this end is called **DOG BEACH** (next to the jetty), a place where German shepherds, Jack Russell terriers, and Afghans romp in the surf. Swimmers, boogie boarders, and body and board surfers congregate at various points along the sand, where cement fire rings are loaded with wooden pallets and logs as groups claim their space for the sunrise and sunset.

NEWPORT AVENUE, running southeast from the beach up into the hills of Point Loma, is OB's main drag. A disreputable cluster of tattoo parlors and bars lines the first block, best known for the presence of **THE BLACK** (5017 Newport Ave; 619/222-5498), one of the last great hippie head shops in San Diego. Incense, lava lamps, Metallica posters, Balinese sundresses, and smoking supplies lure nostalgic boomers and eager pre-teens through the doors of this mysterious haunt. The next block is home to coffeehouses, hair and piercing salons, Mexican restaurants, and the **STRAND THEATRE** (4950 Newport Ave; 610/223-5210), a revered neighborhood movie house awaiting a much-needed revival. Antiques malls have gained hold over mom-and-pop shops through the rest of the four-block downtown stretch, much to the dismay of those who loved walking from home to pick up stationery supplies, five-and-dime trinkets, and current magazines. Still, the blocks are packed with great Greek, Chinese, Mexican, and all-American cafes, and regulars beat the beach crowds to breakfast most every morning.

Newport intersects Sunset Cliffs Boulevard, which leads past mini-malls to **SUNSET CLIFFS**, a scenic wonder of golden sandstone ridges over rock-strewn coves. Surfers haul their boards down the cliffs to the few safe entry points into the sea; only the best tangle with the high waves crashing against boulders and caves. Still one of the priciest neighborhoods in San Diego, Sunset Cliffs is home to the plantation-style pink 1926 **MILLS MANOR**, a true tribute to excess.

Other pockets of OB are also well worth exploring. Down by the beach, **QWIGG'S BAR & GRILL** (5083 Santa Monica Ave; 619/222-1101) and **CECIL'S CAFE & FISH MARKET** (5083 Santa Monica Ave; 619/222-0501) restaurants are beloved for their burgers, salads, and fresh fish dishes served within view of the sun setting behind the pier (see reviews in Restaurants chapter). **OB PEOPLE'S NATURAL FOODS** (4765 Voltaire St; 619/224-1387) is a flash-to-the-past, a 1960s food co-op that has maintained a faithful following for three decades. Where else can you listen to Joni Mitchell while picking up carrot juice, tabbouleh salads, organic grains, and veggies? Grab a snack, then drive to the top of Naragansett or Newport Streets and gaze down upon OB. Wouldn't you want to live here? *Map:MM6*

LA JOLLA

Mediterranean in design and ambience, La Jolla is genteel and trendy, reserved and brash, yet always refined. Artists, writers, musicians, and wealthy landowners have been drawn to the "Village" ever since founders Frank Bosford and George Heald laid out its floor plan in the late 1880s. Ellen Browning Scripps, the mother of San Diego's garden landscape, played an integral role as landscape designer and benefactor into the twentieth century. Her benevolence is memorialized in **ELLEN BROWNING SCRIPPS PARK** (1180 Coast Blvd at Ocean St; 858/221-8900)

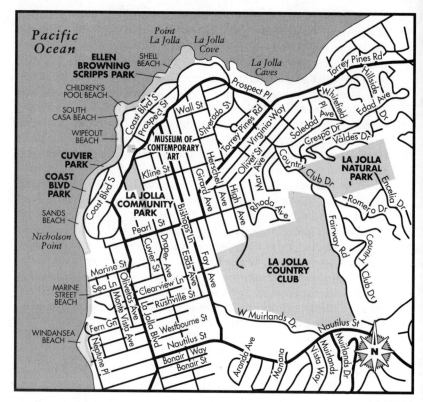

LA JOLLA

with its fringe of century-old Washington palms edging the waterfront (see Beaches and Parks in this chapter).

Prospect Street, overlooking the sea from a slight hill, may well have the highest-priced real estate in the county. Pink as a flamingo, the **LA VALENCIA HOTEL** (1132 Prospect St; 858/454-0771) has presided like a gracious grande dame over Prospect since 1926, housing movie stars in rooms overlooking the sea. More modest but equally precious is Scripps's Wisteria Cottage, which has housed **JOHN COLE'S BOOK SHOP** (780 Prospect St; 858/454-4766) since 1966. Heavy lavender blossoms dangle from a 60-foot-long trellis in spring, enhancing the beauty of architect Irving Gill's beach cottage design. Gill and Scripps were also responsible for the 1916 estate that has become the **MUSEUM OF CONTEMPORARY ART SAN DIEGO (MCA)** (700 Prospect St; 858/454-3541). Art galleries line Prospect Street; be sure to check out the sculptures and paintings at **TASENDE GALLERY** (820 Prospect St; 858/454-3691). Essential to the La Jolla experience is dinner at one of San Diego's finest restaurants. **TOP O'**

THE COVE (1216 Prospect St; 858/454-7779) is consistently rated the most romantic spot in town, while **GEORGE'S AT THE COVE** (1250 Prospect St; 858/454-4244) is *the* place for a sunset dinner with a view, either in the rear dining room or rooftop cafe (see reviews in Restaurants chapter).

Girard Avenue intersects Prospect Street, continuing the shopping and dining scene several blocks inland. A few homegrown treasures stand out amid the designer-name shops. The **COVE THEATRE** (7730 Girard Ave; 858/459-5404) is one of the last neighborhood theaters in San Diego; **ADELAIDE'S FLOWERS AND GIFTS** (7766 Girard Ave; 858/454-0146) displays a riot of colorful tulips, lilies, daffodils, and roses along the sidewalk. Book lovers head to **WARWICK'S** (7812 Girard St; 858/454-0347) and the **WHITE RABBIT** (7755 Girard St; 858/454-3518); clothes hounds rattle hangers at **ARMANI EXCHANGE** (7802 Girard Ave; 858/551-8193), **THE ASCOT SHOP** (7750 Girard Ave; 858/454-4222), and the ever-classic **TALBOT'S** (7817 Girard Ave; 858/551-1144). Artworks with a utilitarian bent are arrayed about the fanciful **GALLERY ALEXANDER** (7850 Girard Ave; 858/459-9433); handblown glass vases and delicate ceramic bowls stand out at **GALLERY EIGHT** (7464 Girard Ave; 858/454-9781); and the drawings of one of La Jolla's most famous denizens, Dr. Seuss (aka Ted Geisel), provide amusement among more staid lithographs by Chagall and Renoir at **FINGERHUT GALLERY** (1205 Prospect St; 858/456-9900). *Map:JJ7*

DEL MAR

Del Mar has always attracted those who love sojourning at the beach. Situated mostly on the sloping western side of a 2-mile-long sandstone mesa, the town of about 5,000 was designed like a row of bleachers oriented toward every spectacular sunset. First plotted in 1885 by founder Jacob Taylor, it quickly attracted vacationers and residents. Many came to frolic in the waves or swim in a unique "natatorium": a concrete-walled enclosure that extended far out into the waves. Today, although the natatorium and other *fin de siècle* beach-resort ventures are gone, Del Mar remains the quintessential beach town. The 2-1/2-mile-long stretch of sand from Torrey Pines State Reserve north to the mouth of the San Dieguito River (near the Del Mar Fairgrounds) is one of the best public strands in Southern California for walking, swimming, surfing, or simply lazing under an umbrella. Most beachgoers access it from the neighborhood between 18th and 29th streets. **SEAGROVE PARK** (5th St and Ocean Ave) overlooking the beach at the foot of 15th Street is perfect for picnicking and sunset watching; small summer concerts and other events are held here.

Del Mar's compact town center lies at the intersection of Camino Del Mar and 15th Street. Walk southward along Camino Del Mar to 12th Street to window-shop at the town's eclectic shops. Notable among the independents are **EARTH SONG BOOKSTORE** (858/755-4254) and

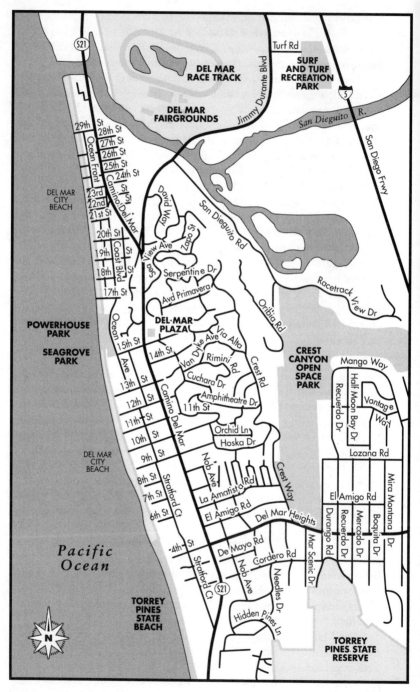

OCEAN SONG GALLERY (858/755-7664), sharing the same space at 1438-1440 Camino Del Mar; one is an excellent neighborhood bookseller with an emphasis on spirituality and self-help, the other an art, gift, and music shop with a Latin American flair. Farther down, **COUNTRY DOWNS INTERIORS** (1302 Camino Del Mar; 858/481-1356) offers beautiful linens, gifts, and furnishings. **VILLAGE CONSIGNMENT** (1150 Camino Del Mar; 858/259-0870) packs several rooms with antiques and collectibles. And **STRATFORD COURT CAFE** (1307 Stratford Ct; 858/792-7433), offers an open-air deck well away from the main coast route's sometimes noisy traffic. **DEL MAR PLAZA** (1555 Camino Del Mar; 858/792-1555), designed to resemble an Italian hill town, shouldn't be missed. Among its upscale shops and restaurants, you'll have to hunt for **ESMERALDA BOOKS & COFFEE** (858/755-2707), but this small shop is a real gem with a grand book selection, a coffee bar serving pastries and light meals, and indoor and outdoor seating. Other superb Plaza shops include **MOONBEAM'S** children's clothing (858/792-9894), **DUPUIS** furniture (858/793-0109), **NEROLI** fine lingerie (858/792-2883), and **SOLE COMFORT** shoes (858/793-7951). The Plaza's grandest feature is its huge terrace overlooking the ocean. You can sit in this public space as long as you please in comfortable Adirondack chairs and feel as though you are on Del Mar's "front porch." The **DEL MAR FAIRGROUNDS** (I-5 at Via de la Valle, main entrance on Jimmy Durante Blvd; 858/793-5555) hosts one of California's best fairs during the last two weeks of June through July 4. The **DEL MAR THOROUGHBRED CLUB** (858/793-5555) hosts a racing season every summer, late July through early September, that's legendary not only for its founder, Bing Crosby, but also a grand slogan: Where the Turf Meets the Surf. **FLOWER HILL MALL** (2650 Via de la Valle; 858/481-7131) warrants a visit for its varied restaurants, theaters, and shops hidden in a cluster of wood-sided buildings. East of Del Mar village lies Del Mar Heights, a housing community that has grown steadily since the 1960s. If you crave hiking, consider a clamber through the Del Mar side of **TORREY PINES STATE RESERVE** (see Top 25 Attractions in this chapter). Parking regulations are rigorously—some say fanatically—enforced. Try the pay lot at Del Mar Plaza. For further information, call or visit the Del Mar Chamber of Commerce (1104 Camino Del Mar; 858/793-5292). *Map:GG7*

RANCHO SANTA FE AND ENVIRONS

Hardly anyone even knew Rancho Santa Fe existed—let alone that it's one of the country's wealthiest enclaves—until 1997, when the Heaven's Gate cult members chose it as the perfect spot for their mass suicide. In fact, this bucolic, eucalyptus-shrouded, super-exclusive community—nestled serenely just several miles north of Del Mar and Solana Beach—has, since the 1920s, been the coveted home to a mainly old-money

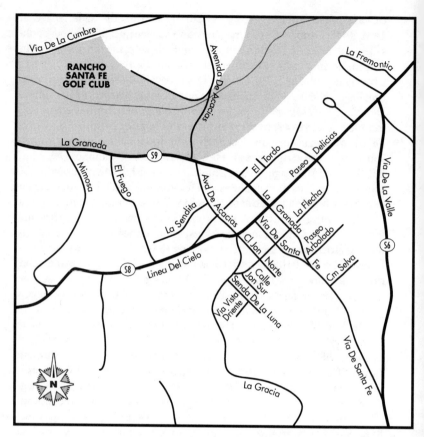

RANCHO SANTA FE AND ENVIRONS

crowd of celebrities, tycoons, politicians, attorneys, and physicians (as well as the rumored smattering of mobsters, CIA informants, and foreign agents). Indeed, this town is so ritzy that stories fly about cold-and-flu-stricken residents dialing 911, beckoning paramedics for middle-of-the-night aspirin and decongestants.

"The Ranch," as it's known to its denizens, had an illustrious beginning and easily grew into its tight-as-a-fresh-face-lift skin. Designed by esteemed architect Lillian Rice, who used Spanish villages as her inspiration, the community evolved into a genteel grouping of Spanish colonial revival buildings surrounded by huge estates (many with fruit groves and horse paddocks), golf courses, and riding trails. In fact, you're apt to see almost as many golf carts and horse riders as Jags and Mercedes. Once you've driven around the winding roads, ogling the mansions and taking in the countrified atmosphere, return to "town" and park your wheels—

this tiny village is best explored on foot. The village hub, quiet as a church (though hardly austere), shelters an array of very chic and elegant boutiques, jewelers, gift shops, and art and antique dealers in and around **PASEO DELICIAS,** the main drag.

Wander over to the historic **INN AT RANCHO SANTA FE** (5951 Linea del Cielo; 858/756-1131), onetime hangout for Errol Flynn, Bette Davis, and Bing Crosby. Obviously, you won't see those faces around town anymore, but you might glimpse resident Shirley MacLaine. The present-day inn was Lillian Rice's first building—a 12-room house constructed in 1922, now incorporated into the peaceful, parklike 20-acre property where guests bed down in private casitas and play croquet on the lawn. The ultra-exclusive, members-only **RANCHO SANTA FE GOLF CLUB** (5827 Via de la Cumbre; 858/756-3094) is the original site of the Bing Crosby Pro-Am, and is ranked one of the top courses in the region. **RANCHO VALENCIA RESORT** (5921 Valencia Circle; 858/756-1123) is another ultra-everything hideaway—this one catering mostly to tennis buffs (it's one of the country's top tennis resorts), with a terrific restaurant and three adjacent golf courses.

For some of the best (and most expensive) French cuisine, book a table at Bernard Hug's **MILLE FLEURS** (6009 Paseo Delicias; 858/756-3085), with its romantic French atmosphere. **DELICIAS** (6106 Paseo Delicias; 858/756-8000) is another good choice, with California cuisine and a country French setting. (See reviews in Restaurants chapter.) Even if you can't afford to eat out, you can buy the same exotic produce, baby veggies, and gourmet herbs as many of the top chefs at **CHINO'S VEGETABLE SHOP** (6123 Calzada del Bosque, at Via de Santa Fe; 858/756-3184). Though it might *look* like just another roadside stand, many of California's culinary artists (including Alice Waters, who started the whole California cuisine commotion) wouldn't dream of hand-picking their ingredients anywhere else when they're in town.

Douglas Fairbanks Jr.'s sprawling old ranch, across the river valley from Rancho Santa Fe, has over the years metamorphosed into **FAIRBANKS RANCH,** a distinctive area of more exclusive estates, golf courses, riding stables, and the accompanying deep-pocket-chasing posh shops, restaurants, and services. The **RANCHO SANTA FE POLO FIELDS** are just a trot away. *Map:EE5*

Museums

Photography, astronomy, natural history, and dozens of other special interests are honored with museums in San Diego. Balboa Park alone has at least a dozen; others are scattered throughout the county. Most are housed in architectural monuments, from the ornate Spanish-style

Museum of Man in the park to the modernistic San Diego Museum of Contemporary Art in La Jolla. Many offer special programs, from lectures to nature hikes.

CHILDREN'S MUSEUM/MUSEO DE LOS NIÑOS / 220 W Island Ave, Downtown; 619/233-8792 The children's museum, at its best, is a hands-on, "kids-are-king" kinda place. At present, it's a rather disappointing collection of exhibits—but there's always room for improvement. Museum leaders are constantly seeking funding and sources for innovative, temporary exhibits to increase the excitement level. Children can create high towers of connectable cardboard boxes and improvise skits or dance on a small stage. One area has blocks and other toys for younger kids; in fact, most of the exhibits seem geared to please children up to about age four. Children can also paint or work with clay. The museum store has a variety of educational toys for sale. Admission is $6 per person. *Tues–Thurs 10am–3pm, weekends 10am–4pm; map:N8* &

GEORGE WHITE AND ANNA GUNN MARSTON HOUSE / 3525 7th Ave, Downtown; 619/298-3142 This lovely example of turn-of-the-century, Arts and Crafts–style architecture is listed in the National Register of Historic Places. Built in 1905 by renowned San Diego architects Irving Gill and William Hebbard, it sits on five acres of landscaped grounds and has a formal English garden. Every room is furnished in the Arts and Crafts style, with Stickley, Ellis, and Roycroft furniture, Tiffany lamps, and Native American art. All visits are by half-hourly guided tours. Admission is $5 for adults; $4 for seniors, military, and students; $2 for ages 6–17. *Fri–Sun 10am–4:30pm; map:N3*

MINGEI INTERNATIONAL MUSEUM / 1439 El Prado, House of Charm, Balboa Park, Downtown; 619/239-0003 Mingei is a combination of the Japanese word *min* (all people) and *gei* (art). The Mingei International Museum promises—and delivers—art by and for and about people. Although the more traditional examples of folk art are decorated utilitarian objects from around the world, some pieces border on aesthetic. Niki de Saint-Phalle's 1999 show of bold, bright statues of polyester resin definitely lean toward the decorative, although designed to be climbed on by kids. There are no permanent galleries; exhibits combine the museum's collection with loaned items.

The museum relocated to Balboa Park's recently refurbished House of Charm in August 1996 after 18 years in University Towne Centre. Six times bigger than its previous space, the contemporary, 41,000 square-foot-facility now also has a theater, research center, and multimedia center. The Collector's Gallery museum store sells unusual jewelry, ethnic artifacts, and contemporary American crafts. Museum admission is $5 for adults, $2 for children 6 to 17 and students with ID; and free the third

Tuesday of the month. *Tues–Sun 10am–4pm; www.mingei@mingei.org; map:O5;* &

MUSEUM OF CONTEMPORARY ART SAN DIEGO (MCA) / 700 Prospect St, La Jolla; 858/454-3541 ▪ 1001 Kettner Blvd, Downtown; 619/234-1001 See Top 25 Attractions in this chapter.

MUSEUM OF PHOTOGRAPHIC ARTS (MoPA) / 1649 El Prado, Casa de Balboa, Balboa Park; Downtown; 619/238-7559 MoPA began as a museum without walls and remained so for nine years, until the City of San Diego gave it a home in Balboa Park in 1982. La Jolla architect David Raphael Singer designed the space for maximum flexibility, with movable walls and lighting. Featured among the museum's 3,600 photographs are some of Ansel Adams' glorious nature stills; MoPA's strength, however, is social documentary, including works by Sally Mann, Weegee, and Margaret Bourke-White. The 1995 "Points of Entry" exhibit generated discussion of U.S. immigration issues among San Diegans; while in 1992, "The Rolling Stone: 25 Years" and "Linda McCartney: the '60s, Portrait of an Era" were well attended by boomers and their kin.

A major expansion currently under way will create a print-viewing room, library, and more galleries. While the museum has typically offered six shows a year (about half featuring work from its own collection), expansion will permit three or four simultaneous shows. And the new, 200-seat theater will show films and videos. The renovation should be completed by the spring of 2000; until that time, MoPA will reside at the Museum of Contemporary Art's downtown location. MoPA's museum store has a good selection of photography books, posters, cards, and frames. General admission is $4, free for children under 12 accompanied by an adult, and free to all the second Tuesday of the month. *Every day 10am–5pm; www.mopa.org; map:O5* &

MUSEUM OF SAN DIEGO HISTORY / 1649 El Prado, Casa de Balboa, Balboa Park, Downtown; 619/232-6203 Exhibits are changed twice yearly at this history museum showing regional art, historical photographs, and memorabilia. Scholars and history buffs can access the nearly 2 million photographic images in the Historical Society's archives (open Thursday through Saturday, 10 to 4), as well as manuscripts, public records, architectural drawings, and oral histories. The San Diego Historical Society, which operates the museum, has an extensive Website with postcards from the 1935-36 California Pacific International Exposition and real-time recordings of oral histories. Museum admission is $4 for adults, $3 for seniors, military, and students, $1.50 for ages 5 to 12; and free to all on the second Tuesday of the month. *Tues–Sun 10–4:30; Edweb.sdsu.edu/sdhs/histsoc.html; map:O5* &

SAN DIEGO AEROSPACE MUSEUM / 2001 Pan American Plaza, Balboa Park, Downtown; 619/234-8291 Though it burned to the ground in 1978, the Aerospace Museum has come back to life even larger than before. Several exhibit rooms contain more than 60 important restored, reproduction, and model aircraft and spacecraft. Check out the original Pietenpol Air Camper, with its 1928 Model-A Ford automobile engine and radiator, and the Piper J-3 Cub, the first "everyman's" airplane, mass-produced in the early 1930s and still in production today. Other originals include the Stearman N2S-3 Kaydet, in which most World War II aviators learned to fly.

Full-size reproductions include the *Spirit of St. Louis*, and there's a full-size model of the Messerschmitt Bf-109G-14, whose brilliant German design cost many Allied aviators their lives in the Second World War. See also the *Mercury*, which put America in the lead in the space race. The Hall of Fame displays oil paintings, bios, models, and memorabilia describing the history of aviation. Admission is $6 for adults, $5 for seniors, $2 for children 6 to 17; and free on the fourth Tuesday of the month. *Every day 10am–4:30pm (winter), 10am–5:30pm (summer); www.aerospacemuseum.org; map:O5* &

SAN DIEGO AUTOMOTIVE MUSEUM / 2080 Pan American Plaza, Balboa Park, Downtown; 619/231-2886 Lovers of vintage cars should not miss this museum, which has some of the world's finest specimens. Exhibitions change at least four times a year, giving devotees the chance to view vintage motorcycles, race cars, stadium trucks, and priceless antiques. See the sexy black 1931 Lagonda, sparkling Model T's, and a 1909 International Harvester "Farm Wagon." The museum's library and resource center are invaluable resources for car aficionados and offer manuals, reference books, vintage car magazines, photos, and vintage films on video. (It's possible to enter the library without paying the museum entrance fee.) Restoration buffs can learn new techniques Thursdays between 9am and 1pm. The museum store carries—you guessed it—automobile-related gifts. General admission is $6 for adults, $5 for seniors and military, $2 for children 6 to 15; free the fourth Tuesday of the month. *Every day 10am–4:30pm (winter), 10am–5:30pm (summer); map:O5* &

SAN DIEGO HALL OF CHAMPIONS SPORTS MUSEUM / 2131 Pan American Plaza, Federal Bldg, Balboa Park, Downtown; 619/234-2544 Sports fans love the interactive exhibits at the Hall of Champions, which moved in the summer of 1999 to the refurbished Federal Building, built for the 1935-36 California Pacific International Exposition. Test your sportscasting skills at the Broadcast Booth, or rate your strength, flexibility, and other athletic abilities in the Sportsability Center. Parents snap their kids' pictures in the Locker Room as the little darlings dress up in different athletic uniforms. See what's happening in the Center Court:

there might be a mini-Chargers' football training camp or a rock-climbing wall demonstration. The art gallery shows work by athlete-artists, including the oil paintings of soccer player and San Diego resident Juli Veee. A theater, meeting and banquet rooms, and gift shop round out the offerings. Admission is $6 for adults, $4 for seniors, military, students, and children 6 to 17; and free the second Tuesday of the month. *Every day 10am–4:30pm; map:O5* &

SAN DIEGO MODEL RAILROAD MUSEUM / 1649 El Prado, Casa de Balboa, Balboa Park, Downtown; 619/696-0199 Kids weary of art or history exhibits revel in this animated museum, which boasts the largest permanent operating scale model and toy train display in the country. Trolleys and narrow- and standard-gauge trains run through landscapes portraying both real and make-believe towns, mountains, rivers, and valleys of the Southwest. While most of the trains are run by overgrown kids belonging to various San Diego model railroad clubs, your little ones can actually run trains and switches in the Toy Trail Gallery near the back of the museum. Throughout the museum, club members patrol the perimeter of their train-filled worlds to answer the questions of both neophytes and model railroad aficionados. The gift shop sells books, videos, and collectibles. Admission is $3 for adults, $2.50 for seniors, free to children 15 or under when accompanied by an adult, and free to all on the first Tuesday of the month. *Tues–Fri 11am–4pm, Sat–Sun 11am–5pm; map:O5* &

SAN DIEGO MUSEUM OF ART / 1450 El Prado, Balboa Park, Downtown; 619/232-7931 The largest visual arts museum in "America's Finest City," the San Diego Museum of Art started off as a small community art gallery over 70 years ago. Its 12,000-piece collection is now presided over by the youthful Don Bacigalupi, wooed from the Blaffer Gallery of Houston in the summer of 1999. The lovely, Spanish colonial revival building houses a California room, Japanese and Chinese art, and an extensive collection of South Asian paintings. Second-floor galleries are home to 14th through 19th century European art, lit by frosted-glass skylights and well-placed track lighting. Explanatory information is in both Spanish and English. Spring brings the well-loved "Art Alive" exhibit, when local professional and amateur horticulturists reinvent some of the museum's best paintings and sculptures in unique floral arrangements. Access the IMAGE Interactive computers to read about your favorite artists or paintings, or to create your very own self-guided tour; free docent-led tours begin daily at 1pm. The museum also sponsors many lectures, performances, and classes. Stop in at the gift shop, which has jewelry, cards, and postcards in addition to a fabulous collection of art books. View the sculptures by Rodin and Miro in the outdoor May S. Marcy Sculpture Court, or relax over lunch or light refreshments in the small adjoining cafe. Admission from Tuesday through Thursday is $7 for adults, $5 for seniors, military, and ages18 to 24, $2 for students 6 to 17, kids under 6 free. Prices are $1 higher Friday through Sunday. All enter free the third Tuesday of the month. *Tues–Sun 10am–4:30pm; www.sandiegomuseum. org; map:O5* &

SAN DIEGO MUSEUM OF MAN / 1350 El Prado, Balboa Park, Downtown; 619/239-2001 See Top 25 Attractions in this chapter.

SAN DIEGO NATURAL HISTORY MUSEUM / 1788 El Prado, Balboa Park, Downtown; 619/232-3821 The three-story museum faces the large fountain on the Prado. Permanent exhibits on the ground floor include the Bug Zoo (with all the favorites: trap-door spider, millipedes, tarantulas, and scorpions) and models and skeletons of whales, North Pacific fish, and California desert animals. If you're really lucky you might even get to hold a California king snake in the Desert Discovery Lab. Exhibits incorporate interactive computer and video stations and walk-through dioramas. Kids love the Wacky Science Sundays, meant to both enlighten and entertain. In the summer, day camps get kids off the couch and into the countryside, and there are camping trips, photo expeditions, and conservation programs for members and nonmembers. This museum's gift shop is one of the park's best, with lots of toys for both kids and adults. Admission price varies with exhibit. Entrance to ground-floor museum only is $3 per person. *Every day 9:30am–4:30pm; www.sdnhm.org; map:O5* &

TIMKEN MUSEUM OF ART / 1500 El Prado, Balboa Park, Downtown; 619/239-5548 Financed by the wealthy Putnam sisters of Vermont, this small, pink-wallpapered museum opened in 1965 on Balboa Park's El Prado, which is Spanish for "a pleasant place to stroll." San Diego's one free art museum, the Timken has a collection of 126 works of art spanning five centuries. The city's only Rembrandt painting is here, part of a collection consisting primarily of European masters and medieval religious paintings. Among the most impressive holdings are the European masterpieces in the International Room, including Niccolo di Buonaccorso's *Madonna and Child*, and two small triptychs that are extremely rare 14th-century pieces of tempera and gold on wood. Also impressive are the Russian religious paintings in the Amy Putnam Icon Room. Admission is free. *Tues–Sat 10am–4:30pm, Sun 1:30–4:30pm (closed Sept); www.gort.ucsd.edu/sj/timken; map:O5* &

Art in Public Places

With 100,000 military personnel stationed at U. S. Navy and Marine facilities, San Diego is home to one of the world's largest military complexes. The presence of the armed forces has always colored San Diego's character, and for all its labels of "kicked-back" and "outdoorsy," the city has an inherent conservatism—it's not as innovative as Los Angeles nor as footloose as Northern California. Such conservatism may be one reason it wasn't until 1990 that the City of San Diego committed to a serious public arts program. Since then, however, its public art policy has been recognized nationally as a model of community development, thanks to an emphasis on involving artists in building and improvement projects from the planning stages up. Unlike the traditional percent-for-art policies of most cities, the city council's plan offers matching grants and other incentives to encourage the grassroots involvement of neighborhoods and communities.

Among the most colorful and talked about projects is bright and whimsical **SEA GODS** (west end of Newport Ave, Ocean Beach; map:B3), painted enamel-on-steel sculptures guarding Ocean Beach's beachfront public parking lot. Local artists Jill Moon and Matthew Welsh created the sculptures in 1995. San Diego's ethnic diversity is celebrated in Jean Cornwell's **TO LIGHT THE WAY**, a colorful tile mosaic on the exterior walls of the **MALCOLM X LIBRARY** (5148 Market St; map:MM3) in southeast San Diego.

While the aforementioned projects have been strictly decorative, the **VERMONT STREET PEDESTRIAN BRIDGE** (map:MM6) is a lovely marriage of artistry and city planning. Designed by Stone Paper Scissors in 1994, the 400-foot bridge connects upper and lower Vermont Streets, providing University Heights residents access to the Hillcrest shopping district by spanning a busy thoroughfare. The bridge's steel panels are laser-inscribed with quotes by the likes of San Diegans Irving Gill, Kate Sessions, and Ted Geisel; the sun shining through the blue Plexiglas behind the panel creates watery blue designs on the concrete footpath. A source of much pride to neighborhood residents, the overpass won both the American Planning Association's Outstanding Planning Award and the AIA's Orchid Award in 1995.

Other public art is more functional, if less centrally located: while your typical Sunday drive might not include a trip to the waste treatment plant, the **METRO BIOSOLIDS CENTER** (5240 Convoy St, Kearny Mesa; map:JJ5) is indeed worth a visit. Richard Turner was one member of the design team that developed the center's landscape and hardscape design, lobby sculptures, and gallery of "informational artwork." Likewise, the **PEÑASQUITOS TRUNK SEWER RELIEF PUMP STATION** (10150 Scripps Poway Pkwy, Peñasquitos; map:HH3) was embellished with stunning mosaics and petroglyphs along its two long retaining walls by project designers Philip Matzigkeit, Fe McQueen, and Alvaro Blancarte. Another water district project developed with design in mind is the

ALVARADO WATER FILTRATION PLANT (5540 Kiowa Dr; map:LL2), off Interstate 8 near the border of Lake Murray and La Mesa. Designed by Manhattan Beach artist Robert Millar, the project will ultimately include an educational gallery, a self-guided tour, a demonstration garden, and a pavilion with portals for viewing the clean, stored water. Overall, since 1992, more than 50 public art projects have been completed, with 41 more either initiated or in the planning stages. For a booklet showing the location of more public art in the city of San Diego, contact the Commission for Arts and Culture at 619/533-3050.

At the opposite end of the artistic spectrum, the long-standing, community-generated murals at **CHICANO PARK** (National Ave at Crosby St, Barrio Logan; map:Q9) embody the spirit of San Diego's Chicano and Latino communities, with huge likenesses of everyday people and heroes from Chicano and Latino cultures. Here more than 40 murals adorn the cement supports of the San Diego-Coronado Bay Bridge, immediately adjacent to the tidelands in Barrio Logan. The murals were originally painted in 1973 by renowned Chicano artists; 13 of the paintings were restored with city funds in 1992. Raw, organic, and powerful, the combination of hope, anger, spirit, and community activism they reflect are a source of inspiration for the adults who sit on the grass and the kids who climb on the playground equipment in the park below.

On Shelter Island other ethnicities have made their mark. Franco Vianello's giant **TUNAMAN'S MEMORIAL** (Shelter Island Dr; map:E7) is a tribute to San Diego's now-extinct tuna fishing fleet, once the pride of Point Loma's Portuguese community. Further west along Shelter Island Drive, near the harbor police substation, the **YOKOHAMA FRIENDSHIP BELL** (Shelter Island Dr; map:E7) nestles under its tiny orange pagoda roof. The cast bronze bell was a gift of San Diego's sister city in Japan in 1960. Adjacent to the friendship bell, at the western extreme of San Diego Harbor's Shelter Island, stands the **PEARL OF THE PACIFIC** (1401 Shelter Island Dr; map:E8), an elegant yet festive monument. Bright mosaic tiles form waves, tigers, dragons, and flowers in a ground-level fountain backed by delicate concrete and iron structures encrusted with ceramics and shells. James T. Hubbell created this monument to intercontinental cooperation in 1998 with the help of architecture students from China, Russia, and Mexico.

The **INSITE** exhibitions, held in San Diego and Tijuana approximately every three years, are another form of intercultural collaboration. Initiated in 1992, this binational partnership between the San Diego-based, nonprofit Installation Gallery and Mexico's National Fine Arts Institute (INBA) is still evolving. The next event will begin at the end of September 2000 and will continue for approximately nine weeks. 30 artists from the United States, Canada, Mexico, and Brazil will create installations throughout San Diego and Tijuana and collaborate with San Diego teachers and students on other projects.

While InSITE installations are always well publicized, some of the city's most-treasured public art remains undiscovered by most San Diego residents, tucked away on the campus of the University of California at San Diego (Gilman and La Jolla Village Dr, La Jolla; 858/534-2230; map:JJ7). A center for conceptual and avant-garde art since its inception in 1960, UCSD's 1,200-acre campus is home to the **STUART COLLECTION**, a thought-provoking series of site-specific sculptures. Alexis Smith's **SNAKE PATH** is a visual representation of the nature-versus-culture conundrum; its 10-foot-wide path meanders 560 feet though the campus, passing a giant book identified as Milton's **PARADISE LOST** and ending at the entrance to the central library. French artist Niki de Saint Phalle's colorful, 14-foot **SUN GOD** (between Mandeville Auditorium and the Faculty Club) is perched atop a 15-foot concrete arch on a grassy knoll. This giant bird (which has at times been dressed by students in cap and gown, sunglasses, and Walkman) was de Saint Phalle's first large outdoor work in the United States. Pick up a walking map of the collection's 14 pieces at the Gillman Drive or North Point information kiosks, or get it on the Web site at http://stuartcollection.ucsd.edu.

Galleries

San Diego's galleries are primarily in La Jolla and downtown, although there are some galleries in Old Town, Balboa Park, and sprinkled throughout the city. A fine time to reacquaint yourself with fine art is during April's ArtWalk, when dozens of downtown galleries host special arts and music programs, and the artists are on hand to talk about their work. Many of the smaller galleries have reduced hours but also show by appointment; call ahead for schedules.

AFRICA AND BEYOND / 1250 Prospect St, La Jolla; 858/454-9983 Once *the* place to buy African beads, this gallery shop now sells Shona sculpture, Ethiopian Coptic crosses, Ashanti fertility dolls, Berber prayer boxes from Morocco, and more. *Every day; map:JJ7*

ALCALA GALLERY / 950 Silverado St, La Jolla; 858/454-6610 Sashay into this small, stylish La Jolla gallery if you're looking for early California art (mid-1800s to 1940s) in fancy gilt frames. The other specialty here is pre-Columbian art, primarily Mayan work and pieces from Mexico's west coast. Additionally, the store sells furnishings, decorative arts, and porcelain. *Every day; map:JJ7*

THE ARTISTS GALLERY / 7420 Girard Ave, La Jolla; 858/459-5844 Longtime La Jolla watercolorist Georgeanna Lipe features the work of more than 30 local artists. This is the kind of a place where a tourist might buy a painting as a keepsake, yet there's enough quality and variety to keep regular collectors interested as well. Most of the work is representational; the atmosphere is low-key and the sales staff friendly. There's also free adjacent parking, always a bonus downtown La Jolla. *Tues–Sat; map:JJ7*

ATHENAEUM / 1008 Wall St, La Jolla; 858/454-5872 La Jolla's lovely music and arts library, built in the 1920s by William Templeton Johnson, has frequent juried fine-art exhibits and also presents lectures and hosts art classes. *Tues–Sat; map:JJ7*

DAVID ZAPF GALLERY / 2400 Kettner Blvd, Downtown; 619/232-5004 The Studio Building, a converted warehouse filled with art studios and galleries, is home to this gallery representing mainly San Diego artists. Works include the colorful, spiritual landscapes of Nancy Kittredge; lushly painted figurative acrylics by David Baze; and the soft, earth-toned photography of Eric Blau. Furniture maker Paul Henry also exhibits here. *Thur–Sat and by appointment; map:M5*

DEBRA OWEN GALLERY / 354 11th Ave, Downtown; 619/231-3030 Debra Owen, formerly of Dos Damas Gallery on Market Street, relocated in 1997 to the ReinCarnation Project. Ubaldo Spagnolo and architect Wayne Buss collaborated to restore the old Carnation Dairy Building in downtown's latest redevelopment district. Owen's L-shaped venue features contemporary art by local artists, including fabulous local painters Maura Vazakas and Marcelina Kim. The multi-use ReinCarnation building is also home to a community media center and outdoor stage, private lofts and art studios, and the Sushi Performance Gallery, which stages avante-garde performance and dance. *Thur–Sat and by appointment; map:O8*

FINGERHUT GALLERY / 1205 Prospect St, La Jolla; 858/456-9900 Right smack in the middle of La Jolla's prominent promenade, this upscale gallery has among its compelling artists Jiang Tiefeng, creator of brilliant stylized serigraphs and oil paintings and one of the originators of the Hunan school of painting. Other artists represented are Joanna Zjawinska, Peter Max, and Ted Geisel (Dr. Seuss). A few etchings and lithos by Chagall, Renoir, Picasso, Rembrandt, and other masters are always on hand for the collector of fine European art. *Every day; map:JJ7*

GALLERY ALEXANDER / 7850 Girard Ave, La Jolla; 858/459-9433 A fanciful art gallery that almost always makes one smile, this is an excellent source for one-of-a-kind gifts, including those with Jewish themes and motifs. A wide range of media are represented: glass, metal, wood, and ceramics by numerous artists are all pressed, carved, and otherwise molded into fabulous utilitarian and decorative objects. Every two or three months the gallery hosts a special showing, of teapots for example, or perhaps objects made of metal. *Every day; map:JJ7*

GALLERY EIGHT / 7464 Girard Ave, La Jolla; 858/454-9781 There's a wonderful feeling of space in this gallery, and every item is beautifully showcased, no matter what the price. In addition to handcrafted jewelry, ceramics, eclectic furniture, and glass, they sell beautiful clothing, and ribbon by the foot. Smaller items reign—it's a great source for graduation, birthday, and new baby gifts. The gallery was started by eight women as a nonprofit to benefit the UCSD International Center, hence the name. It's now strictly a business venture, with two of the founding artists still involved. The entire inventory goes on sale in late January, at 25 percent off. *Mon–Sat; map:JJ7*

INDIA STREET ARTWORKS / 2305 India St, Middletown; 619/234-1251 Owner Michael Borrelli is a master cabinet and furniture maker, and this workshop gallery showcases his work. Borrelli's kitchen designs have won more than one award, including Best Small Kitchen Design from *San Diego Decor & Style* and Best Kitchen Designed by Owner from *San Diego Home/Garden Lifestyles*, both in 1997. Contemporary-style offices and kitchens are made to order for clients or customized in collaboration with some of San Diego's top interior designers. Although you'll often find the gallery open during off-hours, it's best to call ahead or make an appointment. *Wed–Fri or by appointment; map:M5*

INTERNATIONAL GALLERY / 643 G St, Downtown; 619/235-8255 This large craft gallery is a fine place to gift-shop, although there's a danger you may be sidetracked by the unusual African and Melanesian folk and primitive art at the front of the store. The owners and buyers also travel to Turkey and stock a good selection of collectible rugs. In the contemporary American department, well-crafted items of unusual design abound. Painted steel statuettes of whimsical and bawdy figures twirl among wooden jewelry boxes, mirrors and clocks, hand-painted ceramic tiles, and lovely blown glass. *Tues–Sun; map:O8*

LA JOLLA FIBER ARTS / 7644 Girard Ave, La Jolla; 858/454-6732 Here you'll find wonderful woven stuff—everything from baskets to clothing, scarves and throws to three-dimensional sculpture and wall hangings. Take, for example, Julie Wolfe's 1999 show of wall hangings, inspired by Florentine color, history, and religion and looking for all the world like beautiful jeweled quilts. *Mon–Sat; www.lajollafiberarts.com; map:JJ7*

PRATT GALLERY / 2400 Kettner Blvd, Downtown; 619/236-0211 Some of the artists represented by Doug Pratt do wonderful plein-air works; others interpret the urban landscape in acrylics or oils. This gallery, along with the Studio Building, takes part in the downtown ArtWalk every spring. *Tues–Fri and by appointment; map:M5*

QUINT CONTEMPORARY ART / 7661 Girard Ave, La Jolla; 858/454-3409 With more than 18 years in the business, Quint is one of San Diego's oldest surviving galleries. Owner Mark Quint was the instigator of the InSITE public art forum, and is considered a San Diego authority on issues of contemporary art. The gallery has monthly exhibtions featuring museum-quality contemporary art by nationally recognized and regional artists. *Tues–Sat; map:JJ7*

SAN DIEGO ART INSTITUTE / 1439 El Prado, House of Charm, Balboa Park, Downtown; 619/236-0011 A friend to the emerging artist, the institute hosts at least 10 juried exhibits a year, each with a different guest juror. Exhibitions feature the work of numerous San Diego artists, each time showcasing a particular artist of special merit. The variety of styles and media include assemblages, mixed media, watercolors, painting, and photography. If the fine art in Balboa Park's museums inspires you to buy, you can stop in here, at the House of Charm, and purchase your own piece at reasonable prices. *Tues–Sun; map:O5*

SAN DIEGO WATERCOLOR SOCIETY SHOWCASE GALLERY / 2400 Kettner Blvd, Downtown; 619/338-0502 San Diego Watercolor Society's gallery, next to David Zapf on Kettner Boulevard, is the place to shop for watercolors and gouaches. Juried group shows change monthly, and although most of the work is representational, there's a nice variety of styles. The Watercolor Society also sponsors workshops. *Wed–Sat; map:M5*

SPANISH VILLAGE ART CENTER / 1770 Village Pl, Balboa Park, Downtown; 619/233-9050 Built for the 1935–36 California-Pacific International Exposition, this artists' enclave now provides work space for more than 50 artists in 35 studios, working on-site in sculpture, painting, jewelry, stained glass, woodcarving, and pottery. Come for the bimonthly shows in the central courtyard or visit individual studios. *Every day; map:O5*

TASENDE GALLERY / 820 Prospect St, La Jolla; 858/454-3691 San Diego's provider of high-end painting and sculpture, Jose Tasende shows modern and contemporary artists of international fame. With an emphasis on large-format sculpture for open spaces, the gallery represents Basque-born Eduardo Chillida, who creates sculpture of steel as well as granite. Other sculptors are England's Lynn Chadwick, who works in bronze, and Niki de Saint Phalle, whose painted polyester sculptures can be seen around San Diego, including on the UCSD campus. Other international talent includes Roberto Matta, the youngest member of Andre Breton's surrealist group, and Mexico's José Luis Cuevas, best known for his pen-and-ink work. So strong is Tasende's international focus that Barbara Weldon's May 1999 show of oils, acrylics, and encaustic paintings represented the first San Diegan showing in the gallery's 20-year history. *Tues–Sat; map:JJ7*

Gardens

San Diego may have originally been a vast, dry wasteland, but designers and developers have consistently scraped away scrubby chaparral and planted tropical landscapes beneath sky-high palms. Even the freeways are edged with bubblegum-pink ice plant, the ubiquitous succulent that turns barren hillsides into vivid fields of delicate blooms. All of San Diego is a garden, which may explain why there are so few public gardens outside Balboa Park. Instead of plotting formal landscapes, San Diegans have always considered the overall scenery. Jacaranda trees shed delicate lavender blossoms along the sidewalks of downtown, Hillcrest, and Mission Valley. Orange trees flavor the air with their sweet scent throughout residential neighborhoods. Startling red poinsettias wave from leggy bushes during the Christmas season—San Diego is one of the country's leading producers of this holiday favorite. Orange and blue bird-of-paradise peer through broad leaves throughout the year. Blue delphinium, white foxglove, and rosy hollyhocks peek above daffodils and violet swaths of lobelia in Coronado's front gardens during the annual Flower Show Weekend in April, where home owners fervently compete for awards.

Agriculture is one of San Diego's leading industries; avocados star in the annual Fallbrook Avocado Festival in North County, while the Grapefruit Queen reigns over the Borrego Springs Grapefruit Festival in the desert. Most major flower and produce shows occur in April and early May. The largest celebration occurs in Carlsbad, where stripes of yellow, red, and white ranunculus buds cover 50 acres at the Flower Fields at Carlsbad Ranch. San Diego has a number of fine plant nurseries that rival any public gardens; see the Shopping chapter for the best. The following public gardens offer year-round delight.

BALBOA PARK / 2125 Park Blvd, Downtown; 619/239-0512 See Top 25 Attractions in this chapter.

CARLSBAD RANCH / East of I-5 at Palomar Airport Rd, Carlsbad; 760/431-0352 A family flower farm turned tourist attraction, Carlsbad Ranch has become one of North County's leading draws in just a decade. Its 50 acres of blooming buttercups attract considerable attention during April and May; historic biplanes and hot air balloons putter and float over crowds of flower fans. The Nature's Wonders gift shop has a good selection of bulbs and gardening paraphernalia. During the spring, when the flowers are in full bloom, the ranch is open from 10am to dusk. Admission for adults is $4. *Every day; www.theflowerfield.com; map:CC8*

**QUAIL BOTANICAL GARDENS / 230 Quail Gardens Dr, Encinitas;
760/436-3036** Eucalyptus groves, native-plant gardens, and one of the
largest bamboo collections in the United States cover 30 acres at San
Diego's largest public garden in coastal North County. Quail Gardens
was established as a county park in 1971; in 1991 it became a private
nonprofit entity with hundreds of plant-savvy volunteers. There are 24
representative gardens, from tropical to desert and everything in
between. A map in the gift shop will direct you to the plants in bloom at
the time of your visit. The annual plant sale in October attracts flocks of
amateur and professional gardeners. Admission is $5 for adults, $2 for
children 5 to 12, free for children under 5. *Everyday 9am–5pm; www.
qbgarden.com; map:EE7*

Beaches and Parks

Gloriously endowed with one of the most temperate climates in the
world, San Diego is the perfect place to spend time outdoors and explore
some marvelous beaches and parks. No matter what your fancy—surfing
(Tourmaline or Windansea), family (Coronado or Ocean), or hip and
happening (Mission or Pacific)—San Diego beaches offer enough variety
to satisfy everyone.

Balboa Park, first established in 1868, is queen of the city's park
system, with 1,200 acres and over 12 million visitors a year. While it may
be the star, it is by no means the whole show. More than 32,000 acres of
developed parks and undeveloped open space serve the neighborhoods
and communities of San Diego. Parks range from kid-friendly (Mission
Bay/Tecolote playground) to recreational (Mission Trails Regional Park)
to just plain beautiful (Ellen Browning Scripps Park). Watch a sunset
from Kellogg Park, ride your horse at Fiesta Island, or quietly scout for
elusive birds at Mission Bay. For more information about parks or
beaches within the city, call 619/221-8900. For information regarding
state parks, call 619/237-6770.

BALBOA PARK / 2125 Park Blvd, Downtown; 619/239-0512 See Top 25
Attractions in this chapter

BELMONT PARK / 3146 Mission Blvd, Mission Beach; 619/491-2988 See
Top 25 Attractions in this chapter.

**BLACK'S BEACH / 2800 Torrey Pines Scenic Dr, at North Torrey Pines
Rd, La Jolla; 858/221-8900** Black's Beach is the unofficial home to nude
sun lovers. Formally unsanctioned yet judicially ignored, nudism prevails
at the northernmost 2-mile-long section of sand beneath towering cliffs
north of La Jolla. Hang gliders launch their colorful craft into the
updrafts from the glider-port atop the cliffs for a swirling ride over the

TIDE POOL TANGO

The small animals that inhabit coastal tide pools are some of the most adaptive and tenacious on the planet. Living in an environment that undergoes tidal changes four times a day, these little creatures are the commandants of compromise. At low tide their watery sanctuary disappears, exposing them to the broiling sun, increased salinity, and hungry predators. To survive, mussels collect seawater inside their bodies, then slowly release it to cool by evaporation. Sea anemones fold inward, trapping tiny drops of water to sustain themselves until the flow of water returns. At high tide, they are once again flooded, with rough swirls of seawater threatening to evict them from their homes. Barnacles hold on to rocks for dear life or risk being hurled up on the beach or out to sea. Sea urchins stay put by burrowing their spines deep into the rocks on which they live. There is also a constant threat of being eaten by a neighbor. Clams, scallops, and oysters are the favored dinner of the carnivorous sea star, which in turn makes a fitting snack for a gull or a crow. If this wet, miniature-scale drama sounds interesting, San Diego has several prime spots for front-row viewing. Put on your rubber-soled tennis shoes and head for **Bird Rock**, the **Cove** in La Jolla, or the tide pools located on the western side of **Point Loma**, near Cabrillo Monument. **Birch Aquarium at Scripps** (see Top 25 Attractions in this chapter) offers classes on tidepooling and can provide information on the best times for viewing. Call 858/534-7336 for more information.

—Susan Humphrey

ocean, where superb swells on the southern end of the beach attract the cream of the surfing crowd. Accessing Black's Beach is a challenge; one obvious way is hiking down the 300-foot-high bluffs. Although there are plenty of strongly worded signs warning people away from the unstable cliffs, scores of people gingerly make their way down every day. A safer approach is to walk along the sand from adjacent beaches to the north and south, but these routes may be obstructed at times by high tides. Although there are no permanent lifeguard stations at this beach, lifeguards are usually on duty during the busier summer months. No rest rooms exist on the beach, nor is there a snack stand or equipment rental establishment in sight. The amenities are absent, but the incredible beauty of the spot more than compensates. Free parking is available at the glider-port and at the public lot at La Jolla Shores. There are also 450 pay-parking spaces at Torrey Pines State Beach. *Map:HH7*

CHILDREN'S POOL BEACH / 850 Coast Blvd, at Jenner St, La Jolla; 858/221-8900 Safeguarded by a man-made seawall and originally intended as a beach for children and the swimming-impaired, this small beach in La Jolla with its beautiful panoramic view is now domain to a large group of federally protected harbor seals. Deemed unsafe for swimming in 1997 because of high bacterial levels, the Children's Pool beach is currently a political hot potato, pitting people against pinnipeds. Fiercely debated within the La Jolla City Council was a proposal to dredge sand from the beach in hopes of discouraging the seals from hanging out at their favorite lounging spots, thereby increasing water circulation and eliminating the current seal-induced pollution problem. Advocates of the seals were delighted when a recent council vote went their way; no dredging is allowed, and the chubby, blubbery mammals can stay. Swimming here is a nonissue, but come for the nature scene. Parking is limited; there are no public lots at the beach, and a vacant place on the street is cause for celebration. *Map:JJ7*

CORONADO MUNICIPAL BEACH / Ocean Blvd at Marina Ave, Coronado; 619/522-7342 Your choice of scenery at Coronado Municipal Beach is varied. You can plop your towel down near the east end and enjoy the fabulous Hotel del Coronado as your backdrop. Or head farther down Ocean Boulevard to the west end of the beach and watch huge airplanes roaring to and from their home at the Naval Air Station at North Island. With 1½ miles of wide shoreline, you are certain to find a patch of sand to call your own. This is a popular place for families to bring their children during the summer; the waves are gentle and the lifeguards plentiful. Even the canine member of the family is welcome at the most westerly end of the beach, near the Navy enclave. Rover can romp joyously amid the clumps of palm trees on ice-plant-covered dunes or in the waves. Sturdier souls enjoy the chilly beach during winter months; with some luck and a good pair of binoculars pointed toward the ocean, you may spot California gray whales migrating south toward Baja California, Mexico. Parking is available on Ocean Boulevard and the residential streets farther inland. *Map:NN5*

ELLEN BROWNING SCRIPPS PARK / 1180 Coast Blvd, at Ocean St, La Jolla; 858/221-8900 One of San Diego's most beautiful landscapes, Ellen Browning Scripps Park hugs the bluffs overlooking the Pacific Ocean in La Jolla near the Cove. Extending from palm-lined Coast Boulevard to a paved walkway paralleling the cliffs, this grassy stretch is a perfect place for a leisurely afternoon picnic or rousing game of croquet. A gentle breeze on a hot summer day makes for a delightful study hall; students come to read, sprawling beneath gnarled cypress trees. Children crowd into the open-air wooden shelters precipitously perched at the park's edge and cautiously peer down at the waves crashing on the rocks below. Plan a barbecue for a Sunday afternoon when the La Jolla Town Council presents one of its summer Sunday afternoon concerts (call 619/645-8115 for scheduling information). As always in this area, parking is a headache.

Your best bet is a vigilant and slow prowl of the residential zones adjacent to the park, or use one of the pay lots in La Jolla Village. *Map:JJ7*

EMBARCADERO MARINA PARK / End of Kettner Blvd, at Harbor Dr, Downtown; 619/686-6200 Located between Seaport Village to the north and the San Diego Convention Center to the south, Embarcadero Marina Park is a green haven between bustling crowds. Take a break from a hectic day of shopping at the Village or a demanding round of meetings at the Center to enjoy a bite to eat while you watch huge ships making their way through San Diego Bay. The view of the San Diego-Coronado Bay Bridge is excellent from here. The park also features basketball courts, gazebos, and bike and jogging paths. There is a large parking lot at Seaport Village; purchase one of the shops gets you two free hours of validated parking. *Map:N8*

FIESTA ISLAND / Fiesta Island Rd, at E Mission Bay Dr, Mission Bay; 619/221-8900 The most undeveloped part of Mission Bay Park, Fiesta Island is a favored launching site for water sports enthusiasts who roar around in their powerboats or zip past on Jet Skis. It is also one of the rare places in San Diego where Fido can roam without his leash. The annual Over The Line tournament is held here over two weekends in July. Not for the faint of heart, it's a raucous, rowdy softball-type event, with team names of a decidedly ribald nature. Don't bring the children! *Map:LL6*

IMPERIAL BEACH / Seacoast Dr, at Palm Ave, Imperial Beach; 619/423-8328 Meandering along the municipal pier at Imperial Beach, you may encounter an unusual sight suggestive of Robin Hood and his followers. It's not the Merry Men, however, but lighthearted fishermen employing bow and arrow to spear their catch. Upon completion of a safety course sponsored by the City of Imperial Beach, this unusual method of sportfishing is permitted from the 1,500-foot pier. Along with the archers, you will find more conventional anglers vying for barracuda, bat rays, or the more ordinary bass and croaker. No license is required to fish. At the foot of the pier, a major renovation is under way, with the addition of picnic tables, a playground, rest rooms, and shops. The beach in Imperial Beach (which bills itself as the "Most Southwesterly City in the Continental United States") is long and wide, with 3 miles of surf breaks; three-quarters of a mile is guarded for swimming. Surfing is allowed in designated areas, with an especially fabled break called the Slough. Always check with the lifeguards before splashing into the spray; unfortunately, the greenish-blue water is often afoul with sewage coming up from Tijuana. In 1998, this otherwise perfect beach was closed for 111 days due to contamination. One of the summer highlights is the annual sand castle competition, usually held in late July. Upward of 200,000 people come to enjoy the weekend of parades, parties, and fabulous creations made from sand. *Map:QQ4*

KATE SESSIONS MEMORIAL PARK / Soledad Rd, at Loring St, Pacific Beach; 619/581-9927 Dedicated in 1957 to San Diego's remarkable gardener extraordinaire and prolific planter of trees, Kate Sessions Memorial Park is a lovely park in the neighborhood of Pacific Beach. People bring their picnic baskets and pooches, as do parents whose children clamber to the top of the rocket-ship slide at the small playground near the bottom of the park. The arboreal collection on the park's 80 acres would do Ms. Sessions proud: clumps of evergreens, giant eucalypti, and hardy pepper trees provide lots of shade on warm summer days. Climb to the top of the grassy slope for a splendid view of San Diego Bay and the Pacific. Summer nights attract fireworks fans, who watch the pyrotechnics exploding from Sea World. Parking here is adequate; finding a spot will not likely be a problem except on the busiest summer weekends. *Map:KK6*

 LA JOLLA COVE / 1100 Coast Blvd, La Jolla; 858/221-8900 See Top 25 Attractions in this chapter.

LA JOLLA SHORES / 8200 Camino del Oro, La Jolla; 858/221-8900 Picture-postcard perfect, La Jolla Shores is what you imagine a beach should be: a mile-long stretch of powdery sand under bright blue skies, crowded with bronzed locals, scads of frolicsome kids, and lissome surfers with bleached-blond hair. The waves here are generally gentle, making this place a favorite with families, although children and weak swimmers should be warned of possible rip currents. The tame waves and the shore's gradual decline draw a plenitude of prospective scuba divers to formal classes. Divers can explore the adjacent San Diego–La Jolla Underwater Ecological Reserve. Scripps Pier and the prestigious Scripps Institute of Oceanography border the north side of the Shores. Small boats, kayaks, and canoes float in the surf at the foot of Avenida de la Playa, the only beachfront boat launch within city limits. A four-wheel-drive vehicle is recommended, as the launch is simply sand. The lifeguard station is at the foot of Calle Frescota, as is the 350-space parking lot teeming with idling autos canvassing for a place to park during the busy summer months. A quarter-mile walkway separates the beach from Kellogg Park, a grassy area lined with tall palms, ideal for picnics, Frisbee tosses, and ogling the mansions on the hillside. Flanking the park are the rest rooms. Bring a sweatshirt and some firewood and stay past sunset; portable containers for beach fires are generally provided during the summer and are available on a first-come, first-served basis. *Map:JJ7*

MISSION BAY PARK / Bordered by I-5, Grand Ave, and Mission Blvd, Mission Bay; 619/221-8900 See Top 25 Attractions in this chapter.

MISSION BEACH / 3141 Ocean Front Walk, at Mission Blvd, Mission Beach; 619/221-8900 Do you enjoy a mass of humankind, lots of noise, sun and surf, and plenty of people watching? Then Mission Beach in mid-July may be the place for you. This section of sand between Pacific Beach and the Mission Bay channel entrance is a local favorite. The 12-foot-wide cement boardwalk that parallels the beach is a hotbed of sizzling activity; bikini-clad women race by on Rollerblades, guys in gravity-defying pants zoom around on skateboards, and bicyclists pedal past. There is an 8 mph speed limit, often ignored. When it's crowded, it's chaos; pay attention as you stroll. Should the frenzied pace of the board-walk be too much for you, wander toward the southern section of the beach and watch a pickup game of volleyball or a variation of softball called "Over The Line." If you forgot your sporting equipment, rental establishments are available to fill your needs. Surfing and swimming are both permitted in the ocean, with clearly delineated and enforced zones. There are plenty of lifeguards, rest rooms, shops, and restaurants. There's even a wonderful refurbished wooden roller coaster at Belmont Park at Ventura Place. Alas, the only thing there is never enough of is parking. Try your luck at the public lots on either side of Belmont Park or at the foot of West Mission Bay Drive. *Map:LL7*

MISSION TRAILS REGIONAL PARK / 1 Father Junipero Serra Trail, Tierra Santa; 619/668-3275 See Top 25 Attractions in this chapter.

OCEAN BEACH / 1950 Abbott Street, Ocean Beach; 619/221-8900 Ocean Beach has the same free and easy air as the community that shares its name. Wedged between the Ocean Beach Pier to the south and the Mission Bay channel entrance to the north, this city beach exudes a come-join-us attitude; there's always room for one more towel or a couple more toddlers at the shoreline. Summertime finds families, surfers, locals, and camera-toting tourists sharing the wide, sandy seashore. Even the family pet is allowed to join in the fun; the most northern part of the beach, aptly called Dog Beach, is the only city beach where dogs can run in the surf without the encumbrance of a leash. Owners are held responsible for the inevitable canine droppings, but it is still wise to watch where you put your bare feet. South of Dog Beach, buff men and women compete in pickup volleyball games and formal tournaments. Showers and rest rooms are located near the main lifeguard station at 1950 Abbott Street. Lifeguards are on duty year-round at this main tower; summer months bring additional crews to staff seasonal towers set up along the sand. They are kept busy with water rescues, as there is a strong rip current off this beach. If you tire of baking on the beach, stroll down the quarter-mile-long Ocean Beach Pier, where you can watch the surfers shoot through the pilings below, or the serious fishermen reeling in surf perch and white sea bass. (No fishing license is required here, but the catch limit is enforced.) Fishermen buy their bait at the small shop near the pier's center, next door to a cafe with a fabulous view. Finding a place to park is a no-brainer at Ocean Beach. There is a 300-car lot off West Point Loma Boulevard and another 110 spaces in the lot near the pier off Newport Avenue. If these are full, you can usually find a spot in the residential areas nearby. *Map:MM6*

OLD TOWN SAN DIEGO STATE HISTORIC PARK / Twiggs St, at Juan St, Old Town; 619/237-6770 See "Old Town" under Neighborhoods in this chapter.

PACIFIC BEACH / 950 Grand Ave, at Ocean Blvd, Pacific Beach; 619/221-8900 Three miles of sand teeming with humanity, Pacific Beach is one of San Diego's most popular beaches. With La Jolla bordering the north and Mission Beach to the south, intersected by the enchanting Crystal Pier at Garnet Avenue, it typifies the Southern California beach scene. In the northernmost section, under towering, tan cliffs, is Tourmaline Surfing Beach, its medium-size parking lot full of cars with surf racks. Wonderfully warm or blustery cold, nearly naked in baggy shorts or shivering in wet suits, the surfers are always here, riding the waves and then rinsing off at the colorfully painted showers at the foot of the parking lot. About a mile south of Tourmaline is Crystal Pier, a public fishing pier and home to the Crystal Pier Hotel. South of the pier are another two miles of Pacific Beach's powdery sand and rolling surf, replete with sunbathers, families with kids, bodysurfers, and boogie boarders. Paralleling the beach is a cement boardwalk, where bicyclists evade joggers and Rollerbladers dodge those on foot. There are rest rooms at Tourmaline Surfing Beach, at the foot of Grand Avenue by the lifeguard station and at Pacific Beach Drive. The beach is well staffed by lifeguards. Aside from the public parking lot on Tourmaline Street, you're on your own with the street parking hunt. *Map:KK7*

PRESIDIO PARK / 2811 Jackson St, Old Town; 619/692-4918 See "Old Town" under Neighborhoods in this chapter.

 SILVER STRAND STATE BEACH / 5000 Hwy 75, Coronado; 619/435-5184 See Top 25 Attractions in this chapter.

SPRECKELS PARK / 601 Orange Ave, at 6th St, Coronado; 619/522-7342 This clean, boxy little park in the heart of Coronado exudes a feeling of America gone by, with its old-fashioned gazebo, luxuriant green lawns, and spreading shade trees. It is still the center of Coronado's family gatherings, much like a central plaza in a Mexican village. Kids gather at the swing sets, parents sip cocktails (served from the disguise of thermoses) at picnic tables, and artists set up their easels in view of memorable scenes. The park is headquarters for frequent art and garden shows. Coronado Promenade Concerts has been putting on shows here for 25 years, with music ranging from jazz to the sounds of the U.S. Navy Concert Band. The series begins in June and runs through August, Sunday evenings at 6pm. Call 619/437-8788 for more information. *Map:NN5*

TIDELANDS PARK / Glorietta Blvd, at 4th St, Coronado; 619/686-6200 Under the jurisdiction of the Port of San Diego, this 22-acre park along San Diego Bay and under the Coronado Bay Bridge has a small beach area, recreational fields, play areas for the kiddies, and a soft sand shore where boaters stash their rafts and rowboats while collecting supplies onshore. A bike path runs under the Coronado Bay Bridge to the edge of the golf course. The Ferry Landing, a collection of shops, restaurants, and sports-rental stands, sits just north of the beach; mainlanders can catch the ferry from downtown and be on the beach in just minutes. Parking is free, but often scarce. *Map:NN5*

TORREY PINES STATE BEACH / 12600 N Torrey Pines Rd, La Jolla; 858/755-2063 Torrey Pines State Beach has 4-1/2 miles of shoreline, stretching from Del Mar past the marshy Los Peñasquitos Lagoon to the lofty sandstone cliffs of Torrey Pines Mesa. Crowning the cliffs like a jewel is the Torrey Pines State Reserve, serving as a beautiful backdrop to the water and sand below. During the cooler winter months, this beach is popular with surfers, especially when the swell arrives in good form from the south. Sun lovers jam the beach during the warmer months, and picnic baskets crammed with goodies dot the tables near the North Torrey Pines Road entrance. The rest rooms and showers are located here too; take the opportunity to rinse off those sandy children before hopping in the car for the ride home. State lifeguards keep vigil year-round. A large parking lot at the north end of the beach will fill your parking needs for a $4 fee. A smaller lot can be found off Carmel Valley Road. Parking on North Torrey Pines Road is free but hard to acquire. *Map:HH7*

TORREY PINES STATE RESERVE / 11000 N Torrey Pines Rd, La Jolla; 858/755-2063 See Top 25 Attractions in this chapter.

WINDANSEA BEACH / 6800 Neptune Pl, La Jolla; 858/221-8900 A Southern California surfing classic, Windansea Beach in La Jolla is for serious board jockeys only. Waves here tend to be bigger than those at other beaches in the area, and an underwater reef makes them break hard at the shore; entrance to the ocean should be accomplished with caution. Local surfers have a reputation for thinly veiled inhospitality toward newcomers who don't know their curls; those who can't appreciate their way around a "left shoulder" might want to try a less challenging surfing spot out of the way of the pros. If you just want to watch, set your beach chair on one of the large sandstone rocks that form much of the shore. Check out the thatched hut built on the sand and lovingly maintained by the Windansea Surf Club. One fully expects to see Frankie Avalon and Annette Funicello snuggling towel to towel beneath the palm fronds. Lifeguards are on duty in the summer but not necessarily in the winter; call to find out the staffing schedule. Other than the lifeguards, this beach is au naturel, with no showers or rest rooms. There is one small parking lot, or you can try your luck on Neptune Place. *Map:JJ7*

Organized Tours

To capture the true spirit of San Diego, start your visit in that wonderful microcosm, Balboa Park, the cultural heart of the city. Free tours encompassing history, architecture, theater, and natural attractions of the area are available; whether you're an avid birder or a culture buff, you'll find a tour geared to your tastes. The **COMMITTEE OF 100**, a nonprofit organization devoted to preserving the Spanish colonial architecture in Balboa Park, gives one-hour tours once a month; call 619/223-6566 for more information. For the thespian-minded, the **OLD GLOBE THEATRE** offers a behind-the-scenes perusal of its three stages, as well as a glimpse into the costume shop and craft areas. Tours are given most Saturdays and Sundays at 10:30am and cost $3; call 619/231-1941 for information. If the great outdoors calls, join a **NATURAL HISTORY MUSEUM'S CANYONEERS'** nature walk. These volunteer naturalists, trained in local flora, fauna, and geology, lead groups through a variety of San Diego's diverse habitats, including mountain, canyon, and desert terrains. The walks range from 1-1/2 to 6 hours long. Call 619/232-3821, extension 7 for scheduling information.

SPECIAL TOURS

The military is a major presence in San Diego, with Navy and Marine facilities and personnel; some interesting and informative public tours are available. **CAMP PENDLETON** in Oceanside, the Marine Corps' largest amphibious assault training facility, offers two types of tours. One is the self-guided driving tour, offered from 7am to 4pm. Show up at the gate with proof of insurance, registration, and a valid driver's license and you will be allowed to motor through the camp. A more up-close tour is available on the third Tuesday of every month, 9:30am to 3:30pm, with advance reservations required for groups of 25 or more. Call 760/725-5569 for more information.

Host ships offer fascinating tours of **NAVY VESSELS** at the Broadway Pier and also at the 32nd Street Pier. Tours are suspended during times of international conflict. Call the Navy Public Affairs Office at 619/532-1430 to find out if tours are available.

ARCO TRAINING CENTER / 2800 Olympic Pkwy, Chula Vista; 619/656-1500 Sports enthusiasts enjoy visiting the ARCO Olympic Training Center, where up to 60 athletes live on-site and many more have access to the facilities. The one-hour guided tour begins with a short video, followed by a walk through the state-of-the-art center. Visitors watch athletes training on the 400-meter track, the world-class field hockey, and soccer fields, and the largest permanent archery range in North America. Tours are offered every day, Monday through Saturday from 9am to 3:30pm, Sunday 12–3:30pm, but tour hours vary with the season. Groups of 10 or more must make reservations four weeks in advance. *www.olympic-usa.org; map:OO2* &

AIR TOURS

BIPLANE & AIR COMBAT ADVENTURES / 6743 Montia Ct, Carlsbad; 800/759-5667 Operating from the McClellan-Palomar Airport, this company offers aerial tours over San Diego's coastline and some of the more interesting sights inland. A 30-minute flight takes you down the coast from Carlsbad to Del Mar, then inland for a swoop over the opulent mansions of Rancho Santa Fe; another soars farther south over downtown and Coronado to the Mexico border and back. If you like stomach-churning aeronautics, the Red Baron Thrill Ride provides a one-hour mock combat adventure. Prices vary, but range from about $150 to $300. *www.barnstorming.com; map:CC8*

CIVIC HELICOPTERS / 192H Palomar Airport Rd, Carlsbad; 760/438-0451 This company, located at the McClellan-Palomar Airport, offers helicopter tours of the area starting at $75 per person for a half-hour flight; customized tours are available. *www.civichelicopters.com; map:CC8*

BOAT TOURS

HARBOR EXCURSIONS / 1050 N Harbor Dr, Downtown; 619/234-4111 or 800/442-7847 One- and two-hour harbor tours are available daily. Mini cruise ships take you under the Coronado Bridge and past huge Navy ships; the longer tour continues past Harbor and Shelter Islands to Point Loma. Departure times are seasonal—call for a schedule. The cost of the one-hour tour is $12 for adults, $6 for ages 4 to 12. The longer cruise costs $17 for adults and $8.50 for the kids. Whale-watching expeditions are also available during the gray whale's migration south (December through April). *www.sdro.com/sdhe; map:M7*

CLASSIC SAILING ADVENTURES / 2051 Shelter Island Dr, Downtown; 619/224-0800 Various boating experiences are offered aboard a 38-foot sailboat, the *Soul Diversion*, with a six-passenger maximum. The afternoon cruise from 1–5pm, sunset champagne cruise from 5:30–7:30pm, and seasonal whale-watching expeditions cost $50 per person. The boat is anchored at the Shelter Island Marina at the Island Palms Hotel. *Map:F7*

BAHIA STERNWHEELERS / 998 W Mission Bay Dr, Mission Bay; 858/539-7779 A Victorian-style stern-wheeler, the *Bahia Belle* features an open-air upper deck and two interior decks with oak walls, etched glass, and deep red curtains. Live music and a dance floor add to the entertainment as the paddle wheeler churns through Mission Bay on Friday and Saturday evenings throughout the year. Wednesday and Thursday tours are added during the summer. Call for exact departure times. *Map:LL6*

MOTOR TOURS

OLD TOWN TROLLEY TOURS OF SAN DIEGO / 2115 Kurtz St, Old Town; 619/298-8687 Tootling all over the city, these open-air red and green motorized trolleys are driven by jocular conductors who provide historical anecdotes on a two-hour jaunt. Passengers can depart the trolley at nine stops for a more thorough investigation, then reboard the next time a trolley rolls by. Trolleys come by each stop every 30 minutes, starting at 9am and ending in early evening; hours vary with the season. Locals who pay for the tour once annually are eligible for a Hometown Pass which allows them to ride free with a paying passenger. Tickets are $24 for an adult, $12 for ages 4 to 12, and free for children 3 and under. *Map:J3*

GRAY LINE SAN DIEGO / 1775 Hancock St, Ste 130, Middletown; 619/491-0011 or 800/331-5077 This company offers several tours, including the San Diego City Tour (adults $25, children 3 to 11 $11); Seaport Village and harbor cruise (adults $25, children $16); and a whirlwind Three-in-One tour including stops at 11 popular sights in San Diego, a one-hour boat tour of the harbor, and a stop in Tijuana for shopping (adults $50, children $22). All tours depart and return from the terminal at Hancock Street. *www.grayline.com; map:K3*

WALKING TOURS

ART TOURS / 5616 La Jolla Blvd, La Jolla; 858/459-5922 or 888/459-5922 For a different perspective on San Diego's scenery, join a five-hour art class and create your own vision of San Diego with guidance from a professional artist. Art Tours provides all the supplies and a gourmet lunch. Budding artists meet at visually appealing spots at Balboa Park, Presidio Park, or La Jolla Cove, among others. The cost is $139 per painter. Call for reservations. *Map:JJ7*

WALKABOUT INTERNATIONAL / 835 5th Ave, Rm 407, Downtown; 619/233-7463 Volunteer guides conduct Walkabout International tours, which include everything from a leisurely loop around Mission Bay to a hardy hike along the trails of Palomar Mountain. Tours are conducted morning, noon, and night and offer enough variety to please walkers of all persuasions and abilities. Call for schedules and tour descriptions. *Map:O7*

GASLAMP QUARTER HISTORICAL FOUNDATION / 410 Island Ave, Downtown; 619/233-4692 This nonprofit corporation promotes the historic and cultural development of downtown's 16-block Gaslamp Quarter, listed on the National Register of Historic Places. The organization offers two-hour tours, rain or shine, through a portion of the restored district every Saturday at 11am; cost is $5. *www.gqhf.com; map:N8*

CORONADO WALKING TOUR / 1110 Isabella Ave, Coronado; 619/435-5892 For a visit to some of Coronado's most interesting historical sites, join the Coronado Walking Tour for a 90-minute stroll that includes the Glorietta Bay Inn (former mansion of sugar baron J. D. Spreckels), the "Hotel Del," and the Cottage of the Duchess of Windsor. Tours leave Tuesday, Thursday, and Saturday at 11am from the Glorietta Bay Inn and cost $6. Call 619/35-5892 for more information. *Map:NN5*

SHOPPING

SHOPPING

We've got everything from Armani suits to zories (a.k.a. flip-flop sandals) up for grabs in San Diego in dozens of shopping zones. The malls and neighborhoods listed below cover most needs, though the best bakeries, camera shops, bookstores, and gift shops are scattered to the far ends of the county. Beach wear and sports gear rule among the coastline; ethnic markets hide in urban and rural areas. To shop like a master, study your options, map your trail, and combine touring with splurging. To help along the way, see the Neighborhoods section in this chapter.

DOWNTOWN SAN DIEGO

It's easy to conquer most of your shopping demands within the confines of downtown and come up with a few rare finds. Seaport Village displays kites and porch swings (great vacation mementos); Horton Plaza runs the gamut from Disney characters to serious designer boutiques; and the Gaslamp District presents a melange of specialty shops. In fact, shopping is everywhere in downtown—just don't miss the side streets. For more information about these three shopping areas, see Top 25 Attractions in the Exploring chapter.

HISTORIC DISTRICTS

A theme-park ambience prevails amid adobe cottages and turn-of-the-century barns in **OLD TOWN**. The historic buildings contain an ensemble of general stores, country-kitsch shops, and southwestern-style boutiques, but the real shopping fervor takes hold in **BAZAAR DEL MUNDO**. A fanciful version of a Mexican town plaza, the bazaar's stucco buildings—jammed with Latin American jewelry, clothing, household items, and gifts—face a central lawn and gazebo where folk art shows attract crowds. Each shop contains covetable works of art, from elaborate tin-framed mirrors to hand-painted Italian pottery.

NEIGHBORHOODS

Trendy shops line the main streets in **HILLCREST**, San Diego's alternative lifestyle neighborhood. Gay men strut their stuff in clothing from shops like International Male; couples browse hand in hand while seeking the perfect objects d'art for their stylish flats. The best shops are located on Fourth and Fifth between Pennsylvania and University; invest in a parking spot in a lot on University or Washington and devote several hours to eyeing books, flowers, clothing, and perfect pierced bods. Nearby **MISSION HILLS** is far more refined, with an emphasis on French country furnishings for the chic elite. Small antique, book, and video shops line **UNIVERSITY AVENUE** and **ADAMS AVENUE** from Hillcrest to Kensington, long an outpost for those who love historic homes buried in jacaranda blossoms.

The beach cities offer a whole different perspective, featuring bikinis, sunglasses, surfboards, and aloha shirts. **CORONADO** favors refined bookshops, florists, high-end sportswear boutiques, and small gift purveyors along Orange Avenue. **LA JOLLA**, the grande dame of style, is practically a six-square-block open-air mall. Virtually all the major international designers are featured in clothing and accessories shops and art galleries, and window-shopping is a lifestyle among locals and guests. Despite the rather snobbish air in the streets, the village also has garnered its fair share of chain stores, from Victoria's Secret to the Gap. Prospect and Girard are the hottest shopping strips; look for one-of-a-kind gift shops on the side streets.

Between the two stylish beaches lie the commoners' enclaves, each with a distinct character. **OCEAN BEACH** has recently lost many of its mom-and-pop shops to a succession of antique malls jam-packed with collectibles all along Newport Avenue. Vintage clothing also has its place here, beside a smattering of storefronts with metaphysical attitudes. Swimming suits, bikes, water toys, and beach togs predominate in shops along Mission Boulevard in **MISSION BEACH**. Chain stores like Pier One and Trader Joe's sit beside tattoo parlors, costume and vintage clothing shops, and used-furniture havens on Garnet Avenue in **PACIFIC BEACH**.

SHOPPING DISTRICTS

Being a tourist town, San Diego has an abundance of shopping/dining/entertainment theme parks filled with specialty shops. **SEAPORT VILLAGE** (Harbor Dr between Market St and 5th Ave, downtown; map:M8; see Top 25 Attractions in the Exploring chapter) has a nautical New England flair, with sidewalks winding past shops featuring hammocks, blown glass, sportswear, and souvenirs in every imaginable theme. **VILLAGE HILLCREST** (Washington St and 5th Ave, downtown; map:N2) specializes in small boutiques; nearby **UPTOWN DISTRICT** (University Ave between Washington and Richmond Sts, downtown; map:O2) has large grocery stores and some specialty shops. **DEL MAR PLAZA** (1555 Camino Del Mar, Del Mar; map:GG7) is beyond upscale, with excellent galleries, home furnishings shops, and clothing boutiques.

MALLS

Nothing compares with downtown's **HORTON PLAZA** (Broadway at 4th Ave, downtown; map:N7; see Top 25 Attractions in the Exploring chapter) when it comes to sheer architectural audacity and state-of-the-art shopping. But San Diego's more traditional malls have taken giant strides to become hip, user-friendly, and entrancing. **FASHION VALLEY** (707 Friars Rd, Mission Valley; 619/688-9113; map:LL5) has the best Nordstrom in town, along with great branches of Gap, Aveda, Crate and Barrel, Pottery Barn, and Godiva. **MISSION VALLEY** (1640 Camino del Rio N, Mission Valley; 619/296-6375; map:LL4) is more mid-brow, with giant branches of Nordstrom Rack, Macy's, and Montgomery Ward. It movie-theater complex is a big draw, as are several trendy restaurants The Golden Triangle and inland La Jolla area have several major shopping malls, **UNIVERSITY TOWNE CENTRE** (4525 La Jolla Village Dr 858/452-7766; map:JJ7), **LA JOLLA VILLAGE SQUARE** (8657 Villa La Jolla Dr; 858/455-7550; map:JJ7), and **COSTA VERDE CENTER** (8650 Nobel Dr; 858/458-9270; map:JJ6).

Shops from A to Z

ANTIQUES

ADAMS AVENUE CONSIGNMENT / 2873 Adams Ave, University Heights; 619/281-9663 Owner Jack Wilson knows his business and is an acknowledged expert within the antiques community. His two converted Craftsman houses, along Antique Row on Adams Avenue, are crammed full of '20s, '30s, and '40s furniture and lighting. If some of the paintings seem overpriced, the merchandise is generally considered a good value. *Tues–Sun; map:LL4*

THE ANTIQUE RADIO STORE / 8280 Clairemont Mesa Blvd, Ste 114, Clairemont; 858/268-4155 Tucked into a small corner of a nondescript shopping center, this store more than 100 styles of old radios for sale. Most have been reconditioned and all work. A Bakelite radio from the 1940s sells for about $75. *Mon, Wed, Sat; map:JJ5*

ARCHITECTURAL SALVAGE OF SAN DIEGO / 1971 India St, Middletown; 619/696-1313 With a background in art and a building contractor father, native San Diegan Elizabeth Scalice had the entrepreneurial savvy to open this fabulous storehouse of vintage and antique building materials in 1996. Since then it has grown in both size and popularity (Scalice expanded to the adjacent property in early 1997) as San Diegans search for leaded glass, claw-foot bathtubs, decorative molding, chandeliers, and old heater grates. There are glass building blocks from the 1940s and '50s and a bucket of rusty, square nails from the 1800s. It's worth a trip just to admire the beautiful collection of doorknobs. *Every day; map:M6*

CIRCA LA JOLLA / 7861 Herschel Ave, La Jolla; 858/454-7962 MaryJo Kalamon sells a mix of antique and vintage furniture and contemporary accessories. A teacher of interior design for 20 years, Kalamon happily answers decorating questions for her customers, helping them integrate antiques and newer furnishings, including custom-made items. *Mon–Sat; map:JJ7*

CORONADO ANTIQUES AND CONSIGNMENT / 1126 Orange Ave, Coronado; 619/435-7797 Located just a block and a half from the Hotel del Coronado, this is not the place to find the super bargains. But it usually stocks an impressive collection of high-end furniture, porcelain, crystal, and miniature portraits on ivory. *Mon-Sat; map:NN5*

D. D. ALLEN ANTIQUES / 7728 Fay Ave, La Jolla; 858/454-8708 With a strong reputation throughout the antiques community, this small store has 18th to 20th century furniture, linens, porcelain, and decorative art. *Every day; map:JJ7*

GLORIOUS ANTIQUES / 7643 Girard Ave, La Jolla; 858/459-2222 This not-for-profit store is one of the few charity outfits that sells antiques, including estate jewelry, linens, and Asian and European collectibles. The beneficiaries of sales are the SPCA and the San Diego Humane Society, making this a worthwhile place to spend your cash. *Mon–Sat; map:JJ7*

THE CORNER STONE / 7501 Girard Ave, La Jolla; 858/456-7517 Described as purveyors of "shabby chic," the owners of this airy boutique sell a unique mix of primitive, rustic, and cottage furniture and garden pieces. You'll find trundle tables that have been repainted and then distressed, and plenty of dressers, cabinets, and seating from the '40s and '50s. Also on hand are antique and vintage garden accessories, Bauer bowls, and other small period pieces. Although some of the inventory verges on country cutesy, the store is definitely worth a look. *Every day; map:JJ7*

JP AND COMPANY / 7844 Herschel Ave, La Jolla; 858/456-7688 Selling both reproductions and antique furnishings and accessories on consignment and outright, this enormous shop has a warehouse feel. It's fun to wander among the enormous cast-metal gorillas and alligators that share the floor with water-buffalo leather couches, animal print settees, and hassocks, lighting, and accessories. Large-format framed art hangs on the wall. *Every day; map:JJ7*

KING AND COMPANY / 7470 Girard Ave, La Jolla; 858/454-1504 Owner Candace King and her associates stock a varied selection of English, American, and Continental furniture and accessories in a warm, unpretentious atmosphere. This long, deep store contains mainly antique furniture and decorative art from the 1700s to early 1900s. The fact that the associates are principally designers and artists themselves makes this a favorite stop for the county's interior design mavens. King and company also offer home consultations. *Mon–Sat; map:JJ7*

OCEAN BEACH ANTIQUES MALL / 4878 Newport Ave, Ocean Beach; 619/223-6170 One of Ocean Beach's many antique stores along Newport Avenue, this one is airy and well-organized, with calming music in the background. You don't get overwhelmed by the sheer volume of merchandise, as happens in some stores. It's a great place for gift shopping, with a large selection of jewelry and porcelain. In fact, the majority of the items are "smalls," including household and kitchen accessories. *Every day; map:B3*

PIED-A-TERRE / 7645 Girard Ave, La Jolla; 858/456-4433 Although this La Jolla shop (French for "second home," or "where your foot rests on the earth") is just a couple of years old, owner Javid Nazarian has been collecting for over 15 years. Treasure hunters will love searching through the overwhelming jumble of 17th- to 19th-century pieces, although claustrophobes may need to dash outside occasionally for air. There's a good mix of lighting, indoor and outdoor furniture, and tchotchkes, mainly Oriental and European. *Mon–Sat; map:JJ7*

UNICORN ANTIQUE MALL / 704 J St, Downtown; 619/232-1696 EMPIRE ENTERPRISE / 704 J St Downtown; 619/239-9216 Friendly Ken Freeman, co-owner of this Gaslamp venue, is both super-knowledgeable and generous with his time. A former elementary school teacher, he has the ability to educate without making you feel dim. The three-story antique mall is home to 100 different dealers and, with 30,000 square feet, is the county's largest. Within the mall, Freeman's Empire Enterprise has 3000 square feet of antiques and period vintage, including a great collection of clocks from the 1800s and later, and an excellent collection of vintage gold and silver jewelry. *Every day; map:O8*

APPAREL

ARIANA / 2754 Calhoun St, Bazaar del Mundo, Old Town; 619/296-4989 This eclectic store sells bold and colorful women's styles with an ethnic flair. Southwest designs are popular, but you're just as likely to find handcrafted dresses from Indonesia or Europe. Hand-painted silks are popular. The prices are surprisingly reasonable. Don't miss Ariana's Bargain Bazaar downstairs, where you can find deals from several of the Bazaar's shops. *Every day; map:J2*

ARMANI EXCHANGE / 7802 Girard Ave, La Jolla; 858/551-8193 Part of an exclusive clothing store district in downtown La Jolla, this branch of the chic national chain is the store to find the casual wear appropriate for a sunny stroll through the upscale community. It features the designer's latest men's and women's weekend sportswear, as well as a full line of belts, bags, and other accessories. *Every day; map:JJ7*

THE ASCOT SHOP / 7750 Girard Ave, La Jolla; 858/454-4222 As the name implies, this iconic La Jolla men's clothing store features traditional and elegant wear. Labels such as Hickey-Freeman and Talbot are featured. But there's more than traditional knitwears; the store stocks everything from socks and underwear to suits and ties, and has an in-house tailor, making this a perfect spot for one-stop shopping. A few blocks away a related store, Ascot Sport, sells sportswear (1251 Prospect St; 858/456-1451). *Mon–Sat; map:JJ7*

DESIGNER SHOPPING

What began as a light-industry neighborhood hidden beside the railroad tracks in Solana Beach has become one of Southern California's premier design districts. The **Cedros Design District** is the offspring of a neighborhood association of merchants who breathed new life into a quarter-mile section of South Cedros Avenue. The district's gateway (signaled by arching signs over the roadway) lies at Lomas Santa Fe Drive, one block east of the main coast route, Highway 101.

Attracted by low rents in a block-long Quonset-like building and light-filled spaces inside a 1950s Moderne-style electronics factory, the Bohemian fringe moved in during the 1980s. Artists, furniture and antique dealers, importers, and high-end gift retailers have now completely taken over the neighborhood. Shedding its blue-collar architectural origins, Cedros Design District has grown into a hip, attractive, and remarkably pedestrian-friendly neighborhood where shoppers stroll beneath vine-covered trellises, wander from shop to shop, and pause to sip coffee and nibble lemon-pecan cookies on the patio of **Cafe Zinc** (132 S Cedros Ave; 858/793-5436) beneath umbrella-like pepper trees. Allow yourself at least two hours to visit some of the district's highlights, including **Kern & Co.** (858/792-7722), Indonesian-made furniture and other designer finds; **Adventure 16** (858/755-7662), expedition-quality outdoor equipment and clothing; **Birdcage** (858/793-6262), casual-chic gifts and decor; and, anchoring it all, the **Belly Up Tavern** (143 S Cedros Ave; 858/481-9022), which has brought headliner bands into town since 1975 when they pioneered the district's makeover. (All located in the neighborhood's longest building at 142 South Cedros Avenue.) On the east side of the street, don't miss **Cassidy West** (112 S Cedros Ave; 858/755-2728), for Southwest furnishings, and **Trios Gallery** (130 S Cedros Ave; 858/793-6040), one of the county's best showcases for fine arts, crafts, and jewelry.

Although not much larger than a large closet, nearby **Mistral La Compagnie De Provence** (146 S Cedros Ave; 858/755-3613) packs every inch of its shop with soaps, oils, and other bathing paraphernalia, all imported from southern France. **The Antique Warehouse** (212 S Cedros Ave; 858/755-5156) packs dozens of small dealers' booths into a tidy mall of collectibles, while **Cedars Trading Co.** (307 S Cedros Ave; 858/794-9016) features multiple independent importers of new crafts and furnishings from Mexico, Africa, Indonesia, and Europe. **Cedros Gardens** (330 S Cedros Ave; 858/792-8640) is a fine little nursery and more—step inside to browse their garden gifts.

—Peter Jensen

ATOMIC TRADING COMPANY / 1036 Garnet Ave, Pacific Beach; 858/272-8822 Owner Eric Kramer describes the store's offerings as "futuristic sport utilitarian." That translates to sporty styles with big pockets for the happening Gen-Xer. Wild plastic light fixtures help give the store a retro look. Some of the nostalgic styles are kitschy, with plenty of references to the '50s and '60s, but it's not novelty wear. Kramer says he aims for "cool and different cuts." Atomic also has the footwear and hip glasses to complete the perfect club-hopping ensemble. *Every day; map:KK7*

ENCORE OF LA JOLLA / 7655 Girard Ave, La Jolla; 858/454-7540 You'd never guess this is a used clothing store; the atmosphere is classic Beverly Hills boutique. But instead of castoffs, it specializes in gently used top designer labels for men and women, including Armani, Chanel, and Versace. There is a plentiful selection of contemporary men's suits. If you're lucky, you'll find heavily discounted Prada bags and Ferragamo shoes. *Every day; map:JJ7*

INTERNATIONAL MALE / 3964 5th Ave, Hillcrest; 619/294-8600 As much a part of the gay Hillcrest scene as it is a place to pick up stylish briefs and jackets, this homegrown shop (with a huge catalog business) seems like a local hangout for male models. The styles tend toward the European cafe/dashing poet look. Prices are outrageous, but it's quintessential for trendy male fashion. *Every day; map:N2*

NICOLE MILLER / 1275 Prospect Ave, La Jolla; 858/454-3434 When La Jolla's society prepares to gather, this is where the women go to dress. Miller, the New York–based high-end designer, specializes in cocktail dresses and evening wear, although many rave about her sportswear too. For something different, check out her men's silk novelty ties. *Every day; map:JJ7*

PILAR'S BEACHWEAR / 3745 Mission Blvd, Mission Beach; 858/488-3056 California bikini styles tend to be a bit more conservative than the daring down-to-there ones on the Caribbean or French Riviera. Pilar's offers a full line of the latest and hottest SoCal designs, as well as many of the big-name international lines such as Oscar de la Renta. It also goes beyond the latest waif-wear to offer a wide variety of sizes. Mission Beach can get crowded, but parking is available in the back. *Every day; map:LL7*

RON STUART MEN'S CLOTHING / 1110 5th Ave, Hillcrest; 619/232-8850 In the downtown area, this well-stocked men's store offers stylish wear for both the afternoon at the country club and the evening dinner party. It focuses on the European styles of such designers as Joseph Abboud and Jhane Barnes, but you can also go more traditional with

Chequers. Best of all, there's a tailor on-site for fashion emergencies. *Mon–Sat; map:N7*

BAKERIES

A LA FRANÇAISE / 4029 Goldfinch St, Mission Hills; 619/294-4425 If you're looking for a quiet spot to pick up a flaky croissant and peruse Le Monde, look no more. Nestled in a corner a block off Mission Hills's main drag, in the heart of a nice little antiques enclave, the shop has a small outside patio that captures the morning sun. The fresh breads, pastries, and strong coffee keep people coming back; so does the array of European desserts. Wholesale rates are available. *Every day; map:M2*

BAKED BY ETTA / 3635 India St, Middletown; 619/291-4074 Don't let the screen door scare you off. Etta Miller is a charming hostess, and she's more than willing to give you a personal tour of her fresh-baked treats. The selection changes every day, based on her whims. Chocolate meltaways and cappuccino caramel cheesecake are among her specialties. During the holidays she prepares special Christmas-tree cookies and cakes. *Mon–Fri; map:L3*

BREAD & CIE / 350 University Ave, Hillcrest; 619/683-9322 As the name implies, this popular spot is known for its crusty bread. Each day 12 to 15 types are baked fresh, including such exotic flavors as rosemary olive oil, kalamata olive, and jalapeño cheese. There is also a full cafe with sweet baked goods (see Restaurants chapter). Limited catering is available. *Every day; map:N2*

CLAYTON'S PIES & BAKERY / 650 F St, Downtown; 619/235-9100 Several area restaurants buy pies from this downtown institution, which bakes 26 varieties every day. The menu includes everything from such traditional stalwarts as Dutch apple and cherry to key lime and butterscotch, along with 10 different quiche flavors. Delivery is available for a small charge. *Every day; map:N7*

EUROPEAN CAKE GALLERY / 3661 Voltaire St, Point Loma; 619/222-3377 Longtime Point Loma residents rave about this old-world bakery, which specializes in special cakes for special occasions. The Swiss Black Forest cake is one of the most popular, along with the German chocolate and carrot cakes. During the holidays, try the special mouth-watering stollen. *Tues–Sat; map:E4*

GROVE PASTRY SHOP / 3308 Main St, Lemon Grove; 619/466-3277 San Diegans have been buying birthday and wedding cakes here since 1953. The whipped-cream icing alone is worth the drive to this inland community about 15 minutes from downtown. *Mon–Sat; map:MM2*

KAREN KRASNE'S EXTRAORDINARY DESSERTS / 2929 5th Ave, Middletown; 619/294-7001 Sure, a slice of cake can run $3 or more, but price be damned: Krasne bakes up the best, and prettiest, desserts in town. Tortes, tarts, even simple oatmeal cookies and lemon bars are made from the finest ingredients. Forget taking wine to your host's dinner; pick up one of these babies and you'll be swamped with invites forevermore. *Every day; map:N4*

SOLUNTO BAKING COMPANY / 1643 India St, Middletown; 619/233-3506 Italian delis all over the city buy their bread from this old-time bakery in Little Italy. Regulars stop by several times a week for that same bread as well as deli sandwiches, cannoli, and a huge variety of Italian cookies. *Mon–Sat; map:M6*

BODY CARE

AVEDA LIFESTYLE STORE / 7007 Friars Rd, Fashion Valley Center, Mission Valley; 619/220-8518 Proudly eschewing nonrenewable resources, Aveda makes beauty products with organically grown herbs and botanicals. Earth-friendly policies include limited packaging, recycling, and no animal testing. One of the two perfume lines was developed to coincide with and stimulate the body's seven chakras. The saleswomen will help you blend your own fragrance, which can then be mixed into a full line of hair, body care, and beauty products. *Every day; map:LL5*

BATH & BODY WORKS / 7007 Friars Rd, Fashion Valley Center, Mission Valley (and branches); 619/294-4549 This U.S. bath and beauty boutique chain (a sister company to Victoria's Secret, which is also owned by Intimate Brands) is positively awash in fruity, bubbly smells. Fifteen different toiletry fragrances emanate from plain pine barrels in the form of lotions and gels, bath powder, and body scrubs. Try the testers scattered throughout the store, and if you get carried away, wash up at the easy-access sink. For gift giving, grab an oversize coffee mug or picture frame netted up with fragrant lotions or soothing bath salts. In addition to the toiletry scents, the store stocks aromatherapy, tropical, and seasonal (Christmas and Mother's Day) fragrances. Buy scented and unscented candles at the Bath & Body Works at Home store next door (Fashion Valley location only). *Every day; map:LL5*

BEAUTY CLINIC-KLINIEK / 3268 Governor Dr, Marketplace Shopping Center, Golden Triangle; 858/457-0191 Linda Anne Kahn, who has traveled the world studying health and beauty treatments, has owned and operated one of San Diego's most popular day spas for more than 16 years. The 5,000-square-foot spa's specialty is aromatherapy, but there are tons of specialized treatments. All bodyworkers are HHPs (holistic health practitioners, with over 1,000 hours of training); all facialists are trained in Europe. At the front of the spa, French bath and body care products are sold; most are botanically based. Lines include Becleor, Yonka, Epicuren, Murad, and MD Formulations. *Every day; www.beauty kliniek.com; map:JJ6*

THE BODY SHOP SKIN & HAIR CARE / 7864 Girard Ave, La Jolla (and branches); 858/459-6006 The Body Shop is known for its attentive sales staff, eager to answer questions and offer suggestions. Although it's not store policy to mix individual perfume oils, some attendants will do so for the interested customer. The ecologically correct store encourages customers to return empty containers for recycling and keeps packaging to a minimum. There's a line of good-quality yet inexpensive cosmetics; the shop also has shampoos, lotions, bath beads and salts in a wide range of scents, and bath accessories. Try the intoxicating mango or nut body butter. *Every day; map:JJ7*

ECOTIQUE AVEDA SALON / 12925 El Camino Real, Del Mar (and branches); 858/794-8991 This salon offers haircuts, massage, facials, and other skin-care treatments at reasonable prices in addition to selling the Aveda line of beauty products. *Every day; map:GG7*

LA COMPAGNIE DE PROVENCE / 3870 5th Ave, Hillcrest; 619/295-8322 Owner Pierre Monnoyer's one-of-a-kind body and fragrance store specializes in bath and body products from the south of France. His suppliers are mainly family-owned businesses from Provence, such as Molinard, which has been fabricating natural soaps since 1849, and Fragonard, a beauty soap maker since 1900. Many products use shea butter, made from nuts from African trees, as their main ingredient; this 100% natural substance is favored in France. Monnoyer also sells candles, tablecloths, and handmade ceramics from southern France. *Every day; www.lacompagniedeprovence.com; map:N2*

PARFUMERIE / 324 Horton Plaza, Downtown; 619/231-4124 The bright red cart, parked in front of Mervyn's on Horton Plaza's third level, looks like an old-fashioned portable puppet stage. In reality it is filled with a variety of brand-name scents and is staffed by agreeable and knowledgeable sales people happy to supply answers and bathe you in scent. You can special-order by calling 800/552-0705. *Every day; map:N7*

SEPHORA / 4545 La Jolla Village Dr, University Towne Centre, Golden Triangle; 858/457-1983 A French company with retail stores around the world, Sephora's first San Diego location opened to much fanfare in April 1999. Its sales techniques are low pressure and hands-on. Products are readily accessible on open shelves and are grouped by type, not by brand name: perfumes are along one wall, while bath products have their own area. In addition to multinationals such as Estée Lauder and Lancôme, Sephora sells its own line of cosmetics, as well as niche brands often unavailable outside their normal distribution areas. A Fashion Valley location is due to open in the winter of 2000. *Every day; www.sephora. com; map:JJ6*

U.S. HOUSE APOTHECARY AND SOAP SHOP / 2765 San Diego Ave, Old Town; 619/574-1115 What at first glance appears to be a cutesy soap shop in historical Old Town is, on closer inspection, a fabulous apothecary. Owner and master soap maker Ruth Ritchart creates all of her own products from scratch, including 26 scented soaps and creams and 10 different soothing varieties of Epsom salts. She began her business selling mail-order and at street fairs, and opened her first shop here in August 1998. A soon-to-open upstairs salon will sell tinctures and other herbal remedies, with an herbalist on-site to make recommendations and prepare concoctions. Don't forget to sniff the herbal pillows in the back room. *Every day; www.ritchartoils.com; map:I1*

BOOKS AND PERIODICALS

BARNES & NOBLE BOOKSELLERS / 7610 Hazard Center Dr, Mission Valley (and branches); 619/220-0175 Yes, B&N is one of the country's largest booksellers and the bane of small shops. But it does have an astounding selection of titles in a comfortable setting with plenty of tables and chairs for browsers. Book signings are held at all branches; look for the big-name authors here. *Every day; map:LL4*

 BAY BOOKS / 1029 Orange Ave, Coronado; 619/435-0070 Don't think about stopping by this entrancing shop unless you have time to spare. The selection of travel tomes, best-sellers, books on tape, and Spanish-language novels is overwhelming. Fortunately, the staff is beyond helpful and customers are welcome to browse through their selections in the quiet reading room. The sidewalk cafe tables are a perfect spot for reading the *International Herald Tribune*. Author signings are held regularly. *Every day; map:NN5*

BLUE DOOR LITERARY BOOKSTORE / 3823 5th Ave, Hillcrest; 619/298-8610 One of Hillcrest's surviving independent booksellers, the Blue Door specializes in gay and lesbian literature, obscure and well-known; the classics are also featured, along with worthwhile selections from small presses. *Every day; map:N2*

BOOKSTAR / 3150 Rosecrans Pl, Point Loma; 619/225-0465 The Loma Theater, once one of San Diego's grandest movie palaces, has been transformed into this enormous bookstore, with magazines and cards packed in the lobby and shelves lining the sloping amphitheater toward the stage. Members receive a discount on all purchases, but the selection is fairly mainstream. *Every day; map:G3*

BORDERS BOOKS & MUSIC / 1072 Camino del Rio N, Mission Valley; 619/295-2201 Even those who boycott most large booksellers can't resist

Borders' excellent selection of books and music presented in a sensible layout. The staff is quite well-informed, and Borders has become one of the main venues in town for signings by top-name and new authors. *Every day; map:LL4*

CASA DEL LIBRO / 1735 University Ave, Hillcrest; 619/299-9331 Spanish-language novels, dictionaries, and classics are stocked at this small shop favored by students and San Diego's large bilingual population. *Every day; map:P2*

CONTROVERSIAL BOOKSTORE / 3021 University Ave, University Heights; 619/296-1560 Feeling metaphysical, psychic, or downright mystical? Stop by this incense-scented shop, which has been in business for more than three decades—well before the New Age movement took off. Tarot cards like you've never seen lie among precious crystals and minerals. Best of all, you'll get sensible advice from those who can separate authentic spirituality from the fads. *Every day; map:MM4*

GROUNDS FOR MURDER MYSTERY BOOK STORE / 3940 4th Ave, Hillcrest; 619/299-9500 Have your reading habits moved far beyond mainstream mysteries into the truly weird? Then this is your store. The owners are devoted to their clientele, offering readings by cult authors and parties where guests work out tangled plots. *Every day; map:N2*

HILLCREST NEWSSTAND / 529 University Ave, Hillcrest; 619/260-0462 Every imaginable social trend is covered in the magazine selection at this busy stand located near several coffeehouses and cafes. It's also close to two large hospitals, and provides a welcome break for visitors seeking diversion or gifts for patients. *Every day; map:N2*

JOHN COLE'S BOOK SHOP / 780 Prospect St, La Jolla; 858/454-4766 Gnarled vines laden with clusters of lavender blossoms twine through the arbor leading to the Wisteria Cottage, the historic home of the Scripps sisters, doyennes of early La Jolla. The Irving Gill architecture alone is worth the trip; the bookstore inside is a romantic's dream. Piles of new and treasured used books tumble about; the section of old Mexico and San Diego travel books is a delight. Bedrooms, dens, and sitting rooms are devoted to art, architecture, and classics. Readers' collectibles are scattered throughout. Zach's Music Corner in a side room is a collector's haven, with rare jazz albums and what's said to be the largest selection of harmonicas on the West Coast. *Every day; map:JJ7*

LIBROS / 2754 Calhoun St, Bazaar del Mundo, Old Town; 619/299-1139 Gorgeous hardbound architecture, art, and travel books line one wall of this shop, where kids can't resist the back room devoted to their interests. Those who collect greeting cards as if they were fine art should plan to spend major bucks here. *Every day; map:I1*

NEWPORT NEWS / 4949 Newport Ave, Ocean Beach; 619/225-2300
Comic books, surfing magazines, and Latin American periodicals attract a colorful clientele to this Ocean Beach shop, which also displays a tempting array of Brazilian foodstuffs. *Every day; map:B3*

PARAS NEWSSTAND / 3911 30th St, North Park; 619/296-2859 The selection of out-of-town and international periodicals here far exceeds your typical public library; homesick newcomers catch up on their news from back home while scouring papers from Seattle to Singapore. Fashion mags from France, travel mags from China—you name it, Paras has it. *Every day; map:MM4*

PSYCHIC EYE BOOK SHOP / 702 Pearl St, La Jolla; 858/551-8877 Gargoyles, crystal balls, indoor fountains, and bowls of beads fulfill this shop's claim to offer "books and supplies for all persuasions." Fifteen-minute psychic readings are available on request; the selection of books on healing and spirituality is excellent. *Every day; map:JJ7*

RAND MCNALLY MAP & TRAVEL STORE / 243 Horton Plaza, Downtown; 619/234-3341 Globes, atlases, and maps galore delight world travelers, who also can't resist highly detailed tomes describing their favorite destinations. The selection of magnifying glasses, compasses, and travel gear is equally impressive. *Every day; map:N7*

UPSTART CROW BOOKSTORE & COFFEEHOUSE / 835 W Harbor Dr, Seaport Village, Downtown; 619/232-4855 Stuck in SD on a rainy day? Claim a cozy armchair in the upstairs reading room and let the hours drift by as you pore over magazines, novels, and mysteries from the bookshelves downstairs. The selection is fairly mainstream, but you'll find plenty of local lore and fellow readers who enjoy lofty conversation. *Every day; map:M8*

WAHRENBROCK'S BOOK HOUSE / 726 Broadway, Downtown; 619/232-0132 Dusty treasures tumble and topple from shelves in this three-story literary paradise beloved by collectors of antiquarian and rare used books. Owner Chuck Wahrenbrock and his staff can point the way to almost anything you need (and some things you didn't know you had to have). They'll also track down titles not in stock. *Every day; map:N7*

WARWICK'S / 7812 Girard Ave, La Jolla; 858/454-0347 Staff members memorize their customers' names and interests at this long-standing neighborhood shop, which first opened in 1896. Generations of La Jollans have established accounts here, relying on the stationery staff to supply perfect party invitations and personalized note cards. The selection by local authors may be the best in the county, and signings by best-selling celebrities attract long lines of fans. *Every day; map:JJ7*

THE WHITE RABBIT / 7755 Girard Ave, La Jolla; 858/454-3518 What a magical hole you fall into after passing a 4-foot-high rabbit at the front door. This wonderland is devoted completely to children's interests, with something for all ages from infant to teen. Devoted aunts and uncles find valuable guidance when seeking the perfect gift; parents delight in the weekly story time and the opportunity to encourage a love of books. Call for a copy of the newsletter—it's a treasure trove of information for young readers. *Every day; map:JJ7*

CANDY AND CHOCOLATE

GODIVA CHOCOLATIER INC. / 7007 Friars Rd, Fashion Valley Center, Mission Valley (and branches); 619/293-7492 Godiva always presents chocolate with flair. It's a world of rich flavors, gold wrap. and elegant gifts—for example, a special-occasion cigar box full of individually wrapped milk-chocolate cigars. Try slipping a ring from one of the mall's jewelers into a Godiva box for a sure-fire romantic gesture. Other locations are in La Jolla (4415 La Jolla Village Dr; 858/638-7337) and in Escondido's North County Fair (200 East Via Rancho Pkwy; 760/743-7414). *Every day; map:LL5*

MAKE MINE SWEET / 4705 Clairemont Dr, Clairemont; 858/273-8234 The first thing identifying this store as a little different are the 10 "candy art" pieces spoofing artistic masterpieces. This is also the place to find a one-of-a-kind line of San Diego chocolate gifts, such as a bottle of champagne made of pure milk chocolate adorned with a label featuring the Coronado Bridge, or a box of meltaway chocolates wrapped in a unique watercolor of the Carlsbad flower fields. Sample the sugar-free specialties. You can buy 200 candies by the pound. *Every day; www.makemine sweet.com; map:JJ6*

SEE'S CANDIES / 107 Horton Plaza, Downtown (and branches); 619/233-5450 They give you a free piece of candy for buying something at this national candy shop chain displaying old-fashioned nut chews, creams, and mints encased in dark and milk chocolate. Gift boxes are flown all over the country during holidays as former San Diegans request caramel lollipops, sour balls, and pounds of assorted candies. Other locations are in the North County Fair, Plaza Camino Real, Fashion Valley, and Grossmont Center malls. *Every day; www.sees.com; map:N7*

COFFEE AND TEA

THE COFFEE BEAN & TEA LEAF / 3865 5th Ave, Hillcrest; 619/293-5908 This California-based company has about 50 stores nationwide, but only one in San Diego. All coffees are the same price, so you can exclude that factor when making a decision. The most popular bean is the Viennese dark roast. A truly astonishing selection of teas from China, Formosa, India, and Ceylon can be boggling. Consider the handpicked Jasmine

Dragon Phoenix Pearl from China, or one of many black, oolong, green, or herb teas. Straightforward brochures give the origin and price of each coffee or tea, and describe its special characteristics. Desserts are provided by local bakeries Le Provence and House of Tudor. The assortment of imaginative coffee and tea accessories make great gifts. For mail order coffee and teas, call 800/832-5323. *Every day; map:N2*

GARDEN HOUSE COFFEE & TEA / 2480 San Diego Ave, Old Town; 619/220-0723 The perfect spot to stop for a hammerhead (double) espresso while exploring Old Town, this small shop is a bit incongruous. Don't expect the owner to recommend a coffee or tea—he doesn't drink the stuff. But he does provide a pleasant respite and a fair selection of bulk beans and leaves. *Every day; map:J2*

PANNIKIN COFFEE AND TEA / 675 G St, Downtown (and branches); 619/239-7891 The downtown branch of San Diego's most tenacious coffee and tea purveyor is located in a turn-of-the-century red brick building in the heart of the city. There are coffees from four continents: dark roasts, espresso roasts, blends, decaf, and organics, in addition to an outstanding collection of black and herb teas. The company roasts its beans here, and the aroma is irresistible. You'll save a dollar per pound by purchasing the coffee of the month. Freestanding open display cases in the airy interior contain an eclectic, well-chosen collection of ethnic baskets, mugs, and small kitchen utensils. Wall shelves hold fine tea towels, tea pots, thermoses, and European coffeemakers. You can buy brewed coffee, tea, and pastries as well. Order beans and teas by calling 800/232-6482. *Mon–Sat; map:N8*

PEET'S COFFEE & TEA / 350 University Ave, Hillcrest; 619/296-5995 ■ 8843 Villa La Jolla Dr, La Jolla; 858/678-0806 Peet's was born in the '60s in Berkeley, California, before gourmet coffee became part of the middle-class lexicon. The espresso counter serves the usual brews, with juice and some baked goods; get a free cuppa joe when you buy a pound of beans. (Soy milk is available for the lactose intolerant.) The airy, open salon—with seating in the form of wooden church pews, polished stone bar tables, and a bar facing the comings and goings along University Avenue—makes for a pleasant rendezvous spot. Nonetheless, the emphasis is on the sale of hand-roasted beans from the Americas, Arabia and Africa, and the Pacific. If you're a coffee neophyte, take Coffee 101: a blend of coffees from the three areas. There's literature aplenty on how to store your coffee and wash your coffeemaker. Bring your own cup and save the planet and a dime. The small but classy selection of Chinese and Japanese teas and coffeepots, mugs, and accessories is perfect if you need a quick housewarming gift. *Every day; map:N2 and JJ7*

STARBUCKS / 3801 5th Ave, Hillcrest (and branches); 619/295-9310
Named after the java-swilling first mate in Melville's *Moby Dick*, Starbucks has definitely become the Martha Stewart of the coffee scene. Although it's easy to poke fun, they do have high standards for freshness and quality; beans that sit in the bins more than a week are donated to charity or sold at discount stores. This locale is in the heart of Hillcrest, home of the Chicken Pie Shop until the early 1990s. The display menus will help you choose the beans that suit your style: Milder Dimensions™ are described as "light, mild, and welcoming," as opposed to Lively Impressions™, which are "flavorful, bright, and inviting." Did someone say Martha Stewart? *Every day; map:N2*

ETHNIC MARKETS

99 RANCH / 7330 Clairemont Mesa Blvd, Clairemont; 858/565-7799
The name may be an enigma, but this complex houses just about every kind of Asian food there is. As you enter, you'll pass several fast-food eateries serving Vietnamese, Taiwanese, and Chinese food and a juice bar offering grass jelly, almond tofu, and coconut milk. The Taiwanese snack shack displays salty duck eggs or simmered seaweed. The store itself has live geoduck clams, Dungeness crab, striped bass, and catfish on ice. In the grocery aisles, you'll find chili bamboo shoots next to Oscar Mayer lunch meats, pickled bitter gourd alongside Pringles. Or try fish sauce, Chinese mustard, duck eggs, cuttlefish balls, fresh frozen grated coconut . . . you get the idea. The produce section has a good variety of unusual greens. *Every day; map:JJ5*

ANDRES LATIN AMERICAN MARKET / 1249 Morena Blvd, Bay Park; 619/275-6523 Devotees of all things Cubano are thrilled with this tiny market, where several brands of black beans, yellow rice, anchovy-stuffed olives, and tamarind paste are displayed amid candles bearing the images of saints. Costa Rican Lizano sauce (a piquant veggie salsa), Mexican cheeses, and candied papaya delight those seeking familiar and foreign tastes. The small restaurant next door serves authentic Cuban sandwiches, with soft rolls packed high with cheese, meat, pickles, lettuce, and secret sauce. *Every day; map:LL5*

ASSENTI'S PASTA COMPANY / 2044 India St, Middletown; 619/239-5117 Opened in 1980 by Adriana Assenti, an immigrant from Italy's Adriatic coast, this wonderful pasta shop is now run by sons Roberto and Luigi. Pastas come in 13 shapes (including fusilli, pappardelle, angel hair, and lasagna sheets) and such exotic flavors as squid ink, black bean, chipotle chili, and onion parsley in addition to more traditional basil and lemon pepper. 12 to 15 combos of flavor and shape are available daily; for more exotic combos, order a few days in advance. Fresh pasta sauces are sold by the pound or half pound. On Valentine's Day, surprise your sweetheart with the handmade, heart-shaped, red-and-white-striped ravioli filled with pine nuts and feta cheese. In addition to the fresh sauces and pastas, Assenti's sells imported and domestic olive oil, cheeses, deli meats, and more. *Mon–Sat; map:M6*

CARAVAN MARKET / 3200 Adams Ave, Ste 101, Normal Heights; 619/280-2330 This small neighborhood market specializes in East European products, including salt cod, sardines in oil, cacao powder, pelmeni (dumplings of meat or potatoes and apples), and Polish deli meats: bologna, salami, and pepper-topped pork loin. They also sell farina, kasha, kefir, farmer's cheese, and jars of taramasalata. If you don't speak Russian or Armenian, well, good luck! *Every day; map:LL4*

FILIPPI'S / 1747 India St, Middletown; 619/232-5094 Although best known for its wonderful pizzas, Filippi's sells cheeses, deli meats, olives, capers, sardines, packaged pastas, olive oil, and wine—both domestic and imported from Italy, Portugal, and Spain. *Every day; map:M6*

HOA HING / 4149 University Ave, East San Diego; 619/280-2132 As you enter this Vietnamese grocery, you get a blast of contradictory smells. The butcher shop at back has stacks of pig's tongues and live shell oysters. The produce section displays mounds of mangoes, fresh eggplant, mint, bamboo shoots, ginger, and more. Fresh and dried rice noodles and all the other necessary ingredients for a Vietnamese feast are spread about the aisles, along with a small section of Mexican ingredients. *Every day; map:MM3*

INTERNATIONAL GROCERIES OF SAN DIEGO / 3548 Ashford St, Kearny Mesa; 858/569-0362 The owners count 45 international communities among their patrons, with some traveling here regularly from as far as Arizona for supplies. For 20 years, International Groceries has sold products from the Middle East, Turkey, India, Europe, and elsewhere around the globe: New Zealand lamb, Indian naan, Persian-style lavash bread (popular for wraps), Turkish and European jams, relishes from Bulgaria, and flavored tobacco from Egypt (as well as the hookahs in which to smoke it). Rich Egyptian hennas, coffee beans, nuts, seeds, grains, beans, lentils, fresh produce, and myriad international spices overwhelm the first-time shopper. This one you have to see to believe, and what's more, prices are low. They even have a video transfer service that copies foreign films to a VHS format. *Every day; map:KK5*

MONA LISA ITALIAN DELICATESSEN / 2061 India St, Middletown; 619/239-5367 One of Little Italy's most authentic Italian delis, Mona Lisa has been selling sambuca and fresh salami since 1973. In addition to imported Italian pastas and olive oil, the Brunetto family sells fresh pizza dough and egg pastas (linguine, fettuccine, and spaghetti) and ready-to-bake, homemade lasagne. At the deli counter, Italian-speaking matrons inspect vats of Cerignola olives and sheets of baccalà (salt cod), as well as other traditional Italian items, including cheeses and proscuitto. Fresh artichoke and octopus salads, antipasto, and deli sandwiches on bread fresh from Solunto's bakery down the street make great take-out meals. Cruise the well-stocked grocery section for breadsticks and biscotti, risotto, wine, beer, and spirits. There's also a small fresh produce section, and they even sell CDs. *Every day; map:M6*

TRADER JOE'S / 8657 Villa La Jolla Dr, La Jolla (and branches); 858/546-8629 One of over a hundred stores in the national Trader Joe's chain, this and other San Diego locations feature imported cheeses, spices, frozen entrees, desserts, and everything you need for an instant party. Regulars find bargains in imported and domestic beers and wines, snatching up cases of their favorites when the price is right. *Every day; map:JJ7*

FLORISTS AND NURSERIES

ADELAIDE'S / 7766 Girard Ave, La Jolla; 858/454-0146 Living works of art are created at this fashionable florist, long the mainstay of La Jolla patrons. Snow-white tulips, fragile ferns, and sprigs of pussywillow are transformed into sculptures so gorgeous they're used as backdrops for wedding portraits. Sprays of fragrant freesias beckon passersby inside the shop, where delicate orchids are amassed in one corner, spiky bromeliads in another. Bet you can't leave without a few blooms for your room. *Every day; map:JJ7*

FLORAL FANTASIA / 4993 Niagara Ave, Ocean Beach; 619/224-6404 The shop may be tiny, but the arrangements designed inside are spectacular. A small selection of emerald, sapphire, and crystal-clear vases inspire creativity, and the young, innovative florists are eager to experiment with colors and shapes, turning a simple bunch of roses into a masterpiece. *Every day; map:B3*

MISSION HILLS NURSERY / 1525 Fort Stockton Dr, Mission Hills; 619/295-2808 Care to present a blooming gardenia bush or Victorian birdbath as a wedding gift? Need a violet wisteria arbor for your yard? Then skip the trays of perennials by the sidewalk and wander the backyard at this historic nursery, first opened by renowned local gardener Kate Sessions in 1910. The Mission Hills neighborhood has some of the most gorgeous old gardens in the city. If you're serious about creating a living Monet in your yard, take several long walks through the area before chatting up the nursery's helpful gardeners. Come back with a truck and an ample line of credit; you'll soon have your own paradise. *Every day; map:L2*

ROXANNE'S WILD ORCHID FLORIST / 1276 Rosecrans St, Point Loma; 619/223-8349 Need a lei for your girlfriend or a fruit basket for your hosts? Stop by this shop stuffed with gift ideas. Nothing is quite so entrancing as a strand of tiny orchids or ginger blossoms tucked around an engagement ring; Roxanne's can create an array guaranteed to elicit a resounding yes. *Every day; map:E6*

WALTER ANDERSEN NURSERY / 3642 Enterprise St, Point Loma; 619/224-8271 Seasonal specials surround wagons and carts at the entrance to this family nursery, which opened in the 1940s. Impeccably healthy pansies, lobelia, snapdragons, and poppies sit ready for planting; baskets of fuchsias in every shade of lavender and pink hang above pure white calla lilies and pale peach Gerber daisies. Cacti, succulents, and herbs abound in the California native plants section, and all about the nursery one finds jungles of tree ferns and jasmine, mini-orchards of citrus trees, and ponds filled with floating plants. Someone is available to answer nearly any question you can devise or suggest unusual combos for your flower patch. *Every day; map:I2*

WEIDNER'S GARDENS / 695 Normandy Rd, Encinitas; 760/436-2194 Seasonal sales at this enormous flower farm attract hundreds of buyers seeking rare fuschias blooming in hanging baskets or cropped into toparies. Geraniums in every imaginable color and scent, begonias like rare tropical plants, and an overabundance of blooms you've never seen keep gardeners returning regularly for a view of Weidner's latest find. *Wed–Mon, Apr–Sept and Nov–Dec; map:EE7*

GIFTS

APACHE TRADING POST / 2802 Juan St, Old Town; 619/ 298-4106 A staple of the touristy Old Town district, this unusual store is packed with interesting, top-quality Native American arts and crafts from throughout the Southwest. You can spend hours examining the handmade moccasins, belts, and woven baskets. It's obvious the work is authentic, especially the pottery, rugs, and bronzes that speak of ancient civilizations. *Every day; map:I1*

BABETTE SCHWARTZ / 421 University Ave, Hillcrest; 619/220-7048 There is a definite flair to a store that combines *Gilligan's Island*-inspired paraphernalia with Mexican Day of the Dead icons. A wide selection of cards and classic toys is also available. *Every day; map:N2*

THE BLACK / 5017 Newport Ave, Ocean Beach; 619/222-5498 In less polite society, this would be called a head shop. But beyond the smoking paraphernalia, the store offers one-stop shopping for counter-culture gifts. Certainly it's one of the few places to find lava lamps, black lights, and a vast selection of classic rock 'n' roll posters. In the back of the store is a rare music and poetry book section. One part of the store is devoted to unusually chic biker-wear and jewelry. Check out the liquor flasks. *Every day; map:B3*

BO DANICA / 7722 Girard Ave, La Jolla; 858/454-6107 A sophisticated contemporary atmosphere permeates this store, open in La Jolla for 30 years. Crafts, art, and pottery from American and European artists are sold, along with fine soaps, candles, and lamps. The fine china and crystal make it a popular bridal registry. *Every day; map:JJ7*

THE COLLECTOR / 7100 Four Seasons Pt, Carlsbad; 760/603-9601 Colorful gemstones beckon from the cases of this unusual jewelry store, once a staple of La Jolla, now located in the Four Seasons–Aviara Resort. There are crystals, geodes, fossils, and stones, some from the store's own tourmaline mine in Mesa Grande. It's a good place to create your own gem art. Lapidary and stone cutting are available. *Every day; map:CC7*

F STREET BOOKSTORE / 751 4th Ave, Downtown; 619/236-0841 Brightly lit and across the street from Horton Plaza, this adult store is full of naughty toys and gifts for lovers, everything from sexual aids to board games. *Every day; map:N7*

FRENCH GARDEN SHOPPE / 3951 Goldfinch Ave, Mission Hills; 619/295-4573 A taste of provincial luxury is the ticket here, with an emphasis on pottery, fluffy towels, soaps, and everything French. Custom floral arrangements are available as well. *Mon–Sat; map:M2*

GALLERY ONE / 7007 Friars Rd, Ste 255, Fashion Valley Center, Mission Valley; 619/688-6588 The range of gifts makes this mall-based store impressive. In addition to fairly standard fare, such as porcelain boxes and candles, it offers Skagen watches, autographed memorabilia, and artistic glass. *Every day; map:LL5*

THE GUATEMALA SHOP / 2754 Calhoun St, Bazaar del Mundo, Old Town; 619/296-3161 Every square inch of the store is crammed with colorful fabrics, figurines, clothes, and toys from Central American craftsmen. The work is usually top quality, and exploration unearths the unusual. The Peruvian whistle statues are popular. *Every day; map:J1*

THE HEALTHY BACK STORE / 1201 University Ave, Hillcrest; 619/299-2225 Your friends with aching backs will love anything you bring them from this store. It stocks everything from ergonomic office chairs and therapeutic mattresses to massage chairs. A car-seat lumbar support makes a perfect gift for a commuter. *Every day; map:O2*

 LE TRAVEL STORE / 739 4th Ave, Downtown; 619/544-005 or 800/713-4260 Joan and Bill Keller have been running a store for "international independent" travelers in San Diego since 1976. Now conveniently located across the street from Horton Plaza, their store is packed with books, backpacks, and essential accessories. A bulletin board in the front of the store serves as a forum for info and tips. A branch of budget specialists

Council Travel is located in the back. *Every day; www.letravelstor com; map: N8*

PANACHE / 7636 Girard Ave, La Jolla; 858/454-4220 A classy gift sho long favored by La Jolla's most stylish, the store lives up to its name wit fine crystal and silver decorations for the home. It also usually feature the jewelry creations of several local artists. A bridal registry is available *Mon–Sat; map:JJ7*

PAPYRUS / 239 Horton Plaza, Downtown; 619/237-5405 This may b part of a chain, but there's an extraordinary selection of paper styles. The store also offers custom printing and calligraphy. Other locations are i the Fashion Valley Center (619/298-9066); University Towne Centr (858/458-1399); and North County Fair (760/ 747-6181). *Every day map:N7*

PATINA / 1310 Rosecrans St, Point Loma; 619/224-1491 The store is a delight to explore, full of scented pillows, jewelry boxes, linens, and books. It is clear the items are specially selected, with little of the fodder typical in gift stores. An alcove holds unusual baby gifts. Gift wrapping is free. *Tues-Sat; map:E6*

SAN DIEGO HARLEY-DAVIDSON / 5600 Kearny Mesa Rd, Clairemont; 858/616-6999 You don't have to ride a chopper to appreciate the cool Harley accessories here. The classic Harley logo appears on everything from key chains and lighters to authentic leathers. *Every day; map:JJ4*

STACEY HIMMEL STATIONERY / 3997 Falcon St, Mission Hills; 619/295-4764 Just when you think you're in a typical stationery store, you find a section with fine leather journals or another area packed with boxes of unusual paper stocks. The in-house printing department can handle all sorts of orders, including custom invitations and announcements. *Mon-Sat; map:M2*

URBAN OUTFITTERS / 665 5th Ave, Downtown; 619/231-0102 The popular chain moved into San Diego with style, taking over one of the historical spaces in the Gaslamp Quarter. In addition to clothes and accessories geared toward young urbanites, the store features everything from inflatable furniture and housewares to platform sneakers and funky jewelry, perfect for the upwardly mobile grunge dude or dudette. *Every day; map:N8*

HARDWARE

HILLCREST ACE HARDWARE / 1007 University Ave, Hillcrest; 619/291-5988 Not just a hard-core hardware store here—you're more likely to find stylish teakettles in the entryway than boxes of nails. The two floors offer plenty of the basics, but there is also a healthy emphasis on home redecoration and fix-it-up suggestions. *Every day; map:O2*

HOME DEPOT / 3555 Sports Arena Blvd, Midway (and branches); 619/224-9200 When you know what you want and you need a lot of it, there's little substitute for the ease of this big warehouse chain. This store is conveniently located just west of the intersections of Interstate 5 and Interstate 8. Other Home Depots are in Clairemont Mesa (4255 Genesee Ave; 619/277-8910) and Encinitas (1001 N El Camino Real; 760/943-9600). *Every day; map:G2*

OCEAN BEACH PAINT AND HARDWARE / 4851 Newport Ave, Ocean Beach; 619/223-3083 This little store on Ocean Beach's main drag has been helping locals fix their toilets and faulty light switches since 1919. It doesn't have a warehouse feel; it's a family-run operation, and the staff will treat you with a smile. You won't find a gardening department or rows of bathroom fixtures, but you will find key items for electrical, plumbing, painting, and other household repairs. *Every day; map:B3*

SAN DIEGO HARDWARE / 840 5th Ave, Downtown; 619/232-7123 San Diego's oldest hardware store is a tourist attraction in its own right, a throwback to a different era with its old wood floors and a Victorian pressed-tin ceiling. It's also fun to explore, offering 50,000 items, including decorative hardware you won't find in Home Depot. The basement is where you'll find the fasteners, chicken wire, and other hardcore supplies. Validated parking is available. *Mon-Sat; map:N7*

HEALTH FOOD

IN HARMONY / 4808 Santa Monica Ave, Ocean Beach; 619/223-8051 Dubbed one of the 10 best herb stores in the United States by *Self* magazine, this place is worth a visit for the aromas alone. It offers more than 250 herbs and spices, many organically grown. The knowledgeable staff will keep you up to date on the latest medicinal and culinary seeds. There's also a wide selection of aromatherapy products. Order herbs by calling 800/51-HERBS. *Mon-Sat; www.inharmonyherbs.com; map:B3*

PEOPLE'S ORGANIC FOODS MARKET / 4765 Voltaire St, Ocean Beach; 619/224-1387 A good ole-fashioned co-op, this market is consistently well stocked with top-quality, organically grown vegetables and herbs. The vitamin selection is one of the best around. For those who would rather do takeout than create, the vegetarian deli doesn't skimp on the sprouts. Beyond food, you can stock up on natural beauty care products, including handmade scented soaps, real herbal shampoos, and a variety of "cruelty-free" products, developed without animal research. *Every day; map:C2*

SUNSHINE ORGANIC FOODS / 3918 30th St, North Park; 619/294-8055 This is an on-line delivery service specializing in natural foods. The "aisles" include hormone- and antibiotic-free beef, freshly frozen fish, gourmet cheeses, and vitamins. For those too lazy to cook, the deli offers

such taste treats as vegetable paella and Thai noodles, and the men
changes daily. They'll deliver as far north as Carlsbad. *Every day; www
sunshineorganics.com; map:MM4*

VEGETARIAN ZONE / 2949 5th Ave, Hillcrest; 619/298-9232 The com
panion gift shop to the popular restaurant (see Restaurants chapter) pri
marily stocks gifts such as crystals and wind chimes; there's also a goo
selection of teas and breads and an excellent range of vegetarian cook
books. *Every day; map:N4*

WHOLE FOODS MARKET / 711 University Ave, Hillcrest; 619/294-280
■ **8825 Villa La Jolla, La Jolla; 858/642-6700** The Hillcrest store is ;
showcase for the fast-growing chain—a colorful sea of fresh vegetable:
and fruits. The deli, offering a variety of salads and vegan dishes, is pop
ular for takeout. Party platters are available. *Every day; map:N2 and JJ7*

HOME FURNISHINGS

CIRCA A.D. / 3867 4th Ave, Hillcrest; 619/293-3328 This marvelous
shop with its large and eclectic array of decorative art, antiques, and
furnishings would inspire anyone to redecorate. Byzantine icons and
Japanese kimonos mix and mingle with handcarved containers, rattan
balls, unique fountains, African masks, laquerware, religious decor, and
an orchard's worth of wooden fruit. And don't overlook the jewelry case.
Every day; www.circaad.com; map:N2

COLUMN ONE / 401 University Ave, Hillcrest; 619/299-9074 This large
corner shop features a terrific collection of fountains (including some in
column and block forms), garden decor, metal sculptures, ornate corbels,
outdoor lights, sun gods, and wind chimes. Statuary runs the gamut from
St. Francis sheltering a bird to reclining cherubs and exhibitionist nudes.
Every day; map:N2

CONCORD LIGHTING / 1176 Morena Blvd, Bay Park; 619/275-2303
Two floors offer a full spectrum of fine lighting. Choose from fine traditional handcrafted Italian fixtures or modern halogen styles. Many one-
of-a-kind pieces have been purchased directly from artisans on the
buyers' worldwide shopping sprees. *Every day; map:LL5*

**EVERETT STUNZ COMPANY LTD / 7624 Girard Ave, La Jolla; 858/459-
3305** Since the early 1960s, this shop has been a prime San Diego source
for beautiful, classy, imported bedding and bath towels. You'll never
count sheep again after laying eyes on one of the classic bedroom ensembles, such as Peacock Alley's white-on-white "Serenade." DUX and
adjustable beds are also for sale. *Mon–Sat; map:JJ7*

GENGHIS KHAN / 1136 Morena Blvd, Bay Park; 619/275-1182 Walking
through the door here is like taking a trip to the Orient. Exotic accent
pieces include stone fountains, stoic Buddhas and various deities in all

sizes, ceremonial tea sets, birdcages, mirrors, carvings, and miniature pagodas. The ornate doors, gates, and relief carvings are particularly fascinating. *Every day; map:LL5*

HIGHLIGHTS / 301 4th Ave, Downtown; 619/232-6064 Light up your life and home with contemporary lamps and fixtures, including a wide range of unique, eccentric, and creative styles. Only the foremost European and American designers and manufacturers are represented, and the staff is happy to assist with selections. Collectors will drool over the Memphis, Venini, and VeArt designs. *Every day; map:N8*

HOME ACCENTS OF LA JOLLA / 7840 Girard Ave, La Jolla; 858/454-0442 ■ 416 University Ave, Hillcrest; 619/299-3858 This very ornate shop displays hand-painted birdcages, hand-carved Arabian trunks, handblown glass scepters, elegant vases, unusual lamps, glyph panels, fringed tassels, tapestry cushions, limited-edition prints, marble turtles, and onyx eggs. Shop chic in La Jolla or save on similar or lower-end merchandise at the Home Accents Outlet Store in Hillcrest. *Every day; map:JJ7 and N2*

LAMP SHADES UNLIMITED / 1022 W Morena Blvd, Bay Park; 619/276-6530 With a stock of more than 10,000 shades, you'll find a suitable covering for any lamp imaginable—from a transformed Chianti bottle to a piece of rare antique porcelain. *Mon–Sat; map:LL5*

MAIDHOF BROTHERS / 1891 San Diego Ave, Old Town; 619/574-1891 Maidhof Brothers claims to be one of the state's longest-operating purveyors of nautical salvage and fine chandlery. Every nautical accessory you could dream of is stashed somewhere within this salty warehouse—genuine *Titanic* posters, engine equipment, old prints, lamps, mastheads, bells, anchors, lanterns, ships inside bottles, and more. *Mon–Sat; map:K3*

MAISON EN PROVENCE / 820 Fort Stockton Dr, Mission Hills ; 619/298-5318 Enter the heavenly world of country France in this enchanting shop filled with such provençal delights as imported French pottery, quilts, cushions, brooms, dishes, crockery, table linens, fine fabrics, and hand-milled and molded soaps. The Barbotine pitchers were created from the original 14th-century molds. *Tues–Sun; map:M2*

JEWELRY

THE GALLERY / 2754 Calhoun St, Bazaar del Mundo, Old Town; 619/296-3161 A perfect spot to pick up examples of traditional Mexican and Native American silver, but there is much more. This shop also features the work of many contemporary designers, such as the whimsical mermaids of Susan Hyde. *Every day; map:J1*

TABOO / 542 5th Ave, Downtown; 619/696-0055 Located inside the hi⁻ toric Stingaree Hotel, this small studio features the work of 60 craft people. The designs, many in silver and turquoise, tend toward th⁻ unusual and contemporary. *Tues-Sat; map:O8*

TIFFANY & CO. / 7007 Friars Rd; Fashion Valley Center, Mission Valle⁻ 619/297-7200 No question, no doubt—you always know what you'r getting from the traditional icon of class. You can find far more tha simple rings and necklaces—everything from silver baby rattles to cryst⁻ vases is offered here. Delivery is also available. *Every day; map:LL5*

THE SILVER DESIGNER / 1201 1st St, Ferry Landing Marketplace Coronado; 619/437-1428 It may look a bit commercial, but this store ⁻ truly unique. All the pieces are designed in-house and crafted speciall⁻ for the store in Taxco, Mexico. The best work is in sterling silve⁻ including earrings and bracelets with semiprecious stones. *Every day map:NN5*

KITCHENWARE

DESIGN CENTER ACCESSORIES / 2754 Calhoun, Bazaar del Mundo, Ol⁻ Town; 619/296-3161 Just about everything that can go on a dinner table is available here—a vast assortment of colorful Guatemalan tablecloths intriguing napkin rings, imported patterned china from top labels, ever⁻ an assortment of variously dangerous hot sauces. *Every day; map:J1*

GREAT NEWS COOKING SUPPLIES / 1788 Garnet Ave, Pacific Beach⁻ 858/270-1582 This is a one-stop shop for professional-level cooking sup⁻ plies. The prices are better than at most of the chains, and the emphasis is on utensils, books, and spices used by real cooks. Staff members know what they're talking about—this is also a cooking school. *Every day; map:KK7*

THE SILVER SKILLET / 2690 Via de la Valle, Flower Hill Mall, Del Mar; 858/481-6710 As soon as you walk through the door, you know how Martha Stewart equips her kitchen. Two floors are stocked with every⁻ thing from terra-cotta tortilla steamers to fondue sets to colorful dinner⁻ ware imported from Italy. Shiny stainless steel pots and pans gleam from the racks. Vases, pillows, and glasses from top European designers are sprinkled among the shelves. Gift wrapping is free; they'll also ship. *Every day; map:GG7*

WILLIAMS-SONOMA / 7007 Friars Rd, Fashion Valley Center, Mission Valley; 619/295-0510 ▪ 4417 La Jolla Village Dr, La Jolla; 858/597-0611 There is simply nothing second-rate in this store. The chain offers its own line of copper cookware; there are also colorful tablecloths, provincial dinnerware, and special cutlery. And don't forget the machines—bread makers, blenders, and assorted other forms of electrical kitchen magic. *Every day; map:LL5 and JJ7*

EAT AND FISH

GONE WILD / 414 W Cedar St, Downtown; 619/696-6677 It may not be for everyone, but this small store features exotic meats from around the world—including buffalo, rabbit, venison, ostrich, and wild boar. Ask about the special game sausages and jerky. *Every day; www.gonewild. com.; map:N6*

KELLY'S SIMPLY FRESH NATURAL MARKET / 4516 Mission Blvd, Pacific Beach; 858/272-8400 Located next to the Crystal Pier, this is an independent neighborhood market that offers only hormone- and additive-free meat and seafood. Because it won't use chemical preservatives, the fish is delivered fresh every day. *Every day; map:KK7*

POINT LOMA SEAFOODS / 2805 Emerson St, Point Loma; 619/223-1109 Locals love to stop by for a quick cup of clam chowder and a calamari sandwich, but primarily this place sells dozens of varieties of fresh fish from all over the world. On a good day, you're likely to find green-lipped mussels from New Zealand, king salmon from the Northwest, and black sea bass from Mexico. You can choose your own shellfish from saltwater tanks. Sushi lovers will appreciate the sashimi-grade ahi. *Every day; map:E6*

SIESEL'S OLD-FASHIONED MEATS / 4131 Ashton St, Bay Park; 619/275-1234 For 31 years Marv Siesel has been preparing choice cuts for meat lovers. He takes pride in offering prime USDA choice, and the helpful staff will gladly make suggestions for the right steak for the right occasion. For something out of the ordinary, try one of the 35 different juicy marinades. *Every day; map:LL5*

SPORTSMEN'S SEAFOOD / 1617 Quivira Rd, Mission Bay; 619/224-3551 Fresh sea bass, shark, cod, and other local delicacies are taken right off the boats and into the cases of this local icon, owned and operated by the Busalacchi family, well-known San Diego restaurateurs since 1960. Sportsmen's is famous for its smoked fish, including smoked albacore and salmon. It also makes its own tuna jerky. *Every day; map:D1*

MUSIC (CDS, RECORDS, AND TAPES)

BLUE MEANNIE RECORDS / 916 Broadway, El Cajon; 619/442-2212 In business for 25 years, this music store sells new and used domestic and imported rock, pop, oldies, blues, and punk. Almost anything in print can be special-ordered in a few days. The huge selection of vinyl includes many 45s. The Meannie buys clean used CDs and cassette tapes along with some vinyl—call to see if your titles are in demand. The store also sells posters, buttons, stickers, and magazines. *Every day; map:KK1*

COW / 5029 Newport Ave, Ocean Beach; 619/523-0236 Owner Gre
Hildebrand lucked out when he scored the entire inventory of Jerry
Records, a few doors below the current location on Newport, for $2,50(
Since then he's turned a good profit selling used vinyl, cassettes, and CD.
New competition in the form of the Music Trader chain up the street ha
Hildebrand offering more collectibles and rare items, such as gatefolc
signed, and promotional albums. Although rock is his biggest seller, h
makes a point of carrying jazz, country, classical, rap, and reggae. As
for a card that turns into a $10 gift certificate after $100 in purchases
Every day; map:B3

**FOLK ARTS RARE RECORDS / 3611 Adams Ave, Normal Heights
619/282-7833** Owner and music historian Lou Curtis has done disco
graphic work for both the Smithsonian and the Library of Congress. Hi
shop offers vintage LPs, 45s, and 78s, with an emphasis on artists from
the teens, '20s and '30s. His personal collection of rare recordings total
an astonishing 90,000 hours of music—favoring but not limited to folk
blues, jazz, and country. Customers can order custom cassettes or reel
to-reel tapes with compilations from the song catalog. Curtis foundec
and coordinated the San Diego Folk Festival (now the Adams Avenue
Roots Festival) and is involved in the yearly Adams Avenue Street Fair
He also has a radio show on KSDS radio, featuring jazz from the '20s
and '30s. *Every day; map:LL3*

**MUSIC TRADER / 1084 Garnet Ave, Pacific Beach (and branches)
619/272-2274** This location buys, sells, and trades used CDs in addition
to selling new CDs. Although CDs are this chain's forte, some of the other
16 San Diego locations sell cassettes and other formats. *Every day; www.
musictrader.com; map:KK7*

**NICKELODEON RECORDS / 3335 Adams Ave, Normal Heights;
619/284-6083** Owners Ruth Bible and Elizabeth Scarborough have been
selling vintage vinyl—specifically 45s and LPs—for 15 years. Although
they keep a little bit of everything in inventory, their specialty is movie
sound tracks and off-the-wall recordings by comedians and personalities
(for example, old TV or movie stars dabbling in music careers—think
Leonard Nimoy crooning to a crowd of Vulcans). Admiring form as well
as function, Bible and Scarborough also go for unusual cover art from
the '50s and '60s. Check out the "smoking section," where each cover
pictures someone smoking. *Every day; map:LL4*

**NOSTALGIA RECORDS AND COLLECTIBLES / 3750 30th St, North Park;
619/543-9930** In business since 1986, Nostalgia buys and sells used
recordings, specializing in '50s through '70s rock albums, with some CDs
and cassettes. The shop also carries music memorabilia (dolls, masks,
magazines, and posters), and collectibles, including autographs from TV,

radio, and music personalities. There are thousands of autographs, costing anywhere from $10 to $800, recently from the likes of the TV *Star Trek* crew. *Fri–Tues; map:MM4*

OFF THE RECORD / 3849 5th Ave, Hillcrest; 619/298-4755 After almost 20 years in business, the original venue near San Diego State University closed in March 1999. The remaining store—a long, deep emporium in the heart of Hillcrest—still sells an excellent, eclectic selection of music, with lots of used CDs, cassettes, and albums. Featured is a wide range of today's musical styles, including techno, gothic, and industrial, which plays at a vigorous volume as you shop. *Every day; map:N2*

SPIN-OFF RECORDS / 435 Broadway, Downtown; 619/236-0413 Selling both new and used CDs and cassettes as well as some vinyl, this relatively new downtown music store specializes in urban tunes, including R&B, hip hop, and soul. *Mon–Sat; map:N7*

TOWER RECORDS / 8657 La Jolla Village Dr, La Jolla (and branches); 858/452-2566 Founded in Sacramento in 1960, Tower Records now has over 200 store locations in 17 countries. Local music professionals as well as fans prefer the La Jolla Village Square location for its great selection of new music. A wide variety of genres is kept in stock; though CDs and cassettes predominate, nightclub DJs will find a smattering of 12-inch vinyl records, mostly hip hop and other nontraditional tunes. You can special-order music on display in the store, and buy concert tickets at the on-site Ticketmaster counter. *Every day; www.towerrecords.com; map:JJ6*

TRADE ROOTS REGGAE / 3804 Rosecrans St, Midway; 619/299-7824 In addition to Bob Marley bumper stickers, incense, and other rockin' paraphernalia, you can get a good selection of reggae music in the form of new CDs, records, and cassettes. *Every day; map:H2*

OUTDOOR GEAR

ADVENTURE 16 OUTDOOR & TRAVEL / 312 Horton Plaza, Downtown; 619/234-1751 A-16 is one of those stores that's easy to love. The sales staff is helpful but not pushy, and always gracious about returns. The company stocks plenty of made-in-America and recycled products, such as Patagonia's PCI "synchilla" alpine hat, made of recycled soda-pop bottles. It's a no-holds-barred camp and travel shop, selling clothing by North Face, Patagonia, and Royal Robbins; luggage (mainly Eagle Creek brand); shoes and Teva sandals; maps, camping equipment such as camp stoves, flashlights, and Nalgene bottles. You can also rent camping equipment (tents, sleeping bags, snowshoes) with an option to buy. The quarterly newsletter keeps you abreast of free and inexpensive activities such as slide shows, clinics, classes, and wilderness trips. *Every day; www. adventure16.com; map:N7*

CAL STORES / 4030 Sports Arena Blvd, Midway (and branches **619/223-2325** They have a little bit of most things, but not a lot of any one type of sports equipment or clothing. But the selection of walking, running, and hiking shoes is huge, and prices on most items are lower than at trendier specialty stores. *Every day; map:F1*

THE DIVING LOCKER / 1020 Grand Ave, Pacific Beach; 858/272-112 Chuck Nicklin opened the Diving Locker in 1959 and since then ha segued from diving instructor to underwater photographer and film maker. You can still get scuba certification through the shop, which also rents, repairs, and of course sells scuba gear. The Nautilus Club sponsors Saturday-morning dives, lectures, photo workshops, kelp-bed and wreck dives, and trips to such exotic destinations as Thailand, Fiji, and Hawaii *Every day; www.divinglocker.com; map:KK7*

GI JOE'S ARMY-NAVY SURPLUS / 555 Market St, Downtown; 619/53 **1910** On the first floor are surplus foul-weather gear, duffelbags, pocket knives, and a limited amount of camping supplies. There's also a: impressive array of straps in varying widths (sold by the foot) and buckles. In the basement you'll find racks of used Wellingtons and regulation leather boots, military shirts, jackets, and trousers. No cash refunds. *Every day; map:O8*

HAMEL'S ACTION SPORTS CENTER / 704 Ventura Pl, Mission Beach **858/488-5050** Brothers Dan and Ray Hamel opened this beachside store 32 years ago, renting Sting Ray bikes, rubber rafts, and giant surfboards for beach and boardwalk fans. Since then they've helped popularize in line skates, being the first in San Diego to rent them and, according to Dan Hamel, doing more in-house repairs than anywhere else in the country. The brothers Hamel now sell and rent a large variety of beach and sports clothing and equipment, including the California Chariot (a kind of adult tricycle with two skateboards at the back), Soap Shoes (for the aggressive in-line skater), baby joggers, beach umbrellas, volleyballs and nets, and old-fashioned roller skates. *Every day; map:LL7*

HOOK, LINE & SINKER / 1224 Scott St, Point Loma; 619/224-1336 Though there are larger sportfishing shops in San Diego proper, this nearby spot is a reliable standby for high-quality rods and reels, videos on major fishing areas around the world, and info on local conditions. *Every day; map:E6*

NORPINE MOUNTAIN SPORTS / 3045 Clairemont Dr, Clairemont Village Shopping Center, Clairemont; 619/276-1577 Owner Jim Foxworthy has been operating for 17 seasons, selling and renting cross country, Telemark, and backcountry ski equipment—no snowboarding or downhill. Since he's dedicated exclusively to ski gear, the shop is open only during the season (usually from the beginning of November though

GROWTH AND DREAMS

California became the 31st U.S. state in 1850. Since then, San Diego's history has been a slow, steady tale of economic dreams and growth. The city's year-round warm climate, the best harbor south of San Francisco, and a brief gold rush in Julian during the 1870s started a constant population gain and intermittent bursts of development.

Perhaps the greatest influence on growth was the arrival of the U.S. Navy's Great White Fleet in 1908. World War II and the Pacific Theater turned San Diego into an anthill of airplane factories and shipping. Today, San Diego Harbor is still home port to tens of thousands of servicemen and -women; hordes of these part-time San Diegans decide to stay when their service ends.

Ultimately, San Diego's most valuable commodity has always been space to grow. By the 1950s, San Diego city and county had become a modern metropolis of freeways, suburbs, and outlying rural areas. New, self-contained cities served as models for other growing states; prime turf was carved into exclusive enclaves. Today developers continue to ride crests; highways and full-scale communities continually reshape the landscape. But San Diego still doesn't feel like Los Angeles, thanks in large part to the natural landscape. Not only is it buffered from Orange County's growth by the huge Camp Pendleton Marine base, but San Diego's many stream-cut canyons and steep-sided mesas make for an endlessly varied topography. The county is really a series of self-reliant, independent districts, towns, and cities intertwined under a unique identity.

—Peter Jensen

the end of April), when gear can also be purchased mail-order. Foxworthy asserts that the majority of cross-country ski equipment sold in the southern half of the state comes from his store, and that on any given Saturday, 75 percent of his customers will be from outside San Diego. *Mon–Sat, Nov–Apr; map:KK5*

PERFORMANCE BICYCLE SHOP / 3619 Midway Dr, Midway; 619/223-5415 ▪ 7582 Clairemont Mesa Blvd, Clairemont; 858/565-6799 This bike shop offers service as well as sales, and will beat any San Diego shop's price on equipment. They have road, mountain, and racing bikes as well as accessories: clothing, pumps, helmets, sunglasses, and watches. Those who spend $200 a year on biking equipment might consider joining Team Performance, wherein a $20 yearly membership fee earns shopper points worth a 10 percent discount on future purchases. Members also receive a quarterly newsletter and invitations to special preview sales. *Every day; www.performancebike.com; map:G2 and JJ5*

PLAY IT AGAIN SPORTS / 1401 Garnet Ave, Pacific Beach; 858/49⬛ 0222 ■ 8366 Parkway Dr, La Mesa; 619/667-9499 Here you can rent buy a wide variety of new and used sports equipment. The stor⬛ strengths include in-line skates, hockey equipment, and golf clubs; it al⬛ rents and sells snowboards, surfboards and boogie boards, snorkels, fir⬛ and masks. About 30 percent of sales are in used items. The La Me⬛ store, across from Grossmont Center, opened in 1997. *Every da⬛ map:KK7 and LL2*

RECREATIONAL EQUIPMENT, INCORPORATED (REI) / 5556 Copley D⬛ Clairemont; 858/279-4400 Now the largest retail co-op in the countr⬛ REI was formed in 1938 in the Pacific Northwest as a way for th⬛ founders to import quality climbing gear. More than 1.5 million men⬛ bers pay a one-time membership fee of $15. The co-op has a super retur⬛ policy, promising a full refund or replacement unless you're 100 perce⬛ satisfied with the merchandise. REI sells outerwear (North Fac⬛ Marmot, Patagonia, and REI labels), foul-weather gear, and a large sele⬛ tion of hiking boots in addition to comfortable, casual clothing. Produ⬛ information guides for gear such as camp stoves and hiking boots a⬛ extremely helpful in determining which brands best suit your needs. Als⬛ sold are mountain bikes, kayaks, canoes, all sizes and styles of packs, an⬛ an excellent selection of camping and climbing gear. Although anyon⬛ can shop here, members receive annual dividends, can rent campin⬛ equipment, and get special prices on some sale items. *Every day; wwu⬛ rei.com; map:JJ5*

SEAFORTH SPORTFISHING / 1717 Quivira Rd, Mission Bay; 619/224⬛ 3383 Stop by in the evening and mingle with anglers headed out on long⬛ range fishing trips in search of tuna, dorado, and the occasional marlin⬛ The shop sells all the gear you could possibly need to jump right on ⬛ boat, from high wader boots to wide-brimmed straw hats and warn⬛ windbreakers. Oh yes, they also have rods, reels, hooks, lures...you nam⬛ it. *Every day; map:D1*

SOUTH COAST SURF SHOP / 5023 Newport Ave, Ocean Beach⬛ 619/223-7017 ■ 740 Felspar St, Pacific Beach; 858/483-7660 Surf shop⬛ have come a long way since long boards and woodies were in style: now⬛ stocked are sunglasses, tons of casual sporting wear, darling bikinis⬛ skateboards, and beach towels in addition to the boards and Sex Wax⬛ Unlike at some other surf shops, the sales clerks at South Coast are gen⬛ erally friendly and willing to help neophytes and other non-hard-core⬛ surfers. Four doors down toward the ocean on Newport, the affiliated⬛ South Coast Long Board Shop is longer on sticks and shorter on acces⬛ sories. *Every day; map:B3 and KK7*

SOUTHWEST SEA KAYAKS AND ROWING / 2590 Ingraham St, Pacific Beach; 619/222-3616 Owner Katie Kampe's original store opened in Point Loma 12 years ago, but since moving to Pacific Beach, she has dedicated 5,000 square feet exclusively to kayaking gear. Supplies include clothing, gloves, paddling books and maps, Patagonia's Capelin underwear, wet suits, jackets, and life jackets. Also for sale are new and used sit-on-top kayaks (for diving and fishing), sea kayaks, whitewater boats, and Maas rowing shells; both kayak styles are available for rent. Kampe's husband, Ed Gillet, is a local fixture among kayakers and leads trips to 15 different Baja California, Mexico, kayaking destinations, including a two-day beginners' jaunt to Estero Beach, Rosarito. Sign up to receive the free quarterly newsletter. *Every day; www.swkayak.com; map:KK7*

ZODIAC SAN DIEGO / 1919 San Diego Ave, Middletown; 619/294-7270 This store sells Venezuelan-made AB inflatable boats in addition to its namesake, the 100-year-old, French-made Zodiac. You can get anything from a 6-foot-7-inch two-person boat to a 33-foot beauty seating 30 people and costing about $70,000. *Mon–Sat (summer), Tues–Sat (winter); map:K3*

TOYS

BRAD BURT'S MAGIC SHOP / 4690 Convoy St, Clairemont; 858/571-4749 Houdini wannabes will find all the basics in this friendly little shop in the Aaron Brothers shopping center. Supplies for the "hidden rope trick" or the "invisible deck" are available, but you'll have to supply your own rabbit for any hat tricks. *Every day; map:JJ5*

DISCOUNT HOBBY WAREHOUSE / 7750 Convoy Ct, Clairemont; 858/560-9636 For 25 years local hobbyists have been flocking to this store for their essential supplies. Model builders will find rare kits, paints, and specialty tools. There is also an impressive selection of remote-control boats, helicopters, and planes. *Every day; map:JJ5*

GEPETTO'S / 7007 Friars Rd, Fashion Valley Center, Mission Valley (and branches); 619/294-8878 The decor may go a little heavy on the old toy-maker theme, but the store comes through with handcrafted wooden puppets and other traditional favorites. There is also a wide selection of other toys, including Steiff teddy bears, books, and unusual puzzles. Other locations are in the Bazaar del Mundo in Old Town (619/291-4606) and at the Hotel del Coronado (619/435-8871). *Every day; map:LL5*

REED'S HOBBY SHOP / 8039 La Mesa Blvd, La Mesa; 619/464-1672 It's a little out of the way, but this little store has everything for the electric-train enthusiast. Besides rare engines and cars in all gauges, there are shelves full of different landscapes, model villages, and tunnels. If they don't stock a tool or a rare caboose, they'll know where to find it. For the hard-core, the employees will custom paint trains. *Mon-Sc* *map:LL2*

THINKER THINGS / 2670 Via de la Valle, Del Mar; 858/755-4488 Ki love to wander the aisles of this playful store, which features few of t alien creatures and gun-toting villains of chain stores. Instead the noo and crannies are packed with fun, creative toys that can fuel a child imagination. In addition to wonderful stuffed animals and dolls, the are intriguing science kits and puzzles. It is also one of the best places t stock up on Lego kits. Free gift wrapping is available. *Every da* *map:GG7*

VIDEO RENTAL AND SALES

BLOWOUT VIDEO SALES / 3026 Midway Dr, Midway; 619/224-0900 business just a few years at this location, Blowout has two claims to fam the biggest selection of adult videos (over 10,000 titles) for sale in th county, and the largest selection of DVDs (both general-interest an adult). All non-adult DVD rentals cost 99 cents; general-interest video are for sale only, no rentals. The large inventory comes from stores goin out of business. *Every day; map:H2*

DISCOVERY CHANNEL STORE / 7077 Friars Rd, Ste 321, Fashion Valle Center, Mission Valley (and branches); 619/297-9010 There are cur rently four Discovery Channel stores in San Diego, offering best-sellin videos from the cable TV channel for both kids and adults. The video get their own section within the store; also sold here are books, toys, an jewelry. *Every day; map:LL5*

KPBS STORE OF KNOWLEDGE / 7007 Friars Rd, Fashion Valley Center Mission Valley; 619/291-7169 About 30 percent of what you see on PB is available on VHS video at the Store of Knowledge. Tapes are sprinkled throughout the store within thematic sections: you'll find *Mozart a; Healer* in the mind, body & soul section, and *Orangutans with Julia Roberts* with the wild animals. Then there's the British humor section with compilations of the kooky sitcoms *Are You Being Served?* and *To the Manor Born*, as well as John Cleese's *How to Irritate People*. The *Love Lucy* show represents American humor. Plenty of tapes for the kids as well. *Every day; map:LL5*

KENSINGTON VIDEO / 4067 Adams Ave, Kensington; 619/584-7725 According to the store's owners, this is the largest video rental store in the county. Sounds plausible enough, as they have 23,000 titles. And where else in San Diego can you expect to find all 14 episodes of *The Jewel in the Crown*? There's a one-time $10 membership fee, well worth it to access the many rare and hard-to-find foreign and domestic films. *Every day; map:LL3*

WINE AND BEER

BARONS / 4001 W Point Loma Blvd, Point Loma (and branches); 619/223-4397 Three shops in San Diego County feature a vast selection of domestic and imported wines, with prices ranging from cheap to exorbitant. Aisles and bins are crammed with picnic items such as cheeses, crackers, nuts, sweets, and other delicacies, plus breads and gourmet coffee. *Every day; map:F2* &

BEER KING / 7150 Clairemont Mesa Blvd, Clairemont; 858/292-9210 Serious party animals head here for kegs and cases of favorite domestic and imported brands. Ice, dry ice, cups, jockey boxes, dispenser rentals, and picnic pumps are all on tap. And best yet, Beer King delivers. *Every day; map:JJ5*

COST PLUS WORLD MARKET / 372 4th Ave, Downtown (and branches); 619/236-1737 The rear of this favorite import store is stocked with domestic and imported wines, champagnes, and beers—most at bargain prices. All the accouterments are on hand, including corkscrews, bottle openers, goblets, flutes, mugs, and steins. *Every day; map:N8*

CREST LIQUOR / 3787 Ingraham St, Pacific Beach; 858/274-3087 In operation since 1947, Crest is well known among locals for the stock of premium wines, spirits, and microbrews housed within its 7,000-square-foot space. If for some reason you can't find that special brand, Crest offers a wine and spirits search service. Cigars, a deli, and catering services are added perks. *Every day; map:KK7*

DICK'S LIQUOR AND DELI / 737 Pearl St, La Jolla; 858/459-3885 This longtime La Jolla shop, highly visible on busy Pearl Street, is a local favorite for domestic and European wines in all price ranges, a good selection of beer, and all the spirits you can conjure. The full deli prepares made-to-order sandwiches, salads, and other noshes. *Every day; map:JJ7*

SPIRITS OF ST. GERMAIN LIQUORS / 3251 Holiday Ct, La Jolla; 858/455-1414 Not a chance you'll go away empty-handed after scouring the stock of around 1,000 bottles of California and European wines, 600 different kinds of spirits, and more than 330 varieties of beer. Wine prices range from an affordable $4 per bottle up to a $250 sky-high splurge. *Every day; map:JJ6*

THE WINE CONNECTION / 2650 Via de la Valle, Flower Hill Mall, Del Mar; 858/350-9292 You'll find a large assortment of high-end domestic and imported wines, fine Cognac and Scotch, Riedel glass, and accessories such as wine bags, iceless chillers, screw pulls, and vacuum stoppers. All case wine purchases are discounted, and temperature-controlled wine storage is available on the premises. *Every day; map:GG7*

WINESELLAR & BRASSERIE / 9550 Waples St, Ste 115, Sorrento Valle **858/450-9557** The location is a bit off the beaten path, but well wor the search. You'll find thousands of bottles of difficult-to-find, han selected wines, including domestic labels, small European producers Bordeaux and Burgundy, and rare classics. Storage, appraisals, and ta ings are part of the service at this highly esteemed fine wine shop. *Eve day; map:II7*

VINTAGE/RETRO

AAARDVARK'S ODD ARK / 979 Garnet Ave, Pacific Beach; 858/27 3597 It seems all the coolest California towns have an Aaardvark: Sa Francisco, Venice Beach, and the original shop, on Melrose in LA, whic opened more than 30 years ago. The San Diego location, just a few yea young, has a wonderful selection of vintage dresses, skirts, blouses, shirt and even some Victorian pieces. Also lots of faded blue jeans, and a sprir kling of new items at the front of the store. Prices are reasonable, but tak note: there are no exchanges or refunds—no exceptions. *Every da map:KK7*

AMVETS THRIFT STORE / 3441 Sutherland St, Midway; 619/297-421 Located near the foot of Washington Street off Pacific Highway, th enormous thrift store sees a few vintage treasures slip in and out, pract cally lost amid the voluminous inventory of today's used clothin *Mon–Sat; map:K3*

BOOMERANG FOR MODERN / 2040 India St, Middletown; 619/239-204 Period originals—mainly from the '50s, '60s, and '70s—are artfull arranged in this light-filled space in Little Italy. Owner David Skelley ma give you a lecture if you confuse his pieces with "retro," which ar modern copies of period pieces. He does represent Herman Miller, sellin reissues of classic designs, but his focus is seating, coffee tables, an dining sets by companies such as Eames and Knoll. Although the inven tory is constantly changing, the store usually has a good selection o Danish modern furnishings, period lighting, rugs, Rosenthal vases, an colorful handcrafted Blenko glassware. *Mon–Sat; map:M5*

BUFFALO EXCHANGE / 3862 5th Ave, Hillcrest; 619/298-4411 ▪ 1007 **Garnet Ave, Pacific Beach; 619/273-6227** Part of a small chain that spe cializes in creating funky-but-clean used clothing stores, the Hillcrest location is always well stocked with everything from formal wear to bowling shirts, all in near-new condition. The store is constantly buying new inventory, and the employees have a good eye for quality. They always seem to find the coolest poodle dresses, surfer shirts, and letter jackets. *Every day; www.desert.net/buffalo; map:N2 and KK7*

CREAM OF THE CROP / 4683 Cass St, Pacific Beach; 858/272-6601 Although the shop sells mainly designer labels sold on consignment, some vintage items creep into the inventory in this women's resale boutique, which has loads of jewelry. Across the street, the boutique of the same name features fashionable used clothing for the male persuasion. Both stores are well-organized and the clothes are in good condition—offering up good things for those who hunt well. *Every day; map:KK7*

FLASHBACKS RECYCLED FASHIONS / 3847 5th Ave, Hillcrest; 619/291-4200 Colored freak wigs decorate one wall and a disc jockey plays his favorite jagged tunes in this secondhand shop in the heart of Hillcrest. Although vintage clothing must share the stage with more recently worn glad rags, there are bubble-plastic purses, funky hats, furry coats, and lots of big, black shoes and boots atop each rock. Test drive the apparel in the dressing rooms at the back of the store, or ask the many red-haired employees for their opinion. *Every day; map:N2*

GOODWILL INDUSTRIES / 939 16th St, Downtown (and branches); 619/232-2083 Easily the best of the big thrift stores in the area. Vintage clothing and glassware sometimes find their way into this large secondhand shop, although for the most part it's a huge assortment of clothing (assorted artistically by color, not size), lots of kitchenware and stuffed animals, and a hodgepodge of furnishing, appliances, and seasonal kitsch. The downtown location even has a play area for kids. *Every day; map:P7*

INDIGO WAY / 437 Market St, Downtown; 619/338-0173 Vintage men's clothing is the order of the day here, including old-fashioned bowling and Hawaiian shirts, sporting attire from the '30s through the '60s, and a large selection of faded Levi's blue jeans and jean jackets. *Every day; map:O8*

KAREN'S CONSIGNMENT GALLERY / 4051 Voltaire St, Ocean Beach; 619/225-8585 The showroom is full of elegant, hardly worn contemporary furniture, but surprises await those willing to hunt through the rooms. There are few real bargains to be found in this gallery, but it has long been a favorite of local interior designers. *Every day; map:D3*

RETREADS / 3320 Adams Ave, Normal Heights; 619/284-3999 The owner buys constantly from area estate sales to keep this 5,000-square-foot store well stocked with furniture, art, rugs, china, and glassware. When you walk in, it's not unusual to find books and knickknacks piled to the ceiling. Large set pieces from the Old Globe Theatre give the store a fantasy atmosphere. Bargains abound. *Every day; map:LL4*

SALVATION ARMY / 901 12th Street, Downtown; 619/232-1378 An amazing amount of merchandise flows through the charity group's main San Diego County thrift store. The "collectible" section, Sally's Attic, is usually well picked over, but it always has new merchandise. To the right of the front entrance is a varied selection of used furniture a step above the former-cat-toy variety. On the best days there's also a good range of working audio equipment and kitchen appliances. The clothing department is better than most Salvation Army fare. *Mon-Sat; map:O7*

SHAKE RAG-EPICENTER / 432 F St, Downtown; 619/237-4955 Underneath Croce's at Fifth and F Streets is 4,000 square feet of nostalgia. There's a great selection of everything vintage, including hard-to-find little kids' clothing. Exposed heating ducts and lilac walls define the large space, and track lighting illuminates the '40s- to '70s-era clothing. *Every day; map:N7*

WEAR IT AGAIN SAM / 3922 Park Blvd, University Heights; 619/299-0185 In business for 20 years, Wear It Again Sam has la crème de la crème of hats, boots, jewelry, accessories, and clothes that make you wonder how and where they found them. Everything from turn-of-the-century through the 1950s is represented, with emphasis (when they can get them) on nice men's suits from the '40s and '50s, plus vintage women's shoes. Prices are moderate, and although they don't sell on consignment, they will happily buy your old glad rags if they're top quality and in good shape. Look in the back room for some sincerely stunning evening wear. Reproduction items include two-tone spectator shoes and felt fedoras. *Every day; map:P2*

PERFORMING ARTS

PERFORMING ARTS

Theater

The theater scene in San Diego is a marvel to behold. It's been booming for the past decade, and shows no signs of slowing down. The La Jolla Playhouse has sent numerous productions to Broadway, garnering several Tony awards and nominations. "The Playhouse keeps setting up new plays as fast as you can enjoy them," says one local critic. The Old Globe continues to challenge and satisfy audiences with world class dramas and musicals, as does the San Diego Rep. Even the Lamb's Players, a small homegrown troupe, made it to Cambridge in 1999 to stage *Till We Have Faces* by C. S. Lewis. All this action is heartily supported by San Diegans and theatergoers from throughout Southern California. If you're determined to see a particular production, buy your tickets in advance. If you're more interested in checking out the overall theater community, purchase last-minute tickets at discounted prices from some theaters (call ahead) and Arts Tix (see "Ticket Alert" sidebar in this chapter).

AVO PLAYHOUSE / 303 East Vista Way, Vista; 760/724-2110 This 382-seat theater is downtown Vista's indoor space for the Moonlight Theater (see below). The building was once a movie house but has been renovated as a venue for musicals and contemporary dramas. *Map:AA6*

CALIFORNIA CENTER FOR THE ARTS / 340 N Escondido Blvd, Escondido; 760/839-4140 or 800/988-4253 This elaborate cultural center was the dream of Escondido civic leaders, who wanted to bring up-to-date plays, musical performances, and art to North County. Classic in style, the California Center for the Arts occupies 12 acres adjacent to historic Grape Park, site of several museums and a yearly parade that at one time was second in size only to the Rose Parade in Pasadena. Its 1,500-seat concert hall easily accommodates music festivals as well as Broadway plays and community gatherings, while the 400-seat Centre Hall is booked for dramas and more intimate musical performances. *www.art center.org; map:CC2* ♿

CORONADO PLAYHOUSE / 1775 Strand Way, Coronado; 619/435-4856 This small theater on Glorietta Bay (across from the Hotel del Coronado) seats 104, cabaret style. It used to be a WAVES barracks during World War II. The plays are musicals, comedies, and mysteries. The management found Friday-night dinner theater buffets ($15 over the ticket price of $15) so successful, they added Sunday brunches. Summer weekends from August to September, the Playhouse stages free performances of Shakespeare's plays on the outdoor grassy area by the bay. *Map:NN5* ♿

TICKET ALERT

Tickets for most of the concert and performing arts venues can be purchased through **Ticketmaster**. Call 619/220-8497 or visit the Web site at www.ticketmaster.com for locations. Many of the Wherehouse and Robinsons-May stores around town have Ticketmaster outlets. The San Diego Performing Arts League's **Arts Tix** booth, just outside Planet Hollywood at Horton Plaza, offers half-price tickets for many San Diego-area theater, music, and dance performances. These tickets are for the date of purchase on a cash-only basis. Call 619/497-5000 for more information. The Arts Tix booth is also a Ticketmaster outlet selling full-price tickets. *—Susan Humphrey*

LA JOLLA PLAYHOUSE / 2910 La Jolla Village Dr, La Jolla; 858/550-1010
Gregory Peck, Dorothy Maguire, and Mel Ferrer liked hanging around La Jolla in the 1940s, and developed a reason to stay by forming the La Jolla Playhouse in 1947. In many ways, they were the inspiration for San Diego's thriving theater scene. Lack of funding caused the Playhouse to close in 1964; it was resurrected as the Mandell Weiss Center for the Performing Arts on the campus of the University of California at San Diego in 1983. There are now two theaters at UCSD under the La Jolla Playhouse banner. The Mandell Weiss Theater, where large productions are presented, and the more intimate Forum. Theater critics from New York and London pay close attention to Playhouse schedules; several local productions have made it to Broadway and beyond.

Des McAnuff, the first director of the current Playhouse, took local productions of *Big River*, *A Walk in the Woods*, *The Who's Tommy*, and *How to Succeed in Business Without Really Trying* to Broadway; then he handed the baton to Michael Greif, best known as director of the Tony- and Pulitzer-winning show *Rent*. Greif brought *Rent* with him for its West Coast premiere, and went on to direct Randy Newman's *Faust*. During Greif's tenure, the Playhouse won the 1993 Tony as America's Outstanding Regional Theater. Anne Hamburger, the founder of New York's En Garde Arts, will take over Greif's position in 2000.

Classical plays, each with an unusual twist, alternate with new productions that are constant surprises. Plays are given elaborate productions, with no theatrical holds barred. Playwrights, musicians, set designers, and stars challenge their boundaries during the May-to-November six-play series. The 1999 season started with the musical *Oo-bla-dee* by Regina Taylor and includes an intriguing staging of a musical *Jane Eyre*. *www.lajollaplayhouse.com; map:JJ6* &

LAMB'S PLAYERS THEATRE / 1142 Orange Ave, Coronado; 619/437-0600 A full-time, long-term company of actors, directors, playwrights, and designers, Lamb's is the only San Diego theater with a year-round repertory company. It performs in the historic Spreckels Building in downtown Coronado, which has no seat more than seven rows from the stage. While the resident theater holds five productions from February through November, the Lamb's Players maintain an active production schedule with 10 to 12 stage productions at other performance venues, such as the Lyceum Theatre in Horton Plaza, the Horton Grand in the Gaslamp Quarter, and the Playhouse on the Plaza in National City.

The company came together in the early 1970s as a Christian street theatre troupe. In its 28 years, it has become one of Southern California's leading professional nonprofit theaters, with a year-round staff of 42 and an annual budget of $3 million. Though no longer Christian based, the troupe aims to please everyone with humorous takes on the human condition such as *Boomers*, *Triple Espresso*, and *Lettice and Lovage*. Productions are geared to the 7,800 subscribers; plays are challenging but not outrageous, and the old image is fast disappearing. *www.lambs players.org; map:NN5* &

MOONLIGHT AMPHITHEATER / 1200 Vale Terrace Drive, Vista; 760/724-2110 After two decades in operation, the Moonlight Theater in Vista has become one of the most important venues in North County. Its 2,000 seats combine proper reserved seats and lawn seating—meaning plenty of grass for picnic blankets. Patrons are encouraged to bring their own alfresco meal or purchase snacks and full-course dinners at the concession stand. The season runs June through September, opening with a youth theater production followed by four full-scale musicals, including one "risky" production (most recently, the rock musical *Chess*). *Map:AA6*

MYSTERY CAFE DINNER THEATRE / 505 Kalmia St, Downtown; 619/544-1600 Dinner guests mingle with actors performing tales of blackmail, deceit, and murder. It's all tongue-in-cheek, but the impact is considerable when you find the person sitting next to you is the killer. You might even have a starring role. Includes a four-course dinner and show with informal group seating Friday and Saturday nights at Imperial House Restaurant. *Map:N5*

NORTH COAST REPERTORY THEATRE / 987-D Lomas Santa Fe Ave, Solana Beach; 858/481-1055 This intimate 194-seat theater has produced more than 110 high-quality plays in 18 seasons. The company focuses on neglected plays of merit, both contemporary and classical, and those that address social issues. An audience of more than 30,000 annually views world-award plays and West Coast premieres of plays not otherwise staged in the area. The theater was founded by Tom and Olive Blakistone with a group of dedicated volunteers and has recently come under the artistic direction of Sean Murray. It now employs a full-time staff of seven, with more than 300 volunteers. Year-round, the schedule aims for seven main-stage plays from June through May. *Map:FF7*

OLD GLOBE THEATRE / El Prado, Balboa Park, Downtown; 619/239-2255 The Old Globe Theatre in Balboa Park has been a San Diego tradition since it opened in 1935 as a charming little replica of the Old Globe in London. At first the performances were hourlong versions of Shakespeare's plays. Today the Old Globe encompasses three theaters (the Old Globe, the Cassius Carter, and the outdoor Lowell Davies Festival Stage), and Shakespeare is only one of many playwrights given a hearing. Works by Edward Albee, Thornton Wilder, Stephen Sondheim, and Neil Simon have had their turn on the stage. Stage and screen actors consider starring at the Old Globe a rite of passage—one worth revisiting. Jon Voight, Sada Thompson, David Ogden Stiers, Victor Buono, and Christopher Reeve have all starred here. The Globe now ranks as the longest-established professional theater in California.

In 1978 the main theater burned to the ground. Some say the fire was set by an actor who disliked the acoustics, which *were* bad. No such problems exist now. The citizens of San Diego devoted millions of dollars and hours to the Globe's reconstruction, and it reopened in 1982 with three distinct structures. The Lowell Davies Festival Stage is especially fun, as the outdoor stage and seats border the zoo. *Night of the Iguana* and *Henry the IV* (with John Goodman) both played well here, with a background of chirping birds. The Festival Theater was destroyed by a fire in 1984, but quickly returned.

In 1981, the Globe established a talented triumvirate to guide the theaters into prominence. Craig Noel (who first acted at the Globe in 1937) became executive producer; Jack O'Brien was named artistic director; and Thomas Hall took the role of managing director. The Globe's revival of *Damn Yankees* soon made its way to Broadway. The theater regularly produces a season of at least 12 main-stage productions. At the height of its season, the company consists of 250 artistic and administrative staff and more than 1,000 volunteers. *www.oldglobe.org; map:O5* ໄ

POWAY CENTER FOR THE PERFORMING ARTS / 15498 Espola Rd, Poway; 858/748-0505 This stunning building is an excellent venue for performances by big-name touring artists, entertainers, and ensembles, as well as a user-friendly environment for community- and school-based productions. It's the result of a joint-use agreement by the Poway Unified School District and the City of Poway. The 815-seat modern theater, designed by Blurock Partnership with consulting architect John von Szeliski, includes multiple dressing rooms, a band/rehearsal room, a green room with patio, and many ramps to service all three public levels as well as the basement orchestra pit and trap room. The interior finish gives the building a southwestern look, and the 30-foot window-wall along the full length of the east side provides views of the surrounding countryside. Recent productions include *Joseph and the Amazing Technicolor Dreamcoat, Guys and Dolls, Brigadoon,* and a variety of big-band performances. *Map:FF2* ఉ

SAN DIEGO CIVIC THEATRE / 202 C St, Downtown; 619/615-4100 This large venue (almost 3,000 capacity, a 123-foot by 60-foot stage) is part of the downtown San Diego Community Concourse which was formally dedicated in 1965, the year the theater played host to the first staging of the San Diego Opera (*La Boheme*). In addition to the five operas presented annually, the San Diego Playgoers (619/231-8995) has presented its shows of late exclusively at the San Diego Civic Theatre. Under the Playgoers banner, San Diegans get everything from rock concerts and dance performances to blockbuster musicals and legitimate drama. The Playgoers have brought more than 150 shows to San Diego since 1976 (formerly using the Spreckels Theater, Copley Symphony Hall, and Golden Hall). The San Diego Civic Theatre benefited from a major redecoration in 1979, receiving new seat covers, carpets, and wall coverings in the key color for performing-arts theaters around the world— Florentine red. *Map:N7* ఉ

SAN DIEGO REPERTORY THEATRE / 79 Horton Plaza, Downtown; 619/544-1000 This energetic nonprofit company is in its 22nd year in San Diego and its 15th at the Horton Plaza Lyceum Theatre downtown. There are two spaces at the Lyceum: the 550-seat Stage and the 260-seat Space. The Rep, as it's called, stages six plays a subscription season (September to June), an annual production of *A Christmas Carol,* and three festivals: the Kuumba Fest, showcasing local African-American performers, the San Diego International Jewish Arts Festival, and the Nations of San Diego International Dance Festival. Artistic Director Sam Woodhouse chooses musicals, comedy, drama, new plays, and classics to fill his demanding schedule. Molière was featured in 1998; Arthur Miller's *Death of a Salesman* was the choice for 1999. Latin playwrights are treated with respect by the Rep, and you can also always count on at least one twisted production each season. *Six Women with Brain Death* was one of the longest-running shows in Rep history, and the intellectual side of Steve Martin was showcased in *Picasso at the Lapin Agile* in 1999. *www.sandiegorep.com; map:N7* ఉ

SLEDGEHAMMER THEATRE / 1620 6th Ave, Downtown; 619/544-1484 The name says it all. Known for powerful, controversial productions, the Sledgehammer professes "an intense dedication to the development of new American voices in the theater." The company's actors spent most of their early years as urban gypsies alternating between sites ranging from San Diego's Old Carnation Milk Factory to a variety of now-abandoned or destroyed warehouses (though it had one fling at New York's Whitney Museum of American Art). Now in its 13th year, Sledgehammer has also provided graduates and undergraduates from the University of California at San Diego with their first professional credits. Notorious productions include a 5-hour uncut *Hamlet, Demonology, Peter Pan* (with a twist), and *Sweet Charity* (with an ultrafeminist slant). Since 1992, Sledgehammer Theatre has made its home in a converted funeral chapel, St. Cecilia's, formerly the Sixth Avenue Playhouse. *Map:O6*

STARLIGHT THEATER / 2005 Pan American Plaza, Balboa Park, Downtown; 619/544-7827 The Starlight Theater in Balboa Park is a San Diego tradition. For 53 years theatergoers have flocked to its 4,000-seat amphitheater, bringing picnic boxes and a thirst for good music and drama. Unfortunately, the theater is directly in the flight path of planes landing at Lindbergh Field. The action freezes onstage when a plane zooms by, then resumes when all is clear. Audiences have become accustomed to this odd method of performance, but Starlight aficionados have long wished for an indoor venue. In the last few years several extra plays a year have been presented at the Lyceum Theatre in Horton Plaza or at the Westgate Hotel on Broadway. Most recently, *Little Shop of Horrors* and *Lucky Stiff* played indoors during winter months; the summer schedule continued with *My Fair Lady* and *Some Like It Hot.* For summer performances (on Wednesay, Thursday, and Sunday), children 12 and under get in free if accompanied by an adult. *Map:O5*

THEATRE IN OLD TOWN / 4040 Twiggs St, Old Town; 619/688-2494 *Forever Plaid* is in its third year at this intimate theater. The plot: four male harmony singers unexpectedly find themselves on the way to heaven. Their response: 90 minutes of popular songs from the '50s and '60s, each with a special zing. It's an "open-ended run," meaning it will play as long as this witty songfest is financially successful. Performances run every night except Monday. *Map:J2* &

UNIVERSITY OF CALIFORNIA AT SAN DIEGO THEATRE / 2910 La Jolla Village Dr, La Jolla; 858/534-4574 The UCSD Department of Theatre and Dance is the third-ranked graduate theaters training program in the nation. It shares facilities with La Jolla Playhouse at the Mandell Weiss Center for the Performing Arts. MFA students in acting, design, directing, and stage management get at least one professional residency with the La Jolla Playhouse company. The department produces 10 main-stage shows a year, with 8 at other venues on campus. The selections are from Shakespeare, Greek tragedy, cutting-edge drama and comedy, and theater/dance. The season is from fall to June. Tickets to UCSD's mainstage shows are a good bargain, and half-price for students. *www-theatre.ucsd. edu; map:II6* &

WELK RESORT THEATRE / 8860 Lawrence Welk Dr, Escondido; 760/749-3448 Yes, it's Lawrence Welk's old haunt, built in 1981. The theater is part of the Welk Resort Center, which includes a hotel, golf course, and shopping center. Until he died in 1992, the champagne-and-bubbles host lived nearby. The 331-seat theater stages five productions a year—four established musicals and one regular Christmas show featuring ex-Welk stars and plenty of music. The cost includes dinner at a local restaurant. *Map:BB4*

Fringe Theaters

San Diego has a number of fringe theaters with loyal audiences. At the **FRITZ THEATER**, (420 3rd Ave, downtown; 619-233-7505; map:N8), with seating for 75 to 100 viewers, audiences can catch the Fritz Blitz of New Plays in June and July—six weeks of new plays by San Diego writers. The rest of the year-round schedule includes new works from off-off-Broadway, ranging from studied intelligence to modest smut. The **SAN DIEGO BLACK ENSEMBLE** (619/297-4761) chooses plays that "speak to the human condition," says cofounder Walter Murray. Having lost their space at 23rd and Broadway, they'll show up at various play-houses around town for the present. The **DIVERSIONARY THEATER** (4545 Park Blvd, downtown; 619/220-0097; map:P1) focuses on gay and lesbian issues. It's upstairs but is wheelchair accessible. Six productions are held annually.

Classical Music and Opera

Classical music fans in San Diego find a diverse assortment of concerts and recitals to choose from—be it a full orchestra in an acoustically sophisticated hall or a small ensemble playing in the park to the backdrop of the Pacific's crashing waves. The San Diego Symphony has made a happy recovery from bankruptcy and is back at home in its own Copley Symphony Hall (750 B St, downtown; 619/235-0804; map:O7), presenting a delightful series of concerts appealing to a broad range of listeners. The San Diego Chamber Orchestra, La Jolla Chamber Music Society, San Diego Early Music Society, and Athenaeum Music & Arts Library also fill the classical roster with concerts and festivals in a wide variety of venues that cater to every budget and lifestyle. You can don your tux and pack a fat wallet for one of the highbrow performances, or slip into your best faded jeans and pack a picnic for an easygoing and affordable night out.

ATHENAEUM MUSIC & ARTS LIBRARY / 1008 Wall St, La Jolla; 858/454-5872 Amid ancient volumes of art and music books and a 7-foot Steinway

THE SYMPHONY IS BACK . . . AND LOOKING GOOD

The San Diego Symphony is back after a tragic bankruptcy and a two-year absence from the scene. It was a world-class symphony with an experienced maestro (Yoav Talmi), applauded in music circles everywhere. There were superstars and a full musical season . . . and an overblown budget. Big spending nearly destroyed the Symphony in 1996. Now, with new hope, a new director (Jung-Ho Pak), and a new focus, the reconstituted orchestra must pursue a more conservative financial path.

When the Symphony finally launched its Summer Pops series in 1998 with "Truly Tchaikovsky!," excited fans rushed to marvel at the virtuosity of Sheryl Staples from the New York Philharmonic. What followed was a season of outstanding music, classics at Symphony Hall and the California Center for the Arts in Escondido, and a new Summer Pops series at downtown's Broadway Pier.

The winter season offered six separate concert series. Hosted by the magnetic young Pak, the Light Bulb Series was a lecture-demonstration program that emphasized community outreach. Others were the Connoisseur Series, the Rush-Hour Concerts, a silent-film series, and family and holiday concerts—all designed to attract a wider, and younger, audience.

Pak conducts without a baton, shaping music with his hands. At 37, he represents the new breed of American conductors, musically versatile but also able to convert and educate new fans. He has kept some veteran musicians on board (they made major financial concessions to keep the symphony viable) but also attracted a group of new musicians into the fold. The San Diego Symphony, recovering from its staggering crisis, is perhaps a model for modern orchestras, forced to reinvent themselves for the changing times. —*Virginia Butterfield*

grand piano, the 100-year-old Athenaeum Library proudly presents classical and jazz concerts, chamber music recitals, and related lectures to a sell-out audience of classy art-and-music aficionados. Stacking chairs and a few upholstered seats hold fewer than 150 enraptured patrons, who cram in for the Sunday Concert Series featuring nationally renowned musicians. If you don't make it in, try the Mini Concerts at Noon, held every other Monday (usually) and with free admission. *Map:JJ7*

LA JOLLA CHAMBER MUSIC SOCIETY / 7946 Ivanhoe Ave #309, La Jolla; 858/459-3728 Established in 1968, La Jolla Chamber Music Society is an offspring of the Musical Arts Society of La Jolla (founded in 1941 by Nikolai Sokoloff) and a major force in both California and San Diego County's classical music presentations. The society's esteemed Revelle Series has offered intimate performances to discriminating music lovers since its inception. Other programs include the Celebrity Series, bringing world-famous artists, ensembles, and symphony orchestras to the San Diego Civic Theatre stage; the Discovery Series, an outreach program performing in city schools, hospitals, senior centers, and other nontraditional venues; and the newer Prodigy and Piano Series. The Society's annual chamber music festival, SummerFest La Jolla, under artistic directors David Finckel and Wu Han, presents local and visiting musicians, as well as a composer-in-residence and workshops for younger musicians. *www.ljcms.org; map:JJ7*

MAINLY MOZART FESTIVAL / 121 Broadway, Ste 374, Downtown; 619/239-0100 The Mainly Mozart Festival, overseen by artistic director and conductor David Atherton, is one of the country's most acclaimed classical music festivals. The concert series usually takes place in June, spilling across both sides of the U.S./Mexico border. It showcases some of North America's finest artists in orchestral, chamber, and choral music. Performances are held at an eclectic variety of sites including historic Spreckels Theater, Point Loma Nazarene College, the California Center for the Arts, La Jolla's Neurosciences Institute, and Santo Tomás Winery in Ensenada, Mexico. For those who crave more than the annual festival, key artists return during the year for recitals, chamber music, galas, and special events. *www.mainlymozart.org; map:N7*

SAN DIEGO CHAMBER ORCHESTRA / 2210 Encinitas Blvd, Ste M, Encinitas; 760/753-6402 Conductor Donald Barra and the San Diego Chamber Orchestra provide the city with high-quality concerts, esteemed guest artists, and a choice of venues catering to varied crowds wearing tuxes and tails or trendy Lycra minidresses. The 35-member ensemble performs October through April, presenting programs such as "Legends," featuring Jian Wang on cello; "Fiesta Español," with renowned guitar soloist Liona Boyd; and Handel's *Messiah*, a Christmas extravaganza accompanied by the 120-voice San Diego Master Chorale. Concert programs include the Escondido Series, featuring matinee performances of four highlights from the season, held at the California Center for the Arts; the La Jolla Series, Monday-evening events in the 500-seat Sherwood Auditorium at the Museum of Contemporary Art San Diego (MCA); the Twilight Series, at downtown's chic yet casual 4th and B club; and the Fairbanks Series, which features Tuesday-evening, pull-out-all-the-stops, black-tie events in an intimate and elegant setting at the Fairbanks Ranch Country Club. *www.sdco.org; map:EE7*

SAN DIEGO EARLY MUSIC SOCIETY / 3510 Dove Ct, Hillcrest; 619/291-8246 Top local and international performers and ensembles fill churches, cathedrals, and other venues with the joyous, playful, and haunting sounds of medieval, baroque, and Renaissance music. Recent concerts have included San Francisco's Musica Pacifica, playing baroque music from Venice; the British Dufay Collective, with a lively mix of medieval songs and dances; Tapestry, a three-woman vocal presentation; and the baroque flute and harpsichord duo of Wilbert Hazelset and Jacques Ogg. *Map:M4*

SAN DIEGO OPERA / Civic Theatre, 202 C St, Downtown; 619/232-7636 San Diego Opera is Southern California's oldest opera company, offering productions of the highest quality. The company has been in existence 34 years, for the last 16 under the direction of Ian Campbell, formerly of the Metropolitan Opera in New York. The company produces five grand operas a year in San Diego's Civic Theatre (January to May), along with concerts and recitals in the Sherwood Auditorium at the San Diego Contemporary Museum of Art in La Jolla. It conducts the largest opera education and outreach programs in the country, aimed at all age levels. *Map:N7*

SAN DIEGO SYMPHONY / 1245 7th Ave, Downtown; 619/235-0804 Zooming back to symphonic stardom after being silenced by financial woes, the San Diego Symphony—under the guidance of esteemed artistic director and principal conductor Jung-Ho Pak—offers a magnificent choice of concerts for any budget and wardrobe. Maestro Pak, who recently stepped down as associate conductor of the Spokane Symphony, maintains careers in both academic and professional fields and concurrently serves as music director of the San Francisco Conservatory of Music, the University of Southern California Symphony, and the Emmy-nominated Disney Young Musicians Symphony Orchestra. His revitalization of the symphony into an accessible and vibrant art form garners plenty of ovations from local music lovers. Series run October through May, and include: the Connoisseur Series, grand-style, elegant orchestral presentations of Beethoven, Chopin, Rossini, et al.; Light Bulb Concerts, classical music in a provocative and interactive format (including "Symphony 101"); Rush Hour Concerts, 1-hour classical masterpieces (shorter versions of the Connoisseur bill) that are both accessible *and* affordable; the Classic Film Series, a wonderful blend of silent movies such as *The Thief of Baghdad* and *Cyrano de Bergerac* with orchestral accompaniment; Family Concerts, an introduction to classical music for the whole family through a variety of fun and interactive programs; and Holiday Concerts, special, lighthearted celebrations designed to fill any holes in the holiday spirit. The symphony's Summer Pops series at Navy Pier is especially popular with locals, who enjoy the music while snacking from picnic hampers in an outdoor setting. Most of the concerts are held at the symphony's own 2,225-seat, state-of-the-art Copley Symphony Hall (the beautifully restored 1929 Fox Theater), while several matinees are performed at the California Center for the Arts in Escondido. *www. sandiegosymphony.com; map:O7*

SPRECKELS ORGAN PAVILION / 1549 El Prado, Balboa Park, Downtown; 619/239-0512 Civic organist Robert Plimpton dazzles Balboa Park visitors with his year-round concerts, 2pm each Sunday, at the Spreckels Organ Pavilion. The magnificent outdoor organ, christened in 1915, features humongous lead alloy pipes (some stretching 32 feet long) on which Plimpton capably plays marches, show tunes, waltzes, and a Beatles number or two. The exquisitely ornate pavilion seats 2,400. In addition to the Sunday performances, the pavilion hosts a 10-week summer festival on Monday nights. *Map:O5*

Dance

San Diego's dance scene, though small compared to the ones in New York, Los Angeles, and San Francisco, is nonetheless a vibrant force in this city of dancing fools. Resident companies, anchored by the prestigious and enduring California Ballet, include a toe-tapping, heel-stomping connoisseur's mix of classical, contemporary, and modern troupes overseen by prominent dancers such as John Malashock. All ensembles perform at various theaters and concert halls around town, including the Civic Theatre, Sushi Performance and Visual Art, San Diego Repertory and Lyceum Theatres, Poway Center for the Performing Arts, East County Performing Arts Center, and stages at the campuses of University of California at San Diego and San Diego State. The universities and community colleges also present visiting dance troupes as well as festivals throughout the year. Palomar College (1140 W Mission Rd, San Marcos; 760/744-1150; map:CC5) has an exceptionally noteworthy dance ensemble, for those who don't mind a bit of a trek, though no one's quibbling about UCSD's dance department now that choreographer Joe Goode is in residence. Big-name visitors such as Mikhail Baryshnikov's White Oak Dance Project, Paul Taylor Dance Company, Riverdance, and Tap Dogs usually take the stage at California Center for the Arts (340 N Escondido Blvd, Escondido; 800/988-4253; map:CC2) or the Civic Theatre (202 C St, downtown; 619/570-1100; map:N7), while cutting-edge performers fit the bill at Sushi Performance and Visual Art (310 11th St, downtown; 619/235-8469; map:O8).

CALIFORNIA BALLET COMPANY / 8276 Ronson Rd, Clairemont; 858/560-6741 The class act California Ballet Company, now in its 30th year, performs under the artistic direction of Maxine Mahon. Four or five traditional and contemporary productions are presented annually at venues throughout the county. The company's flagship, *Nutcracker*, runs from Thanksgiving through Christmas, and is staged at downtown's Civic Theatre. Other standout productions include *Coppelia*, a tale of a mysterious dollmaker, a young woman, and her sweetheart that is rife with romance, suspicion, magic, and revenge. *Map:JJ4*

MALASHOCK DANCE & COMPANY / 1363 Old Globe Way, Downtown; 619/235-2266 The company celebrated its 10th anniversary in 1999, and founder and artistic director John Malashock has emerged from semiretirement to re-enter the performance arena. Many say this former Twyla Tharp dancer is better than ever. The regulars such as Tammy Dunsizer are still in force, though once up-and-coming Jeffrey Crawford seems to have left town. In residence at the Old Globe Theatre, Malashock & Company perform various modern and contemporary works—some Malashock originals and new pieces, some collaborations (like "Nerve Endings" with Nick Nodovsky), as well as premieres of new works by other choreographers. *www.malashockdance.com; map:O5*

SAN DIEGO BALLET / 5304 Metro St, Ste B, Bay Park; 619/294-7378 Don't be surprised if the San Diego Ballet becomes a regional dance company for the Southwest. At least that's the plan—no pipe dream when you see the push being made by this capable company under the direction of Robin Sherertz Morgan and Javier Velasco. The recent acquisition of husband-and-wife team Thor Sutowski (associate artistic director) and Sonia Arova (associate artist) brings aboard the expertise of alumni of the 1970s version of the San Diego Ballet, making it seem more and more like a no-lose proposition. Works range from experimental "Preludes and Poetry" to "Opas Swing," a tribute to big bands. The annual benefit in October features excerpts from the company's repertoire as well as the season's previews. *Map:LL5*

Film

Although San Diego movie theaters (and the films shown within) tend to be of the multiplex variety, foreign and artier films are shown regularly at **THE KEN CINEMA** (4061 Adams Ave, Kensington; 619/283-5909; map:LL3); **HILLCREST CINEMAS** (3965 5th Ave, Hillcrest; 619/299-2100; map:N2); and **THE COVE** (7730 Girard Ave, La Jolla; 858/459-5404; map:JJ7). And though the city lost two of its historic cinemas (the Guild and the Park), North County's 1920s **LA PALOMA** (471 S Coast Hwy, Encinitas; 760/436-7469; map:EE7), is still showing a mix of art and commercial films. Multiplex fiends should head for Mission Valley, where you can choose from the **AMC FASHION VALLEY 18** (7037 Friars Rd; 619/296-6400; map:LL5) or **AMC MISSION VALLEY 20** (1640 Camino del Rio N; 619/296-6400; map:LL4).

AIRPORT ART

The San Diego Port Authority jumped on the public art bandwagon in 1996, designating three-eighths of one percent of yearly projected port revenues (or $160,000, whichever sum is greater) to go toward public art in the airport and marine areas. The program has generated some controversy, criticized for lacking verve and for missing opportunities. The Port Authority spent $2 million on art as part of the recent expansion at **San Diego International Airport**. Some of the 14 installations are quite pleasing, including Christopher Lee's **Water and Sun**, a lovely aqua pyramidal fountain of flowing water, and **Sea Rhythms**, Terry Thornsley's circular fountain with bronze sea lions and fish cavorting in seaweed. The cheerful, colorful tile mosaics of Mary Lynn Dominguez, collectively called **SeeShells**, are interestingly placed at the entrance to 12 rest rooms.

But much of the art or its placement is dismissed by professional critics. In a July 1997 article in *Art in America*, San Diego writer Leah Ollman compared the works of art to airport food, calling them "convenient, overpriced, and not very nourishing." Some of the pieces are indeed timid, and some are misplaced. A case in point is Gary Hughes's statue of immobile, overladen passengers, **At the Gate**. Although whimsical, the white-resin and fiberglass piece looks temporary and lost at the west end of the baggage claim area. The monumental **Los Voladores/The Sun Fliers**, by Julian Quintana and Mario Torero, also loses its impact because of poor location near Terminal One's parking lot. Joan Irving's **Paper Vortex**, a panel of etched and painted glass that forms part of the Terminal Two security checkpoint, might as well be invisible. People in transit hurry by, too worried about whether their belt buckles will set off the security alarm to even notice the glass panel. Tradition prevails with the bronze sculptures **In Search of Wilderness,** by Les Perhacs, and **Lindbergh: The Boy and the Man**, by Paul Granlund, both outside Terminal Two. Other port art installations include the extremely traditional bronze statues at the navy fleet landing site (Harbor Dr at G St): **Aircraft Carrier Memorial** (even the name is boring), by T. J. Dixon and James Nelson; **Homecoming**, by Stanley Bleifeld; and **Battle of Leyte Gulf Memorial**, by Kim Moon.
—*Jane Onstott*

Every now and then, a token non-mainstream film is squeaked onto one of the screens at **UNITED ARTISTS HORTON PLAZA 14** (457 Horton Plaza, downtown; 619/234-4661; map:N7); **HAZARD CENTER** (7510 Hazard Center Dr, Mission Valley; 619/291-7777; map:LL4); and **LA JOLLA VILLAGE CINEMAS** (8879 Villa La Jolla Dr; 858/453-7831; map:JJ7).

University of California at San Diego hosts the **SAN DIEGO INTERNATIONAL FILM FESTIVAL** from February through May, screening San

Diego premieres of more than 18 international films, as well as short subjects (Mandeville Auditorium, UCSD; 858/534-8497; map:II7). Animated film aficionados make a beeline for the annual **FESTIVAL OF ANIMATION**, held April through May, at the Museum of Contemporary Art's Sherwood Auditorium (700 Prospect St, La Jolla; 858/454-3541; map:JJ7). Sherwood Auditorium is also the setting for the annual **PACIFIC COAST FILM FESTIVAL**, usually held one weekend in February. This event showcases about 45 films, produced by up-and-coming filmmakers (many in attendance at the festival), in categories including underwater, animation, student, and short films. Audiences get to select the prizewinners. The **SAN DIEGO MUSEUM OF ART** (Balboa Park, downtown; 619/696-1966; map:O5) presents various films from January through July, including a **DOCUMENTARY SERIES** and **CHINESE FILM SERIES**.

During summer months, revival films can be enjoyed alfresco at **GARDEN CABARET** (4040 Goldfinch St, Mission Hills; 619/295-4221; map:M2) and in August, mainstream to classic films are projected on screens on barges floating in bays throughout the city; movie buffs gawk from the shore. For movies and barge locations, call 619/280-1600. **MOVIES BEFORE THE MAST**, another water-based series that runs April to October, are bounced off a "screensail"on the 1863 windjammer *Star of India* (1306 North Harbor Dr, downtown; 619/234-9153; map:M7). The IMAX screen at the **REUBEN H. FLEET SPACE THEATER AND SCIENCE CENTER** affords views of everything from Alaska and Mount Everest to outer space and race-car driving (1875 El Prado, Balboa Park, downtown; 619/ 238-1233; map:O5)

Literature

Unfortunately, San Diego is nearly devoid of anything resembling a literary arts scene. The large bookstore chains such as Barnes & Noble, Waldenbooks, and Borders Books and Music regularly sponsor readings and signings by both local and touring authors, in a variety of genres from New Age guru Deepak Chopra to Holocaust survivor David Faber. Refreshingly, it's the independent booksellers that seem willing and able to snag top literary figures, at least for one night. Wordsmiths Timothy Leary, Allen Ginsberg, Amy Tan, and Isabel Allende have all read their own printed pages at either **WARWICKS** (7812 Girard Ave, La Jolla; 858/454-0347; map:JJ7), **D. G. WILLS** (7461 Girard Ave, La Jolla; 858/456-1800; map:JJ7), or **ESMERALDA BOOKS AND COFFEE** (1555 Camino del Mar, Del Mar; 858/755-2707; map:GG7). One of San Diego's crowning moments in literary history was the night that Ginsberg read at D. G. Wills. The bookstore was predictably packed and the crowd had overflowed onto chic Girard Avenue, so Ginsberg used a microphone. As the

staid, wealthy La Jollans took their evening constitutional, they were treat
to Ginsberg's amplified meanderings about the rear ends of young boys.

During the academic year, a variety of resident and visiting intell
tuals, philosophers, writers, and poets take the podiums at the Univers
of California at San Diego (858/534-4090) and San Diego State Unive
sity (619/594-5200); most of these events are open to the public.

ARTISTS ON THE CUTTING EDGE, a "cross-fertilization" literary an
music series under the artistic direction of author and UCSD profess
Quincy Troupe, features such exciting and provocative novelists and poe
as Dorothy Allison, Russell Banks, Colleen McElroy, Abraham Rodrigu
Jr., and Marge Piercy with authors' book-signings following each progran
The seven-night series is held mid-March through April at the Museum
Contemporary Art (700 Prospect St, La Jolla; 858/454-3541; map:JJ7).

NIGHTLIFE

Nightlife by Feature

ALTERNATIVE
Brick by Brick
Casbah
The Crow Bar
Empire Club
Java Joe's
Plan B
Winston's Beach Club

BLUES
Belly Up Tavern
Blind Melons
Buffalo Joe's
Harmony on Fifth
Humphrey's
Patrick's II

CABARET
Harmony on Fifth

CELTIC
The Field

COCKTAIL LOUNGES
E Street Alley
Humphrey's
Kensington Club
MiXX
Pacific Shores
Red Fox Steak House
Top of the Hyatt

COMEDY
4th & B
The Comedy Store
Flick's
Harmony on Fifth

COUNTRY
In Cahoots

**DANCING/DANCE
FLOOR**
4th & B
Barefoot Bar & Grill
Belly Up Tavern
Brick by Brick
Café Sevilla
Club Montage
E Street Alley
Harmony on Fifth
In Cahoots
Live Wire
Marisol

Plan B
Rich's
SOMA Live

DRINKS WITH A VIEW
Barefoot Bar & Grill
'Canes
Sunshine Company
    Saloon Limited
Top of the Hyatt
Top of the Park

FOLK/ACOUSTIC
Belly Up Tavern
Café Sevilla
Java Joe's

GAY/LESBIAN
Club Montage
Rich's
Top of the Park
Wolfs

JAZZ
Buffalo Joe's
Croce's Jazz Bar
E Street Alley
Harmony on Fifth
Humphrey's

OUTDOOR SEATING
Aero Club
Barefoot Bar & Grill
'Canes
Dick's Last Resort
Humphrey's
Sunshine Company
    Saloon Limited

PIANO BARS
Mille Fleurs
Plaza Bar
MiXX
Red Fox Steak House

POOL/BILLIARDS
Aero Club
Blind Melons
Brick by Brick
Casbah
E Street Alley
Flick's
Gaslamp Billiard Palace
The Jewel Box

Kensington Club
In Cahoots
Live Wire
Pacific Shores
Society Billiard Cafe
Sunshine Company
    Saloon Limited
The Tower
The Waterfront
Wolfs

PUBS/BREWERIES
Aero Club
The Field
Karl Strauss Brewery &
    Grill
Princess Pub & Grille

**REGGAE/SKA/
    WORLDBEAT**
Belly Up Tavern
Café Sevilla

ROCK
4th & B
Barefoot Bar
Belly Up Tavern
Casbah
The Crow Bar
E Street Alley

ROMANTIC
Harmony on Fifth
Karen Krasne's
    Extraordinary
    Desserts
Mille Fleurs
Plaza Bar
Top of the Hyatt

SPORTS BARS
Sunshine Company
    Saloon Limited
Trophy's

SWING
Harmony on Fifth
Patrick's II

**UNDERAGE/
    NO ALCOHOL**
Empire Club
SOMA Live

Nightlife by Neighborhood

Y PARK
MA Live

ULA VISTA
risol

WNTOWN
& B
ffalo Joe's
fé Sevilla
oce's Restaurant &
Jazz Bar
ck's Last Resort
Street Alley
e Field
slamp Billiard Palace
rmony on Fifth
e Jewel Box
trick's II
aza Bar
p of the Hyatt
e Waterfront

LLCREST
ick's
ne Living Room
Coffeehouse
iXX
ch's
op of the Park

ENSINGTON
ensington Club
he Tower

LA JOLLA
The Comedy Store
Karl Strauss Brewery &
Grill

MIDDLETOWN
Aero Club
Caffe Italia
Casbah
Club Montage
The Crow Bar
Gelato Vero Caffe
Karen Krasne's
Extraordinary
Desserts
Princess Pub & Grille

MISSION BAY
Barefoot Bar & Grill

MISSION BEACH
'Canes

MISSION HILLS
Espresso Mío

MISSION VALLEY
Brick by Brick
In Cahoots
Trophy's

NORTH PARK
Empire Club
Red Fox Steak House
Wolfs

OCEAN BEACH
Java Joe's
Newbreak Coffee Co
Pacific Shores
Sunshine Company
Saloon Limited
Winston's Beach Club

PACIFIC BEACH
Blind Melons
Plan B
Society Billiard Cafe

POINT LOMA
Pannikin Cafe

RANCHO SANTA FE
Mille Fleurs

SHELTER ISLAND
Humphrey's

SOLANA BEACH
Belly Up Tavern

UNIVERSITY HEIGHTS
Live Wire
Twiggs Tea & Coffee

NIGHTLIFE

The sun rules in San Diego; only the young stay out past midnig
Hence, the nightlife scene ebbs and flows with current trends and cl
drift out of sight regularly. Fortunately, a handful of stalwart mu
venues, dive bars, clubs, and pubs withstand the vagaries of local tast
Even those who only rarely go out on the town know exactly wh
they'll feel comfortable when they do. A 1998 state ban on smoking
bars created quite a furor among owners and barflies, and a few addi
still light up in their favorite dives. But frequent patrols by the police a
vigilant nonsmokers result in hefty fines for smokers; now the sidewa
are littered with cigarette butts. Some clubs have opened outdoor pati
for those who need consistent nicotine fixes, and nonsmokers a
delighted to be able to hear their favorite bands without going hor
smelling like an ashtray.

Listed below are the tried-and-true haunts, along with the latest h
spots. Phone numbers, opening hours, and other particulars change li
the tides. Check the *San Diego Reader* (the largest free paper, whi
comes out on Thursdays), and the Night and Day section of the S
Diego Union Tribune (also out on Thursdays) for updated informatio

Music and Club

4TH & B / 345 B St, Downtown; 619/231-2131 A clever developer h
transformed a '70s-style bank into the top music venue in the city. Abo
1,500 people can fit into the club's eight bars, posh balcony, and theate
Most nights, the comedy and live music (B. B. King, Judas Pries
Squeeze, and George Thorogood) alternate with private parties, includ
ing cigar and martini parties for corporate functions. Check the paper
for the eclectic music schedule, which sometimes includes Hawaiian an
Latin bands. *Full bar; AE, MC, V; no checks; every day; www.4thandb
com; map:N7* &

BELLY UP TAVERN / 143 S Cedros Ave, Solana Beach; 858/481-814
For 25 years the BUT, as it is locally known, has been considered one o
the best live music venues in the county, with performances every nigh
of the week. Local music is showcased on Tuesdays; more famous band

appear on Thursday or Sunday. Bonnie Raitt used to play here frequently
before she hit the Top 40; these days bands like Too Cynical to Cry and
the Zydeco Bluez Patrol keep the crowds happy. Come early for a grea
table and order dinner from the bar, or dine at Wild Note Cafe next door.
With a great dance floor, an interesting blues photo collection, free sodas
or juice for the designated driver (in a party of two or more), and a con-

sistently safe environment, The BUT is one of our best. *Full bar; AE, DC, DIS, MC, V; no checks; every day; www.bellyup.com; map:FF7*

BLIND MELONS / **710 Garnet Ave, Pacific Beach; 858/483-7844** Just steps from the beach and pier, this classic blues bar hosts live bands every night. Pool tables at the back add to the down-home ambience, but it's the music that keeps the soul churning. There is a cover charge when groups are playing. *Full bar; MC, V; no checks; every day; map:KK7*

BRICK BY BRICK / **1130 Buenos Ave, Mission Valley; 619/275-5483** This hip 20- to 30-something club in the warehouse district feels like a bachelor's garage, decorated with posters and a sexy female mannequin. Local bands play six nights a week, each bringing an entourage of dancing fools. Morphine, Helmet, REM, and Sonic Youth have all played here. Off-the-wall locals seek audience votes for quirky performances during the "battle of the bands." Although earplugs might come in handy, the noise doesn't stop the diverse crowd along the mazelike bar from chatting. Other entertainment includes four pool tables and a pinball machine. *Full bar; AE, MC, V; no checks; Mon–Sat; www.brickbybrick.com; map:LL4* ⅃

BUFFALO JOE'S / **600 5th Ave, Downtown; 619/236-1616** Formerly a country bar, Buffalo Joe's has adapted to the times and become one of the leading-edge clubs in the Gaslamp Quarter. Alternately jazzy, funky, or down with the blues, visiting bands tease audiences with new combinations like ska/funk. Expect to stand in line. *Full bar; AE, MC, V; no checks; every day; map:O8*

CAFÉ SEVILLA / **555 4th Ave, Downtown; 619/233-5979** Café Sevilla is an all-in-one night out. At street level, the lively Spanish restaurant (see Restaurants chapter) and tapas bar hosts dueling acoustic guitars that take advantage of the house's extraordinary sound system. Head to the cavelike basement for samba and lambada lessons on Sundays after 8pm, or for Latin music and salsa dance lessons on Tuesdays. *Full bar; AE, DC, DIS, MC, V; no checks; every day; www.cafesevilla.com; map:O8*

CASBAH / **2501 Kettner Blvd, Middletown; 619/232-4355** What appears to be a humble hodgepodge of rooms is actually the critical mass of San Diego's groovin' music scene. Local bands Three Mile Pilot, Rocket from the Crypt, and Drive Like Jehu open for touring acts; owner Tim Mays boasts that treating bands right has attracted such headliners as Nirvana, Smashing Pumpkins, and Alanis Morissette. On afro night, wear an afro, get in free. There are a few seats—good luck getting one. *Full bar; MC, V; no checks; every day; www.casbahmusic.com; map:M5*

CLUB MONTAGE / **2028 Hancock St, Middletown; 619/294-9590** Dazzling light shows and psychedelic video projections make this multistoried,

fog-filled labyrinth of rooms, balconies, and dance pads all the m
interesting. Montage is one of the few clubs open three hours after liqu
sales cease. The crowd is primarily straight, but on Fridays and Saturd;
gay San Diego also parties here, and candy-striper drag queens strut th
stuff on the rooftop patio. The crowd tops out at 1,500—naturally, t
pickup action is lively. *Full bar; cash only; Thurs–Sat; www.clubmc
tage.com; map:J3*

THE COMEDY STORE / 916 Pearl St, La Jolla; 858/454-9176 This ol
time venue attracts seasoned comics including Pauly Shore and Tomn
Davidson, local DJs and comics perfecting their shticks, and open-mi
nights for the brave at heart. There's a two-drink minimum; the cov
charge varies with the act. *Full bar; AE, MC, V; no checks; every da
map:JJ7*

CROCE'S RESTAURANT & JAZZ BAR / 802 5th Ave, Downtow
619/233-4355 Ingrid Croce, wife of the late Jim Croce, is the doyenne
two of the Gaslamp Quarter's most popular clubs. The Jazz Bar hos
greats including Maynard Ferguson and Hollis Gentry. The adjace
CROCE'S TOP HAT BAR & GRILL (818 5th Ave; 619/233-6945; map:O
features jazz and blues bands, including frequent appearances by A.
Croce, son of Ingrid and Jim and a mean piano player in his own righ
*Full bar; AE, DIS, MC, V; no checks; every day; www.croces.con
map:O7*

THE CROW BAR / 2812 Kettner Blvd, Middletown; 619/692-1080 ,
painting entitled *T. J. Elvis*, created by infamous black-light artist Ne
Fredrix, is the only thing left from the Crow Bar's dark past as a hove
for ornery punks. The current owners have pumped thousands into ren
ovation and turned the club into a dark dive showcasing top-notc
music. Bands from liberal clubs in San Francisco and Los Angeles mak
frequent appearances, bringing innovative musicians, some playing fun
on a stand-up bass. Tuesdays, the Downs Family plays pub music and
Wednesday is open jam night—the Crow Bar provides the instrument
and the results are mighty loud. *Beer and wine; cash only; Tues–Sat
map:L5*

EMPIRE CLUB / 4225 30th St, North Park; 619/640-8689 Intense band:
contradict the trancelike attitude of the under-age crowd in this win-
dowless gothic chamber. Bands are raw and play refreshingly new hard-
core and punk sounds. *No alcohol; cash only; Thurs–Sat; map:LL4*

E STREET ALLEY / 919 4th Ave, Downtown; 619/231-9200 An underground space with a maze of lounges and bars, E Street is a one-stop-fits-
all club where jazz bands play in a comfy lounge, pool balls clink in the
bar, dancers let loose, get down and boogie to music driven by crowd-

LOCAL GOLD

Jewel is currently San Diego's most famous musical resident, but the top-selling singer-songwriter is just one of many luminaries who live in or around America's sixth-largest city. Other notable locals range from Indian music legend **Ravi Shankar** and crooner **Frankie Laine** to jazz sax great **James Moody** and fast-rising punk-pop band **Blink-182**. Vista, in San Diego's North County, is home to two world-class musicians: English electric-guitar master **Allan Holdsworth** and recently transplanted Nashville violin virtuoso **Mark O'Connor**. Latin-rock superstar **Carlos Santana** cut his teeth playing in nightclubs in nearby Tijuana, where his mentor, guitarist **Javier Batiz**, now owns and performs at Casa del Blues. **Jack Tempchin**, whose songs have been hits for the Eagles, Jackson Browne, and others, lives near Del Mar, while **Steve Poltz**, Jewel's frequent songwriting collaborator and band member, is a Bird Rock resident.

Other notables in the area include former-porn-star-turned-singer **Candye Kane**, who usually concludes her shows by playing piano with her breasts; chart-topping pop-reggae band **Big Mountain**; neo-swing band **Big Time Operator**, and piano-playing singer **A. J. Croce**, whose next album will mess around with songs written by his famous deceased dad, Jim. Then there's Pulitzer Prize–winning contemporary classical composer **Roger Reynolds**, rock and soul legend **Ike Turner**, longtime Kingston Trio member **Nick Reynolds**, and such nationally acclaimed jazz stars as **Charles McPherson, Arthur Blythe, Mike Wofford, Bob Magnusson**, and the husband-and-wife team of **Jeannie** and **Jimmy Cheatham**. And don't overlook 1999 Grammy Award-winner **Patti Page**, bluesy singer-songwriter **J. J. Cale**, or the members of such vital bands as **Rocket from the Crypt** and **Buck-O-Nine**. Musicians who left San Diego to further their careers include Pearl Jam singer Eddie Vedder; Eric Clapton/Phil Collins bassist Nathan East; Christian-pop vocal star Sandy Patti; R&B songstress Chante Moore; Michael Jackson/Jeff Beck guitarist Jennifer Batten; Chicago bassist/singer Jason Scheff; jazz sax dynamo Harold Land; avant-garde diva Diamanda Galas; and singer-songwriters Tom Waits, Stephen Bishop, and Michael Franks. Nearly all of them regularly return to the city where they came of musical age. And who can blame them? —*George Varga*

pleasing DJs. Expect lines on weekend nights. *Full bar; AE, D, MC, V; no checks; every day; map:N7*

HARMONY ON FIFTH / 322 5th Ave, Downtown; 619/702-8848 A real cabaret club has finally opened in the Gaslamp Quarter, and it's a raging hit. Jazz, swing, and blues bands play nightly as diners feast on Pacific Rim cuisine. Cushy oval booths face the stage and dance floor, considered the

slickest and best wooden base for swing-dancing the night away. The
are evening and late-night shows on Fridays and Saturdays; weekd
shows run from 9–11pm (make reservations to guarantee a seat). Amo
the stars onstage is local singer Romy Kaye, one of the best blues a
ballad crooners anywhere. Hip jazz, swing, comedy, and plenty of au
ence participation fill out the cabaret shows. Strap on your high heels a
best dancing duds and join the fun. *Full bar; AE, DIS, DC, MC, V;*
checks; every day; map:O8 &

HUMPHREY'S / 2241 Shelter Island Dr, Shelter Island; 619/224-35
Best known for its summer series of outdoor concerts, Humphrey's also h
live music from Thursday through Saturday at the indoor lounge. Ja:
swing, and piano-bar musicians rotate through the schedule, which ten
to change with the whims of the times. Call ahead for schedule. The ou
door concert series attracts big-name bands (see Performing Arts chapter
Full bar; AE, DC, DIS, MC, V; no checks; Thurs–Sun; map:F7 &

IN CAHOOTS / 5373 Mission Center Rd, Mission Valley; 619/291-118
The most fun you'll have with your boots on, guaranteed. The plac
looks like a barn, perfect for long lines of dancers doing the Tush Push
Copper Head Row, or the Stomp. Novices can mimic the moves in a fe'
classes before joining the crowd. Like its counterpart in Sacramento, I
Cahoots offers more to the country crowd than dancing, including si
pool tables and three bars. Pick up a beer at the bar by the front doo
then search for seating—try for a stool at the wraparound upper dec
with good views of the dance floor and DJ. The crowd is amiable for th
most part, though the occasional beer-hall battle keeps security guard
on their toes as well. The one-dollar-off cover charge coupon, availabl
on the Web site, is also a plus. *Full bar; AE, DIS, MC, V; no checks*
every day; www.incahoots.com/homepage.htm; incahootssandiego@
msn.com; map:LL4 &

MARISOL / 2638 Main St, Chula Vista; 619/429-8045 Down by th
border near Mexico, Marisol features Mexican big brass bands, mari
achis, and south-of-the-border rock. The building is stark, but the neighborhood's OK, and there's no better place to watch couples salsa in
cowboy boots and spike heels. The bar is packed on Friday nights when
the best bands are playing. *Full bar; cash only; every day; map:PP3* &

MILLE FLEURS / 6009 Paseo Delicias, Rancho Santa Fe; 858/756-3085
Best known as one of the finest restaurants in the county (see Restaurants

chapter), Mille Fleurs also draws a moneyed crowd to its classy piano
bar. Pianist Randy Beecher has been at the keyboard since the early
'90s, and he plays his fans like a finely-tuned Steinway. Though the clientele is decidedly refined in dress and attitude, they don't mind belting
out "Don't Cry for Me Argentina" or the '70s classic "American Pie."

There's no better place for the ultimate splurge in dining and entertainment. *Full bar; AE, DC, MC, V; no checks; every day; www.millefleurs.com; map:EE5*

PATRICK'S II / 428 F St, Downtown; 619/233-3077 This narrow sidestreet bar is one of downtown's oldest and best places for drowning your sorrows to a guitar, zydeco, or swing beat. Patrick's has long been known for its support of local blues bands and is a favorite hideout for locals. *Full bar; AE, MC, V; no checks; every day; map:N7*

PLAN B / 945 Garnet Ave, Pacific Beach; 619/483-9920 In Pacific Beach, every Saturday summer night seems like spring break, with Plan B at the epicenter. Dance on the small black-lit dance floor to alternative rock accompanied by state-of-the-art lights and lasers. Bring two picture IDs if you don't have a California driver's license. *Full bar; cash only; Tues–Sun; map:KK7*

PLAZA BAR (WESTGATE HOTEL) / 1055 2nd Ave, Downtown; 619/238-1818 Classy and comfortable, the Plaza Bar is downtown's best spot for sipping Drambuie and humming (or taking center stage to sing) "I Gotta Be Me" à la Sinatra. Pianist Kristi Rickert is the star of the show Wednesday through Saturday, leading her fans on a sentimental journey. The Westgate's French Renaissance theme enhances the feeling. Settle into an upholstered armchair or banquette and twirl a crystal brandy snifter in the candlelight. *Full bar; AE, D, MC, V; no checks; every day; map:N7* ♿

RICH'S / 1051 University Ave, Hillcrest; 619/497-4588 Club Hedonism, held at Rich's every Thursday night, is a blast of groove and tribal rhythms in an industrial-style pad. It's the only straight night at an otherwise gay club in the heart of Hillcrest. On Fridays, drool over multiple go-go boys. Beer is cheaper than chewing gum on Sundays from 7–10pm. *Full bar; cash only; Thurs–Sun; www.richs-sandiego.com; map:O2* ♿

SOMA LIVE / 3505 Metro St, Bay Park; 619/296-7662 Formerly a mainstay club favored by raucous teen rockers, SOMA moved in the early '90s from a downtown dungeon to its new haunt near Mission Bay. Now in Bay Park, SOMA is still an underground club, occasionally mainstream, and refreshingly techno. It's also an all-ages club featuring performers from Fugazi to Cake. Watch for bodies flying off the stage; it's otherwise safe on the 2,000-square-foot dance floor. You can't drink here, but nearby JC's and Tio Leo's serve liquor. Get concert tickets at Ticketmaster or, to avoid the service charge, at the box office (open Fridays and Saturdays 6–8pm). *No alcohol; DIS, MC, V; no checks; Fri–Sat; map:LL5* ♿

Bars, Pubs, and Taver▮

AERO CLUB / 3365 India St, Middletown; 619/297-7211 Workers fr▮ nearby aerospace factories once claimed this seedy neighborhood bar their own. Today the club has been transformed from a smoky dive i▮ a welcoming, airy place serving dozens of draft beers and bottled impo (along with more potent libations). On sunny afternoons young revel▮ show off their smiles at the sidewalk counter. Lenny Kravitz, Ir Maiden, Lauryn Hill, B-Side Players, and local bands croon from t jukebox, adding a backdrop to pool games and lively conversation. *B(and wine; cash only; every day; map:L4*

BAREFOOT BAR & GRILL / 1404 W Vacation Rd, Mission Bay; 858/27▮ 4630 Boogie your brains out on the sand at this open-air Mission B landmark in the massive Paradise Point Resort. It's quite a scene, whe copper-toned locals pick up on vacationers on the big outdoor patio. T▮ calypso beat takes over by mid-afternoon, and mai tais and frothy pi▮ coladas introduce the cocktail hour. (They're a better bet than beer; you shell out $3.50 for a plastic cup of Bud in the evening.) The Barefoot good anytime, but extra-special when the music, crowd, and weather a all in blissful sync. *Full bar; AE, DIS, MC, V; no checks; every da map:LL6*

'CANES / 3105 Ocean Front Walk, Mission Beach; 858/488-178▮ People-watching and sunbathing are sports at 'Canes, located right c the boardwalk in Mission Beach. Its two-block-long rooftop is a prin place to do both, or to get a burger, salad, or pasta. At night, the regu lars fade away and 'Canes comes alive with punk rock fans. The cove charge is steep but the singles scene is worth it—Saturday nights ar packed. If you don't have a California driver's license, bring two pictur IDs (bouncers in Pacific and Mission beaches are firm on this). *Full bar AE, DC, DIS, MC, V; no checks; Tues–Sat; www.canesbarandgrill.com map:LL7* &

DICK'S LAST RESORT / 345 4th Ave, Downtown; 619/231-9100 Thi giant old warehouse has been converted into an All-American bar tha draws crowds of college students and conventioneers. You'll find beer hall seating and a large outdoor patio, buckets of good food (see Restau rants chapter), big-screen TVs, and a pervading trademark irreveren rudeness. The service can be appalling and the clientele crude (it's part o the charm). Still, Dick's is a nonstop celebration, feting everything from Cinco de Mayo to St. Patrick's Day. Curiously, this is also a popular spot for children's birthday parties and tour groups during the day. *Full bar AE, DC, DIS, MC, V; no checks; every day; map:O8* &

THE FIELD / 544 5th Ave, Downtown; 619/232-9840 The Field is arguably the best Irish pub in San Diego. It's packed from floor to rafters with real Irish rummage and collectibles. This bar offers fine whiskeys and all the traditional fare, along with cozy short stools near the faux fire and fiddlers on its small stage. Get there early before the throngs of singles. *Full bar; AE, DIS, MC, V; no checks; every day; map:O8* &

FLICK'S / 1017 University Ave, Hillcrest; 619/297-2056 High-tech video jockeys play today's vogue flicks on four large screens. If you tire of the show, there's a pool table and, on the last Thursday of each month, live stand-up comedy with a gay theme. *Full bar; cash only; every day; map:O2*

GASLAMP BILLIARD PALACE / 379 4th Ave, Downtown; 619/230-1968 An old-time feeling quickly settles over patrons at this pool hall and neighborhood bar. Don't be fooled by the airy, bright decor—if smoking were allowed in San Diego bars a fog bank would exude from the front door. On weeknights the Palace is a good place to unwind over a drink and shoot a game or two at the tables. Crowds take over on the weekend, and a second-story pool hall handles the overflow. There are 35 tables in all; on weekend nights all could very well be claimed by 9pm. *Full bar; AE; MC; V; no checks; every day; map:O8*

THE JEWEL BOX / 805 16th St, Downtown; 619/236-8685 Owner Alan Yorkman garnered a Downtown Partnership award for remodeling and reviving this watering hole in the warehouse district way beyond the trendy Gaslamp. Don't go looking for ferns and fine art; this is still a dive bar at its best, with free pool in the afternoons, a few tabletop shuffleboard games, three TVs, and a mixed clientele. Worker bees from downtown offices stop by to gossip; bikers proudly park their machines under the sign reading "Harley Parking Only—All Others Will Be Crushed." *Full bar; cash only; every day; map:P7*

KARL STRAUSS BREWERY & GRILL / 1044 Wall St, La Jolla; 858/551-BREW San Diego's favorite home brew is served straight from the vat at this friendly bar, where patrons expound on the merits of amber versus light while downing burgers and salads (see Restaurants chapter). You can buy Karl Strauss beer at nearly every liquor store in the county; impress the locals by swearing it's the best you've ever quaffed. *Beer and wine; AE, MC, V; no checks; every day; map:JJ7*

KENSINGTON CLUB / 4079 Adams Ave, Kensington; 619/284-2848 One of San Diego's best-kept secrets since it opened in 1933, the Ken leads a double life: it's a dark, loungelike dive by day and a trendy club by night. A back room was recently added to accommodate thirsty moviegoers from the Ken Cinema, next door. On weekends, bands thump in the red-lit, booth-strewn back room, rattling the nerves of old-timers accustomed to desultory discourse. In the front, DJs play cha-cha and '80s music f the Gen-Xers. *Full bar; cash only; every day; map:LL3*

LIVE WIRE / 2103 El Cajon Blvd, University Heights; 619/291-7450 Li Wire comes off as clique-ish, but the crowd is really friendly. On accepted by the regulars, you'll be included in a host of recreation events, from boisterous bus tours of the city's dives to river rafting a jaunts to Las Vegas. Back at the saloon, DJs spin rare '70s funk, ol school rap, and hip-hop, punctuated by cartoons on the TV. Know bands like Rocket from the Crypt and Three Mile Pilot rock this sm; bar some weekends, and there's never a cover charge. Pool, pinball, ar Pac-Man are also featured. *Full bar; cash only; every day; map:Q1*

MiXX / 3671 5th Ave, Hillcrest; 619/299-6499 Best known as one of tl most exciting restaurants in town (see Restaurants chapter), MiXX also a great place for a drink. The piano bar is one of the most popul; in town, thanks to the see-and-be-seen attitude among the clientele. Wel dressed straights and gays gather in the lounge, where the walls are cov ered with contemporary art (good for a conversation starter). Sip martini and take in the scene—as upscale hip as San Diego gets. *Full ba; AE, CB, DC, DIS, MC, V; no checks; Thurs–Sat; map:N3* &

PACIFIC SHORES / 4927 Newport Ave, Ocean Beach; 619/223-7549 Pa Shores has a unique underwater atmosphere with black lights and n windows. Big, comfortable booths line the wall below neon portraits o sea creatures. College kids and old-timers meet around the jukebox an the small pool table in the tiny back room. *Full bar; cash only; every day map:B3*

PRINCESS PUB & GRILLE / 1665 India St, Middletown; 619/702-302 Bartenders prepare perfect black and tans in this classic pub, wher Princess Di is still much revered and photos of royalty decorate the walls Guinness, Bass, and all the best brews are on tap, and the accents among the drinkers are enough to transport you to the shores of the Thames *Full bar; DIS, MC, V; no checks; every day; map:M6*

RED FOX STEAK HOUSE / 2223 El Cajon Blvd, North Park; 619/297- 1313 There are old bars, and there are bars like the Fox with old things. Its wooden walls date from the 16th century, brought by a Brit who insisted on importing her favorite singing room (the acoustics are great). These days Shirley Allen and her backup band provide low-key entertainment; grab the mike if you know the song. The piano bar is a favorite among aficionados, and other local crooners take the stage when Shirley gets a day off. This is a good place to actually converse over a drink without having to shout over the music. *Full bar; AE, DC, DIS, MC; no checks; every day; map:Q1* &

SOCIETY BILLIARD CAFE / 1051 Garnet Ave, Pacific Beach; 858/272-7665 Huge streetside windows provide passersby with a full view of pool players in action. The 15 regulation tables provide plenty of action for pool sharks, and a good selection of salads and sandwiches keeps their energy from flagging. There's a private party room perfect for bachelor parties and offbeat wedding showers. *Full bar; MC, V; no checks; everyday; map:KK7*

SUNSHINE COMPANY SALOON LIMITED / 5028 Newport Ave, Ocean Beach; 619/222-0722 Smokers disgruntled with the 1998 smoking ban find solace on the open-air rooftop patio here, filled with scantily clad beach babes and surfer dudes. A palm tree juts up through a hole in the ceiling to shade the second-story covered patio and bar. Multiple TVs blast simultaneous sporting events, while shuffleboard, pool, and video games provide more involved alternatives. Sample the local microbrews—there are 12 in all. *Full bar; cash only; every day; map:B3*

TOP OF THE HYATT / 1 Market Place, Downtown; 619/232-1234 This 40th-floor bar has the view from heaven, not to mention good spicy peanuts. On a clear night the million twinkling lights of Mexico add to the panoramic views of downtown, Coronado, and the San Diego Bay. The hallway has an equally interesting photo collection of San Diego dating from the late 1800s. Since the Hyatt is close to the convention center, the bar is often packed with out-of-towners. But locals still brave the crowds on weekends, or take advantage of less-packed weekday evenings when they can loosen their ties, sip a frosty martini, and watch the sunset. *Full bar; AE, DC, DIS, MC, V; no checks; every day; map:M8* ⅃

TOP OF THE PARK / 3167 5th Ave, Hillcrest; 619/296-0057 Gay party men flock here on Fridays to map out a weekend plan of attack over a superb view of San Diego. Although the bar is huge, standing room is at a premium by 8pm. It takes 10 bartenders to satisfy the troops; by 10pm the crowd is off to pillage the party scene. The dropped ceiling on the top floor adds a *Jetsons* look to this historical brick hotel, built in 1926. *Full bar; AE, DC, DIS, MC, V; no checks; Fri only; www.parkmanorsuites. com; map:N3* ⅃

THE TOWER / 4757 University Ave, Kensington; 619/284-0158 Until recently, the king of San Diego dives was also a vibrant display of public art. In 1995, the city commissioned artists to paint the unusual geometric concrete tower atop this ovoid bar, creating a real eye-catcher and a source of neighborhood pride. The tower started leaning precariously in 1999, and was taken apart bit by bit. The art now rests in the parking lot, but the owner swears he will provide all the necessary reinforcements to reinstall the famous tower. Inside, cheap beer and complimentary peanuts flow freely during the bar's dart games and twice-monthly pool tournaments. The jukebox plays nonstop; it's happy hour from 4pm–7p *Full bar; AE, MC, V; no checks; every day; map:MM3*

TROPHY'S / 7510 Hazard Center Dr, Ste 215, Mission Valley; 619/2⁹ 9600 Both a restaurant and a sports bar, Trophy's has sports memorabi everywhere—even lining the walls up to the ceiling. Televisions abour there's a view of some screen from every seat in the dining areas and bar pick your seat by scanning the screens for your favorite sport. The bar is far from Qualcomm Stadium, and it's on the trolley line, so sports fa stop by before and after local games. Those eschewing the hassle of act ally watching the Chargers and Padres at the stadium gather at Trophy to cheer on their teams. Call ahead for reservations for parties of eight more, and get there three hours before a game for a good seat on t enclosed patio. *Full bar; AE, MC, V; no checks; every day; map:LL4*

THE WATERFRONT / 2044 Kettner Blvd, Downtown; 619/232-96 Though set in the middle of a major redevelopment project that will a⁆ 45 lofts to the ever-more-trendy Little Italy district, the Waterfront is de tined to remain one of San Diego's best neighborhood bars. Worke from the now-defunct Convair airplane factory on Pacific Highwɛ began congregating at this dive bar in the 1930s. Neighborhood barfli⁀ and Waterfront fans from throughout the city still pack the small bɛ which, by the way, is blocks away from the water and has no view. N matter, the pool tables, hefty burgers, amiable crowd, and jukebox a keep patrons happy. *Full bar; AE, MC, V; no checks; every day; map:M*

WINSTON'S BEACH CLUB / 1921 Bacon St, Ocean Beach; 619/222-380 A well-loved hole-in-the-wall with live music nightly, Winston's is an O⁋ landmark. Local bands are featured on Wednesday nights; on Tuesday⁋ hop aboard the free shuttle bus bound for Blind Melons in Pacific Beacl and catch a bit of the blues. *Full bar; DIS, MC, V; no checks; every day map:B2* ⅃

WOLFS / 3404 30th St, North Park; 619/291-3730 The clientele of thi dark, mysterious gay bar is into minimal and bizarre attire; the under wear party on the fourth Saturday of the month is hugely popular. The same goes for the second Saturday of the month, when the boys do⁋ leather or go shirtless to get in the back room. Pool tables, pinbal machines, dart boards, and video games offer a different sort of compe tition. Proceeds from the sale of 50-cent keg beer (available after midnight⁾ benefit a local AIDS charity. Closes at 4am. *Beer and wine; cash only⁾ every day; map:MM3*

Desserts, Coffees, and Teas

CAFFE ITALIA / 1704 India St, Middletown; 619/234-6767 There's a wonderful European air here, with classical music in the background and plenty of foreign and domestic mags and newspapers for sale. A local artist made the small brushed stainless steel tables; an Italian did the interior design. Out on India Street, dark green umbrellas provide shade for sipping a Vietnamese coffee or other specialty drinks. There are sandwiches and salads, tiramisu, gelato, and the popular Sam's Cheesecake. *No alcohol; cash only; every day; map:M6*

ESPRESSO MÍO / 1920-B Fort Stockton Dr, Mission Hills; 619/296-3037 Owners Ron and Carol Penney opened this clean, cozy neighborhood cafe in early 1998 and have been in the black ever since. Ron Penney takes great pride in serving Batdorf & Bronson coffee as well as pastries from the French Pastry House, Pies by Clayton, Sam's Cheesecake, Baked by Etta, and House of Tudor. Snag a table on the tiny back balcony for a canyon view. *No alcohol; no credit cards; local checks OK; every day; map:K2*

GELATO VERO CAFFE / 3753 India St, Middletown; 619/295-9269 This tiny venue at the foot of Washington Street has coffee and tea in addition to its namesake, a rich and creamy gelato. The space is cramped or cozy, depending on your frame of mind, with a few alfresco tables along India Street. Try the delicious gelato milk shakes. *No alcohol; AE; no checks; every day; map:K3*

JAVA JOE'S / 4994 Newport Ave, Ocean Beach; 619/523-0356 Admittedly a total dive, this coffee joint nonetheless features electric music most evenings by local talent such as Gregory Page and the Troubled Sleepers and Steve Poltz of the Rugburns. Even San Diego resident Jewel has shown up to jam a couple of times. The building began life as a church but has been used by a bank, a surf shop, and lots of other businesses before its current incarnation as a grubby but popular OB coffeehouse. Live music commences most nights at 9pm; Monday's open mike night starts at 7:40pm. *No alcohol; cash only; every day; map:B3*

KAREN KRASNE'S EXTRAORDINARY DESSERTS / 2929 5th Ave, Middletown; 619/294-7001 If you've always believed dessert is the main event, Extraordinary Desserts is a slice of heaven. Cordon Bleu-trained chefowner Karen Krasne raises sweet treats to haute cuisine with tarts, tortes, and cakes that are bona fide works of art. This is no common bakery, but a Zenlike temple. Line up with the other blissed-out sugar junkies to peruse the fresh offerings. Splurge on an Extraordinary Brownie (flourless chocolate cake dressed up with shards of chocolate, edible gold dust,

ON THE SMALL SCREEN

San Diego stars in several television series (though few have made a splash on the major networks). *Simon & Simon*, an offbeat detective series with a cult following throughout the 1980s, was set in San Diego, while the old police headquarters near the harbor served as a stand-in for *Silk Stalkings*, a low-grade *Miami Vice*-style series that ran for seven years on USA Network in the '90s. *Renegade* brought Lorenzo Lamas and his trusty motorcycle to the far reaches of the county from 1992–1996, and the *Baywatch* babes occasionally stop by for a shoot.

San Diego hit the big time with *A Killing in Beverly Hills: The Menendez Story*, a CBS miniseries filmed in La Jolla, Rancho Santa Fe, and downtown San Diego in 1994. These days, James Brolin is spotted about town during the filming of *Pensacola*, with San Diego once again mimicking Florida. Occasionally, the star's bride, Barbra Streisand, can be spotted in upscale restaurants. —*Virginia Butterfield*

and flowers) or a White Chocolate Linzer Torte. Too much? Even smaller items, such as slice of chocolate sour cream loaf or a cherry chocolate chip cookie, will satisfy a finicky sweet tooth. All of this is best accompanied by fresh-brewed Hawaiian Lion Coffee or imported Mariage Frères tea steeped in a heavy Japanese teapot. The surroundings are as delightful as the food. At night, blond-wood tables gleam by candlelight, but for privacy, scope out one of the taupe-upholstered booths or sit on the patio. Don't come if you're in a hurry; service is leisurely, even when it's quiet. What's more, the pretty young things behind the counter can be a tad snooty—they're serving the best sweet stuff in town, and sometimes they feel compelled to let you know it. *No alcohol; MC, V; checks OK; every day; map:N4* &

THE LIVING ROOM COFFEEHOUSE / 1417 University Ave, Hillcrest (and branches); 619/295-7911 Settle in with your journal or a good book in this pleasant space in the middle of Hillcrest. It has the same warm, homey feeling as the other San Diego locations, with vintage couches, floor and table lamps, and framed prints on the walls. The coffee and tea list is long and varied. The San Diego State University venue is even cozier, albeit not centrally located; the newest location, on Rosecrans Street, opened in February 1999. *No alcohol; MC; local checks OK; every day; map:O2*

NEWBREAK COFFEE CO / 1830D Sunset Cliffs Blvd, Ocean Beach; 619/226-4471 Throughout the day, the regulars retrieve their personalized mugs from a wrought-iron wall rack. You can get a sandwich on fresh-baked focaccia bread, or a juice combo with a choice of two healthful additives (we're talking bee pollen, lethicin, oat bran . . .). Some of the colorful, computer-generated artwork adorning this small space was created by autistic youngsters and is for sale. *No alcohol; cash only; every day; map:B3*

PANNIKIN CAFE / 3145 Rosecrans St, Point Loma (and branches); 619/224-2891 Modern jazzy music drifts up toward the high ceiling at this popular cafe, where business execs, gangs of moms with toddlers, and loners tapping on laptops set out to drink some serious coffee. Pebble-gray Formica tables rest on a floor of distressed cement; seats from the legendary Loma Theater (now the Bookstar bookstore) line the walls, where large windows let in lots of natural light. They make a great cup of straight coffee here. For breakfast there are steamed scrambled eggs; for lunch or dinner order salads, soups, quiche, and yummy sandwiches. The store sells fresh-roasted beans; bulk and bag teas; and a really great collection of coffee, tea, and kitchen accessories. *No alcohol; AE, DIS, MC, V; no checks; every day; map:H3*

TWIGGS TEA & COFFEE / 4590 Park Blvd, University Heights; 619/296-0616 Multipaned windows shed light on comfortable couches surrounded by coffee and end tables, fresh flowers, and potted plants. There are also tables for two or four inside and out along Park Boulevard. In early 1999 the owners introduced a welcome line of tasty homemade baked goods, sandwiches, and salads. The staff is perky, friendly, and professional; ambient music tends toward the classical. *No alcohol; no credit cards; local checks OK; every day; www.twiggs.info.com; map:P1*

ITINERARIES

ITINERARIES

Want to play for a day—or a week—in San Diego? Listed below are suggested itineraries that give a sample of the best the city has to offer.

More information on most of the places highlighted may be found in other chapters (Restaurants, Lodgings, Exploring, Shopping, Day Trips, and so on) throughout this book. You can get around without a car on Days One and Two by using city buses; for route information call the **TRANSIT STORE** (102 Broadway, downtown; 619/234-1060). **OLD TOWN TROLLEY TOURS** (2115 Kurtz St, Old Town; 619/298-8687) is another good option; a ticket allows you unlimited stops at most of central San Diego's attractions. Still, wheels come in handy for Days Three through Seven.

DAY ONE

If you have just one day in San Diego and are staying downtown, splurge on a waterfront suite in the **SAN DIEGO MARRIOTT HOTEL AND MARINA** (333 W Harbor Dr; 619/234-1500 or 800/228-9290). Spend as much time as possible at the tropical lagoon pool or on the waterfront walkway running to the Convention Center and Seaport Village.

MORNING: Walking the waterfront is an essential beginning to the day. Start early and walk west toward **SEAPORT VILLAGE** (849 W Harbor Dr; 619/235-4013). Stop to admire the yachts in the marina, the early-morning light on the water, and the seagulls announcing the morning like roosters. Continue north along West Harbor Drive past fishing boats and sprinklers adding a sheen to the green lawns until you reach the ticket office for the **SAN DIEGO–CORONADO BAY FERRY** (San Diego Harbor Excursions; 619/234-4111) to Coronado. Board the first boat at (9am) and float across the water beside the arching blue Coronado Bridge. Rent a bike at **BIKES AND BEYOND** (at the Ferry Landing; 619/435-7180) or board the Hotel del Coronado shuttle service from the Ferry Landing. If you're on bikes, cruise down First Street to the **KENSINGTON COFFEE COMPANY** (1106 1st St; 619/280-5153) for an almond croissant and a latte. Suitably fortified, pedal or walk down Orange Avenue, the most beautiful main drag in San Diego. Admire the trees, gazebos, and lawns at **SPRECKELS PARK** (601 Orange Ave; 619/522-7342) and the series of early 20th century neoclassical buildings and Victorian houses leading to the **HOTEL DEL CORONADO** (1500 Orange Ave; 619/435-6611 or 800/HOTEL-DEL).

AFTERNOON: For a taste of royal pampering, have lunch at the Del's sumptuous **CROWN ROOM** or sip piña coladas and dine on seafood salad at the **OCEAN TERRACE** by the pool. Stretch your legs on the beach, then pedal or ride the shuttle back to the Ferry Landing and return downtown. Die-hard shoppers will find it hard to resist the shops at Seaport Village.

KIDS' PLAY

Sea World, Legoland, White Water Canyon, the Wild Animal Park, the San Diego Zoo—what kid wouldn't be happy in San Diego? You might need a brand-new credit card before you're done—or, on the other hand, you could be creative and discover all the fun stuff to do that's free. The young ones get a kick out of building sand castles at Ocean Beach or the Silver Strand and sliding and swinging at Tecolote Park in Mission Bay. The 8 to 18 set all enjoy searching under rocks for starfish and sea anemones during low tide—the best hiding spots for the sea's clever creatures are at Bird Rock, the Cove in La Jolla, or the tide pools of Point Loma near Cabrillo Monument. There are endless bike and roller-skating trails in Mission Bay Park, and everyone enjoys watching the free fireworks show from Sea World while sitting at a bonfire at Ocean Beach, Fiesta Island, or Crown Point. One of the most fascinating adventures for kids of all ages is the Rueben H. Fleet Space Theater and Science Center in Balboa Park; they charge admission fees, but they're still far cheaper than the theme parks. A ride on Belmont Park's Giant Dipper roller coaster is a must, as is a burger at in the Volkswagen booth at Hodad's in Ocean Beach. Fly a kite at Ellen Browning Scripps Park in La Jolla; take the ferry to Coronado; buy a Frisbee and carry it everywhere. The kids will have a great time.

—*Maribeth Mellin*

If you're too tired to choose between kites, toys, T-shirts, and souvenirs, hide out at **UPSTART CROW BOOKSTORE & COFFEEHOUSE** (835 W Harbor Dr; 619/232-4855) where you can settle into a plush couch and write postcards in the upstairs reading room.

EVENING: Slip into your dining duds and head up Fifth Avenue to the **GASLAMP QUARTER**. Wander around Fifth and Fourth Avenues, stopping by **LE TRAVEL STORE** (739 4th Ave; 619/544-0005) for any forgotten necessities, and browse through the shops at **HORTON PLAZA** (entrances on Broadway, 4th Ave, G St, and 1st Ave; 619/238-1596) a fantasyland mall. Then choose a quiet table at **LA PROVENCE** (708 4th Ave; 619/544-0661), and order cassoulet and a fine bottle of wine. After a long, leisurely dinner, hail a horse-drawn **CINDERELLA CARRIAGE** (619/239-8090) for a romantic ride back to your hotel.

DAY TWO

If you only have two days, you must spend the second one exploring the heart of the city, **BALBOA PARK** (2125 Park Blvd, downtown; 619/239-0512)

MORNING: Fuel up on a hearty breakfast at your hotel, then board the **OLD TOWN TROLLEY** or a city bus to the incomparable **SAN DIEGO ZOO** (2920 Zoo Dr; 619/234-3153). Go ahead and pose for photos by the zoo's flamingo pond (everyone does), then board a double-decker bus for a 40-minute tour past elephants, brown bears, and tigers. After the ride, hoof it to the zoo's newest enclosures: Tiger River, Ituri Forest, Gorilla Tropics, the Polar Bear Plunge, and Hippo Beach. Ride the Skyfari aerial tramway back to the entrance; keep an eye out for the tiled dome of Balboa Park's California Tower rising above the trees.

AFTERNOON: Stop for a quick hot dog and ice cream at one of the takeout stands by the monkey enclosure, then leave the zoo and walk past the carousel to **EL PRADO** and the park's museums. Stop by the **VISITOR'S CENTER** (619/239-0512) in the House of Hospitality and purchase a Passport to Balboa Park coupon book, valid for one week and good for admission to 12 museums. You won't be able to hit all the museums in one afternoon, but if you're in town for a few more days, you'll want to come back. On your first round, be sure to see the **MUSEUM OF MAN** (1350 El Prado; 619/239-2001) under the California Tower, the **SAN DIEGO MUSEUM OF ART** (1450 El Prado; 619/232-7931), and the **BOTANICAL BUILDING** (across from the House of Hospitality; no phone), where tree ferns stretch toward the sky under a lath roof. Take a break on the grass by the **LILY POND**, then head to the **REUBEN H. FLEET SPACE THEATER AND SCIENCE CENTER** (1875 El Prado; 619/238-1233), beloved by children of all ages. Play with the gadgets in the Science Center, catch the latest spectacle at the Space Theater, and don't even try to resist the gizmos in the North Star Science Shop. When you're utterly exhausted, board the trolley or bus and ride back to your hotel.

EVENING: After such a strenuous day, you deserve to splurge on dinner at **STAR OF THE SEA** (1360 Harbor Dr; 619/ 232-7408), the finest seafood restaurant downtown. End the night at the **TOP OF THE HYATT** (1 Market Pl; 619/232-1234), sipping a cognac on the 40th floor of the hotel while gazing at the lights on Coronado.

DAY THREE

Now it's time to head to Mission Bay and the beach. Unless you plan on spending the entire day at Sea World, it's best to have a car.

MORNING: If you're traveling with the family, submit to your kids' pleas and head out for **SEA WORLD** (500 Sea World Dr; 619/226-3901) at the edge of Mission Bay. Given the staggering admission fee, you may want to devote a full day to the aquatic park. Don't miss the **PENGUIN ENCOUNTER**, the sharks, and the trademark **SHAMU SHOW**, with its awesome and gorgeous Orca whales. There are plenty of places to eat at the park; try the newest restaurant, the **SHIPWRECK CAFE**.

AFTERNOON: If you're done with animal acts, pile in the car and cruise around **MISSION BAY PARK** (bordered by I-5, I-8, Grand Ave, and Mission Blvd; 619/221-8901). Check out the fishing boats at **SEAFORTH SPORTFISHING** (1717 Quivira Rd; 619/224-3383) and consider paddling about in a kayak or canoe at Santa Clara Point. Rentals are available at **MISSION BAY SPORTCENTER** (1010 Santa Clara Pl; 619/488-1004).

EVENING: Watch the sun settle into the sea as you dine on fresh fish and burgers at **QWIIGS BAR & GRILL** (5083 Santa Monica Ave, Ocean Beach; 619/222-1101); arrive early and claim a window table for a view of surfers riding the waves under rosy skies. After dinner, take a walk on the **OCEAN BEACH PIER** (at the foot of Niagra St). During the summer, fireworks explode from Sea World nightly at 9:30 pm. You can see the whole show from the pier as you listen to the surf pounding the pilings.

AY FOUR

Next head up the coast to La Jolla, the ritzy Mediterranean-style village by the sea. A car is a necessity.

MORNING: To truly appreciate La Jolla, you must stay in a view room at the **LA VALENCIA HOTEL**, or "La V" as the villagers say (1132 Prospect St; 858/454-0771 or 800/451-0772). The 1926 pink palace overlooking the water is an absolute charmer, from its domed roof to the gardens by the pool. Breakfast on fruit and French toast at the hotel's Mediterranean Room Patio, then keep the refined attitude going with a trip to the Wisteria Cottage, aka **JOHN COLE'S BOOK SHOP** (780 Prospect St; 858/454-4766) and the **MUSEUM OF CONTEMPORARY ART SAN DIEGO** (700 Prospect St; 858/454-3541).

AFTERNOON: Have lunch on the rooftop terrace at **GEORGE'S AT THE COVE** (1250 Prospect St; 858/454-4244) and gaze at the palms and lawns fronting La Jolla's rocky coastline. Return to the hotel, don your swimsuits, pack up your beach toys, and walk down Girard Avenue to the expansive cliffside **ELLEN BROWNING SCRIPPS PARK** (1180 Coast Blvd; 858/221-8899). Toss a Frisbee on the lawns for a while, then walk down the stairway to **LA JOLLA COVE** (1100 Coast Blvd; 858/221-8900), one of the prettiest beaches (and the best snorkeling spot) in all of San Diego.

MISTER HORTON BUILDS A CITY

Horton Plaza, downtown's mall-cum-amusement center, is named, fittingly enough, for downtown San Diego's founder. Alonzo Erastus Horton, the ultimate entrepreneur, came to town in 1867. He promptly decided that downtown San Diego should be located by San Diego Bay and bought 960 acres of waterfront property. Much of the Gaslamp District and critical modern buildings lie within Horton's original city plan. His dreams are honored at Horton Plaza, a "city square" with a fountain dedicated to his inspiration in 1910. Horton was also one of the masterminds who created Balboa Park and the surrounding neighborhoods; his name can be found on hotels, taverns, theaters, and businesses around downtown. —*Maribeth Mellin*

EVENING: Stuff your wallet with cash and credit cards and tou▮ the village's exclusive shops and boutiques. Dine amid the utterly roman▮ tic ambience at **TOP O' THE COVE** (1216 Prospect St; 858/454-7779; then finish the night with a brandy in the ever-so-genteel **WHALING BA**▮ at the La V.

DAY FIVE

Today you'll continue north along the coast, driving by the sea into North County.

MORNING: Start the day with lox and eggs at **SAMSON'S RESTAU RANT** (8861 Villa La Jolla Dr; 858/455-1461) in La Jolla. Drive north from La Jolla to **TORREY PINES STATE RESERVE** (11000 N Torrey Pines Rd; 858/755-2063) above Torrey Pines State Beach. Wander about the reserve for a bit, admiring the gnarled and twisted trees, found few places elsewhere in the world. The view of the sea from atop sandstone cliffs is breathtaking; if you stop by in the winter months, you may see whales spouting offshore. Though the beach is mighty tempting, continue on the Coast Highway through funky Leucadia to Encinitas. Take a detour from the coast to **QUAIL BOTANICAL GARDENS** (230 Quail Gardens Dr, Encinitas; 760/436-3036) and listen to the wind rattle through bamboo forests. Head back to the sea and drive through Encinitas to Solana Beach, one of the trendiest enclaves on the coast.

AFTERNOON: Shoppers won't want to miss the **CEDROS DESIGN DISTRICT** (S Cedros Ave, Solana Beach; see "Designer Shopping" in the Shopping chapter), filled with interior design and gift shops. Fortunately, the district contains a fine vegetarian restaurant, **CAFE ZINC** (132 S Cedros Ave; 858/793-5436). Meat addicts should expand their horizons with a hefty veggie burger or a mushroom-topped nouvelle pizza. The sidewalk patio is the perfect place to sip an herbal iced tea while waiting for the shoppers to return. Pile the shopping bags into the trunk and continue on to Carlsbad. If you've got young kids along, reward their patience with the excitement of **LEGOLAND** (1 Lego Dr, Carlsbad; 760/918-LEGO). No kids? Head inland to the **FOUR SEASONS RESORT AVIARA** (7100 Four Seasons Pt, Carlsbad; 760/603-6800 or 800/332-7100). Afternoon tea in the Lobby Lounge is the ultimate luxury; better yet is a night in an utterly perfect room with a private deck beside parks, gardens, and a faraway view of the sea. Golfers take heed: if you're going to play only one course in the county, tee off here.

EVENING: No matter where you're staying, finish the day with dinner at **BELLEFLEUR WINERY & RESTAURANT** (5610 Paseo del Norte, Carlsbad; 760/603-1919). The restaurant anchors a discount shopping mall, but it's tastefully decorated, and the nouvelle American menu has something for everyone—go for the barbecued ribs and the chocolate peanut torte.

DAY SIX

Now you must settle in for a long day's drive packed with exciting stops as you cruise from the coast up into the mountains and down to the Anza-Borrego desert. Consider booking a room for the night at **THE ARTISTS' LOFT** (4811 Pine Ridge Ave, Julian; 760/765-0765) or **LA CASA DEL ZORRO** (3845 Yaqui Pass Rd, Borrego Springs; 760/767-5323 or 800/824-1884).

MORNING: If you're staying downtown or along city beaches, head east on Interstate 8 at dawn. The city landscape soon gives way to a horizon filled with giant boulders and mountain peaks. Turn north on Highway 79 and follow the winding mountain road through the Cuyamaca Mountains, past turnoffs for campgrounds and hiking trails. Pass the Cuyamaca Reservoir and keep going until you reach Julian. Now it's time to stretch your legs and tour **JULIAN PIONEER MUSEUM** (2811 Washington St; 760/765-0227) and **PIONEER CEMETERY** (at the top of A St off Main St). Mountain-grown apples are Julian's biggest claim to fame; be sure to pick up an apple pie at **MOM'S PIES, ETC.** (2119 Main St; 760/765-2472) in case hunger strikes on your ride.

AFTERNOON: After lunch at the **MINER'S DINER** inside the **JULIAN DRUG STORE** (2134 Main St; 760/765-0332), head east on Highway 78 and descend the Banner Pass, an incredible steep grade to the 600,000-acre **ANZA-BORREGO DESERT STATE PARK**. It's an ear-popping ride back to ground zero (actually 280 feet above sea level), where heat rises from the desert floor in shivering waves. Keep driving till you reach **BORREGO SPRINGS**, an enclave for desert lovers who've created a mellow community with golf courses, hotels, and a smattering of hotels and shops. The state park's **VISITORS CENTER** (200 Palm Canyon Dr; 760/767-5311; 760/767-4684 for recorded information) is just outside town. Cool off in the small theater while watching a slide show about the park, then walk the center's nature trails around cactus gardens—watch out for lizards basking in the sun. Pick up an ice cream at one of the cafes on Palm Canyon Drive before cruising back through the desert.

EVENING: If you're not staying at one of Borrego's fine resorts, drive back to the city on county highway S22 east (to avoid climbing the Banner Grade), then follow Highway 79 south to Interstate 8 west, stopping occasionally to photograph cacti and palm-fringed oases. Stop at **RICKY'S FAMILY RESTAURANT** (2181 Hotel Circle S; 619/291-4498), just off Interstate 8, for a down-home meal, or splurge on room service at your hotel. And remember, you've got that pie in your trunk for dessert.

DAY SEVEN

You're due for a day of rest, preferably at the beach. We're fond of all our beaches, but if you have only one day to pack in all your ocean action, your best choice is **PACIFIC BEACH** (950 Grand Ave at Ocean

Blvd). Ideally, you'll plan ahead and book at least one night in a cottage perched over the surf at the **CRYSTAL PIER HOTEL** (4500 Ocean Blvd 858/483-6983).

MORNING: Cruise by **HAMEL'S** (704 Ventura Pl; 858/488-5050) to rent boogie boards, fins, and any other play equipment you desire. Then drive to the intersection of Garnet Avenue and Mission Boulevard and start hunting for a parking spot. Submerge yourself in the surfer scene at **KONO'S CAFE** (704 Garnet Ave; 858/483-1669) for a hearty egg and pancake breakfast. Then arrange your towels, chairs, and gear on the beach near one of the lifeguard towers, toss a Frisbee around till you've worked up a sweat, and dive into the waves to cool off.

AFTERNOON: When you suddenly realize you've also worked up an appetite, claim a rooftop table at the **FIREHOUSE BEACH CAFE** (722 Grand Ave; 858/272-1999) and scarf down burgers and chilled iced tea. Return to the sand for a nap or a few chapters of Tom Wolfe's *The Pump House Gang*, a classic surf novel set in San Diego. Stroll along the boardwalk for complete submersion into the local bikini scene. Hang around on the sand until late afternoon.

EVENING: Return your rentals and walk over to **BELMONT PARK** (3146 Mission Blvd; 619/491-2988) for a sunset ride on the Giant Dipper roller coaster. Return to your hotel for a bracing shower, lather on moisturizer, and don your best sundress or polo shirt and shorts. Dine on frosty margaritas and chicken with spicy mole sauce at **EL AGAVE** (2304 San Diego Ave; 619/220-0692) in Old Town. Wander past the shops and cafes till you spot a group of mariachi. Go ahead and ask them to play "La Bamba"—it's the perfect song for a perfect play day.

DAY TRIPS

DAY TRIPS

North Coas

23 miles north of downtown on Interstate 5 (approximately 45 minutes
Take the Solana Beach exit, and travel along Highway 101 (also calle
S21) for 7 miles.

San Diego County's historic Coast Highway 101 between Del Mar an
Carlsbad seems an odd sort of back road. In the 1970s, Interstate
opened in the hills to the east, and this once-bustling stretch between LA
and San Diego slipped into a slumber. Few travelers used it other tha
surfers in search of a better break, locals on errands, or curious travelers
Leucadia, Encinitas, Cardiff-By-The-Sea, and Solana Beach fell into
hippie-ish beach funk. Surfboard shops and used-record stores took over
Tie-dye and airbrush-art T-shirt shops hung their wares in the open ai
(a few shops still do) to catch the eye of tanned and sandaled shoppers
Leucadia and Encinitas, especially, took on a countercultural flavor.

Today a drive along this same route (about 7 miles) offers a look a
the offbeat north coast of San Diego County, an area undergoing rapid
transformation. The towns now sport hip cafes, ethnic eateries, shops
galleries, and—alas—a few chain stores and restaurants.

SOLANA BEACH blossomed with the opening of a new train station
in the 1990s at N Cedros Avenue and Lomas Santa Fe Drive. Designed
by architect Rob Quigley, it has gained a good deal of international
renown for its Quonsetlike roof and a tower reminiscent of local lifeguard stands. The **CEDROS DESIGN DISTRICT** (see "Designer Shopping"
in the Shopping chapter) is Solana Beach's main draw. Not all the new
activity in Solana Beach is confined to Cedros Avenue, however: Highway
101 from Lomas Santa Fe south to the Del Mar Fairgrounds has a
number of interesting shops and trendy centers (most notably Beach-
walk, at 437 S Hwy 101) along its west side. The east side of 101 is bordered only by a bike path adjacent to the train tracks (which run out of
sight in a deep trench). One of the north coast's most intimate beach
parks is at the foot of Lomas Santa Fe Drive. **FLETCHER COVE BEACH
PARK** (858/793-2564 for information), bounded by tall cliffs, is a gem for
safe swimming and beach walking, especially at low tide. During each
day's ebb, you can walk a mile or more in either direction beneath wind-
and wave-sculpted cliffs. Notice the ancient layers of fossilized oyster
shells several feet thick and millions of years old, a reminder of a time
when most of the San Diego coast was the bottom of a shallow sea.

SAN ELIJO LAGOON separates Solana Beach from Del Mar (see
Neighborhoods in the Exploring chapter). Fresh water and tidewater
meet at the mouth of a seasonal river, creating a life-rich shallow environ-

ment alive with fish, insect life, and wading birds like herons and curlews. Thousands of migratory wildfowl drop in every winter as they ply the Pacific Flyway to Central and South America. The county's best lagoon-side hiking trail skirts San Elijo's southern edge; reach its trailhead by turning north off Lomas Santa Fe Drive onto Rios Avenue and driving to the end. The trail leads (in less than a mile) to a spectacular grotto of eroded sandstone cliffs, a kind of mini–Bryce Canyon hidden behind a eucalyptus grove.

CARDIFF-BY-THE-SEA, borrowed its name from Wales; the developer also gave most of the streets British Isles place names. Cardiff's main attraction, SAN ELIJO STATE BEACH (S Hwy 101 at Chesterfield Dr; 760/753-5091) offers excellent camping, swimming, and tide pooling along a wide beach beneath crumbling bluffs. A parking lot at the north end of the camping area is available for day use only, so you don't have to abandon your car on busier Highway 101. Prowl around the little town by taking Chesterfield Drive east one block from San Elijo State Beach. SEASIDE MARKET (2087 San Elijo Ave; 760/753-5445) is a real find for pre-made beach picnic necessities like salads, sandwiches, and cold cuts.

Highway 101 continues north to ENCINITAS. At the south edge of town, the SELF-REALIZATION FELLOWSHIP (215 W K St; 760/753-2888) shimmers like an Eastern mystic's vision with its lotus-blossom-shaped towers and mysterious inner gardens. Visitors are welcome—the gardens are quite beautiful. Surfers gave a park on a coastal point just south of the Fellowship grounds the somewhat irreverent, but now accepted, local name of SWAMI'S (1298 Old Hwy 101; 760/633-2880), after Indian yogi Paramahansa Yogananda, who founded the Fellowship in 1920. Swami's has stairs to the beach, and it's a great place to watch a sunset.

Take a detour inland on Encinitas Boulevard to QUAIL BOTANICAL GARDENS (230 Quail Gardens Dr; 760/436-9466), which showcases thousands of plants from around the world, all thriving in this mild coastal climate. Then head back to downtown Encinitas, which hasn't changed much since the 1930s. Cars still park at an angle, and a classic theater, the LA PALOMA (471 S Hwy 101; 760/436-7469), hosts everything from movies and surf film festivals to folksingers. ACANTHUS FINE ANTIQUES (1010 S Hwy 101; 760/633-1515) features one of the region's finest selections of vintage furnishings, and THE BLACK SHEEP (1060 S Hwy 101; 760/436-9973) attracts weavers and seamstresses with its selection of hand-spun yarns, beads, and notions from around the world. HANSEN'S SURFBOARDS (1105 S Hwy 101; 760/753-6595) may be San Diego's largest clothing, ski, and surf shop, and can be a good introduction to surf culture. BUILDER'S TRADING CO. (202 N Hwy 101; 760/634-3220) sprawls through a converted Spanish-style house on the northwest corner of Encinitas Boulevard and First Street (Hwy 101);

wander through its inventory of architectural fragments, new and old–sometimes exotic, often hand-carved.

LEUCADIA'S spectacular window of giant eucalyptus trees para leling Highway 101 recalls the community's reputation among a grou of British spiritualists who named it "the sheltered place" (from th Greek). **LOU'S RECORDS** (434 N Hwy 101; 760/753-1382) holds fort as one of the finest (and funkiest) independent new and used record store in the country (yes, we do mean the entire United States), with a huge col lection of everything from jazz and folk to hard-core thrash-rock Nearby, the **PANNIKIN** (510 N Hwy 101; 760/436-0033), a coffeehouse gallery, and gift shop tradition for three decades, occupies the origina Victorian Leucadia train station.

The new north coast is most evident in the city of **CARLSBAD**. The arrival of **LEGOLAND** (see Top 25 Attractions in the Exploring chapter) ha brought the region's fastest-growing city fame and fortune. Carlsbad is no longer part of the old Highway 101 scene; its nexus is Interstate 5. If you want a quick drive back to the city, head south here. Otherwise, turn around and head south the way you came; the drive is worth a round-trip.

Carlsbad and Environs

35 miles north of downtown (approximately 45 minutes). Drive north on Interstate 5 to the Carlsbad Village Drive exit and turn left. Turn right onto Carlsbad Boulevard.

Situated along the coast, about 35 miles north of San Diego, this low-key coastal community was originally named for its mineral water which is akin to that of Europe's popular 19th-century Karlsbad spa. **ALT KARLSBAD HAUS** (2802 Carlsbad Blvd; 760/434-1887) is the site of the original well discovered by retired sea captain John Frazier as he was drilling away on his homestead back in the 1880s. Frazier is also credited with naming the town (quite benevolently, since it had been known as "Frazier Station" beforehand) and inspiring its Bavarian styling. It wasn't long before Carlsbad became a favorite turn-of-the-19th-century stopover for the ailing public who came to "take the waters." These days, you can literally take the waters—bottled and sold in local convenience stores and even delivered to local homes.

NEIMAN'S (300 Carlsbad Village Dr; 760/729-4131) 1887 Victorian mansion, formerly owned by Gerhard Schutte (who bought the well from Frazier), is now a delightful restaurant with a fine dining room, cafe, lunch buffets, nightly entertainment, and a renowned Sunday brunch. The **SANDBAR** (3878 Carlsbad Blvd; 760/729-3170), is a more "get down" nightspot with a thirst-quenching happy hour and live entertainment ranging from reggae and blues to rock and swing.

BEAUTIFUL VIEW

The second-largest city in San Diego County, Chula Vista is blessed with the pleasant climate of communities located on San Diego Bay. Just 7 miles from the Mexican border, this city is a good stopping point for travelers heading down the coast to visit our neighbors to the south. Chula Vista means "beautiful view" in Spanish, and anyone strolling near the 900-slip Chula Vista Marina enjoying an evening sunset would have to agree.

There's much to keep you entertained in the South Bay's fastest-growing community. Visit the **Chula Vista Nature Center** (1000 Gunpowder Point Dr; 619/422-2473), a fully-accredited living museum, located on the Sweetwater Marsh National Wildlife Refuge. Bent on preserving California's diminishing coastal wetlands and its unique wildlife, the center seeks to educate its visitors with informative and interactive exhibits. Where else will the kids get a chance to pet a shark and a stingray? If you like your water without marine company, take the family and head to **White Water Canyon** (2052 Otay Valley Rd; 619/661-7373), an aquatic theme park just east of downtown Chula Vista. Open daily during the summer, weekends in the spring and fall, and closed during the winter, this fun water park features Otay Bay, a half-million-gallon wave pool; Tykes Trough for the wee ones; and speed slides for the more adventurous in the group. Next door to White Water is the **Coors Amphitheatre** (2050 Otay Valley Rd; 619/671-3600) a newly constructed music venue that sits like a giant space station on the outskirts of town. This arena was constructed with music in mind and has the acoustics to prove it. John Mellencamp, Paul Simon, Bob Dylan, and San Diego's own Jewel have rocked the house, with 10,000 reserved seats and 10,000 more on the upper lawn area. Also in Chula Vista is the U.S. Olympic Committee's $65 million **ARCO Training Center**, worth a visit for die-hard sports fans (see Organized Tours in the Exploring chapter). When hunger strikes at the end of the day, check out the **Baja Lobster Restaurant** (730 H St; 619/427-8690), specializing in Puerto Nuevo cuisine from Baja California. Twenty-five dollars will get you a large lobster, just like they serve up in Mexico. If your stomach can't handle a whole crustacean, try the Camarones Rancheros, spicy shrimp best accompanied by a cold beer or soda. If there's still some pep in your step, stop by **Jake's** (570 Marina Pkwy; 619/476-0400) for an after-dinner drink or dessert and enjoy a wonderful view of the waterfront. —*Susan Humphrey*

Carlsbad's "village" area—just a few blocks from the beach—is filled with shops, cafes, and restaurants, and **STATE STREET** is a popular prowl for antique hunters. The nearby 1887 Santa Fe Depot is now home to the **CARLSBAD CONVENTION & VISITORS BUREAU** (400 Carlsbad Village Dr; 760/434-6093), the perfect place to pick up maps and other tourist information. History and architecture buffs should visit **ST. MICHAEL'S**

EPISCOPAL CHURCH (1896), **HERITAGE HALL** (1926), and **MAG▮ HOUSE** (1887), all located near Garfield Street, between Beech a▮ Cypress Avenues. The seawall near the village is a great spot for watchi▮ the ocean's ebb and flow, while three lagoons afford plenty of bir▮ watching, fishing, and nature-walk opportunities. **SNUG HARB◖ MARINA** (Agua Hedionda Lagoon; 760/434-3089), on an inlet waterwa offers water-skiing, Jet Skis, kayak and canoe rentals, Waverunners, a▮ water bikes, as well as a pro shop, equipment rentals, and instruction▮

Serious shoppers won't want to miss **CARLSBAD COMPANY STOR▮** (on Paseo del Norte, off I-5 between Palomar Airport and Cannon R◖ 760/804-9000). Although this complex seems like an innocent Medite▮ ranean village, it actually houses a credit-card-defying complex of outl▮ stores (including Donna Karan, Joan & David, Gap, Fila, Barney's Ne▮ York, Oshkosh B'Gosh, and Royal Doulton), along with fine dinin▮ art galleries, fast food outlets, and—naturally—Starbucks. Tuscan-sty▮ **BELLEFLEUR WINERY AND RESTAURANT** (5610 Paseo del Nort◖ 760/603-1919; see Restaurants chapter) is the first known "shoppin▮ center" winery; it offers fine dining, wine tasting, a barrel aging room demonstration vineyard, and guided tours all under one roof.

If you visit anytime from mid-March to early May, you'll be in syn▮ with the blooms of the famous **FLOWER FIELDS AT CARLSBAD RANCE** (Paseo del Norte, off I-5 at Palomar Rd; 760/431-0352), one of Cali▮ fornia's major commercial flower-growing centers. In March and April you'll be knocked out by the thousands of vibrantly colored buttercup▮ covering more than 50 acres of hillsides; you can also spot many othe▮ varieties, including gladiolus and Star of Bethlehem. In May, the scen◖ changes to a hippie heaven when visitors stroll through the fields and tak◖ photos of their babies amid 20,000-plus Teddy Bear Sunflowers. During the December holiday season, Paul Ecke Ranch in nearby Encinitas sparks spirits with a virtual blaze of scarlet poinsettias arranged in the shape of a 166-foot star. Stock up on flowers (like Carlsbad's official flower—the bird of paradise—first developed commercially here), bulbs, plants, and other unique products at the gift shop by the flower fields.

Long before the buzz of new development and remodeling, Carlsbad was home to renowned **LA COSTA HOTEL AND SPA** (2100 Costa del Mar Rd; 760/438-9111) a celebrity and tycoon hideaway in a tranquil setting with two PGA championship golf courses, a golf school, large tennis center, bevy of restaurants, and world-famous full-service spa. The resort is in full swing during February's **ANDERSEN CONSULTING MATCH PLAY CHAMPIONSHIPS** golf tournament, and August's **TOSHIBA TENNIS CLASSIC**. In the mood for pampering? The **FOUR SEASONS RESORT–AVIARA** (7100 Four Seasons Pt; 760/931-6672), overlooking Batiquitos Lagoon, is one of the county's most luxurious resorts, with opulent rooms, amenities galore, several restaurants (including the highly praised **VIVACE**), and the Arnold Palmer-designed **AVIARA GOLF CLUB**.

Carlsbad's newest attraction is the **LEGOLAND** theme park (1 Lego Dr, off I-5 at Cannon Rd; 760/918-5346; see Top 25 Attractions in the Exploring chapter), the Danish-made monument to Lego interconnecting blocks. The 128–acre park incorporates about 30 million Lego bricks in its innovative family rides, interactive exhibits, mazes, restaurants, shops, landscaping, and even a "driving school"—with many more "Lego-isms" planned for the future (watch out, Disneyland!). Nearby **CAMP PENDLETON** (in Oceanside, at the county's northwest border; 760/725-5566), established in 1942, is the Marine Corps' largest amphibious training base. Visitors can take a self-guided driving tour (call for hours before you visit, since the base is sometimes closed to outsiders). **MISSION SAN LUIS REY** (4050 Mission Ave; 760/757-3651), established in 1798, is the largest of the Franciscans' fabled 21 missions, and includes a retreat, museum, and chapel.

Other events to watch for in Carlsbad are January's **SAN DIEGO MARATHON**, with its beginning and ending point at the Plaza Camino Real Shopping Center and participants numbering around 5,000, and March's **CARLSBAD 5000**, a premier 5K race with more than 10,000 competitors. The **CARLSBAD STREET FAIRES**—held the first Sundays in May and November—are California's largest street festivals, bringing hordes of people to the downtown area to browse hundreds of booths laden with arts and crafts. Throughout the summer, the city also hosts free **JAZZ CONCERTS** at city parks for a mellow picnic-and-blanket crowd.

Escondido and Environs

33 miles northeast of downtown (approximately 45 minutes). Drive north on Highway 163, which merges into Interstate 15 N. Take Interstate 15 to the Valley Parkway exit for downtown Escondido. Turn right onto W Valley Parkway, which becomes W Grand Avenue. To reach the Wild Animal Park take Interstate 15 to the Highway 78 exit E (San Pasqual Valley Road).

The English translation of Escondido is "hidden valley," though this burgeoning city is anything but hidden these days. Situated about 30 miles northeast of downtown, the once-sleepy little community has become firmly entrenched in nouveau San Diego's space-sucking urban sprawl. Though Escondido has a prestigious arts center, some superb restaurants, and one of the largest shopping malls in the country (**NORTH COUNTY FAIR**, at I-15 and Via Rancho Pkwy; 760/489-2332), many San Diego residents and out-of-towners think of the city only in the vaguest terms—mainly as the turn-off to San Diego's famous **WILD ANIMAL PARK** (15500

San Pasqual Valley Rd; 760/747-8702; see Top 25 Attractions in t Exploring chapter).

Nearby **SAN PASQUAL BATTLEFIELD STATE HISTORIC PARK AI MUSEUM** (15808 San Pasqual Valley Rd; 760/489-0076), commemorat soldiers, including Kit Carson, who in 1846 fought here during a hi point of the Mexican-American War. Stop by the visitor center for a m: of the self-guided nature trail, which encompasses native plants and wide valley view.

One of the things that makes this mini-metropolis a cultural stan out is the prominent **CALIFORNIA CENTER FOR THE ARTS** (340 N Escoi dido Blvd; 760/738-4100), which showcases plays, dance performance and concerts including such diverse talents as the Afro-Cuban All Sta: and Turkey's Whirling Dervishes. Noteworthy restaurants withi walking distance of the arts center include **SIRINO'S** (113 W Grand Av 760/745-3835) for excellent Italian specialties (try the signature veal pro sciutto ravioli with cognac); and **150 GRAND CAFE** (150 W Grand Av 760/738-6868), well-regarded for its California-French cuisine an lovely setting. The **VINTAGE TEA ROOM AT THE GILDED LILY** (217 Grand Ave; 760/743-1292) is a delightful stop for traditional English te; finger sandwiches, and puddings.

Though bandleader Lawrence Welk has flown off to that big cham pagne bubble in the sky, his 1000-acre-plus, circa-1960s **WELK RESOR CENTER** (8860 Lawrence Welk Dr; 760/749-3000) still flourishes. Asid: from the plethora of hotel amenities and recreation options (including three golf courses), the resort boasts a museum laden with Welk memo rabilia and a 330-seat dinner theater that presents first-rate musicals and variety shows. **DEER PARK** (29013 Champagne Blvd; 760/749-1666) is an odd—but wonderful—combination car museum and winery. Drool over more than 120 vintage convertibles, then mellow your envy at a wine tasting. Other Escondido area wineries offering tours and tastings are **ORFILA WINERY** (13455 San Pasqual Valley Rd; 760/738-6500), near the Wild Animal Park; and **FERRARA WINERY** (120 W 15th Ave, between Maple and Juniper Sts; 760/745-7632), a historical facility that began wine production in the early 1930s.

Though spa resorts are now common throughout the country, the **GOLDEN DOOR** (777 Deer Springs Rd; off I-15; 760/744-5777) is a long-time classic. Established in the 1950s by mastermind Deborah Szekely, this operation is still a favorite get-fit getaway with the really, really rich and famous, who jet and limo in and pay thousands for a week of peace, privacy, and pampering.

The small community of **FALLBROOK**, about 20 miles northwest of Escondido, is the self-ordained "avocado capital of the world" with some 6,000 acres of the luscious fat-laden fruit, as well as macadamia nuts and other delights. **OLD MAIN STREET**, in the village center, is fun to explore by foot, peeking into antique and collectible shops and old-fashioned stores.

Rancho Bernardo, south of Escondido, an ever-growing bastion of early California-style suburbia and high-tech conglomerate, houses a golfer's paradise, the **RANCHO BERNARDO INN** (17550 Bernardo Oaks Dr; 858/675-8500). In keeping with the environment, the 287-room inn is a low-lying sprawl of adobe and Spanish flair, with a championship 18-hole golf course, driving range, putting green, 12 tennis courts, myriad activities, and the award-winning restaurant **EL BIZCOCHO** (see Restaurants chapter).

Heading back toward the coast from Escondido, take Via Rancho Parkway south for about five miles until **LAKE HODGES** appears below. Turn down toward the lake, where you'll find *very* non–suburban-type cottages and cabins tucked into the woodsy hillside. **HERNANDEZ HIDE-AWAY** (19320 Lake Dr; 760/746-1444), at the bottom of the hill, has been an off-the-beaten-path favorite since 1972, serving up Mexican cuisine, Sunday brunch, cerveza, and Margaritas in its lakefront setting.

Palomar Mountain and Julian

62 miles northwest of downtown (approximately 1½ hours). Drive north on Interstate 15 to Highway 76, then head east to County Road S6 (South Grade Road) and follow this twisting "Highway to the Stars" to the top of Palomar Mountain. From Palomar Mountain, drop back down County Road S6 to Highway 76 and continue southeast to Highway 79. Follow Highway 79 south to the crossroads town of Santa Ysabel, then take Highway 78/79 into Julian.

Sandwiched between San Diego's golden beaches to the west and the vast Anza-Borrego Desert State Park to the east, pine-scented mountains offer an easy day escape from the hurly-burly of the city. Life in the mountain towns of Palomar, Santa Ysabel, and Julian moves at a slower pace—heck, you can't even find current magazines for sale in Julian. It's just too much trouble to haul them up to this Old West hamlet. You can combine Palomar Mountain and Julian into one day trip—if you hit the road early. But there's plenty to see and do in both places, so you may want to devote a day to each. Each is about an hour and a half from the heart of San Diego, but most of the driving is on scenic two-lane country roads.

The S6 road runs right into the parking lot of the **PALOMAR OBSERVATORY** (760/742-2119). Admission is free to this white-domed observatory that rises from the meadow like a nuclear mushroom cloud. The 200-inch **HALE TELESCOPE** remains one of the largest scientific instruments in the world. While visitors can't peer through it, they can admire

this marvel of engineering from an observation deck. To learn m
about some of the celestial discoveries astronomers have made throu
the telescope, as well as the tremendous efforts that went into buildin;
on this remote mountaintop, stop at the **GREENWAY MUSEUM**. Yoɪ
pass it on the walk from the parking lot to the observatory.

As you wind back down S6, you can't miss the commercial hub
Palomar Mountain at the junction of S6 and S7. For a little down-hoɪ
sustenance, maybe a cup of hot chocolate or a bowl of chili, stop
MOTHER'S KITCHEN (760/742-4233). Or pop into the **PALOMAR MOU**
TAIN GENERAL STORE & TRADING CO. (760/742-2496) for groceriɛ
camping supplies, and a fine selection of jewelry, small decorative objec
and books from around the world.

PALOMAR MOUNTAIN STATE PARK (1 mile west on S7 from the ʃ
junction; 760/742-3462) is a pristine, 1,683-acre paradise of hikiɪ
trails, campgrounds, and picnic sites. Check out the kid-friendly hikiɪ
trails, especially the easy **DOANE VALLEY NATURE TRAIL**. Little ones mɛ
spot mule deer among the ponderosa pines, cedar, and spruce. The paɪ
is most popular in winter when it's blanketed in snow. Thanks to a 6,00ɛ
foot-plus elevation, Palomar Mountain gets plenty of snow and raɪ
every year.

From Palomar Mountain, continue southeast to the roadside hamlɛ
of Santa Ysabel at the intersection of Highways 78 and 79. It's a goo
place for a pit stop. Few San Diegans can drive past **DUDLEY'S BAKER**
(30218 Hwy 78, at the intersection with Hwy 79; 760/765-0488) witɪ
out pausing for a loaf of date-nut-raisin bread or a few doughnuts. Juʃ
up the street, the **SANTA YSABEL ART GALLERY** (30352 Hwy 78; 760/765
1676) showcases first-rate work by local artists in a light-filled setting
Prices are pretty good too.

It's just a short haul up the hill into the mountain town of Julian
which looks like an Old West movie set. There really was a short-liveɛ
gold rush in the 1870s, but 19th-century gold mines have given way tɛ
apple orchards that attract hordes of day-trippers on fall weekends. The
come to sip cider and sample the apple pie sold in every cafe and bakery
Everyone claims to have the best pie, but we think it's a toss-up betweeɪ
MOM'S PIES, ETC. (2119 Main St; 760/765-2472) and the **JULIAN PIE**
CO. (2225 Main St; 760/765-2449). For other grub, belly up to the
marble counter at the **MINER'S DINER** inside the **JULIAN DRUG STORE**
(2134 Main St; 760/765-0332). Another good bet is the **JULIAN CAFE &**
BAKERY (2112 Main St; 760/765-2712), which serves hearty vittles amid
an impressive collection of cowboy memorabilia.

Walk off the pie by exploring Julian and its environs. The **JULIAN**
PIONEER MUSEUM (2811 Washington St; 760/765-0227) is filled to the
rafters with odds and ends donated by local residents. You'll find every-

thing from vintage clothes to rusty mining tools and old photos. You also can hike up to the old **PIONEER CEMETERY** (at the top of A St off Main St) to check out the headstones of Julian's founding fathers.

Once you begin exploring, you may want to spend the night in pine-scented air. Book a room at **THE ARTISTS' LOFT** (4811 Pine Ridge Ave, Julian; 760/765-0765). Choose a room in the main house or a cabin in the woods and snuggle up by one of the many fireplaces. With more time to wander, you can check out the surrounding area.

The hike up the **VOLCAN MOUNTAIN WILDERNESS PRESERVE** (off Farmers Rd; 760/765-2811) is steep but short; views overlooking town, the surrounding meadows, and the Cuyamaca Mountains are ample reward. You can also explore Volcan Mountain on a trail ride with **JULIAN STABLES** (760/765-1598). Drop-in visits are discouraged; call ahead for reservations. If driving is your preferred mode of touring, head south on Highway 79 through the Cuyamaca Mountains and stretch your legs on any of the many marked trails (Green Valley Falls is especially nice). Then end the day with samples of locally made chardonnay and sauvignon blanc at Julian's **MENGHINI WINERY** (1150 Julian Orchards Dr; 760/765-2072).

Anza-Borrego Desert and Borrego Springs

78 miles northeast of San Diego (approximately 2 hours). Take Interstate 8 east to Highway 67 and go north to Ramona. Follow Highway 78 to Santa Ysabel. Go north on Highway 79 to Highway S2. Go east on Highway S2 and travel approximately 5 miles to S22, which takes you through the small town of Ranchita and into the Anza-Borrego Desert State Park and Borrego Springs.

Some teasingly call them desert rats—those people who love the hot, dry air and xeric habitat of the American Southwest. With daytime temperatures hovering over 105° for weeks at a time (sometimes reaching 120°), a stoic tolerance for heat is a boon to those 3,500 residents who call the community of Borrego Springs home. If you find that sort of heat unbearable, delay your drive to this part of the country until October through May, when the weather is downright perfect—warm and arid with clear blue skies. The town is also home to the headquarters for the **ANZA-BORREGO DESERT STATE PARK** (760/767-4684), covering 600,000 acres (1,000 square miles) from Riverside County (north of San Diego) down to Mexico along the eastern border of San Diego County. The park is a wild wonderland where roadrunners dash across the asphalt dodging cars and trucks; golden eagles soar in the sky; kit foxes, mule deer, and bighorn sheep hide in isolated habitats; and desert iguanas and four species of rattlesnake slither about the desert floor.

GAMBLING GOES NATIVE

For thousands of years, Indians hunted small game and gathered acorns from the California oak in the rich coastal and inland areas of San Diego County. Today, three local bands, the Barona, Viejas, and Sycuan, are raking in the dough from Vegas-style casinos in the eastern part of the county, all just 30 minutes from downtown. The circus-themed **Barona Casino** (1000 Wildcat Canyon Rd, Lakeside; 619/443-2300) is one of the largest Indian gaming facilities in California, with over 1,000 video gaming machines, a 1500-seat bingo hall, and 20 tables for card playing. Tribal leaders recently announced a $120 million expansion that will double the size of the casino and add an 18-hole golf course and hotel. Also on the premises is the Barona Speedway, a dusty track where tiny dwarf cars and motorcycles race on the weekends. At **Sycuan Casino** (5469 Dehesa Rd, El Cajon; 619/445-6002) those feeling lucky can gamble at poker, bingo, blackjack, or the video machines. Off-track satellite wagering on the ponies is available in the 450-seat Hall of Champions. And you can stuff yourself silly at the all-you-can-eat buffet for less than $10.

The only casino with a license to sell liquor, the **Viejas Casino & Turf Club** (5000 Willows Rd, Alpine; 800/84-POKER) features Indian blackjack, poker tournaments, and 950 video terminals. There's nightly entertainment in the Dreamcatcher Showroom, sometimes with no cover charge, and those who like to belt out a tune or two can check the schedule for karaoke night. If you win a bundle in the poker room, make your way across the street to the stylish outlet center, home to more than 30 stores, including Liz Claiborne, Tommy Hilfiger, Linen Barn, and the Gap. —Susan Humphrey

Begin your desert experience at the park's **VISITORS CENTER** (200 Palm Canyon Dr; 760/767-4205, 760/767-4684 24-hour information line) in Borrego Springs. The facility is open every day from October through May, from 9am to 5pm, and weekends and holidays only from June through September. You'll find desert exhibits, a slide show, and an excellent gift shop with maps showing desert trails. Outside, the fascinating desert garden provides an overview of bizarre and beautiful cacti and wildflowers, all identified for the edification of novices. Pupfish, who survive in oases and small puddles of water, thrive in the garden's ponds. Signs lead to the easy 1½-mile **PALM CANYON TRAIL** from the Visitors Center. The trail leads up a slight incline to palm groves, a seasonal stream, and a waterfall, which tumbles over boulders during the winter rainy season. Blooming cacti and wildflowers bring visitors by the thousands from January through March, creating traffic jams along the highways and in Borrego Springs. Try to visit during the week; weekend hordes detract from the wild, lonely feel of the desert.

There are several ways to explore the region without getting lost on hiking trails. In fact, unless you are an experienced hiker, you're best off sticking close to the road or joining a guided tour. One of the best options is a wild ride with **DESERT JEEP TOURS/OUTBACK TOURS** (760/767-0501); call in advance for reservations. Tours in their air-conditioned four-wheel-drive Jeeps range from $60 to $90 per person; all include pickup and return to any location in Borrego Springs, a well-versed guide, and drinks and snacks. Find fossils in the Badlands or visit an ancient Indian site. There are also specialized tours; if you're not claustrophobic you may want to explore some mud caves on the "spelunking tour."

Self-guided driving tours are another sensible option; maps outlining routes and stops are available at the Visitors Center. The **SOUTHERN EMI-GRANT TRAIL** runs 26 miles from Scissors Crossing at Highway 78 and County Road S2. The Emigrant Trail was one of the few year-round routes into California in the mid-1800s. Spanish explorers, Kit Carson, the Mormon Battalion, Sonoran gold seekers, and the Butterfield Overland Stage all passed along this historic route. The **EROSION ROAD TOUR** runs 18 miles from the Visitors Center on S22 and provides an overview of the desert's geology. It includes 10 stops that demonstrate the geologic forces that create mountains, canyons, alluvial fans, and earthquake faults; the best part is the overlook with endless vistas over the Borrego Badlands to the Salton Sea.

There are several restaurants and cafes in town; our favorite is the **KRAZY COYOTE SALOON AND GRILLE** (2220 Hoberg Rd, Borrego Springs; 760/767-7788), open daily for lunch and dinner. Homemade soups, gourmet pizzas, thick steaks, and great desserts make it a favorite hangout for locals; reservations are recommended. The restaurant is part of the Palms at Indian Head resort. Just outside the door is a 1½-mile self-guided nature trail with waterfalls, streams, and native fan palms around an oasis. Bighorn sheep can sometimes be spotted on cliffs around the resort. For desert memorabilia, check out **TUMBLEWEED TRADING COMPANY** (526 Palm Canyon Dr; 760/767-4244).

Don't miss seeing the desert at night. Stars and planets that are utterly invisible in the city shine bright in a midnight-blue sky. Critters scuttle about in the sand. Silver cholla cacti seem to shimmer in moonlight. And the silence is nearly overwhelming. Our favorite desert hideaway is **LA CASA DEL ZORRO** (3845 Yaqui Pass Rd, Borrego Springs; 60/767-5323 or 800/824-1884). Though it's somewhat expensive, the resort's pools, restaurant, and rooms with fireplaces are worth the splurge. The **BORREGO VALLEY INN** (405 Palm Canyon Dr, Borrego Springs; 760/767-0311) has 14 rooms with fireplaces, kitchenettes, and private patios; rates include a buffet breakfast, and there are two pools.

If camping is more your style, the park has two developed cam grounds, at Borrego Palm Canyon and Tamarisk Grove. Make reser tions by calling Park Net (800/444-7275). There is also a sm campground at Bow Willow and a horse camp located at the mouth Coyote Canyon. Elsewhere in the park, backcountry camping is p mitted with the purchase of a $5 daily park use permit; ask about rules at the Visitors Center.

Temecul

60 miles northeast of downtown (approximately 70 minutes). Dr north on Highway 163, which merges into Interstate 15 N. Contin north to the Highway 79 S exit toward Temecula, and continue to Front Street exit.

Just over the county line in neighboring Riverside County, Temecula is blend of the mundane and the marvelous. What began as a bedroo community of affordable housing is now coming into its own as weekend escape for urban San Diegans. This metamorphosis is due part to the area's nascent wine country. Temecula's "Rainbow Gap with its cool morning mists and sun-drenched afternoons, gives it th ideal climate for cultivating grapes. As yet, the wineries are no match size or cachet to those in Northern California's Napa Valley, or even th Santa Ynez Valley of the central coast. Therein lies its charm, becaus Temecula doesn't put on airs. Spend the morning browsing antiqu shops, pass the afternoon sampling vintages at roadside tasting room then kick up your heels line-dancing into the night.

In typical Southern California fashion, you'll need wheels to explor Temecula and its environs; it's about 60 minutes from downtown Sa Diego, driving north on Interstate 15. Call the **TEMECULA VALLEY VINT NERS ASSOCIATION,** (800/801-WINE or 909/699-3626) for a free ma of local vineyards.

With its tract-home subdivisions, Temecula seems like the epitom of a spanking-new Southern California planned community. In fact, it roots stretch back to 1858, when it was a stop on the Butterfield Over land Stagecoach route. The community indulges its nostalgia in Ol Town Temecula, a 6-block-long shopping district just west of Interstat 15 (exit west on Rancho California and turn left on Front Street). Ir 1998, the city spent $5.2 million on a lavish facelift to enhance the Ol West theme with spiffy wooden sidewalks and old-timey benches anc light fixtures. There's plenty here to entice you stay for a spell, including more than two dozen antique shops. Among the best are **NANA'S ANTIQUES** (28677 Front St; 909/699-2389) for vintage art-deco clothing and Victorian knickknacks, and the **CHAPARRAL ANTIQUE MALL** (28465

Front St; 909/676-0070), which houses 19th-century hardware alongside '60s kitsch. Up the street, you can two-step the night away at **TEMECULA STAMPEDE** (28721 Front St; 909/695-1760). The cover charge at this enormous country-western nightclub is $5 per person and includes live music and a chance to test your skill on the mechanical bull.

The nostalgia of Old Town Temecula isn't manufactured. Many of the district's buildings date back to the community's early days, and the **TEMECULA VALLEY MUSEUM** (in Sam Hicks Park between 6th St and Moreno Rd; 909/676-0021) houses an intriguing display of local historical tchotchkes. You also can peer in the window of the dinky **TEMECULA JAIL** (just off Main St), originally built as a wine cellar using granite mined from the Temecula Quarry, and glimpse a couple of mannequins posed as drunken Old West rascals. Old Town also has some of the best dining options for kids: casual **ROSA'S CANTINA** (28636 Front St; 909/695-2428) serves Mexican fare; for burgers and sandwiches, check out the very affordable **SWING INN CAFE** (28676 Front St; 909/676-2321). More adventurous young eaters may prefer the Greek dishes at **CONSTANTINO'S SILVER SPOON RESTAURANT** (28690 Front St; 909/699-1015).

For more nouveau California pleasures, spend the afternoon exploring the wineries that dot Rancho California Road just outside of town. Most have small tasting rooms open to the public (samples range from free to $6, depending on the winery). Once you drive past the new malls boasting every imaginable fast-food outlet, you're surrounded by bucolic vineyards carpeting the hillsides. **THORNTON WINERY** (32575 Rancho California Rd; 909/699-0099) is best-known for its *methode champagnoise* sparkling wines made under the Culbertson label. Just across the street is **CALLAWAY VINEYARD & WINERY** (32720 Rancho California Rd; 909/676-4001), Temecula's largest wine producer with more than 700 acres. Continuing northeast on Rancho California Road, you'll see signs for other wineries. The staff at **MAURICE CARRIE WINERY** (34225 Rancho California Rd; 909/676-1711) pours free samples in a charming farmhouse tasting room. Just off the main road, **TEMECULA CREST WINERY** (40620 Calle Contento; 909/676-8231) sits high on a hill with a commanding view of the valley. For the best picnic site, head to **MOUNT PALOMAR WINERY** (33820 Rancho California Rd; 909/676-5047), where you can sample vintages in the tasting room, pick up goodies from the gourmet deli, and then follow a short path from the parking lot to a hilltop picnic area. Magnificent views of the vineyards and citrus groves may have you asking: Is this Temecula or Tuscany?

Temecula also has some winning eateries to accompany their wine. Thornton Winery's **CAFE CHAMPAGNE** (32575 Rancho California Rd; 909/699-0099) serves a seasonally inspired menu in an elegant dining

room or on a patio with vineyard views. You can practically reach
and snatch a grape from one of the al fresco tables at Callaway's **VI
YARD TERRACE** restaurant (32720 Rancho California Rd; 909/3
6661). **BAILEY WINE COUNTRY CAFE** (27644 Ynez Rd; 909/676-95
offers a menu of fresh, California-cuisine-style fish, chicken, and pas
accompanied by a wine list consisting entirely of local vintages.

No need to do any driving after all that wine tasting; Temecula
a couple of terrific places to spend the night. Fragrant vineyards surrou
you at the six-room **LOMA VISTA BED & BREAKFAST** (33350 La Sere
Way; 909/676-7046). Rooms at the Mediterranean-style villa ov
looking the valley run $100-$150 a night, including breakfast. The 8
room **TEMECULA CREEK INN** (44501 Rainbow Canyon F
800/622-7335 or 909/694-1000) boasts a 27-hole golf course, ten
courts, and spacious rooms for $120-$195 per night.

Disneylan

*94 miles north of downtown (approximately 2 hours). Drive north
Interstate 5 to the Katella Avenue exit. Turn left on E Katella Avenue, l
on W Freedman Way to Disneyland entrance.*

The "Happiest Place on Earth" has become—difficult as it may be
believe—even *happier*, thanks to recent renovations, spiffed-up attra
tions, and fresh entertainment. **TOMORROWLAND** has undergone mar

enhancements and should be first on your list (unless you're with sma
children, who will insist that Fantasyland gets top priority). Shedding i
stuck-in-the-1950s time warp (which was making it seem almost
archaic as Frontierland), it's now appropriately high-techified for a slic
glide into the next millennium.

All the customary offerings are still there too. Hop one of four choo
choos that circle the park or get a heavy dose of exercise as you walk t
and from eight theme areas—1890s Main Street USA, Adventurelanc
Fantasyland, Frontierland, Tomorrowland, Critter Country, Ne
Orleans Square, and Mickey's Toontown. With more than 60 majo
rides, myriad smaller amusements and arcades, 30 restaurants, and 5
shops, all bets are on: you *will* leave Disneyland with a pair of mouse ear
and a souvenir photo with some fairytale character!

Those old favorites—**SPACE MOUNTAIN** and **STAR TOURS**—are sti
there, but the new attractions are real doozies. The Leonard da Vinci
inspired **ASTRO ORBITOR**, at Tomorrowland's entrance, lets you zoo
and zip the cosmos in your own starship, practically swiping orbitin
planets. Too tame? Try your wits on the futuristic **ROCKET RODS**, the
fastest and longest thrill ride in the park's history. Gutless guests migh
be happier experiencing 3-D life in "**HONEY, I SHRUNK THE AUDIENCE,**"

where the most frightening moment is when the floor rises four inches—still, it's pretty cool. Even cooler is **INNOVENTIONS**, housed in the former Carousel Theater. This gigantic playground appeals to technology fiends, savvy kids, and the rest of us low-techies who are mesmerized by the whole-body interactive experiences designed to show how technology is making the world a better place. The two-story revolving building offers five exploration zones: entertainment, home, transportation, sports and health, and the InfoZone. Control the body movements of a mannequin garbed in Yamaha's sensor-laden Miburi suit; give household commands to "Debbie," the voice (and slave) inside the Home Automated Living 2000 System; take a virtual reality road trip in dramatic climate conditions . . . you get the idea.

Everyone loves a parade and, thankfully, Disneyland has brought in some new marching blood. Goodbye, *Lion King*. Hello, *Mulan*! Inspired by Disney's more recent animated feature, The Mulan Parade is a colorful event filled with special effects, Chinese circus performers, a giant horse-drawn carriage, choreographed martial arts performances, and a 30-foot inflated villain, all celebrating heroine Mulan and ultimate victory. The after-dark schedule makes it even more of a standout.

Along with the parades, other entertainment options have changed and expanded. If you're into fireworks and light shows, check out **FANTASMIC** on the Rivers of America—a Mickey-and-friends battle against villainous characters fought out with synchronized pyrotechnics, stunts, music, and laser-projected images. Or catch **FANTASY IN THE SKY** fireworks over Sleeping Beauty Castle. Carefully choreographed pyrotechnics blaze in sync with patriotic tunes and Disney hits. The kids will be amused by **ANIMAZEMENT—THE MUSICAL**, a live musical revue with songs from Disney favorites, held in the remodeled Fantasyland Theatre. For vaudeville-style entertainment and toe-tapping banjo tunes, catch the **GOLDEN HORSESHOE VARIETY SHOW** in Frontierland.

The **DISNEY GALLERY**, located above the Pirates of the Caribbean, offers interesting exhibits, including sketches, renderings, models, and photographs. To delve even further into this incredible dream-come-true, join one of the designated tour guides for an insider's peek into the fascinating life and times of Mr. Walt Disney, dreamer extraordinaire.

Like Tomorrowland, each of the theme areas has its own unique crowd pleasers. Not to be missed are Adventureland's **JUNGLE CRUISE** and **INDIANA JONES ADVENTURE**; the **HAUNTED MANSION** in New Orleans Square; Critter Country's **SPLASH MOUNTAIN**; **BIG THUNDER MOUNTAIN RAILROAD** and **TOM SAWYER'S ISLAND** in Frontierland; **MICKEY'S TOONTOWN** and **FANTASYLAND**, a favorite with the little ones and home of the **MATTERHORN** bobsled coaster.

Though the Anaheim area is jam-packed with hotels, motels, a
motor inns that feature all price ranges, part of the Disneyland "expe
ence" is a stay at one of the Disneyland Resort Hotels—a complex co
prising the **DISNEYLAND HOTEL AND DISNEYLAND PACIFIC HOTEL.**
a snap to whisk over on the connecting Monorail from the park, a
you'll be treated to more shows, characters, fantasies, odysseys, and od
ities than you can imagine, as well as arcades, shops, lounges, and resta
rants. Try **DISNEY'S PCH GRILL**, in the Disneyland Pacific Hotel, t
newest restaurant with an imaginative new-wave fusion menu. **YAMABU**
also in the Disneyland Pacific, features traditional Japanese cuisine,
sushi bar, and special children's menu. Or stick to all-American favorit
such as french fries, burgers, and thick shakes, at Disneyland Hote
pseudo-1950s diner, the **MONORAIL CAFE.** (For more information abo
Disneyland, phone 714/781-4565, or log on at www.disney land.com

BAJA

NORTH COAST OF BAJA

AJA

Baja California, Mexico

The busiest border crossing in the world lies just 18 miles south of downtown San Diego at San Ysidro, California, and Tijuana, Mexico. Locals from both sides of the border cross frequently to visit family and friends, attend concerts and sporting events, shop for groceries and gifts, and dine in favorite restaurants. Travelers to Tijuana and San Diego can't resist visiting another country for at least one day; once inducted, they almost always want more.

Tijuana is just the beginning of a fascinating journey into Mexico's Baja California Peninsula. The 1,000-mile-long strip of stark desert and mountains is firmly anchored between the Pacific Ocean and the Mar de Cortés. The peninsula was divided into two states—Baja California and Baja California Sur—in 1974. The northern portion is one of the fastest-growing parts of Mexico. Tijuana, in fact, is that nation's fourth-largest city. Development has spread south from Tijuana to the coastal community of Rosarito and on to the port city of Ensenada. Hundreds of U.S. citizens live in this portion of Mexico; hundreds more have vacation homes in private communities.

The Baja side of San Diego is an attraction few cities can claim, and one well worth exploring. Go over the options described in each section below, and choose the cities that best fit your time frame and interests. See "Border Sense" in this chapter for information on transportation, money, health, and safety. *Felíz Viaje*—have a happy trip.

Tijuana

18 miles south of San Diego, off US Interstate 5

Tijuana's influence over San Diego is evident for miles before you reach the border. Signs on roadways and storefronts combine Spanish and English instructions and descriptions. Soon the spoken language slips into Spanglish, a combination of the two languages with its own special slang. The border itself assaults the senses with congested traffic, a significant police presence, and entirely foreign sights and smells. The aromas of meat, onions, and chilies sizzling on grills at taco stands immediately set the stomach growling. Shops and souvenir arcades get fingers twitching. And the eyes are constantly challenged by fascinating distractions. Beyond the obvious tourist attractions, Tijuana has a busy international airport, a thriving arts and culture scene, and hotels and restaurants befitting business travelers and wealthy Mexican families. It also is gaining a reputation as a major hub for drug cartels from both sides of the border.

So unless you're a seasoned and highly savvy foreign traveler, stick w
the tourist zones described below, and keep a close hold on your poss
sions at all times.

AVENIDA REVOLUCIÓN, the traditional tourist zone, is lined w
shopping arcades, fast-food franchises, and a few truly Mexican resta
rants. Its bars have always catered to a rowdy crowd. These days, slea
topless clubs (usually down a dark stairway) compete with rock-and-r
bars (usually up a stairway to a rooftop terrace).

The real reason Revolución is often crowded to the max is its sho
ping opportunities. The avenue, from Calle 1 to Calle 8, is lined wi
shops selling trinkets, mementos, and crafts from cheap and tacky to el
gant and expensive, including silver jewelry, serapes (cotton blanket.
embroidered dresses and blouses, carved figures of onyx or woo
huaraches (leather sandals), and more. Bargaining is expected on tl
streets and in less formal shops, but not in the nicer stores. Shopkeepe
throughout Tijuana generally speak excellent English and accept dollar

Some shoppers find the hawkers, shills, and touts who loudly beckc
and proclaim from outside the storefronts a little disconcerting. The:
folks may feel more comfortable in the mini-malls and modern arcade
BAZAR DE MEXICO (Av Revolución at Calle 7; tel. 66/86-5280) is clea
(it even has decent public rest rooms) and packed with vendors. Simil:
shops and stands fill the **MEXICOACH TERMINAL** (Av Revolució
between Calle 6 and 7; tel. 66/85-1470). **SANBORNS** (Av Revolución :
Calle 8; tel. 66/88-1462), a classy coffee shop/restaurant popular wit
middle- and upper-class Mexicans, also has folk art from throughout th
county, excellent books and CDs, and a delectable assortment of choc
lates, cakes, and pastries. **TOLÁN** (Av Revolución between Calles 7 an
8; tel. 66/88-3637) is a high-end arts and antiques boutique with cerami
eggs by artist Sergio Bustamante, beautiful Christmas ornaments an
decorations, Talavera pottery from the state of Puebla, and lots of othe
elegant and rustic items from throughout Mexico. Artisans' stands lin
Calle 1 between the border and Revolución.

More orderly shopping is available at **PLAZA RÍO TIJUANA** (A
Paseo de los Héroes 96-98; tel. 66/84-0402), a full-scale mall witl
department stores, restaurants, and a multiplex theater. **PLAZA FIEST/**
(Av Paseo de los Héroes 9415; tel. 66/84-2714) is home to a collectior
of unique boutiques, as is **PUEBLO AMIGO** (Vía Oriente 9211; tel. 66/84
2714), whose stuccoed walls are painted in a variety of pastel hues. Her
you'll find Ley, a grocery that sells real Mexican delicacies such as can
died papaya and fresh spicy sauces for seafood and meat.

If you'd like to see a real Mexican market (where you can practice
your Spanish), head for the **MERCADO HIDALGO** (Avs Independencia and
Sanchez Taboada, 5 blocks east of Revolución). The souvenirs here are

of a practical bent—sandals, piñatas, soaps and potions with intriguing labels—and the market is a great place to people-watch or take discreet photos and see life outside the tourist zone.

To reward the kids for putting up with your shopping spree, take them to Mundo Divertido (Av Paseo de los Héroes at Calle Velazco; tel. 66/34-3213; weekdays noon–9pm, weekends 11am to 10pm), with its miniature golf course, batting cages, roller coaster, and enormous video-game hall. Rides are inexpensive and there are stands selling fast food.

The amusement park and several of the city's finer restaurants are located in the Zona Río (between Blvd Agua Caliente and the border) along Avenida Paseo de los Héroes. The avenue runs parallel to the dry Tía Juana River and is a main thoroughfare with large statues of historical figures, including one of Abraham Lincoln, in the center of the *glorietas* (traffic circles). The heart of the Zona Río is the **TIJUANA CULTURAL CENTER** (Centro Cultural, Av Paseo de los Héroes at Av Independencia; tel. 66/84-1111 or 66/84-1125; open every day 9am to 8pm). The museum ($2) gives an overview of Mexican history, and the Omnimax Theater ($3.50), with its 180-degree screen, shows a variety of interesting films—with at least one daily in English. These often complement the center's rotating art and culture exhibits. The bookstore has a good selection of books in both Spanish and English.

As in San Diego, sports play a big part in the Baja experience. Many visitors enjoy watching fast-paced **JAI ALAI**, a game originally from the Basque country in northern Spain. Similar to racquetball but using a long, sickle-shaped basket instead of a racquet, it's played in the Moorish-style **PALACIO FRONTÓN** (Av Revolución and Calle 8; tel. 66/38-4308; 800/PIK-BAJA in the U.S.). Wagering is permitted. Day games are Monday through Friday starting at noon; night games are played Tuesday through Saturday beginning at 8pm; admission is $5. Next door at the **CALIENTE SPORTS BOOK**, folks can wager on satellite-imported sports and horse-racing events. **BULLFIGHTS** are held at El Toreo de Tijuana (Av Agua Caliente outside downtown; tel. 66/85-2210) May through October, generally on Sundays at 4pm. During summer months you can often see fights at the Plaza de Toros Monumental (Playas Tijuana area, near the U.S. border, Ensenada Hwy; tel. 66/85-2210). Admission cost depends on seat location and the matador's fame. For less bloodthirsty entertainment, take a tour of the **L. A. CETTO WINERY** (Cañon Johnson 8151, at Av Constitución; tel. 66/85-3031 or 66/85-1644; closed Monday). Cost is $1 per person, $2 including tastings. Pick up souvenirs and vintages at the winery gift shop.

Even if you only spend a few hours in Tijuana, you must have an authentic Mexican meal. If you prefer an elegant and (by Mexican standards) expensive meal, **CIEN AÑOS** (Av José María 1407 in the Zona Río;

BORDER SENSE

Many leaders and citizens on both sides of the border speak of San Diego and Tijuana as an enormous binational metropolis. A cross-border language, cuisine, and culture has emerged over the last century, and the two cities will forever be entwined. As a result, traveling to northern Baja is almost as easy as heading north to Los Angeles. But there are some differences. Here are some tips you should heed to be sure of a comfortable and rewarding journey.

Getting There: The San Diego Trolley line ends in San Ysidro at the border. Pedestrians either walk over the border on a seemingly endless bridge, or board a Mexican bus or cab and ride through the border (a 10-minute trip across Interstate 5 to the Mexican entry). Drivers park in lots at the end of Interstate 5 near Mexican customs and walk through a few gates, or follow the often long lines of vehicles feeding past the border guards.

Getting Back: Pedestrians and drivers pass through customs' booths, where they must declare their citizenship and describe what they're bringing back into the United States. Adults are allowed 1 liter of alcohol and 1 carton of cigarettes—don't load up on tequila for souvenirs. Cuban cigars are also forbidden. Anyone can be pulled aside for secondary inspection, which can last minutes or hours.

Money: The peso is the official currency in Mexico, but dollars and U.S. credit cards and traveler's checks are readily accepted.

Paperwork: Everyone crossing the border must have proof of citizenship. A U.S. driver's license usually suffices; travelers from countries other than the States must have their passports. Mexican tourist cards are not required for Baja visits unless you plan to stay in the country more than 72 hours. If you need a tourist card, stop by the immigration office just inside the border. U.S. car insurance does not cover travel in Mexico. Stop at one of the many Mexican auto-insurance booths on the San Ysidro side of the border and purchase a policy covering your vehicle during your stay. Most rental companies do not allow their cars to be taken into Mexico; always ask agents about their company's regulations.

Telephones: To call Mexico from the United States dial 011-52 before the numbers in this chapter. Within Mexico, phoning can be quite confusing. Within a city, dial only the 6- or 7-digit local phone number; between cities first dial 01. The area codes for the cities in this chapter are: Tijuana (66); Rosarito (6); Puerto Neuvo (6); Ensenada (6); Bajamar (615).

Tours and Reservations: Without a doubt, the easiest way to visit Mexico is to join a tour. Several excellent options are available in San Diego. **Baja California Tours** (7734 Herschel Ave, La Jolla; 858/454-7166) offers a fascinating array of day and overnight trips, some featuring cultural and recreational themes. **Mexicoach** (Av Revolución between Calle 6 and 7, Tijuana; tel. 66/85-1470) offers several organized tours and shuttle buses to Tijuana and Rosarito. **Baja Information** (7860 Mission Center Ct, Mission Valley; 619/298-4105, 800/522-1516 in CA, NV, and AZ, or 800/225-2786 in the rest of the U.S. and Canada) is a great overall source of information, and can arrange hotel reservations.   —*Maribeth Mellin*

tel. 66/34-3039) offers exotic cuisine from mainland Mexico. Traditional ingredients such as *huitlacoche* (a fungus grown on corn), nopal cactus, papaya, and tamarind are combined just so to produce interesting and delicious dishes. For Spanish tapas (appetizers) in a noisy, lively environment, belly up to the bar or choose a table at **LA TABERNA ESPAÑOLA** (Plaza Fiesta, Av Paseo de los Héroes 10001; tel. 66/84-7562) among the hip set. The umbrella-shaded tables outside are a good spot to people-watch and escape the sometimes dense clouds of cigarette smoke. Within Pueblo Amigo, **SEÑOR FROG'S** (between Av Paseo Tijuana and Via Oriente; tel. 66/82-4964), of the Carlos Andersen chain, dispenses lots of loud laughter, cerveza, and shots of tequila along with tasty, somewhat Americanized Mexican food and barbecued chicken and ribs.

Avenida Revolución is packed with restaurants. Our favorite for inexpensive, authentic Mexican cooking and ambience is **LA ESPECIAL** (Ave Revolución 718; tel. 66/85-6654), which opened in 1952. The enchiladas, carne asada, and puerco adobado are excellent; few meals cost more than $6. Another old-timer, **CHICKI JAI** (Av Revolucion at Calle 7), opened in 1942 in a tiny tiled building near the Palacio Frontón. The cuisine is pure old-world Basque—try the calamari *en su tinto*—and every table holds a hunk of blue cheese and crusty bread.

Well-off Mexicans frequent the fancy **FOUQUET'S DE PARIS** restaurant in the elegant **CAMINO REAL HOTEL** (Av Paseo de los Héroes 10305; tel. 66/33-4000, 800/722-6466 in the U.S.). Ideally situated close to shopping and the cultural center, this five-star hotel has amenities such as direct-dial phones and fax service, but no pool or hot tub. Also within the Camino Real, **AZULEJOS** restaurant offers less formal dining and excellent, extensive breakfast and lunch buffets Monday through Saturday. If you want to treat yourself to an overnight in Tijuana, consider the **HOLIDAY INN VITA SPA AGUA CALIENTE** (Av Paseo de los Héroes 18818, Zona Río; tel. 66/34-6901, 800/522-1516 in CA, AZ, NV, 800/225-2786 elsewhere in U.S. and in Canada). Although sandwiched between two busy thoroughfares, the building straddles an underground thermal spring—the same ones that fed the glamorous Agua Caliente Spa (now a school) in the 1920s. San Diegans check in not for the rooms but for the **VITA SPA**, with hot tubs fed directly from the mineral springs. Y can sign up for a facial, massage, or mud wrap as well.

Tijuana still merits its reputation as a serious party town, and se eral discos carry on long and hard, especially on Saturday nights. One the best is **BABY ROCK** (Calle Diego Rivera 1482, Zona Río; tel. 66/3 2404), the trendy baby sister of the original Acapulco disco, which has hip, well-heeled, and generally youngish following. Thursday is ladie night, Friday is generally given over to special events (to which the publ is sometimes invited), and Saturday it's no-holds-barred dancing cumbia, rock, salsa, and "dance" music. **COMO QUE NO** (Av Sanch Taboada 9590, Zona Río; tel. 66/84-2791; Mon–Thurs 12pm–2am, F and Sat 12pm–4am) is popular with the sophisticated disco set, while t adjacent **DIME QUE SÍ** (tel. 66/84-2791; Tues–Thurs 6pm to 2am, Fri–S 6pm to 4am) is a romantic piano bar. **RODEO SANTA FE** (Via Rapida Or ente at Castellano #9, Pueblo Amigo, Zona Río; tel. 66/82-4967) featur country and disco music, generally canned but occasionally featuring li norteño bands; the scene includes a live indoor rodeo on weekend night Casual dressers beware: Tijuana's discos usually have strict dress codes– no T-shirts, jeans, or sandals allowed.

Rosarit

24 km (15 miles) south of Tijuana, on the Tijuana-Ensenada Toll Road

Rosarito Beach, as it's most commonly called, is northern Baja's newes boomtown. Its population, which now surpasses 100,000, continues t grow steadily. So does its reputation as party central among die-hard young fans of dancing, drinking, and general rabble-rousing. MT touted Rosarito as a perfect spot for the spring break party scene, an college kids raced down to test the waters—and the fire waters. The wil party scene during spring break of 1998 precipitated a government-spon sored advertising blitz the following year to warn young revelers of th consequences of too many tequila shooters. One imagines the city budge swelling with proceeds from drunk driving and public intoxication fines

The young and the restless aren't the only ones attracted to Rosarito whose 5-mile-long beach stretches without interruption from the power plant at the town's northern border all the way to the Hotel Rosarito Beach. Surfers have their favorite breaks, and snowbirds flock to private residences, trailer parks, condos, and favorite hotels in search of respite from Canadian and midwestern winters. Twentieth Century Fox built a permanent studio south of town in 1995, which it used as a base for filming the megahit *Titanic* in 1996 and 1997. Future filming at the new studio will no doubt bring more stars, money, prestige, and growth.

Despite recent hobnobbing with Hollywood glamour-pusses, Rosarito isn't synonymous with sophistication or culture. It's about sun and sea, relaxing and boogying. The town careens haphazardly along both sides of the Old Ensenada Highway, also known as Boulevard Benito Juárez. The street is strewn with restaurants, bars, and shops in an alarming mix of building styles and degrees of completion. Although you can visit Rosarito on a day trip from San Diego, many adopt the Mexican mañana attitude and delay their return home for one or more days. It's certainly worth considering, since there's enough shopping, outdoor activities, and good restaurants to keep you busy throughout the day and on into the night.

The traditional holiday headquarters is the **ROSARITO BEACH HOTEL** (Blvd Juárez, south end of town; tel. 6/612-0144, 800/343-8582 in the U.S. and Mexico). Built in the 1920s as an elegant hotel and gambling palace, the hotel has seen better days. But it still has a glassed-in pool area, a long beach, spa, tennis court, and playground in addition to several restaurants and a happening bar. Although the rooms themselves are unimpressive, services of the Casa Playa Spa (which offers massage and beauty treatments and has exercise equipment, saunas, and hot tubs) are a draw. One of Rosarito's few other beachfront hotels is **LOS PELÍCANOS** (Calle Cedros 115 at Calle Ebano; tel. 6/612-0445 or 6/612-1757). Ask for a room with a balcony overlooking the beach. Although there's no pool, rooms are pleasant and airy, and the second-story restaurant and bar are a great place to watch the sun set. Golfers should check out the secluded, all-suites **MARRIOTT REAL DEL MAR RESIDENCE INN** (km 19.5, Ensenada toll road; tel. 66/31-3670, 800/228-9290 in the U.S.) overlooking the sea 10 kilometers (6 miles) north of Rosarito Beach. All units have fireplaces and kitchens, and the hotel's **PEDRIN'S** restaurant has reliable seafood dishes and Mexican favorites. Vacation packages include green fees at the 18-hole golf course. Before your game you can stretch out in the exercise room, or take a post-play dip in the property's pool.

If golf's not your bag, there are other recreational possibilities. The best **SURFING BEACHES** near San Diego are south of Rosarito on the old Ensenada Highway, which runs parallel to Mexico Highway 1. Beaches are usually designated by kilometer signs. Locals and Southern Californians habitually check the waves at Popotla (km 32.5), Calafia (km 35.5), and just beyond at Costa Baja (km 36). **TONY'S** (Blvd Juárez 312; tel. 6/612-1192) is a rather informal surf shop where you can usually buy or rent surf gear and get the latest on local swells. For horseback riding on the beach, look for signs along Blvd Juárez, or clumps of horses standing in the shade on the beach. Cost is about $10 per hour.

If the thought of all this exercise has made you hungry, take heart: there are lots of good restaurants in Rosarito, some serving traditional

Mexican favorites. At **LA FLOR DE MICHOACÁN** (Blvd Juárez 291; t 6/612-1858), grilled meats rule the day, served in the style of Michoac state—with guacamole, lots of fresh salsa, and stacks of homemade t tillas. Tacos and tostadas round out the menu of this casual eatery (clos Wednesday). The busy **FESTIVAL PLAZA** (Blvd Juárez 11; tel. 6/61 0842) has several bars and good restaurants in addition to its hot rooms, villas, and penthouse suites. Among the best of the restauran here is **EL PATIO** (tel. 6/612-2950), another great spot to relax over bona fide Mexican meal. Rather than the typical tacos and tostadas, loc for spicy chiles rellenos (batter-fried chilies stuffed with cheese or groun meat), grilled quail, and savory crepes, as well as bar drinks and bee Just across the street from the sometimes rowdy Festival Plaza, L **TABERNA ESPAÑOLA** (Blvd Juárez across from Festival Plaza) provides slightly more tranquil atmosphere, with at least the possibility of cor versation. There's a rooftop terrace, as well as dining rooms on the fir and second floors.

After a large Mexican midday meal, many will opt for a relaxing na in a hammock or air-conditioned hotel room. The stalwart, howeve will opt to shop. Consumer opportunities have multiplied like unglaze ceramic rabbits over the last 10 years, and Rosarito now has a respectabl number of stores selling indoor and outdoor furniture, pottery, and othe decorative items. Small souvenir shops are sprinkled all along Boulevard Juárez, and the larger hotels have shopping arcades and crafts stores Within **QUINTA DEL MAR PLAZA** you'll find Interiores del Rio Casa de Arte y La Madera (tel. 6/612-1300), with an irresistible selection of Mex ican folk art and home furnishings treasures, and **TAXCO CURIOS** (tel 6/612-1877), which features lovely handblown glassware. Just down the street, **APISA** (Blvd Benito Juárez 2400; tel. 6/612-0125) sells fancy fur nishings and iron sculpture from Guadalajara. Watch carvers create lovely rustic wooden furniture right on the premises at **CASA LA CAR-RETA** (km 29, Old Ensenada Hwy; tel. 6/612-0502).

For entertainment, Rosarito has boisterous bars, piano lounges, and more sedate restaurant/bars. Drinking-and-driving laws are strictly enforced—take a cab or assign a designated driver if you plan to imbibe. Within Festival Plaza (see above), **EL MUSEO CANTINA TEQUILA** (tel. 6/612-0842) is a venerable tequila museum where you can literally choose your poison; there are more than 125 brands of the agave-based liquor at this fun bar frequented by party-hungry locals and tourists. You can get both food and drink at **ROCK & ROLL TACO**, also within the plaza. You'll find a mixed crowd of old and young revelers at the Rosarito Beach Hotel (see above), which has live music on weekend nights. The nearby **PAPAS AND BEER** (Blvd Juárez; tel. 6/612-0244 or 6/612-0444) generally attracts a boisterous younger crowd. For a sunset cocktail, nothing beats **CALAFIA** (km 35.5, Old Ensenada Hwy; tel. 6/612-2211, 877/700-2093 in the U.S.), where the small tables are set down the cliff—each overlooks the ocean on its own miniature terrace. Live music is sometimes performed near the base of the cliffs. It's a 10-minute ride south of Rosarito by car or cab.

Puerto Nuevo (Newport)

12 km (7½ miles) south of Rosarito, at km 44 on the Old Ensenada Highway

Twenty years ago this collection of restaurants was a tiny outpost of local gastronomy along the road to Ensenada. The menu was—and still is—simple: fresh lobster, boiled and then grilled; lard-laced refried beans; mountains of Spanish rice; and all of the homemade tortillas and salsa you can eat. Over the years these seafood shacks became legendary, then mainstream. The once-rutted entry road has been partially paved, and souvenir shops mark the entrance to dozens of restaurants. Most aficionados have their favorite haunts among the dozens of lobster houses, which are almost identical in menu and price if not in character and service. Poke your head into several restaurants, check out the vibe (and the bar, if you're a drinker; some have beer and wine only). Then pull up a chair—painted, varnished, plastic, or otherwise. Of all the restaurants in this enclave, **ORTEGA'S** is one of the oldest and most established; it now has three branches here and one in Rosarito Beach. **COSTA BRAVA** is among the fanciest, with tablecloths and a window opening onto the sea below. Lobsters are almost universally priced by size, with a medium-size lobster, with all the trimmings, running about $15. Lobster season in these parts is October through March; lobster is imported year-round, however, as the supply cannot keep up with the demand. Most places are open for lunch and dinner.

Entrepreneurs have finally noticed a marketing niche and established a few hotels at the site, solving the drinking-and-driving dilemma. **HOTEL NEW PORT BAJA** (km 45, Old Ensenada Hwy; tel. 6/614-1188, 800/582-1018 in the U.S. and Canada) is situated just south of the lobster shanties. Heaters warm the guest rooms on cool evenings, and many rooms have a small balcony overlooking the surf. The hotel has its own restaurant and bar, as well as a swimming pool, two tennis courts, and an exercise room. Substantial discounts are available midweek. About 9 miles south of Newport, **LA FONDA** (km 59, Old Ensenada Hwy; tel. 6/628-7352 or 6/628-7353) has been luring Southern Californians for decades. The 26-room inn is decorated with carved wood furniture and folk art. Many rooms have an excellent view of the sea and, in a rare reprieve from technology, no television or telephones. If you get lonely in your seaside

room, head for the boisterous and friendly bar, quite the happening pla
on weekend nights. Speaking of Saturday and Sunday, the weekend brunc
is definitely worth investigating. The rest of the week you can enjoy su
culent steaks on the restaurant's outdoor patio overlooking the beach.

Ensenad:

75 km (47 miles) south of Rosarito, 104 km (65 miles) south of Tijuan

The toll road (called Ensenada Cuota) from Tijuana, completed in 197?
is a faster ride than the old Mexico Highway 1 (also called the Old Roa
to Ensenada). The two roads run beside each other from Rosarito t
Ensenada. The old highway provides the best access to the small fishin;
communities en route. Mexico Highway 1 becomes Boulevard Coster(
at the northern entrance to Ensenada.

One of Mexico's largest seaports, Ensenada (Spanish for "cove" o,
"inlet") has grown slowly but steadily since the bay on which it lies
Bahía de Todos Santos (All Saints' Bay), was first seen by Portugues(
explorer Juan Rodríguez Cabrillo. Since then the town has supportec
ranchers, gold miners, wineries, and a prosperous fishing fleet and fish-
processing industry. Along the boulevard fronting Ensenada's perfect,
fish-hook-shaped harbor you'll find boat repair docks, fishing vessels,
and commercial shipping warehouses.

There are no beaches in Ensenada itself, and the burgeoning beach
facilities and accommodations to the north at Rosarito over the last 15
years have siphoned off a substantial amount of Ensenada's tourist trade.
Most of those who choose Ensenada over Rosarito or other beach destinations are seeking a glimpse of the "real Mexico" as close to the U.S.
border as possible. Others feel the need to experience the legendary **HUS-
SONG'S CANTINA** (Av Ruíz 113; tel. 6/174-0720). The large, long saloon
opened over a century ago and is apparently in no danger of closing—
ever! Although during morning and early afternoons you might find just
a handful of locals sitting at the bar, by eventide things are heating up.
Roving mariachi and ranchera musicians add to the cacophony produced
by party animals from north of the border. Believe it or not, there are
some who make Hussong's the point and focus of their pilgrimage. More
traditional pilgrims may find succor at the city's cathedral, **NUESTRA
SEÑORA DE GUADALUPE** (Av Floresta at Av Juárez), which honors
Mexico's patron saint, Our Lady of Guadalupe.

Although Ensenada can be visited as a day trip, many choose to
spend one or more nights in this bayside city. If you're looking for a luxurious property with loads of amenities, check out the **HOTEL CORAL &
MARINA** (km 102, Tijuana-Ensenada toll road, No. 3421 Zona Playitas;
tel. 6/175-0000; 800/862-9020 in the U.S.), built in 1995. With a marina

THE WHOLE ENCHILADA

Please don't eat at Burger King or McDonald's when you're in Mexico; you'll miss half the reason for being there. All the restaurants described in this chapter take extra precautions with food preparation and use purified water for cooking. If you're really wary, take a swig of Pepto-Bismol or another stomach-coating salve, and stick with cooked foods. Never drink water from the tap. Some of the most popular south-of-the-border treats include:

Burritos: Flour tortillas wrapped around a wide range of fillings, from refried beans and cheese to grilled meats with guacamole.

Carne Asada: Marinated and grilled strips of beef served in tacos and burritos or as part of a combo plate with beans, rice, guacamole, and tortillas.

Carnitas: Marinated pork served as above.

Chiles Rellenos: A large semispicy green chili stuffed with cheese, coated with batter, fried, and covered with sauce.

Enchiladas: Corn tortillas wrapped around cheese, chicken, or beef and baked in a semispicy sauce.

Flan: This custard-like dish with a caramel flavor is quite possibly the most popular in Mexico. Some chefs prepare it with tropical fruits or fancy sauces.

Guacamole: Some novices call it "that green stuff"; few retain their aversion. Mashed avocados are mixed with lime, onions, tomatoes, cilantro, and all matter of ingredients following family recipes. Usually served with corn chips or in a dollop with entrees.

Huevos Rancheros: Fried eggs on corn tortillas topped with a spicy, tomato-based sauce.

Huitlacoche: It's a black fungus grown on corn, but don't let that scare you. The taste is like an earthy mushroom, especially good in quesadillas and crepas (crepes).

Mole: This blend of spices used for sauces on chicken, pork, and enchiladas comes in several varieties. Black mole includes bitter chocolate and chilies; yellow mole is seasoned with pumpkin seeds. Mole is an acquired taste worth sampling.

Pan Dulce: Sweet breads sold in bakeries, or *panaderias*. Cookies, muffins, Danish pastries, and fruit breads all taste different in Mexico; in the bakeries, preservatives are shunned and lard and butter are the favored fats. Stop by a bakery, grab a metal platter and a pair of tongs, and stockpile your snacks for the day.

Sopa de Tortilla: Tortilla soup is wonderful when made properly. The best ones have a spicy chicken broth and are served with a platter of crumbled cheese, chopped avocado, cilantro, and crisp tortilla strips.

Tacos: Fried or soft corn tortillas stuffed with every imaginable ingredient. Baja specialties include fish tacos and tacos *al pastor,* made with thin slices of rotisserie pork.

Tamales: Beef, chicken, or fruit fillings mixed with cornmeal and wrapped in corn husks.

Torta: A sandwich made on a thick, crusty roll called a *bolillo*.

—Maribeth Mellin

that can accommodate 600 boats, the resort is frequent host to fishir tournaments and boat races. Its 147 suites are found in three eight-stor towers; all have balconies with ocean view, cable TV, and direct-di phones. For recreation, there are several tennis courts, an exercise roor three pools (one indoor), and two hot tubs. Diving and fishing tours ca be organized on-site. The more intimate **LAS ROSAS** (Mexico Hwy 1, miles north of Ensenada; tel. 6/174-4320; 800/522-1516 in AZ, CA, N 800/225-2786 elsewhere in U.S. and Canada) is true to its name: "th Rose" hotel is delicate and pink. Elegant touches are found throughou the lobby: marble floors, windows overlooking the sea, and a green glas ceiling above the atrium. All of the 32 well-appointed rooms overloo either the pool and hot tub or the ocean; some have fireplaces. **PUNT. MORRO** (Mexico Hwy 1, 3 km/2 miles north of town; tel. 6/178-3507 800/526-6676 in the U.S.) is a secluded hideaway as recommended fo its charming restaurant overlooking the ocean as for its 30 suites, all wit kitchenettes and terraces facing the bay. Although this isn't an idea swimming beach (the surf is rough), the setting is cozy and romanti (some rooms have fireplaces) and has great views of the bay. The prop erty also has a bar, pool, and hot tub. Golfers gravitate toward **BAJAMAF** (km 77.5, Old Ensenada Hwy; tel. 615/5-0151; 615/5-0161 for tee times). Revamped in late 1993, this challenging 18-hole course is set high on the cliffs overlooking the ocean (there's a 9-hole course near the beach). Onsite, the **SIERRA PLAZA BAJAMAR** hotel (tel. 615/5-0152, 800/225-2418 in the U.S.) has the requisite restaurant, bar, and pool along with a few tennis courts. The property is peaceful and has some nice decorative touches, although some guests have complained of lack-luster maintenance.

South of Ensenada you'll find the moderately priced **ESTERO BEACH RESORT** (Mexico Hwy 1 between Ensenada and Maneadero; tel. 6/176-6235 or 6/176-6925), a comfortable place favored by families. It's located right on a calm estuary and beach about 6 miles south of Ensenada. Some rooms have kitchenettes, perfect for keeping soft drinks cold and cooking simple meals. Ask for a room right on the sand, and inquire about midweek discounts. There are tennis courts, pool, horseback riding, volleyball, and a children's playground. Nonguests can use the hotel's facilities for a small fee.

Whether spending the night or just the day, start your tour of Ensenada's waterfront at the **FISH MARKET** (north end of Blvd Costero). Here you'll find stands selling Ensenada's legendary fish tacos (born in this region and copied at fast-food Mexican restaurants throughout San Diego and beyond). These original Baja beauties are made of fresh, piping-hot corn tortillas, fresh grilled or deep-fried fish, chopped cabbage, a squeeze of lime, and salsa. Of course, you might actually be here to haggle for the tuna, dorado, marlin, snapper, and other local species for sale at the oceanfront market. Continue south along the coast road to the **SPORTFISHING PIER** (Blvd Costero at Av Alvarado), from whence fishing and whale-watching boats depart regularly. Tried-and-true **GORDO'S SPORTFISHING** (Blve Costero at Av Alvarado; tel. 6/178-3515, 6/178-2377) has charter boats, group boats ($35 for a half day or $100 for a full day), and whale watching in season. If you want to book before arriving, contact **BAJA CALIFORNIA TOURS** (858/454-7166). The best fishing is generally April through November.

South of the sportfishing pier, admire the sculptures of Mexican heroes Benito Juárez, Miguel Hidalgo, and Venustiano Carranza at the **PLAZA CÍVICA** (Blvd Costero at Av Riveroll). Continue on to the **CENTRO ARTESIAN DE ENSENADA** (Blvd Costero 1094), where trade ebbs and flows as the cruise ships dock and decamp. Some tenants have fled as traffic has been diverted from the area in recent years; others, such as **GALERÍA DE PÉREZ MEILLÓN** (tel. 6/174-0394), stick it out. In business for 11 years, this small store carries museum-quality folk art, including rustic but elegant pottery from Mata Ortiz, Chihuahua; pit-fired pottery made by the PaiPai Indians; and willow baskets made by the Kumeyaay.

For a taste of Prohibition-era luxury and style, continue south to **RIV-IERA DEL PACÍFICO** (Blvd Costero and Av Riviera; tel. 6/176-4310 or 6/176-0594). Although this former gambling palace, hotel, restaurant, and bar closed shortly after its inauguration when gambling was out-lawed, it's now a cultural center and a glamorous reminder of Ensenada's past. Tour the mansion's ballrooms, visit the flower gardens, and stop in at the **MUSEO DE HISTORIA DE ENSENADA**.Visitors can walk through every day for a small admission fee.

If you're ready to relax over a cerveza and a regional barbecue, head for **EL CHARRO** (Av López Mateos 475; tel. 6/178-3881) where locals and visitors chow down on rotisserie chicken, beans, rice, and tortillas. Patrons sniff the air hungrily as they watch the chicken rotate slowly above the open wood fire. If you prefer seafood, the ocean-view **CASAMAR** (Blvd Lázaro Cárdenas 987; tel. 6/174-0417) is an old favorite known for its lobster or shrimp prepared *al mojo de ajo* (sautéed in butter and garlic). For an elegant dinner visit **EL REY SOL** (Av López Mateos 1000; tel. 6/178-1733). This enduring favorite, where light dances through stained-glass windows, has delighted visitors as well as locals since the 1950s. French and Mexican dishes feature vegetables grown in the Santo Tomás Valley, and the patisserie turns out excellent baked goods. All three are open daily.

If you want souvenirs of your trip, Ensenada's shopping zone is found just one block east of the coast road. It begins at the foot of the Chapultepec Hills and runs for about eight blocks south along Avenida

López Mateos. Here restaurants and bars share the sidewalk with sho
selling silver and shell jewelry, blankets, knitted shawls, brightly embro
dered dresses, and ceramic piggy banks. Among the nicest shops a
ARTES DON QUIJOTE (Av López Mateos 503; tel. 6/176-9476), which h
a good selection of crafts from Oaxaca and throughout the interior. L
CASTILLO (Av López Mateos 815; tel. 6/176-1187) sells a nice selecti
of silver jewelry from Taxco.

LAS BODEGAS DE SANTO TOMÁS (Av Miramar 66; tel. 6/178-25(
or 6/178-3333) in downtown Ensenada is Baja California's oldest winer
LA ESQUINA DE BODEGAS (tel. 6/678-2509), across the street from t
winery, is one of the hippest cafes, galleries, and shops in the city. Brow
in the upstairs rooms for glassware, pottery, and books, have a fres
salad in the cafe, and purchase a fine vintage red wine for a souvenir.

If you prefer to escape the city, take the afternoon to explore th
coast south of Ensenada. Drive or take a cab to **LA BUFADORA** (Hwy 2
west of Maneadero, 36 km/22 miles south of Ensenada), an impressiv
blowhole at the point known as Punta Banda, where the mountains com
crouching down over the sea. The blowhole shoots up nearly 80 feet i
the air every few minutes, spraying excited children and their parents a
they stand behind a protective fence. Just before you reach the point, yo
can buy a variety of cooked foods and souvenirs, and sometimes locall
grown olives or garlic, at roadside stands. There is a small fee to par
near the blowhole.

RECREATION

RECREATION

Outdoor Activitie

Forget your shopping, your wining and dining, and all your other indo
pursuits. When it comes to the number-one favorite local pastime, ou
door recreation is where it's at. San Diegans practically live outdoors, an
resent rain and chilly fog for impeding fun in the sun. We bike to wor
skate, run, and walk at lunch; surf at dusk and dawn. Mental-health da
(a.k.a. sick days) are spent in the fresh air; after all, there's nothing like
boat ride on the sea to clear the brain. The county's varied terrain offe
unlimited opportunities, from surfing to desert hiking. Activities a
overseen by an amalgamation of volunteer and governmental organiza
tions as outlined in the categories below. And please remember, if yo
lack skills or experience, don't participate in any of these sports withou
getting training or guidance first.

BICYCLING

San Diego is a perfect cycling region, thanks to its enviable dry, mild cl
mate and wide range of scenery and terrain. An essential tool for seriou
cyclists is the **SAN DIEGO REGION BIKE MAP** (Ridelink Bicycle Informa
tion; 619/231-BIKE). The map clearly illustrates bike lanes, paths, trails
and routes, highlighted in different colors. Follow the red lines if you're
interested in casual rides; teal if you want to cover vast distances. You
can also get information on renting bike lockers (favored by cycling com
muters) when ordering the map. There are bike racks on some city buses
including those stopping at major tourist sites; for specifics call or stop
by the Transit Store (102 Broadway, downtown; 619/234-1060; map:N7).

Several cycling organizations lead casual bike rides and organized
tours. The **SAN DIEGO COUNTY BICYCLE COALITION** (619/685-7742;
www.hobbes.ucsd.edu/sdcbc.html) is a good source of overall biking information and can direct you to contacts for cycling clubs, along with bike eti-
quette and safety classes. Seasoned roadies gravitate toward **CYCLO VETS**
(619/670-0626; www.cyclo-vets.org), a robust clan of over 300 cyclists
nationwide, including more than 100 national and international champions. The recreational cyclist enjoys the cultured **KNICKERBIKERS**
(858/450-0373; www.znetwork.net/knickerbikers), which schedules rides
about the city on Tuesdays, Saturdays, and Sundays and also arranges
national and international tours. The **RAINBOW CYCLISTS OF SAN DIEGO**
(619/294-INFO; www.lanz.com/rainbowcyclist/) holds frequent fund-
raising rides for the gay and lesbian community. The **SAN DIEGO TANDEM
CLUB** (bcnet@san.rr.com; www-cse.ucsd.edu/~esimon/ tandem/SDTC.html)
hosts weekend rides and monthly events for tandem enthusiasts. Once a

month the club also pairs up members with people who have physical or mental disabilities for short rides around Lake Miramar or Mission Bay.

San Diego is the site of several annual racing events, most of which have a festive party spirit. A case in point is the **MIDNIGHT MADNESS** (619/645-8068) fund-raising ride, during which thousands of cyclists dressed in their pajamas and fancy lingerie race around the streets of downtown. The 20-mile ride is held each August in the wee hours; prizes are given for most interesting nighttime attire. Another party-on-wheels is the twice-yearly **ROSARITO TO ENSENADA RACE**, sponsored by Bicycling West, Inc. (619/583-3001), which draws 8,000 to 10,000 fun-minded people (all with different levels of expertise) to career 50-some miles from Rosarito to Ensenada along Baja's coast. Coastal streets along the route are closed; riders speed by tossing candy to children running alongside. Rides take place each April and September, when temperatures are pleasant. The scenery is superb, but gravel on the downhills, along with the occasional drunken cyclist, can make the ride hazardous.

Some of the area's other standout rides are listed below.

CORONADO / End of 10th St near the Hotel del Coronado, Coronado Many Sunday biking enthusiasts bring their wheels aboard the San Diego–Coronado ferry to cruise around Coronado's classy neighborhoods, past historic mansions and modernistic condos. Pedaling along the streets past flower gardens and beaches is great fun. Take the ferry from downtown and rent a cruiser, tandem, or baby-seat bike from **BIKES AND BEYOND** (619/435-7180) at the Ferry Landing and marketplace, and pedal along paths beside Tidelands Park, under the San Diego-Coronado Bay Bridge, and along the golf course and waterfront to Glorietta Bay. *Map:NN5*

FIESTA ISLAND / Fiesta Island Rd between E Mission Bay and Sea World Drs, Mission Bay; 619/276-8200 Fiesta Island is a fun, flat, albeit dusty place to ride with the family while speed boats, Jet Skis, Wave Runners, and water skis zip around in the bay. Traffic is light and although the paved road must be shared with vehicular traffic, the 25-mph speed limit makes for a comfortable ride. *Map:LL6*

MISSION BAY PARK / Bounded by Mission Bay and Sea World Drs, Mission Bay; 619/276-8200 Large chunks of this 4,600-acre park are accessible to bikers, with concrete paths running over grassy slopes and along the beach and the bay. Expect to share the path, however, with walkers, runners, and babies in strollers. Start at De Anza Cove, near the end of E Mission Bay Drive, where there is plenty of free parking, and ride the paths south past the Hilton Hotel and Tecolote Shores Park. From this path you can access Fiesta Island (see above), Sea World Drive, and bike paths along the San Diego River flood control channel. From Crown

Point Shores Park (Corona Oriente Dr at La Playa Ave) you can ride pavement all the way around Sail Bay and down to the southern tip West Mission Bay. *Map:LL6*

MISSION TRAILS REGIONAL PARK / 1 Father Junipero Serra Tr. Tierra Santa; 619/668-3373 About 10 miles northeast of downtov this urban park offers everything from gut-wrenching mountain b climbs to a pleasant roll around Lake Murray. The wide cement path th nearly circumvents the lake is shared by moms pushing baby-jogger ca riages, dedicated bladers, runners, walkers, and bikers. It's a flat 7 mil in and out (3.5 miles each way). For a more challenging ride, stop in the recreation center on the north side of the lake for maps and infc mation. Free parking and rest rooms. *Map:JJ2*

MISSION AND PACIFIC BEACHES / North and south of Belmont Par Mission Beach; 619/221-8900 For more of a cruise than a bike ride, hea for the boardwalk at Belmont Park. Bike rentals are abundant (check o **HAMEL'S ACTION SPORTS CENTER**, 704 Ventura Pl; 619/488-505(map:LL7) and it's reasonably uncrowded—midweek in the dead c winter or when it's pouring rain, that is. Most other times, the boardwal is as clogged as a freeway during rush hour. You can escape the crowc by riding south along the boardwalk to the Mission Bay Channel (sepa rating Mission Beach from Ocean Beach) or jump into the melee b heading north along the boardwalk to Crystal Pier. *Map:LL7—KK7*

NORTH TORREY PINES / N Torrey Pines Rd from Genesee Ave to De Mar Heights Ave, Del Mar Thrills await those with hardy thighs an(calves along one of the county's most scenic routes. A heart-poundinç steep hill descends from the Torrey Pines Mesa (next to Torrey Pines Statc Reserve) to sea level at Torrey Pines State Beach. The road then climbs again toward Del Mar. True devotees continue on up the coast along paths, frontage roads, and Highway 101 through North County beach communities. *Map:II7—GG7*

POINT LOMA / Voltaire St in Ocean Beach to the Cabrillo National Monument, Point Loma The drudgery and traffic at the beginning of this ride quickly give way to some of the coast's most spectacular scenery as you pedal the Point Loma Peninsula past Navy facilities, Fort Rosecrans National Cemetery (a good spot to stop and take in the awesome views), and on to Cabrillo Monument. *Map:LL6—OO6*

SAN DIEGO BAY / W Harbor Dr at the foot of Broadway, Downtown; 619/686-6200 This is a relaxing, flat, 4.5-mile ride along the picturesque bay, where sailboats moored offshore provide a painterly foreground and downtown's skyscrapers loom large behind them. The route follows bike paths and sidewalks, passing the historic clipper ship *Star of India*, now part of a floating maritime museum. This ride is best in early morning or late evening, when pedestrian traffic is light. There are metered parking lots in the area, and bike racks are near the tourist attractions. *Map:NN4—NN6*

SAN DIEGO VELODROME / 2221 Morley Field Dr, Balboa Park, Downtown; 619/692-4919 This regulation outdoor velodrome, or bicycle racing track, is open to the public daily, except when the **SAN DIEGO VELODROME ASSOCIATION** (619/296-3345; www.sdva.org/) is holding its biweekly track events; spectators are welcome. *Map:P3*

SILVER STRAND / Strand Way to Silver Strand Blvd to Imperial Beach, Coronado Cyclists let loose on a 7-mile straightaway along lagoons and the Coronado Cays with views of the Pacific across the road. A wide path runs the length of the ride; cyclists, skaters, and pedestrians have room to share the road—though those moving slowly should stay to the right and listen for speed-freaks headed their way. Beware: the ride back can take twice as long, as you battle ocean winds all the way. *Map:QQ4*

SOLEDAD MOUNTAIN / Nautilus St and Soledad Mountain Rd, Pacific Beach This challenging 5.8-mile hilly ride provides a million-dollar view of practically all of San Diego and La Jolla. *Map:KK6*

MOUNTAIN BIKING

The rough, hilly trails are there for cyclists seeking a dusty, hard ride; although most of these are outside the city limits, you can find decent thrills even in Balboa Park. **TEAM SPOKEY DOKES** (858/538-8352; www.members.home.com/lotsubo/) of the North County Cycle Club organizes rides along the numerous mountain bike paths in remote parks. The **R&B BICYCLE CLUB** (760/765-2200; julian.bikes@juno.com; www. julianbikes. com) sponsors several annual races and festivals in the Julian area. Special events include the **JULIAN FAT TIRE FESTIVAL** one weekend in May, including an off-road ride, barbecue, hill climbs, desert night ride, and a leisurely roll to the Menghini Winery for a wine tour and tasting. In September, the club sponsors the **TOUR DE JULIAN**, which includes several road-racing events in addition to a 22-mile mountain-bike event beginning at Jess Martin Park and following pavement, singletrack paths, and dirt roads to Banner, returning to Julian in a 1,300-foot climb.

In search of a gnarly ride? Try these off-road trails:

FLORIDA CANYON / 1700 Morley Field Dr, east side of Balboa Park, Downtown; 619/239-0512 The east side of Florida Canyon is largely undeveloped, and the trails are tough going because of rocks and brush. This 2-mile, moderately difficult ride takes you through some of Florida Canyon's eucalyptus and pepper tree groves. Turn right into Morley Field's tennis complex, make an immediate right, and start down the trail off the lower parking lot south of the tennis courts. *Map:P3*

LAKE HODGES / 20102 Lake Dr, at Via Rancho Pkwy, Escondi
619/465-3474 An 8-mile tour of this canyon lake winds through the ╒
road trails on the northern shores near a small stream, and usually ta╒
about an hour round-trip. On Wednesdays, Saturdays, or Sundays, st
from the boat launch parking lot, which is only open those days. ╒
other days, park on Lake Drive and bike around a gate at the p╒
entrance. The stretch along Lake Drive from Del Dios Highway to ¥
Rancho Parkway is scenic as well. *Map:CC2*

BOATING

The mouth of **SAN DIEGO BAY** separates Coronado Island and the tip
Point Loma at Cabrillo Monument. The bay curves south past Shel╒
and Harbor Islands to the downtown Embarcadero, where antiq
sailing vessels join navy freighters and cruise ships at dock. This banan╒
shaped bay flows under the San Diego-Coronado Bay Bridge to Cor
nado's tiny **GLORIETTA BAY** (map:NN4), located near the storybo╒
Hotel del Coronado. Surrounded by green parks and the municipal g╒
course, this bay has a good public boat launch.

SHELTER ISLAND (map:F8) also has a 24-hour boat ramp; angle
wait in line to launch when the fishing's good offshore. Boaters tourir
the bay can take in the shores of Point Loma and Coronado and variou
Navy installations, the airport, the cruise ship terminal, and the Sout
Bay all the way to the Chula Vista Nature Center.

MISSION BAY PARK's boating areas include Sail Bay, Fiesta Bay, an
Mariners and Quivira Basins. An excellent map of Mission Bay Par╒
showing bike paths, launch sites, water recreation areas, and the like ca╒
be obtained free at the main lifeguard station (2581 Quivira Ct, Missio╒
Bay; 619/221-8899; map:C1). Following are some good places to launc╒
your craft or board someone else's boat:

DANA LANDING MARINA / 2590 Ingraham St, Mission Bay; 619/224
2513 One of Mission Bay's major boat launches also has an outboar╒
repair shop, fuel dock, and kayak launch site. Boat slips are rented by th╒
day or month. Within the marina you'll find The Market, where you car
get a fishing license, a bag of ice, and a cheese sandwich before climbing
aboard your rented electric or motor boat, Jet Ski, catamaran, or other
sailing vessel for a tour of the bays or the open ocean. Free parking lot.
Map:LL6

DE ANZA COVE / Northern end of N Mission Bay Dr, Mission Bay;
619/221-8900 This public boat launch at the northwestern point of the
bay provides access to Fiesta Island, Ski Island, and Crown Point. As
throughout the park, there are free public parking lots and rest rooms.
Map:LL6

LAKE HODGES / 20102 Lake Dr, at Via Rancho Pkwy, Escondido; 619/465-3474 The lake is only open Friday, Saturday, and Sunday (sunrise to sunset) March through October, and it gets crowded with fishermen angling for bass when the season first opens. You can rent a motorboat or a rowboat for the day (or a canoe by the hour). The store here has food and drink as well as bait and tackle. Free parking. *Map:EE3*

LAKE JENNINGS COUNTY PARK / 10108 Bass Rd, Lakeside; 619/466-0585 About a half-hour drive north from downtown San Diego, Lake Jennings offers some excellent views of the El Capitan preserve and the San Diego River Valley; unfortunately, waterskiing and swimming are prohibited. There's a boat launch fee; rowboats and motorboats are available for rent by the day or half day. Free parking.

LAKE MURRAY COMMUNITY PARK / 5540 Kiowa Dr, at Lake Murray Blvd, La Mesa; 619/465-3474 Boats can be rented for use on this urban lake on Wednesdays, Saturdays, and Sundays. Fee for boat launch and fishing; free parking. *Map:LL2*

QUIVIRA BASIN / Quivira Rd at W Mission Bay Dr, Mission Bay Though it lacks a public boat ramp, Quivira Basin is a great spot for admiring private yachts in the marina and boarding fishing boats. *Map:LL6*

SANTA CLARA POINT / Santa Clara Pl off Mission Blvd, Mission Bay; 619/221-8900 This tiny point juts into the aptly named Sail Bay, where windsurfers and sailors practice their skills. The Mission Bay Aquatic Center (1001 Santa Clara Pl, Mission Bay; 858/488-1036) offers rentals and lessons for nearly any water sport. *Map:LL7*

SEAFORTH BOAT RENTAL / 1641 Quivira Rd, Mission Bay; 619/223-1681, 888/234-2628 Seaforth rents powerboats up to 20 feet, sailboats up to 30 feet, Jet Skis, and ocean kayaks by the hour, half day, and full day. It also runs sportfishing trips (see Fishing, below). Good meals are available at the Landing (1729 Quivira Rd, 619/222-3317) and Sportsmen's Seafoods (1617 Quivira Rd, 619/224-3551). *www.seaforth boatrental.com; map:LL6*

SKI BEACH / Between North and South Ingraham St Bridges, Mission Bay; 619/221-8900 On the northeast side of Vacation Isle is a long, sandy takeoff and landing area for water-skiers north of the boat launch and near rest room facilities. This area gets heavy use on weekends (the parking lot fills up fast) and gives good access to all of Mission Bay. *Map:LL6*

SOUTH SHORES / South Shores Dr at Sea World Dr, Mission Bay The newest part of Mission Bay Park, South Shores opened in 1998. It has a wide boat ramp with plenty of parking and rest rooms, all open 24 hours. *Map:LL6*

DIVING/SNORKELING

The underwater realm off San Diego holds wonders well worth explor for both snorkelers and scuba divers. Wet suits are a must in winter ₂ essential year-round for deep divers, though you can snorkel in swimsᵣ when the water's warm, especially in August and September. Local div celebrate the first Wednesday in October with particular glee—it ma the opening of lobster season. The season lasts until the first Wednesₒ in March; sport divers capturing the crustaceans must have a fishₕ license and follow set limits regarding size and catch. Contact **CA FORNIA FISH AND GAME** (4949 Viewridge Ave, Mission Valley; 619/4₆ 4201; map:KK4) or any dive shop for a license and list of regulations. F gear rentals and sales, lessons, and offshore dive trips, try Ocean Entᵣ prises (7710 Balboa Ave, Kearny Mesa; 619/565-6054; www.oceaneᵣ com; map:JJ5), OE Express (2158 Ave de la Playa, Clairemont; 858/45 6195; www.oeexpress.com; map:JJ7), and The Diving Locker (10: Grand Ave, Pacific Beach; 858/272-11200; www.divinglocker.coᵣ map:KK7). Some of the best underwater spots accessible from shore or ₑ a short boat ride are listed below.

LA JOLLA COVE / 1100 Coast Blvd, La Jolla; 858/221-8900 Snorkeleₛ need only submerge their faces to spot golden garibaldi, blue neons, aₙ angelfish in this sheltered cove, part of 6,000-acre San Diego-La Joₗ Underwater Park. Divers swim beyond the cove to find bass, lobsteᵣ moray eels, bat rays, smelt, and other creatures along rocky points. Theᵣ are no rentals at the cove; the nearest shop is OE Express (see above *Map:JJ7*

LA JOLLA SHORES / 8200 Camino del Oro, La Jolla; 858/221-890ₒ Scuba classes are often held at this ideal spot, where divers can enter thₑ water from shore and quickly access the underwater park. *Map:JJ6*

MISSION BAY PARK ARTIFICIAL REEFS / Off South Mission Beach, Misₛ sion Bay Several sunken ships and concrete rubble form a chain of artᵢ ficial reefs from North County to the border. The Mission Bay reef is thₑ easiest to reach from central San Diego, though you still need to arriᵥₑ by boat. The *Yukon*, a worn-out Navy vessel, will sink in the area in latₑ 1999; soon mussels, clams, barnacles, and baby abalone will cling to itₛ hull. (Contact dive shops above for more information.) *Map:LL6*

SALTWATER FISHING

Anglers think they've died and gone to a watery heaven when they beginᵣ to explore San Diego's fishing options. They cast lines from the beach oᵣ shores of freshwater lakes, dangle hooks from ocean piers, and chaseᵣ their quarry on everything from rubber rafts to massive yachts.

Saltwater anglers follow the sea's calendar, chasing tuna in springₛ and summer, dorado in autumn, halibut and cod in winter. Several fishing

WEIRD SPORTS

Given the local passion for recreation, San Diegans tend to go a bit over the line with their enthusiasm. Case in point—the annual **Over The Line** (OTL)Tournament held July at Fiesta Island (see Calendar of Events in the Planning a Trip chapter). A beach version of back-lot softball, OTL consists of three-player teams batting and catching the ball before it flies over a line in the sand. Teams from Southern California beach towns like this annual competition quite seriously (despite the general revelry). They can be spotted practicing on Fiesta Island for weeks before the event.

Frisbees are essential play gear. The pros carry half a dozen discs of various weights and sizes when playing **Disc Golf** at Balboa Park's Morley Field Sports Complex (2221 Morley Field Dr, downtown; 619/298-0920). Playing the 18-hole course is a hoot as long as you're not teamed up with hotshots. Wire baskets serve as the golf holes; players must loft their disks over canyons and above trees to reach their targets. The course is free and open daily from sunrise to sunset.

Fanatics with pets compete at the **Canine Frisbee Championships** in Balboa Park; some of the hounds put most humans to shame. Also in Balboa Park, players queue up for the Petanque Courts. Archery Range, and Casting Pool, where fly-fishermen practice their casts. In the more modern arena, corporate groups work out their tensions and kids run amok at **Ultrazone** (3146 Sports Arena Blvd, Loma Portal; 619/221-0100). This indoor laser-tag playground is a dark, foggy underground city with ramps, mazes, and secret passageways; teams chase each other about, zapping the competition.

Naturally, the ocean harbors all sorts of strange happenings. Scuba divers carve pumpkins underwater in an annual Halloween spectacle; they also brave the chilly water to watch squid spawn in January. Master swimmers stroke through waves during the **La Jolla Rough Water Competition** (the largest such competition in the United States) at La Jolla Cove in September. And above it all, hang gliders lift off from the Torrey Pines Glider Port (2800 Torrey Pines Scenic Dr, La Jolla; 858/452-9858) and soar above the ocean while strapped to what look like enormous kites—talk about ultimate thrills.

—*Maribeth Mellin*

companies offer half day, full day, and overnight trips, along with long-range expeditions lasting a few nights or many weeks. Most shops sell fishing licenses and are well-acquainted with the laws. For other information contact **CALIFORNIA FISH AND GAME** (4949 Viewridge Ave, Mission Valley; 858/467-4201; map:KK4). For reputable operators try: Fishermans Landing (2838 Garrison St, Ocean Beach; 619/221-8500; www.fishermanslanding.com; map:E6); Point Loma Sportfishing (1403 Scott St, Ocean Beach; www.pointlomasportfishing.com; map:E7), H&M

Landing (2803 Emerson St, Ocean Beach; 619/222-1144; www.hmland
com; map:E6); Seaforth Sportfishing (1717 Quivira Rd, Mission F
619/224-3383; map:D1), and Islandia Sportfishing (1551 W Mission
Dr, Mission Bay; 619/222-1164; www.islandiasport.com; map:D1).

MISSION BAY offers various opportunities for fisher folk. The w
side of VACATION ISLE (between N and S Ingraham St Bridges) is a gc
site for shore fishing. There are decent parking and rest room facili
here, and it's one of the better picnicking areas on the bay. Many peo
fish from the rocky shores of SHELTER ISLAND (Shelter Island Dr
Rosecrans Ave; map:F7), HARBOR ISLAND (Harbor Island Dr, acr
from the airport; map:J6), and QUIVIRA BASIN (Quivira Wy and Quiv
Rd, South Mission Bay; map:D1).

Fishing is allowed from piers at OCEAN BEACH, PACIFIC BEAC
and IMPERIAL BEACH. Catches include halibut, croaker, bonito, s
perch, sand bass, jacksmelt, shark, and rays. Pay attention to warnir
of water pollution broadcast on local news and in the papers (see "Cc
tamination Blues" in this chapter).

FRESHWATER FISHING

Inland lakes provide fly-casters and boat anglers with excellent opport
nities for snagging catfish, bass, and trout. The following lakes pern
fishing; info on licenses is available at the rental offices at the lakes.

LAKE HENSHAW / 26439 Hwy 76, Santa Ysabel; 760/782-3501 This ar
spot about 60 miles northeast of San Diego is rather desolate, but tl
fishing is good (although the lake is no longer stocked with catfish
Nearby Lake Henshaw Resort rents cabins and has RV hookups and te
camping; a no-frills cafe is open daily. Open year-round exclusively fc
fishing, the lake tempts anglers with crappie, bluegill, bass, bullhead
and channel catfish.

LAKE HODGES / 20102 Lake Dr, at Via Rancho Pkwy, Escondide
619/465-3474 The main draw at this pleasant lake is bass fishing, an
bad boys weighing up to 20 pounds have been snagged by crafty angler:
Nestled in a chaparral-covered canyon just 30 miles north of San Diegc
the lake tends to be most crowded at the beginning of the season, whic
runs March through October; it's open Friday, Saturday, and Sunda
only (sunrise to sunset) during those months. The bait shop sells som
food and drink as well, and there's a small picnic area. There are motor
boats, rowboats, and canoes for rent. Free parking. *Map:EE3*

LAKE JENNINGS COUNTY PARK / 10108 Bass Rd, Lakeside; 619/466
0585 About a half hour's drive from downtown San Diego, Lake Jennings offers a respite from city stresses and some excellent views of the
San Diego River Valley and surrounding mountains. Trout is stocked
October to May, blue and channel catfish from June to September. You'l

also find largemouth bass and sunfish. Tent camping and RV hookups permit overnighting for first-thing-in-the-morning fishing. (Make your reservations several weeks in advance; 858/565-3600.) The lake is open for fishing on Fridays, Saturdays, and Sundays. During catfish season, night fishing is permitted with electric trolling motors and running lights. There's a fee for fishing and a boat launch charge; motorboats and rowboats are for rent. Free parking.

LAKE MIRAMAR / 10710 Scripps Lake Dr, at Scripps Ranch Blvd, Miramar; 619/465-3474 This small lake, in the foothills near Scripps Ranch about 20 miles north of San Diego, has a fantastic view of Mount Sledded and the Pacific Ocean. Fishing and boating are allowed Saturday through Tuesday, but no swimming. Although bass skulk about, most often caught are trout, which you can fish for both winter and summer. Free parking. *Map:HH3*

LAKE MURRAY COMMUNITY PARK / 5540 Kiowa Dr, at Lake Murray Blvd, La Mesa; 619/465-3474 Set among rolling grass hills and hillside homes not far from downtown La Mesa, this urban lake has bass, catfish, and crappie in the summer and trout from November to May. Motorboats are available for rent, or you can fish from shore year-round on Wednesdays, Saturdays, and Sundays. The bait store sells permits and fishing licenses. Fee for boat launch and fishing; free parking. *Map:LL2*

LAKE POWAY RECREATION AREA / 14644 Lake Poway Rd, Poway; 858/679-5466 Situated in the foothills of Poway, this is the place for trout fishing—especially from November through April, when 1,200 pounds of rainbow trout are stocked weekly. Fishing and boating are permitted Wednesday to Sunday, with night fishing during the summer (Friday and Saturday only), when channel catfish abound. The Trout Derby (held early to mid-February) is free for kids, and the largest catfish wins a prize, too. Large bass have been caught here, as well as bluegill and sunfish. Rowboats and electric motorboats are rented; private boats are not permitted (there's also no swimming, waterskiing, or windsurfing). Near the dam, the Lake Poway Wilderness Campground has barbecues, picnic tables, and rest rooms, but no showers (it's a hike in of about 1 mile; contact 858/679-4342 for reservations). Pay parking. *Map:FF2*

GOLFING

San Diego has nearly 50 public courses, some overlooking the sea, others in Mission Valley, along the San Diego River, or in the East County near Escondido, Temecula, Jamul, and El Cajon.

BALBOA PARK GOLF COURSE / 2600 Golf Course Dr, Downtown; 619/239-1632 Designed for the 1915–16 Panama-California Exposition, this municipal course tends to be uneven. It's short, with plenty of opportunities to get into trouble—great for the straight hitter. Well-located near downtown and the airport, getting a tee time is fairly easy. There's an hole championship course and a 9-hole executive course. Twenty-se holes, 6,267 yards, PNGA 69.8. *Map:Q6*

CARLTON OAKS COUNTRY CLUB / 9200 Inwood Dr, Santee; 619/4 4242 Despite the name, this country club traversed by the San Di River has more sycamore and cottonwood trees than oaks. It's a cl lenging course, with five sets of tees and an undulating green. Facili include a driving range and two practice chipping and putting gree packages can be arranged for stays at the attached lodge. The club ho free youth clinics on weekends as well as inexpensive two-hour lesse for adults. Eighteen holes, 7,088 yards, PNGA 74.6. *Map:JJ1*

CORONADO GOLF COURSE / 2000 Visalia Row, Coronado; 619/4 3121 This wonderful course is inexpensive for both residents and out-towners—it's one price for all. A flat course favored by walkers, known to be fun and easy (President Clinton claimed it was the first ti he broke 80). It's a great location with several holes right on the wa and views of the Coronado Bridge and Glorietta Bay. Eighteen hol 6,633 yards, PNGA 71.8. *Map:NN5*

FOUR SEASONS RESORT–AVIARA / 7447 Batiquitos Dr, Carlsba 760/603-6900 Despite the high green fees, it can be a challenge to get tee time at this lovely course overlooking Batiquitos Lagoon and t Pacific. Arnold Palmer designed the course and its fast, true greens. Ma golfers stay at the luxurious resort to attend the golf academy or take p vate lessons. Eighteen holes, 7,007 yards, PNGA 74.2. *Map:CC7*

LA COSTA RESORT / Costa del Mar Rd, Carlsbad; 760/438-9111 Golfe of all abilities appreciate the traditional design of this course, site of th World Gold and Andersen Consulting Match Play Championship Three-day or three-afternoon instruction packages are available, and c course green fees at this luxury resort are high. Open to members an resort guests only. Thirty-six holes. North course 6987 yards, PNG, 74.8; South course 6,894 yards, PNGA 74.4. *Map:CC7*

MOUNT WOODSON COUNTRY CLUB / 16422 N Woodson Dr, Ramona 760/788-3555 This is a fine, short, target-oriented golf course wit extreme changes in elevation, bunkers strategically placed within fai ways, and plenty of water. It's a challenging one, favoring skill ove strength. Eighteen holes, 6,113 yards, PNGA 68.3.

RANCHO BERNARDO INN & GOLF COURSE / 17550 Bernardo Oaks D Rancho Bernardo; 858/675-8470 Designed by Ted Robinson, this cham pionship course has a signature 18th: a 522-yard par-5 with a three-tiered green, a creek, and a lake. Eighteen holes, 6,458 yards, PNGA 70.6 women's course 5,448 yards, PNGA 71.2. *Map:FF3*

SINGING HILLS GOLF RESORT / 3007 Dehesa Rd, El Cajon; 619/442-3425 or 800/457-5568 This reasonably priced course has been family-owned since it was created in the 1950s. It's part of a 450-acre resort that's rated "women friendly" by *Golf For Women* magazine, and offers golf and tennis packages. The Pine Glen course is an easy, 3-par layout; the regulation courses are a lot of fun, with a double green, a few neat water holes, and at least one blind tee shot. Willow Glen Course, eighteen holes, 6,605 yards, PNGA 72.0; Oak Glen Course, eighteen holes, 6,597 yards, PNGA 71.3. *Map:KK1*

STEELE CANYON GOLF & COUNTRY CLUB / 3199 Stonefield Dr, Jamul; 619/441-6900 This challenging, hilly Gary Player Signature Course has three championship nine-hole courses, one of which received a four-star rating from *Golf Digest*. Each has a different feel. Twenty-seven holes, 6,741 yards, PNGA 72.5.

TORREY PINES MUNICIPAL GOLF COURSE / 11480 Torrey Pines Rd, La Jolla; 858/452-3226 Rated among the 50 "must play" courses in the nation by *Links Digest* magazine, this course is home to the Buick Invitational in February and the Junior World Championship in July, as well as the San Diego City Amateur Golf Championship every June. The views from atop the cliff overlooking the ocean are fantastic. The south course is more scenic but requires length off the tee. Green fees for locals are very reasonable; tee times are hard to come by. Eighteen holes; south course 7,055 yards, PNGA 74.6; north course 6,647 yards, PNGA 72.1. *Map:HH7*

HIKING

Outdoor lovers in San Diego County have plenty of hiking opportunities, what with all the mountains, deserts, coastal canyons, bays, and beaches to explore. You'll find urban hikes suitable for the casual hiker, as well as challenging rural assaults for the zealot intent on pushing his or her personal envelope. See the calendar section of the San Diego Weekly Reader for information about current physical phenomena worth investigating, such as grunion runs and desert flower blooms (sometimes included or featured on guided hikes), along with listings of group hikes led by area organizations. In the same publication, Jerry Schad's Roam-A-Rama column recommends a different outdoor destination each week. Schad's softcover tome *Afoot and Afield in San Diego County* is an invaluable guide to outdoor adventures, from coastal San Diego to the mountains and deserts. The local chapter of the **SIERRA CLUB** (3820 Ray St, East San Diego; 619/299-1743; www.sierraclub.org/chapters/sandiego/; map:MM4) offers wilderness training courses as well as hiking and backpacking outings. **WALKABOUT INTERNATIONAL** (835 5th Ave, downtown; 619/231-7463; map:O7) offers day hikes and backpacking trips of varying degrees of difficulty, as do outdoor gear suppliers **ADVENTURE 16** (312 Horton Plaza, downtown; 619/234-1⁊ www.adventure16.com; map:N7) and **REI** (5556 Copely Dr, Clairem⸱ 858/279-4400; www.rei.com; map:JJ5). Those wanting informat⸱ easy-to-moderately paced guided hikes of San Diego's canyons can ⸱ the **SAN DIEGO NATURAL HISTORY MUSEUM** outings on weekend mc ings. Call 619/232-3821 for more information.

San Diego's city dwellers appreciate the proximity of **MISSI** **TRAILS REGIONAL PARK** (1 Father Junipero Serra Trail, Tierra Saⁱ 619/668-3275; map:JJ2) for the accessibility of hiking trails and **COWᵖ MOUNTAIN,** which at 1,592 feet above sea level offers a 360-degree vⁱ of the city. This moderately challenging hike has an elevation gain ⸱ almost 900 feet; the trailhead is approximately 75 yards down Barᵇ Way (on the left) off Boulder Lake Avenue. Also within the park, the ⸱ toric **OLD MISSION DAM** is a starting point for hikes into Oak Canyᶜ the East Fortuna Mountain region, the Father Junipero Serra Trail, a⸱ the San Diego River. All these are good for bird-watching, and the S⸱ Diego River walk is wheelchair accessible.

San Diego's vast desert is a world unto itself. The **ANZA-BORREᵍ DESERT STATE PARK** is composed of more than 600,000 acres of desᶜ scrub and badlands punctuated with surprising palm-studded oases. ⸱ the summer heat is scorching, the best time to visit the desert is frᵒ October through May; remember to bring a hat and drinking water fᵉ even the shortest hike. For an overview of the desert flora and fauna aⁱ suggested hikes, visit the Anza-Borrego Desert State Park **VISITᶜ CENTER** (200 Palm Canyon Dr, Borrego Springs; 760/767-4205; wwᵛ anzaborrego.statepark.org) It's open daily October to May, but only o⸱ weekends and holidays during the summer months. Don't go wanderⁱⁿ about in the desert without checking in at the visitor center and gettin⸱ a map of marked trails.

CUYAMACA RANCHO STATE PARK / 12551 Hwy 79, Descanso; 760/76⁵ 0755 Once the summer home of California Indians, and later the prop⸱ erty of Mexicans granted the land in 1845, this 30,000-acre park noᵛ attracts picnickers, hikers, equestrians, and to a lesser extent backpackerˢ The park extends from chaparral-covered lowlands through treeless mesa⸱ interspersed with groves of sycamore, alder, and willow. In the highesⁱ elevations, black and live oak thrive, as do white fir and ponderosa pines Because the state park lies just about 40 miles from the coast and is splⁱ by the well-trafficked Highway 79, it receives lots of visitors anxious tᵒ flee city life, if only for the day. Trailheads line Highway 79, leadinᵍ hikers into the wilderness on treks of varying difficulty. For more inforⁱ mation and specific hikes, contact the park's Interpretive Association.

LAGUNA MOUNTAIN RECREATION AREA / Sunrise Hwy, mile 23.5, Mt. Laguna; 760/445-8341 Between the Cuyamaca Mountains and the desert lie the Laguna Mountains, drier than the former but not nearly as dry as the latter. At around 6,000 feet, Laguna Crest is the highest point in San Diego County accessible by road. There are more than 70 miles of hiking trails in the Laguna Mountains; most trails are part of the Pacific Crest Trail. On summer weekend nights, visitors can view the heavens through the Mount Laguna Observatory's 21-inch telescope. Also in the summer, rangers and volunteers offer interpretive walks and special events. For information on these events, or to obtain maps of the area hiking trails, contact the Visitor Information Office.

YAKING/CANOEING

Mission Bay has excellent opportunities for kayaking. During the summer, music fans launch along the bayside shores of Shelter Island, head around the point past the harbor police station and into the yacht basin, then tie up near Humphrey's Concerts by the Bay (2241 Shelter Island Dr, downtown; 619/224-3577; map:F7) to enjoy a night's outdoor entertainment for free.

DANA LANDING MARINA / 2590 Ingraham St, Mission Bay; 619/224-2513 Right at one of Mission Bay's major boat launches you'll find Southwest Kayak (619/222-3616), where you can buy or rent a sea kayak for a tour of the bays or the open ocean. Lessons and tours are available. The marina has a kayak launch site and free parking lot. *Map:LL6*

LAKE MIRAMAR / 10710 Scripps Lake Dr, at Scripps Ranch Blvd, Miramar; 619/465-3474 Although there's no swimming here, this pretty little lake is open Saturday through Tuesday for canoeing and fishing (you can hike or picnic here daily). Located near the foothills of Scripps Ranch, it's convenient to central San Diego. Water-skiing and jet-skiing are not permitted, meaning canoe enthusiasts can explore the lake's small bays and coves in relative tranquility. Free parking is available. *Map:HH3*

MISSION BAY AQUATIC CENTER / 1001 Santa Clara Pl, Mission Bay; 619/488-1036 Kayaking, water-skiing, sailing, surfing, and rowing are taught at a summer camp for kids ages 6 to 17 and in year-round classes for adults. Rental equipment is available but restrictions apply; call ahead for information. *Map:LL6*

MISSION BAY SPORTCENTER / 1010 Santa Clara Point, Mission Bay; 619/488-1005 The center rents sea kayaks and teaches kids a variety of sea sports at a summer camp for kids 6 to 17. *Map:LL6*

ABOVE IT ALL

When the traffic jams are in full swing, it's a perfect time to take to the skies. Colorful **hot air balloons** lift off from Del Mar for dusk and dawn panoramas of the rising or setting sun, the Pacific Ocean, the backcountry, and the far-away-from-it-all freeway congestion below. Floats last about an hour, and are followed by champagne or other celebratory refreshments. Balloon companies include California Dreamin' (760/438-9550) and Skysurfer Balloon Company (858/481-6800). **Torrey Pines Glider Port** (2800 Torrey Pines Scenic Dr, La Jolla), poised on the cliffs 300 feet above the Pacific affords hang gliders one of the most exquisite jumping-off-the-edge spots in the world. Lessons as well as tandem rides are available from the on-site **Hang Gliding Center** (858/452-9858). Live out wartime or *Out of Africa* fantasies in vintage aircraft with open cockpits—where the term "backseat driver" takes on new meaning—with **Barnstorm Biplane Adventures** (760/438-7680). Planes take off from Carlsbad's McClellan-Palomar Airport for 20-minute to one hour scenic or mock combat flights. For a **whirlybird** tour of the coast, sign on with Corporate Helicopters of San Diego (619/291-4356).

—*Marael Johnson*

PACIFIC WIND DESIGN AQUATIC CENTER / At Lake Hodges near Date Ln and Lake Dr, Escondido; 619/272-3275 In business in San Diego since 1985, PWD Aquatic Center rents canoes and kayaks—tandem, touring, and recreational—by the hour or day. Group kayaking lessons (beginner and intermediate) are given at summer camps for kids ages 6 to 16 by the day or week; lessons are also available for adults. The lake is open March through October, Friday through Sunday from sunrise to sunset. *Map:DD4*

ROLLER-SKATING/IN-LINE SKATING

Follow the running/biking paths in Mission Bay and Mission and Pacific Beaches (see Running below) for nearly unlimited, relatively flat skating. You can rent equipment (including ever-important knee-pads) at Hamel's Action Sports Center (704 Ventura Pl, Mission Beach; 619/488-5050; map:LL7). Other excellent flat, scenic venues are found along SPANISH LANDING (N Harbor Dr near the Sheraton Hotel on Harbor Island; map:I6) and in Coronado, where trails lead through TIDELANDS PARK on the west side facing downtown, and along Strand Way and Silver Strand Blvd to Imperial Beach.

ROWING

MISSION BAY AQUATIC CENTER / 1001 Santa Clara Pl, Mission Bay; 858/488-1036 The Center teaches classes in basic sweep rowing—crew teams of 8 to 30 people—and individual sculling. Rentals are available but restriction apply; call ahead for details. The coed **MISSION BAY ROWING ASSOCIATION** (858/280-2881) meets here on Mondays and Wednesdays at 5:45pm, Sundays at 7:30am. Cost is $100 for 6 months, and some experience is required. Novice rowers are encouraged to take classes at the center first. The **SAN DIEGO ROWING CLUB** (1220 El Carmel Pl, Mission Beach; 619/683-3810; map:LL6) emphasizes both recreation and competition and hosts training camps during the summer months. *Map:LL6*

NNING

San Diego's weather provides little in the way of excuses for not keeping in shape, and plenty of scenic places to occupy your eyes as your feet pound the dirt or pavement. There are neighborhood parks for those who prefer a flat, grassy surface; state parks offering a change of elevation for runners who want more of a challenge; concrete footpaths along the bay; and wide beaches perfect for running year-round. **SURF** (858/456-5725), a.k.a. San Diego Ultra Running Friends, is a group of long-distance runners that holds social functions and training runs.

City races are beginning to get noticed around the country, and the **AMERICA'S FINEST CITY HALF MARATHON** (619/297-3901), now in its 22nd year, was rated one of the best races in the country by *Runner's World* magazine. Every August up to 6,000 runners take to the San Diego streets, beginning at scenic Cabrillo Monument in Point Loma and winding their way along Harbor Island and the Embarcadero to end in historic Balboa Park; there's a 5K walk/run as well. The **SUZUKI ROCK 'N' ROLL MARATHON** (858/450-6510) draws over 15,000 runners, encouraged in their endeavors by live music on 26 stages along the way, with everything from world beat to country rock, alternative to oldies. Pre-marathon concerts are held at the San Diego Concourse. Equally important yet less strenuous is the annual **UNION-TRIBUNE DR SEUSS RACE FOR LITERACY**, whose "magic mile" race for kids and 8K races benefit the San Diego Council on Literacy (888/850-7323).

Here are several other running opportunities:

LAKE MIRAMAR / 10710 Scripps Lake Dr, Miramar; 619/465-3474 A flat, paved loop of just under 5 miles circles this reservoir. Along part of the route there's a trail parallel to the road, but if you run there, keep an eye out for rattlesnakes. From the west end of the loop, near the top of the dam, you can watch planes take off and land at nearby Miramar Air Station. *Map:HH3*

MISSION BAY / Bordered by I-5, I-8, Grand Ave, and Mission Blvd; 619/221-8900 Many activities are popular at this large, loopy aquatic park, and jogging is one of them. From De Anza Cove (where there's plenty of parking) you can follow the path south past the Hilton and

Fiesta Island to the flood control channel; return the same way. Anot
popular path connects Crown Point to the Mission Bay Channel, skirt
Sail Bay and Riviera Drive—smooth sailing and great bay views all
way. Park at either end and go as far as you like before returning alc
the same path. *Map:LL6*

MISSION BEACH AND PACIFIC BEACH / Between S Mission Beach a
Crystal Pier, Pacific Beach Along this stretch of boardwalk join
South Mission Beach and Pacific Beach, you'll have the ocean on yc
left as you run north, sharing the path with bladers, strollers, skaters, a
cyclists. If you get thirsty, this strip is fronted by bars, restaurants, a
burger shacks, most of which have outdoor patios for observing the scer
Map:LL6–KK6

MISSION TRAILS REGIONAL PARK / I Father Junipero Serra Tra
Tierra Santa; 619/668-3275 This 5,760-acre park has many trails wi
small-to-moderate hills suitable for short or lengthy runs. Stop in at t
visitor center to select your trail; maps there show trails' lengths ar
degree of difficulty. Within the park, **LAKE MURRAY** (619/463-4015)
popular with joggers, although since the concrete path doesn't form
loop all the way around the lake, you must return the way you came. Th
trail is 3.5 miles start to finish, or 7 miles total. You can watch the boat
the people fishing, and the waterfowl on weekends, although with all (
the wheeled and foot traffic, you'd best keep your eyes on the wide pat
Also within the park, **COWLES MOUNTAIN** proves a challenging rur
with a 900-foot change in elevation up to the 1,590-foot peak. A fire roa
down the mountain's backside starts just to the left of the monument a
the summit; either way it's 1.5 miles between the trailhead and the top
The trailhead is off Navajo Road, about half a mile to the east of Jackso
Road near the rest rooms. Wear a hat and bring water, especially i
summer months when temperatures climb. Various running clubs trai
here on weekend mornings. *Map:JJ2*

SILVER STRAND STATE BEACH / 5000 Hwy 75, Coronado; 619/435-518
If you like to run on the beach, this wide, white sand beach stretches fo
2.5 miles. There's a large pay parking lot. *Map:NN5*

TORREY PINES STATE PARK / 12600 N Torrey Pines Road, La Jolla
858/755-2063 Great single tracks here have views of the Pacific Ocean and
the tall pines for which the park was named. The hilly trails are a mixture
of sand and clay, which can get slippery when it rains. The Broken Hill
trail is a popular loop heading down to the beach, then north along the
beach for about a mile, and finally uphill on the park road. *Map:HH7*

SAILING

San Diego Bay is the main harbor for both the city of San Diego and
North Island's military machine. It's interesting to sail among the behe-

moth aircraft carriers and other floating war machines and to explore the coast south to the **CHULA VISTA NATURE CENTER** (1000 Gunpowder Point Way, Chula Vista; 619/422-2473; map:OO3). Coronado's **GLORI-ETTA BAY**, located across from the landmark Hotel del Coronado, is a small bay within San Diego Bay, surrounded by lush parks and the municipal golf course. Rent a sailboat at **SEAFORTH BOAT RENTALS** on Shelter Island (2803 Emerson St; 619/224-1681 or 888/234-2628; www. seaforthboatrental.com; map:E6) or downtown (333 W Harbor Dr; 619/239-2628; map:M8) and venture into San Diego Bay. There's a public boat launch and limited free parking at both Glorietta Bay and Shelter Island. If you need instruction before setting sail, **HARBOR SAIL-BOATS** (2040 Harbor Island Dr at N Harbor Dr, Point Loma; 619/291-9568; map:G6) offers sailing and navigation classes for landlubbers as well as tips for dry-docked sailors; they also rent boats.

On Mission Bay, **SANTA CLARA POINT** and **SAIL BAY** are alive with sailboat activity. Both **MISSION BAY AQUATIC CENTER** (1001 Santa Clara Pl; 858/488-1036; map:LL6) and **MISSION BAY SPORTCENTER** (1010 Santa Clara Pt; 858/488-1005; map:LL6) rent sailboats and offer classes for children and adults. There are some restrictions; call ahead for information. The bayside megaresort **HYATT ISLANDIA** (1441 Quivira Rd; 858/224-1234; map:C1) rents 14- to 30-foot sailboats, as well as powerboats, kayaks, canoes, and paddleboats. The **SAN DIEGO HILTON** (1775 E Mission Bay Dr; 858/275-8945; map:LL5) rents catamarans, Hobie Cats, and 14- and 16-foot monohulls as well as kayaks, Wave Runners, Jet-Skis, sailboards, and powerboats. **DANA LANDING MARINA** (2590 Ingraham St; 619/224-2513; map:LL6) rents boat slips by the day or month. Within this marina, **THE MARKET** (619/226-2929) rents lots of different sailboats for a tour of the bays or the open ocean. **PACIFIC WIND DESIGN AQUATIC CENTER** (Lake Hodges near Date Ln at Lake Dr, Escondido; 619/272-3275; map:DD4) rents 14-foot monohull sail craft for up to four adults and gives group and private lessons for beginning sailors. **SOUTH SHORES** (South Shores Dr at Sea World Dr; map:LL6) is a 24-hour boat ramp with a large parking lot and new rest rooms.

WIMMING

The ocean is fine for some swimmers, but others prefer warm, fresh water for their laps. Most San Diegans rely on backyard pools and fitness clubs for their aquatic work-outs, but there are a few fine public pools in the area. Call ahead for schedules and fees, as they vary with the season.

The **MISSION BEACH PLUNGE**(3115 Ocean Front Walk, Mission Beach; 858/488-3110; map:LL6), is a 175-foot long enclosed swimming pool that has entranced water lovers since 1925. Swimmers have dozens of lanes to choose from; other areas are sectioned off for kids and classes. The **KEARNS MEMORIAL POOL** (2229 Morley Field Dr, Balboa Park, downtown; 619/692-4920; map:P3) offers recreational swimming and classes. The indoor pool at the downtown **YMCA** (500 W Broadw 619/232-7451; map:M7) is also open to the public. For information neighborhood pools operated by the San Diego City Park and Recreat Department, call 619/685-1322.

SURFING

San Diego surfers take their art seriously, and cool ocean temperatu tend to discourage dabblers. The best surfing beaches often have riptic that could and should discourage weak swimmers. Not that tourists a first-timers can't enjoy the surf—but a modicum of caution can h avoid a catastrophe. **TOURMALINE SURF PARK** (Tourmaline St and Jolla Blvd, Pacific Beach; 619/221-8900; map:KK7) is where beginne go to learn, and where older surfers go to enjoy themselves and avoid cu throat competition. **SAN DIEGO SURFING ACADEMY** (6335 Camini Telmo, downtown; 619/565-6892 or 800/447-7873; www.surfSDSA.co map:LL5) provides year-round group or private longboard lessons. Cc includes surfboard and wet suit rental. **MISSION BAY AQUATIC CENT** (1001 Santa Clara Pl, Mission Bay; 858/488-1036; map:LL6) has summ surf camp for ages 6 to 17 and year-round classes for adults. Less deman ing than a short or long fiberglass board, body boards (such as the Mor Boogie Board) can be used at many San Diego beaches for safe, ente taining rides on San Diego's swells (but remember, you can get crunche on a body board as well). Body boards, fins, and longboards can l rented daily at **PLAY IT AGAIN SPORTS** (1401 Garnet Ave, Pacific Beach 619/490-0222; map:KK7); **HAMEL'S ACTION SPORTS CENTER** (70 Ventura Pl, Mission Beach; 858/488-5050; map:LL7) rents body board short boards, and longboards by the day or the hour. If you want t watch pro bodysurfers make the sport look easy, check out the **ANNUA WORLD BODYSURFING CHAMPIONSHIP** (760/966-4535) each August a the Oceanside pier.

Here's a survey of prime surfing spots:

BIRD ROCK / Bird Rock Ave and Dolphin Pl, between South Cas Beach and Pacific Beach; 619/221-8900 This uncrowded beach, with a rocky shore, tide pools, lots of little coves, and very little sand at high tide, is accessed by a stairway at the foot of Bird Rock Avenue. South Bird has an inconsistent swell that's fast and fun when it works. It's best at low to medium tide, although often ruffled by onshore winds. North Bird breaks less frequently, usually on a south or southwest swell. No rest rooms or lifeguards; parking on adjacent streets. *Map:KK7*

CONTAMINATION BLUES

Sad to say, water pollution is an ever-increasing unnatural phenomenon in San Diego. Leaks from sewage facilities sometimes make parts of the ocean off Point Loma very unhealthy for surfers and swimmers. Runoff from the San Diego River and sewage lines sometimes shuts down parts of Ocean Beach. Wise locals don't eat fish from San Diego or Mission Bays. And Imperial Beach and much of South Bay is off-limits nearly year-round, thanks to flooding from the Tijuana River and a lack of cooperation on the issue between Mexico and the United States. Die-hard surfers ignore contamination warnings and pick up all sorts of nasty infections, from ear diseases to hepatitis.

San Diegans try to protect the ocean by participating in beach and ocean cleanup days, keeping oil and toxins out of sewage lines, and painting warnings on street curbs by storm drains. But regular contamination warnings are inevitable. Obey the signs posted at beaches and bays and stay out of the water. —*Maribeth Mellin*

BLACK'S BEACH / 2800 Torrey Pines Scenic Dr, at N Torrey Pines Rd, La Jolla; 858/221-8900 Swells abruptly hitting La Jolla's submarine canyon make Black's the best beach break in San Diego, surfable year-round. It's not recommended for the novice, as there are strong riptides and big, powerful waves. Black's is at its finest when fall or winter Santa Ana winds combine with a northwest swell. There are no regular life-guards or rest rooms, although there are portable toilets and a shower at the top of the cliffs. Parking is usually plentiful; there is also limited parking on surface streets. *Map:II7*

CARDIFF STATE BEACH / Old Hwy 101 at Manchester Ave, Cardiff-By-The-Sea; 858/221-8900 Almost any swell brings longboarders to Cardiff Reef at the north end of this beach. There are rest rooms here, and life-guards are on duty during the summer months. Limited parking along Highway 101 tends to fill up quickly; there's also a pay lot. *Map:EE7*

GARBAGE BEACH / Sunset Cliffs Dr at Ladera St, Ocean Beach; 619/221-8900 Both North and South Garbage have reliable reef waves that work best on a medium to low tide. Easy access makes the breaks popular with longboarders. As at many Sunset Cliffs surf spots, the locals dominate the scene and tend to intimidate outsiders. There's on-street parking, or park in the lot at the top of the hill. Stairs at the bottom of Ladera Street lead to the beach, although at high tide with a big swell, these are inaccessible. There are no rest rooms or lifeguards, but there's a shower across the street from the top of the stairs. *Map:A7*

MARINE STREET / 300 Marine St, La Jolla; 858/221-8900 This wi
clean beach tends to fill up during the summer, although bodyboard
and bodysurfers come year-round for the easily accessed waves. The l
of rest rooms and parking lots (look for a spot on Marine Street or
Lane) keeps some beachcombers away. There is lifeguard service dur
the peak summer months. *Map:JJ7*

**NEWBREAK / Sunset Cliffs Dr at Cornish Dr, Ocean Beach; 619/2
8900** This reliable spot, largely protected from winds, is just as fierc
protected by local surfers, who don't appreciate sharing their realm w
novices. Although it breaks with all tides and swells, it's best at medi
to low tide, though the latter can be dangerous for all but advanc
surfers. Parking is available at Sunset Cliffs Natural Park lot at the e
of Cornish Drive. Walk toward Point Loma College, turn right after t
softball field, and watch to see where others descend the cliffs. Newbre
is to the south. No lifeguards or rest rooms. *Map:A7*

SWAMI'S / 1298 Old Hwy 101, Encinitas; 760/633-2880 Tucked belo
the gold and white Self-Realization Fellowship church, this beach bre
is always fun and therefore always crowded. It's most rewarding at lo
or medium tide; swell size is no object. Free parking and nearby re
rooms. *Map:EE7*

TENNIS

The pros often make their way to San Diego for major tennis tourna
ments at private courts affiliated with resorts including La Costa and th
Rancho Bernardo Inn. But there are plenty of amateurs whacking at bal
in public courts throughout the county. The **BARNES TENNIS CENTE
**(4490 W Point Loma Blvd, Ocean Beach; 619/221-9000; map:D2) is
great tennis venue, especially for kids under 18, who always play free (n
membership dues). In addition to 20 hard and four clay lighted courts
there are full-size basketball courts, a sand volleyball pit, and banque
and meeting rooms. The center is open daily 8am to 9pm.

The **BALBOA TENNIS CLUB** (Morley Field Tennis Complex, Balboa
Park, downtown; 619/295-9278; map:Q3), one of the most popula
venues in the city, was formed in 1939 and encourages competitive play
The club maintains the Morely Field Tennis Complex, with 24 courts, 12
of which are lighted. Reservations accepted.

Other public courts include:

LAKE MURRAY TENNIS CLUB: 7003 Murray Park Dr, Kensington; 619/469-3232; map:LL2
PACIFIC BEACH TENNIS CLUB: 2639 Grand Ave, Pacific Beach; 619/273-9177; map:KK7
PENINSULA TENNIS CLUB: 2525 Bacon St, Ocean Beach; 619/226-3407; map:C2

NDSURFING

A board, a sail, strong arms, and a great sense of balance are all you need to skim across the water while windsurfing. Sounds easy, right? Don't count on it. Try pulling a sail upright while treading water, then climbing on your board without turning the contraption upside down. Still want to windsurf? Take a few classes at one of the centers described below.

MISSION BAY AQUATIC CENTER / 1001 Santa Clara Pl, MIssion Bay; 858/488-1036 Classes in windsurfing are available at this full-service water sports center on a quiet section of the bay. *Map:LL6*

PACIFIC WIND DESIGN / Southwest end of Lake Hodges near Rancho and Lake Drs, Escondido; 619/756-8221 This outfit runs a school for windsurfing and kayaking at Windsurf Beach on Lake Hodges. Summer youth camps teach the skills to kids ages 6 to 16; adults can take individual or group lessons April through October. The lake is only open Friday through Sunday (sunrise to sunset), March through October. *Map:EE4*

SAN DIEGO HILTON / 1775 E Mission Bay Dr, Mission Bay; 619/275-8945 Well-situated on East Mission Bay's tranquil Pacific Passage, the Hilton boat yard rents sailboards as well as other toys and sailing and powerboats. *Map:LL5*

Spectator Sports

Although reasonably dedicated to their major-league baseball and football teams, San Diego's support of other major sports has been lackluster. Despite a winning record, the indoor San Diego Soccers disbanded in 1996, and the Clippers basketball team moved to Los Angeles after the 1983–84 season even though that city already had a NBA team, the Lakers. With so much sunshine and so many outdoor opportunities, San Diegans seem to prefer participating in sports to watching them live or on TV. Die-hard sports fans get their kicks from the fledgling minor-league soccer team the San Diego Flash and hockey's San Diego Gulls; both teams show great promise.

DEL MAR RACETRACK / Hwy 5 at Via de la Valle on the Del Mar Fairgrounds, Del Mar; 858/755-1141 This lovely racetrack "where the turf meets the surf," in operation since 1939, has seen many a thoroughbred speed by during the annual 43-day summer meeting, which begins mid-July and ends in early September. Opening day is a must-do event for many San Diegans, when normally bareheaded women stage an informal competition for the finest hat. Among the major stakes races, the track's signature event is the $1 million, 1.25-mile Pacific Classic, usually held near the end of the season. Two years of physical improvements in the early '90s, costing about $80 million, replaced the 50-year-old grandstand with a modern six-story structure; that overhaul may have helped p vent lagging attendance. According to Del Mar Thoroughbred Cl CEO Joe Harper, the track has ranked first or second nationally average daily attendance for the last seven years. Special post-race eve: such as the Jazz at Del Mar concerts (now in its eighth season), Fam Fun Days, and the Sports and Fitness Festival, also draw crowds. The events are free with track entrance and occur after the last race, usua on the track's grassy infield. *www.dmtc.com; map:GG7*

SAN DIEGO CHARGERS / Qualcomm Stadium, 9449 Friars Rd, Missi- Valley; 619/874-4500 San Diegans readily remember the fabulous tear of the late '70s and early '80s—Dan Fouts's elegant and effective pass to Kellen Winslow and Charlie Joiner and the powerful running Chuck Muncie are indelibly etched in our memories. This offense, led I the innovative Coach Don Coryell, took the team to three consecuti division championships (they won the AFC West in 1979–81). Rece: years have seen a strong defense under the leadership of Junior Seau, ar a disappointing (some might say nonexistent) offense. Head coach Mil Reilly, recruited for the 1999–2000 season, hopes to put together a wir ning team with the help of talented yet unproved young quarterbac Ryan Leaf. *www.chargers.com; map:LL4*

SAN DIEGO FLASH / 7250 Mesa College Dr, Clairemont; 858/581-212 Papo Santos, head coach of this A-league professional outdoor socce team, has put the fledgling team near the top of the field. In its inaugura year, the Flash won the 1998 Pacific Division Championship and nov looks to have a bright future. The 1999 season, which runs April t August, is the second for this fledgling team of the Florida-based Unitec Soccer League *www.sdflash.com; map:KK5*

SAN DIEGO GULLS / San Diego Sports Arena, 3500 Sports Arena Blvd Midway; 619/224-4625 San Diego's very impressive ice hockey tean belongs to the four-year-old West Coast Hockey League. This minor- league team won the Taylor Cup Championship for the first three years of the league's existence, beginning in the 1995–96 season, losing in the 1999 finals to the Tacoma Sabercats. The season runs from October to March. *Map:G2*

SAN DIEGO PADRES / Qualcomm Stadium, 9449 Friars Rd, Mission Valley; 619/280-4636 Although they were National League Champions in 1998 and 1984, the Pads have never conquered the World Series. They lost 0–4 in 1998 to the unstoppable New York Yankees, but so besotted the San Diego fans by their brush with greatness that the voters conceded to their demand for their very own multimillion-dollar stadium, to be located in downtown San Diego. Since the voters approved the deal, the winning Padres of 1998 have lost many of their best players to free agency. Slugger Ken Caminiti went to the Houston Astros; Steve Finley to the Arizona Diamondbacks; and Greg Vaughn, the outfielder who hit 50 home runs in the 1998 season, to the Cincinnati Reds. Luckily, Tony Gwynn—who's held the National League batting title for the past eight years—has no desire to relocate. In addition to being a record-breaking hitter, Gwynn is a super role model for kids and a major player in the game of community philanthropy. *www.padres.com; map:LL4*

CONFERENCES, MEETINGS, AND RECEPTIONS

CONFERENCES, MEETINGS, AND RECEPTIONS

Many hotels, inns, and restaurants in the San Diego area have facilit available for private special events. Virtually every museum and facil in Balboa Park is also available for meetings. For more information Balboa Park offerings, contact individual museums or Balboa Pa Administration (Facility Usage, 2150 West Pan American Rd, San Die 92101; 619/235-1103; map:O5).

AMERICA'S FINEST YACHT CHARTERS / 2005 Calle Cantora, El Cajo 619/286-3900 or 877/990-9100 A full-service water event planne America's Finest Yacht Charters considers itself a floating concierg "Anything you can do on land we can do on water" is their compar motto. Over 60 boats, mostly private luxury yachts up to 150 feet, a available for groups from 6 to 1,000 for dinner cruises, cocktail cruise casino action parties, receptions, or meetings afloat. Mariachis, jaz combos, and magicians can also be arranged. *Map:KK1*

BAHIA STERNWHEELERS / 998 West Mission Bay Dr, Mission Bay 619/539-7720 Two authentic paddle-wheel boats cruise the waters o Mission Bay, both outfitted in 19th century American style. The large *William D. Evans* showcases a lovely stained-glass ceiling and ca accommodate up to 550 on two levels for receptions, 310 for banquets The *Bahia Belle* can hold up to 350 on two levels for receptions or 12(for banquets. Live or canned music can be arranged, and the *Bahia* doe full catering. *Map:LL6*

HERITAGE PARK VICTORIAN VILLAGE / Juan and Harney Sts, Old Town 619/694-3049, for reservations: 619/565-3600 Six historic Victorian homes were moved to this site and are now operated by the County of San Diego Department of Parks and Recreation. Among them is the restored historic Temple Beth Israel, built in 1889 and capable of accommodating 150 people. San Diego's first synagogue, it is now used for weddings as well as nondenominational services. The lawn in front is also available for weddings and receptions for up to 200. Amplified music is not permitted. *Map:J1*

HOTEL DEL CORONADO / 1500 Orange Ave, Coronado; 619/435-6611 A national historic landmark, the oceanfront Hotel del Coronado was built in 1888 and retains a sumptuous Victorian ambience. The site of many local senior proms and charity balls, the Grand Ballroom is a luxurious space with crystal chandeliers, tapestry draperies, and a semicircular stage and can serve 950 for banquets. The Promenade Deck is an outdoor facility that overlooks a fabulous beach. The Duchess of Windsor Cottage is a special place for smaller gatherings. *Map:NN5*

MARINA VILLAGE CONFERENCE CENTER / 1936 Quivira Wy, Mission Bay; 619/222-1620 Located on San Diego's largest marina, this Mission Bay venue offers 27 conference rooms and 13 special-event rooms. The Sunset Room has the best views of the marina. The Bay View Room also has a direct water view; both seat about 200. The Baja Room is the largest and can seat 350. Outdoor ceremony sites are the North or South Lawn or the Arbor, the latter available only with room rental. Rates range from $175 to $2,000. *Map:D1*

MARINE CORPS AIR STATION MIRAMAR / Interstate 15 and Miramar Wy, Miramar; 858/577-4814 The birthplace of the military ranking "top gun," and the site of the movie of the same name, the Marine Corps Air Station Miramar is now home to F/A-18 Hornets, the KC-130 Hercules, the CH-46E Sea Knight, and the CH-53E Super Stallion. Settings available for rental include the famed Miramar Officers' Club (holding 90 to 400) as well as flight-line hangars complete with aircraft (with room for up to 5,000). This is your chance to peek into the cockpit of an F/A-18. Events are catered by Semper Fi Special Events and renters must have a military sponsor—someone in active duty or officially retired. *Map:II3*

MOUNT HELIX AMPHITHEATER / Top of Mount Helix Dr, La Mesa; 619/694-3030 An open-air theater that offers rows of stone benches and a stage area surrounded by boulders, this site has a sweeping vista of East County. Renters can bring in food and beverages, but there are no kitchen facilities or running water. It is a popular site for weddings, especially next to the giant cross that stands behind the amphitheater. Operated by the county parks department, it's available for a $25 permit, quite a bargain. Be advised, however, that parking is a problem. *Map:LL2*

PALOMAR CHRISTIAN CONFERENCE CENTER / 34764 Doane Valley Rd, Palomar; 760/742-3438 or 800/833-1444 Home of the famed 200-inch Hale Telescope, Palomar Mountain tops out at about 5,000 feet above sea level in a beautiful forest of tall trees. The conference center is next to Palomar Mountain State Park. The center itself offers a chapel, several meeting rooms, two large fire rings, a swimming pool, and dormitory and motel-type accommodations. Buffet-style catering service is available. The entire facility can host up to 330. Summers are usually booked by the preceding fall.

QUAIL BOTANICAL GARDENS / 230 Quail Gardens Dr, Encinitas; 760/436-3036 A beautiful garden oasis in the center of bustling North County, Quail Botanical Gardens is a favorite wedding site. The Victorian Gazebo, with its large lawn framed by flowering plants, is the largest spot, holding up to 200. The Walled Garden, like an English country

garden, is more intimate, with room for 85 guests. The Waterfall V
Deck overlooks a 3-story waterfall surrounded by palms, orchids, a
other tropical plants; it holds 20 people. Weddings may be conduc
during daytime park hours, but receptions or other special events
allowed only after hours, from 7–10pm following a 5–7pm sunset we
ding, for example. The Garden requires use of its own caterer. Fees ran
from $250 for a daytime event for 50 or fewer to $1,500 for a sun
wedding and reception package. *Map:EE7*

RANCHO GUAJOME ADOBE / 2210 N Santa Fe, Vista; 760/724-4082
state and national historic landmark, the Rancho Guajome Adobe h
been carefully preserved and restored to its 1853 splendor. A popul
place for weddings and special events, the adobe itself is a museum, ava
able for tours. Weddings may be conducted in the chapel, which hol
150 people; the Adobe Arches outside can accommodate 200. The Vi
torian Garden may also hold up to 300, and tables and chairs for 100 a
available. Music is no problem here, and renters may bring in their ow
caterers. The chapel or arches may be rented alone for $400; with use
the garden for receptions, the fee climbs to $1,000. *Map:AA6*

**SAN DIEGO AEROSPACE MUSEUM / 2110 Pan American Plaza, Balbo
Park, Downtown; 619/234-8291** Construction on the best party site
this museum is due to be completed in December 1999, when the ope
courtyard—featuring the PBY Catalina, a World War II patrol bombe
built in 1943—will be able to accommodate a sit-down dinner for abou
400. Stand-up space for about 1,000 will be available in the museum an
the courtyard. Until construction is completed, stand-up reception spac
for 300 or sit-down dinner space for about 120 can be found indoors
This museum features 67 aircraft on display, including a replica of the
Spirit of St. Louis (the original was built in San Diego). *www.Aerospace
Museum.org Map:O5*

**SAN DIEGO MARITIME MUSEUM / 1306 N Harbor Dr, Downtown;
619/234-9153** The museum's showpiece, the *Star of India*, sits next to its
other gem, the *Berkeley*, the latter the most popular site for special
events. Built in 1898 as a ferryboat plying the bay from Oakland to San
Francisco, the *Berkeley* is a beautifully restored Victorian two-level ferryboat. Catering and DJs are available through the museum. The
Berkeley is usually rented for five hours on weekends at $1,000 for up to
100 guests, $5 per head above 100; it has a capacity for 600. Weekday
rates are lower. *Map:M7*

**SAN DIEGO MUSEUM OF ART / 1450 El Prado, Balboa Park, Downtown;
619/696-1924** The beautiful and imposing rotunda in this classic
museum in Balboa Park has hosted many an elegant gala. There is room
for 700 for receptions, 300 for banquets. The outdoor Sculpture Garden

and Cafe feature 16 large-scale sculptures. Copley Auditorium, with a capacity for 350, is another multiuse space with audiovisual capabilities. *Map:O5*

SAN DIEGO ZOO / 2920 Zoo Dr, Balboa Park, Downtown; 619/685-3259 Several areas, both enclosed and open, are available for private functions at the world-famous zoo. The Rondaval room in a bamboo garden can seat 80; the Treetops room with attached deck and waterfall view can accommodate 150; Treehouse Decks in the heart of Gorilla Tropics can handle 500; and the outdoors Zoofari Party Area can host up to 3,500 for receptions or 1,000 for banquets. *Map:P4*

ZLAC ROWING CLUB / 1111 Pacific Beach Dr, Pacific Beach; 619/274-0661 A private women's rowing club since 1892, ZLAC rents its marvelous 1930s clubhouse to nonmembers for special events. A favorite spot for weddings, the clubhouse sits on the sand of Mission Bay and can hold up to 135 seated (250 unseated) inside and outside on its barbecue patio. No hard liquor and no hard rock bands are allowed, and all music must stop at 10pm. Current fees are $1,000 for four hours. Patrons may bring in their own caterers. *Map:KK7*

Française, 169, 215
rdvark's Odd Ark, 242
nthus Fine Antiques, 289
Hardware, Hillcrest, 228
ams Avenue, 172–74, 208
Street Fair, 16
ams Avenue Bookstore, 172
ams Avenue Consignment, 210
am's Steak & Eggs, 44
elaide's, 225
venture 16 Outdoor & Travel,
213, 235
hiking, 334
ro Club, 270
rospace Museum, San Diego,
184, 350
ica and Beyond, 189
show, 16
tours, 203. See also balloon
rides; biplane rides;
helicopters/whirlybirds
planes
biplane rides, 117, 203, 336
charter or private, 3
San Diego Aerospace
Museum, 184, 350
scheduled, 2
See also gliding
irport (San Diego International
Airport at Lindbergh Field), 2
art, 258
lodgings near, 121
transportation to and from,
3
Aladdin Mediterranean Cafe, 44
Alcala Gallery, 189
Alfonso's, 44–45
Alt Karlsbad Haus, 290
American Indian Cultural Days,
159
America's Finest City Half
Marathon, 337
America's Finest Yacht Charters,
348
Amtrak, 3
amusement parks
Belmont Park, 119, 161–62,
286
Mundo Divertido, 309
Sea World, 148–49, 282
White Water Canyon, 291
Amvets Thrift Store, 242
Anaheim (Disneyland), day trip,
302–04
Andres Latin American Market,
223
Antique Radio Store, The, 210
Antique Warehouse, 213
antiques, 210–12. See also vintage
apparel and furnishings

Antiques Row, 172
Anza-Borrego Desert State Park,
285, 297–300
camping, 300
hiking, 298, 334
day trip, 297–300
itinerary, 285
Apache Trading Post, 226
Apisa, 314
apparel, 212–15
vintage/retro, 242–44
aquariums
Birch Aquarium at Scripps,
160–61, 195
Sea World, 148–49, 282
Architectural Salvage of San Diego,
210
architectural tour, Committee of
100, 202
ARCO Training Center, 291
tour, 203
area codes, 9
Ariana, 212
Armani Exchange, 212
art
festivals and events, 13
galleries, 189–92. See also
individual galleries
museums. See museums
in public places, 186–89
at San Diego International
Airport, 258
walking tour, 204
Art Alive, 13
Art Tours, 204
Artes Don Quijote, 320
Artists Gallery, The, 189–90
Artists' Loft, The, 138, 285, 297
Artists on the Cutting Edge, 260
Arts Tix, 247
Artwalk Festival, 13
Ascot Shop, The, 212
Assenti's Pasta Company, 223–24
Athenaeum Music & Arts Library,
190, 252–53
Athens Market Taverna, 45
Atomic Trading Company, 214
Auto Impound, 24
automobiles. See cars
Aveda Lifestyle Store, 216. See
also Ecotique Aveda Salon
Avenida Revolución, 308
Aviara Golf Club, 293, 332. See
also Four Seasons
Resort–Aviara
Avo Playhouse, 246
Azul La Jolla, 45
Azulejos, 311
Azzura Point, 46

B

Babette Schwartz, 171, 226
Baby Rock, 312
Bahia Resort Hotel, 127
Bahia Sternwheelers, 204, 348
Bai Yook Thai Cuisine, 46
Bailey Wine Country Cafe, 302
Baja (northern), 305–20
Ensenada, 316–20
map, 306
Puerto Nuevo (Newport),
315–16
Rosarito, 312–15
Tijuana, 307–12
useful information, 310–11
Baja California Tours, 310–11, 319
Baja Information, 311
Baja Lobster Restaurant, 291
Bajamar, 318
Baked by Etta, 215
bakeries, 215–16. See also
individual bakeries
Balboa Park, 117, 142–44
itinerary, 281–82
map, 144
Mingei International
Museum, 182–83
Museum of Photographic
Arts, 183
Museum of San Diego
History, 183
Old Globe Theatre, 202,
249
Reuben H. Fleet Space
Theater & Science
Center, 156, 350
San Diego Aerospace
Museum, 184, 350
San Diego Automotive
Museum, 184
San Diego Hall of
Champions Sports
Museum, 184–85
San Diego Model Railroad
Museum, 185
San Diego Museum of Art,
143, 185–86, 350–51
San Diego Museum of Man,
159
San Diego Natural History
Museum, 186, 202, 334
San Diego Zoo, 144–46,
351
Starlight Theater, 251
Timken Museum of Art, 186
Balboa Park Golf Course, 331–32
Balboa Park Inn, 116–17
Balboa Tennis Club, 342
Bali Authentic Indonesian, 46–47
ballet, 256–57
balloon rides, 117, 336

banks, 25–26
Barefoot Bar & Grill, 270
Barnes & Noble Booksellers, 218
Barnes Tennis Center, 342
Barnstorm Biplane Adventures, 336
Barnstorming Adventures, 117
Barona Casino, 298
Barons, 241
bars, 270–74
baseball: San Diego Padres, 344–45
Basilica San Diego de Alcalá, 10
Bath & Body Works, 216
Bay Books, 218
Bay Club, The, 123
Bay Park, 170
  nightlife, 263
Bayou Bar and Grill, 47–48
Bazaar del Mundo, 157, 166
  shopping, 208
Bazar de Mexico, 308
Beach Haven Inn, 129
beaches, 194–202
  Black's Beach, 194–95, 341
  Children's Pool Beach, 195–96
  Coronado Municipal Beach, 196
  Estero Beach Resort, 318
  Fiesta Island, 147, 197, 323
  Fletcher Cove Beach Park, 288
  Imperial Beach, 197–98
  La Jolla Cove, 160, 195, 328
  La Jolla Shores, 198, 328
  Mission Bay Park, 146–47, 323–24, 326, 328
  Mission Beach, 162–63, 199, 324, 338
  Ocean Beach, 174, 199–200
  Pacific Beach, 200, 285–86
  Rosarito, 312, 313
  San Elijo State Beach, 289
  Silver Strand State Beach, 161, 325, 338
  Torrey Pines State Beach, 201
  Windansea Beach, 201–02
Beauty Clinic-Kliniek, 216–17
beauty salons, 29. See also body care; spas
Bed & Breakfast Inn of La Jolla, The, 130
beer, 241–42. See also pubs
Beer King, 241
Belgian Lion, 48
Bella Luna, 48
Bellefleur Winery & Restaurant, 49, 284, 292
Belly Up Tavern, 213, 264–65
Belmont Park, 161–62, 286
  Giant Dipper, 117, 162

Mission Beach Plunge, 162, 339
Berta's Latin American Restaurant, 47
Best Western Hacienda Suites–Old Town, 124
Best Western Island Palms Hotel & Marina, 124
bicycling, 24–25, 322–25
  clubs and organizations, 322–23
  events, 323
  map, 25, 322
  rentals, 25, 324
  routes and rides, 323–25
  See also mountain biking
Big Kitchen, The, 49–50
Bikes and Beyond, 323
billiards, 273
Biplane & Air Combat Adventures, 203
biplane rides, 117, 203, 336
Birch Aquarium at Scripps, 160–61, 195
Bird Rock, 195
  surfing, 340
Birdcage, 213
Black, The, 175, 226
Black Sheep, The, 289
Black's Beach, 194–95
  surfing, 341
Blind Melons, 265
blowhole, 320
Blowout Video Sales, 240
Blue Door Literary Bookstore, 171, 218
Blue Meannie Records, 233
Blue Point Coastal Cuisine, 50
Bo Danica, 227
Boardwalk, The, 162–63
boat parades, 17
boat tours, 150–51, 203–04
boating, 326–27
  rentals, 327
  See also kayaking/canoeing; rowing; sailing
body care, 216–18. See also salons; spas
Body Shop Skin & Hair Care, The, 217
bodysurfing, 340
  championships, 16, 340
Bombay, 50–51
books and periodicals, 31–32, 218–21. See also individual bookstores and newsstands
Bookstar, 218
Boomerang for Modern, 242
Borders Books & Music, 218–19
Borrego Springs, 285, 299–300
  day trip, 297–300
  lodgings, 139–40
Borrego Valley Inn, 139, 299
Brad Burt's Magic Shop, 239
Bread & Cie, 51, 215

Brick by Brick, 265
Brigantine, The, 51
Buffalo Exchange, 242
Buffalo Joe's, 265
Builder's Trading Co., 289–90
bullfights, 309
Bully's North, 51–52
bus tours
  Mexico, 310–11
  San Diego and environs, 204
buses
  to and from airport, 3
  to and from San Diego, 3
  San Diego Transit Company, 23
business services, 28
butchers, 233

C
Cabrillo Festival, 16
Cabrillo National Monument, 14
Cafe Athena, 52–53
Cafe Champagne, 301–02
Cafe Del Mar, 53
Cafe Japengo, 53
Cafe 1134, 167
Cafe Pacifica, 54
Café Sevilla, 54, 265
Cafe 222, 52
Cafe Zinc, 55, 213, 284
Cafe Zucchero, 55
Caffe Italia, 275
Cal Stores, 236
Calafia, 315
calendar of events, 12–17
Caliente Sports Book, 309
California Ballet Company, 256–57
California Center for the Arts, 246, 294
California Cuisine, 55–56, 171
California Fish and Game Department, 328, 329
California Tower, 142
Callaway Vineyard & Winery, 301. See also Vineyard Terrace
Camino Real Hotel, 311
Camp Pendleton, 293
  tour, 202
camping: Anza-Borrego Desert State Park, 300
candy, 221
'Canes, 270
Canine Frisbee Championships, 14, 329
canoeing/kayaking, 335–36. See also rowing
Canyoneers' nature walks, 202, 334
Caravan Market, 224
Cardiff-By-The-Sea, 289
  restaurants, 38
Cardiff State Beach, surfing, 341

...bad
day trip, 290–93
lodgings, 137
restaurants, 38
See also individual businesses and attractions
...sbad Company Stores, 292
...sbad 5000, 293
...sbad Ranch, 193
flower fields, 12, 292
...sbad Street Faires, 293
...ton Oaks Country Club, 332
...ousels, 143, 154
...age rides, 117, 154
..., 3–4, 24
parking, 24
San Diego Automotive Museum, 184
See also driving tours; freeways
...a de Bandini Restaurant, 166
...a de Pico, 157
...a del Libro, 219
...a la Carreta, 314
...samar, 319
...sbah, 265
...inos, 298. *See also* gambling; individual casinos
...ss Street Bar & Grill, 56
...ssidy West, 213
...tamaran Resort Hotel, The, 129
...) stores, 233–35
...ecil's Cafe & Fish Market, 56
...edars Trading Co., 213
...edros Design District, 213, 288
...edros Gardens, 213
...hameleon Cafe, 57
...naparral Antique Mall, 300–01
...hart House, 57
...harters
airplanes, 3
yachts, 348
...heese Shop, The, 57–58
...hez Loma, 58
...hicano Park, 188
...hicki Jai, 311
...hilango's Mexico City Grill, 58
...hildren
activities and adventures for, 281
traveling with, 8
See also toys; individual businesses and attractions
Children's Museum/Museo de los Niños, 182
Children's Pool Beach, 195–96
Chinese New Year, 12
Chino's Vegetable Shop, 181
chocolate, 221
Christmas on the Prado, 17
Chula Vista, 291
nightlife, 263
Chula Vista Nature Center, 291
churches, 26

Cien Años, 309–11
Cilantro's, 59
Cinco de Mayo, 13–14
Cine Café, 32
Circa A.D., 230
Circa La Jolla, 210
City Delicatessen & Bakery, 171
Civic Helicopter, 203
Clairemont, 170
restaurants, 38
Classic Sailing Adventures, 203
classical music, 252–56
Clayton's Coffee Shop, 167
Clayton's Pies & Bakery, 215
climate, 5
clothing, appropriate, 6. *See also* apparel
Club Montage, 265–66
clubs, 264–69
Coaster, 3
Cody's at the Cove, 59
coffee
houses, 275–77
retail, 221–23
Coffee Bean & Tea Leaf, The, 221–22
Collector, The, 227
Column One, 171, 230
Comedy Store, The, 266
Committee of 100 architectural tour, 202
Como Que No, 312
computers, repairs and rentals, 29
concerts
classical music, 252–56
jazz, 293
See also individual venues and events
Concord Lighting, 230
conference facilities, 347–51
Constantino's Silver Spoon Restaurant, 301
construction, 31
Controversial Bookstore, 219
Convention Center, construction, 31
Coors Amphitheatre, 291
copy services, 28
Corner Stone, The, 211
Coronado, 167–69
bicycling, 323
lodgings, 121–23
map, 168
restaurants, 38
shopping, 209
See also individual businesses and attractions
Coronado Antiques and Consignment, 210–11
Coronado Bakery, 167
Coronado Beach Historical Museum, 167
Coronado Flower Show Weekend, 13
Coronado Golf Course, 332

Coronado Independence Day Celebration, 15
Coronado Municipal Beach, 196
Coronado Playhouse, 169, 246
Coronado Walking Tour, 205
Cortez Hill, construction, 31
Corvette Diner Bar & Grill, 171
Cost Plus World Market, 241
Costa Brava, 315
Costa Verde Center, shopping, 210
costs, 6–7
county fair, 14
Cove Theatre, 177
Cow, 234
Cowles Mountain
hiking, 334
running, 338
Cream of the Crop, 242–43
Crest Cafe, 59–60
Crest Liquor, 241
Croce's Restaurant & Jazz Bar, 266
Croce's Top Hat Bar & Grill, 266
Crow Bar, The, 266
Crystal Pier, 162–63
Crystal Pier Hotel, 130, 163, 286
currency exchange, 11. *See also* banks
Cuyamaca Mountains, itinerary, 285
Cuyamaca Rancho State Park, hiking, 334

D

D. D. Allen Antiques, 211
D. G. Wills, 259–60
D. Z. Akin's, 60
Dana Inn, 128
Dana Landing Marina, 335, 339
boating, 326
dance, 256–57
dancing. *See* clubs
David Zapf Gallery, 190
Day at the Docks, 13
day trips, 287–304
Anza-Borrego Desert and Borrego Springs, 297–300
Carlsbad, 290–93
Disneyland, 302–04
Escondido, 293–95
North Coast, 288–90
Palomar Mountain and Julian, 295–97
Temecula, 300–02
See also Baja; itineraries
De Anza Cove, boating, 326
Debra Owen Gallery, 190
Deer Park, 294
Del Mar, 22, 175–77
lodgings, 135
map, 178
restaurants, 38
See also individual businesses and attractions

Del Mar Fair, 14
Del Mar Fairgrounds, 179
Del Mar Pizza, 61
Del Mar Plaza, 179, 209
Del Mar Racetrack, 15, 343–44
Del Mar Thoroughbred Club, 179
delicatessens, 171, 224, 241. See
    also ethnic markets; restaurants
Delicias, 60–61
dental services, 27
Desert Jeep Tours/Outback Tours,
    299
Design Center Accessories, 232
designer shopping, 213
desserts, 275–77
Dick's Last Resort, 270
Dick's Liquor and Deli, 241
Dime Que Sí, 312
disabilities, local information for
    people with, 8
disc golf, 329
Discount Hobby Warehouse, 239
Discovery Channel Store, 240
Disneyland, day trip, 302–04
Diversionary Theater, 252
Diving Locker, The, 236
diving/snorkeling, 328
    Underwater Pumpkin
        Carving Contest, 17
    See also San Diego–La Jolla
        Underwater Park
Doane Valley Nature Trail, 296
Dobson's Bar & Restaurant, 61
Dog Beach, 174
dogs
    Canine Frisbee
        Championships, 14, 329
    dining with, 45
    Dog Beach, 174
    off-leash areas, 9
Don's Country Kitchen, 62
Doubletree San Diego Mission
    Valley, 126
downtown
    itinerary, 280–81
    lodgings, 116–20
    nightlife, 263
    restaurants, 38
    shopping, 208.
    waterfront, 150–52
    See also individual businesses
        and attractions
Downtown Johnny Brown's, 62
drama. See theater
driving tours, 299
drugstores, 27
dry cleaners, 28
Dudley's Bakery, 296

E

E Street Alley, 266–67
Earth Day, 13
Earth Song Bookstore, 177
East San Diego, 170

Ecotique Aveda Salon, 217. See
    also Aveda Lifestyle Store
El Agave, 62–63, 286
El Bizcocho, 63
El Charro, 319
El Cordova Hotel, 121–22
El Cortez Hotel, construction, 31
El Indio Shop, 63–64
El Museo Cantina Tequila, 314
El Patio, 314
El Rey Sol, 319
Ellen Browning Scripps Park, 160,
    175–77, 196–97
Embarcadero, 20
Embarcadero Marina Park, 197
Embassy Suites San Diego Bay,
    117
Embers Grille, 64
emergency telephone numbers,
    33–34
Empire Club, 266
Empire Enterprise, 211
Encinitas, 289.
    restaurants, 38
    See also individual businesses
        and attractions
Encore of La Jolla, 214
Ensenada, 316–20
Epazote, 64
Erosion Road Tour, 299
Escondido, 170
    day trip, 293–95
    restaurants, 38
    See also individual businesses
        and attractions
Esmeralda Books & Coffee, 179,
    259
Espresso Mío, 170, 275
Estero Beach Resort, 318
ethnic festivals and events, 12–17.
    See also individual festivals and
    events
Ethnic Food Fair, 14
ethnic markets, 223–25. See also
    delicatessens
European Cake Gallery, 215
events and festivals, 12–17
    film, 258–59
    fishing, 13
    food, 14
    golf, 292
    literary, 259–60
    mountain biking, 325
    music, 254, 293
    running, 14, 293, 337
    skiing, 12
    surfing, 340
    tennis, 292
    See also individual events and
        festivals
Everett Stunz Company Ltd, 230
exploring, 141–205
    art in public places, 186–89
    beaches and parks, 194–202
    galleries, 189–92

    gardens, 193–94
    museums, 181–86
    neighborhoods, 166–8
    Top 25 attractions, 142–
    tours, 202–05

F

F Street Bookstore, 227
Fairbanks Ranch, 181
Fairouz Restaurant & Gallery, 6
fairs, 14. See also street fairs
Fallbrook, 294–95
families, local information for, 8
    See also children
Fashion Valley, shopping, 209
Father Luis Jayme Museum, 16
ferries, 25, 151
Ferry Landing Marketplace, 16
Festival Plaza, 314
festivals and events. See events
    and festivals
Fidel's, 65
Field, The, 271
Fiesta Island, 147, 197
    bicycling, 323
Filippi's Pizza Grotto, 65–66, 2
film(s), 257–59
    made in San Diego, 131
Fingerhut Gallery, 177, 190
Fio's Cucina Italiana, 66
Firehouse Beach Cafe, 66, 286
fish, fresh, 233, 318–19
Fish Market, 318–19
Fish Market Restaurant, 67
fishing
    Crystal Pier, 162–63
    Ensenada, 319
    festivals and events, 13
    freshwater, 330–31
    license, 329
    Ocean Beach Pier, 163
    saltwater, 328–30
    See also Grunion Festival
Flashbacks Recycled Fashions, 24
Fleet (Reuben H.) Space Theater
    & Science Center, 156, 350
Fletcher Cove Beach Park, 288
Flick's, 271
Floral Fantasia, 225
Florida Canyon, mountain biking,
    325
florists, 225–26
Flower Fields at Carlsbad Ranch,
    12, 292
Flower Hill Mall, 179
flowers
    shows, 12
    viewing, 12, 292
    See also florists; gardens;
        nurseries
flying, 336. See also air tours
Folk Arts Rare Records, 234
food
    costs, 7
    festivals, 14

health, 229–30
See also bakeries;
    delicatessens; desserts;
    ethnic markets; grocery
    stores; restaurants
all: San Diego Chargers, 344
gn visitors, services for, 11
uet's de Paris, 311
Seasons Resort–Aviara, 137,
34, 292–93
    golfing, 332
& B, 264
ways, 4–5
ch Garden Shoppe, 169, 227
ch Pastry Shop, 67
water fishing, 330–31. See
so saltwater fishing
e theaters, 252
ee Championships, Canine,
4, 329
Theater, 252

ería de Pérez Meillón, 319
leo Café, 143
lery, The, 231
lery Alexander, 177, 190
lery Eight, 191
lery One, 227
eries, art, 189–92. See also
individual galleries
bling, 298
    Caliente Sports Book, 309
    See also casinos
rbage Beach, surfing, 341
rden Cabaret Cinema, 171,
259
rden House Coffee & Tea, 222
rdens, 193–94. See also flowers;
nurseries; Self-Realization
Fellowship; individual gardens
aslamp Billiard Palace, 271
aslamp Plaza Suites, 117
aslamp Quarter, 20–21, 152–53
    walking tour, 204–05
aslamp Quarter Historical
Foundation, 204–05
aslamp Stadium 15, 153
ays and lesbians
    information and
        organizations, 9–11
    Lesbian & Gay Pride Parade,
    15
    nightlife, 262
Gelato Vero Caffe, 275
Genghis Khan, 230–31
George White and Anna Gunn
Marston House, 182
George's at the Cove, 68, 283
Gepetto's, 239
GI Joe's Army-Navy Surplus, 236
gifts, 226–28. See also individual
gift shops
gliding, 336
Glorietta Bay, boating, 326

Glorietta Bay Inn, 122
Glorious Antiques, 211
Godiva Chocolatier, 221
Golden Door, 294
Golden Hill, 170
    restaurants, 38
Golden Triangle, 170
golfing, 331–33
    disc, 329
    events, 292
    See also individual golf
        courses and country clubs
gondola rides, 117
Gone Wild, 233
Goodwill Industries, 243
Gordo's Sportfishing, 319
Gourmet Bagger, 68
Grande Colonial, The, 131
Grant Grill, The, 69
Gray Line San Diego, 3, 204
Great News Cooking Supplies, 232
Greek Islands Cafe, 69
Greek Town Restaurant and
Taverna, 69–70
Green Flash, The, 162
Greenway Museum, 296
Greyhound Bus Lines, 3
grocery stores, 27. See also ethnic
markets; health food
Grounds for Murder Mystery
Book Store, 219
Grove Pastry Shop, 215
Grunion Festival, 15–16
Guatemala Shop, The, 227
Gulf Coast Grill, 70

H
Hacienda Suites–Old Town (Best
Western), 122–23
Hamburger Mary's, 70
Hamel's Action Sports Center,
236, 286, 324, 340
Hanalei Hotel, 126
Hang Gliding Center, 336
Hansen's Surfboards, 289
Harbor Excursions, San Diego,
150, 203
Harbor Island, 170
Harbor Sailboats, 339
harbor tours, 150–51, 203
hardware stores, 228–29
Harley-Davidson, San Diego, 228
Harmony on Fifth, 267–68
Harvest Festival, 17
health food, 229–30
Healthy Back Store, The, 227
helicopter/whirlybird tours, 203,
336
Heritage Park Inn, 125
Heritage Park Victoria Village, 166,
348
Hernandez Hideaway, 295
Highlights, 231
hiking, 333–35

Anza-Borrego Desert State
    Park, 298, 334
    clubs and organizations,
    333–34
    Palomar Mountain State
        Park, 296
    San Elijo Lagoon, 288–89
    tours, 204, 333–34
    Volcan Mountain Wilderness
        Preserve, 297
Hillcrest, 171–72
    nightlife, 263
    restaurants, 38
    shopping, 208
    See also individual businesses
        and attractions
Hillcrest Ace Hardware, 228
Hillcrest Cinemas, 172
Hillcrest Newsstand, 219
Hilton Beach and Tennis Resort,
San Diego, 128–29, 343
Hilton La Jolla Torrey Pines, 132
historic districts, shopping, 208
history, 10–11
    museums. See museums
Hoa Hing, 224
Hob Nob Hill, 71
hobby shops, 239–40
Hodad's, 71
Holiday Inn Vita Spa Agua
Caliente, 311
Home Accents of La Jolla, 231
Home Depot, 229
home furnishings, 230–31
Hook, Line & Sinker, 236
horse racing, 15, 179, 343–44
horseback riding, 297
horse-drawn carriage rides, 117,
154
Horton, Alonzo Erastus, 283
Horton Grand Hotel, 117–18, 152
Horton Plaza, 20, 152–53,
154–56
    background, 283
    shopping, 209
hospitals, 27
hot air balloons, 117, 336
Hotel Circle Inn, 126–27
Hotel Coral & Marina, 316–18
Hotel del Coronado, 122
    conferences/meetings/
        receptions, 348–49
    lunch, 280
    as a tourist attraction,
        149–50
Hotel New Port Baja, 315
Hotel Parisi, 133–34
Huddle, The, 169
Humphrey's, 268
Hussong's Cantina, 316
Hyatt Islandia, sailing, 339
Hyatt Regency La Jolla, 132–33
Hyatt Regency San Diego, 117
    construction, 31
    Top of the Hyatt, 273

I

ice hockey: San Diego Gulls, 344
Ichiban PB/Ichiban, 71–72
Il Fornaio, 72
Imperial Beach, 197–98
In Cahoots, 268
In Harmony, 229
Independence Day, 15
India Street Artworks, 191
Indian Fair, 14
Indigo Way, 243
information centers, 22–23
in-line skating/roller-skating, 336
Inn at Rancho Santa Fe, The, 136, 181
InSITE, 188–89
International Gallery, 191
International Groceries of San Diego, 224
International Male, 214
Internet
    access, 32–33
    information, 11
Island Palms Hotel & Marina (Best Western), 122
itineraries, 279–86
    Anza-Borrego desert, 285. See also Anza-Borrego Desert State Park
    Balboa Park, 282–82
    Cuyamaca Mountains, 285
    downtown, 280–81
    La Jolla, 283–84
    Mission Bay, 282–83
    North Coast/County, 284–85
    Pacific Beach, 285–86
    See also day trips

J

jai alai, 309
Jake's, 291
Jake's Del Mar, 73
Jasmine, 73
Java Bar & Garden Cafe, 173
Java Joe's, 275
Jewel Box, The, 271
jewelry, 231–32. See also vintage apparel and furnishings
Joe's Crab Shack, 73–74
John Cole's Book Shop, 176, 219
Jose's Courtroom, 74
Joseph Tabler Books, 171
JP and Company, 211
Julian, 285, 296–97
    day trip, 295–97
    lodgings, 138–39
Julian Cafe & Bakery, 296
Julian Drug Store, 285, 296
Julian Fat Tire Festival, 325
Julian Pioneer Museum, 285, 296–97
Julian Stables, 297
Junipero Serra Museum, 167
Jyoti Bihanga, 74

K

Kaiserhof, 75
Karen Krasne's Extraordinary Desserts, 216, 275–76
Karen's Consignment Gallery, 243
Karl Strauss Brewery & Grill
    La Jolla, 271
    Sorrento Valley, 75
Kate Sessions Memorial Park, 198
kayaking/canoeing, 335–36. See also rowing
Kearns Memorial Pool, 339–40
Kearny Mesa, 170
    restaurants, 38
Kelly's Simply Fresh Natural Market, 233
Kemo Sabe, 75–76
Ken Theater, 174
Kensington/Adams Avenue, 172–74
    map, 173
    nightlife, 263
    restaurants, 38
    shopping, 208
Kensington Club, 271–72
Kensington Coffee Co., 173
Kensington Grill, 76, 172
Kensington Video, 174, 240
Kern & Co., 213
Ki's, 76–77
King and Company, 211
kitchenware, 232–33
Kono's Cafe, 77, 286
Korea House, 77
KPBS Store of Knowledge, 240
Krazy Coyote Saloon and Grille, 299

L

L. A. Cetto Winery, 309
L'Auberge Del Mar, 135
La Bufadora, 320
La Casa de Estudillo, 166
La Casa del Zorro, 139–40, 285, 299
La Compagnie de Provence, 217
La Costa Hotel and Spa, 292
    golfing, 332
La Especial, 311
La Especial Norte, 77–78
La Esquina de Bodegas, 320
La Flor de Michoacán, 314
La Fonda, 315–16
La Fresqueria, 78
La Jolla, 22, 173–75
    itinerary, 283–84
    lodgings, 130–34
    map, 176
    nightlife, 263
    restaurants, 38
    shopping, 209
    See also individual businesses and attractions
La Jolla Chamber Music Society, 253–54

La Jolla Cove, 160, 195
    diving/snorkeling, 328
La Jolla Cove Suites, 133
La Jolla Easter Hat Sidewalk Promenade, 13
La Jolla Fiber Arts, 191
La Jolla Playhouse, 247
La Jolla Rough Water Competition, 329
La Jolla Shores, 198
    diving/snorkeling, 328
La Jolla Village Square, 210
La Mesa, 170
    restaurants, 38
La Paloma, 289
La Panaderia, 157
La Pensione Hotel, 118
La Provence, 78–79
La Salsa, 79
La Taberna Española, 311, 314
La Vache & Co., 171
La Valencia Hotel, 133, 176, 2
Laguna Mountains, 20
Laguna Mountain Recreation A hiking, 335
Lahaina, 162
Lake Henshaw, freshwater fishi 330
Lake Hodges, 295
    boating, 327
    fishing, 330
    mountain biking, 326
    See also Pacific Wind Desi, Aquatic Center
Lake Jennings County Park
    boating, 327
    fishing, 330–31
Lake Miramar
    fishing, 331
    kayaking/canoeing, 335
    running, 337
Lake Murray, running, 338
Lake Murray Community Park
    boating, 327
    fishing, 331
Lake Murray Tennis Club, 342
Lake Poway Recreation Area, freshwater fishing, 331
Lambs Players Theatre, 169, 247–48
Lamp Shades Unlimited, 231
Las Bodegas de Santo Tomás, 32
Las Posadas, Old Town's, 17
Las Rosas, 218
laser tag, 329
laundromats, 28
Laurel Restaurant & Bar, 79–80
Le Fontainebleau, 80
Le Travel Store, 32, 227–28
legal services, 28
Legoland California, 159, 293
Lemon Grove, 170
Les Artistes, 135
lesbians. See gays and lesbians
Lestat's Coffee House, 173

...dia, 290
...estaurants, 38
...es, 30–31. See also books
... periodicals
..., 219
..., fishing, 328
...ouse, 148
...ergh Field. See airport
...ure/literary events, 259–60.
... also books and periodicals
...taly, construction, 31
...Wire, 272
...Room Coffeehouse, The,
...6
...ers, diving for, 328
...gs, 113–38.
... airport area, 121
... Borrego Springs, 139–40
... Carlsbad, 137
... Coronado, 121–23
... Del Mar, 135
... downtown, 116–20
... Julian, 138–139
... La Jolla, 130–34
... Mission Bay, 127–29
... Mission Valley, 126–27
... Old Town, 124–25
... Pacific Beach, 129–30
... Point Loma/Shelter Island,
...   123–24
... Rancho Bernardo, 137–38
... Rancho Santa Fe, 136
...   See also day trips; itineraries
...ws Coronado Bay Resort, 123
...na Vista Bed & Breakfast, 302
...Castillo, 320
...Pelícanos, 313
...'s Records, 290
...eum Theater, 155

...gic shops, 239
...idhof Brothers, 231
...inly Mozart Festival, 254
...ison en Provence, 169, 231
...ke Mine Sweet, 221
...lashock Dance & Company,
...257
...lls, 209–10, 293
...aps
... Baja (northern), 306
... Balboa Park, 144
... Coronado, 168
... Del Mar, 178
... Kensington, 173
... La Jolla, 176
... Mission Bay, 146
... Rancho Santa Fe, 180
...arathons, 14, 293, 337
... half, 337
...   See also running
...arina District, construction, 31
...arina Village Conference Center,
...349

marinas
    Best Western Island Palms
        Hotel & Marina, 122
    Dana Landing Marina, 326,
        335, 339
    Hotel Coral & Marina,
        316–18
    San Diego Marriott Hotel &
        Marina, 118–19
    Shelter Pointe Hotel and
        Marina, 122
    Snug Harbor Marina, 292
Marine Corps Air Station Miramar,
    conferences/meetings/
    receptions, 349
Marine Room, The, 80–81
Marine Street, surfing, 342
Marriott Hotel & Marina, San
    Diego, 118–19
Marriott Mission Valley, San Diego,
    127
Marriott Real del Mar Residence
    Inn, 313
Marisol, 268
Maritime Museum, San Diego, 150
    conferences/meetings/
    receptions, 350
Market Cafe, 81
markets, ethnic, 223–25. See also
    delicatessens
Maurice Carrie Winery, 301
meat, fresh, 233
medical services, 27
meeting facilities, 347–51
Menghini Winery, 297
Mercado Hidalgo, 308–09
messenger services, 28
Mexican food, definitions, 317
Mexico
    entering and leaving, 310
    money, 310
    paperwork required in, 310
    telephones, 310
    touring, 310–11
    See also Baja
Mexicoach, 311
    Terminal, 308
Middletown, 170
    nightlife, 263
    restaurants, 38
Midnight Madness, 323
Midway
    restaurants, 38
Miguel's Cocina, 167
Mille Fleurs, 81–82, 268–69
Mimmo's Italian Village, 82
Miner's Diner, 285, 296
Mingei International Museum,
    182–83
Miramar Air Show, 16
Mission Basilica San Diego de
    Alcalá, 10, 26, 164–65
Mission Bay
    itinerary, 282–83
    kayaking/canoeing, 335

lodgings, 127–29
map, 146
nightlife, 263
running, 337–38
sailing, 339
    See also Mission Bay Park
Mission Bay Aquatic Center, 335,
    336–37, 339, 340, 343
Mission Bay Boat Parade, 17
Mission Bay Park, 146–47
    artificial reefs, 328
    bicycling, 323–24
    boating, 326
Mission Bay Sportcenter, 335, 339
Mission Beach, 22, 199
    bicycling, 324
    Boardwalk, 162–63
    nightlife, 263
    restaurants, 38
    running, 338
    shopping, 209
    See also Belmont Park;
        Mission Bay Park
Mission Café & Coffee Shop, 82
Mission Hills, 169–71
    nightlife, 263
    restaurants, 39
    shopping, 208
Mission Hills Cafe, 83
Mission Hills Market Cafe, 83,
    169–70
Mission Hills Nursery, 169, 225
Mission San Luis Rey, 293
Mission San Luis Rey de Francia,
    165
Mission Trails Golf Course, 164
Mission Trails Regional Park,
    163–64
    bicycling, 324
    hiking, 334
    running, 338
Mission Valley, 170
    lodgings, 126–27
    nightlife, 263
    restaurants, 39
    shopping, 209–10
    See also businesses and
        attractions
Mistral La Compagnie de
    Provence, 213
MiXX, 84, 272
Mom's Pies, Etc., 285, 296
Mona Lisa Italian Delicatessen,
    224–25
Montanas, 84
Moonlight Amphitheater, 248
Morton's of Chicago, 84–85
Mother's Kitchen, 296
motor tours, 204, 299
    Mexico, 310–11
Mount Helix Amphitheater,
    conferences/meetings/
    receptions, 349
Mount Palomar Winery, 301

Mount Woodson Country Club, 332
mountain biking, 325–26
    clubs and organizations, 325
    routes and rides, 325–26
    See also bicycling
movies, 257–59
    "dive-in," 162
    See also individual movie theaters
Movies Before the Mast, 259
Mundo Divertido, 309
Museo de Historia de Ensenada, 319
Museo de los Niños/Children's Museum, 182
Museum of Contemporary Art San Diego (MCA), 165
Museum of Photographic Arts (MoPA), 183
Museum of San Diego History, 183
museums, 179–84
    Children's Museum/Museo de los Niños, 182
    Chula Vista Nature Center, 291
    Coronado Beach Historical Museum, 167
    Deer Park (cars), 294
    El Museo Cantina Tequila, 314
    Father Luis Jayme Museum, 165
    George White and Anna Gunn Marston House, 182
    Greenway Museum, 296
    Julian Pioneer Museum, 285, 296–97
    Junipero Serra Museum, 167
    Mingei International Museum, 182–83
    Museo de Historia de Ensenada, 319
    Museum of Contemporary Art San Diego (MCA), 165
    Museum of Photographic Arts (MoPA), 183
    Museum of San Diego History, 183
    San Diego Aerospace Museum, 184, 350
    San Diego Automotive Museum, 184
    San Diego Hall of Champions Sports Museum, 184–85
    San Diego Maritime Museum, 150, 350
    San Diego Model Railroad Museum, 185
    San Diego Museum of Art, 143, 185–86, 350–51

San Diego Museum of Man, 159
San Diego Natural History Museum, 186, 202, 334
San Pasqual Battlefield State Historic Park and Museum, 294
Temecula Valley Museum, 301
Tijuana Cultural Center, 309
Timken Museum of Art, 186
music
    classical, 252–56
    jazz concerts, 293
    festivals and events, 14–15, 16, 17
    nightlife, 264–69. See also individual clubs
    stores, 233–35. See also individual stores
Music Trader, 234
musicians, local, 267
Mystery Cafe Dinner Theatre, 248

N

Nana's Antiques, 300
Natural History Museum, San Diego, 186
    Canyoneers' nature walks, 202, 334
nature trails and walks
    Doane Valley Nature Trail, 296
    San Diego Natural History Museum, 202, 334
Naval Air Station at North Island, 148, 167
Navy vessels, tour, 202
neighborhood(s), 166–81
    Coronado, 167–69
    Del Mar, 177–79
    Hillcrest, 171–72
    Kensington/Adams Avenue, 172–74
    La Jolla, 175–77
    Mission Hills, 169–71
    nightlife, 263
    Ocean Beach, 174–75
    Old Town, 166–67
    Rancho Santa Fe, 179–81
    restaurants, 38–39
    shopping, 208–09
    small, 170
    See also individual neighborhoods
Neiman's, 290
Newbreak, surfing, 342
Newbreak Coffee Co, 276–77
Newport Avenue, 174–75
Newport News, 220
newspapers, local, 30
newsstands, 219, 220
Nickelodeon Records, 234
Nick's at the Beach, 85

Nicole Miller, 214
nightlife, 261–77
    bars, pubs, and taverns 270–74
    desserts, coffees, and te 275–77
    music and clubs, 264–6
    neighborhood listings, 2
    nightclubs, 264–69
    special features, 262
99 Ranch, 223
Normal Heights, 170
    restaurants, 39
Norpine Mountain Sports, 236–37
North Coast/County
    day trip, 288–90
    itinerary, 284–85
North Coast Repertory Theat 248–49
North County Fair, 293
North Island Naval Air Station 148, 167
North Park, 170
    nightlife, 263
North Torrey Pines, bicycling,
Nostalgia Records and Collectibles, 234–35
Nuestra Señora de Guadalupe 316
nurseries, 225–26

O

OB People's Natural Foods, 17
OB Street Fair, 14
Obelisk Books, 11
observatories, Palomar Observatory, 295–96
Ocean Beach, 22, 174–75, 199–200
    nightlife, 263
    Pier, 163, 174
    restaurants, 39
    shopping, 209
    See also individual business and attractions
Ocean Beach Antiques Mall, 21
Ocean Beach Kite Festival, 12
Ocean Beach Paint and Hardwa 229
Ocean Beach Pier, 163, 174
Ocean Beach Pier Cafe, The, 16
Ocean Song Gallery, 179
Off the Record, 235
off-leash areas, 9
Old Globe Theatre, 249
    tour, 202
Old Mission Dam, hiking, 334
Old Point Loma Lighthouse, 148
Old Town, 10, 166–67
    Bazaar del Mundo, 157, 166, 208
    lodgings, 124–25
    Las Posadas, 17
    restaurants, 39

hopping, 208
ee also individual businesses
    and attractions
wn Mexican Cafe, 166
wn San Diego State
oric Park, 157, 166
wn Trolley Tours of San
go, 204
enice Italian Restaurant Caffe
ar, 85–86
adrid, 86
e Border, 86–87
rand Cafe, 87, 294
, 252–56
rd Hill Country Inn, 136–37
  Winery, 294
al Pancake House, The, 87
a's (Ocean Beach), 88
a's (Puerto Nuevo), 315
ack Tours/Desert Jeep Tours,
9
or activities, 322–43
  bicycling, 322–25
  boating, 326–27
  diving/snorkeling, 328
  fishing, freshwater, 330–31
  fishing, saltwater, 328–30
  gliding/hang gliding, 336
  golfing, 331–33
  hiking, 333–35
  kayaking/canoeing, 335–36
  mountain biking, 325–26
  roller-skating/in-line skating,
    336
  rowing, 336–37
  running, 337–38
  sailing, 338–39
  surfing, 340–42
  swimming, 339–40
  tennis, 342
  unusual/weird, 329
  windsurfing, 343
door gear, 235–39
er The Line (OTL)
ournament, 15, 329

ific Beach, 22, 200
  bicycling, 324
  Boardwalk, 162–63
  itinerary, 285–86
  lodgings, 129–30
  nightlife, 263
  restaurants, 39
  running, 338
  shopping, 209
  See also individual businesses
    and attractions
cific Beach Tennis Club, 342
cific Shores, 272
cific Wind Design Aquatic
  Center, 335, 339, 343
cifica Del Mar, 88
cking, 6
lacio Frontón, 309

Palisades Park, 163
Palomar Christian Conference
  Center, 349
Palomar Mountain, day trip,
  295–97
Palomar Mountain General Store
  & Trading Co., 296
Palomar Mountain State Park, 296
Palomar Observatory, 295–96
Pamplemousse Grille, 88–89
Panache, 228
Panda Inn Chinese Restaurant, 89
Pannikin (Leucadia), 290
Pannikin Café (Point Loma), 277
Pannikin Coffee and Tea
  (downtown), 222
Papas and Beer, 314
Papyrus, 228
parades
    Lesbian & Gay Pride Parade,
      15
    Mission Bay Boat Parade, 17
    St. Patrick's Day Parade, 12
    San Diego Harbor Parade of
      Lights, 17
Paradise Point Resort, 128
Paras Newsstand, 220
Parfumerie, 217
Parkhouse Eatery, 89
parking, 24
parks, 194–202
    Anza-Borrego Desert State
      Park, 285, 297–300, 334
    Balboa Park, 117, 142–44,
      281–82
    Belmont Park, 117, 161–62,
      286
    Chicano Park, 188
    Cuyamaca Rancho State
      Park, 334
    Ellen Browning Scripps Park,
      160, 175–76, 196–97
    Embarcadero Marina Park,
      197
    Fiesta Island, 197, 323
    Fletcher Cove Beach Park,
      288
    Kate Sessions Memorial
      Park, 198
    Lake Jennings County Park,
      327, 330–31
    Lake Murray Community
      Park, 327, 331
    Mission Bay Park, 146–47,
      323–24, 326, 328
    Mission Trails Regional Park,
      163–64, 324, 334, 338
    Old Town San Diego State
      Historic Park, 157, 166
    Palisades Park, 163
    Palomar Mountain State
      Park, 296
    Pioneer Park, 169
    Presidio Park, 166–67

San Diego–La Jolla
    Underwater Park, 160
San Pasqual Battlefield State
    Historic Park and
    Museum, 294
Seagrove Park, 177
Spreckels Park, 200–01
Swami's, 289, 342
Tidelands Park, 201
Torrey Pines State Park, 338
Torrey Pines State Reserve,
    164
Tourmaline Surf Park, 340
Volcan Mountain Wilderness
    Preserve, 297
See also beaches; gardens
Patina, 228
Patrick's II, 269
Pearl of the Pacific, 188
pedicabs, 154
Pedrin's, 313
Peet's Coffee & Tea, 222
Penguin Day Ski Fest, 12
Peninsula Tennis Club, 342
Peohe's, 167
People's Organic Foods Market,
    229
Performance Bicycle Shop, 237
performing arts, 245–60
    classical music and opera,
      252–56
    dance, 256–57
    film, 257–59
    fringe theaters, 252
    literary readings, 259–60
    theater, 246–52
pets
    dining with, 45
    local information for people
      traveling with, 9
    services, 29
    See also dogs
pharmacies, 27
Phil's BBQ, 170
photography
    equipment and services,
      28–29
    Museum of Photographic
      Arts (MoPA), 183
    Photo Caravan, 158
Piatti, 90
Pied-a-Terre, 212
Pilar's Beachwear, 214
Pioneer Cemetery (Julian), 285,
    297
Pioneer Park, 169
Pizza Nova, 90
Pizza Port, 90–91
Plan B, 269
Play It Again Sports, 238, 340
plays. See theater
Plaza Bar (Westgate Hotel), 269
Plaza Fiesta, 308
Plaza Río Tijuana, 308
Plunge, Mission Beach, 162, 339

Point Loma, 22, 168, 195
  bicycling, 324
  lighthouse, 148
  lodgings, 123–24
  nightlife, 263
  restaurants, 39
  See also individual businesses
    and attractions
Point Loma Seafoods, 91, 233
police, 26–27
polo, Rancho Santa Fe Polo Fields,
  181
pool/billiards, 273
pools. See swimming
Porkyland, 91–92
post offices, 27
Poway
  Lake Poway Recreation
    Area, 331
  Center for the Performing
    Arts, 249–50
Pratt Gallery, 191
precipitation, average, 5
Presidio Park, 166–67
Primavera Ristorante, 92
Prince and the Pauper, 172
Prince of Wales Grill, The, 92
Princess Pub & Grille, 272
Psychic Eye Book Shop, 220
pubs, 270–74
Puerto Nuevo (Newport),
  315–16
Punta Morro, 318

Q

Quail Botanical Gardens, 117,
  194, 289
  conferences/meetings/
    receptions, 349–50
Quicksilver Stained Glass &
  Antiques, 172
Quint Comptemporary Art,
  191–92
Quinta del Mar Plaza, 314
Quivira Basin, boating, 327
Qwiigs Bar & Grill, 92–93

R

races
  bicycling, 323
  running, 14, 293, 337
  swimming, 329
radio stations, 32
Rainwater's, 93
Ramada Limited Old Town, 125
Rancho Bernardo, 295
  lodgings, 137–38
  restaurants, 39
Rancho Bernardo Inn & Golf
  Course, 137–38, 295
  golfing, 332
Rancho Guajome Adobe,
  conferences/meetings/
    receptions, 350
Rancho Santa Fe, 177–79

  lodgings, 136
  map, 180
  nightlife, 263
  restaurants, 39
Rancho Santa Fe Golf Course,
  181
Rancho Santa Fe Polo Fields, 181
Rancho Valencia Resort, 93–94,
  136, 181
Rand McNally Map & Travel Store,
  220
readings, 259–60
Real del Mar Residence Inn
  (Marriott), 313
reception facilities, 347–51
record stores, 233–35
recreation, 321–45
  outdoor activities, 322–43
  spectator sports, 343–45
  See also individual activities
    and sports
Recreational Equipment,
  Incorporated. See REI
recreational gear, 235–39
Red Fox Steak House, 272
Red Sails Inn, 94
Reed's Hobby Shop, 239–40
Refindery Antiques & Collectibles,
  172
REI (Recreational Equipment,
  Incorporated), 238
  hiking, 334
rentals
  bikes, 25
  boats, 327
  cars, 24
  computers, 29
  kayaks/canoes, 335–36
  sailing, 339
  windsurfing, 343
  See also charters; individual
    sports and activities
rest rooms, public, 25
restaurant(s), 35–111
  features and food types,
    40–43
  neighborhood listings,
    38–39
  pet-friendly, 45
  romantic, 42
  seafood, 104
  star ratings, 36–37
  See also bakeries;
    delicatessens; desserts;
    taverns; individual
    restaurants
Retreads, 243
retro apparel and furnishings,
  242–44
Reuben H. Fleet Space Theater &
  Science Center, 156, 350
Rich's, 269
Ricky's Family Restaurant, 94, 285
Riviera del Pacifico, 319
Roberto's, 94–95

Rock & Roll Taco, 314
Rock 'n' Roll Marathon, 14
Rodeo Santa Fe, 312
roller coaster, 117, 162. See
  amusement parks
roller-skating/in-line skating,
romantic suggestions, 117
Ron Stuart Men's Clothing,
  214–15
Roppongi Restaurant, Bar, an
  Cafe, 95
Rosa's Cantina, 301
Rosarito, 312–15
Rosarito Beach Hotel, 313
Rosarito to Ensenada Race, 3
rowing, 336–37
  clubs and organizations,
  events, 12
Roxanne's Wild Orchid Floris
  225–26
Roxy, 95
Rubio's, 96
Ruby's Diner, 96
running, 337–38
  clubs and organizations,
  races, 14, 293, 337

S

safety, 26–27
Saffron Noodles and Saté, 96–
sailing, 338–39
  Classic Sailing Adventure
    203
  lessons, 339
  See also boating
St. James Bar at Triangle, 101
St. Patrick's Day Parade, 12
Sally's, 97
salons, 29
saltwater fishing, 328–30. See c
  freshwater fishing
Salvation Army, 243–44
Sammy's California Woodfired
  Pizza, 97
Samson's Restaurant, 98, 284
San Diego
  bus service, 23
  construction, 31
  cost for lodging and food,
  economy, 6–7
  exploring, 141–205
  facilities, businesses, and
    services, 25–28
  films made in, 129
  growth of, 237
  history, 10–11
  local resources, 30–34
  neighborhoods, 166–81
  on television, 276
  passing for a local, 21
  orientation, 20–22
  packing to visit, 6
  places of worship, 26
  time zone, 6
  transportation within, 23–2

sitor information, 22–23
weather, 5
web sites, 11
see also individual
    businesses, attractions,
    and activities
ego Aerospace Museum,

conferences/meetings/
    receptions, 350
ego American Indian
    tural Days, 159
ego Art Institute, 192
ego Automotive Museum,
4
ego Ballet, 257
ego Bay, 20
bicycling, 324–25
boating, 326
sailing, 338–39
Diego Bay Ferry, 25, 151
iego Black Ensemble, 252
Diego Chamber Orchestra,
4
Diego Chargers, 344
Diego Civic Theatre, 250
Diego–Coronado Bay Ferry,
, 151
Diego–Coronado Bridge, 21
Diego County Fair, 14
Diego Crew Classic, 12
Diego Early Music Society,
54–55
Diego Flash, 344
Diego Gulls, 344
Diego Hall of Champions
ports Museum, 184–85
Diego Harbor Excursion
oats, 150–51, 203
Diego Harbor Parade of
ights, 17
Diego Hardware, 229
Diego Harley-Davidson, 228
Diego Hilton Beach and
ennis Resort, 128–29
    windsurfing, 343
Diego International Airport at
Lindbergh Field, 2
    art, 258
    lodgings near, 119
    transportation to and from,
    3
Diego–La Jolla Underwater
Park, 160
Diego Marathon, 293
Diego Maritime Museum, 150
    conferences/meetings/
    receptions, 350
Diego Marriott Hotel &
Marina, 118–19
Diego Marriott Mission Valley,
127
Diego Model Railroad
Museum, 185

San Diego Museum of Art,
    185–86
    conferences/meetings/
        receptions, 350–51
    Sculpture Garden Cafe &
        Bistro, 143
San Diego Museum of Man, 159
San Diego Natural History
    Museum, 186
    hiking, 202, 334
San Diego Opera, 255
San Diego Padres, 344–45
San Diego Police Department,
    26–27
    Auto Impound, 24
San Diego Repertory Theatre,
    250
San Diego State University, literary
    events, 260
San Diego Street Scene, 16
San Diego Surfing Academy, 340
San Diego Symphony, 255–56
    background, 253
San Diego Transit Company, 23
San Diego Trolley, 23
San Diego Velodrome, 325
San Diego Watercolor Society
    Showcase Gallery, 192
San Diego Zoo, 144–46
    conferences/meetings/
        receptions, 351
    See also Wild Animal Park
San Elijo Lagoon, 288–89
San Elijo State Beach, 289
San Pasqual Battlefield State
    Historic Park and Museum, 294
Sanborns, 308
sand castle competition, 15
Sandbar, 290
Santa Clara Point, boating, 327
Santa Ysabel, 296
Santa Ysabel Art Gallery, 296
Santé Ristorante, 98
Science Center, 156
Scripps, Birch Aquarium at,
    160–61, 195
Scripps Inn, 134
Scripps (Ellen Browning) Park,
    160, 175–77, 196–97
Sea Lodge, 134
Sea World, 148–49, 282
seafood
    fresh, 233, 318–19
    restaurants, 104
Seaforth Boat Rental, 327, 339
Seaforth Sportfishing, 238
Seagrove Park, 177
Seaport Village, 20, 151, 153–54
    shopping, 209
Seaside Market, 289
See's Candies, 221
Self-Realization Fellowship, 289
seniors, local information for, 8
Señor Frog's, 311
Sephora, 217–18

services
    business, copy, and
        messenger, 28–29
    computers, 29
    for families with children, 8
    for foreign visitors, 11
    for gays and lesbians, 9, 11
    legal, 28
    medical/dental, 27
    for people with disabilities, 8
    for pet owners, 9
    pets and stray animals, 29
    photography, 28–29
    for seniors, 8
    for women, 9
Shake Rag-Epicenter, 244
Shakespeare Pub and Grille,
    98–99
Shelter Island, 170
    boating, 326
    lodgings, 123–24
    nightlife, 263
    public art, 188
    restaurants, 39
Shelter Pointe Hotel and Marina,
    124
Sheraton Harbor Island San
    Diego, 121
shopping, 207–44
    antiques, 210–12
    apparel, 212–15
    bakeries, 215–16
    body care, 216–18
    books and periodicals,
        218–21
    candy and chocolate, 221
    coffee and tea, 221–23
    designer, 213
    districts, 209
    downtown, 208
    ethnic markets, 223–25
    florists, 225–26
    gifts, 226–28
    hardware, 228–29
    health food, 229–30
    historic districts, 208
    home furnishings, 230–31
    jewelry, 231–32
    kitchenware, 232–33
    malls, 209–10, 293
    meat and fish, 233
    music, 233–35
    neighborhoods, 208–09
    nurseries, 225–26
    outdoor gear, 235–39
    toys, 239–40
    video rentals and sales, 240
    vintage/retro, 242–44
    wine and beer, 241–42
    See also individual
        businesses,
        neighborhoods, and
        towns
Sierra Club, hiking, 333
Sierra Plaza Bajamar, 318

Siesel's Old-Fashioned Meats, 233
Silver Designer, The, 232
Silver Skillet, The, 232
Silver Strand State Beach, 161
    bicycling, 325
    running, 338
Singing Hills Golf Resort, 333
Sirino's, 294
Ski Beach, boating, 327
skiing festival, 12
Sky Room, The, 99
Sledgehammer Theatre, 250–51
snorkeling. See diving/snorkeling
Snug Harbor Marina, 292
soccer: San Diego Flash, 344
Society Billiard Cafe, 273
Solana Beach, 288
    nightlife, 263
    restaurants, 39
    shopping, 288
    theater, 248–49
Soledad Mountain, bicycling, 325
Solunto Baking Company, 216
SOMA Live, 269
Sorrento Mesa, 170
Sorrento Valley, 170
    restaurants, 39
Souplantation, 99–100
South Beach Bar and Grill, 100
South Coast Surf Shop, 238
South Shores, boating, 327
Southern Emigrant Trail, 299
Southwest Sea Kayaks and
    Rowing, 239
Space Theater, 156
Spanish Village Art Center, 192
spas, 29
    Golden Door, 294
    Holiday Inn Vita Spa Agua
        Caliente, 311–12
    La Costa Hotel and Spa, 292
Spices Thai Cafe, 100–01
Spin-off Records, 235
Spirits of St. Germain Liquors, 241
sports
    ARCO Training Center, 203,
        291
    San Diego Hall of
        Champions Sports
        Museum, 184–85
    spectator, 343–45
    See also outdoor activities;
        individual sports
Sportsmen's Seafood, 233
Spreckels Organ Pavilion, 256
Spreckels Park, 200–01
Stacey Himmel Stationery, 228
Star of the Sea, 101–02
Starbucks, 223
Starlight Theater, 251
Steele Canyon Golf & Country
    Club, 333
stern-wheelers, Bahia
    Sternwheelers, 204, 348
Store of Knowledge (KPBS), 240

Strand Theatre, 175
Stratford Court Cafe, 179
stray animals, 29
street fairs, 14, 16, 293
Sunshine Company Saloon
    Limited, 273
Sunshine Organic Foods, 229–30
surfing, 340–42
    events, 340
    lessons, 340
    Rosarito, 313
Sushi Deli/Sushi Deli Too, 102
Sushi on the Rock, 102–03
Suzuki Rock 'n' Roll Marathon,
    337
Swami's, 289
    surfing, 342
swimming, 339–40
    Mission Beach Plunge, 162,
        339
    races, 329
    White Water Canyon, 291
Swing Inn Cafe, 301
Sycuan Casino, 298
synagogues, 26

T

T's Cafe, 107–08
Taboo, 232
tapes, records, and CDs, 233–35
Tasende Gallery, 176, 192
Taste of Thai, 103
taverns, 270–74
Taxco Curios, 314
taxis, 3, 24
tea
    houses/rooms, 275–77, 294
    retail, 221–23
telephone
    area codes, 9
    numbers, useful, 33–34
television
    shows filmed in San Diego,
        276
    stations, 32
Temecula
    day trip, 300–02
    shopping, 300–01
    wineries, 300, 301
Temecula Creek Inn, 302
Temecula Crest Winery, 301
Temecula Stampede, 301
Temecula Valley Museum, 301
Temecula Valley Vintners
    Association, 300
temperatures, average, 5
tennis, 342
    events, 292
Thanksgiving Dixieland Jazz
    Festival, 17
    theater(s), 246–52
    fringe, 252
    tickets, 247
    tour, 202
    See also individual theaters

Theatre in Old Town, 251
Thee Bungalow, 103–04
Thinker Things, 240
Thornton Winery, 301. See ⟨
    Cafe Campagne
thrift stores, 242–44
Ticketmaster, 247
tickets, 247
tide pools, 195
Tidelands Park, 201
Tierra Santa, Mission Trails
    Regional Park, 163–64
Tiffany & Co., 232
Tijuana, 22, 307–12
    transportation to, 310
Tijuana Cultural Center, 309
time zone, 6
Timken Museum of Art, 186
Tip Top Meats, 104–05
Tolán, 308
Tony's, 313
Tony's Jacal, 105
Top o' the Cove, 105
Top of the Hyatt, 273
Top of the Market, 67
Top of the Park, 273
Top 25 attractions, 140–63
Tori Tori New Japanese Cuisir
    106
Torrey Pines, north, bicycling,
Torrey Pines Glider Port, 336
Torrey Pines Municipal Golf
    Course, 333
Torrey Pines State Beach, 201
Torrey Pines State Park, runnin,
    338
Torrey Pines State Reserve, 16
Tour de Julian, 325
Tourmaline Surf Park, surfing, 3
tours, 202–05
    air, 203
    Anza-Borrego Desert Sta
        Park, 297–300
    architectural, 202
    ARCO Training Center, 2
    balloons/biplanes, 117, 33
    Coronado, 167
    boat, 203–04
    driving, 299
    helicopter/whirlybird, 336
    Mexico, 310–11
    motor, 204, 299
    walking/hiking, 202, 204–(
        333–34
Tower, The, 273–74
Tower Records, 235
toys, 239–40
Trade Roots Reggae, 235
Trader Joe's, 225
trains
    Amtrak, 3
    San Diego Model Railroad
        Museum, 185
translators, 11

...rtation
...rplanes, 2
...o and from airport, 3
...icycles, 24–25
...uses, 3, 23
...ars, 3–4, 24
...erries, 25, 151
...o and from San Diego, 2–4
...axis, 3, 24
...o and from Tijuana, 310
...rains, 3
...rolleys, 23
...ria Acqua, 106
...ria Mama Anna, 107
...ers Aid, 2
...Gallery, 213
...rs
...Old Town Trolley Tours of
   San Diego, 204
...San Diego Trolley, 23
...y's, 107, 274
...ieweed Trading Company, 299
...nan's Memorial, 188
...upper Club, 108
...Mare Ristorante, 108
...s Tea & Coffee, 277
...ght in the Park, 14–15
...s, 109

zone, 329
...erwater Pumpkin Carving
  ontest, 17
...orn Antique Mall, 211
...on-Tribune Dr Seuss Race for
  iteracy, 337
...ed Artists Theatre (Horton
  laza), 155
...Customs, 310
...5. Grant Hotel, 119–20
...5. House Apothecary and Soap
  hop, 218
...5. Open Sand Castle
  Competition, 15
...versities, 33. See also San
  Diego State University;
  University of California at San
  Diego
...versity Avenue, shopping, 208
...iversity City, 170
...iversity Heights, 170
  nightlife, 263
  restaurants, 39
...iversity of California at San
  Diego
  art on campus, 189
  film festival, 258–59
  literary events, 260
  Theatre, 251
...niversity Town Centre,
  shopping, 210
...ostart Crow Bookstore &
  Coffeehouse, 220
...ptown District, shopping, 209
...rban Outfitters, 228

V

Vegetarian Zone, The, 109, 230
Velodrome, San Diego, 325
Venetian, The, 109–10
Vermont Street Pedestrian Bridge,
  172, 185
Via Italia Trattoria, 110
video rentals and sales, 240
Viejas Casino & Turf Club, 298
Vigilucci's, 110
Village Hillcrest, shopping, 209
Village Theatre, 169
Vineyard Terrace, 302
vintage apparel and furnishings,
  242–44
Vintage Tea Room at the Gilded
  Lily, 294
visitor information, 22–23
Vita Spa Agua Caliente (Holiday
  Inn), 311
Volcan Mountain Wilderness
  Preserve, 297

W

Wahrenbrock's Book House, 220
Walkabout International, 204, 333
walking/hiking tours, 202, 204–05,
  333–34
Walter Anderson Nursery, 226
Warwick's, 220, 259
waterfront, downtown, 150–52
Waterfront, The, 111, 274
water-skiing. See boating
Wear It Again Sam, 244
weather, 5
Web information, 11
Welk Resort Center, 294
  Theatre, 252
Westgate Hotel, The, 120
  Plaza Bar, 269
Westin Harbor Island, 121
Westin Hotel at Horton Plaza, 120
Whaley House, 166
Whaling Bar, The, 111
When in Rome, 111–12
whirlybird tours, 336
White Rabbit, The, 221
White Water Canyon, 291
Whole Foods Market, 230
Wiedner's Gardens, 226
Wild Animal Park, 157–58
wildflowers, viewing, 12, 13
William Heath Davis House, 152
Williams-Sonoma, 232–33
Windansea Beach, 201–02
windsurfing, 343
wine, 241–42. See also wineries
Wine Connection, The, 241
Wine Lover, 172
wineries
  Callaway Vineyard & Winery,
    301. See also Vineyard
    Terrace
  Deer Park, 294
  Ferrara Winery, 294

  L. A. Cetto Winery, 309
  La Esquina de Bodegas, 320
  Maurice Carrie Winery, 301
  Menghini Winery, 297
  Mount Palomar Winery, 301
  Orfila Winery, 294
  Temecula, 300, 301
  Temecula Crest Winery, 301
  Thornton Winery, 301. See
    also Cafe Campagne
Winesellar & Brasserie, 112, 242
Winston's Beach Club, 274
Wolfs, 274
women, local information for, 9
World Bodysurfing
  Championships, 16, 340

Y

yacht charters, 348
YMCA, swimming, 340
Yokohama Friendship Bell, 188
Yoshino, 112–13

Z

ZLAC Rowing Club,
  conferences/meetings/
  receptions, 351
Zodiac San Diego, 239
Zoo Founder's Day, 16
zoos
    San Diego Zoo, 144–46,
      351
    Wild Animal Park, 157–58

We Stand By Our Reviews

⬛uatch Books is proud of *San Diego Best Places*. Our editors and contribu-
⬛go to great lengths and expense to see that all of the restaurant and lodging
⬛ws are as accurate, up-to-date, and honest as possible. If we have disap-
⬛ted you, please accept our apologies; however, if a recommendation in this
⬛dition of *San Diego Best Places* has seriously misled you, Sasquatch Books
⬛ld like to refund your purchase price. To receive your refund:

1. Tell us where and when you purchased your book and return the book
   and the book-purchase receipt to the address below.
2. Enclose the original restaurant or lodging receipt from the establishment
   in question, including date of visit.
3. Write a full explanation of your stay or meal and how *San Diego Best
   Places* misled you.
4. Include your name, address, and phone number.

Refund is valid only while this 1st edition of *San Diego Best Places* is in
⬛t. If the ownership, management, or chef has changed since publication,
⬛quatch Books cannot be held responsible. Tax and postage on the returned
⬛k is your responsibility. Please allow six to eight weeks for processing.

Please address to Satisfaction Guaranteed, *San Diego Best Places,* and send to:
Sasquatch Books
615 Second Avenue, Suite 260
Seattle, WA 98104

San Diego Best Places Report Form

d on my personal experience, I wish to nominate the following restaurant,
e of lodging, shop, nightclub, sight, or other as a "Best Place"; or confirm/
ect/disagree with the current review.

(Please include address and telephone number of establishment, if convenient.)

REPORT

se describe food, service, style, comfort, value, date of visit, and other aspects
our experience; continue on another piece of paper if necessary.

m not concerned, directly or indirectly, with the management or ownership
this establishment.

GNED

DDRESS

IONE   DATE

Please address to San Diego Best Places and send to:
SASQUATCH BOOKS
615 SECOND AVENUE, SUITE 260
SEATTLE, WA 98104
Feel free to email feedback as well: **BOOKS@SASQUATCHBOOKS.COM**